CAREER
OPPORTUNITIES
in the

MUSIC INDUSTRY

CAREER OPPORTUNITIES in the

MUSIC INDUSTRY

Sixth Edition

SHELLY FIELD

Checkmark Books®
An imprint of Infobase Publishing

Career Opportunities in the Music Industry, Sixth Edition

Checkmark Books
An imprint of Infobase Publishing
132 West 31st Street
New York NY 10001

Library of Congress Cataloging-in-Publication Data

Field, Shelly.
  Career opportunities in the music industry / Shelly Field. — 6th ed.
    p. cm.
  Includes bibliographical references and index.
  ISBN-13: 978-0-8160-7801-1 (hardcover : alk. paper)
  ISBN-10: 0-8160-7801-7 (hardcover : alk. paper)
  ISBN-13: 978-0-8160-7802-8 (pbk. : alk. paper)
  ISBN-10: 0-8160-7802-5 (pbk. : alk. paper) 1. Music—Vocational guidance. 2. Music—Economic aspects. I. Title.
  ML3795.F497 2009
  780.23'73—dc22   2009030498

Checkmark Books are available at special discounts when purchased in bulk quantities for businesses, associations, institutions, or sales promotions. Please call our Special Sales Department in New York at (212) 967-8800 or (800) 322-8755.

You can find Infobase Publishing on the World Wide Web at http://www.infobasepublishing.com

Cover design by Takeshi Takahashi

Printed in the United States of America

MP Hermitage 10 9 8 7 6 5 4 3 2

This book is printed on acid-free paper.

This book is dedicated to my parents,
Ed and the late Selma Field,
who gave me every opportunity,
supported all my decisions,
and always let me be me.

CONTENTS

HOW TO USE THIS BOOK

From the time I was very young, my dream was to work in the music business. While at the time, no one really thought the music industry was a viable career option, I knew they were wrong, and I decided to pursue my dream.

When I tried to enter the industry, I found there were numerous obstacles. To begin with, there was not a lot of information about career choices in music. Additionally, not only could I find very few people who knew anything about the business, but most of those who did, did not want to share their knowledge. I promised myself that if I ever got into the music business, I would help everyone else who wanted to work in the industry to get the job of their dreams too.

With a lot of hard work, some creativity, and a bit of luck, I was finally successful in entering the music business, working in public relations and publicity. And I never forgot my promise.

While I now give seminars and workshops and personal consultations and coaching sessions about entering and succeeding in the industry, the first edition of *Career Opportunities in the Music Industry* was written as part of the deal I made with myself to help others who wanted to be in the music business.

When the first edition of *Career Opportunities in the Music Industry* was published in 1986, there was no single source describing the major job opportunities in music presented in a clear and simple fashion. Over the years, the book has emerged as one of the leading volumes for helping individuals in their quest for success in the music field. Today, six editions later, *Career Opportunities in the Music Industry* is still help-ing people who aspire to work in the music business to develop a game plan.

Since the book was first written, the music industry has continued to explode. Thousands of people are currently working in the music industry in the business and talent areas, and there are literally thousands upon thousands of people who want to get in.

Most people have no idea how to enter the industry. Many dream of becoming recording stars or yearn to write songs that will remain with people through the years. Others want to work in the business end of the industry, helping others to climb the ladder of success.

This book can help you discover your options. It can help you learn what it takes to prepare yourself so that you can enter and succeed in the industry, no matter what path you select.

Advances in technology and the music industry have made it easier than ever to launch a satisfying and successful career in the talent end of the music business. There are now a greater number of smaller, independent record labels in existence than ever before, with new labels springing up around the country. VH1, MTV, Country Music Television, and a host of other video television and cable programs make it possible to generate hit CD's almost instantly. Similarly, Youtube, MySpace, and other Internet outlets make it possible for new and established acts to get their material heard. And, of course, programs such as *American Idol* can create recording stars overnight.

Affordable electronic musical instruments, such as keyboards, guitars, and drums, in addition to computer hardware and software and new computer technology, allow people to play, write, and record music with unprecedented ease. Affordable audio and video equipment make it easy to create both demos and videos at a relatively low cost.

Career Opportunities in the Music Industry was written for anyone who dreams of working in the music industry but does not know how to turn that dream into reality. The 96 jobs discussed in this book encompass all aspects of careers in the music industry. Almost every category of work can be found in the music business. The industry needs secretaries, receptionists, publishers, tour managers, teachers, therapists, librarians, attorneys, accountants, executives, writers, publicists, salespeople, webmasters, and more.

You may have to be creative to find your niche. The trick is to identify your skills and use them to get you in the door. Once in, you have a good chance of moving into other positions as you climb the career ladder.

Read through this book and find out what you are qualified to do, or how you can obtain training in your field of interest. You can then work toward one of the most rewarding and exciting careers in the world—one in music!

What's New in the Sixth Edition

The sixth edition of *Career Opportunities in the Music Industry* is chock full of updated information. All salaries, employment and advancement prospects, training and educational requirements, and unions and associations for each job profile have been reviewed and updated when necessary. The information in every appendix has been updated as well, giving you the most up-to-date names, addresses, phone numbers, and Web sites of colleges and universities, trade associations, unions and other organizations, record labels, distributors, booking agencies, music publishers, public relations and publicity firms, and entertainment industry attorneys and law firms. New books and periodicals complete the bibliography.

Three new appendixes have been added. The first is a listing of useful Web sites relating to the music industry. The second, with a listing of job and career Web sites, makes it easier for you to find more job opportunities. The third new appendix lists relevant workshops, seminars, conferences, and conventions.

While the first five editions of *Career Opportunities in the Music Industry* were very comprehensive in the coverage of careers and key jobs, eight new job profiles have been added to the this edition of the book. This brings the total number of career opportunities to 96.

Sources of Information

Information for this book was obtained through interviews, questionnaires, and a wide variety of books, magazines, newsletters, and other written material. Some information was gleaned from personal experience working in the industry. Other data was obtained from friends and business associates in various branches of the music business.

Among the people interviewed were individuals involved in all aspects of the music industry. These include record company executives, radio station personnel, tour managers, personal managers, booking agents, accountants, attorneys, church musicians, songwriters, performing artists, and recording artists. Employment agencies were contacted, as well as schools, personnel offices, unions, trade associations, orchestras, operas, and other relevant organizations.

Organization of Material

Career Opportunities in the Music Industry is divided into 13 general employment sections. These sections are Recording and the Record Business; Radio and Television; On the Road; Music Retailing and Wholesaling; the Business End of the Industry; Instrument Repair, Restoration, and Design; Publicity and Advertising; Support Services for Recording Artists; Symphonies, Orchestras, Operas, Etc.; Arenas, Facilities, Halls, and Clubs; Education; Talent and Writing; and Church Music. Within each of these sections are descriptions of individual careers.

There are two parts to each job classification. The first part offers job information in abbreviated form. The second part presents information in a narrative text. In addition to the basic career description, you will find information on unions and/or associations and tips for entry into the profession.

Twelve appendixes are offered to help locate information that you might want or need to enter in the music business. You can use these reference sections to locate colleges, schools, workshops, and training seminars. There are lists of names and addresses for music-oriented unions, trade associations, record companies, booking agencies, music publishers, rights societies, public relations and publicity firms, record distributors, entertainment industry attorneys, music related Web sites, and career and job Web sites. There are suggestions for books and periodicals to read and a glossary to help you learn the lingo.

The music industry holds widespread appeal. Nearly everyone dreams of reaching a star. For some, that star might be a successful career as a popular recording artist, while for others, the goal might be recognition as a songwriter. Still others who love music, whatever the genre, might aspire to work in the recording business or in music education.

With talent, training, the right opportunities, a few connections, and a little bit of luck, or a combination of all these, you can reach your star in the music business.

Persevere! I know if you do, you will make it.

Shelly Field
www.shellyfield.com

ACKNOWLEDGMENTS

I would like to thank every individual, company, union, and association that provided information, assistance, and encouragement for this book.

I acknowledge with appreciation my editor, James Chambers, for his continuous help and encouragement. I would also like to express my sincere gratitude to Sarah Fogarty, the project editor, for her assistance.

In addition, I also thank Kate Kelly, who, as my initial editor, provided the original impetus for *Career Opportunities in the Music Industry* and a number of other books in the Career Opportunities series.

As always, I gratefully acknowledge Ed Field for his assistance and ongoing support in this and every one of my projects.

I must take a moment to acknowledge Jeff Serrette. Many years ago when I was first attempting to enter the music industry, I called *Billboard* to try to get some advice from anyone who would give it. No one in editorial would talk to me, and I was transferred to the advertising department.

I was lucky enough to end up with Jeff on the other end of the phone. I told him what I was trying to do and that I didn't really want to buy an ad; I just wanted some advice. His advice was something to the effect of "invest in yourself."

While I don't remember all the details, I do remember Jeff explaining how to develop copy for a very small classified ad I could afford. I recall, too, that he told me that ads didn't have to have a lot of words, but the words used in the ad needed to be effective. I placed a very, very small ad. Soon after it came out, I received a call from a potential client that gave me the confidence to go after others. My business took off.

Although Jeff has always been quick to say I would have experienced success without his help, I can't be sure. What I do know is that had my business not taken off, I might never have had the chance to work in the industry I loved, to write this book, or do any of the other wonderful things I have had the opportunity to do in my career. Jeff, who is still at *Billboard,* is a senior account manager. I am sure there have been many others whose careers Jeff has helped during his tenure, and I am most grateful for the advice he gave me then and for his continued advice over the years.

Others whose help was invaluable include the Academy of Country Music; Ellen Ackerman; Harrison Allen; Julie Allen; Alverno College; American Federation of Musicians; American Guild of Musical Artists; American Guild of Variety Artists; American Music Therapy Association; American Society of Composers and Publishers; American Society of Music Copyists; American Symphony Orchestra League; Arista Records; Association of Theatrical Press Agents and Managers; John Balme; Dan Barrett; Lloyd Barriger; Allan Barrish; Warren Bergstrom; Eugene Blabey; Steve Blackman; B'nai B'rith Vocational Service; Linda Bonsante; Broadcast Music, Inc.; Theresa Bull; Al Bumanis; Earl "Speedo" Carroll; Cantors Assembly; Catskill Development; Anthony Cellini, Town of Thompson supervisor; Brandi Cesario; Patricia Claghorn; Janice Cohen; Dr. Jessica L. Cohen; Norman Cohen; Robert Cohen, Esq.; Community Employment Training Center, Las Vegas, Nevada; Fred Coopersmith; Jan Cornelius; Crawford Memorial Library staff; Margaret Crosslsey; Robert Crothers; Meike Cryan; Daniel Dayton; W. Lynne Dayton; Carrie Dean; Scott Edwards; Michelle Edwards;

Cliff Ehrlich, Catskill Development; Ernest Evans; Julie Evans; Sara Feldberg; Deborah K. Field, Esq.; Greg Field; Lillian (Cookie) Field; Mike Field; Robert Field; Selma Field; Finkelstein Memorial Library staff; Jack Furlong; Richard Gabriel; David Garthe, CEO, Graveyware.com; John Gatto; Sheila Gatto; Morris Gerber; Larry Goldsmith; Sam Goldych; Gail Haberle; Lillian Hendrickson; Hermann Memorial Library staff; Joan Howard; Hudson Valley Philharmonic; Jo Hunt, DeLyon-Hunt & Associates; International Alliance of Theatrical Stage Employees; International Association of Auditorium Managers; International Brotherhood of Electrical Workers; Julia Jacobs; Jimmy "Handyman" Jones; Dave Kleinman; Janice Kleinman; K-LITE Radio; Dr. John C. Koch; Bruce Kohl; Las Vegas Review Journal; Karen Leever; Bob Leone; Liberty Central School; Liberty Public Library staff; Ernie Martinelli; Robert Masters, Esq.; Richard Mayfield; June E. McDonald; Phillip Mestman; Rima Mestman; Metropolitan Opera; Beverly Michaels, Esq.; Martin Michaels, Esq.; Monticello Central School High School Library staff; Monticello Central School Middle School Library staff; Jennifer Morganti; Music Business Institute; Music Educators National Conference; Florence Naistadt; National Association for Music Therapy; National Association of Broadcast Employees and Technicians; National Association of Broadcasters; National Association of Music Merchants; National Association of Recording Merchandisers; National Association of Schools of Music; National Music Publishers Association; Earl Nesmith; Nevada Society of Certified Public Accountants; Jim Newton; New York State Employment Service; Nikkodo U.S.A., Inc.; Ellis Norman, UNLV; Heather Dawn O'Keefe; Ivy Pass; Ed Pearson, Nikkodo USA; Barbara Pezzella; Piano Technicians Guild; Anita Portas, IATSE; Practising Law Institute; Public Relations Society of America; Doug Puppel; Ruth Qualich; Harvey Rachlin; Ramapo Catskill Library System; John Riegler; Reverend Brace Rentz; Doug Richards; Susan G. Riley, ASOL; Sheldon Rosenberg; Gary F. Roth, BMI; Diane Ruud; Bob Saludares; Michael Seiter; Joy Shaffer; M.D. Smith; Raun Smith; Smith Employment Agency; John Sohigian, Orange County Choppers; Songwriters Guild; Aileen Spertell; Laura Solomon; Debbie Springfield; Matthew E. Strong; Sullivan County Community College; Sullivan County Performing Arts Council; The Teenagers; Thrall Library staff; Marie Tremper; David D, Turner, Music Business Institute of Atlanta; United States Department of Labor; Brian Vargas; Brian Anthony Vargas.; Sarah Ann Vargas; Pat Varriale; Amy Vasquez; Pat Vasquez; Kaytee Warren; Marc Weiswasser; Dr. Ray Williams; Carol Williams; John Williams; John Wolfe; Dr. Diana Worby; Rachel Worby; Henry J. White; Johnny Worlds; WSUL Radio; WTZA; WVOS Radio; and George Wurzbach.

In addition, much material was provided by sources who wish to remain anonymous. My thanks to them all the same.

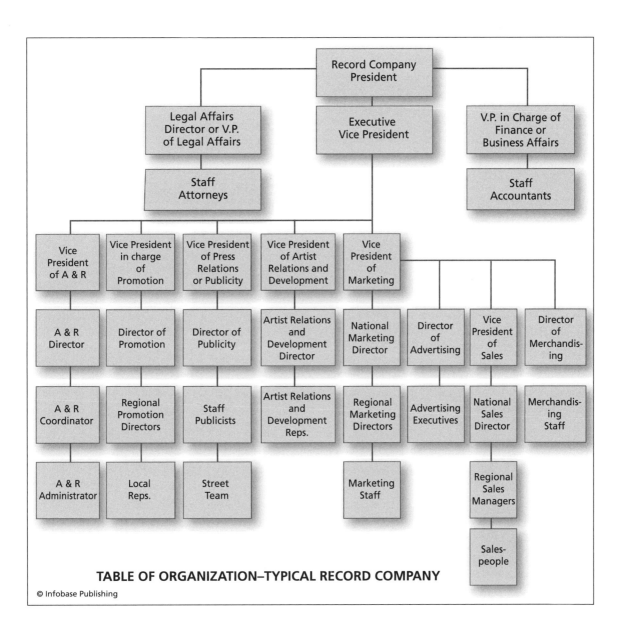

TABLE OF ORGANIZATION–TYPICAL RECORD COMPANY

© Infobase Publishing

INTRODUCTION

Music is often described as the universal language. It has existed for as long as anyone can remember. It may not always have taken the sophisticated forms that we know today, but it was music just the same.

Throughout history, people made music for different purposes. Primitive people used drums to send messages. Drums also accompanied dance in ceremonies and celebrations. People sang for joy and in sadness. Some people sang to make time go by more quickly or to take their minds off the drudgery of hard, tedious work.

Music means different things to different people. To some, it is healing; to others, it is pure entertainment. Music often elicits memories. Hearing an old song, for example, might evoke memories of a particular time and place. It might remind you of an especially enjoyable day or even a day on which something sad occurred.

Whatever else music is, today it is a multibillion-dollar business. Thousands work in every aspect of the music industry, from talent to business to education to retail and everything in between. Many more reap the rewards and pleasures of music.

As you read over the various sections in this book, searching to find the "perfect job," keep in mind that there is no one way to get into the music business. There are many avenues. I have given you the guidelines. You have to do the rest.

Within each section of this book you will find the necessary information to get acquainted with most of the important jobs in the industry. A key to the organization of each entry follows.

Alternate Titles

Many jobs in the music business, as in all industries, are known by alternate titles. The duties of these jobs are the same; only the name is different. Titles vary from company to company.

Career Ladder

The career ladder illustrates a normal job progression. Remember that in the music business there are no hard-and-fast rules. Job progression may not necessarily follow a precise order.

Position Description

Every effort has been made to give well-rounded job descriptions. Keep in mind that no two companies are structured exactly the same. Therefore, no two jobs will be exactly the same. For example, note figure 1. This illustrates the organization of a typical record label. However, another company might have a different structure with different personnel reporting to different executives, or with or without some positions on the chart.

Salary Ranges

Salary ranges for the 96 job titles in this book are as accurate as possible. Earnings will be dependent on a number of factors. These include the size, prestige, and geographic location of the specific company for which an individual works, as well as his or her experience, education, and professional reputation. Compensation in the talent end of the industry is often also based on the talent and popularity of an individual.

Employment Prospects

If you choose a job that has an excellent, good, or fair rating, you are lucky. You will have an easier time finding work. If, however, you are interested in a job that has a poor rating, do not despair. The rating only suggest that the job is difficult to obtain—not impossible.

Advancement Prospects

Try to be as cooperative and helpful as possible in the workplace. Do not attempt to see how little work you can do. Be enthusiastic, energetic, and outgoing. Go the extra step that no one expects. Learn as much as you can. When a job advancement possibility opens up, make sure that you are prepared to take advantage of it.

A variety of options for career advancement are included. However, you should be aware that there are no hard and fast rules for climbing the career ladder in the music industry. While work performance is important, advancement in many jobs is based on experience, education, training, employee attitude, talent, and, of course, individual career aspirations.

Many companies in the music industry promote from within. The best way to advance your career is to get your foot in the door and then climb the career ladder.

Education and Training

This section presents the *minimum* educational and training requirements for each job area. This does not mean that you should limit yourself. Try to get the best training and education possible.

A college degree or background does not guarantee a job in the music industry, but it might help prepare you for life in the workplace. Education and training also encompass courses, seminars, programs, on-the-job training, and learning from others.

Special Requirements

This section covers any special licensing and credentials that may be required for a specific job.

Experience, Skills, and Personality Traits

These will differ from job to job, but getting started on any career path you choose will probably take a great deal of perseverance. Being an outgoing individual helps. Contacts are important in all facets of the music business. Make as many as you can. These people will be helpful in advancing your career.

Volunteer work, internships, and even helping out in family businesses can enhance your résumé.

Best Geographical Location

You will note that most jobs in major record companies and the business end of the industry are located in the major music capitals, such as New York City, Los Angeles, and Nashville. Smaller and independent labels and businesses are located throughout the country.

While jobs and opportunities in talent and performing can be found in culturally active areas, they also are available from coast to coast and everywhere between. Opportunities in teaching, retailing, wholesaling, and related fields can be located almost anywhere in the United States.

Unions and Associations

This section offers other sources for career information and assistance. Unions and trade associations offer valuable help in obtaining career guidance, support, and personal contacts. They may also offer training, continuing education, scholarships, fellowships, seminars, and other beneficial programs.

Tips for Entry

Use this section to gather ideas on how to get a job, gain entry into the area in which you are interested, or to excel in a current position. When applying for any job, always be as professional as possible. Dress neatly and conservatively. Do not wear sneakers. Do not chew gum. Do not smoke. Do not wear heavy perfume or cologne.

Always have a few copies of your résumé with you. These, too, should look neat and professional. Have them typeset and presented well, and check and recheck them for grammar, spelling, and content.

If asked to fill out an application, complete the entire application, even if you have a résumé with you. Print the information neatly.

When applying for jobs and filling in applications, be prepared. Make sure that you know your Social Security number. Ask people in advance whether you can use them as references. Make sure that you know their full names, addresses, and telephone numbers. Secure at least three personal references and three professional references.

The ability to go online, whether from your home computer, or one in a school or public library, puts you at a great advantage. No matter which aspect of the music industry piques your interest, you need to be computer literate. Whether required or not, it is always a plus.

Record labels, publishers, and other music-related companies as well as newspapers and magazines, feature Web sites that might be helpful in your quest to find the perfect job. You can also obtain information online about companies and their current job opportunities, industry news, or even the classified sections from newspapers in areas where music-related companies are located.

The Internet can also provide a wealth of opportunities to jumpstart and promote your career, whether you are an aspiring singer, songwriter, recording artist, or other talent.

Use *every* contact you have. Do not become fixated on the idea that you want to get a job on your own. If you are lucky enough to know someone who can help you to obtain the job you want, take advantage of this opportunity. You will still have to prove yourself at the interview and on the job. Nobody can do that for you.

Once you get your foot in the door, learn as much as you can. Do that little extra bit of work that is not expected. Be cooperative. Be a team player. Do not burn bridges; it will hurt your career. Ask for help. Network. Find a mentor.

The last piece of advice in this section is to be on time for everything. This includes job inter-views, phone calls, work, and meetings. People will remember when you are habitually late, and it may hinder you in advancing your career.

Remember that the music business is just that; a business. It may be fun; it may be glamorous; it may be exciting; but it is still a business. It is essential that you treat it as such.

Some people spend their lives wishing that they could have a job that they love going to every day; one that is interesting, exciting, and never the same. If a career like this is your dream too, you do not have to wish anymore. You have taken the first step to getting the career of your dreams by picking up this book.

Have fun reading it. It will help you prepare for a career you will truly love. Do not get discouraged and do not give up on your goal. Every job and every experience you have teaches you something and is a stepping stone to the job of your dreams.

Have faith and confidence in yourself. You will make it in music eventually, but you must persevere. In many instances, the individual who did not make it in the music business is the one who gave up too soon.

When you do get the job you have been dreaming of, become a mentor, share your knowledge, and help others fulfill their dreams too.

We love to hear success stories about your career and how this book helped you. If you have a story and want to share it, go to www.shellyfield.com. I hope to hear from you!

Good luck.

Shelly Field

RECORDING AND THE RECORD BUSINESS

A & R COORDINATOR

Duties: Find talent for a record company to sign; locate tunes to match with specific artists on the label's roster

Alternate Title(s): A & R Representative; Artist and Repertoire Coordinator, A & R Staffer; Talent Acquisition Rep

Salary Range: $29,000 to $150,000+

Employment Prospects: Poor

Advancement Prospects: Fair

Best Geographical Location(s) for Position: New York City, Los Angeles, and Nashville are music capitals

Prerequisites:

Education or Training—High school diploma is a minimum requirement; college degree may be required or preferred by major labels; see text

CAREER LADDER

A & R Director

A & R Coordinator

A & R Administrator;
A & R Assistant or Trainee

Experience—Experience in music or record business

Special Skills and Personality Traits—Foresight; ability to see past "raw" talent; self-confidence; enjoyment of music; ability to deal well with people; good verbal and written communication skills

Position Description

An A & R (Artist and Repertoire) Coordinator or rep performs a variety of functions depending on the record company he or she works with and its size.

The main duty of the A & R Coordinator is to find talent for the company to sign up. He or she may do this in a number of ways. The A & R Coordinator may visit clubs and/or showcases checking out new talent. The individual may listen to tapes and demo records and/or watch videocassettes of acts performing. The A & R Coordinator may also try to sign up existing talent, such as individuals currently signed with another record label. In cases such as this, the A & R Coordinator might either wait for the act's contract to expire, or, in rare cases, try to buy out an existing contract. When A & R Coordinators are vying for an established act to sign with their company, they do everything in their power to make their contract more attractive than competing companies' contracts.

The A & R Coordinator has another important duty. He or she is often responsible for finding (or helping to find) songs for the artists signed to the record label. These can be located in a number of ways. One is by going through the masses of tapes and demos of new tunes that are mailed or brought to the record company by would-be song writers. Another method is to listen to old hit records or classics that might be arranged in a new or current fashion. The A & R Coordinator might

put a staff writer of the record company together with the artist in an effort to come up with that all-important hit tune. The new artist might also be a writer and have a healthy supply of his or her own material from which a potential tune might be selected.

Once a tune is picked, the A & R Coordinator locates a producer who will work well with the act. The A & R Coordinator might also help an unmanaged or poorly managed act find a management team, lawyers, business managers, accountants, etc.

The A & R Coordinator works very closely with the act from the moment they are signed with the label. He or she takes the act under his or her wing and tries to build it into a total artistic, creative, and commercial success.

If an act is unhappy about anything, whether it be a CD not selling well or difficulties with an assigned producer, the act would talk to their A & R Coordinator.

The A & R Coordinator works closely not only with the act, but also with the various other departments in the company to assure the act the best possible chance of attaining success.

The A & R Coordinator is usually responsible to the vice-president in charge of A & R, the vice-president in charge of talent acquisition, or the A & R director. It depends on how the particular record company is structured.

The hours for the A & R Coordinator are often irregular and long as a result of late nights at clubs seeking out talent and the nature of the job.

Salaries

Depending on the size of the record company, salaries can be quite high for this position. Salaries can range from $29,000 to $150,000 plus annually. Salaries at the lower end of the scale are paid to individuals working in smaller, independent labels. In addition, A & R Coordinators are often given bonuses for signing existing "superstar" talent or an artist who makes it big.

Employment Prospects

There are many people who want to work as A & R Coordinators. As a matter of fact, there are more people than there are positions.

If a record company requires an A & R Coordinator, they will usually try to find a qualified individual within the ranks of the company. Exceptions are made, however, when an A & R Coordinator has worked at another company and proved him or herself by finding artists who consistently hit the top.

Employment prospects are increasing with the growing success of smaller, independent labels.

Advancement Prospects

Once an individual gets into a record company, he or she has the opportunity to move up the career ladder. As an A & R Coordinator, the individual may move into the position of A & R director. The person may also be hired by a bigger, more prestigious company for the same position. To move ahead, the individual must prove him or herself by signing acts that hit the top of the charts.

Education and Training

An A & R Coordinator must usually have at least a high school diploma. Major labels generally prefer that their staff members hold a college degree.

Degrees or courses in music merchandising, the music business, communications, marketing, advertising, etc. are useful. In addition, there are a number of seminars, workshops, and programs put together by associations and organizations that are helpful both for their educational value and for the opportunity they provide for developing contacts.

Experience, Skills, and Personality Traits

A & R Coordinators usually have worked in the music business, the record business, and/or radio prior to accepting their positions.

The A & R Coordinator must have a unique type of foresight that comes into play when watching a new act or listening to a new tune. He or she must have that special ability to see past the raw talent to the potential talent an act or record could have. The individual must have the self-confidence to stand by his or her decision and not be swayed.

Unions and Associations

A & R Coordinators may belong to the National Academy of Recording Arts and Sciences (NARAS) as associate members. They might also be members of the Country Music Association (CMA) or the Gospel Music Association (GMA).

Tips for Entry

1. If you are interested in getting into an A & R position, try to get a job in a record company performing any task possible. Many companies promote from within. An energetic, talented, bright individual can move up.
2. You might want to begin your career by checking out local talent. If you can recognize talent, you might very well find it in a local act. You might want to work with this act as a manager or agent. You will be gaining valuable experience.
3. Read the trades and books or magazines on trends in the music and record business. Trends often repeat themselves over a period of years. This information may be useful to your career.
4. Look for a position as an intern with a record company. This will help you gain needed experience and make contacts in the industry.

A & R ADMINISTRATOR

Duties: Plan budgets for artists signed to the record label; deal with clerical functions and administration of the A & R department

Alternate Title(s): Artist and Repetoire Administrator; A & R Administration Representative

Salary Range: $27,000 to $65,000+

Employment Prospects: Poor

Advancement Prospects: Fair

Best Geographical Location(s) for Position: New York City, Los Angeles, and Nashville are music capitals

Prerequisites:

    Education or Training—High school diploma; college degree may be required or preferred by some companies

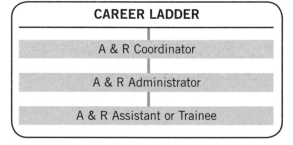

CAREER LADDER

A & R Coordinator

A & R Administrator

A & R Assistant or Trainee

    Experience—Experience in record company is useful; bookkeeping positions are helpful

Special Skills and Personality Traits—Ability to budget; good with numbers; enjoyment of music; written and verbal communication skills; organization; ability to multitask

Position Description

An A & R (Artist and Repetoire) Administrator works in the A & R department along with the A & R coordinators. If the record label is a small one, he or she might assume the duties of both A & R administration and coordination. In a large record label, however, the A & R Administrator is responsible for much of the clerical functions of the department.

The individual is responsible for planning budgets for the artists who are signed to the label. Working on the annual or semiannual budget for the coming year is one of the more important functions of the A & R Administrator. He or she must analyze previous budgets, current acts, and projected estimates of costs. The A & R Administrator must then come up with a working budget for the recording of the acts.

As the year progresses, the individual working in A & R administration keeps an eye on the budget in relation to the expenses. Staying within a budget means that the A & R Administrator is doing his or her job. The individual might work exclusively with one or two studios in order to build up a great volume of studio time. With this volume, the A & R Administrator can often receive discounts on time.

The A & R Administrator keeps track of all monies spent for recording studio time, session musicians, talent, and miscellaneous expenses. These costs are all logged. It is through this log that expenses for each recording act can be tracked.

The A & R Administrator also submits bills and purchase orders to the proper individuals in the accounting department. He or she must make sure that these bills are submitted and paid on time. Union regulations stipulate certain time limits for musicians' payment schedules. A late bill could result in a union dispute.

The A & R Administrator works with the A & R coordinator in monitoring the progress of a label's recording acts in order to determine how much of a project has been recorded, when the record will be ready for release, the amount the recording has cost to date, whether the act is within budget, etc. This information is compiled into reports that are given to various department heads in the recording company.

If the act is receiving tour support from the record company, the A & R Administrator must keep records of all monies laid out on behalf of the group. This is often recouped later from record sale monies.

The A & R Administrator is additionally responsible for obtaining all pertinent information that will be on the completed record packaging. This information includes the name of the group, the members of the group, other musicians who played on the record, producers, tunes, lengths of songs, how the songs will be sequenced on the recording, and any other additional material the act, its management, and the producer want on the packaging.

The A & R Administrator might have to apply for copy-right materials and applications for any songs, tunes, CD covers, etc. that it owns. The A & R Administrator might be responsible for applying for any mechanical rights licenses that are necessary. He or she must make sure that all this is on file.

The A & R Administrator must be very organized. He or she must keep excellent records. The individual is responsible to different people and department heads depending on the company. He or she might be responsible to one of the company's vice-presidents in charge of A & R, or might be responsible to an A & R administrator supervisor.

Salaries

Salaries for A & R Administrators will vary depending on the size of the record label and the qualifications and duties of the individual. Earnings can range from $27,000 to $65,000 plus per year for individuals in these positions.

Employment Prospects

The A & R department is one of the most popular departments in which to work. There are more people who desire jobs in this area than there are openings.

Record companies often promote from within. If an individual is considering a position in an A & R department, he or she may have to enter through a lower-paying job in a different department.

Possibilities for employment also exist at smaller, independent labels that are springing up throughout the country.

Advancement Prospects

Advancement prospects are fair for A & R Administrators working at record labels. Openings often occur as individuals receive promotions, change jobs, obtain new jobs, or move to other labels. As that happens, A&R Administrators may be promoted to A & R coordinators at the same label or land a position at a larger, more prestigious label.

Education and Training

Many record companies require a college degree for this position. Others just ask for a high school diploma. It depends on the label.

College courses or majors that might prove useful include business, accounting and administration. There are colleges around the country with curriculums in the music business.

There are also many seminars, programs, and workshops put together by record companies, associations, organizations, and colleges that are helpful both for their educational value and for the opportunity they provide to develop contacts.

Experience, Skills, and Personality Traits

The individual working in A & R administration must have the ability to plan budgets for recording artists. Certain acts that the company feels will sell more records will have bigger budgets. Newer or lesser known acts must have budgets developed for them that are considerably smaller.

Since most of the job is budgeting or checking bills, the ability to work with numbers is a must. Other areas of the job require the individual to write reports and to keep other departments of the company informed. The A & R Administrator, therefore, must also be able to communicate both on paper and verbally.

Individuals need to be organized people who can multitask effectively.

Unions and Associations

A & R Administrators may belong to the National Academy of Recording Arts and Sciences (NARAS) as associate members. They might also belong to the Country Music Association (CMA) or the Gospel Music Association (GMA), depending on their musical interests.

Tips for Entry

1. Record companies promote from within. If you want to work in the A & R department, try to get a job in a record company doing any type of work you can. Be enthusiastic and ask questions.
2. Read the trades and any other material you can lay your hands on regarding trends in the music business, record deals, etc.
3. If you are in college, see if the school has a summer internship program with a record company for which you can get college credit.
4. There are some minority training programs available at some record companies that can help you get your foot in the door. Check with the personnel departments of individual record companies.

PROMOTION MANAGER

Duties: Supervise promotion department of a record label; obtain airplay for label's records

Alternate Title(s): Promotion Director; Director of Promotion

Salary Range: $27,000 to $95,000+

Employment Prospects: Fair

Advancement Prospects: Fair

Best Geographical Location(s) for Position: New York City, Los Angeles, and Nashville for larger labels; other cities throughout the country for smaller labels

Prerequisites:

Education or Training—High school diploma, minimum for most positions; some jobs require college background or degree

Experience—Working as a promotion rep or in promotion or related department in record company

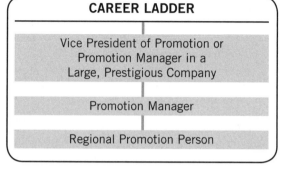

CAREER LADDER

Vice President of Promotion or Promotion Manager in a Large, Prestigious Company

Promotion Manager

Regional Promotion Person

Special Skills and Personality Traits—Ability to sell; communications skills, knowledge of music; supervisory skills; organized; ability to multitask; creativity

Position Description

The Promotion Manager of a record company supervises all the employees in the promotion department. The prime function of everyone in this department is to obtain airplay for as many of the record label's singles and albums as possible.

This is not an easy task. Hundreds of new records are released each week. The promotion department must bring new tunes to radio stations and ask them to review them in hopes of having them added to stations' playlists. As a rule, stations only add a few new songs to their list each week. Most stations play the hits of the week interspersed with a limited number of other songs. These other tunes that are aired may be oldies or potential new hits. The promotional people vie to place their new releases in these slots.

Music television is now also a very viable venue for selling records. The promotion department is in charge of attempting to obtain airplay for music videos, too.

In order to get the stations to listen to and play the label's tunes, the Promotion Manager works with the regional and local representatives who call and visit the program directors or music directors of the radio stations. The Promotion Manager is in charge of deciding where a record should be "broken." It is up to this individual to outline a plan of action. Should the record

be broken in New York City or should it be tried out first in a key market in the South? The individual must know what areas are good for what types of songs. The person must also be aware of what formats are available at which radio stations in all given markets.

The Promotion Manager is responsible for devising any type of promotion that he or she feels will help get the records aired. The individual may work with other departments in putting these together. These might, for example, include the merchandising department. Using this department, the Promotion Manager could have T-shirts, tour jackets, bumper stickers, pins, etc., designed and made up on behalf of an act or its album. The Promotion Manager might arrange interviews, television appearances, promotional appearances, or press conferences through the publicity department.

The manager of this department may also work with the advertising department. This, too, is an important method of getting potential airplay. The Promotion Manager may feel that a group needs a little extra push that could be gained through some advertising exposure. The department heads decide together how much should be spent on this project, how to go about the task, and the route they want to take in gaining the exposure.

The manager of the promotion department is in charge of scheduling regular meetings with the staff. At these meetings, any problems will be discussed and suggestions given for rectifying difficulties. This may also be the time when statistics on the label's records are given out, for example, how many of which records are selling, which record was added to what stations' playlists, reviews of records in the trades, etc.

In this position, the individual will work closely with, and reports to, the vice-president of the department. In smaller companies, the person might also be the vice-president and be responsible to the president or CEO. Together they create overall promotional campaigns that can be put into motion. They also discuss which methods of promotion have worked and which have failed.

Success in this position is shown by how many of the label's records are on major stations' playlists. The Promotion Manager at a record label works long hours trying to attain this success, often under quite a bit of stress.

Salaries

Annual earnings of Promotion Managers will differ depending on the size, prestige, and location of the record label as well as the experience and duties of the individual. Salaries can range from $27,000 at one of the new, smaller independent labels to $95,000 plus at a large, well-known one.

Employment Prospects

It is difficult to obtain a position as a Promotion Manager at one of the very large, well-known labels. Those who aspire to do this must first work as promotion reps and regional managers for these labels.

It is possible to locate a position, however, after a bit of experience in some of the smaller independent labels that are springing up. While the salaries are low, the experience gained can make it worthwhile.

Advancement Prospects

Advancement possibilities are fair for Promotion Managers in record companies. The most frequent career path taken is usually that of finding a similar position in a larger, more prestigious company. Other possibilities for career advancement for the Promotion Manager include becoming the vice-president of the promotion department or heading up a related department.

Education and Training

Educational requirements vary from label to label. The minimum educational requirement for a Promotion Manager at most labels is a high school diploma.

Depending on the position and the label, that might be sufficient. Jobs at major labels usually require a college degree.

Experience, Skills, and Personality Traits

The Promotion Manager must know not only how to do his or her job, but also how to supervise others in the department. This individual is often in charge of many people. He or she must have the ability to guide them and direct their work.

Most Promotion Managers in this field are good sales-people. They know how to persuade people at radio and music television stations to listen to their records and watch their videos. They also know how to convince stations to add those records to their playlist.

In this job, the individual must stay well-informed on all types of music, other records, target markets, etc. The Promotion Manager should also be creative and personable.

Unions and Associations

A Promotion Manager in a record company may belong to a number of organizations and associations. He or she may be a member of the Country Music Association (CMA) or the Gospel Music Association (GMA), among others. The individual might also be an associate member of the National Academy of Recording Arts and Sciences (NARAS).

Tips for Entry

1. Many of the larger record labels, as well as a number of the smaller ones, have internship programs. Ask to work in the promotion department.
2. If there is not an internship program at the label of your choice, call or write to the promotion manager or vice president of promotion to see if you can create one. Keep in mind that the pay in an intern program is minimal, if there is any salary at all. You might, however, be able to get college credit.
3. Colleges with music merchandising and music business programs often have work-study programs within the industry. This is another excellent way to get experience.
4. Employment agencies in larger cities that host some of the better-known labels often seek out personnel for these types of positions.
5. Openings may be advertised in any of the trade magazines or in local newspaper display or classified sections. Look under heading classifications of "Music," "Records," or "Promotion."

PROMOTION STAFFER

Duties: Visit and call radio station program directors; try to get airplay for the label's albums

Alternate Title(s): Promotion Man (or Woman); Regional Staff Promotion Person; Local Promotion Person; Record Promoter; Promotional Representative

Salary Range: $27,000 to $65,000+

Employment Prospects: Fair

Advancement Prospects: Fair

Best Geographical Location(s) for Position: New York City, Los Angeles, and Nashville for positions with major record companies; other locations for independent promoters (reps may work in various locations)

Prerequisites:

Education or Training—Minimum of high school diploma; college degree may be required or preferred; see text

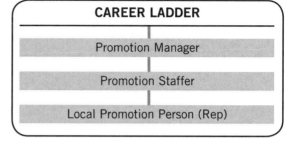

CAREER LADDER

Promotion Manager

Promotion Staffer

Local Promotion Person (Rep)

Experience—Sales jobs helpful; working in music business, radio, etc., useful; see text

Special Skills and Personality Traits—Sales skills; personable; music knowledge; aggressiveness; communications skills; organization

Position Description

A Promotion Staffer working at a record label has one prime function: to get airplay for the label's albums and/or music videos. To accomplish this, the Promotion Staffer or representative visits and calls radio and music station program directors and music directors.

Promotion Staffer may be assigned a certain category of music—for example, R & B, pop, gospel, rap, etc. They are also assigned territories. There are a number of different markets in which Promotion People generally work. This is where they hope to "break" records.

Promotion Staffers work closely with program directors, music directors, and disc jockeys in these markets. The first thing the Promotion Staffer does is to set up appointments with these station people. When the label's Promotion Staffer goes on appointments he or she will bring a number of the label's new releases. He or she also brings along a supply of promo or press material and videos about the artists who made the CDs.

The individual will sit with the radio station personnel and listen to the new releases. The Promotion Staffer hopes that the program director or the music director will like the song well enough to add it to the station's playlist. The staffer may leave copies of the CDs with the radio station staff to listen to at their leisure.

Individuals visit a number of stations in each area covered.

In this position, the individual might do quite a bit of socializing. Promotion Staffers often take key radio and music television personnel out to lunch, dinner, or for drinks. They might also bring a program director to a club to listen to a group play a song live and gauge audience response.

The individual must do research in order to get stations to play records or music videos. He or she may talk to Promotion Staffers in other markets to determine how a specific tune is doing. The individual must also check with various record stores to see what kind of sales a CD has in a specific area. He or she may check into the total sales of the CD in the label's sales department. Any number of other methods to develop information on the reason a radio station should play a record may be employed.

At certain times, the promotion people will use the phone and mail to reach disc jockeys, program directors, and music directors. This system of mailing promotional copies of CDs, videos, and press material to stations and then following up with phone calls is frequently used in smaller areas. These smaller locations usually do not have the market potential to justify visits, but may be important just the same.

Salaries

Salaries for Promotion Staffers will vary depending on the size of the record company and the experience and duties of the individual. Salaries range from $27,000 to $65,000 plus annually.

Employment Prospects

Employment prospects are fair for those people who can obtain entry into a record company. There are usually quite a number of Promotion People working for each major company. Individuals who have built up a good reputation in other record companies working in this position generally will not find any problem getting a job. Other individuals may gain entry in local promotion positions. Individuals may also find openings at smaller, independent labels.

Advancement Prospects

Advancement prospects are fair for Promotion Staffers. Individuals who have a good track record for getting radio stations to listen to CDs and put them on their playlist may land a better job at a larger, more prestigious label. A Promotion Staffer who has proven him or herself may also be promoted to the position of director of promotion at the label.

Education and Training

Educational requirements vary for positions as Promotion Staffers. While a college degree doesn't guarantee a job in the music industry, it certainly doesn't hurt. It also helps in career advancement. Smaller, independent labels may just require a high school diploma. Major labels often require or prefer a college degree.

Experience, Skills, and Personality Traits

Individuals working in the promotion field are generally interested in music, records, and radio. Some of these individuals have worked in one of these three areas at a prior time while others have been involved with product sales or a variety of different positions.

Promotion Staffers need to be able to sell. While they may not be selling a product directly, they are selling the sound of a CD. Promotion Staffers are judged on how many CDs or videos they can get radio or music television stations to add to their playlists. In order to do this, it is necessary for the Promotion Staffer to stay on top of the music and the record industry and be well-informed about all phases of it. The individual must additionally be pleasantly aggressive and articulate.

Unions and Associations

Promotion Staffers may belong to the Gospel Music Association (GMA), the Country Music Association (CMA), or other similar associations depending on the type of music they promote. Additionally, they may belong to the National Academy of Recording Arts and Sciences (NARAS) as associate members.

Tips for Entry

1. There are internship programs available in many record companies. Check directly with the various companies.
2. It helps to have contacts to get into a position in a record company. If you have any, this is the time to use them.
3. There are minority training programs available in some record companies. If you qualify, check these out.
4. Enter the record company in any way possible. Apply for a position as a secretary, receptionist, mailroom clerk, etc. These companies promote from within.
5. Check out the classifieds in *Billboard* magazine. You might see an opening.

DIRECTOR OF PUBLICITY

Position Description

The Director of Publicity at a record label is in charge of the entire publicity and/or press relations department of the label. As director, he or she supervises all the work that is performed by the staff of the department.

The director assigns to the staff publicists the various acts that the label has signed. He or she then works with the act, its management, and the staff publicists, developing a viable publicity campaign.

Once the campaign is put into motion by the staff publicist, the director oversees all aspects of that campaign. In certain cases, the Director of Publicity will handle personally the publicity requirements of a number of the label's "top" artists.

With the current influx of smaller, independent record labels in the music industry, the Director of Publicity may be the only person in the publicity department or may work with a secretary and/or an administrative assistant. In these cases, the individual will handle all publicity functions.

The Director of Publicity meets regularly with members of the publicity staff, discussing strategies, media, and problems that have occurred. He or she also meets regularly with other department heads of the record label to talk about publicity campaign strategies for various acts on the label. The individual additionally works closely with the label's marketing and artist relations departments as well as the A & R and promotion departments.

The Director of Publicity gathers information from staff members in the form of publicity reports concerning each act they are assigned to. These reports are then submitted to various executives of the company.

At times, the individual works with an act's private publicist or public relations firms, trying to work together to produce as much good press as possible.

The Director of Publicity is in charge of approving major expenditures for publicity projects such as major press parties, photo sessions, press giveaways, etc. Depending on the structure of the company, these expenditures must usually be approved for the Director of Publicity by other department heads.

As Director of Publicity, the individual will ensure that all campaigns are on schedule. He or she might see that an act is not receiving as much publicity as it should. In this case, the director must determine why. Perhaps the act is uncooperative. Possibly the publicist assigned to the act is not doing a good job. There are any number of problems that may arise. It is the director's job to identify the difficulty and resolve it.

The favorable publicity each act receives helps achieve the ultimate goal of selling records.

The Director of the Publicity Department will often attend press parties and other functions for both the label's artists and others as well. In this way, the Director can mingle and talk with the press on a range of subjects.

A Director of Publicity must evaluate persons working on the publicity staff. If one of the staffers is not working up to par, the director may find it necessary to fire the individual (or recommend that the person be let go). On the other hand, the director might also have the authority to promote (or recommend for promotion) a talented individual.

The Director of Publicity at a record company works long hours. After everyone else has gone home, he or she might still be making calls to publicize the label's acts.

Salaries

Salaries for Directors of Publicity working in a record company will vary greatly depending on the size and the prestige of the label. Individuals working for very small individual labels might earn from $35,000 to $40,000 annually. Those working in larger companies with more and better-known acts will earn between $40,000 and $55,000 per year. The Director of Publicity who is employed by a major record label can earn between $50,000 and $100,000 plus per year.

Employment Prospects

Competition for all jobs in record labels is high and this position is no exception. Prospects are better because of the many independent labels springing up around the country. It is not easy to find a position as the Director of Publicity for a major record label without some type of experience. Major record companies want to have people on staff in this position who have proven themselves either at their company or at another.

Those who seek this position will have an easier time breaking in at smaller or independent labels. These companies are springing up throughout the country.

Advancement Prospects

Advancement prospects for the Director of Publicity in a record company are fair. Individuals may move up the career ladder by being promoted to the position of vice president of press relations and publicity. This would mean more responsibility as well as a higher salary. The individual may also be promoted to any of a host of other top executive positions.

Other possibilities for advancement for the Director of Publicity include finding similar positions in larger, more prestigious record companies. The individual may also open up his or her own publicity firm, handling publicity and public relations for music industry clients.

Education and Training

Different labels have different educational requirements. Many, especially some of the newer, independent labels, do not specify the necessity of a college degree, although most Directors of Publicity have attended college.

A degree or courses in public relations, communications, publicity, marketing and/or music merchandising is useful. There are also a number of seminars and/or courses offered in public relations and publicity by colleges and organizations such as the Public Relations Society of America (PRSA).

Experience, Skills, and Personality Traits

Directors of Publicity for record companies usually have worked in publicity positions prior to their appointment. A great deal of the time, they worked in a publicity department of a record company. Many individuals also worked as music critics, journalists, or for independent publicity or public relations firms.

The Publicity Director at a record label must have the basic public relations and publicity skills of writing and communicating. He or she must also have the ability to supervise others.

It is helpful to enjoy the type of music that the label's clients play (although it is not a necessity) because the individual has to listen to so much of it.

Unions and Associations

Directors of Publicity at record companies are not usually members of any union. They might, however, belong to a number of organizations and associations. One of these is the Public Relations Society of America (PRSA). There are also a number of music associations that the individual might join, including the Country Music Association (CMA), the Gospel Music Association (GMA), and the National Academy of Recording Arts and Sciences (NARAS). These groups all work to promote a specific type of music. Some of them provide internships, scholarships, seminars, and other practical help.

Tips for Entry

1. Positions are often advertised in the classified sections of newspapers in the major music capitals. Look under "Music," "Record Label," or "Public Relations" heading classifications.

2. Get experience at a small, independent record label where it is easier to get your foot in the door. You might be the only person in the department, but it will give you wide-ranging experience in the field that will look impressive on your résumé.

3. Send your résumé and a cover letter to record company personnel departments. If a position isn't open at the time, request that your résumé be kept on file.

4. If a job requirement specifies experience with a record label publicity department and you don't have it, don't let that discourage you from applying for the job. You must, however, have something to spark the interest of the person who might interview you or accept your application. For example, you might bring a portfolio of press clippings for an act you worked with in a private firm or while you were self-employed.

5. Openings may be advertised in the classified section of trade publications such as *Billboard*.

6. Don't forget to check for openings online. Record label Web sites often list job openings.

STAFF PUBLICIST

CAREER PROFILE

Duties: Handle the publicity and press needs of acts signed to a label

Alternate Title(s): Press Agent

Salary Range: $25,000 to $80,000+

Employment Prospects: Fair

Advancement Prospects: Fair

Best Geographical Location(s) for Position: New York City, Los Angeles, and Nashville are music capitals; smaller labels located throughout the country

Prerequisites:

Education or Training—College degree or background in journalism, communications, music business, or music merchandising helpful

Experience—Positions in music- or nonmusic-oriented publicity and public relations

Special Skills and Personality Traits—Ability to write; creativity; persuasive manner; ability to work under pressure; enjoyment of music; creativity; communication skills

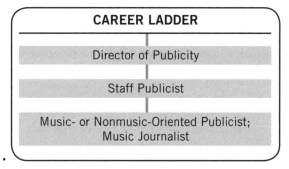

CAREER LADDER

Director of Publicity

Staff Publicist

Music- or Nonmusic-Oriented Publicist; Music Journalist

Position Description

Publicists on staff in record companies perform many different functions. The main goal of the department is to get as much good publicity for the artists signed to the label as possible. Publicity helps the label sell records and that is the primary way the company produces income.

A beginning Staff Publicist may do just clerical types of work, such as assembling press kits. He or she may start by gathering information for the press kits or by writing simple press releases.

As the Staff Publicist gains more experience, he or she will be writing more creative press releases. Eventually the publicist will work with the act on developing publicity strategies for their press campaign.

As a Staff Publicist, an individual must be able to get an artist's name in the news (magazines, trades, TV, radio, online, etc.) as often as possible. This is accomplished by writing press releases, sending them to the correct media, talking to media about acts, arranging interviews, etc.

The Staff Publicist often arranges a series of print interviews, radio interviews, and TV appearances in conjunction with the release of a new record.

He or she may either keep the information on the group going to the media in a shotgun approach or release information selectively. This would depend on the type of campaign that has been chosen for the act prior to the record's release.

When Staff Publicists have something very important going on with one of their artists, they usually plan a press party or press conference to announce it. These press parties and conferences must only be used for special events. If this caution is not heeded, the media might not be interested on the next occasion, although the publicist may really have something important to unveil. In addition, because of the great expense of these press functions, executives usually like them limited in frequency.

Staff Publicists are on the phone a great deal of the time, calling media and trying to interest them in what is happening with their acts. When they are not on the phone or writing releases, publicists are often at parties or functions meeting with the press and other people important to their clients.

Staff Publicists are usually the first ones to send out promotional copies of new records and other important materials to the media. After a new record is released, the publicist might work with the A & R department or the promotion department on a showcase booking of the group. The publicist might then decide that this is the proper time for an all-important press party.

The Staff Publicist working for a record company often works closely with an act's personal publicist or P.R. firm. (Acts hire personal publicists and P.R. firms because they want more attention than a label publicist can give them.) Label Staff Publicists often work with up to 10 acts each. As a rule, label publicists zero in on creating publicity that will potentially sell more records. Personal publicists work to create an image for the artist that will help to sustain him or her in the business longer.

The Staff Publicist's hours are not the regular nine to five most people work. Publicists work a long regular day and then go out to parties, clubs, and other functions to mingle with the press or to listen to acts they represent.

It is also the Staff Publicist's job to set up interviews and appearances with the media when the act goes on tour. During big tours the publicist works with a tour publicist and other tour personnel, coordinating tour publicity.

The Staff Publicist is usually responsible to the director of publicity at the label. All the Staff Publicists meet regularly with this individual to map out strategies and handle any problems that come up.

Salaries

Salaries for Staff Publicists vary depending on the size of the record label one is working for and the amount of experience the publicist has. Salaries can range from $25,000 for a beginning publicist or a publicist at a small label, to $55,000 at a bigger label. Salaries for Staff Publicists can go up to $80,000 or more yearly if the publicist is experienced, working at a big label, and has a great deal of responsibility. This salary level is rare, though. The average salary range for a Staff Publicist would be from $40,000 to $60,000 annually.

Employment Prospects

If an individual can write well and is creative, he or she has a decent chance of landing a position in the publicity department at a record label.

There is a fairly high turnover of people in this department because individuals move around to various record labels. Bigger labels sometimes have an entry-level position in publicity. However, the individual might only fill press kits. As one gets more experience, he or she is usually given less tedious work and more interesting projects.

It is sometimes easier for an individual to find a job as a Staff Publicist in a record company (because you can start out in an entry-level position and move out of it fairly quickly), than as a publicist in a music-oriented P.R. firm.

Advancement Prospects

As noted throughout this section, most positions in the record business allow for advancement fairly routinely. This is especially so in nonsupervisory capacities.

Staff Publicists who do well at their jobs move into better positions in the department, such as supervising others or handling more prestigious clients.

Publicists with a proven track record at one label can usually find a job at another label without too much trouble.

Staff Publicists also often gain experience at a label and then strike out on their own as independent publicists or with a P.R. firm.

Education and Training

Different positions in publicity require different amounts and types of education. Not all positions at record companies require college degrees or backgrounds. However, these applicants are often preferred.

College courses or majors that might prove useful in this type of position include public relations, marketing, advertising, music merchandising, journalism, and communications.

In addition, there are a number of seminars offered by different organizations, associations, and colleges on publicity, promotion, and public relations as related to the music business.

Experience, Skills, and Personality Traits

A Staff Publicist working in a record company must be able to work under pressure, as deadlines must be met on a constant basis.

Publicists must have the ability to write well. Creativity is a plus; it helps to come up with new angles for acts. The Staff Publicist must constantly make new media contacts, as these people can make or break an act.

As the Staff Publicist must go out after working hours quite frequently, he or she must have a lot of stamina and not mind having a business life and social life wrapped in one. Enjoying and appreciating music, especially the music of the acts being promoted, is helpful, too.

Unions and Associations

Staff Publicists working in a record company may belong to the Public Relations Society of America (PRSA). This organization is one of the best-known in the publicity and public relations field. It offers seminars, booklets, a magazine, and other helpful information to members.

The individual might also belong to the National Academy of Recording Arts and Sciences (NARAS) as an associate member.

Tips for Entry

1. Find out if the record company has an internship program and try to get into it. It's worth working

for nothing (or a small salary) or even college credit for a summer or a short period of time if you can gain entry into one of these programs. Not only is the experience worthwhile, but you also have an excellent chance of being hired after the internship ends.

2. Prepare your résumé and a few samples of your writing style. Send these with a cover letter to personnel departments or publicity directors of record companies.

3. There are a number of employment agencies specializing in public relations and publicity jobs. Call or write to them about openings in the record companies.

4. There are also a limited number of employment agencies specializing in jobs in the music business. Check these out.

5. If you have any contacts in the record business, this is the time to use them. See if they will help you get your foot in the door.

6. Openings are often advertised in trade publications such as *Billboard*.

7. Check out record label Web sites for employment openings.

ARTIST RELATIONS AND DEVELOPMENT REPRESENTATIVE

Duties: Act as a liaison between a record company and one or more of their signed artists

Alternate Title(s): Artist Relations and Development Staffer

Salary Range: $29,000 to $68,000+

Employment Prospects: Poor

Advancement Prospects: Fair

Best Geographical Locations for Position: New York City, Los Angeles, and Nashville are music capitals; smaller labels may be located throughout the country

Prerequisites:

    Education or Training—High school diploma minimum; college degree may be preferred; see text

    Experience—Experience in public relations, publicity, or artist management helpful

CAREER LADDER

Artist Relations and Development Director

Artist Relations and Development Representative

Publicist/P.R. Counselor; Intern

Special Skills and Personality Traits—Knowledge of music and record business; ability to deal effectively with people; organized; detail oriented; personable

Position Description

The Artist Relations and Development Representative is a position that is not present in every record label. Certain companies either are too small to retain people in this position, or they delegate the responsibilities normally taken care of by the Artist Relations and Development Representative to other departments.

Duties of the Artist Relations and Development Representative differ, too, depending on the company. If the record company does have this department, most often it is the representative's responsibility to act as a liaison between the company and its artists. The representative makes sure that the artist feels that the record company is treating him or her specially. For example, the Artist Relations and Development Rep might send roses on behalf of the record company to a singer whose record just went gold. The rep might make sure that a group is sent champagne before kicking off a prestigious tour. In essence, the Artist Relations and Development Representative makes sure that there is a good relationship between the artists and the record company, not only businesswise, but socially, too. The record business is unique in that business life and social life often blend into one.

The Artist Relations and Development Representative keeps in close contact with the act and its man-

agement. He or she listens for potential problems that might involve the record company. When the individual hears of any developing problems, he or she takes care of them (or, if unable to solve the problems, brings them to the attention of someone who can).

The Artist Relations and Development Representative works with the act and its management to help build the act's career. The reps work with all the different departments of the record company, such as planning promotional concert tours in conjunction with CD releases. The rep makes sure that the tour coincides with the CD release. If it turns out that a tour has to begin three weeks later than anticipated, the rep might discuss the option of holding up the release for a short time with the record company executives.

The Artist Relations and Development Representative might also work with the publicity department or the group's P.R. firm in coordinating television, radio, and promotional public appearances.

At times, the individual will attend an act's concert and review the performance. He or she might make suggestions on how the act could improve the performance or stage presentation.

The Artist Relations and Development Representative usually becomes quite friendly with the act and its management team. He or she might remain friends with the act long after its recording contract has expired and the group has moved on to another company.

This is another position in the record industry in which long, irregular hours are maintained. To be successful at this job, an individual must really love both music and people.

Salaries

An Artist Relations and Development Representative has a salary range of $29,000 to $68,000 or more annually. The salary of the individual will depend on the size of the record company he or she is working with. Salary is also dependent on the individual's duties and qualifications.

Employment Prospects

Since not every record label has this position, it is often difficult to find openings. Once again, there are many people who want to work in this department of a record company and a limited number of positions.

Individuals who cannot find work in this position might want to look for jobs in publicity and public relations. Then, when an opening is located, the individual will already have experience in the field.

Advancement Prospects

As in most positions in a record company, once an individual gets his or her foot in the door, there is a fair chance for advancement and promotion. In order to be promoted, there must be an opening in an advanced position. Individuals may direct their careers into other departments for advancement.

Education and Training

Educational requirements vary for positions as Artist Relations and Development Representatives. Smaller, independent labels may require only a high school diploma. Majors labels generally require or prefer a college degree. Even if a label does not require a college degree, having one might be the one thing that distinguishes one applicant from another. Good choices for majors include music merchandising, music business, public relations, marketing, communications, or related fields.

Courses, workshops, and seminars in publicity, promotion, journalism, and communications will be help-

ful. Workshops and seminars directed toward any area of the music business will be especially useful both for the educational value and the opportunity to develop important contacts.

Experience, Skills, and Personality Traits

Most individuals who work in the artist relations and development department have had some type of experience in promotion, publicity, or public relations. Others have worked in artist management.

The successful Artist Relations and Development Representative must have a knowledge of both music and the record business. He or she must attend many shows and concerts, concentrating on other acts and their stage appearances, concerts, performances, etc.

He or she must not only have the ability to deal with people, but like to do so. Since record companies cannot comply with every request an act has, the Rep must have the ability to deny some requests and still keep the group relatively happy.

Unions and Associations

The Artist Relations and Development Representative in a record company might belong to the Country Music Association (CMA) or the Gospel Music Association (GMA), depending on the variety of musical artists he or she represents. The individual may also be an associate member of the National Academy of Recording Arts and Sciences (NARAS).

Tips for Entry

1. Attend as many seminars and programs as you can to learn the business and develop contacts.
2. As with many other record company jobs, you might have to accept an entry-level position to get to the position you want. People are promoted if they have the drive and the qualifications.
3. Try to find a record company with either a summer internship program or a college internship program and request to be placed in this department. This way you will have an "in" when you finish school.
4. You might also want to check into label-sponsored minority training programs.
5. Check out record label Web sites for possible job openings.

MARKETING REPRESENTATIVE

Position Description

A Marketing Representative for a record company may work on a local or regional level. The prime function of the marketing department in the record company is to develop various ways to market and sell the company's CDs. The Marketing Representative will help execute this function.

Depending on the position held, the Marketing Representative oversees marketing activities in a certain area. A local rep will oversee specific markets. The regional rep will oversee entire regions. For example, a local rep may be in charge of the marketing in Philadelphia. The regional Marketing Representative or director would be in charge of the entire northeast section of the United States, which would include Philadelphia.

Regardless of territory, the individuals have the same function and duties. The first, mentioned above, is to oversee the marketing of the CDs. To accomplish this, the reps will work under the supervision of the director of marketing to assist in implementing such marketing strategies as delivering displays for a number of the label's hot acts to record shops or setting up window displays in the record stores. Other ideas might not involve stores directly. The concepts might revolve around radio station giveaway contests with the label's new CDs or T-shirts, bumper stickers, posters, etc., as prizes. The marketing department often offers radio stations and record shops in a specific area joint pro-

motions, such as promotional appearances in a record shop by a hot group combined with radio station CD giveaways. Similarly, the marketing department may work on promotions with various music-oriented Web sites or online stores.

The Marketing Representative is also responsible for calling and/or visiting record stores in a specific area to make sure that they have sufficient products on hand to meet possible demands. This often occurs after a group has won an award or a gold record or before a concert in the city.

The Marketing Representative gets reports of record sales from the various shops and stores in the specific market. He or she will call these in to the radio stations, music television stations, major trades, and tip sheets. This is the method many record stores and radio stations use to develop the music charts.

The Marketing Representative reports directly to his or her supervisor; in most cases, that is the director of marketing. The local rep may also report to the regional director of marketing. Hours are irregular. There is often a great deal of travel associated with this job.

Salaries

Salaries for Marketing Representatives vary according to the positions they hold and the companies they work for. A marketing rep can expect $27,000 to $50,000 or more annually.

Employment Prospects

Employment prospects are fair for those seeking positions as Marketing Representatives. Major record labels hire a fairly large number of people in this position. One of the better ways of getting a job in the marketing department is by working as in intern for the department.

Advancement Prospects

Marketing Representatives can advance their careers by becoming regional reps or regional directors of marketing. The individual may be promoted to the position of marketing director or a specific type of music, such as country or adult contemporary music, gospel music, etc. The rep can further advance his or her career by becoming the national marketing director of a label.

Education and Training

Educational requirements vary for record label Marketing Representatives. While smaller labels may require individuals to hold only a high school diploma, major labels generally require their Marketing Representatives to hold a college degree.

Good majors might include marketing, advertising, and communications. There are also a number of colleges offering music-business or music-merchandising degrees. While these degrees do not guarantee a job, they are helpful in preparing for a career.

No matter what the major, courses in marketing business, advertising, and so forth will be useful.

Experience, Skills, and Personality Traits

Experience in a record company is useful for work in this field. One of the best ways to get this experience is to look for an intern position in the department. These jobs give the individual an invaluable hands-on learning experience.

Marketing Representatives must also be literate, articulate, and good with numbers. Creativity is a plus. Understanding of the music business and a complete knowledge of the record industry is essential.

Unions and Associations

Marketing Representatives may belong to a number of associations. These include the Country Music Association (CMA), the Gospel Music Association (GMA), the National Academy of Recording Arts and Sciences (NARAS), and a host of others.

Tips for Entry

1. Try to find an internship in a record company's marketing department. This opportunity might come through either the record company or a college.
2. If you already have a job in a record company, possibly in the clerical end, volunteer to do some work for the marketing department. Learn the business.
3. Get a job in a large record store and make contacts with Marketing Representatives who visit and/or call the store. They might be able to get you an appointment for an interview.
4. Positions are often advertised in trade publications such as *Billboard*.
5. Openings may also be listed on record label Web sites.

CONSUMER RESEARCHER

Duties: Research and analyze consumer buying practices for the record company

Alternate Title(s): Market Researcher; Market Analyst

Salary Range: $24,000 to $47,000+

Employment Prospects: Fair

Advancement Prospects: Fair

Best Geographical Location(s) for Position: New York City, Los Angeles, and Nashville offer the most opportunities

Prerequisites:

    Education or Training—Bachelor's degree in business usually preferred; master's degree sometimes required

    Experience—Working as a research assistant or trainee in any field; conducting interviews and opinion polls

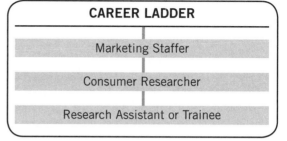

Special Skills and Personality Traits—Knowledge of research and analytical methods; ability to write reports; knowledge of music business and record industry

Position Description

The marketing and/or sales departments of record companies hire Consumer Researchers. These people have interesting jobs. Their main function is to research consumer buying practices for the record company. After the data have been compiled, they must be analyzed by the Consumer Researcher. With this information the marketing and/or sales department can develop a better understanding of the various types of records people want to buy through examination of what has been previously purchased.

The Consumer Researcher—or market researcher, as he or she is sometimes referred to—may secure information on the record-buying public in a number of ways. The first step the individual usually takes is to decide the method or methods that will be used in finding information. The Consumer Researcher may collect facts from the record company and its various departments. Information sought out includes the types of records that have sold previously; the number of CDs of each style that were sold during a certain time period (e.g., pop, classical, country, adult contemporary, etc.); and the geographical location in which each variety sold well.

The individual might then research facts about records that were sold on other labels. This is usu-

ally much more difficult, as companies seldom like to disclose sales information to their competitors. However, the Consumer Researcher may talk to distributors, record shops, rack jobbers, etc., to gather such data.

Another method of checking out consumer buying practices is to prepare a survey. An interview might be given by the individual directly, or he or she might train a number of people in a variety of markets to handle the project. The Consumer Researcher might also choose to interview consumers by phone on their buying habits. Today many companies do research by surveying people's music buying habits on the Web. All of the different methods may be used to secure results.

After the surveys or the interviews have been completed, the Consumer Researcher will have to tabulate and analyze the data collected. From these surveys, the individual very often can obtain information about customer opinions and tastes in record buying. This tells the marketing and/or sales department what type of records to market, the best sales locations, and more effective ways to do the job.

The Consumer Researcher in a record company must be very knowledgeable about records, target markets, the music business, and the recording industry in order to know the types of questions to ask in a survey or opinion poll. Individuals in this field work closely with the marketing director and the department staff. The Consumer Researcher may recommend test marketing of certain records in specific areas. In other situations, the individual may recommend for or against the release of a certain record in an area because of his or her test marketing. The head of the marketing department has the option of listening to recommendations or ignoring them. The amount of authority the Consumer Researcher has, of course, depends on the position and the structure of the department.

Salaries

Consumer Researchers working for record companies may earn $25,000 to $47,000 plus annually. Salaries will depend on the size of the record company, its location, and the qualifications and duties of the Consumer Researcher.

Employment Prospects

Those who are qualified have a fair chance of obtaining a job as a Consumer Researcher in a record company. Marketing and/or sales departments of major labels usually hire a good number of Consumer Researchers. Smaller labels frequently hire a limited number, too.

There is competition in every phase of the record company, especially in larger labels. The more qualified an individual is for this job, the better his or her chances for employment.

Advancement Prospects

Consumer Researchers may advance their careers in a number of ways. The individual may assume responsibility for bigger and better projects. He or she might move into a supervisory position in the research department. Another possibility for advancement is for the individual to become a member of the marketing staff—a marketing coordinator or vice president of marketing. As in all positions in record companies, advancement really depends on the individual and on the structure of the company.

Education and Training

A good education is necessary for this type of job. A bachelor's degree is usually required. A master's degree is sometimes preferred. Majors may be in business administration, marketing, or any related field. Courses in computer technology or data processing are extremely helpful.

Experience, Skills, and Personality Traits

Individuals who aspire to get into the marketing end of the recording industry may be interested in consumer research. Those who become Consumer Researchers need the know-how to delve into consumer buying habits. The Consumer Researcher must know how to analyze the data and render an understandable final report for supervisors. In order to excel at this type of job, a thorough knowledge of the music business and recording industry is essential.

Unions and Associations

Consumer Researchers may belong to advertising associations, such as the American Advertising Federation (AAF) or the American Marketing Association (AMA). Both of these organizations provide information and assistance to people in this field.

Tips for Entry

1. Get experience in consumer research in any field.
2. Become a pollster for a new product, a corporation, a new service, etc.
3. This is one of the jobs in which a good education really helps. The more qualified you are, the better your chance of employment.
4. These jobs are often advertised in the classified sections of newspapers in the major music capitals.
5. You also might be able to locate openings online. Check the traditional job search sites like monster.com and hotjobs.com and go from there.

ADVERTISING ACCOUNT EXECUTIVE

Duties: Develop advertising campaigns for a record label's products

Alternate Title(s): Account Representative

Salary Range: $29,000 to $60,000+

Employment Prospects: Fair

Advancement Prospects: Fair

Best Geographical Location(s) for Position: New York City, Los Angeles, and Nashville offer the most opportunities

Prerequisites:

Education or Training—College degree in advertising, marketing, or a related area preferred

Experience—Copywriter; advertising executive in nonmusic-related agency

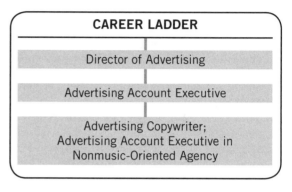

CAREER LADDER

Director of Advertising

Advertising Account Executive

Advertising Copywriter; Advertising Account Executive in Nonmusic-Oriented Agency

Special Skills and Personality Traits—Creativity; ability to work under pressure; knowledge of advertising skills and technology; cognizance of music and record industry

Position Description

An Advertising Account Executive in a record company develops advertising campaigns for the label's products. The main purpose of the advertising campaign is to make the public aware that a certain album has been released and is in the stores. If people know about an album, it is hoped, they will buy it.

The Advertising Account Executive or representative, as he or she may be called, is usually assigned a certain number of acts and/or records to work with. This assignment generally comes from the director of the advertising department.

A lot of work goes into planning an advertising campaign for a new album. The Advertising Account Executive may study other campaigns used for the specific artist and/or record or might look over other programs. The individual will consider the act's public image and decide what type of people the advertising should target. For example, if the account executive is developing a campaign for a rap recording act, the individual will gear the advertising to young people. If an act has put out a hard rock album, the Advertising Account Executive will gear the advertising to that audience.

Depending on the size and the structure of the record company, the Advertising Account Executive may not only have to develop advertising campaigns for the new records, but may also have to do the artwork

and/or copywriting, too. The advertising representative may also have to negotiate contracts for advertising space or air time.

The Advertising Account Executive in the record company must have a total understanding of the recording industry and the acts and/or records for which he or she is developing campaigns. The individual needs to work with many of the other departments in the record company to obtain useful information and ideas for an advertising program. For example, the account representative may work with the promotion or publicity departments, putting together a total campaign that includes advertising, promotional appearances in record stores, and television and radio interviews.

In this position, the individual must have the ability to know which types of advertising will be most effective for the money. He or she must decide whether ads should be run on TV or radio, in newspapers, magazines, or trades, or on billboards, etc. Decisions must also be made as to which ads should be run locally and which ads should be run nationally. Often, when a large record store or chain advertises a specific record or group of records, the label picks up the cost of the ad. With more and more online stores selling CDs and records, the Internet must also be considered a viable advertising medium.

It is very important for the Advertising Account Executive to be able to stay within the budget allocated to each record.

Advertising Account Executives have frequent meetings with the director of the department. During these sessions new concepts, problems, and budgets are discussed. It is also during these times that the effectiveness of the campaigns are evaluated.

The individual in this job works long hours. He or she is responsible to the director of advertising.

Salaries

Advertising Account Executives in a record company earn from $29,000 to $60,000 plus annually. Salaries vary depending on the size of the record company and the experience and duties of the individual.

Employment Prospects

Employment prospects are fair for an individual who is trained and qualified in this area. Those who are knowledgeable about both advertising and the recording industry have better prospects. The Advertising Account Executive who has proven him- or herself in this field should be able to find employment. Large and mid-size record companies usually have advertising departments. Many of the smaller labels use the services of an outside advertising agency.

Advancement Prospects

Prospects are fair for an Advertising Account Executive working in a record company. To move up the career ladder, the individual can seek out the same type of position in a larger, more prestigious company. This type of advancement means more responsibility and a higher salary. The individual may move into the position of director of advertising in a record company. Many Advertising Account Executives obtain jobs in advertising agencies not affiliated with music.

Education and Training

A college degree in advertising, marketing, or a related area is usually preferred by most record companies. Degree programs in these fields may be found in many colleges and universities around the country.

There are many seminars, workshops, and additional courses in advertising and the music and recording industry that are beneficial to an Advertising Account Executive.

Experience, Skills, and Personality Traits

The person working in this position must be very creative. He or she must have the ability to come up with unique, effective advertising campaigns for new records. The Advertising Account Executive must be knowledgeable about all advertising skills and technology, including copywriting, the use of audiovisuals, graphics, etc. An ability to work under intense pressure is necessary.

Many record companies prefer that the staff of their advertising department has prior experience in the field. Other companies prefer to train staff themselves.

Unions and Associations

Advertising Account Executives working in record companies may belong to the National Academy of Recording Arts and Sciences (NARAS) as associate members. Individuals might also belong to the American Advertising Federation (AAF).

Tips for Entry

1. Look for an internship in the advertising department of a record company. This is one of the best ways to learn about the business. Chances of landing a paying job with the label after the internship are good, too.
2. Get a good education or solid training. Many of the things you will need to know for this type of position are taught in a school setting. You're better off making any major mistakes working on an advertising project for school than directly on the job.
3. If you can't find a job in a record company's advertising department, look into an advertising job in a nonmusic-oriented advertising agency. After you obtain some experience, try the record labels again.
4. Openings are often advertised in the classified section of newspapers located in areas hosting record labels.

REGIONAL SALES MANAGER

Position Description

A Regional Sales Manager of a record company is in charge of selling the label's products to wholesalers and/or retail outlets in the specific region assigned. Depending on the structure of the company, regions might be divided into different segments of the country. The most popular divisions include the northeastern region, the southeastern region, the southwestern region, the midwest region, and the western region. It is in these markets that the greatest concentration of selling occurs. The popularity of new online outlets has also created major new sales opportunities. Depending on the company, online outlets may be considered part of a geographic region or may be assigned a specific sales manager.

The Regional Sales Manager must see to it that a specific amount of merchandise is sold each month. These sales quotas can run into hundreds of thousands of dollars. This "demand" selling can lead to a lot of pressure. In order to meet these huge quotas, the individual must work closely with both the national sales director and the salespeople in the region.

In this position, the individual is in charge of creating sales campaigns for his or her region. The Regional Sales Manager designs these campaigns with the help of the national sales director. Together, all the Regional Sales Managers and the national director work out the

sales policies they will use in selling the product. These programs include merchandise return policies, the number of records one is required to buy in order to qualify for discounts, etc.

As a Regional Sales Manager or director of sales, the person may be responsible for interviewing, hiring, and training salespeople. Each company has different methods and techniques for selling their product, and new employees must be instructed accordingly.

The Regional Sales Manager must keep a close watch on how salespeople in his or her region are producing. The region usually consists of a number of cities; for example, the northeast region might include Baltimore, Boston, Hartford, New York City, Philadelphia, and surrounding areas. The Regional Sales Manager must supervise each salesperson in each of these cities.

If sales activity slacks off in any particular area, the individual must check into it, find out what is wrong, and correct the situation. It may be that the city requires additional promotion. In that case, the Regional Sales Manager would contact the promotion department. It could be that a certain record needs more of an advertising push in a specific area. The individual must know whom to contact in case of a problem and do so rapidly. Loss of sales for even one week will negatively affect the monthly sales quotas.

At times, the Regional Sales Manager may feel that the salespeople in an area just aren't doing a good job. It is up to him or her to talk to the individuals, give them some pointers or a pep talk, and get them selling again.

The Regional Sales Manager is also responsible for making sure that the salespeople in the various areas are servicing all accounts. That means that all accounts must be called upon on a regular basis, phone calls returned, and orders filled rapidly. If this is not happening, the sales manager is not doing a competent job.

The Regional Sales Manager works long hours, travels extensively, and works under a great deal of pressure to meet sales quotas.

Salaries

The Regional Sales Manager of a major recording company will do quite well financially. In addition to a regular salary, the individual often receives commissions on the products sold in his or her region.

Those working in smaller companies will earn considerably less than their counterparts from the major labels.

The Regional Sales Manager earns $40,000 to $90,000 plus per year.

Employment Prospects

Employment prospects for Regional Sales Managers in major record companies are limited. There are only a few major record companies and each has only a certain number of sales manager positions. Jobs are difficult to come by, but are obtainable.

Opportunities are better with smaller companies or independent labels located throughout the country.

Advancement Prospects

Advancement is slow. To move up the career ladder, one would probably want to become the national sales director of a label. These jobs are more limited than Regional Sales Manager positions.

Another advancement opportunity might be a similar position at a bigger or more prestigious label. One may also obtain a better and bigger region as a form of career advancement.

Education and Training

There are many Regional Sales Managers of record companies with just a high school diploma. It is really all that they require. There are some positions, however, that require a bachelor's degree. For those who are currently planning on attending college, thought should be given to the new courses and degrees in music business and/or music merchandising. These degrees and courses will not obtain a job for the individual, but they will certainly help with some background and knowledge about the industry. This extra know-how might prove helpful. Many of the schools also offer internships in cooperation with record companies.

Experience, Skills, and Personality Traits

A Regional Sales Manager for a record company must be familiar with the entire record industry and have a basic knowledge of the music business. The individual must have proven that he or she was a superb salesperson. An ability to lead and direct others is necessary to succeed in this business. The individual must also be able to work effectively under pressure, as it is a constant in this position.

Unions and Associations

Regional Sales Managers working for record companies may belong to the National Association of Recording Merchandisers (NARM). This organization provides a forum for people in the recorded music industry. Individuals might also be members of the Country Music Association (CMA) and/or the Gospel Music Association (GMA).

Tips for Entry

1. These positions are generally not advertised. As a rule, the Regional Sales Managers are chosen from the ranks of salespeople working for the company. The first step to take is to obtain a job in the sales department.
2. This is another of the jobs in which contacts help. If you have them, use them to help you get an interview.
3. Sales experience in any field will be beneficial.

SALESPERSON

CAREER PROFILE

Duties: Sell the company's albums; service accounts

Alternate Title(s): Sales Representative

Salary Range: $30,000 to $50,000+

Employment Prospects: Fair

Advancement Prospects: Fair

Best Geographical Locations for Position: New York City, Los Angeles, Nashville, Atlanta, Chicago, Philadelphia, Jacksonville, Miami, Detroit, etc.

Prerequisites:

Education or Training—High school diploma minimum; some positions require bachelor's degree; see text

Experience—Retail and/or wholesale jobs helpful

CAREER LADDER

Regional Sales Manager

Salesperson

Salesperson in Related or Unrelated Field

Special Skills and Personality Traits—Good sales skills; aggressiveness; reliability; knowledge of music and records; ability to work under pressure

Position Description

A Salesperson at a record company sells the label's CDs, DVDs, and videos. He or she does this by physically visiting accounts, mailing out letters and other information, and/or making phone calls. The person's accounts may include retail stores, online outlets, rack jobbers, and one-stops. In order to meet the sales quota usually imposed by regional managers, the Salesperson must constantly service his or her accounts competently.

The individual should be totally knowledgeable about the company's catalog. Although a good number of records, tapes, CDs, etc., sold are new releases, the Salesperson must be aware of the label's older releases, too. This is especially true as older releases come out on CD. The retailer, rack jobber, online store, and one-stops might ask the Salesperson questions regarding a new release's sales in other areas of the country. The individual, therefore, should stay informed about as many record-related matters as possible.

After discussing any questions the buyer might have and talking about the new releases available, the Salesperson will take the order. He or she will let the purchaser know what the costs are, the types of discounts available, and how much of the product it is necessary to purchase in order to qualify for the discounts. The Salesperson may also talk about any special promotions that are available to the retailer.

The Salesperson will probably visit a number of accounts each day. Certain days may be set aside for handling correspondence and/or phone work. Depending on

the structure of the company, the Salesperson might have other duties in retail shops. These duties might include taking inventory of the company's CDs and videos, suggesting which products should be reordered, setting up in-store displays or window displays, etc.

Once a Salesperson has received an order, the individual must call it in to be filled. The individual must check back periodically to make sure that orders have been received on time. If they have not, the individual must bring the matter to the attention of the regional sales manager and have it taken care of.

The Salesperson talks to and/or sees the regional sales manager on a regular basis. The Salesperson must attend periodic sales and strategy meetings.

Salaries

Salespeople are compensated in various ways. They may earn a straight salary, a salary plus a commission on sales made, or a commission against a basic salary.

It is difficult to estimate the yearly earnings of a Salesperson in a record company because of the different salary structures, the sizes of various record companies, and the amount of product sold.

Generally, earnings for a Salesperson working for a record company might range from $30,000 to $50,000 plus.

Employment Prospects

Employment prospects are fair for those interested in working as a record company Salesperson. Good salespeople are hard to find in any industry, and this includes the record business. The opportunities for people to work for major companies in locations other than the three major music capitals expands the prospects. Major and independent record companies employ large numbers of salespeople in all the music markets, which include New York City, Los Angeles, Nashville, Memphis, Atlanta, Philadelphia, Chicago, Jacksonville, Miami, Detroit, Baltimore, and a host of others.

Advancement Prospects

If a Salesperson shows superior selling skills, he or she may be promoted to regional sales manager or another supervisory position. Selling skills are proven to management when Salespeople meet and exceed their monthly quotas, obtain new accounts, and service old ones well.

Education and Training

Educational requirements vary for record label salespeople. While smaller labels may require individuals to hold only a high school diploma, major labels generally require their salespeople to hold a college degree.

Good majors might include marketing, advertising, and communications. There are also a number of colleges offering music-business or music-merchandising degrees. While these degrees do not guarantee a job, they are helpful in career preparation and advancement.

Experience, Skills, and Personality Traits

Salespeople working for record companies need many of the same skills and/or experiences found in other sales jobs. The person may find that retail and/or wholesale selling experience is helpful.

A good Salesperson has good sales and interpersonal skills. He or she should be aggressive, articulate, and reliable. The individual needs to be able to work under heavy pressure to meet sales quotas. The person working in this situation also needs a knowledge of music and records to be effective on the job.

Unions and Associations

Salespeople working for a record company might be members of the National Association of Recording Merchandisers (NARM). NARM is an association that provides a forum for those in the recorded music business.

Tips for Entry

1. Apply to a field office of a major record company. These may be located in Philadelphia, Jacksonville, Miami, Chicago, Detroit, Baltimore, or one of a host of other cities, depending on the structure of the record company.
2. Send a résumé and a cover letter directly to the record company. You might want to send one to the national sales director and one to the personnel department to make sure the proper person sees it.
3. If you do send your résumé or a letter, try to find out the person's name to whom you are sending it. Try to send it to a specific name, such as Mr. John Jones, Director of Sales, etc.
4. Remember to include all your sales achievements, not just music-oriented ones. If you had a 90% conversion rate selling vacuum cleaners door to door, chances are you will be a great Salesperson for any product.
5. Visit record label Web sites to see if they list employment opportunities.

FIELD MERCHANDISER

CAREER PROFILE

Duties: Distribute and explain merchandising promotions to record shops and departments in specific markets

Alternate Title(s): Merchandising Rep; Field Rep

Salary Range: $27,000 to $42,000+

Employment Prospects: Fair

Advancement Prospects: Fair

Best Geographical Locations for Position: Major markets are New York City, Los Angeles, and Nashville; the individual may also work in other cities, including Atlanta, Memphis, Miami, San Francisco, Philadelphia, Boston, Chicago, Detroit, and others

Prerequisites:

Education or Training—High school diploma minimum; major labels may require a college degree; see text

Experience—Some type of sales experience helpful

Special Skills and Personality Traits—Pleasant personality; knowledge of music and/or the record industry; communications skills; good rapport with people

Position Description

A Field Merchandiser works for the record company in the marketing, merchandising, sales, or promotion department, depending on the structure of the company. The individual in this position travels to record stores and the record departments of stores in his or her territory. The Field Merchandiser distributes promotional displays, posters, contests, and merchandising aids to these locations. Displays might include CD holders, posters, window displays, pictures, or CD covers. Additional possibilities would be contest entry blanks, T-shirts, buttons, bumper stickers, and other merchandising items relating to the label's acts.

The individual may physically set up the displays or just give the owner or manager of the shop or department advice on how to set it up, describe where it would be most effective, etc. If there is a promotion under way, such as an album giveaway, the Field Merchandiser will explain the promotion in detail to the manager or owner. If the record company has set up an in-store appearance or a promotional concert in the area, the individual may bring in concert tickets, flyers, posters, or other items and make sure that everything is moving according to schedule.

The Field Merchandiser travels for the majority of his or her working days. The individual keeps in close contact with the supervisor of the department. The Field Merchandiser is also required to attend staff meetings. At these meetings, new promotions and merchandise are discussed. The talk may also turn to which retailers are using the merchandising displays and which ones are not. Ideas are often exchanged concerning better methods to entice shop owners and managers into using the merchandise.

The individual in this position may also check the store's inventory of the label's merchandise while attending to other tasks. If a supply is low, the Field Merchandiser will contact the salesperson or sales manager responsible for servicing the area.

Salaries

Field Merchandisers can expect to earn a salary of $27,000 to $42,000 or more per year. Salaries will vary for individuals depending on the size of the record company, the location, the experience of the Field Merchandiser, and his or her exact duties.

Employment Prospects

Employment prospects are fair for Field Merchandisers. The individual has opportunities to work not only in the major markets of New York City, Los Angeles, and Nashville, but in other regions as well. These might include Atlanta, Memphis, Miami, San Francisco,

Philadelphia, Boston, Chicago, Detroit, Baltimore, and Houston, among others.

Advancement Prospects

A Field Merchandiser may move up the career ladder to be a marketer, a merchandising coordinator, a salesperson, a sales manager, etc. The possibilities are limitless.

Education and Training

Educational requirements vary for record label Field Merchandisers. While smaller labels may just require individuals to hold only a high school diploma, major labels generally require their Field Merchandisers to hold a college degree.

Good majors might include marketing, advertising, and communications. There are also a number of colleges offering music business or music merchandising degrees. While these degrees do not guarantee a job, they are helpful in career preparation and advancement.

Experience, Skills, and Personality Traits

It helps a Field Merchandiser to have some type of sales experience prior to taking the job, although it is not always necessary. Possessing a pleasant personality and establishing a good rapport with people makes the job easier. Being articulate is a plus. A knowledge of the music and/or record industry is essential.

Unions and Associations

Field Merchandisers may belong to the National Association of Recording Merchandisers (NARM). This organization represents people who work in recorded music. While regular membership is open to record shops, distributors, rack jobbers, etc., associate membership is open to others who work in the industry.

Tips for Entry

1. Try to obtain a job in a large record store in a major market for a short time. In this position, you will often have the opportunity to meet Field Merchandisers, salespeople, promotion people, etc. Get to know them and ask about the proper person to talk to about a job in the company.

2. If you do work in a record shop or department that deals directly with record company personnel, your boss (the store owner or manager) might be able to help you. Ask the management person whether they would make a call on your behalf to the company person they deal with from the record label to inquire about setting up an interview for you.

3. If there is an opportunity open to obtain an internship in the marketing or merchandising department of a record company, grab it.

4. Send your résumé and a short cover letter to the director of personnel of record labels.

INTERN

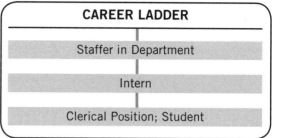

Position Description

An Intern working in a record company will perform many of the same duties as other people on staff. The Intern works under the direction of a department head, manager, or director. One of the advantages of obtaining an Intern position in a specific department is that the individual has the opportunity to learn the ropes from experienced people.

There are Interns in almost every department of a record company. In certain companies, one becomes an Intern in a specific department. In others, the individual's internship involves working in various departments of the company. Duties will depend on the department to which one is assigned. For instance, an Intern working in the publicity/press relations department may address envelopes for invitations to press parties, make calls to check whether various people will be attending press parties, and help make arrangements for the press function. As he or she gains experience the Intern might begin writing press releases, attending meetings to work out publicity campaigns, calling the media to discuss a good story, etc.

An Intern working in the marketing department might work on consumer research surveys, tabulate data, and/or call radio stations and the trades with information about the number of records sold in a specific market. As time goes on, the Intern may learn to develop marketing campaigns, go out with field reps, or help the director create a sales incentive program.

The Intern usually begins by handling a lot of the tedious work that no one else wants to do. As he or she becomes more experienced, the individual learns how to perform more difficult tasks. Only the simplest of projects is performed without direct supervision.

Whether or not the Intern is getting paid a salary, he or she is expected to function like a paid employee. This includes arriving at work on time and not taking time off unnecessarily. It is to the Intern's advantage to learn as much as possible through instruction, asking questions, and just working in a hands-on situation.

The individual is responsible to the supervisor or department head to whom he or she is assigned. If the Intern is using the program as part of a college credit experience, a paper on the work experience might be expected.

A good Intern has a fairly good chance of becoming a member of the company staff after internship has concluded.

Salaries

Interns may work and not earn a penny. If they do earn a salary, it is usually quite small. An individual who has obtained an internship through a college might get college credit for his or her work. If the person is working as an Intern and is lucky enough to receive a salary, it probably would range from $1,500 to $3,000 or more.

Employment Prospects

Despite the low pay or even lack of a salary, many people want to work as Interns. Individuals seeking internships can find them in almost every department of every major record company. Smaller labels tend to offer fewer opportunities.

Although many of these internship programs may be located directly through the record company, there are a number that can be obtained through schools and colleges in return for college credit and hands-on experience.

Advancement Prospects

One of the major reasons so many people try to become Interns in this industry is that it almost guarantees a job in the record company. After all the training and instruction given to the individual, the company most likely will want to keep the Intern in its employ. The person must, of course, be a good employee and learn the trade. Interns can advance their careers very quickly in most departments. They may first be promoted to staffers, and then become coordinators, supervisors, or directors in various departments.

Education and Training

To become an Intern in a record company the only educational requirement may be a high school diploma. If an individual is currently in college, he or she may be able to have the school set up an internship program with a company for college credit. The person may be working toward a degree in any subject that can be made relevant to a semester or summer in a record company. Majors might include business, advertising, music, communications, journalism, the social sciences, pre-law, etc.

Experience, Skills, and Personality Traits

Interns do not really need any experience. What is required is the desire to enter the record industry and an eagerness to learn all about it.

Individuals who are chosen to be Interns generally are bright and aggressive and have pleasant personalities. A knowledge of music and/or the recording business is a plus.

Unions and Associations

Interns do not usually belong to any union while working in a record company. They may, however, join associations relevant to the department in which they are working.

Tips for Entry

1. If you are in college, the school may know of some Intern positions in record companies. If the school has a music business or merchandising degree or offers courses in one of these areas, they might have an internship program already established with a record company.
2. Contact record labels to see if they conduct intern programs or if you can develop an internship.
3. If you live in one of the music capitals, you might want to visit the record companies personally to see if you can get an internship in one of the departments.
4. Interns are often chosen from the ranks of clerical workers in the office. Talk to the head of the department with which you want to work.
5. Internship openings may be advertised in *Billboard* or other trade publications.

CAMPUS REPRESENTATIVE

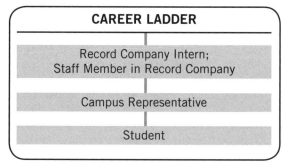

Position Description

A Campus Representative is a student who is hired by a record label to promote that label's products on the campus. The student may work with or without pay. Products promoted may include the company's records, merchandising material, or concerts.

The student usually does his or her work in the campus bookstore, record shop, or student union. The individual will set up a display provided by the record company. There are a variety of displays or booths the Campus Representative might set up. One might be a merchandising booth. This would be loaded with merchandising material related to the label's acts. It might include T-shirts, bumper stickers, pins, buttons, and posters. Another type of display might be a point-of-purchase exhibit. This might be set up in a record store or bookstore and contain the label's CDs, videos, and merchandise. These displays are often quite elaborate.

The student may be responsible for checking the inventory of the CDs in the campus shop or in the shop's surrounding area. When stock gets low, the rep notifies the distribution department. Conversely, if stock is not moving, the Campus Representative might let the label know, so they can do some extra promotion in the area.

Depending on the specific label, individual duties may vary. The Campus Representative may, for example, interview other students to find out how they feel about the label's CDs, acts, etc. This information would be relayed back to the correct department of the company.

Another duty of the Campus Representative might be to sell concert tickets for the label's acts when they perform on campus or in the immediate area. He or she might also put up posters or flyers in the area to promote the show. The individual may line up interviews with specific media personalities for the acts when they come to the college for a concert. The rep could even interview the act him- or herself for the campus paper, a local paper, or a radio station.

The job of Campus Representative is sought out by individuals aspiring to get into the recording industry. A position like this allows a person to pay dues while still in school. The position almost guarantees entry into a record company.

Salaries

Campus Representatives may work with or without payment. When they do earn a salary, it usually isn't very high. A salary for a student in this position runs between $2,000 and $7,000 or more a year.

The reason most people vie for this type of job is that it often leads to a position in the record company after graduation.

Those individuals who do not receive a salary will usually get free CDs, T-shirts, posters, and concert tickets.

Employment Prospects

The position of Campus Representative is not easy to obtain, but it's possible. The problem is that not all labels use the services of such individuals. Once one finds a company that has a college department, though, prospects get better.

A person may also try to create a position such as this with any record company, even if it does not currently have Campus Representatives.

Advancement Prospects

Advancement prospects are fairly good for those who are Campus Representatives. Once a person works for a label, he or she has an excellent chance of obtaining a job after graduation. The label feels that the person has proven him-or herself and is part of the company.

People who have worked in this job may advance to almost any position in the record company. It is important to remember that the hard part of getting a job in a record company is getting in. Advancement is easier to accomplish, especially if the individual is bright and aggressive and wants to move up the career ladder.

Education and Training

Campus Representatives, as a rule, are concurrently attending a college or university and earning a degree. There are many different fields an individual might be studying; majors helpful for a career in this field include communications, music, business, finance, journalism, advertising, marketing, or music merchandising.

Experience, Skills, and Personality Traits

Record companies usually choose bright, aggressive people to fill these positions. As many of these jobs pay either nothing or only a small salary, the person must really want to get into the record business. A knowledge of the industry and the music business, even if only basic, is helpful. An ability to work without direct day-to-day supervision is necessary.

Unions and Associations

Students interested in the music business often belong to the student union or activity board of the college, work on school concert committees, and might represent the school at the National Association for Campus Activities (NACA). This organization works to help all parties involved in booking concerts on campuses.

Tips for Entry

1. Campus Representative jobs may be obtained through the record company's college department. Call or write and inquire about these positions. If you do call, follow up with a letter and your résumé.
2. If the company does not have a college department, write to the public relations department, personnel director, or president of the company asking about Campus Representative positions.
3. In the event that a label does not use the services of a Campus Representative, don't let this stop you. Call, write, and/or set up an appointment for an interview to create a job for yourself. It sometimes works.

ARRANGER

Duties: Determine voice, instrument harmonic structure, rhythm, tempo, etc. of a song; arrange songs for musical artists

Alternate Title(s): Adapter; Transcriber; Transcripter

Salary Range: $22,000 to $200,000+

Employment Prospects: Fair

Advancement Prospects: Fair

Best Geographical Location(s) for Position: New York City, Los Angeles, and Nashville for recording positions or music positions; other cities for other positions

Prerequisites:

Education or Training—Training in music theory, orchestration, composition, harmony, etc., required

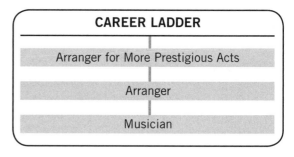

CAREER LADDER

Arranger for More Prestigious Acts

Arranger

Musician

Experience—Writing music; playing one or more instruments; copying charts

Special Skills and Personality Traits—Ability to read music; good musical "ear"; proficiency as a musician; creativity

Position Description

An Arranger's main function is to arrange the various parts of a musical composition. This is accomplished by determining voice, instrument, harmonic structure, rhythm, tempo, and tone balance to achieve the desired effect.

A talented Arranger can take a song and, through creative arranging, turn it into a hit tune. A good Arranger will be aware of current music trends.

One of the functions of the Arranger is to transcribe a musical composition for an orchestra, band, choral group, or individual artist in order to adapt the tune to a style different from the one in which it was originally written.

The Arranger may, in addition to working on new tunes, work on new arrangements of some old hits or classics. Arranged well, these tunes (sometimes called "cover records") often outsell the original versions.

The Arranger who works for a recording artist will work closely with the act and the producer. He or she will be on hand before recording even begins to hear how his or her arrangements sound in rehearsals. Last-minute changes are not uncommon.

In addition to working with recording artists, Arrangers may work with artists arranging music for concerts. Other Arrangers work with such services as Muzak, which arranges and orchestrates much of the music heard in dentists' offices, doctors' offices, and department stores.

Music Arrangers who work for music publishers are responsible for developing new and/or different ways to write and play music. The music Arranger might even go into television. In this type of job, the individual might be responsible for putting together music for skits or musical guests on comedy or variety shows.

As a music Arranger one might get into the motion picture business, scoring and/or arranging music for the title tune and the music throughout the film. The opportunities are endless once the Arranger gets in the door.

Most Arrangers work freelance. Therefore, the more jobs they get, the more they earn. Hours for this type of position are extremely irregular. Recording sessions do not usually go from nine to five (although they might run from 9:00 P.M. to 5:00 A.M.).

Staff Arrangers employed by music publishers have a more regular workday.

Arrangers are usually musicians first. Many Arrangers perform with an act and arrange much of the act's material. They might also write much of the music the act records.

Salaries

Arrangers who have not yet hit stardom and success may make so little arranging that they must work other jobs to make ends meet. Once an Arranger gets his or her foot in the door, he or she can expect to make from $22,000 to $30,000 yearly.

Others who have attained more success in arranging may earn up to $45,000 annually. Salaries depend, of course, on how much work one gets. Fees for Arrangers of movies, television, or recordings are usually paid to the scale set by the American Federation of Musicians (AFM).

In some instances, Arrangers are paid a royalty on each piece of music or record sold, in addition to their fee.

Top Arrangers may demand and receive fees well over scale payments, as well as royalties. These people can earn between $75,000 and $200,000 plus yearly.

Employment Prospects

It is not difficult for an Arranger to break into the profession on a small scale. Arranging tunes for groups who have not yet made it is a good example of the work one may do. Money for this type of employment is usually low. It does give the aspiring Arranger a start, though.

Arrangers have opportunities to work for the recording industry, TV, motion pictures, shows, music publishers, or print-music licensees. Other opportunities include working for individual artists or groups of artists, arranging materials for recordings or concerts.

Advancement Prospects

Advancement as an Arranger comes in working for more prestigious acts. As the individual's talent is recognized, he or she will have more opportunities. Composing and arranging one's own material for a Broadway show or a top group is probably a situation most Arrangers hope for.

Education and Training

No formal education is required to become an Arranger. Some type of training is usually necessary, however. This training can be garnered in a conservatory or college or through private study.

The Arranger must be knowledgeable and be able to implement all phases of orchestration. He or she must be educated (either formally or informally) in areas of composition, harmony, arranging, and theory.

Most people aspiring to be an Arranger have studied at least one instrument, privately, at conservatory or in college classes, or through a combination of both.

Experience, Skills, and Personality Traits

Arrangers begin as musicians. They need to play at least one instrument well. The ability to play more than one is a plus.

Quite frequently, Arrangers have tried composing on some level, either amateur or professional. The Arranger must have the ability to read and write music. Talented Arrangers—those who become most successful—are creative individuals who can develop their ideas into musical arrangements.

A good musical "ear" is a necessity, as are versatility and familiarity with current musical trends.

Unions and Associations

Arrangers may belong to the American Federation of Musicians (AFM). This is a bargaining union that sets payment scales for arrangements.

Arrangers may also be members of the National Academy of Recording Arts and Sciences (NARAS). This organization gives out the Grammy awards each year.

Many Arrangers additionally belong to the American Society of Music Arrangers.

Tips for Entry

1. As a member of the American Federation of Musicians (AFM), you will receive their publication, *International Musician*. This paper has a number of opportunities and openings listed in it.
2. Hanging around recording studios might help you learn about the profession and develop contacts.
3. Write as much music as you can. Write for up-and-coming groups, yourself, etc.
4. You might want to arrange some tunes and try sending them to publishers.
5. You might want to form your own group and arrange for them.
6. Any type of experience in this field helps. Consider donating your talent (writing and arranging) to a local production or school or college musical.

RECORD PRODUCER

Position Description

The Record Producer's main job is to produce a CD. If the individual is very successful and lucky, he or she will come out of a recording session with a hit album. There are a number of different responsibilities within this job classification, some creative and others business-oriented.

The Record Producer first helps a group or artist select the tune or tunes to be recorded. Once an act has rehearsed and is ready to record, the producer will locate a suitable studio in which to record and arrange for studio time. The producer may then choose an engineer, hire an arranger, and contact a contractor who will find background musicians and vocalists for the job.

The Record Producer will make sure that all those hired arrive at the studio on time. The individual is also in charge of making sure that those who have been hired are paid promptly.

During the recording session the Record Producer will work closely with the engineer. The person in this position advises the engineer of any specific sounds or feelings he or she is trying to create. The producer will supervise the entire recording session, making decisions about when to do a take over, what takes to use, etc.

The Record Producer usually adds a personal touch to the recording. This is sometimes a special sound effect or the way a tune is ended. Often, it is a blend of instruments or vocal harmony. It is not unusual for a producer to place his or her trademark on records.

It is up to the Record Producer to try to keep the recording within the budget agreed upon. Going over budget often costs the label or artist thousands of dollars extra.

After the recording has been made, the producer is often in charge of "mixing" it to perfection. Although the producer doesn't always do this job personally (special engineers or mixers are often hired), he or she always supervises this function. Success or failure in the mixing process can be what makes or breaks a CD.

If the tunes recorded are for an album, the Record Producer may help choose the order in which they are placed on the CD. He or she will also help to choose the single from the album.

The producer is involved with all aspects of the CD. When the recording and mixing have been completed, the producer's job does not end. Though the creative process is almost over, the Record Producer must attend to many of the business aspects of producing.

The Record Producer is responsible for clearing mechanical licenses, making sure that all copyrights are checked, and providing completed consent forms and releases from artists, engineers, photographers, etc., who worked on the project (if they are to receive credit on the record). At this point the producer must also submit receipts and paid bills to the record company.

The Record Producer may work on staff for a label or be an independent producer, freelancing his or her talent. The producer on staff at a record company is responsible to the A & R department head. The producer who freelances may be responsible directly to the label or to the artist. This depends on the arrangement made beforehand.

Salaries
Record Producers on staff at a record company may earn a salary plus royalties on records produced.

Producers who freelance as independents are paid a fee for their services by either the label or the artist. In addition, they are always paid royalties on works they produce. The amount of the royalties differ from producer to producer. Successful Record Producers can negotiate for larger royalty payments. This money is often advanced to the individual.

Staff Record Producers may earn $27,000 to $75,000 plus, depending on the label. Very successful independent producers may earn up to $1,000,000 or more annually.

Employment Prospects
All records and CDs have producers. They are sometimes produced by a member of the group recording them. At other times, records may be produced by the engineer. Records and CDs may also be produced by a staff producer working at a record company or by an independent producer who freelances his or her talent.

On some records there is more than one producer. For example, there may be an executive producer and a coproducer. Another possibility is for an artist to produce part of the record in conjunction with the executive producer.

There are quite a few possibilities for employment in this field. However, one must first get in the door.

Advancement Prospects
The way a producer advances in the recording industry is by working on records that become hits. As a producer's efforts yield records that hit the charts, he or she becomes more valuable.

When a Record Producer attains success, many different options open. The producer may go to a position at a better label, demand more money, work with more prestigious acts, or freelance as an independent producer.

Education and Training
There is no college requirement to become a Record Producer, although many producers do possess college degrees. Music training is useful. Some people attend a sound recording school for a short period to learn more about the recording process.

This is another of the careers in which a knowledge of the music business is quite helpful, as it makes it easier to get into the industry. This knowledge can be obtained through formal education or by working in various jobs in the music business.

Experience, Skills, and Personality Traits
The most important qualification for a Record Producer is the ability to pick hit tunes. Every recording group or artist wants a number one song; that is how they gain recognition and make money. Record Producers who can, indeed, pick the tunes and have a proven track record doing so will be successful.

Record Producers must have a good musical "ear" and the ability to know what will sound good. Naturally, the producer must love music, as he or she will be listening to it for a good part of the day.

The Record Producer must be able to hear raw talent and have the ability to foresee how it will sound if properly arranged and recorded.

Unions and Associations
Record Producers may be active or associate members in the National Academy of Recording Arts and Sciences (NARAS). This is the association that gives out the Grammy awards each year.

Record Producers might also belong to any of the music associations, including the Country Music Association (CMA) and the Gospel Music Association (GMA).

Tips for Entry
1. Try to find a job in a recording studio as a floor manager, engineer, studio set-up worker, receptionist, etc. to gain opportunity to watch producers at work.
2. One way of getting into producing is to find a group with a song they want to record. Put some of your own money into the recording of a master you produce and try to sell both the record and the group to a major label.
3. As with many careers in the music business, you should check with some recording studios or even a major label to see if you can intern or apprentice in return for learning the skills.

RECORDING ENGINEER

CAREER PROFILE

Duties: Operate the sound board and other electrical equipment during the recording of music

Alternate Title(s): Mixer, Recording Assistant

Salary Range: $27,000 to $150,000+

Employment Prospects: Fair

Advancement Prospects: Fair

Best Geographical Locations for Position: New York City, Los Angeles, and Nashville

Prerequisites:

Education or Training—College or technical school background in sound engineering or recording technology; apprenticeship in studio in lieu of schooling

Experience—Experience in studio necessary

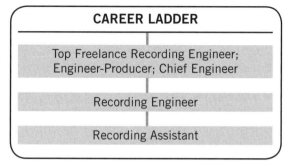

CAREER LADDER

Top Freelance Recording Engineer; Engineer-Producer; Chief Engineer

Recording Engineer

Recording Assistant

Special Skills and Personality Traits—Good musical "ear"; electronic and mechanical inclination; appreciation of music; stamina; ability to work under a great deal of pressure

Position Description

It is the Recording Engineer's job to operate the sound board and all the other electrical equipment necessary when making a recording.

This is not, however, the only responsibility of the Recording Engineer. In a large studio there are usually a number of engineers working on a session. These include the recording assistant or set-up worker, the main Recording Engineer, and possibly another engineer who helps with the mixing after tracks have been recorded.

Prior to a recording session, one of the engineers (usually the recording assistant) prepares the studio before the act arrives. As recording time is booked by the hour (and it is very expensive), no one wants to waste time waiting for the instruments to be set up or the mikes to be placed, turned on, and checked.

The Recording Engineer must discuss with the act and/or his or her producer how they want the end product to sound. It then becomes the engineer's responsibility to make the record into the sound image the act wants.

He or she does this during the recording session by operating the sound board and the other electrical equipment and electronic devices. The different audio controls used create different sounds.

After a track has been recorded, the engineer plays it back. The Recording Engineer, the act, and the producer then discuss the recording and any changes they

would like. For example, the recording might need more base, more treble, a faster or slower tempo, etc. This information is noted for later use.

After all the tracks have been recorded, the engineer will mix them down to either two or four tracks. Mixing is not just a skill, but an art the Recording Engineer must learn. He or she decides how loud or soft a specific track should be and then balances it correctly. The individual might feel that another instrument is needed. The engineer would talk over this suggestion with the producer to get his or her opinion. If the producer agrees, another track with the instrument is recorded. This new track is then mixed down with the others to become, eventually, the master tape.

Through the entire recording process the Recording Engineer works closely with the producer and the act. He or she discusses the sound with these individuals and tries to put their ideas into the final product.

In certain studios, the Recording Engineer must not only know how to work the equipment, but also how to repair it when it breaks down. As a rule, many Recording Engineers know how to take apart and put together most of the equipment they work with.

Recording Engineers keep up with the latest electronic and recording technology. They are constantly striving to improve their talent in the engineering process.

Recording Engineers work long, irregular hours. Many engineers begin work at 9 or 10 P.M. and work until the next morning with one act. In the afternoon, they often have to return to the studio with another client. The job requires a lot of stamina.

Recording Engineers must have the ability to work with people with whose musical ideas they disagree. The Recording Engineer is usually responsible directly to the producer and act or to the chief engineer in the studio.

Recording Engineers can be on staff at a record company or a recording studio. They can also work by the hour. Better-known Recording Engineers work freelance. Their business is obtained through word-of-mouth.

Salaries

Salaries vary for Recording Engineers according to the situation for which they have been hired. Recording Engineers who are just beginning (called recording assistants or studio set-up workers) usually make close to the minimum wage.

As the Recording Engineer gains experience he or she will be better compensated. A lot depends on whether the individual is on staff, paid by the number of hours per week that he or she works, or a freelance engineer.

Salaries for those individuals who are on staff range from $27,000 to $50,000 per year. Recording Engineers who are well-known and freelance often make up to $75,000 annually. In addition to being paid a fee by the act or record company he or she is working with, the individual is also usually paid a percentage of the monies given to the recording studio for renting the studio time. This percentage varies.

Top Recording Engineers who work with popular recording acts can make $150,000 plus annually.

Employment Prospects

As with most jobs in the recording industry, things are very competitive. However, if an individual doesn't mind starting at the bottom, he or she may eventually get a job in a recording studio. A person with talent, personality, patience, and perseverance may obtain a position as a Recording Engineer, or at least as an assistant.

Advancement Prospects

It is often necessary to knock on a lot of doors, make a great number of calls, and mail many résumés before you get your foot in the door. Once this is done, however, a person who works hard and has a lot of talent and a little bit of luck will advance his or her career.

Recording Engineers select different roads for advancement. One is to become a chief engineer. This individual is in charge of the entire studio and supervises all recordings that take place in that studio.

Another method of advancement is for the individual to become a top freelance Recording Engineer. Top recording groups, record companies, and producers will usually seek such a person out to work with them on sessions.

Another method of advancement selected by engineers is to become an engineer-producer. This individual will produce records as well as engineer them.

Education and Training

There are a variety of ways to train for a position as a Recording Engineer: through college courses in sound engineering, for example, or in a technical or training school course in sound engineering or recording technology.

A third method of training for this position is to work as an apprentice in a recording studio. Many times, the individual in this position does not get paid or is paid a minimal salary. He or she learns the business from the bottom up. By being in this environment and asking questions, he or she will pick up the major engineering methods. Eventually, he or she will become a recording assistant and learn even more.

Experience, Skills, and Personality Traits

As noted above, experience in a studio is one method to becoming a Recording Engineer. In addition, the engineer must have a good musical "ear" to be effective at his or her job.

The ability to work under a great deal of pressure is important to the Recording Engineer. He or she might have to work with three or four different recording acts a day. Each act usually is set on how the record should sound. The engineer must be able to communicate and translate their verbal ideas into tape.

Unions and Associations

Recording Engineers may be active members of the National Academy of Recording Arts and Sciences (NARAS). This is the association that gives out the Grammy awards each year.

Depending on the type of music the individual works with, he or she might be a member of the Country Music Association (CMA) or the Gospel Music Association (GMA). These associations work to promote their specific variety of music.

Recording Engineers may represent a recording studio as a member of the Society of Professional Audio Recording Studios (SPARS).

Tips for Entry

1. If you can afford to, you might consider offering your services free to a recording studio in exchange for learning the business. When they feel you know enough, they might put you on salary.
2. Check to see what organizations are offering in the way of seminars for Recording Engineers. These seminars might help you make important contacts as well as learn more about the industry.
3. Check with various record companies (the larger ones) to see if they offer an internship program in the recording engineering department. It isn't uncommon for the record company to hire an intern after the internship ends.
4. Look for minority training programs sponsored by record labels.

RECORDING STUDIO SET-UP WORKER

CAREER PROFILE

Duties: Arrange sound recording equipment in studio before recording begins

Alternate Title(s): Recording Assistant; Assistant Engineer

Salary Range: $19,000 to $25,000+

Employment Prospects: Fair

Advancement Prospects: Fair

Best Geographical Location(s) for Position: New York City, Los Angeles, and Nashville offer the most opportunities

Prerequisites:

Education or Training—Technical school background in sound recording may be helpful, but not required; on-the-job training

Experience—Prior work with electrical equipment useful

Special Skills and Personality Traits—Knowledgeable in electronics; dependable; mechanically inclined; appreciative of music; able to get along with people

CAREER LADDER

```
          Engineer

Recording Studio Set-Up Worker

   Clerk in Recording Studio
```

Position Description

Recording Studio Set-Up Workers do as the name implies—they set up equipment. Individuals employed in this type of position have the responsibility of physically setting up the recording studio before a recording session takes place.

As recording time is usually very expensive, companies and/or individuals renting the studio do not want to waste their own time setting up their instruments, mikes, etc. The Recording Studio Set-Up Worker handles this task.

Once a block of time is booked by an act, the Recording Studio Set-Up Worker goes to work. He or she receives work orders indicating which instruments will be used, where they will be placed, how many mikes will be needed, etc.

Using this work order as a guide, the set-up worker begins. In addition to setting up the instruments and mikes, the individual must position other pieces of equipment, such as consoles, isolation booths, tape machines, amps, music stands, and chairs.

Some of this equipment is moved by hand. The rest is loaded onto dollies and handtrucks. Each piece must be in the correct position before the recording session begins.

The Recording Studio Set-Up Worker helps connect all the equipment to the correct electrical lines, following instructions. If there is a breakdown of any particular piece of equipment during the session, the studio set-up Worker will replace it or fix it as quickly as possible. If there is a short in any of the electrical lines, the set-up worker may help repair the problem.

After the recording session is completed, the set-up worker dismantles all the equipment, instruments, and mikes and puts them in their proper places. If anything has broken or is not in good working order, he or she either fixes it or reports it as broken so that it can be repaired or replaced.

In some studios the set-up worker is also responsible for maintaining the tape library. In this job, the set-up worker needs to be totally organized. A lost tape can create a real problem for a studio.

The Recording Studio Set-Up Worker may assist the engineer during a recording. He or she is usually responsible to that individual.

Salaries

Salaries for Recording Studio Set-Up Workers are considerably lower than those of engineers. The set-up worker often earns only a minimum salary. Beginning set-up workers may only earn around $19,000 yearly. With added experience, the individual may earn up to $25,000 annually. Salaries do not usually go much over this figure.

Employment Prospects

A Recording Studio Set-Up Worker may find it easier to obtain a job in a studio than an engineer would. In some small studios, set-up worker positions are considered entry level. In others, individuals must begin as clerks, receptionists, or gofers.

Advancement Prospects

If a Recording Studio Set-Up Worker watches what is going on in the studio and asks questions, he or she has a reasonable chance for promotion to an assistant engineer or engineer. The main thing that is necessary for advancement is skill.

Education and Training

People spend a great deal of money to rent recording time and do not always want to use their time and money to train an aspiring engineer. Many individuals in the industry feel that because a certain degree of training and skill are required, the person who wants to get into engineering should attend a technical school or college in order to learn the basics of the craft.

There are others who feel that on-the-job training is the best way to learn. A Recording Studio Set-Up Worker with virtually no experience in recording may obtain a job in a studio and by watching and asking questions receive the same, if not better, training.

Experience, Skills, and Personality Traits

Many Recording Studio Set-Up Workers first walk into a studio and obtain jobs as receptionists, secretaries, gofers, etc. After a short time, if someone leaves and a position opens, the person who is in the right place at the right time gets the job. Others enter the engineering field as studio set-up workers.

Set-up workers do need to know the basics of electronics and to be mechanically inclined. As they are around music on a constant basis, an appreciation of music helps. Dependability and getting along well with those who book studio time can help the Recording Studio Set-Up Worker advance his or her career.

Unions and Associations

Recording Studio Set-Up Workers do not usually belong to any union or specific trade association at this point in their career.

Tips for Entry

1. Check different studios to see if the opportunity to learn the business can be gotten in exchange for working free in the studio. After you have learned enough, they may put you on salary.
2. Some of the larger recording companies offer internship programs in recording. If you are a beginner, they'll start you as a set-up worker, and you can move up the career ladder from there.
3. Certain recording associations and organizations give seminars on different facets of the recording business. Check this out.
4. Positions may be located in the classified section of newspapers in areas hosting recording studios. Look under headings such as "Studio Set Up Worker," "Recording Studio Set-Up Worker," or "Recording."
5. Knock on the door of as many recording studios as you can. Be persistent.

ORCHESTRATOR

Duties: Transpose music from one instrument or voice to another in order to accommodate a particular musician or group; write scores for an orchestra, band, choral group, individual instrumentalist, or vocalist

Alternate Title(s): None

Salary Range: Earnings depend on how much orchestrating is done; it is impossible to estimate earnings

Employment Prospects: Fair

Advancement Prospects: Fair

Best Geographical Location(s) for Position: New York City, Los Angeles, Boston, and other cultural and/or metropolitan areas

Prerequisites:

Education or Training—Training in music theory and notation

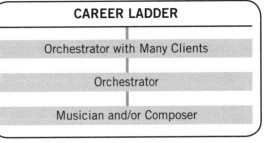

CAREER LADDER

Orchestrator with Many Clients

Orchestrator

Musician and/or Composer

Experience—Experience copying music and/or arranging

Special Skills and Personality Traits—Knowledge of music theory; ability to transpose music; accuracy; reliability; neatness; understanding of music

Position Description

An Orchestrator's prime function is to write the scores for an orchestra, band, choral group, individual instrumentalist, or vocalist. In this position, the person transposes the music from one instrument or voice to another to accommodate a particular musician or musical group. For example, an Orchestrator might be asked to transpose a score for a song into a key more suited to a vocalist.

When accomplishing this function, the individual does not usually alter the musical quality, harmony, or rhythm. He or she just scores the composition so that it is consistent with the instrumental and vocal capabilities of the artists. This is sometimes done with special computer software.

Although many Orchestrators work with the compositions of composers and arrangers, sometimes the individual is asked to work as the arranger. For instance, the Orchestrator may be asked to transcribe a composition while adapting it to another style of music. An example is when an individual changes the style of a pop tune to an "easy listening" instrumental version. This type of work often requires additional knowledge or training.

The Orchestrator may also function in the capacity of a copyist, transcribing musical parts onto staff or manuscript paper from a score written by an arranger.

The individual performing as an Orchestrator can work full-time or part-time. He or she may be responsible for orchestrating, arranging, and/or copying as part of a job.

Salaries

Salaries for Orchestrators will vary depending on how much work they do and under what conditions. Orchestrators belonging to the American Federation of Musicians (AFM) will be paid minimum rates according to fees set by the union. In certain situations, the individual may be paid by the hour. These situations include work where the Orchestrator must do adjustments, alterations, additions, or takedowns of the score. Time rates are also used when page rates are not practical.

Individuals are urged to contact the AFM for specific rates.

Rates will vary for work done by the page depending on the type of arrangement orchestrated and what needs to be done.

Employment Prospects

Employment prospects are fair for Orchestrators. They may work for orchestras, bands, choral groups, individual instrumentalists, or vocalists. Individuals may work for, with, or as arrangers in the recording field.

They may also do orchestration for television, films, and theater.

Advancement Prospects

Advancement for an Orchestrator may occur when the individual becomes so well known that he or she is constantly busy. People in this job may become successful composers and musicians in their own right. They may also go on to work in the music publishing field as music editors.

Education and Training

As in many music jobs, there is no formal education required in order to become an Orchestrator. The individual must know how to write scores for orchestras, bands, choral groups, etc., and/or how to transpose them from one instrument to another. This knowledge might be acquired at a conservatory, college, or university, or through private study. The skills needed might also be self-taught.

Experience, Skills, and Personality Traits

As an Orchestrator, an individual must have a thorough knowledge of music theory. He or she needs the ability to transpose music. The person must be accurate and have neat handwriting. As noted previously, Orchestra-

tors may perform their job with the help of computers and special software; computer literacy is therefore becoming necessary. Reliability is a must for success in this job. Additionally, the Orchestrator must have a good understanding of music.

Unions and Associations

Orchestrators may belong to the American Federation of Musicians (AFM). This union sets the minimum rate scale for Orchestrators.

Tips for Entry

1. These positions are often advertised in the classified section of newspapers in major cultural centers.
2. Put up your business card or a flyer in music and instrument repair stores.
3. Talk to the orchestra(s) in your area to see if they have part- or full-time work.
4. If you are just beginning, volunteer to do some work for a local theater putting on a musical. It will give you invaluable experience and will add to your résumé.
5. Join the American Federation of Musicians.
6. You might consider looking for job openings or projects online.

COPYIST

CAREER PROFILE

Duties: Transcribe musical parts onto staff paper from scores

Alternate Title(s): None

Salary Range: It is impossible to estimate salary; earnings vary depending on the amount of copying done

Employment Prospects: Good

Advancement Prospects: Fair

Best Geographical Location(s) for Position: Major cultural and music centers for most jobs; other cities may also have positions

Prerequisites:

Education or Training—Training in music notation and theory

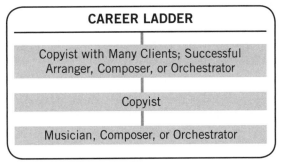

CAREER LADDER

Copyist with Many Clients; Successful Arranger, Composer, or Orchestrator

Copyist

Musician, Composer, or Orchestrator

Experience—Music background useful; writing music helpful

Special Skills and Personality Traits—Knowledge of music notation; knowledge of music theory; neatness; accuracy; computer skills

Position Description

A music Copyist transcribes musical parts onto staff or manuscript paper from a score. This score may have been done by an arranger, composer, or orchestrator. The Copyist reproduces the various parts of instruments and/or voices.

The individual utilizes his or her knowledge of music notation and experience and background in music to accomplish this task. The function of the Copyist is to make it easier for the musician or vocalist to play or sing his or her part. It is important for the person copying the music to do so neatly and accurately. If not, it will be extremely difficult for the artist to perform properly. In many cases Copyists now utilize computer hardware and software to do this job.

At certain times, the individual will be asked to copy a corrected or changed score. At other times, the individual may copy various parts for different instruments. A very talented individual may be asked to write the music from a record or tape onto paper without seeing a copy of the music. This is a very difficult feat and requires a thorough knowledge of music theory, notations, harmony, composition, and orchestration.

The music Copyist may work full-time, either independently or for a music publisher, or part-time. As a music Copyist, the person is responsible to the individual or organization using his or her services. If that person or organization feels that the work is inaccurate,

messy or illegible, or is not done on schedule, the music Copyist will not be hired again. As the amount of music work in any given area is limited, the word will get around and the individual will not be able to obtain more copying work.

Salaries

The American Federation of Musicians (AFM) sets minimum fees and wages for music Copyists. There are different fees depending on the type of work done.

Copyists are usually paid by the page copied in relation to the score page. They are usually remunerated per page and a half produced. Rates vary depending on the parts copied.

In certain situations, the Copyist may be paid by the hour. Individuals are urged to contact the AFM for current rates.

Employment Prospects

Employment prospects are good for music Copyists. There are opportunities for individuals who can perform this function in major music and cultural centers as well as in smaller cities. There are many groups, writers, composers, arrangers, and orchestrators who require this service.

Many Copyists do the job part-time while pursuing a career as a musician, singer, composer, etc. There are also many students who perform copying services while in school.

Advancement Prospects

Copyists may advance their careers by becoming well-known arrangers, composers, orchestrators, singers, etc. There are Copyists who go on to become music editors for music publishing companies.

Many individuals prefer to stay in copying and develop a clientele.

Education and Training

There is no formal educational requirement to become a Copyist. Individuals must know how to transcribe musical parts onto manuscript paper. They must have a knowledge of music notation, music theory, etc. This knowledge may be obtained in high school or college or at private music lessons. It might also be a self-taught skill.

Experience, Skills, and Personality Traits

As noted above, the Copyist must know how to transcribe music parts onto manuscript paper. The person must know and understand music notations and should be cognizant of music theory. The individual must write neatly and be accurate. Copyists who perform their job with the help of computers and special software will need computer skills.

Many Copyists are musicians and aspiring songwriters and arrangers. The person performing this function usually has a great interest in music.

Unions and Associations

Copyists may belong to the American Federation of Musicians (AFM) and/or the American Society of Music Copyists.

Tips for Entry

1. You may wish to advertise your skill in a newspaper or entertainment magazine in your area.
2. Put up signs in the music stores, record shops, and showcase clubs in your area.
3. Occasionally there are positions requiring the skill advertised in the help wanted sections of newspapers.
4. You may consider talking to local acts and groups and letting them know you provide this service. They might be interested.
5. Join the American Federation of Musicians. It is a valuable resource to your career.

WEBMASTER

Position Description

Most companies today have a presence on the World Wide Web. Record labels are no exception. Web sites are an important part of the way labels promote themselves and their artists.

The individual in charge of creating and putting together the Web site is called the Webmaster. The record label Webmaster has many responsibilities. Depending on the situation, he or she may work alone or may assign tasks to assistants, content producers, copywriters, graphic artists, etc.

One of the first things the Webmaster must do is find a host for the site. In order for a label (or any company) to have a Web site, they must rent a space or location on the Web. This may be done by obtaining a host. The label pays the host for the right to place their site online on the host's space. In some instances, the label and the host are one and the same.

In order for individuals to be able to locate the record label's Web site, it must have a Web address. This is called the domain name. The Webmaster works with the label management to develop a Web address that people can remember and that is available. Most often the Web address is the label's name.

The Webmaster's duties depend to a great extent on the size and structure of the label, the importance it puts on the Web site, and whether or not the Web site has already been set up.

The Webmaster is expected to discuss the direction the label wants the Web site to take and the goals of the Web site. Does the management just want a Web site to maintain a Web presence? Do they want people to be able to buy products while online? Will there be separate sites for each recording artist? Should Web site visitors be able to listen to snipets of songs or watch music videos online? Does the label want to sell advertising to other companies to increase revenue? Once the Webmaster understands what label management wants, he or she can get to work.

The Webmaster is responsible for developing and creating the label's Web site on the World Wide Web. He or she must design the site so that it is exciting and easy to use. The Webmaster must be sure that each webpage on the site opens easily and quickly. If they do not, people will often leave the site and surf to another location.

The Webmaster will develop the site, adding photos of the label's artists, and products; animations or other graphics; and perhaps sound. In creating the site, the Webmaster may manipulate images to the proper size and format. If this is not done correctly, an image may either be too large, slowing down the loading of a webpage, or too small, making it difficult to see clearly.

The Webmaster develops the site's search function so that people can search for something specific on the site. He or she may program pop-up windows, features, shopping carts, secure payment systems, the ability to hear artists' songs or see their videos, and a variety of other functions. The Webmaster may also build in technology so the label knows how long people stay on a specific webpage, which part of the site is most popular, how many hits the site gets, etc. Developing and designing the Web site is just one part of the job of the Webmaster. He or she is additionally responsible for the continued management and maintenance of the site. In order to keep a Web site fresh and timely, the Webmaster may change the homepage and update other parts of the site. Sometimes the site content changes daily. The Webmaster must make changes and remove out-of-date content.

Web sites are created in special languages so they can be displayed on the Internet. Text, for example, is converted into a language called HTML, or Hypertext Markup Language. Other languages may be used as well. The Webmaster must know how to format the special languages. Part of the job of the Webmaster is to monitor the site on a continuing basis. Every time new content or a link is added, the individual or one of his or her assistants must be sure everything on the site is working and all links are accurate.

The record label Webmaster is expected to make sure that the site is user-friendly. When there are problems with the site, the individual is responsible for handling them. This may include responding to inquiries from browsers having problems with the site.

Salaries

Earnings for Webmasters working for record labels may vary from approximately $32,000 to $150,000 or more annually. Variables include the geographic location, size, and prestige of the label and the specific site, as well as the responsibilities, experience, and reputation of the individual.

Webmasters who have a proven track record for developing creative sites that attract attention will earn the highest salaries.

It should be noted that some smaller labels hire consultants to handle their Web sites. These individuals may earn between $50 and $200 or more per hour.

Employment Prospects

Employment prospects for Webmasters aspiring to work at record labels are good. Depending on experience, individuals may work for major labels or may find employment at smaller independent labels. As noted, in some cases, individuals may work on a consulting basis.

Advancement Prospects

Webmasters who build Web sites that consistently attract visitors will have no trouble climbing the career ladder. Webmasters working for record labels may advance their careers in a number of ways. The most common method is locating similar positions with larger or more prestigious labels. This results in increased responsibilities and earnings. Some Webmasters decide to strike out on their own and start a consulting firm.

Education and Training

Education and training requirements vary for Webmasters working at record labels. Many Webmasters are self-taught. Some have taken classes. Others have college backgrounds or degrees in computers, programming, languages, graphics, Web authoring, and the Internet.

However it is learned, Webmasters must know HTML. It is also necessary to know other programming languages, such as Cold Fusion, PERL, and Active Server Pages. Knowing how to integrate databases is a plus.

It is essential that Webmasters update their skills by self-study and/or classes, seminars, and workshops to keep up with changes in technology.

Experience, Skills, and Personality Traits

Experience requirements depend, to a great extent, on the size and prestige of the label. Smaller independent labels just starting a Web site may not require Webmasters with a great deal of experience as long as they can prove that they can do an effective job. Larger, more prestigious labels will generally want their Webmasters to have a proven track record and experience.

Webmasters need excellent communications skills, both verbal and written. Creativity is essential. A knowledge of the music industry is helpful.

Individuals must have a total competence with Web dynamics, HTML authorship, and other programming languages. While some graphics work is outsourced or done by graphic designers within the company, graphic talent is necessary.

Unions and Associations

Individuals interested in learning more about careers in the field may obtain additional information by contacting the Internet Professional Publishers Association (IPPA) and the World Organization of Webmasters (WOW).

Tips for Entry

1. Look for internships at record labels. These will give you on-the-job training, experience, and the opportunity to make important contacts. Contact labels to see what they offer or talk to your college adviser.

2. Positions may be located in the classified section of newspapers. Look under heading such as "Webmaster," "Record Label," "Music Industry," "Web Careers," etc. Also look for ads under specific record label names.

3. Many labels also advertise openings on their Web sites. You might want to check them out.

4. Look for a job online. Start with the more popular job sites, such as www.hotjobs.com and www.monster.com, and go from there.

5. Get experience putting together Web sites for not-for-profit organizations or civic groups. Don't forget to add your name as the creator and Webmaster.

6. Send your résumé and a short cover letter to record labels at which you are interested in working. You can never tell when an opening exists.

7. Don't forget to read trade publications. *Billboard* often has advertisements for labels with openings in this area.

WEB SITE MARKETING MANAGER

Special Skills and Personality Traits—Creativity; good verbal and written communications skills; Internet savvy; understanding of music industry

Position Description

The music industry is very competitive. Record labels, like most other businesses today, need to find as many ways as possible to market their company and their products. As a result most record labels are now utilizing the Internet as a marketing tool.

A record label's Web site can be a very effective way to promote the label as well as the label's artists. The end result of a successfully marketed Web site can be thousands, if not millions, of products sold. This means money in the pocket of the label and the recording artist.

The music industry has changed from the day when the only way to get exposure for a new tune was to listen to the radio. While radio is still a huge way to push a new album, many people also listen to the "radio" via the Web. Others watch music television. Marketed correctly, fans will use the site to get information on their favorite artists, new CDs, and appearances.

With online buying becoming more and more popular, label Web sites can additionally generate income by selling the label's product's directly with no middleman. Additional income is often earned through selling commercial space to other complimentary companies on the site.

There are literally thousands of Web sites on the Internet. Some are companies who had well-known names and reputations prior to their Internet presence. Others are less well known. With so many sites available, how does any Web site attract visitors? As in traditional business, a Web site must market its presence.

The Web Site Marketing Manager for a record label has an important job. He or she is responsible for finding ways to market the site, the label, and its artists to current and potential fans.

Responsibilities may vary, depending on the size and structure of the label and its Web site. At some labels, a marketing director and one or two assistants handle all the marketing functions, including the Web site. Increasingly, however, record labels are hiring Web Site Marketing Managers whose sole job is marketing the label's Web site. The individual in this position can mean the success or failure of the site.

The Web Site Marketing Manager is responsible for developing the concepts and campaigns that will determine how the site will be marketed. The individual is expected to determine the most effective techniques and programs to market the site and its contents. To do this, the individual will work closely with the label's marketing director.

As part of this job, the marketing manager must plan and coordinate the site's marketing goals and objectives. How will people know the Web site is online? How will they know its Web address? Who will the site be marketed toward? Who is the label trying to attract? Marketing a Web site is slightly different than marketing a traditional business. Visitors to online sites can come from virtually anywhere in the world.

Additionally, many record labels have mini-sites within the main site for each of the label's artists. In these cases, the marketing manager may be responsible for marketing each mini-site as well.

It is essential that the marketing manager find ways to include the Web address in as many places as possible. This includes all CDs, artist promo material, advertising, etc. The more people hear a Web address, the more likely they are to remember it and visit to see what's happening on the site. The label's Web address must be added to all television commercials, print advertisements, billboards, stationery, etc. This helps keep the name and address of the label in the public eye.

The Web Site Marketing Manager is often expected to do research to obtain information about people visiting the site. He or she may prepare questionnaires or surveys to be placed on the site. In order to entice people to answer questionnaires, the Web site may offer a gift or entry into a sweepstakes.

Often Web Site Marketing Managers advertise their site on other Web sites via banner ads. An individual need only click on the banner ad to be taken to the site of the advertiser. In many instances, the label Web Site Marketing Manager partners with another company to obtain more exposure. For example, a record label may partner with record store chains, radio stations, etc.

Record label Web Site Marketing Managers are expected to develop innovative ideas to try to attract new fans and visitors to the site. In many situations, the Web Site Marketing Manager may work with the label's promotion department to develop contests, sweepstakes, and other promotions which can be entered online. People will then have an incentive to go to the label Web site. The more people who visit the Web site, the more exposure for the label's artists, which results in more sales.

Once people log on to a label's Web site to enter contests, the hope is they will return to the site to browse, read about an artist, find out about appearances, or buy products. To accomplish this, many marketing managers run sweepstakes that individuals can enter daily. This means visitors have an incentive to visit the label's Web site daily and hopefully be attracted to something of interest on the site.

Another reason Web Site Marketing Managers use sweepstakes is to help build mailing lists. When people enter sweepstakes, they usually provide their name, address, phone number, age, and e-mail address. Additional information may be gathered as well, which may be helpful in targeting specific visitors to the site and finding ways to sell CDs, T-shirts, photographs, videos, tickets to shows, etc.

Marketing managers also use sweepstakes to build lists for e-mail newsletters. These newsletters are useful for informing fans about new CDs, videos, artist events, and appearances. Sometimes these lists are also used when new videos are being shown on music television.

Many label Web Site Marketing Managers create online fan clubs and chat rooms. The idea is to keep a constant interest in the label's artists.

The marketing manager who can come up with innovative and creative ideas might get the attention of media journalists or others doing stories on interesting Web sites. Depending on which media show a story appears, the exposure can lead to thousands of Web site hits.

Depending on the size and structure of the label, the Web Site Marketing Manager may work with the label's main marketing, advertising, public relations, or promotion department. In some situations, the Web Site Marketing Manager may also be responsible for handling the public relations and advertising functions of the Web site as well.

Salaries

Annual earnings for record label Web Site Marketing Managers can range from approximately $27,000 to $65,000 or more. Variables affecting earnings include the geographic location, size, and prestige of the specific label and its Web site, as well as the experience and responsibilities of the individual.

Employment Prospects

Employment prospects for this position are good. In addition to major labels located in music capitals such as New York, Los Angeles, and Nashville, there are many independent labels located throughout the country. Web sites give independent labels, or "indies" as they are often referred to, an opportunity to gain local and global exposure for their artists.

Advancement Prospects

Record label Web Site Marketing Managers have a number of options for career advancement. Some individuals get experience, prove themselves, and move on to similar positions at larger or more prestigious labels. This results in increased responsibilities and earnings.

Other individuals may climb the career ladder by moving into positions as label marketing directors. Still other individuals strike out on their own to start a marketing firm.

Education and Training

Generally larger, more prestigious, or well-known labels will require their Web Site Marketing Managers to hold a minimum of a four-year college degree. Good choices for majors include public relations, advertising, business, journalism, marketing, liberal arts, English, communications, and business. While smaller, lesser-known labels may prefer a college degree, it might not be a requirement.

Courses and seminars in marketing, public relations, publicity, promotion, the music industry, and Web marketing are also helpful.

Experience, Skills, and Personality Traits

Record label Web Site Marketing Managers must be tech savvy. Communications skills, both written and verbal, are essential to success in this field. Individuals should be creative, innovative, ambitious, articulate, and highly motivated. Marketing managers also need the ability to handle many details and projects at one time without getting flustered and stressed.

A knowledge of publicity, promotion, public relations, and advertising as well as research techniques is also necessary.

Unions and Associations

Record label Web Site Marketing Managers may belong to a number of trade associations providing support and guidance. These include the American Marketing Association (AMA), the Marketing Research Association (MRA), and the Public Relations Society of America (PRSA). Individuals might also belong to the National Academy of Recording Arts and Sciences (NARAS) or genre-specific associations, such as the Country Music Association (CMA) or the Gospel Music Association (GMA).

Tips for Entry

1. Positions may be advertised in the classified section of newspapers. Look under headings including "Marketing," "Marketing Manager," "Web Site Marketing," "Record Label Marketing," "Recording Industry," and "Record Label Marketing Manager."
2. Send your résumé and a cover letter to record labels at which you are interested in working. Ask that your résumé be kept on file.
3. Look for jobs online. Check out popular sites, such as www.hotjobs.com and www.monster.com, to get started. Go from there.
4. Take seminars and courses in marketing, promotion, public relations, publicity, and Web marketing. These will give you an edge over other applicants as well as help you hone your skills and make valuable contacts.
5. Many labels advertise openings on their Web sites. Check them out.

WEB SITE CONTENT PRODUCER

CAREER PROFILE

Duties: Develop and create content for record label Web site; research and write articles for Web site

Alternate Title(s): Web Site Content Editor

Salary Range: $29,000 to $80,000

Employment Prospects: Fair

Advancement Prospects: Good

Best Geographical Location(s) for Position: Music capitals such as New York City, Los Angeles, and Nashville for major record labels; other areas hosting record companies

Prerequisites:

Education or Training—College degree required

Experience—Writing and editing experience necessary

Special Skills and Personality Traits—Good command of the English language; excellent writing

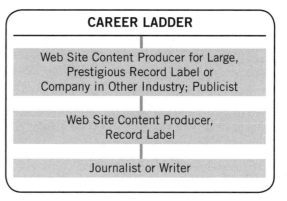

CAREER LADDER

Web Site Content Producer for Large, Prestigious Record Label or Company in Other Industry; Publicist

Web Site Content Producer, Record Label

Journalist or Writer

skills; creative; understanding of the music industry; Internet savvy

Position Description

Web sites give a record label exposure on the Web and another avenue for showcasing their artists. Just as print newspapers and magazines need writers and editors, many Web sites have content producers.

The main function of the Web Site Content Producer is to create and develop interesting and unique content for a label's site. Individuals in this position are responsible for researching and writing engaging articles and blurbs in a variety of areas. Depending on the specific label and the structure of the site, there might be artist bios, stories about upcoming tours, announcements regarding new CDs, and features about label artists.

If the record label Web site is large, there may be more than one content producer. For example, one content producer may handle the webpages of two or three of the label's major artists, while another might handle the content on the webpages of the label's newer artists. One may handle events or be responsible for developing the copy for on-site contests and promotions. Another may be responsible for the content on the home page.

Labels hosting large Web sites often have a senior or executive Web Site Content Producer. He or she may be responsible for overseeing the work of the other content producers.

The label Web Site Content Producer often oversees on-staff copywriters and graphic artists. Some content producers are also responsible for finding and retaining freelancers to write articles on specific subjects. A content producer in charge of an entire label Web site may, for example, find writers to do stories in cities where one of the label's artists is touring. Once stories come in, the content producer edits them and gets them ready for the Webmaster to put online.

The record label Web Site Content Producer may be responsible for interviewing label artists and obtaining photos to make the online stories interesting. He or she may develop eye-catching headlines for each article or blurb.

One of the great things about the Internet is that it can be interactive. The Content Producer may develop surveys, questionnaires, or other pieces to involve those visiting the site. In this manner, the label can gather information such as what track fans like best of a new CD. The Content Producer may also develop online chats, where fans get a chance to talk in cyberspace to their favorite artists.

The Web Site Content Producer works closely with the label's promotion and publicity department in order to get as much important information out as possible. With the Internet, items can be posted online almost instantly. If news breaks, the content producer need only develop a story and get it online.

The Web Site Content Producer is often responsible for acquiring pictures, animation, and other graphics to make the content more appealing. He or she may utilize the services of graphic artists, photographers, or others to accomplish this task. The individual may work with the webmaster to find just the right images which will look good, but not affect the ease of opening the site.

It is essential for record labels to keep their Web sites fresh, or else they risk losing return visitors. The Web Site Content Producer is often responsible for daily updates. He or she may post artist events or daily news.

Salaries

Annual earnings for record label Web Site Content Producers can vary from approximately $29,000 to $80,000 or more annually. Variables include the geographic location, size, and prestige of the label and the specific site, as well as the responsibilities, experience, and reputation of the individual.

It should be noted that some smaller labels hire consultants to handle the content on their Web sites. These individuals may earn between $15 and $50 or more per hour or may be paid on a per-project basis.

Employment Prospects

Employment prospects are fair for record label Web Site Content Producers and are getting better every day. Depending on the experience of the individual, he or she might work for a major label or an independent label in cities throughout the country.

An interesting fact to note is that due to the nature of the Web Site Content Producer's job, some employers may allow individuals to telecommute all or part of the time. Individuals may also find part-time or consulting positions.

Advancement Prospects

Record label Web Site Content Producers may advance their careers in a number of ways. The most common method of advancement is locating a similar position at a larger, more prestigious record label, resulting in increased responsibilities and earnings. Individuals who are working on a specific area of a label's Web site may be promoted to executive content producer. Some Web Site Content Producers find similar positions in other industries. There are also some Web Site Content Producers who move into positions in the publicity or public relations department of the label.

Education and Training

Most record labels require that people in this position have a minimum of a four-year college degree. Good choices for majors include journalism, communications, English, public relations, marketing, and liberal arts.

While it may not be required, individuals who know HTML may have a leg up on other candidates. Courses, workshops, and seminars in public relations, writing, promotion, journalism, and the music industry will be helpful in honing skills and making new contacts.

Experience, Skills, and Personality Traits

Web Site Content Producers working for record labels generally need some type of writing and editing experience. Some individuals have journalism backgrounds, while others have worked in publicity or public relations. Experience requirements depend on the size and prestige of the label.

Web Site Content Producers should have a good command of the English language, great writing skills, and creativity. Editing skills are also necessary. A knowledge of the music industry is helpful.

Web Site Content Producers should have the ability to multitask and work under pressure without getting flustered. People skills are mandatory in this position. Those who are Web savvy will have an advantage.

Unions and Associations

Individuals interested in learning more about careers in the field may obtain additional information by contacting the Internet Professionals Association (IPA) and the World Organization of Webmasters (WOW). Record label Web Site Content Producers may also belong to various music-related associations, such as the National Academy of Recording Arts and Sciences (NARAS) or genre-specific associations, such as the Country Music Association (CMA) or the Gospel Music Association (GMA).

Tips for Entry

1. Internships at record labels are a great way to get your foot in the door, learn skills, and make important contacts.
2. Positions may be located in the classified section of newspapers. Look under headings such as "Record Label Web Site Content Producer," "Web site Content Manager," "Record Labels," and "Web Careers."
3. These types of jobs may be found online. Many labels advertise openings on their Web sites. Also

check out the more popular job sites, such as www. hotjobs.com and www.monster.com.

4. Get as much writing experience as you can. Consider a part-time job with a local newspaper. If you are still in school, get involved in your school newspaper and/or Web site.

5. Don't forget to read trade publications. *Billboard* often has advertisements for labels with openings.

6. Send your résumé and a short cover letter to record label personnel departments. Ask that your résumé be kept on file if there are no current openings.

RADIO AND TELEVISION

PROGRAM DIRECTOR

Duties: Select format, programs, and schedule for radio station; may also act in the capacity of the music director

Alternate Title(s): P.D.

Salary Range: $27,000 to $100,000+

Employment Prospects: Fair

Advancement Prospects: Fair

Best Geographical Locations for Position: Local communities for small market stations; New York City, Los Angeles, Chicago, Atlanta, etc., for major market stations

Prerequisites:

　Education or Training—Some stations may prefer college degree or broadcast school training

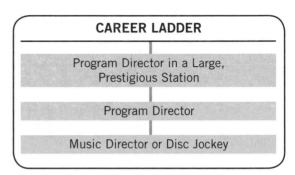

Experience—Hands-on training in radio station helpful

Special Skills and Personality Traits—Knowledge of radio stations; understanding of music industry; ability to supervise, hire, and fire; responsible

Position Description

The Program Director of a radio station holds a very important position. He or she is responsible for selecting the station's format and programs. The individual is also responsible for scheduling the programs at times when they will reach the largest audience.

In certain stations, the Program Director also works as the music director, selecting music for the playlist. The Program Director might also have his or her own show, working as a disc jockey or an on-air personality.

Most Program Directors begin their career in radio as disc jockeys, although there are a small number of individuals who move into the position having had other jobs at a radio station.

The Program Director or P.D., as he or she is sometimes referred to, is responsible for everything that is said or played at the station. If a station is sold or is not doing well, the Program Director may have to revise the station's format. There are a number of formats that can be selected, including Top 40, MOR (middle of the road), A/C (Adult contemporary), oldies, classical, talk, news-oriented, jazz, country, dance-oriented music, U/C (Urban contemporary), or a combination.

The Program Director must have a thorough knowledge of the community his or her station serves and must recommend the type of format likely to attract the most listeners. The larger the audience, the higher the ratings. Ratings determine advertising and commercial rates, which is how radio stations derive income.

The Program Director decides what kind of public-service shows should be aired, who should host them, and when they should be on. The P.D. also decides how many times the news, weather, and community affairs announcements will be read and when they will air.

The P.D. is often responsible for hiring, supervising, and firing disc jockeys. It is his or her job to communicate to the disc jockeys the image the station wants to project.

One of the more important responsibilities of the Program Director is to develop a segue. The segue is the way that records are rotated in relation to other records, commercials, and announcements. For instance, a station might play a ballad, then a Top 40 tune, have a commercial, another Top 40 tune and an oldie-but-goodie; then the cycle would start over again. A good segue can keep an audience interested and excited. A boring segue can prompt listeners to switch to another station.

P.D.s also spend time with record promotion people, who visit the station in hopes of getting their clients on the station's playlist. The program director usually makes up a new list every week or two.

In general the P.D. is responsible to the station manager or owner. He or she will usually work long hours. There are many times when a P.D. must come in early, work late or come in on days off because of special station promotions. However, a special sense of pride can be derived from boosting a station's ratings.

Salaries

Salaries for Program Directors vary depending on the size of the station, its location, its popularity, and the experience and responsibility of the individual. Salaries can range from $27,000 to $100,000 plus annually. The lower salary would be for an individual without a great deal of experience working in a small station. The higher salary would go to those working in large stations in major markets.

Employment Prospects

Almost every radio station in the country has a Program Director. However, the Program Director's job might be combined with that of music director or disc jockey.

Employment prospects are fair for an individual seeking a position in a small station in a sparsely populated community. Experience helps attain a job in a middle or major market, although finding such a position becomes more difficult relative to the station's size and audience.

Advancement Prospects

Opportunities for advancement are fair. The best career path to advancement in this type of position is for the individual to seek a job as Program Director at a larger, more prestigious station, which will in turn provide a higher salary and more responsibility. The Program Director might also advance his or her career by moving into the position of the station's general manager. Opportunities for this type of career advancement, however, are poor.

Education and Training

Educational requirements vary for positions as Program Director. Some stations prefer a college degree in communications or broadcasting, but that will not guarantee an individual a job.

There are a number of radio broadcasting vocational or trade schools located around the country. Many of these schools are good ones. It is wise to look into the school through the state's Attorney General's office and/or the Department of Consumer Affairs.

Experience, Skills, and Personality Traits

Most Program Directors begin their careers as disc jockeys. Often they have had experience working at college radio stations or other stations before obtaining their position.

Program Directors must have the ability to understand the type of market their station is trying to reach.

The Program Director must have a great deal of knowledge about music and be up on trends. He or she is responsible for the station's programming and cannot let personal music preferences affect decision making.

Unions and Associations

Program Directors may belong to the National Association of Broadcasters (NAB). They may also be members of the American Federation of Television and Radio Artists (AFTRA). As Program Directors, individuals may also belong to the National Association of Broadcast Employees and Technicians (NABET).

Tips for Entry

1. Work in a college radio station and/or a local station as a disc jockey to gain experience.
2. Certain larger stations have college credit internship programs. It is not unusual for a station to hire an intern after graduation.
3. There are positions advertised in most of the radio and record-oriented trades, including *Radio and Records, Billboard,* and *Broadcasting,* to name a few.
4. Openings and positions are also often advertised in the classified sections of newspapers. Look under "Radio," "Broadcasting," "Program Director," and "Music" heading classifications.
5. Openings can be located online. Check out radio station Web sites and job search Web sites.

MUSIC DIRECTOR

Position Description

The Music Director of a radio station is responsible for selecting music for specific programs aired on the station. The individual works closely with the program director. In certain stations, the Music Director is also the program director. The Music Director might also have his or her own show, working as a disc jockey.

Music Directors as a rule began their careers in radio as disc jockeys. During the time they were D.J.'s they proved that they had expertise in selecting CDs and putting shows together.

The Music Director's duties vary depending on what type of format is being used by the station and the duties of the program director. He or she may spend time with the record label promotional people, screening tunes for the program director to listen to. The two then discuss the CDs that could potentially hit when they air them in their market.

Music Directors assist the program director in most music-oriented activities. The individual helps the P.D. research the market, determine the kind of audience the station plays to, learn what the people want to hear, and get a feel for station listeners' likes and dislikes.

The individual often meets with or talks to the managers of major record stores in the area. Through these meetings, he or she can find out what's hot in record releases.

The Music Director, along with the program director, might help train new disc jockeys and help them adjust to the station's procedures. This is often done by listening to air checks, which are short tapes of the different on-air personalities recorded at various times.

The Music Director is responsible directly to the program director. He or she works long hours. When the station is short of on-air personnel, the program director might assign the Music Director to take another shift. In addition, the Music Director often takes part in special appearances or promotions. These special shows usually take place during a weekend or at night.

Salaries

Salaries for Music Directors vary depending on the size of the radio station, its location, its popularity, the duties of the Music Director, and his or her experience. Salaries tend to be highest in major markets, such as New York City, Los Angeles, Chicago, etc.

Music Directors' salaries can range from $25,000 to $95,000 or more annually. In addition, many jobs offer other benefits.

Employment Prospects

Employment prospects are fair for Music Directors. It should be noted that in some stations the job of Music Director is combined with the job with that of the program director.

The best place to look for a position is in a small to midsized station. The individual can then gain experience, making it easier to find a position at a bigger station.

Advancement Prospects
A Music Director can advance to the position of program director at a radio station. The individual may also advance his or her career by becoming a Music Director at a better or bigger station.

Education and Training
There is no formal educational requirement for a job as a Music Director. Many stations prefer or require a college degree or broadcasting school training. If the individual does attend college, he or she should take courses in communications, journalism, music, and broadcasting. He or she should also work on the school's radio station. This will give the individual hands-on training.

There are many radio broadcasting vocational and trade schools located around the country. Although a majority of these schools are good ones, some are not. Check into the school's reputation through the state's Attorney General's office and/or the Department of Consumer Affairs.

Experience, Skills, and Personality Traits
Most Music Directors begin working in radio stations as disc jockeys. If they've been to college, they also have experience working on their college radio stations.

Music Directors, as a rule, like music. They enjoy listening to records and have the knack of knowing what will be hot.

Individuals in this position must be responsible people who have the ability to supervise others.

Unions and Associations
Music Directors may belong to the National Association of Broadcasters (NAB). Depending on the job situation, they might also belong to the American Federation of Television and Radio Artists (AFTRA). Music Directors may additionally belong to the National Association of Broadcast Employees and Technicians (NABET).

Tips for Entry
1. Work in a college radio station and/or a local station to gain experience.
2. Certain larger stations have college credit internship programs. It is not unusual for a station to hire an intern after graduation.
3. Openings and positions are often advertised in the classified sections of newspapers.
4. There are also positions advertised in most of the radio- and record-oriented trades, including *Radio and Records, Billboard,* and *Broadcasting.*
5. Search for openings online. Radio station and job search Web sites may list openings.

DISC JOCKEY

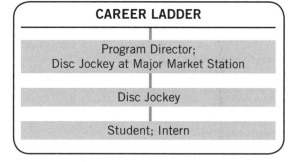

Position Description

A Disc Jockey's main responsibility is to introduce the CDs, commercials, news, and public announcements that are aired on a station. The Disc Jockey is expected to have some sort of style or personality to project over the air waves. This personality is what makes a Disc Jockey successful and gives him or her a following.

Disc Jockeys work in time shifts. Shifts vary, but usually range from three to five hours in length. D.J.'s are usually assigned the same shift every day. Popular Disc Jockeys receive the most listened-to shifts, such as the morning drive, afternoon drive, or early evenings slot.

Depending on the size of the station and its makeup, the jock has additional responsibilities. Sometimes the D.J. is responsible for picking out the music for his or her show. This usually occurs in small market stations that have small staffs. They must, however, choose records from an approved playlist put together by the station's program or music director.

Sometimes the Disc Jockey is also the acting music or program director. This, once again, depends on the size of the station and how it is staffed. If the station is small, the Disc Jockey might also be responsible for putting the records on the turntable and working the sound controls.

During the course of his or her shift, the D.J. sometimes comes up with comments, ad libs, the weather, or information about the records he or she is introducing.

Disc Jockeys have other activities besides performing on the air. As the Disc Jockey becomes a celebrity of sorts (even in small markets), he or she may make public appearances for store promotions, station promotions, or charity events. He or she also might do voice-overs on commercials for radio or television. In addition, Disc Jockeys might act as live jocks at clubs or discos, or even host concerts in large or small facilities.

The Disc Jockey is responsible to the program director, music director, or station manager.

Salaries

Salaries for Disc Jockeys vary according to a number of factors, including the size of the station, the market, the experience of the jock, and his or her appeal.

Salaries can start at approximately $25,000 a year for a beginner in a small market station. A Disc Jockey who is very popular may earn $225,000 plus annually. In addition, Disc Jockeys may make additional income from personal appearances, voice-over commercials, and doing club D.J. work. There are some Disc Jockeys who earn $1,000,000 or more through a combination of salary, personal appearances, and endorsements.

Employment Prospects

Employment prospects in small market stations are fair. There is a large turnover at many of these stations because pay is so low and people want to move on to better positions.

Employment prospects get tougher as the station's market gets larger.

Advancement Prospects
The Disc Jockey at a small market station has an opportunity to advance to the position of program director or music director at that station or a similar station. He or she also has the option of trying to locate a position at a better station in a bigger market.

Education and Training
Educational requirements vary for the position of Disc Jockey. Many stations prefer or require their employees to have a college degree, background, or vocational training. If the individual is considering college, courses in communications and broadcasting are useful. Working on the college radio station is also valuable experience. This gives the individual hands-on training.

If the person is planning on attending a broadcasting vocational or trade school, he or she should check out the reputation of the school. This can be accomplished through the state's Attorney General's office and/or the Department of Consumer Affairs. Although most of these schools have good reputations, some do not.

Experience, Skills, and Personality Traits
Many Disc Jockeys begin their careers by participating in a high school radio club. They then move on to a college station and learn many additional radio jobs.

A Disc Jockey must have a good speaking voice and the ability to project his or her personality over the air.

The Disc Jockey must be responsible and dependable. He or she must consistently show up on time for his or her air shift.

Disc Jockeys must obtain a license from the FCC (Federal Communications Commission). This is obtained by having a letter sent to the FCC by the prospective employer stating that the individual has a job in the broadcasting field. An application must also be filled in and submitted.

Unions and Associations
Disc Jockeys may be members of the American Federation of Television and Radio Artists (AFTRA). Individuals might also belong to the National Association of Broadcasting (NAB) or be an associate member of the National Academy of Recording Arts and Sciences (NARAS). Disc Jockeys may additionally belong to the National Association of Broadcast Employees and Technicians (NABET).

Tips for Entry
1. Positions may be advertised in the classified sections of newspapers. Look under key words such as "Disc Jockey," "Radio," or "Music."
2. Other openings may be advertised in the radio and record trades, such as *Billboard, Broadcasting,* and *Radio and Records.*
3. See if you can get into a college internship at a radio station.
4. Work on your high school or college radio station for experience.
5. Make a demo tape and send it along with your résumé to a station's general manager or personnel director (depending on the station size). Make sure you make a few copies of the tape and always keep one.
6. Search for openings online. Radio stations may advertise openings on their Web sites. You might also find openings on job sites such as hotjobs.com, monster.com, and simplyhired.com.

VIDEO JOCKEY

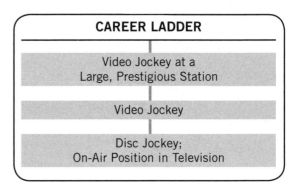

Position Description

Video Jockeys are similar in many ways to radio disc jockeys. The main difference is that instead of introducing records on radio, the Video Jockey introduces music videos on television.

Previously, it took a certain amount of time for new tunes to become hits. Today success can be almost instantaneous. Now a new tune can be aired via a music video to the entire country on network and/or cable television. Within minutes, radio stations will start getting calls to play the record and a hit is made.

Video Jockeys, or V.J.'s, as they are often called, are the people who announce to the viewing audience the music videos they will be seeing. The individuals may talk about the video or its performers.

The V.J. is expected to project a particular style or personality. It is this style and personality which will determine the success and popularity of the individual. Very successful V.J.'s can develop followings which in turn may lead to better show slots or opportunities at larger, more prestigious stations.

Video Jockeys have varied responsibilities depending on the size of the station or the popularity of the show that they are involved with. The Video Jockey

may work in specific time shifts if he or she is hosting a live show or may tape a number of video shows in a given period of time.

The Video Jockey may be expected only to introduce music videos or may have additional duties. For example, the individual may host an entire show during which he or she interviews music acts, reviews new videos, lists Top 10 videos, etc. The V.J. may be in charge of choosing which videos will be shown on his or her show or may just comment on videos that have been suggested by a program director.

Major music video networks will usually have a program director or station executive view new videos and decide when and if they should be included on the station's playlist. If the V.J. is hosting a show on a local or cable station (i.e., not on a music video network, such as VH1 or Country Music Television) the individual may be responsible for reviewing videos to see if they fit the format of the particular show.

Video Jockeys, even those appearing on small market or local cable stations, often become celebrities in their viewing area. They may be expected to make public appearances for station promotions, functions, or charity events. In some situations, the Video Jockey may also work as a D.J. on a radio station or at a live event. The individual might also be asked to host concerts or act as M.C. for acts touring the city.

At smaller stations the Video Jockey may be expected to fulfill other obligations in other areas. He or she may, for example, be asked to help with the copywriting of scripts for commercials or even to sell advertising. The individual may also be the entertainment or music reporter for the station. In larger stations, the individual usually would not have to perform these tasks.

The Video Jockey may be responsible to the program director or the station's general manager. He or she may work regular hours or may tape all his or her shows in a given time period. Many V.J.'s working in small local or cable stations do just one or two shows a week.

Salaries

Salaries for Video Jockeys can range greatly depending on a number of variables. These include the size of the television station, its location, and the type of show. Other variables include the experience and responsibilities the individual has, as well as his or her popularity. At certain stations the Video Jockey will be represented by a union. In these cases, the union will set minimum earnings that individuals may be paid. Stations in smaller markets will usually have the lowest salaries because individuals in these positions are just entering the job market. Individuals working on music television oriented stations or those working for major market stations or networks will be earning the most. Salaries can range from $25,000 for those who have shows on small local stations to $250,000 plus a year for V.J.'s who have large followings. Individuals may also earn additional income by doing personal appearances and endorsements. These individuals may earn $500,000 or more.

Employment Prospects

Employment prospects for individuals seeking jobs as Video Jockeys in television are poor but are increasing. With the current surge in new local, syndicated, and cable television stations around the country, there will be more and more employment opportunities in the coming years. Opportunities will present themselves as more local and cable television shows begin to air music video shows.

It is easier for individuals with little or no experience to enter the job market in smaller stations. In these situations they may often get the job just by suggesting a video show as a possibility for a program format.

Advancement Prospects

Advancement prospects are poor for Video Jockeys but are getting better as music expands. Individuals may climb the career ladder in a number of ways. The V.J. may obtain a following and command a higher salary or he or she may look for employment at a larger, more prestigious station.

The individual may find that he or she can find better employment in radio and become a disc jockey at a larger station, thereby increasing his or her earnings. The individual might also go into broadcast news or reporting outside the realm of the music industry.

Education and Training

While no formal education may be required to obtain a position as a Video Jockey, it must be remembered that the music and broadcast industries are extremely competitive. Those who aspire to become successful may want to be as prepared as possible. A college degree with a major in television, broadcasting, or the music business may be helpful in climbing the career ladder.

Experience, Skills, and Personality Traits

A Video Jockey should have a pleasant or distinctive appearance. This is important because the V.J. will be seen by an audience. The individual should be comfortable around television cameras, microphones, and lights.

The Video Jockey should have a good speaking voice and be articulate. He or she should be personable and have the ability to project his or her personality over the air.

An understanding of television production is useful. Knowledge of camera angles, directions, lighting, etc., is helpful, but may not be necessary, depending on the situation.

The Video Jockey should have a good understanding of music and keep abreast of current trends, acts, etc. It is imperative that the V.J. is responsible and dependable. He or she must be punctual. For those who are scheduled to host live broadcasts, being late can be a disaster. Arriving late for a taping can cause problems in scheduling and will cost the station additional funds, as well.

Unions and Associations

Depending on the situation, station, and the responsibilities of the individual, the Video Jockey may be a member of the American Federation of Television and Radio Artists (AFTRA), the National Association of Broadcast Employees and Technicians AFL-CIO (NABET), or be an associate member of the National Academy of Recording Arts and Sciences (NARAS).

Tips for Entry

1. Try to choose a college with a television station, and get involved in as many facets of its operation as possible.
2. If your college does not have a television station, get involved with the school radio station. You need experience on the air.
3. Consider working as an intern or a secretary at a local station part time or for the summer. Hands-on experience in the field is helpful.
4. Positions in this field may be located in the display or classified section of newspapers under "V.J.," "Broadcasting," or "Television" heading classifications.
5. Larger stations often offer training programs or internships. Try to locate these opportunities.
6. A job in radio as a disc jockey will help you make valuable contacts.
7. Have a short video demo made to show your talent to potential station managers.
8. Keep an eye out for casting calls for V.J.'s often advertised on music television.

ON THE ROAD

TOUR COORDINATOR

Duties: Coordinate the many facets of an act's tour

Alternate Title(s): None

Salary Range: $35,000 to $175,000+

Employment Prospects: Poor

Advancement Prospects: Fair

Best Geographical Location(s) for Position: Most major tours are planned from booking agencies or management firms in New York City, Los Angeles, and Nashville

Prerequisites:

Education or Training—No formal educational requirement; college background required or preferred; see text

Experience—Travel and touring experience with music acts as road manager, tour publicist, etc.

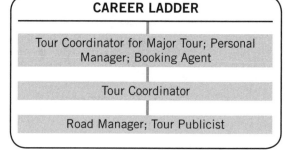

Special Skills and Personality Traits—Ability to assert authority; freedom to travel; communications skills; organized; responsible; detail oriented

Position Description

The position of Tour Coordinator is one of the most important jobs on the road. The individual in this position is responsible for coordinating all of the many facets of an act's tour. He or she oversees everything that is done by all members of the tour staff while the act is on the road. It is the duty of the Tour Coordinator to supervise not only the road personnel but the act as well.

The Tour Coordinator's job starts well before the tour leaves for its first destination. He or she works with the act's management, booking agents, and publicists. The individual maps out the location of concerts and their dates and times. He or she then discusses with the publicist or tour publicist other appearances that have to be made, including radio interviews, television spots, print media interviews, special promotions, stops at record shops, etc. These are added to the list of times, dates, and locations.

The Tour Coordinator may work out what transportation will be used by which members of the entourage. Often, for example, the singers travel by plane, the musicians by private bus, and the equipment crew by truck. In instances where the group must travel 2,000 miles in a day, the logical transportation would be an airplane. The Tour Coordinator must decide if a chartered jet would be better than a commercial flight. The individual finds the best routes to take, makes reserva-

tions at hotels, and rents cars, limos, buses, and planes. As a rule, the Tour Coordinator tries to make the best arrangements as economically as possible.

The Tour Coordinator also plans the tour day by day—sometimes hour by hour—to use time as well as possible. He or she tries to get everyone where he or she is supposed to be with the least amount of effort. The road gets grueling, and sometimes the Tour Coordinator must weigh the price of flying against traveling a cheaper way and having the act come in too exhausted to put on a good show.

Once the tour leaves, the Tour Coordinator really goes into action. He or she must coordinate all the activities of the entourage. The problems of the entourage, the act, and the promoters often become the problems of the Coordinator.

The Tour Coordinator works closely with the Tour Manager, as many of their responsibilities are interchangeable. Sometimes he or she is also the road manager. Tour Coordinators also keep in close contact with the act's management and agents. He or she lets them know if everything is going according to schedule or if the act will be late for a particular date.

If a car or bus breaks down, it is the Tour Coordinator's responsibility to make sure another means of transportation is found. If a member of the backup band gets sick while on the road, the Tour Coordinator must find a replacement. If the act has a major problem during the tour, the individual must deal with it or at least delegate someone to handle the situation.

Tours can be long (no matter how short they really are). Life on the road is not for everyone. The Tour Coordinator must be able to deal with the responsibilities of the job and the road while everyone around is under tremendous pressure. Most tours average six to eight weeks, although there are shorter and longer ones; hours are long and irregular. The Tour Coordinator is always on call, not only for the act and the entourage, but also from management, agents, the act's family, etc.

Tour Coordinators often come off the road and are so physically and mentally exhausted that they must take a few weeks off and do nothing.

The one thing all Tour Coordinators, road managers, and road personnel have in common is a love of music and of life on the road.

Salaries

Salaries of Tour Coordinators are usually high. An individual could start at $700 per week. However, the remuneration is usually much higher. The average is between $850 and $2,000 per week plus either expenses or a per diem.

Experienced Tour Coordinators who work on prestigious tours often earn $3,500 or more per week plus expenses and bonuses.

Tour Coordinators are not always on staff and therefore may not work every week. There are some situations where the Tour Coordinator is paid a reduced salary while a group is not actively working in order to retain his or her services.

Employment Prospects

The outlook is not good for Tour Coordinators. There are few jobs in this area and more potential Tour Coordinators than positions.

With the current high price of touring, there are tours that go out with fewer personnel, using road managers instead. Those who prove themselves may find opportunities with major acts as well as lesser known acts who are on the way up.

Advancement Prospects

As a Tour Coordinator, an individual can advance his or her career by becoming a Tour Coordinator for a better-known group or for a major, prestigious tour.

There are a few Tour Coordinators who go into personal management or booking after their experience as Tour Coordinators.

Education and Training

There is no formal educational requirement for this position. However, a college background often helps with the job. Courses in accounting, bookkeeping, psychology, publicity, and the music business are useful.

Experience, Skills, and Personality Traits

Many Tour Coordinators were roadies, road managers, and publicists prior to their current position. There are Tour Coordinators who worked as travel agents or travel escorts but always had a love of music.

The most important trait a Tour Coordinator can have is a love of the road and travel. The individual in this position has to like living out of a suitcase. He or she also must be responsible, dependable, and able to supervise an entourage of people. The Tour Coordinator must be organized. A disorganized person can make a shambles of a tour. He or she must also have the ability to deal effectively with a crisis.

Unions and Associations

There is no union or association specific to Tour Coordinators.

Tips for Entry

1. This is another of the positions in the music business that you get through contacts. If you have any, use them. If you don't, develop some.
2. Advertise your availability in a small display or classified ad in one of the music trades.
3. Experience helps. If you have put together a tour for anyone, even an unknown show group, put it on your résumé.
4. Send your résumé to the personnel department of major record labels.

ROAD MANAGER

CAREER PROFILE

Duties: Handle problems that occur while act is traveling; supervise equipment, sound, and light personnel

Alternate Title(s): Tour Manager

Salary Range: $25,000 to $125,000+

Employment Prospects: Fair

Advancement Prospects: Fair

Best Geographical Locations for Position: Major tours are usually planned in New York City, Los Angeles, and Nashville; positions may be available throughout the country

Prerequisites:

Education or Training—No formal education required

Experience—Positions as roadie or equipment manager helpful

Special Skills and Personality Traits—Responsibility; ability to work under pressure; dependability; ability to supervise; freedom to travel; ingenuity

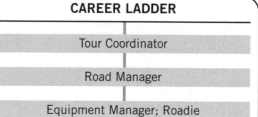

CAREER LADDER

Tour Coordinator

Road Manager

Equipment Manager; Roadie

Position Description

The Road Manager of a group is the group's management representative while the act is on the road. He or she is responsible for handling many of the problems that occur while an act is traveling. The main job is to get everybody and everything where they are supposed to be and on time. Everything must be accomplished as easily as possible with the fewest problems possible.

The Road Manager is directly responsible to either the tour coordinator, the group's management, or the group itself, depending on advance arrangements made.

At times the Road Manager is also the tour coordinator. In these situations, he or she is responsible for all the problems on the road and for supervising not only the equipment, sound, and light personnel, but also the tour publicist, the tour photographer, the musicians, the security, and anyone else working on the tour.

It is the Road Manager's duty to make sure that the act is up in the morning, gets to any public appearances, interviews, or television or radio spots. He or she must make sure they arrive at rehearsals and concerts on time.

He or she is responsible for getting the equipment to the concert hall on time and getting it set up properly. The Road Manager supervises the sound checks, light checks, and security checks for the performances.

The Road Manager is often the liaison between the act and the promoter of a concert or club date. He or she has the responsibility of collecting any monies owed

to the act before and/or after the show. The individual must make sure that riders have been followed and the promoter satisfied.

He or she may be in charge of paying the entourage and all bills on the road. The Road Manager must keep all receipts, vouchers, etc., from the tour to give to the group or its management. All money must be accounted for.

The Road Manager often has to deal with problems between members of the entourage or help a member of the entourage take care of personal problems. Long road tours put stress on most people. The Road Manager must be the one who keeps a cool head no matter what happens.

If an individual has responsibilities that must be dealt with at home, road managing is definitely not the job to look for. Road Managers must like travel and must be free to be away from home for weeks or even months at a time.

Hours are long. Road Managers may work twenty hours or more a day. They are always on call. While most of the entourage is fast asleep, the Road Manager is often working throughout the day and long into the night.

Salaries

Salaries of Road Managers vary greatly according to the popularity and success of the groups they work with. Road Managers are usually paid weekly salaries. They may, however, be paid a flat rate for each tour they complete. In addition, Road Managers are paid a per diem for living expenses while on tour. In some groups, the Road Manager's room and board are paid for and the per diem is used for personal expenses. In other situations, the Road Manager's room and board must be paid out of the per diem.

A Road Manager for a touring (but not recording) group might make approximately $400 per week. A Road Manager for a top recording group often makes $1,500 to $2,500 per week or more plus bonuses. Road Managers' salaries are often reduced by a percentage when the act is not working. This reduction keeps the Road Manager under salary with the group. Some Road Managers do not receive any salary when their act is not on tour, and may work for other groups.

Employment Prospects

Although most touring groups employ Road Managers, positions often go to nonmusical friends of a group. The Road Manager position is one for which you have to be at the right place at the right time. In addition, you need a lot of contacts in the business to find open positions. Groups and their management tend to use individuals who have a proven track record in road management for major tours.

Individuals may find employment with lesser known groups, recording acts, touring acts, and other types of entertainers.

Advancement Prospects

Road Managers advance either by moving into the position of tour coordinator or by acting as Road Manager for a more prestigious tour. Often an individual has more clout as Road Manager for a prestigious tour than he or she would have as tour coordinator for a tour starring lesser-known musicians.

To advance, the Road Manager must prove him- or herself. Management has to be totally convinced that the Road Manager is completely reliable, responsible, and effective as their representative on the road.

Education and Training

There is no formal educational requirement for the position of Road Manager. There are Road Managers who have not even completed high school. The more successful Road Managers, however, have. There are also Road Managers who have college degrees in everything from business to psychology.

Experience, Skills, and Personality Traits

Most Road Managers start out as roadies. Some begin their careers as equipment personnel or tour publicists.

The Road Manager must be able to deal with problems effectively, especially when he or she is under pressure. He or she must have the capability to supervise not only the group's road crew, but also union crews present in many concert halls.

The most important trait that a Road Manager can have is responsibility. It is his or her responsibility to get personnel and equipment where and when they are supposed to be. In addition, the Road Manager must be dependable.

Unions and Associations

There are no major associations specific to Road Managers.

Tips for Entry

1. This is a position most often gotten through contacts. If you have any, use them.
2. You might want to try to get a position by putting a small ad in one of the music trades.
3. Many groups starting out have a nonmusical friend act as Road Manager. This might be a way to gain experience.
4. Check the trades to see what tours are going out. These are usually printed well in advance. Send résumés to these groups, their management, and/or their record companies.
5. Send your résumé to the personnel department of record companies.

TOUR PUBLICIST

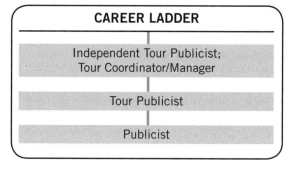

Position Description

A Tour Publicist is a trained publicist who goes on tour with a recording act or artist. He or she is in charge of making sure that both the act's fans and the media know that the group or artist is coming to town to perform a concert.

Certain Tour Publicists set up media interviews with local television, radio, newspaper, and magazine editors before the group leaves their home base. They might also arrange press parties and press conferences. Other times a staff publicist takes care of these details. The Tour Publicist's main function occurs on the road. When the group leaves on tour, the Tour Publicist is automatically part of the entourage.

On the road, he or she attends all interviews, photography sessions, concerts, press parties, and press conferences along with the act. In addition, the Tour Publicist accompanies the act to all radio interviews or television appearances. The Tour Publicist usually spends a few minutes with the show's producer, talent coordinator, or host to discuss what he or she would like the act to talk about during the interview.

At concerts, it is the Tour Publicist who is responsible for issuing press passes to disc jockeys, music editors, photographers, etc. He or she also issues the important backstage passes. All interviews and photo sessions must be approved in advance by the Tour Publicist. He or she usually sets a specific time before or after each show for additional interviews and photo sessions.

The Tour Publicist works closely with any sponsoring radio or television stations. He or she tries to make sure the employees of the station are happy. This might entail arranging special interviews or autograph sessions, presenting records or T-shirts, etc.

The Tour Publicist, who works for a record company or publicity firm, usually calls his or her office at least once a day. The Tour Publicist is responsible to his or her superiors at the record company or the publicity firm. An independent Tour Publicist is responsible directly to the act and its management team.

Tour Publicists work for the duration of the tour. It is not a nine-to-five job. While the act is still sleeping at 10:00 A.M., the Tour Publicist has already been up for a few hours making calls and discussing arrangements for the upcoming day. The Tour Publicist might still be up at 3:00 A.M. at a party thrown in the act's honor. The Tour Publicist must have a lot of stamina and a great love for the job to survive on the road.

Salaries

The salary for a Tour Publicist is usually higher than that for a home-based publicist because he or she must travel for long periods of time. Tour Publicists who work for a record company or publicity firm generally receive a weekly salary plus a daily or weekly stipend to cover personal expenses. Travel expenses are paid by the act or its management firm.

Independent Tour Publicists receive a weekly or monthly fee plus all expenses. These expenses may include food, lodging, phone, and other amenities. All work-related expenses, such as printing, long-distance phone calls, mailings, etc., are paid for by the group, record company, etc.

Salaries for Tour Publicists vary according to the employer, the act, and the amount of experience that the Tour Publicist has. A beginning Tour Publicist usually makes no less than $500 per week plus expenses. An average salary for a Tour Publicist working for a fairly established music group is between $40,000 and $85,000 or more per year plus expenses. There are Tour Publicists who are very much in demand who can command $2,000 and up per week for certain tours.

Employment Prospects

With the expenses of traveling going up many groups cannot go on tour as often as they used to. There are also few groups that can afford the services of a Tour Publicist. These positions are available, but only on a very limited basis. However, there are not many people who like to or can travel constantly.

Advancement Prospects

A good Tour Publicist can advance to the position of Tour Coordinator or Tour Manager. If the Tour Publicist has worked for a major record company or has experience working with a publicity firm, he or she has the option of becoming an independent Tour Publicist.

Education and Training

A Tour Publicist position usually requires much the same training as a home-based publicist. A college degree with a major in communications, journalism, English, public relations, or music merchandising is preferable. Seminars on music-oriented publicity are also helpful.

Experience, Skills, and Personality Traits

The Tour Publicist must have the ability to travel and must enjoy being on the road for long stretches at a time. Tour Publicists work under more pressure than home-based publicists. Road tours sometimes create stress for people. Toward the end of a tour, for example, the entire entourage may get jumpy. They just want the tour to end. The Tour Publicist must make sure that this attitude is not displayed to the media or the fans.

The Tour Publicist must maintain a list of national media contacts to call upon while his or her client is touring.

Unions and Associations

There are a number of organizations and associations Tour Publicists can belong to. The best known is the Public Relations Society of America (PRSA), which has local chapters in major cities in the United States.

Tips for Entry

1. Place an ad in one of the music trades (classified or display) describing the type of position you're looking for. Professionals in the business read these trades and might be looking for someone to fill this type of position.
2. Openings for this type of position might also be advertised in the trades, such as *Billboard*.
3. If you're working in a music-oriented public relations firm or a record company, talk to your superiors about this position. Often they need someone for this position. Many publicists in a company may not be free to travel for great lengths of time.
4. Send your résumé with a cover letter to record companies or music-oriented public relations firms asking about openings for Tour Publicists.

SOUND TECHNICIAN

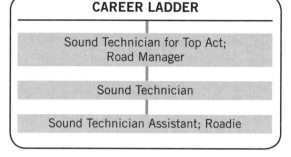

Position Description

The Sound Technician working on the road has a good deal of responsibility. The main area he or she must be concerned with is good quality sound during a show.

The Sound Technician usually arrives at a concert hall or club earlier than the performers. Along with the rest of the road crew, he or she unloads, sets up, and positions the equipment and the instruments. (In certain union situations, such as union halls, union employees must unload the equipment. In cases like this, the Sound Technician will supervise placement of equipment.)

The equipment and the instruments must be placed on the stage in such a way that the sounds of the instruments and the vocals will blend well. In addition, everything must be situated so that the sound is good and those on stage can both see and hear what goes on during the show.

After everything is set up, the musicians and the vocalists will arrive. The Sound Technician must then prepare for the all-important sound check. During this time the Sound Technician works with the talent. Each person will play his or her instrument or sing, and the technician must listen to determine whether the sound is coming through properly. Sometimes this takes a great deal of time because acoustics are different in every hall. During this period as many adjustments as possible are taken care of. Minor

adjustments will take place just before the show when the hall fills up.

During the show the Sound Technician works the sound board. He or she can adjust the volume of voices while changing the volume of instruments. Instruments can be made to sound more bass, treble, etc. The sound must constantly be balanced so that all the instruments and vocals blend together. The Sound Technician is usually situated somewhere in front of the stage during the performance. This is where the true sound can be heard the best.

After the show, the Sound Technician may be responsible for watching the loading and packing of the sound equipment. Big tours sometimes have an entire truck designated to haul only the sound equipment.

The Sound Technician might also be responsible for checking out the equipment after a show to see what needs repair or replacement. Many Sound Technicians know how to fix much of the equipment they work with. This is a plus, especially if the equipment breaks down just before or during a show.

Sound Technicians are responsible to the head road manager or tour coordinator. It depends on the acts they work with.

Sound Technicians do not always work on a constant basis. They might work a six week tour with one act and have a month off before the next tour starts with another group. There are instances where the Sound

Technician might go on a reduced salary while not on tour in order to make sure that he or she is available to a particular group.

Sound Technicians who work on the road must have the freedom to travel. In addition, they must be able to deal with long periods on the road and living out of a suitcase.

Salaries

Salaries for Sound Technicians vary greatly. Sound people working for a local band on its way up may make minimum wage or less. They may get the same percentage of the pot as each of the band members.

As Sound Technicians move up and work for better-known acts, their income increases. Salaries run from $27,000 to around $65,000 plus yearly. The higher salary would, of course, go to a Sound Technician on the road with a very well-known act.

Sound Technicians working on the road usually receive a per diem to pay for living expenses while traveling.

It is important to note that if the Sound Technician free-lances, he or she will probably not work 52 weeks a year.

Employment Prospects

A Sound Technician has a fair chance of finding employment with a local or well-known regional band. Possibilities of finding work decrease as the popularity of the group with which one aspires to work increases.

Advancement Prospects

Advancement is difficult for Sound Technicians. They may find work with a more popular band or act, but this is not easy.

Sound Technicians may also advance to the position of road manager or tour coordinator if they exhibit sufficient drive, responsibility, and competence.

Education and Training

No formal education is required for the position of Sound Technician. Many individuals in this job picked up the basics by watching someone else work the board.

Other people do have some training in electronics or sound, possibly from attending a recording or broadcasting school.

Experience, Skills, and Personality Traits

As noted above, many Sound Technicians pick up the basics of the work from watching someone else do it. They might occasionally assist or ask questions of a working Sound Technician.

Talented Sound Technicians usually have gathered a lot of experience. The more they work on the sound board, the better they get at balancing the sound.

As individuals in this field usually have to travel extensively, it is a must for the person to have the flexibility to travel and to enjoy it. Not everyone likes living out of a suitcase for weeks on end.

Certain Sound Technicians start out as roadies, helping or filling in with sound work along the way. Eventually they either fill an opening or apply for a job as a Sound Technician with another group.

Unions and Associations

Touring Sound Technicians do not usually belong to any union, although they could be members of the International Alliance of Theatrical Stage Employees (IATSE).

Tips for Entry

1. If you are interested in working in this field, hang around clubs and bars that provide live entertainment. Most of the Sound Technicians working in this type of atmosphere will answer any questions you have. You might even offer to work for nothing. The experience you gain may pay you back with a job.

2. Working as a roadie for a short stint might not only train you, but also land you a job when the Sound Technician leaves.

3. You might consider taking out an advertisement (classified or display) in a trade magazine or a newspaper read by acts or managers requiring sound services.

4. Positions may be advertised in the classified section of newspapers. Look under headings such as "Sound Technician," Sound Man," "Sound Woman," and "Audio Technician."

5. Search for openings online. You might search traditional job sites, such as monster.com or hotjobs.com and go from there.

ADVANCE PERSON

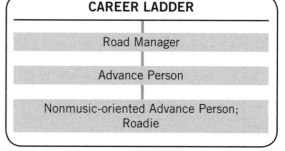

Position Description

The Advance Person goes out on the road before a tour. He or she leaves the home base before any of the entourage does and always arrives before the group; usually the Advance Person is gone by the time the act or group arrives at the destination.

When an Advance Person gets to a city in which an act is booked to perform, he or she will make sure that everything is set up as planned. He or she will check to see that posters and billboards are up. If they aren't, he or she might put them up or hire a crew to do it.

The Advance Person may bring in concert tickets. This happens rarely, though, because most concert halls utilize the services of a ticket service agency, such as Ticketron or Ticket Master. The Advance Person might bring in and hand-deliver any press passes issued by the publicist and/or management team.

The Advance Person will also hand-deliver press packages, photos, and promotional copies of records to press and promoters in each city.

Often the Advance Person checks out the acoustics of the hall or auditorium where the concert is to be held. He or she checks to see the location of electric outlets and types of electrical service available. This information is relayed back to the tour manager or coordinator. The Advance Person might also check out seating and exits and entrances of halls, making diagrams for the road personnel to use later.

Depending on the position, the Advance Person might measure mileage and check routes between concert cities. He or she might see what options are available for transportation in each city. All this information is relayed back to the tour manager, coordinator, or management office.

Certain groups have tremendous fan clubs that organize events in honor of the act's arrival in town. The Advance Person might contact the fan club president and deliver press passes or group memorabilia.

To be an Advance Person, an individual must be very dependable and responsible. No one is looking over the individual's shoulder. He or she must be able to structure his or her own day in order to get everything accomplished.

He or she must also be personable and articulate. Much of the job involves talking to people about the concert tour. As an Advance Person, an individual represents the group or act he or she is working for. The Advance Person must also like to travel and not mind being alone most of the time.

The Advance Person is responsible to the management, booking agency, or act that retained his or her services.

Salaries

Salaries vary depending on the group or management team that the Advance Person is working with and may range from approximately $25,000 to $48,000 or more.

Salaries usually start at about $450 per week and go up to $900 or more weekly. Advance People always receive either a per diem or reimbursement for their traveling expenses.

Advance people are usually paid by the week for the time that they work. Weeks that they are not on the road, they might have a reduction in salary, no salary, or might be kept on a retainer.

Employment Prospects

Employment prospects for this position are poor. With the new overnight delivery systems, many management firms just mail what they need delivered and make phone calls for any information. Furthermore, not every act uses an Advance Person.

Advancement Prospects

If a person does obtain a position as an Advance Person, he or she might eventually become a road manager or even a tour manager. It all depends on the type of organization the individual works with.

The Advance Person also has the option of working for bigger acts and better, more prestigious tours.

Education and Training

There is no formal educational requirement for this position. The individual might, however, be required to have a driver's license.

Special Requirements

An Advance Person will often be required to hold a driver's license with a clean driving record.

Experience, Skills, and Personality Traits

The Advance Person must like to travel and must not mind traveling alone. Advance People in the music business often have held positions as Advance People in other parts of the entertainment industry or for convention management.

The individual in this job must be extremely organized. He or she should be responsible and dependable. The Advance Person should also be personable and articulate.

Unions and Associations

There is no major association specific to Advance People.

Tips for Entry

1. This is a position you either get by contacts or by being in the right place at the right time. Pass along the word to musicians, groups, management, and booking agencies that you're looking for this type of job.
2. Advertise your availability in a small display or classified ad in one of the music trades.
3. Experience helps, whether it be experience as a nonmusic-oriented Advance Person or a travel agent, roadie, etc. Put in your résumé everything that might be of value to a potential employer.

MUSIC RETAILING AND WHOLESALING

MUSIC SHOP MANAGER

Position Description

The position of Music Shop Manager can be an exciting one for a person who likes to be around musical instruments. The main function of the individual in this job is to manage and run a retail music shop. There are many duties within the job classification.

Naturally, the manager must oversee the day-to-day activities of the music shop. He or she is responsible for hiring and supervising employees. The manager is in charge of putting together a work schedule for those who are employed by the shop. The individual assigns staff to perform specific duties and trains them, if necessary.

The Music Shop Manager works closely with the store owner (or he or she may be the store owner). Together, they decide what policies will be used for the store regarding payment, layaway, instrument returns, special orders, music lessons, etc. They may work out a marketing, advertising, or promotional campaign together, too.

The Music Shop Manager is in charge of seeing that instruments are ordered and purchased. The individual will select the equipment, supplies, and/or sheet music the store will stock. He or she is responsible for making sure that orders come in, bills are paid on time, and internal problems with distributors or sales representatives are minimized.

If there is a problem with an instrument or piece of equipment that a customer has purchased in the music store, it is up to the manager to resolve the difficulty.

The manager must try to keep customers happy and uphold the reputation of the store.

The Music Shop Manager may act as a salesperson, selling instruments, equipment, or other supplies to customers. The individual may be called on to explain in detail differences in quality or variations among instruments.

He or she assumes the responsibility for maintaining operating records of all daily transactions. Cash income must be reconciled with the day's receipts.

This type of position usually has fairly regular retail hours. The manager is responsible to the store owner or department store manager.

Salaries

Those who manage music shops or departments may expect salaries ranging from $27,000 to $48,000 plus yearly. Salaries may consist of weekly salaries, bonuses, commissions, etc. The larger earnings go to individuals who are very experienced in managing music shops. The salary of a Music Shop Manager is also dependent on the location and size of the store.

Employment Prospects

Employment prospects for people seeking to be Music Shop Managers or department managers are good. There are many opportunities for individuals in all sections of the country. People may find work in large stores, small shops, music store chains, or the instrument/sheet music department of a variety store.

Advancement Prospects

Music shop or department managers move up the career ladder in a number of ways. They may advance by obtaining a job in a music store instead of a music department. An individual might move to a position in a larger, more prestigious store as a means of advancement. The other opportunity for a Music Shop Manager is to open his or her own music shop.

Education and Training

Music shops often prefer their managers to hold bachelor's degrees or at least have some type of college background. The exception would be an owner of a music shop who is also managing it. Even in such a situation, however, people find it helpful to have an education.

Music Shop Managers often hold degrees in business, liberal arts, music, retailing, music education, or music performance. A music background is necessary to successfully run a music store. This background may be obtained through the standard educational process, such as college or conservatory training, or might come from experiences dealing in music.

Experience, Skills, and Personality Traits

The Music Shop Manager needs to have an understanding of retail business management. He or she must possess the ability to hire, fire, and train personnel. The manager will have to supervise the shop and the staff on a day-to-day basis.

The individual in this position needs knowledge of a wide variety of musical instruments. The person should be capable of playing or demonstrating most instruments in the store, or should find someone else who can handle this part of the enterprise.

Unions and Associations

Music Shop Managers may belong to the National Association of Music Merchants (NAMM).

Tips for Entry

1. Jobs for Music Shop Managers are advertised in the classified sections of newspapers. Look under headings such as "Music Shop Manager," "Manager-Retail," and "Retail Opportunities."
2. Job openings may also be posted in shop windows.
3. People working in music shops are often promoted. Many Music Shop Managers started working as salespeople in the shop they currently manage.
4. Send résumés and cover letters to music shops and request that they keep them on file.

MUSIC SHOP SALESPERSON

Position Description

A Music Shop Salesperson sells instruments, musical accessories, equipment, supplies, and/or sheet music to customers in a retail store. The individual may specialize in selling brass, percussion, stringed, or woodwind instruments.

The salesperson might act as a cashier, making a sale, totalling up the customer's purchases, arranging for lay-aways, taking money, and giving change.

The Music Shop Salesperson may perform a wide spectrum of other duties, depending on the job. A specific duty might be to assist customers in choosing the correct instruments for their needs. For example, someone may come into the store to buy a guitar. The salesperson must find out a few things about the individual: Is the guitar going to be used for pleasure or to play in a band? Is the band a school group or a famous recording act? Does the customer want an electric guitar or an acoustic instrument? What size guitar: standard, three quarters, or child's size? What price range and brand is the customer considering? These are some of the questions the salesperson needs answered in order to help a customer choose an instrument.

In this sales position, the individual might demonstrate a few different instruments to help a customer decide which has a better tone, sound, etc. The salesperson talks to the potential buyer about the variables in the instruments versus the prices.

Salespeople or clerks in music shops may clean or repair instruments in addition to their sales duties. Depending on a person's talent, he or she might tune pianos, too.

The salesperson in a music shop will take special orders for instruments not in stock. The individual often talks to schools in the area about their musical requirements and may try to solicit orders.

Salespeople in music shops frequently receive commissions on instrument sales as well as salaries. This gives them extra incentive to try to make additional sales.

Depending on the range of duties, the Music Shop Salesperson may take inventory of existing merchandise and keep a list of what has been sold. He or she might send to call orders in to instrument sales representatives or companies.

In certain stores, the salesperson also gives music lessons on various instruments. This depends on the competence of the individual teaching. The person is usually paid extra for this duty.

In a music shop, the salesperson either works regular store hours or a particular shift. The job can be full- or part-time. The individual in this position is responsible directly to the store owner or manager.

Salaries

Salespeople working in music shops may be paid in a number of ways. The Music Shop Salesperson may receive a straight salary, a commission on instruments sold, or a combination of the two. The salary range for Music Shop Salespeople is approximately $20,000 to $30,000 plus annually. The lower figure represents the earnings of an individual working in a small shop with little or no experience. The higher figure is for a person who is working in a large music store in a city. That person probably has quite a bit of experience in the field.

Music Shop Salespeople who have the ability to play certain instruments well and can teach may make extra money by giving lessons.

Employment Prospects

Employment prospects for Music Shop Salespeople are good. Those who have the ability to play more than one instrument and can demonstrate them to prospective customers may have even better prospects. Opportunities for work exist in major cities, smaller cities, and large towns. Individuals may find work in large stores, small shops, or in the music sections of department stores.

Advancement Prospects

Individuals might find openings as salespeople in larger stores. Working in a larger shop could mean that the Music Shop Salesperson would be earning a higher salary and/or commissions.

Those working as Music Shop Salespeople might climb the career ladder by advancing to music shop managers or music department managers.

The Music Shop Salesperson may get experience, learn the business, and then open his or her own store.

Education and Training

Educational requirements vary for salespeople working in music shops. Some shops hire part-time salespeople who are still in high school. Others require their salespeople to hold a high school diploma.

In larger, more prestigious music stores, management and/or owners may require or prefer that their staff has college degrees or backgrounds. Individuals who hold music degrees often have an advantage over applicants who do not hold similar degrees.

It is helpful for the Music Shop Salesperson to be trained to play at least one instrument. Playing more

than one instrument is a plus. It is also useful for the individual to have a knowledge of music theory and be able to read music. This training may be obtained in school, conservatories, colleges, private study, or on one's own.

Experience, Skills, and Personality Traits

The Music Shop Salesperson generally has had some type of retail sales experience prior to obtaining the music shop position. He or she must work well with people, making them feel comfortable purchasing in the store. The salesperson must not pressure customers, but should be helpful and give honest, concise information about instruments and accessories.

The Music Shop Salesperson who can play and/or demonstrate various instruments is a valuable commodity in a music shop. The individual may also teach students who have purchased instruments from the store. Therefore, an ability to teach is a plus.

The individual must understand how the instruments work and be able to identify their various parts.

Unions and Associations

Depending on the store where an individual works, a Music Shop Salesperson may or may not belong to a bargaining union. The union might be an in-house union or may be a union that encompasses the job classification.

Music Shop Salespeople or the shops they work in might also belong to the National Association of Music Merchants (NAMM). This trade organization provides educational materials, training sessions, conferences, etc., for its members.

Tips for Entry

1. Jobs for Music Shop Salespeople are advertised in help wanted sections. Keep an eye on such headings as "Salesperson Wanted," "Instrument Sales," "Music Shop Clerk," etc.
2. Jobs may be posted in shop windows as well.
3. You might consider sending résumés with cover letters to a number of stores. Follow up with a phone call.
4. Ask to see the store owner or manager and ask to fill out an application to be kept on file.

RECORD STORE
(OR DEPARTMENT) MANAGER

CAREER PROFILE

Duties: Manage and run a record store or department on a day-to-day basis

Alternate Title(s): Record Shop Manager

Salary Range: $24,000 to $48,000+

Employment Prospects: Good

Advancement Prospects: Good

Best Geographical Locations for Position: All locations have possible positions available

Prerequisites:

Education or Training—High school diploma minimum; some positions require or prefer college degree or background

Experience—Retail sales experience, preferably in record store or department

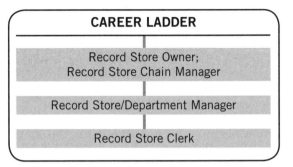

CAREER LADDER

Record Store Owner;
Record Store Chain Manager

Record Store/Department Manager

Record Store Clerk

Special Skills and Personality Traits—Salesmanship; good administration; knowledge of retail record business; cognizance of customers' musical tastes

Position Description

Record Store Managers work in record stores or in department stores in the record and video department. Their basic function is to manage and run the record shop or department on a day-to-day basis. The manager may work for a private store owner, a record chain, a department store, or may be the actual shop owner.

Daily duties for the Record Store Manager include the supervision of other employees in the store or department, development of work schedules, and assignment of employees to specific duties. He or she may be responsible for the hiring and firing of personnel.

The Record Store Manager works in close contact with other employees, pitching in where needed. He or she may perform sales duties on a regular basis or assign these duties to clerks. The individual is responsible for taking care of any problems that arise with customers. These might include faulty merchandise, questions about orders, or difficulties with store personnel. It is up to the manager to deal with problems and complaints in a fair manner but according to store policy. At times, the manager may feel the need to go against store policy in order to keep a customer or to maintain good store relations. This is the individual's prerogative.

As the Record Store Manager, the person is in charge of ordering merchandise. To do this, he or she

must know what is hot. Managers of record shops must keep up with the current musical trends and customers' musical tastes.

The Record Store Manager must take and/or supervise inventories of stock on hand. Certain CDs, videos, and DVDs sell out as soon as they come in. Requisitions must be prepared to replenish the stock. Merchandise that does not sell can often be returned to the distributor. Data must be kept on what comes in, from what distributor, and on what date.

A variety of other merchandise and products may be ordered in addition to CDs, DVDs, and records. These might include music videos, blank cassettes, blank CDs; blank DVDs, music magazines, posters, etc.

It is the responsibility of the Record Store Manager to make sure that operating data are kept, daily postings of transactions are prepared, and cash is reconciled with sales receipts.

Depending on the store, the manager may have to coordinate sales promotion activities and prepare advertisements and merchandising displays. The Record Store Manager may perform any of these functions or supervise or direct other employees to do so.

The Record Store Manager's hours vary, but are usually fairly regular. The manager is responsible to the storeowner, record chain supervisor, or department store manager. If the manager owns the store, he or she is responsible only to him or herself and to any investors.

Salaries

Salaries for Record Store Managers fluctuate, depending on the size of the store, the location, and the experience of the individual.

Starting salaries are usually around $24,000 per year. Earnings for more experienced record shop managers of very large stores may range from $30,000 to $48,000 annually. Monies can come in the form of salaries, commissions, and/or bonuses.

Many Record Store Managers own the shop they run and receive a percentage of the profits.

Employment Prospects

There are openings for Record Store Managers and record department managers across the country. Individuals who have had sales experience in record shops and know how a store works are qualified for the many positions available.

With the growth of online music stores, many brick-and-mortar record stores are closing. Individuals interested in these positions may have more luck in the music departments of department or chain stores.

Advancement Prospects

Advancement prospects for Record Store Managers are good. Individuals may upgrade their careers in a number of ways.

One method is to obtain a position at a larger store with additional responsibilities and greater earnings. Others advance their career by moving from a job at a department store as a manager of the record department to a job as manager of a record shop. There are individuals who begin as Record Store Managers and go on to manage whole chains of record stores. Of course, there are those people who promote themselves by buying their own record shops.

Education and Training

Record Store Managers must usually have a minimum of a high school diploma. Some positions require or prefer a college degree or background. There are degree programs available in retailing, business administration, and music merchandising that can prove useful.

Experience, Skills, and Personality Traits

Record Store Managers generally have worked in a retail sales position previous to their appointment. Usually, they have worked in a record store as a clerk for a period of time. The duration of this experience varies from person to person. However, managers generally have worked long enough in a clerical position to learn how the retail record business is run. Depending on the geographical area of the record shop, managers must know the type of customers they will be servicing and what their musical tastes are. The Record Store Manager must be reliable, honest, and hardworking. Besides this, he or she must be a good administrator, capable of hiring and firing employees.

Unions and Associations

Record Store Managers or the shops they manage may be members of the National Association of Recording Merchandisers (NARM). This organization is a trade association for people in the recording business.

Tips for Entry

1. These positions are often advertised in the help wanted sections of newspapers.
2. There are employment agencies that occasionally look for people to fill jobs as managers of record shops. Depending on the agency and the job, you might have to pay a fee if you obtain a position. Check it out first.
3. Many record stores like to promote from within. If you are working as a clerk in a store and impress the owner, you may be able to advance your career.
4. Record shops often advertise openings on their front window. Keep a lookout for these signs.

RECORD STORE CLERK

Duties: Sell records and tapes in record shop or department; assist customers

Alternate Title(s): Record Shop Clerk; Record Shop Salesperson

Salary Range: $17,000 to $25,000+

Employment Prospects: Good

Advancement Prospects: Good

Best Geographical Location(s) for Position: Positions may be located nationwide

Prerequisites:

Education or Training—High school diploma (or high school student)

Experience—Retail sales experience helpful, but not required

CAREER LADDER

Record Store Manager

Record Store Clerk

Student; Other Retail Sales Job

Special Skills and Personality Traits—Sales ability; ability to work well with others; dependability; enjoyment of records and music

Position Description

Record Store Clerks work in record stores or music departments selling CDs, records, tapes, and assorted music-oriented merchandise to customers. Other goods might include blank CDs, DVDs, CD cases, recording maintenance equipment and supplies, music videos, posters, and music magazines.

The Record Store Clerk or salesperson may perform a variety of functions. One of these is to assist customers. Patrons may need help locating records, deciding what album would be suitable for a gift, or deciphering price codes on CDs.

The clerk may be responsible for totalling a customer's purchases, taking money, giving change, and packaging or wrapping the merchandise. The salesperson will take down information for special orders that are not in stock. The clerk will pass the information on to the store manager to order.

Under the supervision of the record shop manager, the clerk may receive new stock into the store from distributors. He or she may count and sort the merchandise and verify receipt of items on invoices. The individual will check that the items arriving are indeed the merchandise that was ordered.

The Record Store Clerk may take inventory of existing merchandise, maintaining lists, and informing the manager of those records selling well and those that have not moved. He or she may pack up items that are being sent back to the distributor.

The Record Store Clerk might stamp, mark, or attach price tags to goods in the store. At times, he or she may stock bins, shelves, etc. Depending on the situation, the individual may help the manager set up advertising displays or arrange merchandise in a manner that will promote sales.

Sales clerks work different shifts. They may work full- or part-time. Individuals in this position are responsible to the shop manager.

Salaries

Earnings for Record Store Clerks vary depending on the experience of the person, the size of the store, and the geographical location. Salaries begin at or slightly above the minimum wage. Clerks working in record shops can expect to earn $17,000 to $25,000 plus yearly. Sales clerks may earn straight salaries or salaries plus commissions on each sale made. Sales clerks might also receive bonuses.

Employment Prospects

Employment prospects are good. This particular job is one in which almost anyone can enter the music business. There are many positions open in record shops, record chains, and department stores in every section of the country.

This is an entry-level position. Young people still in high school or college often apply for jobs in record shops to learn about the record business.

Advancement Prospects

Those who wish to advance have good prospects. Record Store Clerks are often promoted to record department managers, record shop managers, or other management positions in the store or chain.

As noted above, many individuals begin working in a record shop as a way of entering the music field. Learning about record sales helps prepare those aspiring to enter the recording industry. It affords them a positive means of entry.

Education and Training

Those working in record shops as clerks are usually required to hold at least a high school diploma. However, most stores will hire young people who are high school students as part-time workers or for summer jobs.

Experience, Skills, and Personality Traits

Although some retail sales experience is helpful, it is often not required. What is required is that the Record Store Clerk be pleasant and helpful to customers. A knowledge of the current records and trends is useful.

Record Store Clerks must work well with others and be dependable and reliable.

Unions and Associations

In very small record shops, clerks usually do not belong to unions. Clerks often belong to unions in larger record shops or while working in the record department of a department store. The union may be an in-house union or a local union that encompasses the job classification.

Tips for Entry

1. Positions for Record Store Clerks are often advertised in the classified sections of newspapers. Look under key words such as "Record Store," "Retail," "Music," or "Clerk."
2. Openings are also often noted in shop windows or on bulletin boards.
3. You may consider going into a record shop and asking to see the manager. This individual will usually let you fill out an application and keep it on file for future reference.

INSTRUMENT SALES REPRESENTATIVE

CAREER PROFILE

Duties: Sell musical instruments to dealers

Alternate Title(s): Sales Rep; Rep; Manufacturer's Representative

Salary Range: $23,000 to $75,000+

Employment Prospects: Good

Advancement Prospects: Good

Best Geographical Location(s) for Position: Instrument manufacturers are located in various areas of the country

Prerequisites:

Education or Training—High school diploma minimum; some positions require college background or degree

Experience—Some sales experience (either wholesale or retail) helpful

CAREER LADDER

```
┌─────────────────────────────────────┐
│            Sales Manager             │
├─────────────────────────────────────┤
│  Instrument Sales Representative     │
├─────────────────────────────────────┤
│          Nonmusic Sales Job          │
└─────────────────────────────────────┘
```

Special Skills and Personality Traits—Sales ability; communications skills; knowledge of music and instruments; ability to play instrument helpful

Position Description

An Instrument Sales Representative sells musical instruments to shops, dealerships, and schools. Usually a sales rep has a specific territory. This area (sometimes called a region or district) may consist of a few cities, counties, or states, or an entire section of the country.

As a sales rep, the individual must know as much as possible about the instrument(s) and the manufacturer. Additionally, it is important for the person to know about instruments manufactured by competing companies. With this information, the individual can speak knowledgeably to dealers about comparisons. Actually, the more knowledge the sales rep has, the better qualified that person is to come up with a good sales pitch. Knowing about the weaknesses of a particular instrument (even if it's made by one's own company) helps prepare the individual to field questions on the subject.

In this position, a person may make sales calls either in person or on the phone or combine the two methods. The individual is responsible for visiting established accounts, seeing what they require and what has been sold since the last visit. The Instrument Sales Representative will probably talk to the dealer for a short while, discussing any problems with instruments sold and under warranty. He or she may review new instru-

ments, products, trends, etc. By the time the Instrument Sales Representative is ready to leave, he or she should have developed a large order for the company.

The rep may also seek out new accounts (places to sell the instruments). To do this, the individual may call in advance to try to set up an appointment, send a letter and some product brochures, or just drop in. The dealer may not buy from the sales representative the first time, but may after a relationship has been established.

As an Instrument Sales Representative, the individual may call or visit schools to find out about their band and orchestra instrument needs. Making a sale in this area could mean a big order. Schools, both public and private, may create a new market for the sales rep.

The Instrument Sales Representative has duties other than selling. He or she must telephone established and new accounts, send letters and brochures, keep up on all the newest instrument technology, and maintain good records. Losing an order or forgetting to call back a potential buyer may mean not only a lost sale, but possibly a lost job.

The Instrument Sales Representative is usually directly responsible to the sales manager of the organization. Hours for this type of position vary. Some jobs offer more flexibility in working hours than others.

Salaries

Remuneration for Instrument Sales Representatives may be made in a variety of ways. Reps may be paid a straight salary, a commission, or a combination of the two. Instrument Sales Representatives additionally may receive bonuses and fringe benefits, including cars, traveling expenses, etc.

Earnings for sales representatives in the musical instrument field range from $23,000 to $75,000 plus. Individuals working on commission basis can do quite well financially. The sky is the limit as far as earnings are concerned.

Employment Prospects

Employment prospects for this field are good. There are many openings for aggressive, talented Instrument Sales Representatives. Those who have a background in music and have the ability to play an instrument or group of instruments have an advantage.

Many positions require the individual to sell in large geographic areas. Those who don't mind traveling will find even greater opportunities.

Advancement Prospects

Advancement prospects for an Instrument Sales Representative are generally good. If the individual has done a good job, met sales quotas, maintained good relationships with shop owners and dealers, and opened new accounts, he or she may be promoted to a sales manager position. This position may be on a local, regional, national, or possibly even international level.

Education and Training

Educational requirements differ with each position. Many companies just require their sales reps to have high school diplomas. Others prefer that their sales staff have college backgrounds or degrees.

Some type of music or instrument training is useful for a better understanding of the product being sold.

Experience, Skills, and Personality Traits

A person who works for a major music manufacturer as a sales representative will usually have had some type of retail or wholesale sales experience. The individual might have had other types of selling jobs unrelated to the music business.

The ability to come up with a good sales pitch is essential. The rep must be aggressive without being annoying. It helps immensely if the individual has the ability to be articulate both on the phone and in person. It is also useful for the Instrument Sales Representative to be knowledgeable about music and about the instrument being sold. The ability to play one or more instruments can also be helpful.

Unions and Associations

Instrument Sales Representatives may belong to the National Association of Music Merchants (NAMM). Depending on the type of instruments the individual sells, he or she may also belong to the Guitar and Accessories Marketing Association (GAMA).

Tips for Entry

1. Get some experience selling before you apply for a job as a sales rep. You might consider finding a job in a music instrument shop. This will give you an opportunity to talk to sales representatives to find out more about the job.
2. When you do apply for a job with a company, know as much about the company, their instruments, etc., as possible. This will help to impress the interviewer with your capabilities.
3. If you do play an instrument, try to find some manufacturers in that family of instruments. The ability to play that instrument is a plus when looking for a job of this type.
4. You might want to look for a job online. Check out company Web sites as well as some of the online job sites.

RACK JOBBER

CAREER PROFILE

Duties: Supply CDs, cassettes, records, tapes, and DVDs to shops whose main business is not the sale of music

Alternate Title(s): Subdistributor

Salary Range: $25,000 to $55,000+

Employment Prospects: Good

Advancement Prospects: Fair

Best Geographical Location(s) for Position: Positions may be located in most cities across the country

Prerequisites:

Education or Training—High school diploma

Experience—Selling experience (both wholesale and retail) helpful

CAREER LADDER

Owner of Record Store; Record Company Distribution Representative

Rack Jobber

Rack Jobber Field Representative

Special Skills and Personality Traits—Good business skills; knowledge of music market; good salesmanship; ability to work with figures and calculations

Position Description

A Rack Jobber supplies CDs, cassettes, records, videotapes, and DVDs to shops that are not primarily in the music or video business. Many of the CD or DVD displays that are seen in supermarkets, department stores, automotive shops, discount stores, book stores, and drug stores are put together by Rack Jobbers. A Rack Jobber, incidentally, may have a number of people working in the business or may work alone.

As a Rack Jobber, the individual selects CDs and DVDs to display and sell in a section of someone else's store or market. He or she receives space and in return either pays a rental fee, a leasing fee, a percentage of record sales, or a combination of these.

The job of a Rack Jobber is much like that of owning a retail record or music store. However, in this instance, the merchandise is in a space that already draws a stream of customer traffic. The Rack Jobber may have space in more than one store.

The Rack Jobber buys records from a distributor. Since he or she has limited space, it is impossible to stock every CD, as a conventional record shop does. The most important records are those that have a high rating on the charts. The charts, in turn, are compiled in part by reports from Rack Jobbers on sales of specific records.

Rack Jobbers offer the store a CD/video/music department. If an item doesn't sell, the Rack Jobber takes it back. This is a no-risk situation for the store's management.

It is the Rack Jobber's responsibility to select the CDs and videos and place those that he or she feels will sell. After making sure that they get to the store, the individual must also make sure that they are displayed properly. This display should be pleasing to the eye and make people want to look at and purchase merchandise. The Rack Jobber periodically comes into the store and takes inventory. He or she takes back merchandise that isn't moving and brings in better sellers.

Depending on the situation, the Rack Jobber must either hire a staff of salespeople (if it is a lease situation) or train and supervise members of the store's existing staff who will be working in the record department. In this instance, a rental fee or percentage may be paid to the store by the Rack Jobber.

In addition, the Rack Jobber supplies the store with advertising and promotional material to help sell the records. The Rack Jobber is in charge of keeping inventory and accounting records for his or her space.

As a Rack Jobber, the individual will get to know the distributors from many of the major record companies. This will enable the Rack Jobber to develop contacts within the recording industry.

The Rack Jobber must keep the stores happy and satisfied or they will not renew their contracts.

Salaries

Salaries for Rack Jobbers vary, depending on the company, its location, how many records are sold, and the type of salary received.

Earnings may be in the form of a straight commission or may be a guaranteed salary against a commission.

Salaries range from $25,000 to $55,000 plus.

Employment Prospects

There are many stores and shops that have record displays and/or record departments serviced by Rack Jobbers. The prospects are good for people who want to find jobs in this field. A person may take over an entire rack jobbing operation or be a field representative. The field representative, incidentally, acts under the instructions of the main Rack Jobber, performing most of the same functions.

Advancement Prospects

Individuals who work as Rack Jobbers or rack jobber field representatives have a fair chance of moving ahead in their careers. If they decide that they like the business, they might open up their own record shops. A Rack Jobber may increase the size of his or her business immensely by broadening the base of operation.

As Rack Jobbers meet and work closely with distributors of major recording companies, they frequently make good contacts in the record industry. As a result, many of these individuals obtain jobs in the distribution department of large labels.

Education and Training

No educational background is required to be a Rack Jobber or to work for one, except possibly having a high school diploma. Individuals who do prefer to go to college will find that courses in business, marketing, merchandising, and related fields will be useful. There are also music merchandising and music business majors available in many schools; these can be useful for individuals desiring to work in this field.

Experience, Skills, and Personality Traits

A Rack Jobber needs a good head for business. He or she must have the ability to sell and to be aggressive in a nice way. Knowledge of the current music market, trends, and the record business is essential to success. Being organized is also helpful.

Unions and Associations

Rack Jobbers may belong to a number of associations. These include the National Association of Music Merchants (NAMM) and the National Association of Recording Merchandisers (NARM). Both these organizations sponsor conventions, meetings, seminars, and conferences for their members. The associations also offer books, pamphlets, and other information useful to those selling or distributing records, CDs, videos, and cassettes.

Tips for Entry

1. If you're looking for a job as a Rack Jobber/field representative, visit various drug stores, department stores, supermarkets, etc. Find out who their Rack Jobbers are. Get addresses and phone numbers and set up interviews.

2. Many of the major department stores around the country have record or home entertainment departments serviced by Rack Jobbers. To begin with, get a job as a clerk. Move up from there.

3. Call the distributor department of a major record company. Try to find out names and addresses of Rack Jobbers in your area. Send them your résumé and a cover letter, and try to arrange an interview.

THE BUSINESS END OF THE INDUSTRY

PERSONAL MANAGER

Duties: Represent act; oversee and guide all aspects of an artist's career

Alternate Title(s): Artist's Representative; Manager

Salary Range: 10% to 50% of artist's earnings

Employment Prospects: Good

Advancement Prospects: Poor

Best Geographical Locations for Position: Managers for major acts are usually located in New York City, Los Angeles, or Nashville; managers for lesser known acts may be located anywhere in the country

Prerequisites:

Education or Training—No formal educational requirement; college background helpful; courses or seminars in business and music industry useful

Experience—Any type of experience in any phase of the music business is valuable

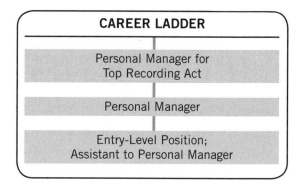

CAREER LADDER

Personal Manager for Top Recording Act

Personal Manager

Entry-Level Position; Assistant to Personal Manager

Special Skills and Personality Traits—Music industry contacts; aggressiveness; knowledge of music industry; ability to see raw talent; ability to work under pressure

Position Description

The main job of the Personal Manager is to represent one or more musical groups or artists. In doing this, the manager oversees all aspects of an act's career.

The Personal Manager, in essence, deals with and advises the act on all business decisions and many of the creative decisions artists must make. In this manner, the manager attempts to guide an artist's rise to the top.

The Personal Manager begins by hearing and/or seeing an artist he or she feels has talent. After discussions with the act, a manager may feel he or she has something to offer the act. The manager should have the know-how to direct a musical career. If a bargain is struck, the two parties usually sign a contract. It is then the manager's job to begin to plan for stardom.

In this position, the Personal Manager is the single most important person (talent notwithstanding) helping the act attain stardom or success. Soon after signing the contract, the manager will begin looking for a record label that is interested in the act. This is accomplished in a variety of ways, including talking to personal contacts, showcasing the act, and/or providing demo tapes and videos.

When the Personal Manager finds a label interested in the act, he or she may negotiate a recording deal or recommend a music industry attorney to negotiate on behalf of the group.

The Personal Manager seeks out booking agents to find engagements for the act. If the act is just starting out, the manager may book dates him- or herself. However, it is illegal in a number of states for an individual to act as both a manager and a booking agent. In other words, the manager cannot usually take both a percentage of the artist's earnings for managing and an additional percentage for booking the act.

The Personal Manager might help the artists polish their act by reviewing tunes, choreography, costumes, and backup musicians. He or she might also help choose musical personnel, producers, engineers, etc., for a recording date.

Representing the artist at all times, the manager advises the act about other personnel to hire and/or fire. Personnel might include both business and talent people. Some examples of support personnel are: public relations firms, publicists, road personnel, producers, musicians, accountants, security people, and merchandisers.

As the Personal Manager, the individual is responsible for advancing the act's career as much as possible. He or she must oversee all the personnel and their jobs in relation to the act. At times, the manager might have to audit books or act as a road manager or even as the heavy in a dispute with a promoter.

A Personal Manager must be willing to work hard for the success of the client. Working hard, however, doesn't always mean the artist will be successful. It is helpful for the manager to have industry contacts. These contacts sometimes help the artist get to the top.

Managers are often given power of attorney for their clients. In some cases, the power of attorney is complete; in others, it is limited. Whatever the case, the manager usually is given authority to approve concert dates and places, monies for concerts, publicity materials, etc.

The individual an act chooses to be its manager must be compatible with the act. He or she must be available on a day-to-day basis to discuss any problems the artist has. In addition, the two parties must meet on a regular basis to discuss new ways to advance the career of the act.

In many cases, the manager puts up money to finance the group or artist hoping to make the money back later. In other cases, the manager might find a financial backer for the group.

The Personal Manager works closely with all members of the act's team. He or she may spend a great deal of time with the act's publicity or public relations firm working on building the image of the act.

The manager will also be in constant communication with the act's booking agent or agency. The manager must make sure that the act is always well represented by others.

The Personal Manager is responsible directly to the act. Although the terms of each artist-manager contract are different, most run for a specified number of years. Some have option clauses that the manager can pick up if he or she desires.

The lifestyle of a Personal Manager in the music business is a busy one. Long hours are spent with the act. More hours are used up dealing on the group's behalf. If a manager is with an artist who makes it financially, he or she usually enjoys the success, too. Since managers can handle more than one client (although they don't usually handle vast numbers at any one time), they can make out quite well financially.

Salaries

Personal Managers receive a percentage of the artist's earnings. This percentage varies with the individual and the manager. It can range from 10% to 50%. The usual amount is 15% to 20% of artist earnings. In certain situations, the percentage goes up as an artist makes more money. For example, the manager may make 10% of all earnings up to $100,000 and 15% on all monies after that.

Personal Managers receive these fees off the top. Fees are received on monies from personal appearances, concerts, television, recording, etc. In some cases, the manager also takes a percentage of merchandising

paraphernalia sold (T-shirts, posters, bumper stickers, pins, etc.).

A Personal Manager working with a band just starting out may earn the same amount of money as the band members until they get on their feet financially. The manager may opt to take nothing until the group starts doing reasonably well.

The Personal Manager often puts up money for the act in excess of his or her salary, temporarily losing money. The manager hopes that the money will be recouped later when the band is successful. (On the other hand, the band may break up or never get anywhere, and the manager may incur a loss.)

A Personal Manager working with a top recording group can make $500,000 plus. Managers often handle more than one act at a time.

Employment Prospects

Employment prospects are good for Personal Managers. As almost anyone can become a manager, all one has to do is find acts to sign up. This is not to say that everyone can be a *good* manager. In order to be successful, the Personal Manager must have contacts and guide the act's career.

There are many groups that are not yet signed with anyone. An individual with an eye for raw talent can certainly enter this field.

Advancement Prospects

There are many Personal Managers around the country and the world. Most of them, however, do not handle major acts. In order to attract a top recording act, a manager must have proven him- or herself in the past. This usually means having a top act or an up-and-coming act signed. One other excellent method is for the Personal Manager to start with a new act and work with them, guiding their career until stardom. Unfortunately, though, as groups begin to attain success they often try to get out of their contracts with smaller managers and sign with better known managers.

Education and Training

There is no formal educational requirement to qualify one for a position as a manager. A college background is helpful, however. There are currently degrees and courses offered in the music business and music merchandising. Other useful majors and/or courses are business, law, communications, journalism, and marketing.

Experience, Skills, and Personality Traits

A very broad knowledge of the entire music business is necessary for success as a manager. Many new managers (those starting out with local acts, for instance) learn the ropes as they go. It is important for the individual to acquire as many useful music contacts as possible. This allows the manager to help an act.

Successful managers are hard-working individuals, always making efforts on their group's behalf. A Personal Manager should have the ability to see raw talent and work with it until it is polished to perfection.

Many managers begin their careers as musicians and find they enjoy the business end of the industry more. Personal Managers should be adept at all the business facets of an entertainer's career. The ability to give positive, constructive advice on the creative end is a plus.

Unions and Associations

Personal Managers may be members of the National Conference of Personal Managers. This organization sets standards for the conduct of Personal Managers.

Tips for Entry

1. Try to break into management on a local level. There are many acts waiting for someone to help them.
2. You might consider working for a management agency as a secretary or assistant to learn the ropes.
3. There are often ads placed in the classified sections of newspapers and trades by groups seeking management. Some of these acts need management to find a backer. Some will want the manager to be the backer, while others may just need to have someone notice their talent. Check it out.
4. Look for an internship program in any aspect of the industry to give you a good background and the opportunity to make contacts.

BOOKING AGENT

Duties: Secure engagements for musical artists and groups

Alternate Title(s): Booking Manager; Theatrical Agent; Booker; Agent; Booking Representative

Salary Range: $20,000 to $1,000,000+

Employment Prospects: Fair

Advancement Prospects: Fair

Best Geographical Location(s) for Position: New York City, Los Angeles, and Nashville for major agencies; other cities may have opportunities

Prerequisites:

Education or Training—No educational requirement

Experience—Experience in various facets of music business; sales jobs; buying talent for college concerts

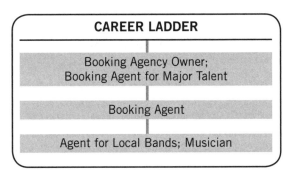

CAREER LADDER

Booking Agency Owner; Booking Agent for Major Talent

Booking Agent

Agent for Local Bands; Musician

Special Skills and Personality Traits—Ability to communicate; knowledge of music business; knowledge of routing; ability to talk on phone for great lengths of time; good salesmanship

Position Description

Booking Agents are also known as booking managers, theatrical agents, bookers, agents, and booking representatives. Whatever name the individual goes by, he or she performs one main job: secure engagements for musical artists and groups.

The Booking Agent works in a number of ways. To start with, an agent needs the talent to book. He or she may send out literature, brochures, pictures, etc., to a variety of clubs and concert halls to obtain bookings for a client. The Booking Agent usually follows up with many phone calls to these places.

If an agent is dealing with a recognized talent (for example, a group with a Top 40 record on the charts) things are different. Under these circumstances, the agent is usually called by clubs and promoters who want the act to appear in their venues. The Booking Agent works very closely with the act's manager and knows what fee to charge. The agent will often negotiate with a promoter or club who wants the act for a lower price.

After a deal has been struck on the phone, the agent sends out copies of contracts to be signed by the promoter or club owner. These contracts include all the information required by the promoter for the show or concert. Included is the name of the group, the date of the concert, the times of the shows, how many performances are required, how much money will be paid for the performance, and in what manner

it will be paid. Agents, as a rule, require a percentage of the money up front. This amount varies, but is usually about 50 percent. The money is due when the contract is signed. The agent collects the money, takes his or her percentage, and pays the group. The rest of the money is usually paid at the performance.

The contracts agents send to people employing their acts may also have a rider attached that stipulates any extras the group is to receive. These extras might include expense money, hotel rooms, food, limousines, or instrumental augmentation, among other things.

In large agencies, agents are often separated into categories. For instance, one agent may handle classical acts, another rock acts, still another R & B acts. Other agencies may handle just one variety of artist.

Agents representing top artists may set up complete concert tours for the acts and deal with promoters all over the country. During these tours, the agent works with the artist's manager and record company, deciding where concerts will be most effective.

In many states, booking agencies and agents must be licensed. These licenses, like those of other employment agencies, are usually obtained through state agencies.

Agents often audition new talent that comes to them seeking representation. In addition, many agents attend showcases, local clubs, etc., looking for talent to book.

Agents may represent a client exclusively or nonexclusively, depending on the circumstances. The agent may also represent a client exclusively in one field (e.g., concerts) and nonexclusively in another (e.g., personal appearances).

Agents can represent as many clients as they can handle. They often book artists who compete with one another in the marketplace. Agents strive to build up a roster of clients. In addition, agents aspire to have clients who command large fees.

The Agent is responsible to the artist and his or her manager. An agent may sign an artist for a specified number of years.

Most of the working day of an agent is spent on the phone trying to sell the acts, talking about the acts, negotiating for the acts, etc. Most agents spend seven to eight hours a day on the phone and use the phone as the vehicle to success.

Salaries

Booking Agents are paid a commission. They receive a percentage off the top of the artist's fee. Commissions vary, but usually range from 10% to 20% of the act's gross income per show.

Agents working in agencies may be paid a salary plus a percentage of the monies they bring into the agency. Agents who make the most money usually handle more than one act. The most successful agent may earn $200,000 to $1,000,000 or more per year. Individuals just starting out in the industry make much less. The variables are too great to estimate the average salary.

Employment Prospects

It is extremely difficult to break into booking on a major scale. Entering on a local level, however, prospects are much brighter. Many aspiring agents begin by booking local talent (or possibly even their own band) in local clubs and bars.

There are also agencies located in most cities. These agencies do not usually book major talent. Instead, they book regional talent. Entry into such an agency is another possibility for the individual looking for a job as an agent.

Most booking agencies that book major talent are located in New York City, Los Angeles, and Nashville. Many of these agencies have offices in other cities around the country.

Advancement Prospects

Agents may advance in a number of ways. They may begin booking a local band that gains some notoriety and go up the success ladder with it.

Another way an agent may advance his or her career is to gain entry into a regional agency. After obtain-

ing experience, the agent might be able to move into a major agency.

Agents frequently become talent buyers for concert halls, clubs, arenas, etc. Other agents build up enough of a client roster to start their own talent agency. There is no one way to advance a career like this. There are a number of Booking Agents and agencies around the country who are making a fortune booking acts on a regional level. Some of these people earn more than Agents who work in a major agency in a music capital.

Education and Training

There is no educational requirement to work as a Booking Agent. There are seminars, workshops, and courses available in booking entertainment. Courses in business may be useful. There are also classes and seminars in contracts and/or contract law offered in many colleges.

Experience, Skills, and Personality Traits

A Booking Agent, in effect, sells a group or an artist. Therefore, first and foremost an agent must possess sales ability.

In order to be a successful agent, one must be aggressive. Much of the selling of acts is done on the telephone. Agents of major groups may stay on the phone pushing their acts for seven to eight hours a day or even more.

As in most jobs in the music industry, agents must be able to work under extreme pressure. Acts constantly call to see if they have new jobs. Managers call to tell the agent they want more money for their acts. Clubs call to negotiate for an act for less money. Even after everything is set up, the group might cancel. The agent must be able to keep his or her cool under these conditions.

Unions and Associations

Major Booking Agents may work under a union contract, such as that of the American Federation of Musicians (AFM), the American Federation of Television and Radio Artists (AFTRA), the American Guild of Variety Artists (AGVA), the Screen Actors Guild (SAG), or the American Guild of Musical Artists (AGMA). These unions specify what percentage an agent can get from an act, how long contracts can run, etc.

Tips for Entry

1. Start booking groups in your area. All groups need work and most can never find enough jobs. Make sure the groups you book know that you will be taking a percentage. This money won't make you rich, but it will give you an opportu-

nity to gain valuable experience in this type of position.

2. You might consider calling clubs in your area, too. Try to set up a meeting with the owner or club manager to see if they need entertainment for their clubs. Indicate that you will hire the entertainment under their direction, taking into account their budget, style of music, etc. Then place an ad for bands looking for work. Always keep a list of possibles in case an act cancels out.

3. In both of the above instances, try to use some form of contract as protection for yourself so that you get your commission.

4. If you want to work in a major agency, you might have to accept an entry-level position as a secretary, receptionist, or mailroom clerk. Once you get in, ask questions and be interested.

5. If you are familiar with the business and have some experience, keep knocking on doors and calling major agencies. They often feel that if you can sell yourself to them, you can certainly sell the acts.

6. Look into the training programs some of the bigger agencies have established. There is a list of major agencies in the appendix.

CONCERT PROMOTER

Duties: Present talent in concert, club, or festival settings; oversee every aspect of putting on a show

Alternate Title(s): Talent Promoter, Promoter

Salary Range: $0 to $1,000,000+

Employment Prospects: Poor

Advancement Prospects: Poor

Best Geographical Location(s) for Position: Large cities for major concerts; smaller cities for other types of shows

Prerequisites:

Education or Training—No educational requirement

Experience—Music business background helpful; booking acts on any level; working as an assistant to

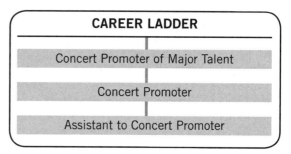

CAREER LADDER

Concert Promoter of Major Talent

Concert Promoter

Assistant to Concert Promoter

a concert promoter or in a promotional company is helpful

Special Skills and Personality Traits—Ability to finance shows; knowledge of music business; knowledge of area where concert is being promoted; stamina; contacts within the industry

Position Description

The Concert Promoter is responsible for putting concerts together. As a promoter, the individual has many duties.

The first thing a promoter needs to do is secure the money required for the venture. In some cases, the Promoter raises and invests the money and is the backer him- or her-self. In other situations, the promoter finds others who share the expenses and profits.

The Concert Promoter must have a definite plan of action. In what city will the concert take place? Which hall (or club, arena, etc.) will be used? When will the show be? How many shows will be promoted? Who will headline?

Creation of a preliminary budget is one of the most important tasks the promoter will undertake. Underbudgeted, the promoter will lose money; overbudgeted, he or she is in a better position. The extra budget funds will often take care of situations that don't go according to plan. The preliminary budget will be reworked after negotiations for the main act have taken place.

Once the promoter has completed the negotiations, signed the headliner and a supporting act, and rented a venue, he or she must go to work to sell tickets.

The Concert Promoter generally must advertise. He or she will decide where the advertising dollar buys most—on radio or TV, or in the print media. The pro-

moter will buy advertising space, keeping in mind the money allocated for advertising in the budget. If, near the show date, and ticket sales are low, the promoter might put extra money into advertising.

The promoter will have posters, flyers, etc., printed and put up around the area. He or she will also need a place for tickets to be sold. This might be the box office of the concert hall, a ticket selling agency, or record stores in the area.

The Concert Promoter may work with the act's record company or the act themselves putting together interviews, publicity stunts, press conferences, etc., in order to build momentum before the concert. The promoter may hire a publicist or public relations firm to help orchestrate these things or may do them him- or herself. The promoter or the publicist also sees that the press releases, press kits, and free tickets are delivered to media people prior to the event.

The Concert Promoter is in charge of supervising any workers, specialists, etc., who have been hired. Depending on the circumstances under which the hall is rented, the promoter may be responsible, additionally, for hiring and/or supervising stage managers, ushers, security guards, lighting technicians, sound technicians, and people to move equipment.

The night of the concert the promoter will go over the final box office receipts, often with the act's manager or road manager in attendance. At this time, the act is usually paid the monies that were not advanced to them on signing the contract.

After the show, the promoter will make sure that the hall is in proper order. At this point, many promoters throw parties, either for the act or for the people who helped pull the event together.

After checking the expenses and the box office receipts, the promoter can tell whether he or she lost money, made money, or broke even on that show. The promoter, incidentally, may promote an act's entire tour or just one concert. This individual may also promote in more than one area.

This career is best suited to those in a position to take financial risks. The promoter must also have incredible stamina and enthusiasm in order to pull off a successful event or try another promotion after one has failed.

Salaries

There are a great many variables that influence the earnings of Concert Promoters. These include the area where they promote shows, the kind of talent used, how successful the talent is, and luck.

If the show is successful, Promoters wind up with a percentage of the profits. It is not unheard of for promoters to lose money on shows they put together. Breaking even is sometimes thought of as a blessing by those in the business.

Promoters who are successful in the business can earn a great deal of money—sometimes hundreds of thousands of dollars a year. The top promoters have earnings topping $1,000,000 or more.

Employment Prospects

It is very difficult to break into the world of concert promotion. Most areas are locked up by promoters who have proven track records in the business. Turnover of these promoters is very slow.

Many agents do not want to take chances and work with new promoters, especially with their major acts.

It is sometimes easier, though, to break into the smaller promotional field of halls and clubs with up-and-coming acts.

Advancement Prospects

It is difficult to advance in the concert promotion field. As noted above, there is not a high turnover of successful Concert Promoters in an area, and in order to promote, agents prefer those with a proven track record. It turns into a "Catch 22" situation.

Advancing by promoting an up-and-coming act which does rise to the top is one method of moving upward in this profession. If one has a great deal of money to promote shows and a lot of good contacts in the industry willing to take a chance, possibilities for success increase.

Education and Training

There is no educational requirement for a Concert Promoter. There are those in the business who have no education whatsoever, and those who hold graduate degrees from leading colleges and universities.

It does help to have some type of business background, either from formal education or from practical experience. Learning the basics of music promotion from a college course or music seminar might help, too.

Experience, Skills, and Personality Traits

The successful Concert Promoters—those who make money most of the time—often have a background in the music business. They have built up a list of contacts and friends in the business with whom they can work.

The most important thing a Concert Promoter needs to get any show off the ground is money. Sufficient funds are required so that if the show loses money or breaks even, the promoter can learn from the experience and try again.

Unions and Associations

Concert Promoters do not belong to any union, although they probably work with a few unions when putting together a concert.

Many Concert Promoters are associate members of the National Academy of Recording Arts and Sciences (NARAS), the organization that gives out the Grammy awards.

Promoters may also belong to other associations, such as the Country Music Association (CMA) or the Gospel Music Association (GMA).

Tips for Entry

1. Try finding a position with an established concert promotion company as an assistant, receptionist, secretary, etc. Watch what is going on in the company and learn the ropes.
2. If you decide to promote on your own, start small. Promote a concert with a small outlay of money instead of an enormous one.
3. Try promoting on someone else's money. Donate your services to a school, church, or organization that will put up the money and give you help. You book the show and take care of the

details. You might not make any money (you won't lose any either), but you will gain invaluable experience.

4. Get on your school's or college's entertainment or concert committee. This is a great way to learn about concert promotion.

5. There are organizations and associations dealing with concert promotion in colleges. They sometimes offer apprenticeships, workshops, or conferences on concert promotion.

MUSIC PUBLISHER

CAREER PROFILE

Duties: Publish music; negotiate royalty agreements with composers; screen songs; print music; acquire copyrights; distribute music; find material

Alternate Title(s): None

Salary Range: $0 to $1,000,000+

Employment Prospects: Fair

Advancement Prospects: Fair

Best Geographical Location(s) for Position: New York City, Los Angeles, and Nashville

Prerequisites:

Education or Training—Educational requirements vary according to position; some jobs require bachelor's degree

Experience—Working in all facets of music business useful

Special Skills and Personality Traits—Understanding of music industry; ability to hear hit tunes; knowledge of copyright laws; business orientation; contacts in music business

CAREER LADDER

Top Music Publisher

Music Publisher

Song Plugger/Professional Manager; Songwriter; Musician

Position Description

Individuals working as Music Publishers are responsible for acquiring the copyrights to songs and publishing them. People in this profession may work in a variety of job situations. They might work for a very large music publishing company and perform one or two specific duties of a Music Publisher. They may work for a relatively small firm and fulfill a variety of functions. Another option for an individual in music publishing is to become an independent Music Publisher, with one's own music publishing firm.

The Music Publisher has many responsibilities. The first is to obtain music to be published. In order to do this, a Music Publisher must listen to demos that are sent or brought into the office. The Music Publisher may also visit clubs, cabarets, showcases, and concerts to locate new material. The purpose is to find potential hit songs. This function may be accomplished by or with a song plugger or professional manager.

In this position, the individual must decide which materials are good and which ones are not. Bad songs must be rejected. Writers of good songs are offered contracts. If the songwriter (or owner of the song) has had prior hits, the publisher may negotiate a contract that is acceptable to both parties. Once the contract is signed, the publisher has the rights to the song. His or her main concern then is to sell it in as many ways as possible. This may mean getting a group to record it,

having it used for motion picture music, sheet music, etc. Every time that musical piece is used in any way, the Music Publisher will make money. This process is called "exploiting the work (or copyright)."

In order to sell the song, the Music Publisher must have a demo to bring or send to potential buyers. The publisher should have contacts in the business. These might include recording groups, record producers, managers, agents, etc. The Music Publisher tries to get as many people as possible to listen to the demo in the hope that he or she will find someone to record it. If a Music Publisher has a song in the catalog that has been recorded previously, that individual will try to get it recorded again and again, in an attempt to turn it into a standard that everyone will want to record.

The Music Publisher will prepare printed music (sheet music, songbooks, etc.) and have it distributed. Before this occurs, the publisher must make sure that the music is technically correct, proofed, and printed. This is another method by which the Music Publisher can collect fees. Before the record industry became as large as it is today, Music Publishers made most of their earnings publishing printed editions.

An important function of the Music Publisher is to file copyright forms on behalf of the song. As the publisher, he or she is responsible for making sure that there is no copyright infringement and/or unauthorized use of the material.

In the position of Music Publisher, the individual may also seek to subpublish any of the music from his or her catalog out of the country. This may be done through a subsidiary of the Music Publisher in a different nation or through a different publishing company in the other country.

Publishing companies make money by exploiting songs. The more the song is recorded, played, distributed as sheet music, etc., the more income the Music Publisher earns. As a Music Publisher, the individual is in charge of collecting fees for the use of the songs. Publishers may collect fees or royalties from a variety of sources. These include performance fees (fees for each time a song is played on the radio, TV, etc.), mechanical royalties (from the sale of each record or tape), printed edition royalties (from songbooks, sheet music, etc.), synchronization fees (from the use of a publisher's song in a movie), and ancillary income (from commercials, advertisements, music boxes, and on such merchandising paraphernalia as toys, clothes, greeting cards, T-shirts, bumper stickers, etc.).

People in this field work under a great deal of pressure, constantly trying to sell songs from their catalogs. Hours depend on the work situation but are often flexible.

Salaries

It is difficult to estimate the earnings of a Music Publisher. Incomes vary widely, depending on the songs the publisher has in his or her catalog, how often they are recorded, the size of the catalog, etc. A Music Publisher who has just one song that hits the top of the charts can make a fortune. Conversely, there are Music Publishers who never have a hit tune in their catalogs. One of the exciting things about music publishing, though, is that a good song can become a hit anytime. This means that a Music Publisher can bring in thousands of dollars anytime. It does take luck, perseverance, and, of course, a good song.

Music Publishers' earnings can range from almost nothing to a million or more dollars a year.

Employment Prospects

Employment prospects for Music Publishers are fair. If an individual cannot find a job, it is not uncommon for him or her to become an independent Music Publisher. Entering this field without experience or knowledge may not be the best idea in the world, but it sometimes works.

Those seeking employment in established firms must have extensive knowledge and experience in the business. Individuals with a good working knowledge of the copyright laws may have a better chance of getting in the door.

Advancement Prospects

The more background in the business one has, as noted above, the better the chances of not only getting into music publishing, but moving up.

The individual who has a proven track record in music publishing will probably have no trouble finding a job. Many people advance their careers in this field by becoming independent Music Publishers or owners of large music publishing companies.

The difficulty in moving ahead in this field, however, is that it is hard to know what will turn into a hit song. Locating these hits and acquiring the copyrights on them is the real key to advancement.

Education and Training

There are many different sizes and kinds of publishing companies. Education for this career varies. There seems to be a correlation between the size of the firm and the educational requirements. The bigger the company, the more education usually required. This stems from the fact that in smaller companies, an individual may perform a variety of functions, while in larger firms, individuals usually perform one or two tasks.

Some publishing companies require their people to hold bachelor's degrees. Others don't care much about the education an individual has as long as he or she has had experience in the music industry and/or music publishing.

There are some schools that offer a major in the music business or music merchandising. These schools usually have courses in music publishing. There are also a number of seminars given on the subject. All these information resources will prove helpful to the aspiring Music Publisher.

Experience, Skills, and Personality Traits

A total understanding of the music industry is needed by a Music Publisher. Contacts in the business are vital, too. The individual must have extensive knowledge of copyright laws and business in general.

As a Music Publisher, one of the most important qualifications is the ability to hear a hit song before it is a hit. The individual must be aggressive enough to sell a song and/or get appointments for it to be listened to. The Music Publisher must also be organized in business. Records must be kept accurately in order for songwriters to be paid properly.

Unions and Associations

Music Publishers may belong to the Music Publishers' Association of the U.S. (MPA) and/or the National Music Publishers' Association. Individuals in this field might also be associate members of the National Academy of Recording Arts and Sciences (NARAS). This is the organization that gives out Grammy awards each year.

Tips for Entry

1. Positions in this field are not usually advertised. If you want to get into this type of work, put together a good résumé, including all experience in the music field. Send it with a cover letter to a number of the larger music publishing companies. These firms are more apt to have openings.

2. You can open your own music publishing firm. However, try to get some experience beforehand. Knowing the ropes can not only make you money, but also save you money.

3. There are a number of music publishing companies owned by record companies. As indicated throughout this book, many of these record companies have internships and minority training programs.

4. Try to be as knowledgeable about the subject as possible. If you can find a course or seminar in music publishing, take it.

PROFESSIONAL MANAGER

Special Skills and Personality Traits—Perseverance; a feel for the right song and act; knowledge of music business; contacts in the industry; salesmanship

Position Description

A Professional Manager, or song plugger, works for a music publisher. Depending on the size of the publishing company, the publisher might also act as the song plugger. This happens most frequently in one-man operations.

In the Professional Manager capacity, an individual has a number of duties. One of these is to perform the administrative functions of the publishing office.

In this role, the Professional Manager must find possible hits to add to the publisher's catalog. Naturally, in order to be good at the job, the individual must have a feel for a good song. The Professional Manager may look for material by attending concerts, clubs, showcases, etc. The Professional Manager also goes through material sent to the publishing company, listening to a piece of each song until one clicks.

The individual also is responsible for finding acts to record songs from the publisher's catalog. The catalog contains all tunes to which the publisher has the rights. Each time the song plugger gets a singer or group to record a tune from the catalog, money is made for the publishing company.

After songs are recorded by one group, the Professional Manager will often try to get the tune covered by another. A tune that is covered enough becomes a standard. Standards make publishers wealthy. A Professional Manager who is good at his or her job is in great demand.

Most song pluggers use to get songs recorded and/or rerecorded through personal contacts. These contacts can make or break a Professional Manager and/or publisher. By contacting people in the industry (such as recording acts, record producers, A & R personnel, personal managers, etc.), the Professional Manager often can get his or her song listened to. A good tune is useless to a Professional Manager or a publisher if it sits idly in the catalog.

The Professional Manager often assists artists with tunes he or she believes in by helping them make professional-sounding demos. These demos help the individual sell the tune. The demos are either delivered in person or mailed to the key people noted above. As a rule, if the Professional Manager is not mailing or dropping off the demo to someone he or she knows, making a phone call and writing a brief note to accompany the tape are customary. It is very rare for a Professional Manager to send a demo tape completely unsolicited.

Salaries

Salaries for Professional Managers vary widely according to a number of factors. These include the size of the music publishing company, the number of songs recorded, and the songs' popularity.

Professional Managers usually receive a weekly salary. When they are successful in getting tunes recorded by known acts, they may also receive bonuses. Individuals in this field earn between $25,000 and $100,000 plus annually.

Employment Prospects

There are innumerable groups looking for material to record and many songs that need to be published. Technically, an individual has a fair chance of becoming a Professional Manager.

The hard part is getting a foot in the door. If one can find the way in, there are quite a few jobs in this field.

Advancement Prospects

Advancement for a Professional Manager comes only when the individual has attained some success. Success means that the Professional Manager or song plugger has picked up one or more tunes that have become hits or that the person has matched a tune in the publisher's catalog with an act that has turned it into a hit. After this happens, the Professional Manager is in a very good position.

Many Professional Managers become the major buyers of songs for prestigious music publishers. Other individuals strike out on their own and form new publishing companies. Individuals who have been acting as Professional Managers in their own companies find success through increased earnings.

Education and Training

Professional Managers are not required to have any specific education. Many people in the profession are former musicians. Other individuals have degrees in areas ranging from business to music to broadcasting.

Professional Managers who desire to move into other phases of the industry would be wise to have some business background. Any seminar or course on music publishing would also prove useful.

Experience, Skills, and Personality Traits

The most successful Professional Managers have had experience in many different phases of the music indus-try. Over time, they have made innumerable personal contacts. These contacts are what help the Professional Manager attain success.

The individual must have a feel for the right song and the ability to put songs and artists together in an effort to get the song recorded. If a person has a good song and believes in it, he or she must have the perseverance to work with it until someone else believes in it, too.

Unions and Associations

Professional Managers may belong to the Music Publishers' Association of the United States (MPA) and the National Music Publishers' Association (NMPA). The organizations provide programs, conferences, seminars, etc., on all aspects of music publishing. The Professional Manager may be an associate member of the National Academy of Arts and Sciences (NARAS).

Tips for Entry

1. Music publishing companies can be small or very large. Send your résumé to some of the larger companies. Make sure you include all your experience in the music business, from writing tunes to working in a record store.

2. Some individuals form their own publishing companies. As indicated above, you can act as a Professional Manager while being a music publisher. Remember, just forming a company does not make money. Acquiring songs and getting them recorded does.

3. Learn which organizations, associations, and schools are putting on seminars or giving courses in music publishing. You should know as much as possible about the entire business, especially if you do not have a lot of experience in the music industry.

BUSINESS MANAGER

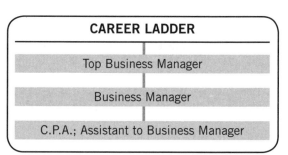

Position Description

A Business Manager handles financial affairs for singers, musicians recording artists, and other entertainers. A person in this position may have one or more clients. Acts that hire Business Managers are usually doing quite well financially.

The Business Manager (or agent, as the person is sometimes called) must oversee the finances of an act or individual in order to maximize the earning potential. The individual is responsible for collecting all monies due and paying all the bills.

The Business Manager performs a number of duties as part of the job. The Business Manager may negotiate with agents and/or representatives for contracts and appearances. He or she might negotiate with union officials, motion picture studios, television producers, concert halls, record companies, merchandising firms, or publishing companies. The Business Manager may seek out firms, companies, and corporations that will pay the artist for endorsements or sponsor a large concert tour. After the act has performed a service, the individual will make sure they are paid in a timely fashion.

The individual is in charge of checking all bills for accuracy. If bills are in order, the Business Manager pays them. The person may be responsible for paying employees of the act, such as road personnel, secretaries, musicians, vocalists, publicists, public relations firms, lawyers, etc. The Business Manager may also pay the artist's personal bills. He or she must keep records of all monies taken in and paid out.

Depending on the requirements of the act, the Business Manager may plan budgets for the group or for individual members. The individual may work with the record company or the booking agent and personal manager in designing budgets for various projects.

The Business Manager might act as a financial or business advisor, counseling the act and its members on good investments, taxes, legal matters, or other income interests.

If the act is experiencing differences concerning contractual rights and obligations with their representatives, the Business Manager may act as a liaison during these difficulties. The Business Manager may also request audits of firms with which the act is or has been doing business. The individual might hire a C.P.A. to conduct these audits.

The person hired as a group's or individual's Business Manager will regularly summarize and send statements of investments, property, and financial status to the client. He or she will also be available for meetings with the act or their representatives to discuss investments, problems, audits, etc.

Salaries

The earnings of a Business Manager vary from individual to individual and from year to year. Individuals just starting out may earn only $25,000. Persons doing well can earn $1,000,000 or more. Variables include the number of clients one has, how well each of them is doing financially, geographical location of the Business Manager, and his or her experience and expertise.

The Business Manager makes money by charging clients fees. Fees can be obtained in a variety of ways. The most common is to charge a percentage of the act's total gross income. This percentage varies from 3% to 10% or more. The individual can also charge a flat retainer or an hourly fee. Some Business Managers charge a combination of a minimum fee against a commission on total monies earned by the client.

It is important to remember that a Business Manager may (and usually does) service more than one client.

Employment Prospects

A qualified individual has a fair chance of becoming a successful Business Manager. The person seeking this type of job will probably have to work in or near one of the music capitals to obtain clients. There are many offices in which a person can work as an administrative assistant to a Business Manager and learn the ropes. Once again, these are usually located in one of the music cities—New York City, Los Angeles, or Nashville.

An individual might also work as a Business Manager or accountant for nonmusic-oriented clients and then actively seek music clients. Most of the time, this must be accomplished through contacts in the music business, although there are Business Managers who advertise in the music trades.

Advancement Prospects

The way a Business Manager advances his or her career is by obtaining more clients. Conversely, the Business Manager can take fewer clients, if they are large ones.

More prestigious clients are obtained by word of mouth. If a Business Manager can advise well and help the act save and make money, that individual will probably become successful.

Education and Training

Although there is no educational requirement for a person in this field, most individuals do have college degrees in business administration, finance, or accounting. Persons who are very successful as Business Managers usually have gone through a graduate program in one of the above fields.

There are some business managers who are C.P.A.s and others who are not. Business Managers might retain the services of C.P.A.s when needed.

Experience, Skills, and Personality Traits

Business Managers should be cognizant of all types of investments. The individual may advise the client on investments outside of the music industry, which are often thought to be safer. The Business Manager must have the ability to negotiate with people in all phases of business. He or she should have a total understanding of the music business in order to negotiate efficiently.

The individual in this position must also have a good knowledge of tax laws. It is beneficial to be able to advise the act how to save money on taxes. The ability to help the artist make money through investments, endorsements, etc., is another valuable commodity.

Unions and Organizations

Business Managers may belong to a number of associations. If they are accountants, they might belong to the American Institute of Certified Public Accountants (AICPA), or the National Society of Public Accountants (NSPA).

Individuals might also be members of the Financial Planning Association (FPA)

If the individual is also a personal manager, he or she could belong to the National Conference of Personal Managers (NCOPM).

Tips for Entry

1. Try to locate some successful Business Managers and apply for a position as an administrative assistant.
2. Make sure you are qualified for a position like this. Big acts will not go near a person who has not yet proven him- or herself. Smaller, lesser-known acts might.
3. This is a position in which contacts in the music business help. Let people know what you are doing (or trying to do).
4. Take seminars on business management, investments, tax shelters, etc. These courses need not be specific to the music business. Many of the investments you advise your clients to make will not be music-oriented. You need to be well versed in a full range of investments.

ATTORNEY, MUSIC INDUSTRY

CAREER PROFILE

Duties: Handling legal matters for clients in music industry; handling contractual matters; negotiating contracts; negotiating deals; providing legal advice and counsel; helping put together an artist's team; litigating

Alternate Title(s): Lawyer

Salary Range: $60,000 to $1,000,000+

Employment Prospects: Fair

Advancement Prospects: Good

Best Geographical Location(s) for Position: Positions may be located throughout country; more opportunities may exist in culturally active cities with larger numbers of record labels, music industry companies, and recording artists, such as New York City, Los Angeles, and Nashville, Atlanta, Philadelphia, Boston, etc.

Prerequisites:

Education or Training—Law degree required

Experience—Experience requirements vary from job to job; see text

Special Skills and Personality Traits—Negotiation skills; knowledge of music industry; ability to

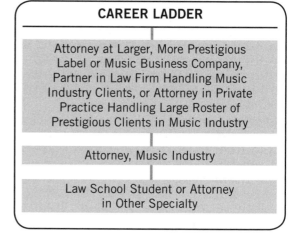

CAREER LADDER

Attorney at Larger, More Prestigious Label or Music Business Company, Partner in Law Firm Handling Music Industry Clients, or Attorney in Private Practice Handling Large Roster of Prestigious Clients in Music Industry

Attorney, Music Industry

Law School Student or Attorney in Other Specialty

read and understand contracts; must be focused and organized; good verbal and written communications skills; an analytical mind; flexibility

Special Requirements—Must pass the bar exam and be licensed in the specific state in which one works

Position Description

While there are Attorneys who have general practices handling a variety of legal issues, a good number of Attorneys specialize in specific fields. An Attorney, may, for example, specialize in corporate law, elder law, family law, criminal law, or a wide spectrum of other fields.

A popular specialty for many individuals interested in entertainment is music or entertainment law. Music and entertainment Attorneys are the individuals who handle the legal needs of those in the music and entertainment industries.

While all Attorneys graduate from a law school, pass a bar exam, and are admitted to the bar in the state or states in which they practice, there are often different areas of speciality. Those who specialize in music and entertainment law must have a complete understanding of the music industry and issues that affect it.

There are many aspects of the music industry that require the services of Attorneys. There are agreements, contracts, and negotiations. There are copyrights,

trademarks, sponsorships, and endorsements . . . and, of course, there are always lawsuits.

Specific responsibilities of Attorneys working in the music industry will depend on the employment situation they are in. Attorneys working at record companies may have responsibilities different from those working at music publishers. Those working with music promoters may have different responsibilities than those working in music or entertainment-oriented law firms. No matter the situation, an Attorney specializing in the music industry is above all responsible for protecting the rights of his or her client.

Many of the responsibilities of Attorneys working in the music industry revolve around contracts. Depending on the specific situation, individuals might negotiate and prepare contracts or review those that others have written. Attorneys may, for example, review a management contract for an up-and-coming artist. They might also be responsible for negotiating new management contracts for established recording artists. Whether actually preparing a contract or reviewing a contract, the Attorney must always be sure that all points that are agreed upon are actually in the document and that the specific wording is clear.

Sometimes Attorneys prepare contracts for individuals who want to form a group. They might, for example, detail how monies are split, what happens if a group member leaves, what is expected of each member, as so on. Conversely, an Attorney might be responsible for negotiating the terms for an individual who wants to leave a recording group in which he or she is currently a member.

Contracts in the music industry have their own language and can often be quite complicated. The Attorney is responsible for explaining all points in a contract to his or her client. In addition, an Attorney is expected to make sure that each contract he or she prepares reflects the points that the client has asked for and approved.

Attorneys must review each contract entrusted to them carefully, whether or not they have actually written it. In some cases, after looking over a contract, an attorney might discover that an artist is giving up more than he or she needs to or that the contract does not reflect what the artist had indicated he or she wanted. In these situations, negotiations to change the contract's wording will have to be undertaken.

Attorneys working at labels may prepare and write contacts for a label's recording artists, songwriters, producers, etc. Depending on the situation, they might also prepare employment contracts for label executives.

As contracts are often amended by one party or another, the Attorney will be responsible for reviewing the amended contracts for changes made by an artist or his or her management team. The change of even one word, if not correct, might potentially mean thousands of dollars to a label or an artist.

Attorneys working with promoters and promotion companies may either prepare performance contracts for artists who appear at their venues or review contracts prepared by either the artist, or his or her manager or agent. These contracts can be fairly extensive. In addition to the name of the venue and the name of the artist, contracts will include the location of the show, times, dates, and length of appearances. They must also include areas such as fees and advances and how payment will be made to the artist. Contracts might include artist billing, the order of appearance of artists if there are more than one in a show; the name of the headliner; size of the artists name on the marquee and in advertisements; the price of tickets; and the amount and type of advertising that will be done.

Many artists add riders to the basic performance contact, specifying additional things they might want or require. Riders may be simple one-page documents or may be more than 100 pages. A simple rider might state, for example, that an act requires a certain type of piano, certain brands of microphones, the type of lighting and sound, rehearsal time, sound checks, amount of publicity the act will undertake and backstage arrangements.

Elaborate riders may state specific types of foods and drinks the act demand's in dressing rooms, specific types of air and ground transportation required, the people to be allowed backstage, and more. Sometimes riders can be demanding and unusual. It is not unheard of for artists to ask for large bowls of M&M candies with the red ones taken out, new toilet seats in dressing rooms, dressing rooms painted a certain color. Riders may include demands such as that the opening act must be approved by the featured artist before billing, the length of the opening act, or the number of complimentary tickets to be distributed. Riders might also include information on the sale of merchandise related to the arist and the percentage (if any) the artist must pay to venue for selling such merchandise. Riders often spell out the type of food that must be served to artists, the times they need to be served, the minimum cost for meals, and any foods that may not be allowed in the dressing rooms.

The Attorney must be sure that each point the artist asks for is in writing in the contract and/or the rider. He or she must also be sure that the contract is signed by both parties in order for the contract to be valid.

Some Attorneys apply for copyrights for new songs or other published material on behalf of the writer, a label, or publishing company. Depending on the situation, they might also apply for trademarks. Additionally, attorneys might handle copyright or trademark infringement suits.

Attorneys working at publishing companies might be responsible for applying for copyrights and working to assure that all copyright laws have been followed. They might also be expected to handle copyright-infringement issues.

Sometimes recording artists find it is necessary to call an Attorney to handle situations where a tabloid or television show allegedly slanders them. The Attorney may handle this him- or herself or refer it to another specialist.

Attorneys can be especially useful at the beginning of an artist's career. They often can bring the artist to the attention of people important to the artist's career. While it may be difficult for a new artist to get to an agent, a manager, or get his or her music listened to on his or her own, an Attorney can often cut through the red tape.

Attorneys specializing in the music industry may also help artists put together their team, including managers, agents, and publishing companies, among others. They may also secure endorsements, tour sponsorships, licensing opportunities, and more.

Salaries

Earnings for Attorneys specializing in the music industry can vary substantially. Attorney's starting out may earn about $60,000 annually. Others who have a great deal of experience or are working for a large and prestigious law firm, a major label, or other music industry company can earn $500,000 or more a year. There are some Attorneys specializing in the music industry who earn more than $1,000,000 annually.

Some lawyers specializing in the music industry are paid a salary. Others earn income dependent upon contracts negotiated. These might related to recordings, publishing rights, endorsements, sponsorships, public appearances, etc. Earnings for Attorneys who are in private practice are based to a great extent on the amount and type of work they perform.

Employment Prospects

Employment prospects are fair for qualified individuals aspiring to work as music industry or entertainment Attorneys. Employment opportunities may be available at record labels, music publishing companies, booking agencies, management companies, and entertainment venues, to name a few. Employment options also exist with promoters and promotion companies, as well as other companies within the music industry. Certain recording artists, songwriters, and entertainers also keep their own personal Attorney on staff.

Some Attorneys work for law firms that specialize solely in the music or entertainment industries; others may work for firms that include one of those areas among their specialties.

Attorneys may also freelance or work on retainer. Many start their own practices.

Jobs and opportunities may be located throughout the country. The greatest number of opportunities, however, will exist in areas where there are large numbers of record labels and other music industry companies, such as New York City, Los Angeles, and Nashville. Other possibilities exist in culturally active cities such as Boston, Philadelphia, Washington, and Atlanta.

Advancement Prospects

Advancement prospects are fair for Attorneys working in the music industry. Individuals can climb the career ladder in a number of ways, depending on their career aspirations. Some find similar positions in larger or more prestigious music-oriented companies. Individuals employed at law firms specializing in the music and entertainment industries may find positions at larger or more prestigious law firms. Others may get more prestigious clients or may even become partners. Some individuals strike out on their own and build their practice with a larger roster of clients.

Education and Training

Attorneys are generally required to have a four-year college degree and three years of law school. Law schools must be approved by the American Bar Association (ABA). In order to apply to law schools, applicants must first take the Law School Admission Test, better known as the LSAT. In order to practice, individuals must pass a written bar exam and be admitted into the bar of the particular state in which they wish to practice.

Those aspiring to work in the music industry should make sure they take courses geared toward the entertainment and music industries. These might include contracts, tax law, business law, and intellectual property and copyright law.

There are a number of law schools that offer special programs or at least a large number of classes in music and entertainment, including at University of California, Los Angeles; University of Southern California; New York University; Columbia; Stanford; Loyola; and California Western. It should be noted that most industry professionals suggest attending the best law school possible, whether or not it specializes in music or entertainment law.

Conferences and symposiums on entertainment and music law will prove useful both for the educational opportunities they offer as well as for the ability to make valuable contacts.

Special Requirements

Like all other Attorneys, attorneys specializing in the music industry, need to pass the bar exam for the state or states in which they will be practicing and be licensed and/or registered in that state.

Experience, Skills, and Personality Traits

Experience requirements for Attorneys specializing in the music industry vary from job to job. Large record labels or other large music companies may want staff Attorneys to have three to five years or more of experience in music or entertainment law. A smaller independent label may require only a little more than a year.

All Attorneys, whether specializing in the music industry or not, need to have good written and verbal communications skills. The ability to think analytically and objectively is essential. In addition, Individuals need to be responsible, organized, and professional, with the highest standard of ethics.

Attorneys specializing in the music industry need a full knowledge of all aspects of the industry. An understanding of the special legal issues that face recording artists, musicians, singers, and songwriters is also essential.

All attorneys often are privy to sensitive information. This is especially true in the music industry. The ability to keep this informational confidential is essential. Discretion is critical. The individual must also be extremely trustworthy.

Unions and Associations

Attorneys specializing in the music industry may be members of the American Bar Association (ABA) and specific state bar associations. Both the ABA and some state bar associations have sections or divisions devoted to entertainment law. There are also professional organizations, such as the International Association of Entertainment Lawyers (IAEL), that bring together attorneys in the entertainment industry to share knowledge and information.

Tips for Entry

1. Get involved in the music industry, whether or not in the legal end. If you are still in school, find an internship at a record company, music publisher, promoter, agent, or manager. You want to be able to demonstrate an understanding and knowledge of the music industry when you are ready to go after the perfect job.

2. Once you have some college under your belt, you might also consider an internship or job as a paralegal at a law firm that specializes in the music or entertainment industries.

3. If you have your law degree, have passed the bar and have a great deal of experience in the music industry but still have not found that perfect job, think about contacting a large law firm that does not yet have an entertainment or music specialty and seeing if they are interested in adding one.

4. Send your résumé with a short cover letter to artist management companies, record labels, booking agencies, promoters, and recording artists. You might get lucky.

5. Positions in this field may be advertised in classified sections of newspapers in areas such as New York City, Los Angeles, and Nashville. Look under headings such as "Entertainment Industry Attorney," "Music Industry Attorney," "Record Label Attorney," "Attorney," "Legal Affairs—Record Label," "Legal Affairs—Music Industry."

6. Trade magazines such as *Billboard* also may advertise openings advertised.

7. Don't forget to check traditional job sites such as monster.com, hotjobs.com, and job sites specific to the music industry.

EXECUTIVE DIRECTOR, MUSIC INDUSTRY TRADE ASSOCIATION

Position Description

The music industry, like other industries, has a large number of trade groups, associations, and organizations geared to promoting their particular segment of the industry. These trade associations cover a wide array of areas, including those dealing with music-related products, services, activities. They may be composed of employees, employers, and educators who work in the music industry. They may also include music- and other entertainment-related restaurants, entertainment venues, retail establishments and more. There are trade associations for songwriters, musicians, record producers, engineers—the list goes on.

Some examples of larger organizations might be the National Association of Recording Arts and Sciences (NARAS), which is known for the Grammy Awards, the National Association of Recording Merchandisers (NARM), and the the Country Music Association (CMA).

The individual in charge of overseeing the operations of a trade association is called the Executive Director. In some instances, he or she may also be called the trade association director.

Trade associations generally are not-for-profit organizations. These groups bring together individuals in a simlar field, support their members, represent their interests, provide them with business support, and often give them a voice in government. Depending on the specific organization, they may also provide educational guidance and professional support and access to benefits.

The main function of the Executive Director is to manage the affairs of the organization. Responsibilities can vary greatly, depending on the specific organization, and its mission, size, structure, prestige, and budget. In smaller organizations, the Executive Director may handle everything him- or herself or, perhaps, with the help of committees of volunteers and interns. In larger trade associations, the Executive Director may have a large staff and assistants to help handle the job's various duties.

The Executive Director works with the board of directors of the organization to establish the direction of the trade association. As part of the job, the individual is expected to determine what types of programs the association will undertake.

The Executive Director is heavily involved in the budget and finances of the organization. One of the responsibilities of the individual may be the preparation of an annual budget. Depending on the size and structure of the organization, this may be difficult, because many of these organizations work with limited budgets.

In order to raise money for the association, the Executive Director is often responsible for fund-raising. He or she may develop, implement, and execute a number of special events during the year to this end. These events may include dinners, membership drives, auctions, galas, golf tournaments, etc. If the association is large, there may a fund-raising director who handles this function.

Grants are another source of funds that trade associations depend on. The Executive Director is responsible for locating grants from federal, state, or local agencies, as well as from private industry. He or she must then write and prepare the grant application. If the individual is successful in securing a grant, he or she must then make sure that all rules and regulations related to the grant are adhered to. In some situations, the Executive Director will oversee a grant writer and administrator who handles these tasks. The Executive Director of a music-related trade association may also solicit donations from private donors as well as corporate donations.

The Executive Director is expected to either personally handle or oversee the association's public relations and advertising. This may include public relations and advertising efforts directed toward the public, as well as within the organization's membership. As part of this responsibility, press releases, calendar schedules, and newsletters must be developed and prepared. In addition, brochures, leaflets, and booklets must be signed and produced to promote the organization. In smaller organizations, the Executive Director may handle these tasks him- or herself. In larger organizations, the Executive Director is responsible for overseeing the public relations and publications departments and staffers.

The Executive Director is expected to find ways to increase the organization's membership. The individual may work with a membership director or handle the task him or herself. The Executive Director may speak at industry events, conduct interviews with the media, or circulate membership materials, among other things.

Many trade associations depend on the help of volunteers within their membership. The Executive Director is responsible for coordinating the efforts of all volunteer groups and committees within the association membership.

A major responsibility for the Executive Director of a trade association in the music business is often scheduling conferences, conventions, and other educational and networking activities. The Executive Director is expected either to handle these activities and events personally, or delegate the duties to a committee or conference coordinator.

The Executive Director of the music industry trade association must be the champion of the organization. He or she is expected to attend meetings and events on behalf of the association. This may include industry events as well as community meetings. The individual will often be the liaison between the association and community groups, often serving on boards of community and civic organizations.

Other responsibilities of the Executive Director of a trade association in the music industry might include:

- Developing new membership drives and handling membership applications and renewals
- Supervising staff
- Dealing with issues significant to the associations
- Attending industry meetings, conferences, and conventions on behalf of the association

Salaries

Annual earnings for Executive Directors of trade associations in the music industry can range from approximately $26,000 to $125,000 or more, depending on a number of factors, including the size, structure, prestige, and budget of the specific trade association. Other Factors affecting earnings include the responsibilities, professional reputation, and experience of the individual.

Employment Prospects

Employment prospects are fair for individuals seeking positions as Executive Directors of trade associations in the music industry. Individuals may find employment in a wide array of areas of the music industry depending on their interests. These areas might include music-related products, services, activities, and genres. They might include the recording industry, instruments, radio, other parts of the entertainment industry, entertainment-related restaurants, entertainment venues, retail establishments, and more. Other associations might encompass employees, employers, and educators who work in the music industry. There are trade associations for songwriters, musicians, record producers, engineers—the list goes on.

It should be noted, that indivuduals may need to relocate for positions.

Advancement Prospects

Advancement prospects are fair for Executive Directors of trade associations in the music industry. Individuals may climb the career ladder in a number of ways. Some may find similar positions at larger or more prestigious associations in the music industry. Often the Executive Director of a trade association may also climb the career ladder by successfully building his or her trade organization into a larger, more prestigious association. In these situations, he she will often have increased responsibilities and earnings.

Some Executive Directors also advance their careers by moving into similar positions in larger or more prestigious associations outside of the music industry. Others gain coveted positions in the corporate end of the music industry through networking.

Education and Training

Most trade associations in the music industry require or prefer that their applicants have as a minimum a four-year college degree. There may, however, be smaller associations that may accept an applicant with an associate's degree or even a high school diploma, coupled with experience.

Courses, seminars, and workshops in fund-raising, grant writing, public relations, business, management, presentation skills, and the music industry will be useful in honing skills and making new contacts.

Experience, Skills, and Personality Traits

Experience requirements depend, to a great extent, on the size, structure, and prestige of the specific trade association. Individuals seeking positions with large, prestigious music industry associations generally will be required to have either a minimum of three years' experience working with trade associations in some manner or working at a high-level corporate job within the industry. Experience in public relations, journalism, fund-raising, grant writing, and working with not-for-profit organizations will also be helpful.

Executive Directors of trade associations in the music industry need to be creative visionaries. They need to be able to think "outside of the box." Individuals must be well spoken with excellent verbal and communication skills. An understanding of grant writing is usually necessary, as is the ability to develop and adhere to budgets. People skills are essential. Management and supervisory skills are also crucial.

An understanding and knowledge of the specific area of the music industry that the association serves is essential.

Unions and Associations

Individuals interested in a career as an Executive Director of a trade association in the music industry may want to contact the Center for Association Leadership. They might also join other professional associations within the music industry in order to make contacts.

Tips for Entry

1. Get experience working with not-for-profit organizations by volunteering with a local civic or community organization.
2. Look for job openings in the classified sections of newspapers. Heading titles might be under key words such as "Trade Association," "Trade Association Executive Director," "Executive Director," "Music Industry Trade Association," or "Association Executive." Jobs may also be advertised under the name of the specific music industry association.
3. Read trade publications; they often advertise openings.
4. Openings may be listed on the Web sites of specific trade associations.
5. Network as much as you can in the industry. Go to conferences, conventions, and educational seminars and workshops to meet industry insiders.
6. Offer to do the publicity or fund-raising for a local not-for-profit organization. It does not matter whether the organization is related to music. If you can do publicity or fund-raising for one organization, you can do it for any type of group.

INSTRUMENT REPAIR, RESTORATION, AND DESIGN

MUSICAL INSTRUMENT BUILDER/ DESIGNER

Duties: Build and/or custom design instruments for sale privately or through a shop or factory

Alternate Title(s): Musical Instrument Master Craftsman (or Craftswoman); Custom Instrument Builder

Salary Range: $25,000 to $150,000+

Employment Prospects: Good

Advancement Prospects: Fair

Best Geographical Locations for Position: Larger cities may have more positions in factories and shops; many custom Musical Instrument Builders/Designers work from their homes in any town or city

Prerequisites:

Education or Training—Training or an apprenticeship in instrument building and designing

Experience—Working with wood and metal (depending on family of instruments the individual designs and/or builds)

Special Skills and Personality Traits—Knowledge of instruments; woodworking; metal working; good musical "ear"; mechanical ability

CAREER LADDER

```
Master Craftsperson; Self-Employed
Instrument Builder/Designer, or Musical
Instrument Builder/Designer at Large,
More Prestigious Company
```

```
Musical Instrument Builder/Designer
```

```
Musical Instrument Builder/Designer
Apprentice
```

Position Description

The Musical Instrument Builder/Designer is a creative person. He or she not only loves instruments but loves to touch them and find new ways they can be shaped or built.

The individual's main function is to take materials and turn them into functioning instruments. He or she does this by watching other instrument builders work, examining other instruments, reading books on the subject, and visiting museums that have collections of instruments from other eras. By noting how these instruments are constructed, the builder/designer can often develop interesting, usable ideas for instruments of today.

The Musical Instrument Builder/Designer usually knows how to play at least one instrument. Sometimes he or she knows how to play almost an entire family of instruments. It is usually that family of instruments that the individual artisan yearns to build and/or design.

The builder/designer has a number of options as to where he or she can work. He or she might choose a position on staff in a music factory or store or the individual might design and build instruments on speculation or from custom orders in his or her workshop.

Musical Instrument Builders/Designers are usually handy people. They have an interest in handcrafts as well as in musical instruments. The ability to work with the hands is essential. They are not only creative, but usually extremely inventive as well.

Although almost any instrument can be built and designed, there is a great market for violins, guitars, dulcimers, harpsichords, banjos, and flutes that are finely crafted and have excellent tones. Many self-employed Musical Instrument Builders/Designers find that they sell as many instruments as they can make, and often they cannot keep up with their orders.

Once instrument builders/designers have been trained as master craftspeople in their field, they are also qualified to teach others who aspire to learn the art.

Salaries

Salaries vary according to the instruments built or designed. The highest salaries go to builders/designers of rarer instruments. Salaries run from $25,000 for a beginner to $150,000 plus yearly by builders/designers in large musical instrument companies. Individuals can also custom design and build instruments for skilled classical musicians and pop/rock stars. Skilled craftsmen may sell their works of art for $2,500–$100,000 plus per instrument. Yearly salaries depend upon the number of custom instruments an individual completes and sells.

Employment Prospects

There are always openings for qualified Musical Instrument Builders/Designers. These individuals can work in factories, shops, or companies or on their own.

Once a builder/designer is qualified, he or she can usually find work and make a good living.

It should be noted that with the current influx of electronic instruments, there is a budding new field that is waiting to be tapped.

Advancement Prospects

As indicated above, qualified individuals can usually find work in the field. Depending upon the individual, it may take years to become a skilled master craftsman (or woman). Talented Musical Instrument Builders/Designers may find similar jobs with larger or more prestigious companies, resulting in increased earnings and responsibilities.

Education and Training

There are courses and technical schools around the country that teach the fine art of building and designing musical instruments. However, they are often difficult to locate.

The best training might be available through working for a qualified builder/designer as an apprentice. To enter into an apprenticeship, one needs a degree of knowledge in woodworking skills. This can often be picked up in high school through industrial arts programs or at an extension course from a community college or other institution. Some knowledge of instrument technology is also useful.

Experience, Skills, and Personality Traits

Musical Instrument Builders/Designers must usually go through an apprenticeship. This apprenticeship helps hone the skills needed for this type of career. The instrument builder/designer needs to know all there is to know about the type and family of instruments he or she is working with.

The individual must also be creative enough to come up with unique ways to put instruments together. A good musical "ear" is necessary. Knowledge of woodworking and/or metalworking is also required.

Unions and Associations

There are no unions for Musical Instrument Builders/Designers. Depending on the types of instruments the individual works with, he or she might belong to the Acoustical Society of America (ASA), the National Council of Acoustical Consultants (NCAC), The Piano Technicians' Guild (PTG), or the Electronic Industries Alliance (EIA).

Tips for Entry

1. To find a person with whom to apprentice, contact a manufacturer of the type of instrument you would like to work with. Tell them what you are looking for and ask for their help.
2. There are a number of associations dealing with specific families of instruments. These associations—the Acoustical Society of America, the National Council of Acoustical Consultants, the Piano Technicians' Guild, and the Electronic Industries Alliance—might also be able to help you find training in your area. In addition, they may know of any seminars or training programs scheduled around the country.
3. Go into your local instrument shop and see if you can get a job for the summer. Try to learn as much as possible about instruments.

INSTRUMENT REPAIR AND RESTORATION SPECIALIST

Position Description

An Instrument Repair and Restoration Specialist usually loves instruments. He or she likes to hear them, play them, and work with them. His or her main function is to take instruments that are damaged, broken, or not in correct working order and repair and/or restore them.

The Instrument Repair and Restoration Specialist can specialize in string and fretted instruments, pianos, organs, brass instruments, percussion instruments, or a combination of the above.

The individual must be familiar with the various parts of many different instruments. In addition, he or she must know where they belong in the instrument and how to get them there. Many parts for older instruments are not even made today. In cases such as this, the repair and restoration specialist must often create and build new parts.

Instrument Repair and Restoration Specialists usually enjoy music and instruments during their school years. Most like woodworking and other industrial arts subjects in high school.

Many repair and restoration specialists know how to play a variety of instruments. This musical knowledge is helpful in repairing or restoring an instrument to its original state.

The Instrument Repair and Restoration Specialist can work on staff in a music store, factory, or school. He or she might also work for a museum, restoring instruments from earlier time periods. If on staff, the specialist may be paid a weekly salary, a commission, or a combination of the two.

As the individual becomes more proficient, he or she might decide to work as a self-employed Instrument Repair and Restoration Specialist. Eventually, he or she might also take on an apprentice and help that individual hone his or her skills.

In areas where the Instrument Repair and Restoration Specialist does not have sufficient work to make a full-time living, the individual might also build, design, or supervise the production of instruments for manufacturers, shops, or individuals.

Salaries

As there is a tremendous shortage of Instrument Repair and Restoration Specialists, salaries can get quite high. Salaries depend on the experience level of the repair and restoration specialist and where he or she works.

Depending on whether the specialist works for him- or herself or is on staff at a music store or factory, the individual may earn between $25,000 and $100,000 plus annually.

Those who work on instruments that are more difficult to repair and for which there are fewer trained specialists command higher wages, some earning $250 or more per hour.

Employment Prospects

As noted above, there is a shortage of qualified Instrument Repair and Restoration Specialists. The prospects of finding a job in this field after apprenticeship are good. The individual would probably have to live in a culturally active location, however, or he or she would not be able to locate work.

Advancement Prospects

After training in the craft of instrument repair and restoration, the individual must find a skilled craftsman (or woman) to work with as an apprentice. Depending on how quick he or she learns, the individual might apprentice for two to five years.

Usually, the Instrument Repair and Restoration Specialist works in a shop or factory for a few years after the apprenticeship. After this, he or she may stay in a shop or factory setting or move on to a self-employed situation.

Education and Training

A successful specialist needs the appropriate training in instrument technology and repair. These courses are given in schools and colleges or through private instruction.

The position also requires a knowledge of woodworking and/or metalworking, depending on the type of instrument in which one specializes. This is often acquired in high school courses. Additional training is available at many technical schools and colleges.

A good Instrument Repair and Restoration Specialist needs to know how to play a variety of instruments. The more instruments with which he or she is musically adept, the more flexible he or she can be.

Experience, Skills, and Personality Traits

To become an Instrument Repair and Restoration Specialist, one must go through an apprenticeship with a talented individual in the field. The apprenticeship can last anywhere from two to five years, depending on the individual. This on-the-job training is often picked up by working in instrument repair shops and factories.

The Instrument Repair and Restoration Specialist needs a good musical "ear." He or she must have a total dedication to learning the craft. The individual must also have a great deal of patience and good mechanical ability.

Unions and Associations

Depending on the type of instruments individuals work on, they can belong to the Acoustical Society of America (ASA), the National Council of Acoustical Consultants (NCAC), the Piano Technicians' Guild (PTG), or the Electronic Industries Alliance (EIA).

Tips for Entry

1. Try to find an instrument repair and restoration shop and get a job there part-time doing anything. Watch, learn, and gain experience. If you can apprentice in a shop such as this, do so.
2. Learn to do minor repairs, such as changing or replacing strings on stringed instruments, becoming skilled in as many repairs as possible.
3. Join professional organizations. These offer opportunities to network.

PIANO TUNER-TECHNICIAN

Special Requirements—Volunteer credentially by the Piano Technicians' Guild

Position Description

A Piano Tuner-Technician's main job is to tune pianos and keep them in tune. After deciding to become a Piano Tuner-Technician and getting the proper training, an individual must usually apprentice in order to hone his or her skills to perfection.

The Piano Tuner-Technician must know the piano inside and out. He or she must recognize the 6,000 to 8,000 different pieces of each instrument. The tuner-technician must know what each of these parts is, where it belongs in the instrument, and what it does.

The individual adjusts the piano strings so that they will be in proper pitch and sound musically correct. There are approximately 220 strings in a standard 88 key piano. After muting the strings on either side, the tuner-technician uses a tuning hammer to tighten or loosen the string being tested until its frequency matches that of a standard tuning fork. The Piano Tuner-Technician tunes the other strings in relation to the starting string. A good musical "ear" is essential in order to attain a perfect pitch, tone, and sound.

The Piano Tuner-Technician often works with electronic tuning devices. These devices are relatively new in the field. Old-time master craftsmen usually do not use these aids and don't encourage their apprentices to use them, either. With these electronic devices, however, Piano Tuner-Technicians can usually take care of more pianos in a shorter period of time. This is important if the individual is being paid per instrument tuned.

The tuner may make minor repairs, such as replacing worn or broken hammers in the piano. He or she may also detect and correct other problems in the instrument that affect its sound. More serious problems that the Piano Tuner-Technician may take care of include realigning hammers that do not strike the strings just right and replacing the felt on hammers. The Piano Tuner-Technician may have to dismantle the piano to find out what is wrong with it and fix the problem.

The tuner-technician may also teach piano to supplement his or her income.

Salaries

Salaries for Piano Tuner-Technicians vary according to the types of jobs they hold. A Piano Tuner-Technician working in a piano factory can earn between $26,000 and $45,000 per year. Tuners working for music dealers can average between $26,000 and $45,000 plus annually.

Tuner-technicians are often self-employed or independent. These individuals charge fees for each piano they work on. Fees vary according to whether or not the individual is a member of the Piano Technicians' Guild. Those who are members will have minimum fees set by the Piano Technicians' Guild.

A tuner can obtain contracts with music conservatories, universities, studios, and/or music groups. Independent Piano Tuner-Technicians, working full time, can earn $80,000 or more annually. Tuner-technicians who are self-employed must pay their own expenses. These might include tools, travel expenses, etc.

Employment Prospects

Piano Tuner-Technicians have the opportunity to work full-time or part-time, for themselves or on staff for dealers, factories, music schools, conservatories, universities, colleges, music shops, music groups, concert halls, or recording studios.

Clients can be obtained by advertising or word of mouth. Satisfied clients can make an independent Piano Tuner-Technician successful.

Large cities with many stores, factories, dealers, etc., offer the best opportunities for tuner-technicians. In smaller communities with limited music outlets, Piano Tuner-Technicians often do other piano-related work, including teaching.

Advancement Prospects

Piano Tuner-Technicians who have been trained well and have apprenticed with skilled tuner-technicians can usually get a position as a staff tuner. After a few years, many individuals find that they prefer to work on their own as self-employed or private Piano Tuner-Technicians. They then have the opportunity to build as large a business as they can handle.

Education and Training

A training program and/or an apprenticeship is required to become a Piano Tuner-Technician. The best type of course to take is one endorsed by the Piano Technicians' Guild. Check the appendix for a list. A good course of study will usually take two to three years to complete.

The individual might opt to take an apprenticeship with a skilled Piano Tuner-Technician. These opportunities are often difficult to locate for those without experience. After completing a training program, however, the individual will probably need to apprentice with an individual or a shop or in a factory.

Special Requirements

Piano Tuner-Technicians may belong to the Piano Technicians' Guild. This organization is open to Tuner-Technicians. Individuals who pass exams given by the guild will be granted the Registered Piano Technician, or RPT, credential.

Experience, Skills, and Personality Traits

To become a Piano Tuner-Technician, an individual must have experience as an apprentice. The tuner must have a good musical "ear." He or she should have a great interest in the piano, a knowledge of the instrument, and the ability to play it.

The Piano Tuner-Technician must have a mechanical ability and dexterity. In addition, he or she must have an enormous amount of patience to obtain a perfect pitch, tone, and sound.

Unions and Associations

Piano Tuner-Technicians may belong to the Piano Technicians' Guild. This association is open to tuner-technicians who pass exams given by the guild. After becoming a member, the Piano Tuner-Technician's fees are set by the guild. Nonmembers are free to charge lower fees.

Tips for Entry

1. Prepare well by obtaining good training. Your best bet is to go to a school endorsed by the Piano Technicians' Guild.
2. Try to find the most skilled person possible to apprentice with. It is during this apprenticeship that you pick up much of the craft.
3. If you are trained in the profession, put your business card up in music stores, record shops, and on supermarket bulletin boards.
4. Remember to check out Web sites of piano factories and music dealers for openings.

BOW REHAIRER AND RESTORER

Duties: Rehair stringed instrument bows and restore old or damaged bows

Alternate Title(s): Bow Restorer; Craftsman

Salary Range: $45 to $200+ per bow

Employment Prospects: Fair

Advancement Prospects: Poor

Best Geographical Location(s) for Position: Major cultural centers, such as New York City, Boston, Cleveland, Philadelphia, Chicago, Los Angeles, etc., offer the most opportunities

Prerequisites:

Education or Training—Training at workshops or seminars on subject; apprenticeship

Experience—Hands-on experience in craft is necessary

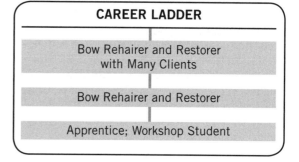

CAREER LADDER

Bow Rehairer and Restorer
with Many Clients

Bow Rehairer and Restorer

Apprentice; Workshop Student

Special Skills and Personality Traits—Fine craftsmanship; dexterity; ability to work with detail; patience; desire to develop the craft

Position Description

Bow Rehairers and Restorers replace the bow hair of stringed instrument bows. They also restore old and/or damaged bows and put them back in working condition.

The work is done using hand tools such as small knives, chisels, short- and long-nose pliers, scissors, and a comb. The individual must disassemble the bow and remove the spent or used hair. (Most bows are made of the hair of horses' tails.) The person then examines the bow to see what condition it is in, check for damage, etc. The rehairer also cleans the various bow parts.

If the bow is old and/or damaged, the individual may restore it. The Bow Rehairer and Restorer may concentrate on a broken bow tip, a cracked frog, or the timber. This restoration, too, is done with hand tools.

People in this line of work require a great deal of manual dexterity. They may have to hand-carve replacement wedges and/or plugs to fit the bow. These parts must fit exactly or it will affect the quality of the sound produced by the bow.

The bow rehairer must select new hairs for the bow. Once this is done, the individual will bind one end with special threads. This bound end will be secured into one end of the bow with the hand-carved wedges.

The bow rehairer will comb the hair neatly and bind the remaining loose ends with the special thread. This end will then be secured with wedges.

The quality of construction and rehairing of the bow affects the quality of tone and sound of the stringed instrument. The rehairer is totally responsible for this task. There are rehairers who are famous for their craft and skill.

The rehairer may work full- or part-time at this job, depending on how many customers he or she can obtain. Many people in this position contact schools, colleges, conservatories, and orchestras to obtain contracts to perform all the rehairing required for the group's stringed instruments.

Hours are flexible. Many rehairers are working or aspiring musicians, usually with an ability to play a stringed instrument.

Salaries

It is impossible to estimate the yearly salary of a Bow Rehairer and Restorer. Individuals who perform this work often do so on a part-time basis while pursuing performance or teaching careers, or careers in instrument building or instrument repairing and/or restoring.

People who rehair and restore may get contracts to take care of all the stringed instruments in a school, college, conservatory, or orchestra. The normal charge for bow rehairing ranges from $45 to $200 or more per bow. Fees for restoring bows depend on the amount and type of damage done to the bow. Restoration fees range from $50 to $300 or more per item.

Employment Prospects

As there are not many people who know how to correctly rehair and/or restore bows, individuals who do have a fair chance of locating work. There are opportunities in the major cultural cities, such as New York City, Boston, Cleveland, Philadelphia, Chicago, and Los Angeles. These locations have symphony orchestras, chamber music groups, etc., that use a large number of stringed instruments. Individuals looking for work in the bow rehairing field might have to relocate to one of these major cities.

Advancement Prospects

Advancement as a Bow Rehairer and Restorer is difficult to achieve. The best way to do it is to obtain a lot of clients. People in this field may open their own music or repair shop.

Education and Training

There is no specific educational requirement for a Bow Rehairer and Restorer, but people must be trained in the craft. This may be accomplished in workshops or seminars given on the subject or through an apprenticeship with a master craftsman.

Experience, Skills, and Personality Traits

To perfect this craft, a person needs hands-on experience in bow rehairing. This may be acquired through an apprenticeship.

The individual doing this type of work needs manual dexterity. The person must also be extremely patient and capable of working on details.

Many who perform this job are aspiring or working musicians who love the sound of good music.

Unions and Associations

If individuals are performing musicians as well as rehairers and restorers, they might belong to the American Federation of Musicians (AFM). Individuals may also belong to the Acoustical Society of America and/or the National Council of Acoustical Consultants.

Tips for Entry

1. Teachers of violin often know of workshops in the art of rehairing bows.
2. Violin or other string players usually know of people in this field. Talk to a bow rehairer and inquire about an apprenticeship.
3. If you already know how to rehair bows, go to schools, colleges, and orchestras to obtain clients.
4. Put up signs, posters, or business cards on the bulletin boards in music stores.

PUBLICITY AND ADVERTISING

PUBLIC RELATIONS COUNSELOR

Duties: Create an image for a musical group, artist, product, place, or company; write press releases; compile press kits; arrange press conferences

Alternate Title(s): Publicist; P.R. Counselor

Salary Range: $25,000 to $200,000+

Employment Prospects: Fair

Advancement Prospects: Fair

Best Geographical Locations for Position: New York City, Los Angeles, Nashville, Philadelphia, and Chicago offer the most opportunities; other areas may have additional possibilities

Prerequisites:

    Education or Training—College degree in communications, journalism, English, advertising, marketing, or public relations

    Experience—Some type of music or nonmusic-oriented publicity position; journalism experience

Special Skills and Personality Traits—Excellent written and verbal communication skills; knowledge of music business; creativity; ability to work under pressure; pleasantly aggressive; ability to think "outside" the box

Position Description

The main function of Public Relations (P.R.) Counselors in the field of music-oriented public relations is to create an image for a group or artist. If the counselor is working in a radio station or concert hall, his or her function is to create a good image of and for the business.

The Public Relations Counselor must begin by evaluating the public's perception or image of the client. Sometimes the client is well-known but has a poor image. In this case, the Public Relations Counselor is often retained to help change this public perception. Sometimes the client is an act or a club that is just starting out and is not known. In this case, the Public Relations Counselor must start from scratch, building the client's image.

The counselor might begin by outlining a campaign for the client. This campaign will vary according to any image problems and to the budget available to accomplish the task.

The P.R. Counselor must know how to write press releases, compile press kits, arrange press conferences and parties, etc. In addition, the counselor must know how to find an angle to arouse media interest.

P.R. Counselors usually spend a great deal of time with a client getting pertinent information. During this period, he or she usually learns some interesting facts

about a client that may be unrelated to the music business. For example, a club might have been the place a famous president stayed during a war. This theme might be the basis of a feature article about the club. Another example is a singer whose hobby is cooking. The counselor could expand the client's image from singer (in music magazines) to singer who likes to cook (gourmet cooking magazines). This gives the singer a more rounded personality. In essence, the P.R. Counselor works on creating a fuller image for clients.

P.R. Counselors usually have a large list of media contacts to call upon and use when they require press for their clients. When calling on this press, the counselor must always try to remain as credible as possible; otherwise, he or she won't be able to use the press effectively.

As with all positions in promotion and publicity, public relations people must be able to work under a great deal of pressure. There are constant demands by clients, deadlines to meet, things to accomplish, and parties to attend.

As a rule, the Public Relations Counselor working in a P.R. firm is directly responsible to his or her supervisor. On occasion, he or she might be responsible to the client. A counselor working in a radio station is usually responsible to the general manager of that station. P.R.

Counselors or directors working in concert halls or arenas are generally responsible to the concert hall director or manager.

The Public Relations Counselor must be willing to work behind the scenes and not expect any public recognition. A successful campaign for a client will yield only personal satisfaction. An unsuccessful campaign will often yield an unhappy client who blames the Public Relations Counselor.

Salaries

Salaries for Public Relations Counselors vary depending on the firm or company, geographical location, and type of job held.

A Public Relations Counselor in a music industry firm can earn anywhere from $35,000 to $200,000 plus. In addition, P.R. Counselors often earn 10% to 15% of all income from clients they bring to the firm. This can add up to thousands of dollars.

A radio station Public Relations Counselor or director might make from $25,000 at a small station to $50,000 plus at a larger station.

A Public Relations Counselor or director working at a concert hall or auditorium would be at the similar income level as the P.R. person working at a radio station. Once again, salaries vary according to the size of the business and the location of the company.

Employment Prospects

Employment prospects are fair for individuals seeking positions as Public Relations Counselors in the music industry. Jobs may be available at music-oriented public relations firms or even firms with one or two music-oriented clients. Other opportunities may be available with music-oriented businesses, such as radio stations, night clubs, concert halls, arenas, music stores, and record labels.

Some individuals may also start their own music-oriented public relations firm or simply act as consultants for recording artists or other music businesses or companies.

Advancement Prospects

Advancement prospects are fair for Public Relations Counselors working in the music industry. To a great extent, advancement will depend on where an individual is currently in their career and where they want to go.

For example, individuals working in public relations firms who obtain more experience may be assigned more responsibility, better projects, or more challenging clients. Some strike out on their own. Others find similar positions in larger or more prestigious P.R. firms.

Individuals handling P.R. at radio stations, concert halls, arenas, or even at record labels similarly may find positions at larger, more prestigious companies or may be assigned bigger projects. Many Public Relations Counselors become self-employed after gaining experience.

Education and Training

A college degree in communications, public relations, journalism, English, advertising, marketing, or music merchandising is preferable. Depending on the firm the individual wants to work with, some positions require a master's degree.

There are numerous public relations seminars given around the country by colleges, universities, and the Public Relations Society of America. These are very useful to one aspiring to be in the public relations field or one who has already landed a P.R. position.

Experience, Skills, and Personality Traits

A good P.R. Counselor must have excellent writing skills. The Counselor must also be creative enough to come up with a really special campaign so the act or product will be a hit.

A good knowledge of the music business is essential to the P.R. Counselor in the music industry. He or she must understand the complexities of the industry in order to be effective in his or her client's campaign.

Many P.R. Counselors in the music industry work in nonmusic-oriented public relations or publicity positions prior to entering the music business. Other aspiring P.R. people work for newspapers or magazines as reporters, critics, or reviewers.

Unions and Associations

Public Relations Counselors can belong to the Public Relations Society of America (PRSA). The association is run by and for public relations people and works to keep ethics in public relations high. The association also prints a magazine and runs seminars throughout the year.

Public Relations Counselors dealing with theatrical productions may also belong to the Association of Theatrical Press Agents and Managers (ATPAM).

Tips for Entry

1. If you can't get the position you want, try to get some experience in the public relations department of a record store, radio station, or concert hall.
2. Attend seminars such as those given by the Public Relations Society of America. They are great opportunities for making contacts as well as learning new skills.

3. Try to attend a music industry convention. There are a number of conventions around the country throughout the year. These conventions also offer great potential for making contacts. It could be worth the price of attending.

4. If you can't locate a position in a music-oriented field, see if you can find a job in nonmusic-oriented public relations (there are many more of these). The experience might be all you need.

5. Openings are often advertised in *Billboard* magazine and other trade publications.

6. Openings may also be located online. Check out the Web sites or music- and entertainment-oriented public relations companies, record labels, concert halls, radio stations, etc. as well as online job sites, such as www.monster.com and www.hotjobs.com.

PUBLIC RELATIONS TRAINEE

Duties: Assist public relations counselor in servicing clients; learn basic public relations techniques

Alternate Title(s): Public Relations Assistant; P.R. Trainee

Salary Range: $23,000 to $28,000+

Employment Prospects: Fair

Advancement Prospects: Fair

Best Geographical Locations for Position: New York City, Los Angeles, Nashville, Chicago, Philadelphia, and other large cities offer most opportunities; other areas may have additional possibilities

Prerequisites:

Education or Training—College degree in public relations, journalism, marketing, English, communications, advertising, or music merchandising preferable

CAREER LADDER

```
        Public Relations Counselor

        Public Relations Trainee

    College Student; Nonmusic-oriented
           Publicity Position;
          Print Media Journalist
```

Experience—Writing experience; attending seminars on music business or public relations helpful

Special Skills and Personality Traits—Good writing skills; knowledge of music business; outgoing personality; creativity

Position Description

A Public Relations (P.R.) Trainee or Assistant usually has little or no experience in public relations. In the music business, however, Public Relations Trainees often have had experience working at nonmusic-oriented publicity firms. People in music business P.R. like to train their people with the music business as a focal point.

The P.R. Trainee learns how to develop a campaign for a musical act or product. He or she learns to talk to a client, gather information, and put together press releases. Once the press release is written, it must usually be approved by the trainee or assistant's supervisor.

The trainee makes the many contacts he or she needs by calling people, following up on press releases or client activities. He or she might also meet media people at a press conference or press party for a client's campaign.

The Public Relations Trainee learns how to put together these important press functions. The individual does this by handling details for the P.R. supervisor.

The Public Relations Trainee often studies previous campaigns put together and implemented by other counselors. Using these programs, he or she learns how to create an angle or "hook" for a campaign.

The P.R. Trainee sits in on many meetings with clients and throws out his or her ideas for the campaign.

As the trainee gains experience, he or she might begin to implement certain facets of the actual campaign.

The trainee responds to many of the calls from clients dealing with details such as dates and times. The assistant/trainee often accompanies the client to interviews or public appearances that have been scheduled. In addition, the trainee accompanies the client to television or radio interviews that have been arranged.

As a public relations assistant, he or she attends many social functions on behalf of his or her firm or company or its clients. It is at these luncheons, dinners, cocktail parties, etc., that the P.R. trainee has opportunities to make new contacts and meet new people in the industry.

A P.R. trainee/assistant working for a concert hall or auditorium might be responsible for showing the press around the facility. At a radio station, he or she might be responsible for introducing media or recording acts to the staff.

Unless the company has a clipping service, the P.R. trainee/assistant might also be responsible for clipping press releases, articles, feature stories, and photographs of the client from magazines, newspapers, trades, etc. These clippings are put together in a client's portfolio with tapes of interviews, advertisements, etc.

The P.R. Trainee is responsible directly to his or her supervisor, who checks most work done by the trainee.

Salaries

Salaries for Public Relations Trainees/assistants in the music field start low. A beginning salary might be around $23,000 for a trainee who has no public relations experience at all. The salary is usually higher for people who have previously worked in the public relations industry. Earnings for P.R. Trainees can go up to $28,000+ or more.

Employment Prospects

Employment prospects are fair for individuals seeking positions as Public Relations Trainees in the music industry. Jobs may be available at music-oriented public relations firms or general firms with just one or two music- or entertainment-oriented clients. Other opportunities may be available with music-oriented businesses such as radio stations, night clubs, concert halls, arenas, music stores, and record labels.

Advancement Prospects

Advancement prospects are fair for Public Relations Trainees working in the music industry. With some experience and training, individuals may become full-fledged public relations counselors or publicists.

Public Relations Trainees may move up in the company in which they are currently working or find better positions at larger, more prestigious companies related to the music industry.

Education and Training

The best education for a Public Relations Trainee is a college degree with a major in public relations, journalism, English, or communications. Courses in music merchandising are useful. As creative writing is one of the important skills required of a Public Relations Trainee, a variety of writing courses should be included in the curriculum.

Experience, Skills, and Personality Traits

A Public Relations Trainee needs many of the same skills as a public relations counselor or publicist. He or she must be a good writer. Experience writing for a college newspaper or reviewing concerts for a local magazine or newspaper is useful.

The trainee must be creative and have an outgoing personality. Many P.R. Trainees in the music field work in nonmusic-oriented positions prior to obtaining their positions in music public relations.

A summer internship is a useful, fun way of learning the different skills needed in a music-oriented P.R. firm, as well as an opportunity to make valuable contacts.

Unions and Associations

Public Relations Trainees may belong to the Public Relations Society of America (PRSA). This organization puts out many useful booklets and a magazine and presents communications seminars throughout the country.

Tips for Entry

1. Try to get into a summer internship position in one of the music-oriented public relations firms. Although they usually are not paid, interns might get positions as trainees in the company after the summer.
2. Write for a local or college paper reviewing concerts and records. Make copies of the clippings and send them with your résumé. This helps prove that you have talent. (Always keep copies of *everything* you have written that has been printed.)
3. On occasion, openings for P.R. Trainees in music oriented P.R. firms are advertised in the classified sections of newspapers.
4. Many record labels have minority training programs in this area. If you qualify, take advantage of these programs.
5. Look for opportunities online. Check out record label Web sites, music- and entertainment-oriented public relations and publicity company sites as well as online career sites.

PUBLICIST

CAREER PROFILE

Duties: Help a group or artist become better known; create buzz for music-oriented client; create a positive image for music group or artist; compile press kits; write press releases; arrange press conferences; deal with media

Alternate Title(s): Press Agent

Salary Range: $25,000 to $200,000+

Employment Prospects: Fair

Advancement Prospects: Fair

Best Geographical Location(s) for Position: New York City, Los Angeles, Nashville, Philadelphia, Chicago, and other large cities offer the most opportunities; other areas may have additional possibilities

Prerequisites:

    Education or Training—College degree in communications, journalism, English, advertising, marketing, public relations, or music merchandising preferred

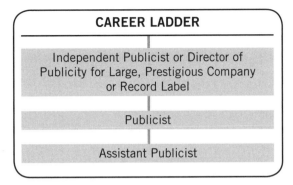

CAREER LADDER

Independent Publicist or Director of Publicity for Large, Prestigious Company or Record Label

Publicist

Assistant Publicist

    Experience—Prior position in music or nonmusic-oriented publicity; newspaper reporter, journalist, or critic experience helpful

    Special Skills and Personality Traits—Creative writing skills; persuasiveness; ability to work under pressure; knowledge of music business; love of music

Position Description

The basic duty of a music-oriented Publicist or press agent is to create ways to make a musical act's name, record, and video better known. The best way to get a group's or artist's name or product in the spotlight is to keep it in the public eye as much as possible. The better the act and the product are known, the more records, DVDs, and concert tickets will sell.

The Publicist must know how to write creative press releases that the press will use. Press kits consisting of press releases, biographies, pictures, and reprints of reviews and articles must be compiled. The Publicist must then see that the press kits are given or sent to music editors, disc jockeys, TV producers, etc., around the country.

The Publicist must know what type of event is important enough to call a press conference for, how to put one together, and how to get the right people to attend.

The Publicist must know how to get through to music editors, disc jockeys, TV producers, etc., in order to place the client on a television or radio show or have a feature story written on the act.

Many times, the press isn't interested in an act until it is so well known that publicity self-generates. In such

a case, the Publicist must be creative enough to come up with a unique angle to get attention for the act from the press and/or radio and television.

There are some acts, on the other hand, that are so well known that every editor and disc jockey wants to interview them. In this case, the Publicist must be selective and decide which interviews are in the best interest of the client. The Publicist has to act as the bad guy and keep the press away from a client if he or she feels it would harm a client's image to give interviews. The Publicist must say no in such a way as to save the media contact without blaming the act.

Publicists are famous for creating hype. Hype is the practice of taking a group or record and super-selling it with media saturation and sometimes exaggeration.

Part of the Publicist's job is attending a lot of parties, luncheons, and dinners on a client's behalf or to make important contacts. The Publicist's social life and business life are frequently rolled into one.

Contacts are important for the Publicist, especially if he or she is working as an independent. One of the ways new clients are obtained is through these musical cocktail parties that "everyone" attends.

The Publicist employed by a record company generally works to help the artists sell their records, videos, and concert seats. He or she is usually responsible to a supervisor. Independent Publicists are usually responsible directly to the client and the client's management team.

A Publicist must have the ability to work under the constant pressure of deadlines. He or she must also be willing to accept the fact that if a publicity campaign is successful, the act will get the credit, while if it fails, the Publicist will most likely get the blame.

Salaries

Salaries vary according to the type of firm or company the Publicist works for and the geographical location of that firm. Firms or companies in New York City, Los Angeles, Nashville, and Chicago tend to pay more. Some Publicists start out at $25,000 per year. Others at more prestigious firms have a starting salary of $35,000 to $45,000. As the Publicist gains more experience and recognition in the field, he or she can make $100,000 to $150,000 or more per year. In addition, Publicists who attract new clients to their firms are often given 10% to 15% of all monies brought in by the new clients. Depending on what the clients pay the firm, this can add up to a great deal of money.

Independent Publicists are paid directly by their clients. Fees range from $850 per month per client to $10,000 plus per week per client. The fees depend on the status of the musical act or artist being publicized. In addition, the Publicist often earns a percentage of any monies brought in from commercials, endorsements, TV, or movies that he or she obtains for the client. Independent Publicists are usually paid their fees as a monthly retainer. They are often reimbursed for out-of-pocket expenses as well.

Employment Prospects

Music-oriented Publicists may work for record companies to promote their acts or any upcoming promotional tours. Record companies generally have a number of Publicists on staff.

Music-oriented Publicists can also find work in firms that specialize in publicity or public relations for the music business. Other opportunities exist at radio stations, concert halls, clubs, arenas, and music stores.

Publicists may also work as independents, which means that they must get their own clients and are paid a fee instead of a salary. Independent Publicists and press agents have to be very good to get and keep clients. They must have a proven track record with clients in order to be successful on their own.

Advancement Prospects

A good Publicist will usually be promoted to better clients, more interesting projects, and less tedious work in a firm or record company. If the Publicist can deliver a good campaign, a lot of TV and radio talk shows, good placement of press releases, and a happy client, he or she will move up. Good Publicists are sought after by other companies, firms, and clients. Although the public doesn't usually know who "made" a star, group, or artist, the insiders usually find out. Competition is keen in publicity positions, so the Publicist must be the best. Some individuals are also promoted to directors of publicity for the company.

Education and Training

Different positions in publicity require different amounts of education. The most qualified person has a better chance of getting the job. A college degree in communications, journalism, public relations, advertising, marketing, English, or music merchandising is helpful in honing the skills needed for a position as a music business Publicist. Courses or seminars in publicity and the music business are also useful.

Experience, Skills, and Personality Traits

A music industry Publicist must be able to work under pressure. The constant stress of deadlines and clients changing their minds about what image they want to project can take its toll.

Publicists must be creative enough to come up with an angle for a client and then be persuasive enough to make the client and his advisers like it, too. He or she must have the ability to make a news release about an ordinary subject into an exciting story the press will pick up. Many Publicists have worked with the press as reporters, reviewers, or talent coordinators. Contacts picked up from other positions are valuable. The Publicist must have a reputation for credibility, however, or all contacts will prove useless.

Unions and Associations

The best-known organization that Publicists can belong to is the Public Relations Society of America (PRSA). This organization offers seminars, booklets, a magazine, and other helpful information.

Publicists working with clients in musical theater might additionally belong to the Association of Theatrical Press Agents and Managers (ATPAM).

Tips for Entry

1. Find out if the record company or public relations firm has an internship program for Publicists.

Internships are one of the best ways to get your foot in the door. Generally, you will either be paid a very small salary or will receive college credit.

2. Prepare your résumé and a few samples of your writing and send them to the record company or publicity firm where you want a job.

3. Work with a local music group as an independent Publicist to get some experience to put on your résumé. (You frequently have to work for a nominal fee.)

4. Openings are often advertised in trade publications such as *Billboard*.

5. Jobs may be located online. Check out record label sites, music- and entertainment-oriented public relations company sites, and online job Web sites such as hotjobs.com and monster.com.

ASSISTANT PUBLICIST

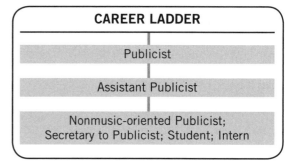

Position Description

The main function of an Assistant Publicist is to help the head publicists in a company sell an act's name, records, and videos. The Assistant Publicist learns from watching and doing. He or she writes press releases and helps compile press kits. It is usual for all of the Assistant Publicist's work to be reviewed and checked for accuracy and content by the individual's superior.

Many Assistant Publicists sit in on meetings with clients, joining the publicist assigned to that client. They often throw in ideas for the act's publicity campaign.

However, as a rule, they are never totally responsible for originating and implementing an entire campaign.

At times, the Assistant Publicist will accompany an act to radio, television, or public appearances. He or she will also be asked to go with the act for interviews or photography sessions set up by the head publicist.

The Assistant Publicist will handle many of the details of press parties the head publicist arranges. He or she may also be responsible for extending invitations to the media and other guests who will be invited.

The Assistant Publicist might also go to dinners, luncheons, and/or cocktail parties on behalf of a client or his or her company.

Responding to a client's calls and answering questions about schedules, dates, etc., is one of the responsibilities of the Assistant Publicist. He or she also

will have to do secretarial work, such as typing press releases, making phone calls, confirming appointments, checking out information, etc.

The individual might also be responsible for clipping press releases from magazines and newspapers. These clippings are put together in the client's portfolio, along with copies of advertisements, photos, and tapes of interviews.

The Assistant Publicist must be ready and willing to work overtime. Deadlines must be met, afterhours functions must be attended, and calls must be made.

Salaries

Assistant Publicist's salaries usually range from $23,000 to $45,000 or more yearly. Earnings depend on the type of firm or company at which the Assistant Publicist is employed. Salaries also vary by geographical location. The highest earnings are usually found in Los Angeles and New York City. Assistant Publicists who work for public relations firms specializing in music acts usually earn more than Assistant Publicists who begin at record companies. The record companies, as a rule, have better benefits.

Employment Prospects

The job market is tight for Assistant Publicists, but there are openings. Individuals may find opportunities at record companies, music-oriented publicity firms, or management companies, radio stations, concert halls, arenas, and record stores.

Advancement Prospects

Advancement prospects are good for Assistant Publicists working in the music business. Once a talented Assistant Publicist gets some experience, he or she can climb the career ladder by becoming a full-fledged publicist. He or she may stay at the same company or may land a job at a different radio station, record label, concert hall, arena, etc.

Education and Training

Assistant Publicists working in the music industry need at least a four-year college degree. Good majors include communications, English, journalism, advertising, marketing, public relations, music merchandising, or the music business. Additional courses, workshops, and seminars in various areas of the music business, publicity, promotion, etc. will be useful.

Experience, Skills, and Personality Traits

Assistant Publicists need to be creative individuals with excellent written and verbal communications skills. The ability to work under pressure without getting flustered is essential. Individuals need good computer skills as well.

Experience working in the publicity department of a record label, or any publicity department for that matter, will help the individual. Many Assistant Publicists interned before landing their job. Internships are useful in helping to learn different publicity techniques and skills as well as giving the individual the opportunity to make valuable contacts.

Unions and Associations

There are a number of organizations and associations an Assistant Publicist may belong to. The best known is the Public Relations Society of America (PRSA). The organization offers many seminars throughout the year on public relations and publicity subjects.

Tips for Entry

1. Find out if the record company or public relations firm for whom you would like to work has an internship program for publicists.
2. Certain record companies and music organizations have minority training programs. Check with the companies you would like to work with to see if these are available.
3. Prove yourself by presenting reviews you have written on concerts or records for local, school, or college newspapers. Send copies of the clippings to the act's record label's publicity department. Make sure you include a short letter telling them your name, address, phone number, qualifications, and the type of position in which you are interested. Persistence and perseverance sometimes land a job.
4. Begin putting together a portfolio of your work to illustrate your talent and creativity.

MUSIC JOURNALIST

CAREER PROFILE

Duties: Write articles, reviews, and critiques on music acts, concerts, shows, records, videos, etc.

Alternate Title(s): Writer; Music Critic; Music Reviewer

Salary Range: $25,000 to $150,000+

Employment Prospects: Good

Advancement Prospects: Fair

Best Geographical Location(s) for Positions: New York City, Nashville, and Los Angeles for major music publications; other large cities with moderate-sized publications and smaller locations for individuals just starting out

Prerequisites:

Education and Training—College degree required or preferred for most jobs

CAREER LADDER

Music Journalist for Major Publication

Music Journalist

Entertainment Journalist for Local Paper; Nonmusic-oriented Reporter or Journalist; Student

Experience—Writing for school paper; reviewing local concerts or records for local papers

Special Skills and Personality Traits—Writing skill; knowledge of music; typing skill; computer literate; objectivity; ability to work under pressure

Position Description

Music Journalists work in many different situations. A Music Journalist might be on staff at a local or small circulation weekly newspaper. In this case, he or she might write a daily, biweekly, or weekly column about happenings in the music business. The Music Journalist would also be responsible for reviewing any concerts, shows, and artists passing through the area. The Music Journalist might review new records or music products on the market. In small circulation newspapers, he or she might write about other entertainment-oriented subjects. A Music Journalist may also have to report on nonentertainment subjects. Many opportunities now exist in online publications or other sites on the World Wide Web.

As Music Journalists move into positions on larger papers or magazines, their jobs become more specialized. For instance, one might be a classical reviewer, a rock writer, a jazz writer, a record reviewer, etc. Some Music Journalists write columns for online publications or Web sites.

The life of a Music Journalist is often exciting. He or she is expected to be knowledgeable about the field of music being covered. Usually the individual also enjoys the music. As a Music Journalist reviewing concerts or acts, the individual might first receive a press kit on the artist. A phone interview may take place for additional background material. Music Journalists receive press passes to the shows covered.

Prior to the event, he or she may have much of the background story developed and written. After the show, the journalist writes a review of the actual act. The ability to work under pressure is a must, as the finished review may have to be completed and handed in just an hour after the show ends to make a deadline. The journalist must also be careful to be as objective as possible. For example, if the journalist is writing a review of a group of which he or she is not particularly fond, this feeling may enter the review. It must not be allowed to color the piece.

Music Journalists interview musical acts for short features or in-depth articles. The ability to delve below the surface to seek information is necessary to Music Journalists. The Music Journalist who will move up and succeed is the one who asks the questions that no one else has thought of and develops a really interesting story.

Reviewers often have to review semiprofessional concerts, such as student symphonies. The reviewer must try to write a review in which the symphony is judged on its own merits and not the same basis as a major orchestra.

Music Journalists gather material in a variety of ways. They may research prior stories about a group in other magazines or publications. They may interview the act either personally or by phone. During the interview, the Music Journalist may either take notes or record the interview session (with the permission of the act). The journalist may talk with people who are close to the act (the manager, a song-writer, family members, friends, etc.). It is important to end up with a factual and interesting story.

Music Journalists may work full-time and part-time. They can work as stringers for publications on a concert-to-concert basis or work on a freelance basis doing stories by commission or writing articles to sell.

A Music Journalist is responsible to the editor of the publication for which he or she writes. Many Music Journalists become editors after a few years in writing.

Salaries

Salaries for Music Journalists depend on where they are employed, how experienced they are, and what they do.

A beginning journalist writing reviews and/or music news for a local paper may earn approximately $25,000 or more annually. As he or she gains more experience, yearly salaries go up to $30,000 or more.

Journalists writing for major publications or newspapers earn between $40,000 and $150,000 plus annually. The higher figure, of course, is for those who have made it in the field. Salaries usually average between $35,000 and $50,000 annually for a Music Journalist working for a good publication.

Employment Prospects

Employment prospects are good for the individual who doesn't mind starting at the bottom and/or moving to a location where a job is available.

Nearly all newspapers have some type of entertainment or music section, including local newspapers and magazines. The reporter-journalist may often have other duties besides writing about music.

After one gains experience writing professionally, he or she may seek employment anywhere. Employers usually require writing samples.

Advancement Prospects

If a Music Journalist has a good writing style, is responsible, and develops good contacts and a good reputation, he or she can advance. Music Journalists generally advance by obtaining positions at more prestigious publications. For example, they can go from a job on a local paper to a position on a regional newspaper. They can advance from this point to a major city newspaper as a music reviewer, reporter, or journalist. Or they can obtain a position at a prestigious music-oriented magazine.

Education and Training

Most jobs on newspapers require a college education. Individuals might, however, be able to obtain a position on a local newspaper without a college degree, but advancement is difficult.

There are journalism degrees offered at many colleges, although this does not have to be the specific degree obtained. A general liberal arts education is usually sufficient. If individuals are interested in this type of career, they should take a variety of journalism, communications, and writing courses.

Experience, Skills, and Personality Traits

Music Journalists usually begin writing for their high school papers. During their college years, they obtain positions on their school papers or part-time for local newspapers reviewing concerts, writing music columns, and critiquing records.

The Music Journalist must have good writing skills as well as a solid knowledge of the type of music he or she is writing about. The journalist must be a responsible individual who can get things done on time. Newspapers and magazines cannot wait for someone to finish articles.

Unions and Associations

Music Journalists might belong to a number of associations or organizations depending on their interests. One of the most important is the Music Critics Association of North America. This organization sponsors seminars, conferences, etc., for those in the industry.

Tips for Entry

1. Get experience locally reviewing music events, concerts, records, etc.
2. You may consider proposing a music column to a local newspaper or magazine that doesn't already have one.
3. Names and addresses of daily newspapers are available in the *Editor and Publisher International Year Book*. This publication is available in many libraries and larger newspaper offices. You might use this as a starting point to send out your résumés and writing samples. Pick a geographical area you want to work in and send your résumé to all the newspapers in that region.

4. There are a number of fellowships, assistantships, scholarships, and internships available in the journalism field. You might have to begin your career in an area of journalism other than music.
5. If you are in college, try to get on the college paper. Every bit of experience is important.
6. The Music Critic Association of North America sponsors seminars and other interesting programs for those in the field.
7. New opportunities may also exist for Music Journalists at online publications.
8. Begin putting together a portfolio of your best work to illustrate your talents.
9. Surf the Web for opportunities. Start with some of the more popular job serach sites, such as monster.com and hotjobs.com.

ADVERTISING ACCOUNT EXECUTIVE, MUSIC-ORIENTED PUBLICATION

CAREER PROFILE

Duties: Selling advertising space in music-oriented periodical or newspaper; meeting with clients; writing orders; developing advertising promotions

Alternate Title(s): Salesman; Saleswoman; Sales Rep; Sales Exec

Salary Range: $21,000 to $125,000+

Employment Prospects: Good

Advancement Prospects: Good

Best Geographical Location(s) for Position: Positions may be located throughout country; more opportunities may exist in New York City, Los Angeles, and Nashville; opportunities may also exist in other culturally active cities with large numbers of music and entertainment oriented companies and venues such as Atlanta, Philadelphia, Boston, Las Vegas, etc.

Prerequisites:

Education or Training—Educational requirements vary; high school diploma, minimum requirement; college degree or background may be preferred or required; see text

Experience and qualifications—Experience requirements vary from job to job; see text

CAREER LADDER

Advertising Account Executive at Larger, More Prestigious Music-Oriented Publication; Advertising Sales Manager; or Marketing Director

↑

Advertising Account Executive, Music-Oriented Publication

↑

Sales Assistant, Advertising Sales Rep Trainee, or Entry-Level Position

Special Skills and Personality Traits—Sales skills; aggressiveness; likeability; strong desire to succeed; organizational ability; independence; ability to deal with discouragement; verbal and written communications skills

Special Requirements—Driver's license and car may be required for some positions

Position Description

There are many music-oriented publications in existence today. Some are geared toward consumers. Others are trade publications directed at industry professionals. These trades specialize in almost every area of the music business. There are also entertainment- and music-oriented newspapers. Some publications are in print form; others are digital with online access.

While publications may make money by selling subscriptions or single copies, the majority of their earnings generally come from the sale of advertising. Advertising Account Executives are the individuals who find advertisers for these music-oriented publications. They may also be referred to as sales reps, salesmen, saleswomen, or sales executives.

While specific duties of Advertising Account Executives may vary, their main responsibility is to sell advertising space in the publication. The Advertising Account Executive may be assigned accounts or may be expected to find potential advertisers on his or her own. Depending on the specific publication, Advertising Account Executives may be assigned accounts with national advertisers or local advertisers. They might also deal with clients themselves or through a client's advertising agency.

Advertising Account Executives selling advertising for music-oriented publications may utilize a variety of methods to sell ads. Some set up meetings and go to visit potential advertisers in person. Others call advertisers. Still others use the Internet and e-mail to prospect for potential advertisers. Many Advertising Account Executives selling advertising space in music-oriented publications send out e-mail blasts in an effort to solicit both new and established advertisers. Some account executives e-mail reader surveys or even articles to potential clients on how advertising in their particular publication has increased another advertiser's business. Individuals may also e-mail advertisers about special promotions and sales the publication is holding.

If the publication is well known, selling advertising space is often easier. In such situations, potential advertisers often are aware of the demographics of the people who read the specific publication and have an idea what placing an ad or series of ads might do for their business. If the publication is new or not very well known, on the other hand, the Advertising Account Executive generally needs to find ways to prove to potential advertisers the importance of advertising in the publication.

In some cases, the publication itself may have advertisements inviting potential companies to advertise. Sometimes potential advertisers may simply contact the publication to get information about advertising opportunities. They may inquire about the publication, demographics, and/or advertising rates. Depending on the structure of the publication and its advertising department, calls may go directly to a sales manager, who in turn will refer callers to the appropriate account executive or may go to an account executive specifically assigned to handle these calls.

The Advertising Account Executive is responsible for sending out advertising or rate kits. This may be done via traditional mail, a delivery service, or through e-mail. These kits may contain rate cards, informational sheets on the publication and its demographics, testimonials from other advertisers, or a copy or two of the publication. They may also contain information on the publication's special issues and promotions.

The Advertising Account Executives must have a complete knowledge of the publication. He or she must know the demographics of the publication's readers, how long the publication has been in existence, the products and services of other advertisers, and competing publications. This information can help the Advertising Account Executive illustrate how advertising in his or her publication can benefit a potential advertiser.

Part of the job of an Advertising Account Executive selling advertising for music-oriented publications is often developing advertising campaigns for their clients. He or she may develop monthly or even annual advertising campaigns designed to increase the client's business. To do this, the account executive must be familiar with the client's products and/or services as well as competition's. After the client places orders for advertisements and the campaign is implemented, it is also the responsibility of the account executive to monitor the effectiveness of the campaign.

Advertising Account Executives frequently brainstorm with clients or their advertising companies to come up with effective advertising ideas. The more effective ads are, the more advertising customers will purchase.

Advertising Account Executives often schedule appointments with potential clients to discuss advertising needs. It is essential that the Advertising Account Executive be aware of all the promotions and up to date on various rates, discounts, and advertising packages offered. He or she must also be able to fully explain all of these to advertisers.

To be successful as an Advertising Account Executive, the individual must find ways not only to sell an advertiser one ad but to build a lasting business relationship. He or she can do this by explaining promotions, putting together the best package possible, and servicing the account well. The individual must continually check with clients to be sure they are happy with their ads and are being billed properly.

One of the major responsibilities of the Advertising Account Executive is bringing in new business. Obtaining new accounts is an essential part of the job for account executives selling advertising at music-oriented publications. Individuals may spend a great deal of time calling new accounts, traveling to meet potential advertisers, and arranging for follow-up meetings

The individual may make what are known as "cold" calls to potential advertisers. These calls may be made to people who have not yet advertised in the publication or who have not advertised for an extended time period. After identifying him- or herself and the publication's affiliation, the Account Executive attempts to set up an appointment to explain more about the publication's advertising opportunities, promotions, and specials to the potential advertiser. Not every call will result in an appointment. The Advertising Account Executives must have the ability to accept rejection without taking it personally.

In order to entice new advertisers to his or her publication, the Advertising Account Executive may offer a variety of promotions and discounts to potential clients. The individual may also offer specials, promotions, and discounts to established accounts in order to tempt them to advertise more often.

Sometimes these promotions, are developed by the sales manager or the publication's marketing manager. In other cases, the account executive may help develop marketing and advertising ideas and campaigns for current or potential customers designed to help increase their business. These may include sweepstakes or co-op ads, among others. For example, the account executive may help develop a joint advertising campaign where a record label and a music store advertise together. Or he or she may develop a promotion as part of an advertisement for an instrument company in a consumer publication whose readers can enter a sweepstakes and win prizes. In many instances, these types of promotions are developed in conjunction with a client's marketing department.

Successful Advertising Account Executives continually find ways to generate revenue for the publication by looking for and negotiating a broad range of advertising deals.

Advertising Account Executives must constantly call on businesses that might buy advertisements. Depending on the specific publication, these might include any business or service that will benefit by having an advertisement in the periodical or newspaper. Even though a publication may be music-oriented, its advertising client may come from the businesses.

An Advertising Account Executive for a local or regional consumer-based music or entertainment magazine or newspaper might contact bands, instrument stores, clubs, restaurants, music stores, department stores, chain stores, doctors, dentists, lawyers, shops of all kinds, movie theaters, concert halls, clubs, etc. An account executive for a music trade publication, on the other hand, might seek out advertisers on a more national level, such as instrument companies, music publishers, record labels, etc.

The Advertising Account Executive is usually assigned a sales territory in which to work. This means that he or she sell ads within certain locality or designated area. Territories may be large or small or might even refer to a specific type of client. For example, an Account Executive might be responsible for soliciting ads from record labels or instrument companies.

Depending on the size of the publication, the account executive might be responsible for actually writing the ads, acting as a copywriter, or even designing and laying out advertisements.

Many music-oriented publications develop special issues designed to attract advertisers. They may, for example, have special issues when someone in the music industry wins an award, a large music venue opens for the season, or to celebrate a musical event. The Advertising Account Executive may call clients to discuss these special promotions that the publication is running to determine if they would like to be associated with the issue by buying advertising space in it.

While Advertising Account Executives work under the direction of sales managers, much of their day involves working on their own. It is up to them to sell as many ads as possible. Often the job is not nine to five, especially if advertisers are on the opposite side of the country. The individual may find that he or she has to make a sales call to a client at eight in the morning or eight at night. No one monitors what the account executive does all day. It is up to him or her to organize his or her time and efforts effectively.

Sometimes the Advertising Account Executive works in the field. At other times the advertising sales representative might be in the office helping clients decide where, when, and how their advertising dollars would be best spent. The individual also spends a great deal of his or her time on the phone locating potential clients or telling current customers about the status of their ads.

Advertising Account Executives working for music-oriented publications are expected to keep accurate records of advertisements sold, billings, and so on. Individuals are responsible for writing orders and making sure each order gets to the appropriate department at the publication.

Salaries

Earnings for Advertising Account Executives working for music-oriented periodicals or newspapers can vary tremendously. There are some individuals who have annual earnings of $21,000 and others who have annual earnings of $125,000 or more.

Individuals may be paid in a number of different ways. Some are paid a straight salary. Others receive a small salary plus commissions. Still others work exclusively on commission. Advertising Account Executives also often receive bonuses when they meet or exceed sales projections.

Factors affecting earnings include the popularity, prestige, and size of the specific publication. As the majority of Advertising Account Executives receive at least part of their income from commissions, other variables include the sales ability and motivation of the individual.

Motivated Advertising Account Executives selling advertising for well-known publications will earn the highest commissions. The greatest thing about selling on commission is that the sky is the limit for earnings.

Employment Prospects

Advertising is how publications make money, so employment prospects are always good for talented, motivated individuals who can sell.

Jobs and opportunities may be located throughout the country in areas hosting music-oriented publications. The greatest number of jobs will be found in areas where there are large numbers of music-oriented publications such as New York City, Los Angeles, and Nashville. Others good locations are cultural centers such as Boston, Philadelphia, Washington, Atlanta, and San Francisco, among others. This is not to say that these are the only areas where music-oriented publications can be found. Regional music and entertainment publications may also be located in any area where there is musical entertainment.

Job possibilities might exist at music-oriented periodicals geared toward consumers or those geared towards professionals in the industry. Other possibilities include music-oriented trade publications as well as music- and entertainment-oriented newspapers.

Advancement Prospects

Advancement prospects are good for motivated account executives selling advertising for music-oriented publications. Individuals may climb the career ladder by locating a similar position at a larger or more prestigious music oriented publication, being assigned a bigger or better territory, or getting bigger accounts. These situations offer the Advertising Account Executive the opportunity for increased earnings and responsibilities.

Some individuals also advance their careers by being promoted to the sales manager or advertising director. Still others become marketing directors for the publication employing them.

Education and Training

Educational requirements vary for Advertising Account Executives working for music-oriented publications. Some publications just require their account executives to hold a high school diploma. Others require or prefer their account executives to have a college background or degree.

Whatever the requirements, courses, workshops, and seminars in salesmanship, advertising, and related areas will be useful.

Special Requirements

Depending on the specific situation, Advertising Account Executives selling advertising may need a driver's license and a car.

Experience, Skills, and Personality Traits

Experience requirements for Account Executives selling advertising for music-oriented publications vary from job to job. In some situations, this may be an entry-level position. Others require or prefer applicants to have three to five years' sales experience.

A knowledge of the area of the music industry in which the publication is targeted is necessary to adequately explain the benefits of advertising to potential advertisers. Advertising Account Executives should have good written and verbal communications skills. They also need to be responsible, organized, and have the ability to multitask without getting flustered.

Sales skills are essential. Individuals who are successful in this line of work are personable and appropriately aggressive. Advertising Account Executives need to be motivated individuals with a strong desire to succeed.

Math skills are necessary. Account executives will need to calculate costs of various advertising packages.

The ability to deal with discouragement is critical. Every prospective client will not buy an ad. Account executives must have a thick skin and learn not to take rejection personally.

Unions and Associations

Advertising Account Executives selling advertising for music-oriented publications often belong to trade associations geared toward the area of the music industry in which the publication is directed. Individuals in the profession also generally belong to business and civic groups in their area. Account executives might also belong to the International Newspaper Advertising and Marketing Executives (INAME).

Tips for Entry

1. If you are still in school, see if you can find an internship in the advertising department of a music-oriented trade magazine, periodical, or newspaper. You will learn a lot and make valuable contacts.

2. Consider sending your résumé and a short cover letter to music-oriented trade magazines, periodicals, and newspapers. You can send it to the human resources department as well as to the advertising sales manager. Be sure to ask that your résumé be kept on file if there are no current openings.

3. Look for seminars and workshops on sales techniques. Whether or not these are geared specifically toward the music industry, these courses will be helpful in honing your selling techniques.

4. Positions may be advertised in the classified section of newspapers under headings such as "Advertising," "Music Trades", "Account

Executive—Music," "Salesperson," "Sales," or "Account Executive."

5. Many music oriented trade magazines, publications and newspapers also advertise openings in their own publication. Check them out.

6. Don't forget to check traditional job search sites such as monster.com and hotjobs.com, as well as job sites specific to the music industry, for openings.

ADVERTISING ACCOUNT EXECUTIVE, MUSIC-ORIENTED WEB SITE

CAREER PROFILE

Duties: Selling advertising on music oriented Web site; meeting with potential customers; sending out advertising and rate kits; developing promotions to help sell more advertising; preparing buy orders; keeping records of sales

Alternate Title(s): Account Executive; Advertising Account Representative; Rep; Sales Rep; Advertising Rep; Sales Representative

Salary Range: $21,000 to $100,000+

Employment Prospects: Good

Advancement Prospects: Good

Best Geographical Location(s) for Position: Positions may be located throughout country

Prerequisites:

Education or Training—Educational requirements vary; minimum of high school diploma; college background or degree required or preferred by many employers; see text

Experience and qualifications—Experience in sales helpful but not always required

CAREER LADDER

Sales Manager or Advertising Account Executive for Larger, More Prestigious Music-Oriented Web Site

↑

Music Oriented Web Site Advertising Account Executive

↑

Entry Level or Sales Position in Other Industry

Special Skills and Personality Traits—Sales skills; persuasiveness; being articulate, self-motivated, appropriately aggressive; personable; having an outgoing nature; having an understanding of music industry

Position Description

Every day, more and more music-oriented companies are gaining a presence on the World Wide Web. Some are commercial, others are not. There are large companies, small companies, and everything in between.

Some Web sites sell merchandise, such as music, CDs, DVDs, magazines, or musical instruments. Other Web sites sell tickets to concerts, music-oriented books, and magazines. Some sell music-branded merchandise, such as tee-shirts, jackets, or hats.

Virtually every music club, arena, and concert hall also now has its own Web site. So do radio stations, music television, and music-oriented television programs. There are recording artist Web sites, fan sites, and songwriter Web sites. Most promoters, agents, management companies, agencies, music publishers, record labels, and other music-oriented service companies also have their own sites.

Whether a Web site is selling merchandise or services, promoting its company or providing information, many are now finding additional ways to use their site to generate income by selling advertising space on the site.

The individual in charge of selling the advertising on the Web site is called the Advertising Account Executive. He or she may also be referred to as an account rep, salesperson, sales rep, advertising account rep, or advertising rep. Depending on the size and structure of the specific Web site, there may be one or more Advertising Account Executives selling ads on the site.

The Advertising Account Executive may be assigned accounts or may be expected to find potential advertisers on his or her own. In some cases, the Web site itself may have a banner or text inviting potential companies to advertise.

If the music-oriented Web site is prominent, potential advertisers may contact the site to get information about advertising opportunities. They may make inquiries about the site's, demographics and advertising rates. Depending on the structure of the Web site, calls may go directly to a sales manager or marketing manager who in turn will refer callers to the appropriate account executive.

Advertising Account Executives at music-oriented Web sites have a number of responsibilities. First and foremost they are responsible for selling advertising. Selling advertising on Web sites may have certain challenges other media may not have. The music-oriented Advertising Account Executive must be able to prove to potential advertisers the popularity of the site and how many "hits" it gets. This is often difficult.

Advertising Account Executives must also be able to demonstrate to potential advertisers the demographics of people who visit their site. They must be able to prove the exposure that the Web site receives and what that exposure can offer a potential advertiser.

Music-Oriented Web Site Advertising Account Executives use a variety of methods to sell ads on their Web sites. Some set up meetings and go to visit potential advertisers in person. Others call advertisers. Still others use the Internet and e-mail to fund prospective for advertisers. Many account executives selling space on music-oriented Web sites for example send out e-mail blasts to solicit advertisers. Some e-mail reader surveys or articles to potential clients on how advertising on their particular site has increased another advertiser's business.

If the site is very well known, selling advertising is often easier. For example, if the Web site is that of an established concert hall that hosts a large number of concerts, the Advertising Account Executive is selling a known commodity. Prospective other advertisers are aware of the sites popularity. If the site is not very well known, the Advertising Account Executive needs to find ways to prove the importance of the site to advertisers.

Once the Advertising Account Executive contacts potential advertisers, he or she is responsible for sending out advertising or rate kits. This may be done via traditional mail or through e-mail. These kits may contain things such as rate cards, informational sheets on the Web site's, demographics, testimonials from other advertisers, etc.

Advertising Account Executives often schedule appointments with potential clients to discuss advertising needs. Because advertisers on the World Wide Web might be found almost anywhere, meetings may be in person, over the phone, or via e-mail. Depending on the specific advertiser, the Advertising Account Executive may deal directly with a client or may deal with the client's advertising agency.

A major responsibility of the music-oriented Web site Advertising Account Executive is bringing in new business. The individual may make what is known as "cold" calls to potential advertisers. These calls are made to people who have not advertised on the site. After identifying him- or herself and the site's affil-iation, the Account Executive attempts to set up an appointment to tell the potential advertiser more about the Web site and advertising opportunities on it. Not every call will result in an appointment. The Advertising Account Executives must have the ability to accept rejection without taking it personally.

The Advertising Account Executives must have a complete knowledge of the Web site. He or she must know the demographics of the visitors to the site, how long the site has been in existence, other advertisers, and so on. This information can help the Advertising Account Executive illustrate how advertising on his or her site can benefit a potential advertiser.

In order to entice new advertisers to their site, Music Web Site Advertising Account Executives may offer a variety of promotions and discounts. They may also offer specials, promotions and discounts to established accounts in order to tempt them to advertise more frequently.

Some of these promotions are developed by the sales manager or the marketing manager. In other cases, the account executive may help to generate marketing and advertising ideas for current or potential customers. These may include sweepstakes or co-op ads. Individuals also often brainstorm with clients to come up with effective advertising ideas. The more effective ads are, the more advertising customers will purchase.

It is essential that that Advertising Account Executive be aware of all the promotions as well as up to date on various rates, discounts, and advertising packages offered. He or she must also be able to explain all of these to advertisers.

To be successful as an Advertising Account Executive for a music-oriented Web site, the individual must find ways not only to sell an advertiser one ad but to build a lasting business relationship. He or she can do this by explaining promotions, putting together the best package possible, and servicing the account well. The individual also must continually check with clients to be sure they are happy with their ads and are being billed properly.

Music-Oriented Web Site Advertising Account Executives are expected to keep accurate records of advertisements sold, billings, and so on. Individuals are responsible for writing orders and making sure that they get to the appropriate department at the Web site

Unlike traditional print ads, Web advertising has limitations and options. In some cases, the Music-Oriented Web Site Advertising Account Executive may offer suggestions to advertisers for copy, ad content, or design. As large graphics may slow down a site, the Advertising Account Executive may, for example, suggest ad graphics be specially sized and created to allow the Web site and the ad to open quickly.

Depending on the situation and the site, the individual may also suggest a banner ad on the site. With this type of ad, a visitor need only hit the banner to be taken to the advertiser's site.

One of the responsibilities of the Web Site Advertising Account Executive is determining how long an advertiser wants to run a specific ad. He or she may also establish when the advertiser wants his or her ad changed. With Web advertising, it is relatively easy to change online ads quickly. It is up to the Advertising Account Executive to know which ads need to be put up on the site and when.

Salaries

Annual earnings for Music-Oriented Web Site Advertising Account Executives can range from $21,000 to $100,000 or more depending on a number of variables. These include the size, prestige, and popularity of the Web site. Other variables include the sales ability of the Advertising Account Executive. Individuals who sell more, earn more. The reason many people love this type of job so much is that the sky is the limit on earnings. Most Advertising Account Executives are paid on a commission basis. This means that for every dollar of advertising that an individual sells, he or she receives a percentage as part of his or her salary. Percentages can vary from company to company and generally range from 10 percent to 20 percent, with the average commission about 15 percent.

Some companies offer a weekly or monthly draw against salary for the Advertising Account Executive. They do this for a number of reasons. It is helpful for beginning Advertising Account Executives to get into the swing of selling. It also adjusts the take-home pay of individuals in the case of their having had a "bad" week or month.

Employment Prospects

Employment prospects are good for Music-Oriented Web Site Advertising Account Executives and it is getting better all the time. Individuals who are sales oriented, appropriately aggressive, and hard working are always in demand for sales positions.

Jobs may be located throughout the country. In some cases, companies allow employees to telecommute either all or part of the time.

Advancement Prospects

Advancement prospects are good for aggressive, hard-working Music-Oriented Web Site Advertising Account Executives. Some individuals climb the career ladder by selling more advertisements, thereby increasing their earnings. Others find similar positions working for larger, more prestigious and more popular music-oriented Web sites. Some become sales managers. Still others move into selling in another industry.

Education and Training

Educational requirements vary from job to job for Advertising Account Executives working for music-oriented Web sites. In general, companies require a minimum of a high school diploma or GED. Many prefer or require a college degree or background.

Educational requirements may be waived by the employer if the applicant is eager, aggressive, and shows potential for selling.

Courses that might prove useful in selling include advertising, sales, business, English, psychology, sociology, writing, and communications. Seminars and workshops in selling and various areas of the music industry will also be helpful.

Experience, Skills, and Personality Traits

Experience requirements vary from company to company. Some Web sites will hire individuals with no experience who illustrate a desire to sell. Other Web sites require their Advertising Account Executives to have sales experience.

Advertising Account Executives working for a music-oriented Web site need to understand the area of the music industry for which the site is geared. Sales skills are critical. Individuals should be articulate, with excellent verbal and written communications skills. An understanding of Web sites, the Internet, and graphics is also necessary.

Advertising Account Executives need to be personable, outgoing, and appropriately aggressive. Self-motivation and the ability to work without constant supervision are mandatory.

Advertising Account Executives must be able to plan out their workday, make appointments and calls, and go to appointments without someone looking over their shoulder.

The ability to work with numbers is helpful in calculating out costs and rates for ads and related packages.

Unions and Associations

Advertising Account Executives selling ads for a music-oriented Web site may belong to a trade association specific to the area of the music industry in which the site is focused. Individuals may also get additional career information from the American Advertising Federation (AAF).

Tips for Entry

1. Get involved in the music industry. If you're still in school, find an internship with a record company, music publisher, promoter, agent, or manager. The contacts you make at this internship can turn into potential advertisers down the line.
2. Many music-oriented Web sites also offer internships. Internships give you on-the-job training, experience, and the opportunity to make the important contacts.
3. Many Web sites advertise openings on their sites. Check them out.
4. Send your résumé and a short cover letter to music-oriented Web sites. Request that your résumé be kept on file if there are no current openings.
5. Trade magazines such as *Billboard* also may advertise openings.
6. Don't forget to check traditional job search sites, such as monster.com and hotjobs.com, as well as job sites specific to the music industry.

SUPPORT SERVICES FOR RECORDING ARTISTS

RECORDING ARTIST WEB SITE CONTENT PRODUCER

Position Description

Recording artists, like others in the music industry, have begun using Web sites as marketing tools. Depending on the recording artist and his or her level of popularity, a Web site devoted to an artist has the potential to receive thousands of hits a day.

In order to keep fans engaged, informed, and, most importantly, coming back, most artists, their management companies, or labels retain Web Site Content Producers. These individuals are responsible for creating and maintaining the content of the artist's Web site.

Web Site Content Producers are expected to develop and execute a strategic online content plan. In order to be successful, they must constantly come up with fresh, innovative content that keeps fans returning to the site.

Recording artists use Web sites for a number of reasons. To begin with, the Web site gives the recording artist a necessary presence on the Web. This presence makes it easy for fans to get general information on the artist as well as timely news, concert dates, and new CD offerings. Artist Web sites also give artists a simple way to sell or promote their CDs and other merchandise.

Web sites also help recording artists build communities of fans. These communities can dramatically help artists increase their popularity and sell concert tickets and CDs.

Artist Web sites also mean that media, talent buyers, or anyone else requiring information can access it with a click of the mouse. In a world where people want information *now*, this can be priceless.

Web Site Content Producers are responsible for the content of every aspect of the Web site. It is essential that the Web sites are informative, user friendly, and make people want to keep coming back. Content producers are responsible for researching and writing engaging stories and articles on a variety of subjects. Their job is similar to that of both a print journalist and editor.

Web Site Content Producers are expected to develop a variety of stories for the Web site that are of interest to fans of the artist. These articles might be about the artist, the music industry in general, or may simply interest those visiting the site. Articles may be short blurbs or longer. The Web Site Content Producer must be sure each article will both catch the eye of those visiting the site and hold visitors' attention.

The homepage is where most people enter an artist's Web site, and it is from there that visitors will be enticed to continue to explore the site. The Web Site Content Producer must be sure the homepage stays fresh and is constantly updated. No fan wants to visit an artist's Web site only to find later that the information is out of date. The homepage may include breaking news about the recording artist, announcements of new concert dates, upcoming CDs, photos, and, of course, links to other information.

Other pages on the site might include bios of the act, profiles of each member of the act (if it is a group), feature stories, reprints of interviews, tour news, discographies, lyrics of songs, forums, photos, and videos. The Web Site Content Producer must be sure all copy is interesting and easy to read.

In an effort to increase interest in the recording artist as well as giving fans a reason to visit the site, Web Site Content Producers may develop blogs, webcasts, chats, and podcasts. These outlets help to get fans involved. This, in turn, often leads to the opportunity to solicit positive reviews or user comments.

Web Site Content Producers often find ways to develop mailing lists of fans. They may accomplish this using a variety of methods, including developing "contact us" forms, surveys, sweepstakes, or fan clubs. These mailing lists can be extremely valuable to recording artists. They can be used to get news out quickly, and to inform fans about concert dates and new CD availability.

Some Web Site Content Producers develop e-mail blasts that they send out to fans of the artist. These may be used to get news out quickly as well. Many recording artists send these e-mail blasts to fans requesting them to call radio stations or music television program on specific days to request a new CD or video. If the artist has developed a large enough e-mail list, these blasts can push an artist's CD onto the charts or, at the very least, draw attention to it.

Depending on the size, structure, and extent of the recording artist's Web site, there may be more than one content producer. One may be a senior or executive Web Site Content Producer who oversees the entire site. Another may develop and monitor blogs. Still another may develop podcasts.

Some Web Site Content Producers are responsible for researching and writing feature stories, articles about the recording act, or conducting interviews. Everything really depends on the size of the site and how comprehensive the recording artist wants it to be.

Web Site Content Producers are often responsible for overseeing staff copywriters, photographers, and graphic artists. Some content producers are also responsible for finding and retaining freelancers to write articles on specific subjects or specific areas.

The content producer is responsible for getting all stories, editing them when necessary, and giving them to the webmaster to put online. He or she may also be expected to arrange for photos and obtain other information, such as music downloads, that might make online stories interesting.

For recording artists, one of the exciting things about the Internet is that it can be interactive. The content producer may develop surveys, questionnaires, or other pieces to involve those visiting the site. In some instances, the interactive part of the site may be related to promotions, concerts, or other happenings.

The Web site Content Producer is often responsible for finding pictures, animation, and other graphics to make the content more appealing. He or she may utilize the services of graphic artists, photographers, or others to accomplish this task. The individual may work with the webmaster to find images that are appropriate and will look good but not affect the ease of opening the site. The Web Site Content Producer may also utilize videos of of interviews with the artist or of the artist in concert.

Recording artist Web sites often also utilize sweepstakes, contests, or other promotions to encourage fans to come back to the site on a regular basis. The individual may develop these promotions him- or herself or may work with the artist's marketing team.

Salaries

Recording Artist Web Site Content Producers can earn between $25,000 and $75,000 or more annually. Factors affecting earnings include the experience, responsibilities, and professional reputation of the individual as well as the popularity and career level of the specific recording artist. Other variables include the size of the Web site as well as the importance the artist places on the particular site.

Web Site Content Producers for well-known recording artists with fairly extensive Web sites will generally earn more than their counterparts handling similar duties for less popular artists. Individuals who work on a consultation basis may be paid a monthly fee ranging from $2,000 to $5,000 or more. Some are also compensated on a per-project basis.

Employment Prospects

Employment prospects are fair for Web Site Content Producers handling Web sites for recording artists.

Individuals may work for well-known, established recording acts or newly established or up-and-coming artists.

Depending on the situation, individuals may be employed directly by the recording artist, his or her management company, or even the artist's record label. It should be noted that even if a label hosts a Web site for an artist, this does not mean the artist does not have his or her own Web site too.

Web Site Content Producers may also work on a consultation basis.

Advancement Prospects

Advancement prospects are fair for Web Site Content Producers working on Web sites for recording artists. To a great extent advancement prospects depend on an individual's current career level.

Web Site Content Producers handling the Web sites for lesser-known acts, for example, can climb the career ladder by finding similar positions with more popular recording artists. This generally results in increased responsibilities and earnings. Those at the top of their field, may find similar positions with even more popular recording artists.

Some individuals move into analagous positions at larger record labels. Others may move into corporate-level public relations jobs at a larger label.

Education and Training

While there may be exceptions, most positions require or prefer individuals to hold at least a four-year college degree. Good choices for majors include journalism, communications, English, public relations, marketing, music-business management, or liberal arts. Courses, workshops, and seminars in public relations, writing, promotion, journalism, the music industry, and Web journalism will be helpful in honing skills and making new contacts.

Experience, Skills, and Personality Traits

Experience requirements depend to a great extent on the specific recording artist or group and the importance they place on their Web site. Up-and-coming acts may require only that an individual be able to demonstrate competency. More successful, popular recording artists, who put a great deal of importance on their Web site, may prefer that candidates have a proven track record and a minimum of two or three years of experience developing, creating, editing, and managing Web and interactive content.

Writing and editing experience will be useful, whether or not it is Web related. Web Site Content

Producers need to be innovative, creative, and organized. An excellent command of the English language is necessary, as are excellent communications skills, both written and verbal.

Web Site Content Producers need to the ability to multitask effectively. A complete understanding and working knowledge of the music industry is essential. Individuals must also be Internet savvy. While it may not be required, individuals who know HTML (a programming language) may have a leg up on other candidates.

Unions and Associations

Web Site Content Producers for recording artist Web sites may belong to a number of music-related associations, such as the National Academy of Recording Arts and Sciences (NARAS), or association related to a specific musical genre, such as the Country Music Association (CMA) and the Gospel Music Association (GMA). Producers may also belong to the Internet Professionals Association (IPA).

Tips for Entry

1. Positions may be advertised in the classified section of newspapers in cities where there may be larger numbers of recording artists. While these areas can be spread throughout the country, the best bets are New York City, Los Angeles, and Nashville. Look under such headings as "Web Site Content Producer," "Web Site Content Manager," "Music—Web site," "Recording Artist—Web site," "Web Sites," and "Web Careers."

2. This is the perfect type of job to look for online. Start with some of the more popular job sites, such as www.hotjobs.com and www.monster.com, and go from there.

3. Jobs openings may also be located on career sites specific to the music industry.

4. Get as much experience writing as you can. If you are still in school, get involved in your school newspaper and/or Web site.

5. If you know an up-and-coming band, offer to put together their Web site. This will give you good experience, a line to add on your résumé, and, if they hit it big, you've got a job.

6. Consider a part-time job at a local newspaper, to get writing experience and to gain your contacts.

7. Look for internships at a record label or a radio station. These will give you on-the-job training, experience, and the opportunity to make

important contacts. Canvas human resource departments to see what they offer.

8. Send your résumé and a short cover letter to the manager or management company of recording artists you might be interested in working with. You can never tell when an opportunity exists.

9. Many acts advertise their openings on their Web site. Look for the section of the Web site that says "employment opportunities," "work for us," "exciting opportunities," or "jobs."

10. Every now and then you might find an opening in the trades. Check out the classifieds on a regular basis in *Billboard* and any local trade publication.

PERSONAL ASSISTANT TO RECORDING ARTIST

CAREER PROFILE

Duties: Ensuring that a recording artist has an easier, more organized personal and/or business life; handling day-to-day details for the artist; acting as gatekeeper; answering phones and screening calls; scheduling meetings; running errands

Alternate Title(s): Assistant; Executive Assistant; CPA; Celebrity Personal Assistant

Salary Range: $35,000 to $100,000+

Employment Prospects: Fair

Advancement Prospects: Fair

Best Geographical Location(s) for Position: Positions may be located throughout the country; more opportunities may exist in areas with larger numbers of record companies, companies related to the music industry, and recording artists, such as New York City, Los Angeles, and Nashville

Prerequisites:

Education or Training—Educational requirements vary; see text

Experience and qualifications—Experience requirements vary from job to job; see text

CAREER LADDER

Personal Assistant for More Prestigious Recording Artist, Music Industry Executive or Personal Assistant in Other Industry

↑

Personal Assistant to Recording Artist

↑

Personal Assistant in Different Field, Executive Assistant, or Other Position in Music or Entertainment Industry

Special Skills and Personality Traits—Organization; verbal and written communications skills; computer skills; creativity; problem solving skills; people skills; ability to multitask; energetic

Special Requirements—Valid passport and/or driver's license may be required depending on the specific position

Position Description

Recording artists, like other professionals in the music industry, are very busy people. Between touring, recording, business, and family and friends, life can become overwhelming. Many recording artists hire Personal Assistants to help take care of some of the day-to-day chores related both to their personal and/or business concerns.

It can be exciting and fun to work as a Personal Assistant to someone in the music business. The PA is right there with the recording artist, helping him or her make life easier and more organized. Personal Assistants to recording artists may rub shoulders with other recording artists and celebrities, eat in the finest restaurants, travel first class, stay in four-star hotels, and attend award shows. Of course, a lot of that depends on the specific recording artist for which the PA is working, the artist's level of success, and the specific job.

Personal Assistants work long hours. Being a PA is not normally a nine-to-five job. Responsibilities can

vary greatly, depending on the specific job and artist. In some situations, the Personal Assistant is primarily responsible for helping the artist with his or her business; in others, the assistant helps the artist with his or her personal matters. Often, the Personal Assistant is responsible for assisting the artist with both.

Duties can run the gamut—from taking the recording artist's children to school to scheduling a recording session or rehearsal, from checking the recording artist's e-mail to buying a birthday gift for his or her mother. The Personal Assistant must assist the recording artist in every aspect of his or her life and career.

Personal Assistants working for recording artists generally are expected to maintain a calendar of the artist's personal and business responsibilities. Assistants may create daily, weekly, monthly, and/or annual calendars of all concerts, travel dates, meetings, interviews, recording sessions, phone calls, and events to which the artist is committed. As activities and events are added, the Personal Assistant updates the calendar. The PA is also expected to keep track of family functions, birthdays, anniversaries, dinners, luncheons, and so on.

The Personal Assistant may schedule and book meetings, interviews, and appointments on behalf of the artist. At times, he or she may also be asked to cancel or reschedule meetings as well.

The Personal Assistant may be responsible for answering phones, screening calls, or making calls on behalf of the artist. Part of the job of the Personal Assistant is often to be a gatekeeper or buffer between the artist and the typically large number of people who want to speak to him or her. Callers might be seeking concert tickets, back stage passes, autographs, or a meeting. Some might want permission to do an interview or for the artist to participate in a nonprofit charity event, or they might simply want the artist to listen to their music. The Personal Assistant must be able to put people off nicely until he or she can establish whether the artist is available.

A PA must determine what each caller or visitor wants and decide whether he or she should be put through to the artist. In some cases, the assistant is given a list of people whom the artist wants to talk to or see. In other cases, he or she may check with the artist each time a call or visitor arrives.

The Personal Assistant is often responsible for travel arrangements. He or she might make plane reservations, hotel reservations, rent limos, or arrange for other car service. Sometimes arrangements might be made only for the artist and his or her entourage. At other times, they might be made for the artists family or friends. Scheduling flight itineraries for recording artists is not always easy. The artist may be performing a concert late into the night in one part of the country and then be schedule to do a television appearance on a different coast the next day. Sometimes the Personal Assistant will book a commercial flights. Other times, he or she may have to arrange for a private jet.

The Personal Assistant is often expected to travel with the recording artist to recording sessions, interviews, events, personal appearances, meetings, and concerts. Depending on the situation, the individual may be asked to take notes or just be on hand to assist the artist if he or she needs anything.

If the artist goes to the Grammys or other award shows, the Personal Assistant may have the opportunity to walk the red carpet. He or she may also accompany the artist to award show parties and events. This can be a very exciting part of the job for PAs, as long as they remember that their job is to assist the artist and that his or her needs must be their number-one focus.

The Personal Assistant is often privy to a great deal of private and sensitive information. It is essential that he or she keep all information confidential. While success, fame, and fortune are things most recording artists strive for, these come with a lot of pressures. Many Personal Assistants, therefore, may also become confidants to the artists for whom they work.

Personal Assistants often go on tour with their employers. While on tour, they may be expected to accompany the artist to sound checks, interviews, meetings, in-store appearances, public appearances, and, of course, concerts. The Personal Assistant may be responsible for checking the artist in and out of hotels, ordering room service, or finding a special food or drink that the artist may want. He or she may be asked to go shopping, pick up personal care items, or even find a hairstylist, physician, or personal trainer to come to the artist's hotel.

The Personal Assistant may be asked to iron, sew on a button or otherwise repair a garment, or even take clothing to a laundromat. He or she may be expected to make sure the artist has clothing to change into after a concert or has at the ready the beverage the artist wants before or after a performance. The Personal Assistant may also be responsible for setting wake-up calls and making sure the artist has everything he or she needs for the day.

The Personal Assistant working for a recording artist may work closely with the individual's management company, agents, publicists, and tour managers. However, his or her main allegiance must always be to the artist.

The Personal Assistant will often be the one carrying copies of the artist's press kits, audio and video materials, and so forth to meetings, distributing them to the appropriate people. He or she is expected to get the names and contact information of those whom the artist promises something or wants to contact at a later date.

A big part of the job of many Personal Assistants working with recording artists is to keep track of all receipts. As many of the expenses that recording artists incur are tax deductible, this is especially important. The Personal Assistant may log expenses and receipts into a computer program or simply turn them over to the artist's manager or accountant.

Personal Assistants are often responsible for opening an employer's correspondence, whether answering letters or checking e-mail. They must respond in an appropriate manner, by phone, e-mail, or standard letter. Depending on the situation, the Personal Assistant may be expected to handle fan mail, directly or through the artist's fan club.

Personal Assistants help the artist manage his or her personal life as well. This might mean finding a babysitter or nanny for the artist's children, planning a party, overseeing the rest of the artist's staff, or paying personal or business bills. It might mean shopping, stopping at the dry cleaners, or scheduling medical appointments.

Personal Assistants working for recording stars may be asked to do simple tasks, such as watering plants or bringing clothing to a tailor or larger tasks, such as researching potential new homes for the artist or negotiating for a new car. PAs may help the artist learn how to use his or her Blackberry or computer or help plan a vacation.

When the recording artist has a problem or wants something done, he or she calls on the Personal Assistant to find a solution. The PA must be able to handle the situation calmly, quickly, and effectively.

While many PAs are surrounded by the glitter, glamour, and gold of the music industry, the one drawback some express with their job is that they must remain in the background. While in reality they have their own identity, in many cases these are lost, and they simply become known as "so and so's assistant." Nevertheless, for those seeking a job in the music industry that is challenging every day, this might be a perfect career choice.

Salaries

Earnings for Personal Assistants working with recording artists can vary dramatically. Some individuals earn $35,000; others earn $100,000 or more annually. Factors affecting earnings include the specific recording artist the individual is working for and the popularity, prestige, and the level of the artist in his or her career. Other factors affecting earnings include the specific responsibilities, experience, and professional reputation of the Personal Assistant.

PAs with numerous responsibilities working for established recording artists at the top of their profession will generally earn more than their counterparts working with less established artists.

Employment Prospects

Employment prospects are fair for qualified individuals seeking positions as Personal Assistants for recording artists. In addition to recording artists signed with major labels, there are many who are signed with independent labels. It should be noted that every recording artist is not at the top of the charts. Some go up and then down again. Some are still trying to make it. All are equally potential employers.

While the greatest number of opportunities exist in areas where there are large numbers of record labels, such as New York City, Los Angeles, and Nashville, independent labels are located throughout the country.

Advancement Prospects

Advancement prospects are fair for talented Personal Assistants. A great deal of advancement possibilities in this area are related to the individual's career aspirations.

Some individuals climb the career ladder by getting some experience and finding similar positions with more popular recording artists. Others stay with the same artist and advance their career by being given additional responsibilities, resulting in increased earnings.

There are also individuals who go on to become Personal Assistants for record company executives as well as others in the music industry. Some Personal Assistants also find positions working with celebrities outside the music industry.

Frequently, as Personal Assistants become known in the industry, other recording artists and people in the industry try to snag them from their current employers.

Education and Training

Education requirements for Personal Assistants working with recording artists vary from job to job. Most employers require a minimum of a high school diploma or the equivalent. A college background or degree may be preferred or required. In most situations, however, educational requirements will generally be waived in favor of experience or the ability to demonstrate competence.

Courses, seminars, or workshops related organizing, the music industry, stress management, time management, party planning, computers, writing, or other skill may be useful in the job.

Special Requirements

As many recording artists travel overseas, the Personal Assistant may be required to hold a valid passport. He or she may also be required to have a valid driver's license. In some cases, depending on the specific client, the individual may also be required to have a reliable automobile with which he or she can do errands.

Experience, Skills, and Personality Traits

Experience requirements vary from job to job. Some employers prefer someone who has held one or more prior positions as a Personal Assistant. Others prefer individuals who have experience in the entertainment or music business. Still others just want someone who can demonstrate that they can do the job. It all depends on the position.

Successful Personal Assistants are professional, responsible, organized individuals who realize that they are doing a job. In this type of position, individuals often are privy to sensitive information the recording artist may not want broadcasted. The ability to keep confidences is essential. The ability to show discretion is critical. The individual must also be extremely trustworthy.

Good communications skills, both verbal and written, are essential to this type of job. Organizational skills are necessary. The ability to be resourceful is helpful.

Good judgment is critical in this type of job, as is the ability to multitask effectively. Organizational skills are also necessary.

Successful Personal Assistants need good problem-solving skills. They also need the ability to remain calm, cool, and collected under all kinds of circumstances.

Unions and Associations

Individuals interested in a career in this field may want to contact the Association of Celebrity Personal Assistants (ACPA), at http://www.celebrityassistants.org.

Tips for Entry

1. Consider a short stint as an executive assistant. This will put some experience under your belt.

2. Prior experience in some aspect of the music or entertainment industry will be helpful. If you are interested in this type of job as a career, consider looking for an internship at a record label or other music-industry company. It will give you good experience and help you to make some valuable contacts.

3. Develop your résumé and send it with a short cover letter to artist-management companies, record labels, booking agencies, entertainment attorneys, entertainment publicists, and recording artists themselves. You might get lucky.

4. Positions in this field may be advertised in the classified section of newspapers in areas such as New York City, Los Angeles, and Nashville. Look under headings such as "Personal Assistant," "Assistant," "Entertainment," "Music Industry," or "Recording Artist."

5. Trade magazines such as *Billboard* also advertise openings.

6. Don't forget to check traditional employment sites such as monster.com and hotjobs.com, as well as job sites specific to the music industry.

CELEBRITY BODYGUARD

CAREER PROFILE

Duties: Overseeing the personal security needs of recording artist or other celebrity in the music industry; keeping artist safe; planning routes for getting artist to and from concerts; crowd control; handling fans; handling stalkers

Alternate Title: Security Specialist; Protection Officer; Security Consultant; Executive Protection Officers

Salary Range: $25,000 to $500,000+

Employment Prospects: Fair

Advancement Prospects: Fair

Best Geographical Locations For Position: Positions located throughout the country; greatest number of positions will be located in areas where there are large numbers of recording artists and celebrities in the music industry, such as New York, Los Angeles, and Nashville

Prerequisites:

Education or Training—Educational and training requirements vary; see text

Experience and qualifications—Experience working in security or as bodyguard; experience in military or police may be helpful

CAREER LADDER

Celebrity Bodyguard for More Prestigious Client or Owner of Security Service Company

Celebrity Bodyguard, Music Industry

Bodyguard in Other Industry

Special Skills and Personality Traits—Integrity; honesty; loyalty; excellent judgment; quick thinking; stamina; physical fitness; verbal communications skills; knowledge and understanding of music and entertainment industry; people skills; discretion

Special Requirements—State licensing may be required; permit to carry firearms may be required; other special requirements vary; see text

Position Description

No matter the celebrity status of individuals in the music business, as soon as they gain recognition, they begin to acquire fans. Normally this is a good thing. Fans can help build the popularity of a recording artist. They are the ones who go to clubs to see the artist, buy the concert tickets, request tunes on radio and music television, and purchase CDs, downloads, music videos, and other merchandise.

As recording artists and other celebrities begin to gain popularity they get more fans and more recognition. Unfortunately, this attention sometimes causes problems. Whether fans just want meet a star, shake his or her hand, or get an autograph, without some security measures, the situation may become dangerous.

Some fans may be obsessed with a recording star; others may believe the star is their girlfriend or boyfriend. There also are people who may want to hurt the star or otherwise gain some notoriety.

The more successful an individual in any field becomes, the more at risk he or she becomes.

Recording artists and other celebrities have unique security needs. While not every recording artist need worry about security risks, recognition can for certain celebrities bring a wide range of concerns. These can include physical threats, harassment by the paparazzi and media, negative publicity, stalkers, potential kidnappers, embezzlement, overzealous fans, and more.

While most people can go out unnoticed, that may not be possible for recording artists or other celebrities in the music industry. For these people, going out to dinner or a nightclub can unleash masses of fans trying to get autographs, shake the artist's hand, simply attempting to meet the artist. People may throw themselves at a star in an attempt to get a date, or paparazzi may try inappropriately to snap a picture.

Going on tour raises a whole new set of security issues. There is constant travel to unfamiliar places and new venues. There may be huge numbers of fans trying to get to the star, and stalkers, the paparazzi, and other unknown persons.

If the artist has a family, he or she may also need to address their safety. Celebrity may bring fortune and fame, but it may bring unusual problems.

Many recording artists and other celebrities use the services of professional bodyguards to help them with their security needs. Responsibilities of Celebrity Bodyguards depend on the specific recording artist and situation. The main function of the bodyguard is, of course, to protect the recording artist.

Some recording artists have only one bodyguard. Others require the services of more than one. Possibly, one main individual might direct security matters, while a number of others handle other duties, as needed.

Some Celebrity Bodyguards accompany the recording artist everyplace he or she goes. Depending on the specific situation, this might mean going to interviews, recording sessions, appearances, meetings, and concerts with the individual. A bodyguard may also go out with the artist when he she goes out to clubs, dinner, or to parties and award shows. Other bodyguards make sure the recording artist is safe in his or her home. Some do both. While individuals may work certain time shifts, this is not generally a nine-to-five job. Individuals who go on tour with recording artists may be on call 24 hours a day.

Bodyguards are expected to stay close to the recording artists they are protecting. They may remain beside them or at least nearby. The Celebrity Bodyguard must have the ability both to blend into his or her surroundings when protecting a client and to show a physical presence when needed. The challenge for most bodyguards is protecting the client while letting him or her work and live as normal a life as possible.

If the client goes out to a restaurant, for example, the Celebrity Bodyguard may either sit at the same table or at the next table. It is up to the bodyguard to decide if people should be allowed near the client when he or she is dining. The individual will generally get an idea of how the client wants to handle such situations beforehand. Some celebrities don't want to be bothered at all while they are in a restaurant. Others don't mind giving autographs and taking pictures after they have finished a meal. During this entire process, the bodyguard must be there yet must be unobtrusive. This situation is similar when the recording artist attends parties. The bodyguard must always be with the individual, yet stay out of the way.

Within the scope of the job, the Celebrity Bodyguard must constantly be alert to potential threats to the artist. If he or she sees a problem, it needs to be addressed quickly and with as little incident as possible. What might happen? Someone might jump out and grab the artist. Someone might pull a gun on the artist.

Fans might rush the stage. Someone might try to extort money. There are any number of different scenarios that might occur.

Bodyguards are often responsible for the security of the recording artist when he or she is at home. The bodyguard might simply be on hand at the home of the recording artist to ensure that no one suspicious comes in and nothing out of the ordinary occurs. It is the bodyguard's responsibility to check everyone who wants to come into the recording artist's home, whether a fan, food delivery person, home repair people, or housekeepers.

Many recording artists, especially those with large homes, may have closed-circuit cameras throughout their house and property, as well as a special security room that needs to be monitored on a constant basis. The bodyguard may be expected to monitor these cameras or oversee a staff of other security consultants who handle that task.

When the recording artist goes on tour, the Celebrity Bodyguard has additional responsibilities. He or she may check out the venue before the artist arrives to make sure he or she knows where all the entrances and exits are located. This is essential to enable the bodyguard to get the artist in an out of the venue quickly and safely.

He or she is expected to find the best routes to and from the venue, make sure a car is waiting, and that there are no stalkers or unwanted people hanging around. The Celebrity Bodyguard must constantly be alert and on the lookout for anyone who may want to harm the artist in any manner either intentionally or unintentionally. If he or she senses something is wrong, the bodyguard must take swift action.

When the artist is onstage, the bodyguard will constantly monitor the audience. If fans jump on stage uninvited, they will be escort off. If there are any problems at the venue during the show, the bodyguard will make sure that he or she safely extricates the artist.

After the show, the bodyguard may stay close to the artist while he or she signs autographs or may rush the artist out of the venue and back to the tour bus or hotel. If the artist is going back to a hotel, the bodyguard may bring him or her in through a back entrance and then check the hotel room to be sure there are no intruders. He or she may additionally stand outside the artist's room or stay in an adjoining room to make sure no unauthorized people get near the artist. He or she may also screen all phone calls and visitors.

Bodyguards often work with local police and other law enforcement agencies as well as the staff of venues and hotels when the artist they are protecting is on tour. In this manner, if the artist needs some help, it is there.

While recording artists often have chauffeur-driven limousines, bodyguards may also drive their clients on occasion. As the paparazzi or fans may want to get to the star, the Celebrity Bodyguard must be aware of suspicious-looking vehicles or those that are being driven erratically. Knowing evasive driving techniques can save the life of the client.

Depending on the specific situation, the bodyguard may have additional responsibilities. He or she may, for example, be responsible for protecting the recording artist's family or be expected to accompany them when shopping or make sure that the artist's children get to and from school safely.

While fans, the media, and, to some extent, the paparazzi can help boost an artist's career, as noted, at times their attention can be problematic. The Celebrity Bodyguard must have the ability to be tactful and diplomatic when dealing with both fans and media.

As bodyguards are with the recording artist so much they often become confidants. Additionally, they may also see and hear things that the recording artist probably does not want leaked to the public.

There may be people from the media and the tabloids who offer the Celebrity Bodyguard a great deal of money for an exclusive story or some dirt on the recording artist. It is critical that the bodyguard have discretion and keep things confidential. Breaking this rule—even just once—can mean the end of a bodyguard's career.

Some Celebrity Bodyguards carry firearms. Many practice various types of martial arts. Whenever possible, the most successful bodyguards are able to handle situations without violence and without incident. This may be accomplished by simply seeing a potential problem before it occurs and obviating it, showing a physical presence, or simply stepping in when necessary.

While Celebrity Bodyguards attend parties, dinners, award shows, and concerts and travel with their clients in order to protect them, it is essential for them to realize that their's is a job. They are not the star nor are they hired merely to have fun. The bodyguard is not there to get photographed with the recording artist. Nor is he or she there to enjoy all the perks. His or her role is to ensure that the recording artist is safe at all times.

All that being said, the life of a Celebrity Bodyguard can be exciting, glamorous, and rewarding. Most who work in the field would never forfeit the experience.

Salaries

Earnings for bodyguards working in the music industry can vary tremendously. Some Celebrity Bodyguards earn of $25,000 annually, while others earn $500,000 or more a year. Factors affecting earnings include the experience and responsibilities of the bodyguard and the prestige and popularity of the recording artist for which he or she is responsible.

Other variables include the specific employment situation in which the bodyguard works. Individuals working for security companies may be paid a weekly salary by the company, no matter what their assignment. Others working directly for a recording artist may be paid on an hourly, weekly, or per project basis.

Bodyguards paid on an hourly basis may earn $100 to $300 or more per hour. Those who travel with the artist or go on tour may have their hourly fee doubled.

Employment Prospects

Employment prospects are fair for qualified individuals seeking to work as bodyguards for recording artists or others in the music industry. They may work directly for recording artists who are at various levels in their career.

Opportunities may also exist with touring companies, promotion companies, record labels and artist-management companies seeking to keep their artists safe. Individuals may also work for either a general security company or a security company specializing in services for celebrities and entertainers.

Advancement Prospects

Advancement prospects are fair for bodyguards working with recording artists or others in the music industry. Individuals who have proven their expertise and can make clients feel safe and comfortable should have no problem climbing the career ladder. It should be noted that advancement is, to a great extent, based on the artist's professional status.

Some start out working as bodyguards for an emerging artist or group. These individuals often climb the career ladder as their employers gain more success and popularity and acquire greater security needs. This generally will result in increased responsibilities and earnings for the Celebrity Bodyguard.

Some individuals may climb the career ladder by locating similar positions with more popular and prestigious recording artists. Others get better assignments. Many individuals working for security companies strike out as consultants or start their own security company.

Education and Training

Educational and training requirements vary for jobs as bodyguards. Some individuals just fall into the job and have no formal education or training. Those who are sought out most, however, generally have gone through some sort of formal training.

Some Celebrity Bodyguards hold degrees in criminal justice. Others have gone through police or military training. There are also schools that specialize specifically in training bodyguards.

Courses, seminars, and workshops in a variety of security and protection areas may be useful. These might include such areas as unarmed combat, tactical driving, firearms, screening and controlling crowds, protective escorting, and electronic surveillance. Other important training may include various martial arts classes.

Special Requirements

There are a number of requirements bodyguards working with recording artists may need. These requirements will, of course, depend on the specific job and employer. In many situations, the Celebrity Bodyguard will need a basic security guard or private investigator's license issued by the specific state in which he or she is employed.

Bodyguards generally also need a valid driver's license, whether or not they are driving for the recording artist. Individuals should additionally have a clean criminal record as well as the ability to pass an extensive background check. Some employers may require their bodyguards to have a physical exam to ensure that they are healthy, physically fit, and have sufficient stamina for the job.

Experience, Skills, and Personality Traits

As noted previously, some individuals just fall into this job. Others, especially those hired by large security companies may have experience in law enforcement, the military, or governmental agencies such as the Secret Service or the U.S. Marshals.

Bodyguards working with recording artists need an understanding of the music industry as it relates to celebrity and fans. The ability to be alert to surroundings and have an almost sixth sense of what might be happening is helpful.

Individuals in this line of work must be honest, loyal, and have a great deal of integrity. Excellent judgment is necessary. The ability to think quickly and make effective decisions is critical. Verbal communications skills are essential. People skills are also a must.

Bodyguards need to be physically fit. They can never tell when they need to run after someone or step in to protect their clients. Bodyguards should be able to adopt an unobtrusive presence, must be assertive when necessary, and unafraid of confrontation.

Unions and Associations

Depending on their situation, Celebrity Bodyguards may belong to a number of trade associations, including the North American Association of Independent Security Consultants (NAAISC) or the National Council of Investigation and Security Services (NCISS).

Tips for Entry

1. Many people begin their career in this field by working with an up-and-coming new act. As the act becomes more successful, the individual often grows in his or her job. If you are interested in this type of job, seek out these up and-coming acts. At the very least, this type of work situation will give you experience and something to put on your résumé.

2. Get some additional experience by finding a short-term job in security at a concert hall, arena, or even during a school concert.

3. Send your résumé and a short cover letter to security companies specializing in celebrity clients. Request that your résumé be kept on file if there are no current openings.

4. Just because you don't see a job advertised, doesn't mean one doesn't exist. The "hidden job market" offers an opportunity to let people know you are available. Contact recording artists and their management companies to check out openings in this area.

5. On occasion, positions may be advertised in the trades, such as *Billboard*. Consult these publications on a regular basis.

SYMPHONIES, ORCHESTRAS, OPERAS, ETC.

CONDUCTOR

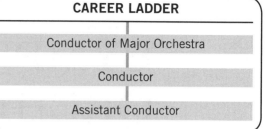

CAREER LADDER

Conductor of Major Orchestra

Conductor

Assistant Conductor

Special Skills and Personality Traits—Ability to communicate musical thoughts; proficiency at piano and at least one other instrument; thorough knowledge of symphonic repertoire

Position Description

The Conductor holds the top musical job in the orchestra. His or her main duty is preparing the orchestra for the finest performance it is capable of presenting. The job is stressful as well as demanding. Hours are long. The Conductor must often put many hours into rehearsals before a performance. When the orchestra is on tour in cities throughout the country or the world, he or she must travel, too.

Top Conductors possess dynamic, charismatic stage personalities. This, plus immense talent, is what makes the difference between a good Conductor and a great Conductor.

As a Conductor, an individual must be proficient in at least one instrument in addition to the piano. He or she must have the ability to sight-read. Most important, the Conductor must know how to communicate musical thoughts and ideas not only verbally during rehearsals, but also through his or her body movements while involved in a performance.

The Conductor is responsible for choosing the orchestra's repertoire. He or she studies the orchestral scores and decides how the works will be played. The same piece of music might sound different depending on which individual conducted it. Each Conductor possesses his or her own style.

A good Conductor with a unique technique is often sought out to make appearances as a guest Conductor with other orchestras. As a guest Conductor, the individual's only responsibility is to prepare for the particular performance.

With his or her own orchestra, the Conductor has many other responsibilities. In addition to preparing the orchestra for individual performances with numerous rehearsals, the Conductor must plan an entire musical season. He or she is responsible for choosing guest soloists, artists, and other conductors to guest or fill in with the orchestra.

The Conductor's job includes advising various section leaders and assisting them when auditions are held for section members. The Conductor of an orchestra is also called on for public and private appearances at fund-raising events on behalf of the orchestra. During summers, many leading Conductors teach at seminars, helping aspiring Conductors to reach their goals.

The Conductor of an orchestra is usually responsible to the board of directors of that orchestra.

Salaries

Conductors' salaries vary widely. In major orchestras the Conductor may earn up to $285,000 plus a year. There are a number of very well-known Conductors who earn

$1,000,000 or more from live performances and recording revenues. In smaller orchestras, the individual may earn between $75 and $500 per service. In between, there are orchestras where Conductors' salaries range from $18,000 to $75,000 plus annually. As a rule, Conductors negotiate their salaries with individual orchestras.

Employment Prospects

Jobs are not plentiful for Conductors. The field is very limited. To get a job as a Conductor or even as an assistant conductor one must have the opportunity to audition. Competition is fierce. Most Conductors work for years as musicians while studying to become Conductors.

Possibilities for work as a Conductor include all varieties of orchestras. Not all positions are full-time jobs. Many successful Conductors have agents and/or managers who seek positions for them.

Advancement Prospects

The Conductor has the top position in an orchestra. Conductors can, however, advance from one type of orchestra to another. For instance, one might obtain a job as a Conductor in a community orchestra and eventually move up to the position of assistant conductor in an urban orchestra. In this profession, advancement occurs as a result of both great talent and a degree of luck.

Education and Training

An individual might have a doctoral degree in conducting and still not land a job as a Conductor. A conservatory or college degree in conducting is not usually required, but may be helpful. Training similar to that received in an educational setting is required, whether it be through seminars or private study.

Summer seminars in conducting are extremely useful to an individual aspiring to be a Conductor. Through these seminars, one can find out if he or she has the talent to be in this field. The best seminars are led by world-renowned Conductors. A seminar given by a skilled Conductor can help an individual bring out his or her own personal style of conducting.

Experience, Skills, and Personality Traits

Any practical experience is useful in becoming a Conductor. Conducting chamber ensembles, small community orchestras, youth orchestras, etc., gives the individual needed experience. Most conservatories and music-oriented schools also offer assistant programs where the student is given an opportunity to conduct.

Summer seminars, such as those held at Tanglewood in Massachusetts, also offer individuals a chance for conducting experience.

Unions and Associations

Conductors may belong to the American Federation of Musicians (AFM) or the American Guild of Musical Artists (AGMA), depending on their situation. For example, if the Conductor plays or played an instrument, he or she probably belongs to the AFM. If the individual was a soloist, he or she might also belong to AGMA. However, many Conductors do not belong to either union.

Tips for Entry

1. Try to attend a summer seminar that has world-renowned Conductors associated with it. Aside from the excellent experience gained at these seminars you can often make important contacts. If you show exceptional talent in the art of conducting a well-known Conductor may help you and guide you up the ladder to success.

2. There are a number of orchestras that offer internships and fellowships in conducting. Check with orchestras to see what programs they offer and whether you qualify.

3. Positions are advertised in many music-oriented publications, including *The International Musician.*

4. Positions may also be advertised in the newspaper classified section. Look under key words such as "Music," "Orchestra," "Conductor," or "Symphony."

CONCERTMASTER/ CONCERTMISTRESS

Duties: Lead the entire string section of the orchestra; solo; tune orchestra

Alternate Title(s): Section Leader; 1st Violinist

Salary Range: $25,000 to $425,000+ full time; impossible to estimate the earnings of individuals working part time and/or paid per service

Employment Prospects: Poor

Advancement Prospects: Poor

Best Geographical Locations for Position: Major cultural centers and other large cities that host orchestras

Prerequisites:

Education or Training—Extensive musical training and/or private study of violin

Experience—Performing as a section member; performing in orchestras and/or chamber music groups

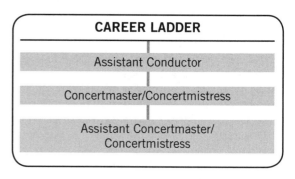

Special Skills and Personality Traits—Good leadership skills; excellent musical ability; ability to deal with stress and pressure; sight-reading skills

Position Description

The position of Concertmaster/Concertmistress is an extremely important one in an orchestra. The person holding this position leads the entire string section of the orchestra during rehearsals and concerts.

At the beginning of every rehearsal or concert, the Concertmaster/Concertmistress is responsible for tuning the rest of the orchestra. For example, the individual will glance at the oboe player, who then gives the "A" note. The rest of the players then tune themselves before the conductor walks out on stage. This procedure takes only 15–20 seconds.

The Concertmaster/Concertmistress usually begins his or her career as a section player. Then if he or she is in the second violin section, the individual can choose to either become section leader in the second violin section or move into the first section as a first section player.

If a player moves into the first section as a section player, he or she then might strive to become the Concertmaster/Concertmistress. This person must show good leadership qualities. Coordination and leadership of the section must be subtle. It must not be obvious to the audience, only to the members of the section.

It is important for the individual to know all the solo literature (music) in the orchestral repertoire. He or she will often have to perform solo during concerts.

The Concertmaster/Concertmistress is also responsible for supervising rehearsals of the string section. The individual may be involved in preliminary auditions for new section members.

A Concertmaster/Concertmistress is directly responsible to the conductor. The job is all-encompassing. The individual is practically considered the section leader of the entire orchestra.

To attain this position, a person must be an extremely accomplished musician and a master of the violin. The Concertmaster/Concertmistress job is competitive; only the best are chosen.

Salaries

Concertmaster/Concertmistress salaries vary depending on the type of orchestra (major, metropolitan, suburban etc.), the number of weeks the orchestra is in session, and the bargaining power of the individual. Minimum earnings are negotiated by the American Federation of Musicians (AFM) local unions for musical members of an orchestra. The Concertmaster/Concertmistress might also be a member of the American

Guild of Musical Artists (AGMA), as he or she may often perform as a soloist. Therefore, minimum earnings might also be set by that union.

The amount of money paid to the Concertmaster/Concertmistress over that paid to the section musicians will vary. In some orchestras the Concertmaster/Concertmistress receives from 10% to 35% over the section members' salaries. In other cases, the individual may negotiate his or her own contract directly with the orchestra management. In a major orchestra, the Concertmaster/Concertmistress may earn from $60,000 to $425,000 plus annually. In smaller orchestras the individual will earn considerably less. As many of the smaller orchestras offer only part-time work, the Concertmaster/Concertmistress may be paid on a per service basis.

Individuals in this position may earn additional income by teaching, participating in recording sessions, or going on the lecture circuit.

Employment Prospects

There are not many opportunities for obtaining a Concertmaster/Concertmistress position with a major orchestra. Opportunities in other types of orchestras are limited too. As there is only one Concertmaster/Concertmistress in each orchestra, competition is always extreme.

Advancement Prospects

The position of Concertmaster/Concertmistress is not entry-level. Once in this position, the individual might want to advance to conductor or assistant conductor. In many orchestras, the assistant conductor position is held simultaneously by the Concertmaster/Concertmistress.

After an individual gets his or her foot in the door by obtaining an orchestral position such as section member, advancement is possible. However, if one holds the position as a Concertmaster/Concertmistress in an urban orchestra, he or she might still have a problem obtaining a position as a Concertmaster/Concertmistress in a major or regional orchestra. The person would probably have to work as a section member in the regional or major orchestra prior to obtaining the Concertmaster/Concertmistress position in a more prestigious orchestra.

Education and Training

Extensive musical training is necessary for the Concertmaster/Concertmistress. This training may be obtained through study at a conservatory, college, with private teachers, or a combination of the above.

Experience, Skills, and Personality Traits

The Concertmaster/Concertmistress begins as a section player. Experience in many different orchestras hones skills. Playing at every opportunity possible helps the musician become more accomplished. It goes without saying that the individual must be an accomplished, talented violinist. Demonstrating leadership skills is important too, as the Concertmaster/Concertmistress leads the entire string section.

Unions and Associations

A Concertmaster/Concertmistress can belong to either the American Federation of Musicians (AFM) or the American Guild of Musical Artists (AGMA). In addition, there are a number of associations that individuals may belong to. Among them are the American Symphony Orchestra League (ASOL) and the National Orchestra Association (NOA).

Tips for Entry

1. Audition for the position of Concertmaster/Concertmistress in your college orchestra.
2. Learn the orchestra's repertoire.
3. Take as many lessons as possible, and practice, practice, practice.
4. Take part in seminars and internships that are available throughout the country.
5. Listings for positions are available through *The International Musician Magazine* (an American Federation of Musicians publication) as well as a variety of other orchestral newsletters, magazines, and publications.

SECTION LEADER

CAREER PROFILE

Duties: Lead a section of the orchestra; supervise any rehearsals with the section; assign parts to players in the section

Alternate Title(s): Principal Player

Salary Range: $25,000 to $95,000+ in full-time orchestras; part-time or per service wages in smaller orchestras

Employment Prospects: Poor

Advancement Prospects: Poor

Best Geographical Locations for Position: Major cultural centers and other large cities

Prerequisites:

Education or Training—Extensive musical training

Experience—Performing as a section member; acting as section leader in youth or college orchestra

Special Skills and Personality Traits—Leadership skills; exceptional musical talent

CAREER LADDER

Concertmaster (if violin)

Section Leader

Section Player

Position Description

Each section of an orchestra has a leader called the Section Leader or the principal player. The Section Leader is responsible to the concertmaster. The main duty of the leader is to lead the section so that the sound is the best that can be produced. It is important that the Section Leader communicate what he or she expects of the section. This is a job that has to be done subtly. It must be obvious only to the section and never the audience.

The string Section Leader, for example, must decide where the bowing should be inserted. The individual must make a decision on the correct phrasing and on who in the section should play the individual parts.

In the wind section, the Section Leader emphasizes such techniques as correct breathing. In certain sections, like that of the oboe, the Section Leader has different responsibilities because there are so few members of that section. Those sections function much more as a personal team than the larger sections do.

To obtain a position as a Section Leader, an individual must audition. Committees are usually set up to listen to these auditions and select the best candidate.

A good stage presence and creative musical ability help place one musician above the rest. A thorough knowledge of the symphonic repertoire is essential. The Section Leader must know how to sight-read and be ready to do so at any time.

At times, the Section Leader has to be able to recognize talent. This individual is on the selection commit-

tee during auditions for the section. The Section Leader, additionally, must supervise any rehearsals within his or her section.

Certain orchestras require their Section Leaders to participate in the orchestra's chamber music group. This is usually specified in the job description.

Salaries

Salaries for Section Leaders in orchestras depend on a number of variables. These include the type of orchestra (major, metropolitan, suburban, etc.), its location, the number of weeks the orchestra is in session, and the seniority of the player.

Minimum earnings are negotiated by the American Federation of Musicians (AFM) local unions. In some orchestras, the Section Leaders receive the same amount of money as other section players. In other orchestras, Section Leaders receive a specific amount of money over the scale set for the section members. In other cases, the Section Leader's salary will be from 10% to 35% over those of section members. Certain Section Leaders negotiate their contracts directly with the orchestra management.

Section Leaders in full-time and major orchestras earn from $25,000 to $95,000 plus. Section Leaders in smaller orchestras earn considerably less. As many of the smaller orchestras offer only part-time work, Section Leaders may be paid on a per service basis.

Section Leaders may earn additional income by teaching or by participating in recording sessions.

Employment Prospects

To become a Section Leader, one must first be a section member of an orchestra. In the ladder of experience, therefore, it is usually the older players with experience in a few different orchestras who obtain these positions. The opportunity does exist, however, to become a Section Leader of a community orchestra or an urban orchestra.

Advancement Prospects

The Section Leader of the violin section can move up to the concertmaster/concertmistress position. However, these positions do not often open up.

The Section Leader of the flute or any of the wind instruments, on the other hand, cannot move up to a concertmaster/concertmistress position. They have the opportunity, though, to train to be conductors or to obtain jobs as a Section Leader or section members in more prestigious orchestras.

Education and Training

As with most symphonic positions, a college degree is not required. Conservatory training or a degree in music performance may help the musician in his or her journey toward becoming a great musician and Section Leader. Years of intensive training and study in the instrument of choice are essential.

Seminars in section leading are also available and often prove to be useful.

Experience, Skills, and Personality Traits

Section Leaders must have experience as section members. Many also play in chamber music ensembles.

Section Leaders often begin playing in youth orchestras. There they gain the experience of acting as Section Leaders. Of course, a Section Leader must be an exceptional musician on his or her instrument.

The Section Leader must be a good leader, able to communicate to the section without being obvious to the audience.

Unions and Associations

Section Leaders must belong to a musician's union. Most belong to the American Federation of Musicians (AFM). This union sets the minimum pay scale for musicians.

Tips for Entry

1. This position is obtained through application and auditions.
2. Prior to applying, take part in as many different orchestral situations as possible.
3. The National Orchestral Association holds training programs for individuals entering the orchestral music field.
4. Take part in seminars and internships offered by orchestras, organizations, colleges, and associations.
5. Positions are listed in music-oriented journals and newsletters such as *The International Musician.*
6. Job openings may also be listed online. Check out orchestra Web sites as well as job search sites.

SECTION MEMBER

CAREER PROFILE

Duties: Play an instrument in an orchestra

Alternate Title(s): Classical Musician; Artist; Section Player

Salary Range: Weekly earnings in orchestra of major musical production, symphony, ballet, or opera company: $800 to $2,500+; weekly earnings in smaller or less prestigious orchestra of musical production symphony, ballet, or opera company: $300 to $750+

Employment Prospects: Poor

Advancement Prospects: Poor

Best Geographical Location(s) for Position: Major cultural centers and other large cities offer the most opportunities

Prerequisites:

Education or Training—Extensive musical training

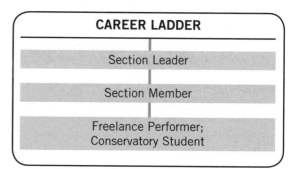

Experience—Performance in chamber music ensembles, youth, college, urban, and/or metropolitan orchestras useful

Special Skills and Personality Traits—Exceptional musical talent; dedication to music; perseverance

Position Description

The Section Members of the orchestra are the people who make up the musical portion of the orchestra. There are different numbers of Section Members in each orchestra.

To be a Section Member, an individual must have exceptional talent with his or her instrument. In addition, the individual must like to perform on stage.

The Section Member must have a full knowledge of the orchestral repertoire. He or she must know the music before going into rehearsal. Rehearsals are mainly for putting together all the parts played by the orchestra.

An important part of the Section Member's responsibility is to play with a group. This is what makes an orchestra sound the way it does.

The Section Member is responsible to his or her section leader. The musician must take cues such as where the correct bowings or phrasing should be (in the string section), correct breathing (in the brass sections), who will play what part, etc.

Section Members must continually practice their instruments and rehearse musical pieces. As a Section Member, an individual must always keep trying to better his or her musical skill.

The Section Member is under contract to perform a specific number of concerts and rehearsals per week. Any rehearsal or concert over that number (the number

differs with various orchestras) and any recording the Section Member participates in qualifies the individual for additional monies.

The Section Member must be available to travel, as orchestras often tour other cities and countries. Travel expenses are paid by the orchestra management.

Section Members who work full-time in major or regional orchestras generally receive at least four weeks vacation, usually when the orchestra takes its break.

Section Members often earn additional income teaching privately. If the individual is a noted member of the orchestra, he or she may also become a speaker on the lecture circuit.

Salaries

Salaries for Section Members depend on a number of factors. These include the type of orchestra (major, metropolitan, urban, etc.), its location, the number of weeks the orchestra is in session, and, in some cases, the seniority of the player.

Minimum earnings are negotiated by the American Federation of Musicians (AFM) local union. Depending on the location, Section Members working in a major orchestra may earn between $800 and $2,500 or more per week. Annual salaries depend on how many weeks per year the orchestra is in session. Major orchestras run from 30 to 52 weeks a year. Salaries may also be contingent on seniority. In addition to salaries, Section Members receive vacation pay and other benefits.

Section Members working in smaller orchestras usually earn considerably less than those playing in major orchestras. Many of the smaller orchestras offer only part-time work. Members are paid on a per service basis. This means that they are paid for each concert in which they perform. In most cases, these individuals are also paid for each rehearsal they attend.

Section Members in youth and college orchestras generally do not get paid and play for the experience.

Section Members might earn additional income by teaching or by participating in recording sessions.

Employment Prospects

Employment prospects for Section Members in major orchestras are limited. There are many more talented and qualified positions than there are openings. Competition for these positions is fierce. That does not mean you can not be successful, just that it is more difficult. Prospects in smaller and less prestigious orchestras are slightly better.

It is interesting to note that many orchestras audition people behind a screen. Using this procedure ensures that there can be no racial or sexual discrimination in the selection process. This procedure was adopted following years of orchestras being dominated by white males.

Advancement Prospects

Once a Section Member obtains a position in an orchestra, the individual has a chance of advancing to a section leader position. The Section Member must be very talented to advance in this manner. Section Members also have the opportunity to advance their careers by trying to land positions as Section Members in more prestigious orchestras.

Education and Training

No college degree is required for a position as a Section Member. However, extensive musical training is essential. This training might be acquired at a conservatory or college, or through intensive private study.

Experience, Skills, and Personality Traits

Any type of performance experience is helpful to an aspiring Section Member. Performing in youth or college orchestras or chamber music ensembles is most useful. Auditioning is useful for the experience.

Section Members must be very dedicated to their music. They must also have the perseverance to keep trying to land a position in an orchestra.

Unions and Associations

Section Members may belong to the American Federation of Musicians (AFM). This union negotiates minimum wages for the musician, maximum number of rehearsals, etc.

Tips for Entry

1. This position is obtained through application and auditions.
2. Prior to applying, take part in as many different orchestral situations as possible.
3. The National Orchestral Association holds training programs for individuals entering the orchestral music field.
4. Take part in seminars and internships offered by orchestras, colleges, and associations.
5. Positions are listed in music-oriented journals and newsletters such as *The International Musician*.

OPERA SINGER

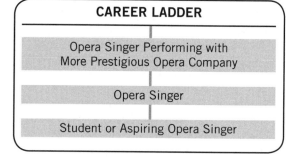
Position Description

Opera Singers are highly trained in classical music. Individuals perform in classical theatrical productions set to music. During these performances, the dialogue is sung instead of spoken. Opera Singers must also act and move on the stage to help bring the story to life.

Traditional operas were written and performed in a number of foreign languages. Opera Singers must either know the language that the opera was written in or be able to learn his or her part in the particular language. Often, the Opera Singer may just learn the part without being able to speak or understand the meaning of the words. Modern operas, written in this country, are usually written and performed in English.

Every opera tells a story. The story is written in a libretto or little book. Operas may be elaborate productions relying on a myriad of costuming, scenery, and lighting.

Individuals may be principal singers in the opera, singing lead, feature, or support roles. They may also sing in opera choruses.

Opera Singers usually audition to obtain jobs. Some individuals have agents or managers who obtain auditions for them. Others find out about openings in shows in a variety of ways, including word of mouth, through the union, or advertisements or notices in trade papers.

Once the Opera Singer obtains a part, he or she is required to attend show rehearsals, become familiar with the opera, and learn the part. Individuals will be fitted with costumes, and have their hair and makeup determined by stylists.

It is the responsibility of the Opera Singer to attend each rehearsal and sing at each performance. Work hours may vary depending on the schedule of rehearsals and performances. Opera Singers often work in the afternoon, evenings, and on weekends.

Salaries

Salaries can vary greatly for Opera Singers depending on a number of factors. These include the type of setting in which the individual sings, the geographic location, and level, size and budget of the opera company. Other factors include the reputation and experience of the individual and the type of part he or she is singing. Individuals may be paid by the performance or on a weekly basis, depending on their specific situation.

Opera Singers can earn between $10,000 and $200,000 or more annually. Variables affecting earnings are, among other things, based on the singer's experience, talent, and popularity.

Aspiring Opera Singers, taking part in an apprentice program, may earn a weekly salary of approximately $300 to $500 or more plus housing. Individuals with additional experience such as those involved in a Young Singer program may earn between $500 and $750 a week. (Young Singer programs are a type of program for up-and-coming young singers similar to apprentice programs.)

Opera Singers are either paid by the performance or on a weekly basis. Individuals also may earn royalties from recordings. Opera Singers working in unionized halls have minimum earnings set by the American Guild of Musical Artists (AGMA). Minimum earnings are based on the type of role an individual is singing as well as the number of rehearsals and performances required.

Employment Prospects

Employment prospects are dependent on talent, determination, and drive. Employment opportunities exist in choruses of operas throughout the country in local, regional, and national companies.

While opera companies exist in most culturally active cities throughout the country and the world, New York City is the opera capital.

Opera Singers often find employment with the help of a manager or talent agent. There are a number of agencies specializing in classical music. Most of them are located in New York City.

Advancement Prospects

Once a talented Opera Singer gets his or her foot in the door, prospects for advancement are fair. Individuals may climb the career ladder by locating a position singing with a more prestigious opera company or by obtaining a lead or solo part in an operatic production.

Education and Training

Individuals must go through years of classical singing and other training to become Opera Singers. Aspiring Opera Singers usually participate in apprenticeship programs with regional or national opera companies before becoming full-fledged Opera Singers.

Generally, Opera Singers attend music conservatories or colleges or universities with majors in classical music. This period is invaluable to individuals for the training and education as well as the opportunities

and practical experience that may not be available elsewhere.

Many individuals take additional classes from private vocal coaches and teachers to supplement their training.

Experience, Skills, and Personality Traits

In order to become successful, Opera Singers must get a great deal of experience singing classical music. This may be obtained through Young Singer and apprenticeship programs sponsored by opera companies.

An Opera Singer must be very talented and have an extraordinary voice. Acting skills are also necessary. Fluency in other languages is useful when singing classic operas in foreign languages or performing in other countries. Familiarity with operas is also helpful.

Success in this field is also dependent on drive, determination, and the willingness to practice long hours. To do this, individuals must have a great deal of physical, mental, and emotional stamina.

Unions and Associations

Opera Singers working in unionized concert halls, theaters, and other venues must be members of the American Guild of Musical Artists (AGMA). This union negotiates minimum earnings for its members as well as minimum working conditions and standards.

Tips for Entry

1. Summer workshops and other similar programs with opera companies are a good way to get excellent training and experience.
2. Internship and apprenticeship programs are invaluable to this career. Contact opera companies for program availabilities.
3. Get the best training you can.
4. Make contacts and get additional experience by finding competitions in opera.
5. Get involved with your local opera company.
6. Attend live operas to learn techniques from other Opera Singers.
7. Many public broadcasting networks and cable stations have operatic productions on television. These are valuable learning tools.

MANAGING DIRECTOR

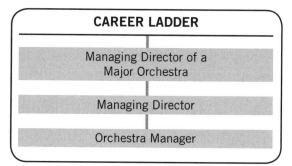
Position Description

The Managing Director of the orchestra holds the top administrative position in an orchestra. It is his or her job to oversee all of the administrative functions of the orchestra and to supervise the administrative personnel.

The individual works closely with the orchestra manager. Together they work with and supervise the development, public relations, business, educational activities, and ticket subscriptions directors and their departments. Both the orchestra manager and the Managing Director must be knowledgeable about these departments, their internal problems, and their activities.

The Managing Director acts as a liaison between the orchestra's board of directors and the administrative departments. It is his or her responsibility to make sure that the policies set up for the orchestra are carried out. The individual attends most of the orchestra board's meetings, working with the board on many of the policies developed. He or she will also report on any administrative problems. Through these meetings, the Managing Director keeps the board members aware of all that is happening within the orchestra.

The Managing Director, or executive director, as he or she is sometimes called, takes part in all labor negotiations involving the orchestra. The individual must

have the ability and the knowledge to effectively negotiate with unions.

The Managing Director of an orchestra usually works in many of the other departments of the orchestra's administration before attaining the Directorship. This experience makes the Director better qualified to handle the details of managing the orchestra.

As the Managing Director, the person is responsible for ensuring that the orchestra meets the needs of the community from a cultural standpoint. He or she might decide that the community needs more children's concerts or a summer concert series. In these cases, the individual will work with the orchestra board and the community to try to put these programs together.

At times, the Managing Director will work with the personnel director. He or she will ultimately be responsible not only for hiring administrative personnel, but also for firing individuals who don't work out.

The Managing Director must work with the development department and the business department, making up budgets and raising money for the orchestra. Some of this money is made available through foundations, corporations, and arts councils. The Managing Director is responsible for locating as much money as possible through this system and bringing it to the attention of the development department.

The Managing Director of the orchestra is responsible to the president of the board of directors and to the board members. His or her days are long, but they are challenging and exciting.

Salaries

Symphony orchestras are classified into different categories according to their size, budget, etc. Salaries will naturally depend on the size, budget, and location of the orchestra. Individuals working as Managing Directors in major orchestras earn more than those working in smaller organizations. Salaries range from $24,000 to over $1,000,000 plus per year.

Employment Prospects

There are a limited number of major and regional orchestras. Employment prospects at that level are limited, too. Positions are more frequently available at the metropolitan and urban levels of orchestras.

Advancement Prospects

The orchestra's Managing Director may advance by obtaining the job of Managing Director with a bigger, more prestigious orchestra. The Managing Director of the orchestra holds the top position in the administrative side of the organization.

Education and Training

A college degree is not always required for this position, although it is usually preferred. Courses in arts administration, music arrangement, business, publicity, and journalism are helpful in handling the job.

Seminars on arts and orchestral administration, given by various colleges and by associations such as the American Symphony Orchestra League (ASOL), are

a bonus to the individual seeking or already holding a position as an orchestra Managing Director.

Experience, Skills, and Personality Traits

The Managing Director must be an enthusiastic type of person. The individual must be personable and congenial, as he or she must deal not only with the orchestra but also with the entire orchestra administration and the board of directors.

The Managing Director must have the ability to supervise and must do so effectively. He or she must be sensitive and understanding toward both the musicians and the administration.

Unions and Associations

The Managing Director of an orchestra may belong to the American Symphony Orchestra League (ASOL). This association sponsors seminars and internship programs in addition to publishing a magazine/newsletter. Many individuals also belong to the Associated Council of the Arts and/or local arts councils.

Tips for Entry

1. Find an orchestra, school, or association that offers an internship program. Interns have a much better chance of obtaining a position.
2. Attend seminars on orchestral management. These seminars are given by colleges, orchestras, and associations such as the American Symphony Orchestra League (ASOL). These will train and educate you and help you develop important contacts.
3. Vacancies are listed in the ASOL newsletter, the Associated Council of the Arts newsletter, and many regional arts organizations' publications.
4. Take a chance and send your résumé with a cover letter to a number of orchestras. One might have an opening for an assistant.

ORCHESTRA MANAGER

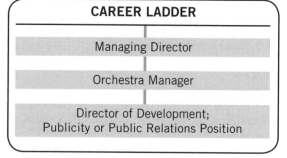

Position Description

The Orchestra Manager is the assistant to the orchestra's managing director. A primary duty is negotiating with the musicians union on behalf of the orchestra. An Orchestra Manager must try to get the best deal for the orchestra management from the union while keeping the players happy.

The Orchestra Manager is also in charge of arranging any concert tours for the orchestra. He or she not only arranges the details of the tour, but also tries to make it easy for the orchestra members who will be traveling. The individual is responsible for any problems that are not directly music-related. These could include anything from a musician's instrument that arrives late to an auditorium, a musician who becomes ill in the middle of the night in a strange town, or a dispute caused by hot tempers that erupt on the road. The Orchestra Manager must deal with crises that occur while traveling. With the pressures of touring, many problems are magnified.

The Orchestra Manager also oversees the orchestra's administrative employees, including the director of development, director of public relations, music administrator, business manager, director of educational activities, and director of ticket subscriptions. He or she must be knowledgeable about these positions and

the problems that might occur. The person must have a broad understanding of the needs of the community or area in which the orchestra is based. As Orchestra Manager, he or she must negotiate contracts for guest soloists and guest conductors.

The Orchestra Manager is responsible to the managing director of the orchestra. The position is not a nine-to-five job. The successful Orchestra Manager loves symphonic music. This makes the job—which involves long hours and hard work—worthwhile.

Salaries

Symphony orchestras are classified into different groups depending on size, budget, and other factors. There are major orchestras, such as the Boston Symphony or the Cleveland Orchestra; there are regional orchestras, like the Birmingham Symphony Orchestra or the Memphis Symphony Orchestra; there are metropolitan, urban, community, college, and youth orchestras. Salaries of Orchestra Managers vary according to the classification and location of the orchestra. Salaries range from $26,000 to $100,000 plus annually. Orchestra Managers of urban, community, college, or youth orchestras often work on an avocational or per service basis.

Employment Prospects

There is a limited number of major and even regional orchestras in the country. Therefore, employment prospects at this level are poor. Positions are sometimes available at the metropolitan, urban, and community levels. However, these jobs are not always full-time.

Advancement Prospects

The position of an Orchestra Manager is not an entry-level job. Positions held prior to Orchestra Manager might include public relations director, fund-raising director, business manager, or an assistant in one of these fields. Once an individual has proven him- or herself in the position of Orchestra Manager, he or she is a valuable commodity to the orchestra and has the opportunity to move up to the position of managing director or to move to an open position in a better orchestra as Orchestra Manager.

Education and Training

A college degree is preferred or recommended for most positions as Orchestra Manager. Individuals may find a few positions without this requirement. These are usually in smaller orchestras.

Courses in music management, administration, and/or business are helpful. Classes in publicity, labor negotiations, fund-raising, and psychology are useful, too. There are also seminars given around the country in arts administration. These seminars put the individual in touch with others already in the field and help develop contracts.

Experience, Skills, and Personality Traits

A good sense of business is important to an Orchestra Manager. An understanding of and sensitivity to musicians and their problems and pressures is almost equally important. To do the job well, one must be able to deal effectively with problems and people under pressure. Hands-on experience is always helpful. Many conservatories and universities have internship programs that provide practical experience. Enjoying music makes it all worthwhile.

Unions and Associations

The Orchestra Manager may belong to the American Symphony Orchestra League (ASOL). He or she might also belong to a local arts council.

Tips for Entry

1. Find an orchestra or school that has an internship in orchestral management. The American Symphony Orchestra League (ASOL) sponsors a variety of internship programs.
2. Attend seminars on orchestral management. Seminars are sponsored by various universities and orchestras in addition to the ASOL.
3. Vacancies are listed in the ASOL newsletter, the Associated Council of the Arts newsletter, and many regional arts organizations' publications.
4. Job openings may also be located on the Internet. Look for specific orchestra sites which often list employment opportunities.

BUSINESS MANAGER

CAREER PROFILE

Duties: Supervise the financial affairs of the orchestra; prepare and distribute payroll

Alternate Title(s): Comptroller, controller

Salary Range: $25,000 to $80,000+

Employment Prospects: Fair

Advancement Prospects: Poor

Best Geographical Locations for Position: Major cultural centers such as Boston, Philadelphia, New York City, Chicago, etc.

Prerequisites:

Education or Training—Educational requirements vary; all positions require at least a high school diploma; many require a college degree

Experience—Bookkeeping experience, accounting positions, etc.

Special Skills and Personality Traits—Skill with figures; accuracy; responsibility; accounting and/or bookkeeping skills; cognizance of orchestral procedures

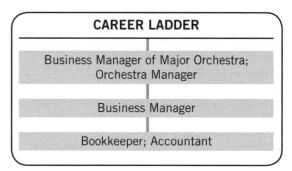

CAREER LADDER

Business Manager of Major Orchestra; Orchestra Manager

Business Manager

Bookkeeper; Accountant

Position Description

The Business Manager of the orchestra is in charge of supervising all of its financial affairs. Depending on the size and the budget of the organization, the Business Manager may work alone or have an assistant and a staff.

The individual in this position must check all bills the orchestra receives. If they are correct, he or she issues checks and pays them. If they are wrong or if there is a discrepancy, the Business Manager or comptroller attempts to rectify the problem. The individual is responsible for paying all bills on time. These may include rentals for music, transportation costs for out-of-town concerts, hotel bills, etc.

The Business Manager may look at comparative prices of various items to make sure that the organization is buying well. For example, the person may check the prices of music stands from four or five companies before purchasing to establish a good price. The individual may work out deals with hotel or motel chains for putting up the orchestra members while on tour. As most orchestras' budgets are extremely tight, the Business Manager will always try to save money for the group.

Accurate records must be kept on all expenditures paid out for the orchestra. Payment dates, check numbers, and lists of items purchased must be kept meticulously. If there are any guarantees or warranties on products purchased, it is usually up to the Business Manager to keep these on file.

The Business Manager is responsible for preparing the payroll and distributing it at the proper times. If a guest conductor or soloist has been employed by the orchestra, the individual must make sure that he or she are paid, too. These payments must be disbursed in accordance with union regulations. The individual must make sure that the proper deductions are taken from everyone's salary and that these monies are correctly deposited and reported to the government.

The person in this position works closely with the director of development. The Business Manager may be responsible for keeping a tally of money raised or for depositing donations. He or she might be in charge of the bookkeeping for the fund-raising department.

The Business Manager also works with the orchestra manager and the managing director in putting together a yearly budget for the organization. After the budget is approved by the board of directors, the Business Manager works to stay within its bounds.

The individual in this position works fairly regular hours. He or she may report to the orchestra's managing director or to the board of directors.

Salaries

The salary of a Business Manager working for an orchestra will vary depending on the classification, size, and budget of the orchestra. Salaries might also vary due to an individual's qualifications and responsibilities. A Business Manager working full time may earn from $25,000 to $80,000 or more annually.

Employment Prospects

Employment prospects are fair for those wanting jobs as business managers in orchestras. Almost every orchestra in the country which has any type of income and/or expenses hires at least a part-time person to fill this position. Larger orchestras may hire a full-time Business Manager and one or more assistants.

Advancement Prospects

Advancement prospects for a Business Manager in an orchestra are poor. The individual may be promoted to orchestra manager, but this may take a long time.

A Business Manager working for a smaller orchestra may, however, advance his or her career by finding employment with a larger or more prestigious orchestra. This usually means more responsibility and an increase in salary.

Education and Training

Education requirements vary greatly according to the orchestra and the position. For example, a Business Manager working part-time in a small orchestra may only be required to have a high school diploma. A major orchestra might, however, require an individual to have a degree in accounting, business, finance, or a related area.

There are many people who work in all phases of the orchestral system who have music performance degrees but cannot get performance-related jobs. A good num-

ber of these individuals take jobs in non-performance areas such as Business Management just to be close to the orchestral setting.

Experience, Skills, and Personality Traits

One of the primary skills a Business Manager needs is an ability with figures. Many people in these positions have bookkeeping experience or accounting skills. Accuracy is essential.

It is helpful, too, for the individual to have a basic knowledge of orchestra procedures.

Unions and Associations

The Business Manager in an orchestral situation does not usually belong to any union. He or she may belong to a number of orchestra-related associations. The most prominent in the field is the American Symphony Orchestra League (ASOL).

Tips for Entry

1. Jobs as Business Managers of orchestras are often listed in the classified sections of newspapers. Most often these jobs open up at the end of a season.
2. Openings are listed in the American Symphony Orchestra League (ASOL) newsletter and various other arts council newsletters.
3. Send a résumé and a cover letter to a few orchestras. They may have openings coming up.
4. Check out the Web sites of orchestras. Many list job opportunities.

DIRECTOR OF DEVELOPMENT

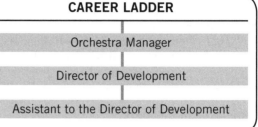

Position Description

Getting people to donate money isn't easy, especially when there are so many causes and organizations soliciting. The Director of Development of the orchestra has one job: to raise money for the orchestra.

He or she does this in a number of ways. The Director of Development will coordinate the annual giving activities, capital campaigns, and deferred giving opportunities for donors and potential donors.

As part of this project, he or she might develop special events and programs to support the orchestra financially. These programs may increase attendance or develop direct financial support.

Activities of a Director of Development might include direct mail campaigns, telephone and telethon fund-raisers, balls, dinners, or cocktail parties.

In order for the Director of Development to reach people who are interested in these fund-raisers, he or she must do a great deal of research. Questionnaires and surveys are used to locate potential supporters.

The Director of Development should have strong public contacts. Through these contacts the Director learns the needs of the community in relation to the orchestra. He or she works closely with both the director of public relations and the orchestra's manager.

The Director of Development usually reports to either the orchestra manager or the managing director, as well as to the orchestra's board of directors.

The Director of Development acts as a liaison between donors, potential donors, and the orchestra's management and board of directors. He or she informs the management and the board of any occurrences affecting donors. The Director of Development also works with the board projecting support programs for fund-raising projects.

At times, the Director of Development may also work with volunteers, getting them involved in such orchestra fund-raising activities as auctions, dinner-dances, etc., to benefit the organization. He or she will reach out to the community for much-needed volunteer support.

The Director of Development creates fund-raising literature and audio-visual materials such as brochures, booklets, pamphlets, programs, volunteer training films, slide shows, and tapes.

A large amount of money for orchestras is raised through grants, foundations, corporations, and endowments for the arts. The Director of Development must keep up with the latest information on these. He or she must know how to apply for grants, how to write proposals, and how to follow up in order to receive the largest gifts possible.

He or she must be an enthusiastic individual. Believing in the cause (financial support of the orchestra) is crucial to the successful Director of Development. Days are long. In addition to regular work hours, he or she must attend community meetings, volunteer meetings, and special events.

Salaries

The Director of Development's salary is commensurate with the size of the orchestra and its fund-raising goals. Directors of Development for small orchestras start out at around $25,000 annually. Individuals working with larger orchestras and with greater responsibility can earn up to $90,000 or more.

Employment Prospects

Directors of Development who can produce results are always in demand. There is a turnover of people in this field. Much of the turnover is a result of an individual's failure to satisfy the board of directors of the orchestra in fund-raising. It takes a number of years to develop a producing program and many boards are impatient, demanding immediate results.

Advancement Prospects

As noted above, Directors of Development who can produce are in demand. An individual who is knowledgeable in coordinating fund-raising and can back up that knowledge with results can move on to a development position with a more prestigious orchestra. He or she may also try to advance his or her career by becoming an orchestra manager.

Education and Training

College degrees are not always required of Directors of Development. However, they are often preferred. There might be several applicants who are qualified, and the difference between them might be a college background or degree.

There are a number of colleges around the country that offer degrees in arts administration or management. If attending a school with such a major is impossible, the individual should take courses in marketing, public relations, and business. These courses will help lay a foundation for a job in the development field.

Experience, Skills, and Personality Traits

Many people get into fund-raising by acting as chairperson for a club or organization. They find that it is a challenge to bring in money for a specific cause or organization. These individuals are enthusiastic about fund-raising and finding ways to get other people to give.

As a rule, Directors of Development are persuasive in an inoffensive way. They not only know the methods to use to bring in potential donations, they know how to get others to volunteer to help. This is important to an orchestra that depends on fund-raising to stay alive financially.

Unions and Associations

Many Directors of Development of orchestras belong to the American Symphony Orchestra League (ASOL), the Associated Council of the Arts, and/or local arts councils.

Tips for Entry

1. There are internship programs in the various positions of orchestral management, including development. These internships are made available through orchestras, colleges, or organizations.
2. There are also many seminars offered in both the development and fund-raising field and specialized orchestral development. These programs are sponsored by major orchestras, colleges, or other organizations. Look into them.
3. Vacancies are listed in the American Symphony Orchestra League (ASOL) newsletter, the Associated Council of the Arts newsletter, and many regional arts organization publications.
4. If you are interested in a position of this type, write to a number of orchestras and ask if you may submit an application to work as an assistant or trainee.

DIRECTOR OF PUBLIC RELATIONS

Duties: Handle press and promotion of the orchestra and its activities; possibly handle advertising (for small orchestra)

Alternate Title(s): P.R. Director; Director of Press Relations; Publicity Director

Salary Range: $26,000 to $75,000+

Employment Prospects: Fair

Advancement Prospects: Poor

Best Geographical Location(s) for Position: Cultural centers hosting major orchestras; other cities that host smaller orchestras

Prerequisites:

Education or training—College degree not always required, but sometimes preferred

Experience—Publicity and public relations experience in orchestral or nonorchestral situation

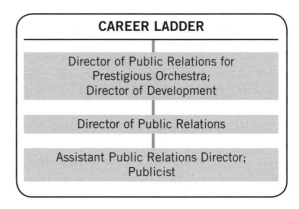

CAREER LADDER

Director of Public Relations for Prestigious Orchestra; Director of Development

Director of Public Relations

Assistant Public Relations Director; Publicist

Special Skills and Personality Traits—Good writing skills; ability to work under pressure; creativity; knowledge of orchestras

Position Description

The Director of Public Relations (P.R.) for an orchestra is in charge of handling the press and promotion of that orchestra and its activities.

Throughout the season, the orchestra puts on a number of concerts. It is the job of the Director of Public Relations to see that the community and the press know of these concerts. Most orchestras also plan special activities, such as children's concerts, educational activities, holiday shows, etc. The P.R. director must make sure that the community is aware of these events.

The way most Directors of Public Relations alert the community to orchestra activities is through publicity. This is attained through press releases and advertising.

P.R. directors must build up a media contact list to which to send out important news items. After writing a news release and sending it out, the P.R. director's job is not complete. He or she must follow up on stories, calling the press to see if they need additional information, photos, interviews, etc.

The Director of Public Relations works with the development department. When that department is trying to raise monies through an annual fund-raising drive, for example, the P.R. department will usually do a story on the activity.

The P.R. director will also put together a number of press parties, press conferences, cocktail parties, and other functions. These affairs are used by the P.R. director to help promote the orchestra.

The Director of P.R. might supervise the writing, layout, and printing of publications prepared for the orchestra, including those used for promotion, education, and fund-raising.

In his or her position, the Director of Public Relations might also work with other organizations or corporations for tie-in possibilities. For instance, the orchestra might work with a shopping mall in a promotion for both the mall and the orchestra.

The Director of P.R. would also do publicity on the hiring of a new conductor. He or she might write press releases on new section members. The individual must put together press packages for the media to use routinely or for special events.

If the orchestra hires a guest conductor, the Director of Public Relations may do a special news release as well as setting up interviews between the conductor and media.

The Director of Public Relations is responsible to the orchestra manager or managing director, depending on the size and structure of the organization. He or she might also be responsible to the orchestra's board of directors.

The Director of Public Relations for an orchestra might supervise a number of people in the organization's P.R. department or might be the sole employee of that department. This depends, of course, on the size and budget of the orchestra.

Salaries

Salaries of Directors of Public Relations for orchestras are usually commensurate with the size of the orchestra.

P.R. directors working for small orchestras might have yearly salaries of $26,000 or more. P.R. directors for these smaller orchestras might also work part-time or on a per-project basis. Fees for specific types of P.R. projects vary.

Directors of Public Relations working in larger orchestras have yearly incomes ranging from $29,000 to $75,000 or more annually.

Employment Prospects

If an individual is interested in working in an orchestral setting and can write and communicate fairly well, this may be the type of position to seek.

Most orchestras employ at least a part-time person for the position of Director of Public Relations or publicist.

Larger orchestras may have five or more people working in their P.R. departments.

Advancement Prospects

There are a number of ways for a Director of Public Relations to advance. The individual may seek a position with a more prestigious orchestra. These are often hard to obtain, as people in these positions do not tend to float from job to job. The individual may also move into the development department, possibly as director of development. Financially, this does not represent that much of a promotion; however, since these two jobs are often interrelated, many people do advance to these positions.

Education and Training

Directors of Public Relations in orchestras are not always required to hold college degrees, although it is sometimes preferred.

Courses in journalism, communications, public relations, publicity, and marketing help. A knowledge of the activities of an orchestra is helpful, too.

There are seminars and programs given by schools, associations, and organizations on public relations and music. These might be useful.

Experience, Skills, and Personality Traits

Any type of writing skill and experience is helpful to a Director of Public Relations. P.R. directors often come from the ranks of newspaper and magazine journalists.

Other P.R. directors work as assistants in the orchestra or with other companies. Still other individuals work as publicists in either music or nonmusic fields.

Whatever the experience, the P.R. director needs sound, creative writing skills. The individual should also have built up or be able to build up a list of media contacts.

As in most jobs in P.R., the director must have the ability to work under tremendous pressure.

Unions and Associations

The P.R. director of an orchestra might belong to the Public Relations Society of America (PRSA). This organization works to uphold the ethics of P.R. people. In addition, the organization offers seminars, a magazine, pamphlets, and other useful information.

The individual might also belong to the American Symphony Orchestra League (ASOL). This organization, too, provides many useful seminars, workshops, and a newsletter.

Tips for Entry

1. There are numerous internship programs in various orchestral management positions, including the public relations department. These internships are made available directly through orchestras, colleges, and organizations.
2. There are vacancies listed for these positions in the ASOL (American Symphony Orchestra League) newsletter, the Associated Council of the Arts newsletter, and many regional arts organization publications.
3. Even if there is not an opening listed, you might want to contact a number of orchestras and send them your résumé plus a few samples of your writing style. Ask the personnel people to keep your résumé on file in case an opening develops.
4. Make sure you check out opportunities online. Orchestras often list openings on their Web sites.

SUBSCRIPTIONS AND TICKET SERVICE DIRECTOR

CAREER PROFILE

Duties: Obtain new subscriptions for orchestra season; renew current subscriptions; keep records of ticket sales

Alternate Title(s): Head of Subscriptions; Ticket Service Director

Salary Range: $24,000 to $49,000+

Employment Prospects: Poor

Advancement Prospects: Fair

Best Geographical Location(s) for Position: Any city that hosts an orchestra, such as New York City, Boston, Memphis, Phoenix, Syracuse, Pittsburgh, Philadelphia, etc.

Prerequisites:

Education or Training—College degree not required for all positions, but may be preferred

Experience—Volunteer work with orchestras; fundraising; prior promotional work helpful; working in box office; ability to multitask

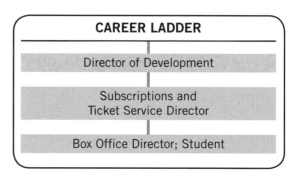

CAREER LADDER

```
           Director of Development

         Subscriptions and
       Ticket Service Director

       Box Office Director; Student
```

Special Skills and Personality Traits—Organization; ability to write; knowledge of orchestras; bookkeeping skills

---

Position Description

The Subscriptions and Ticket Service Director is responsible for selling and keeping track of tickets and subscriptions for the orchestra season.

In this position, the individual must put together programs to obtain new subscribers for the upcoming season. Although part of the income of the orchestra is derived from grants and funding, much of it comes from subscriptions. In order to procure these new subscriptions, the director of this department often runs a variety of campaigns directed toward locating potential subscribers. These programs might include mass telephoning, mailings, or telethons. Additionally, the individual runs advertisements and sends out press releases on the subject. Some of these functions might be handled in conjunction with the public relations department.

Depending on the orchestra, the Subscriptions Director may work with a number of volunteers who help run the above events. In a major orchestra, the director of the department may have a paid staff.

The Subscriptions and Ticket Service Director must also keep track of current subscribers. Renewal forms

have to be sent out at the appropriate time. In certain instances, these renewal forms must be followed up with phone calls. At times, the director of the department will ask a board member to make a follow-up phone call or visit a subscriber regarding a renewal.

The person in this position is in charge of coordinating the sales of individual concert tickets. Records must be kept on how many tickets are sold at each location. Tickets may be sold at the box office, schools, stores, or a ticket service. If a ticket service (such as Ticketron) is used, the Director must make sure they receive monies owed to them for ticket sales.

The individual in this job must keep precise records of everything in the department. He or she has to know at a glance who was sent what, when it was sent, when a follow-up call was made, etc. Records must also be maintained on monies arriving for subscriptions and tickets.

The Director of Subscriptions may be called upon to speak to groups or to attend functions on behalf of the orchestra. He or she usually works fairly regular hours. The director of this department is responsible to the orchestra manager and/or the board of directors.

Salaries

Salaries range widely for Subscriptions and Ticket Service Directors. In very small orchestras, the position may be a voluntary one. In large orchestras, an individual may earn from $24,000 to $49,000 or more yearly, depending on the size of the orchestra and its budget.

Employment Prospects

Employment opportunities in this type of position are not bountiful. There are only a limited number of orchestras employing a full-time paid person to do this job.

Individuals will find that only the larger orchestras, such as major and regional ones, have these jobs. Additionally, there is not a large turnover in this department.

Advancement Prospects

Advancement is difficult but possible. Individuals in this field may find employment in the same position in larger, more prestigious orchestras, or they may advance their careers by becoming directors of development.

In order to advance in the current organization, he or she may need additional training or education.

Education and Training

As in many positions in the music industry, educational requirements vary widely. In larger major orchestras, the position of Subscriptions and Ticket Service Director may require or prefer a college background or degree.

In a smaller orchestra the individual may need only bookkeeping experience and training.

Experience, Skills, and Personality Traits

A Subscriptions and Ticket Service Director must be a totally organized individual. He or she needs the ability to keep accurate records. A good memory is a must.

Additionally, the person seeking this job should have the ability to write well and creatively. The individual must possess a talent for supervising both staff and volunteers. Knowledge of bookkeeping is essential. The Subscriptions Director must be fully cognizant of the way an orchestra functions.

Unions and Associations

A Subscriptions and Ticket Service Director may belong to the American Symphony Orchestra League (ASOL), the Associated Council of the Arts, or any number of local arts councils.

Tips for Entry

1. If you think you might be interested in a position of this type, try volunteering. Go to an orchestra and ask if it would be possible to help out on a ticket subscription campaign.
2. Check with various orchestras and colleges to find out if they offer internships programs.
3. Openings are found in the American Symphony Orchestra League (ASOL) newsletter and various other arts council newsletters. On occasion, an orchestra may advertise an opening for a job of this type in the local newspaper.
4. Send a résumé and a cover letter to orchestras you might want to work with.
5. Check out openings online. Orchestra Web sites often advertise openings.

DIRECTOR OF EDUCATIONAL ACTIVITIES

Duties: Coordinate activities for students; design young people's concert series; plan learning activities relating to orchestra

Alternate Title(s): Education Director

Salary Range: $24,000 to $50,000+

Employment Prospects: Poor

Advancement Prospects: Poor

Best Geographical Location(s) for Position: Major cultural centers offer most opportunities

Prerequisites:

Education or Training—Bachelor's degree required or preferred for most positions

Experience—Experience in orchestra administration and business helpful

Special Skills and Personality Traits—Writing skills; knowledge of orchestra & music; public relations skills; communications skills

CAREER LADDER

Director of Educational Activities for Major Orchestra; Director of Public Relations, Fund-Raising, Development, Etc.

Director of Educational Activities

Assistant Director of Educational Activities; Publicist; Student

Position Description

The Director of Educational Activities in an orchestra is responsible for coordinating all orchestral activities for students and other young people in the community.

One of the main functions of this individual is to keep in close contact with the schools in the area surrounding the orchestra's base of operations. The director may call or meet with school district music supervisors, music teachers, etc.

At times, the orchestra may offer concerts to the schools. They might bring the entire orchestra or just parts of it directly into the school to perform. Other educational activities might include offering the conductor or other orchestra members as speakers at school assemblies or at career days.

The individual in this position works closely with the music administrator, managing director, and/or orchestra manager designing young people's concerts. These concerts may be coordinated with school visits by members of the orchestra.

As the director of this department, the individual may recommend reduced prices for student tickets. Additionally, the individual is responsible for making sure that students, parents, and administrators are aware of the special activities, ticket prices, etc. This may be accomplished by the director designing and sending brochures or posters to the schools, placing them in the surrounding areas, sending out press releases to newspapers, and mailing notices to current subscribers. This function may be accomplished with the help of the public relations director.

The Director of Educational Activities may plan tours for students of the orchestra hall, backstage, rehearsals, and/or business offices. He or she may prepare booklets dealing with the different career opportunities in the orchestral field. This person might counsel or find appropriate people to counsel students on educational requirements and/or training needs of various positions in the field.

It should be noted that this position is not found in all orchestras. In smaller orchestras, responsibilities of this job overlap into other areas such as public relations or the ticket subscription department.

The Director of Educational Activities may be responsible to the orchestra manager, the managing director, or the organization's board of directors.

Salaries

The Director of Educational Activities in an orchestra may work on a part-time or full-time basis, depending on the size of the orchestra. Part-time workers work by the project or by the hour.

Full-time people in this position have salaries that range from $24,000 to $50,000 or more annually. Salaries vary according to the size and budget of the orchestra and the specific duties of the individual.

Employment Prospects

This is a hard position to locate. Jobs are very limited. In smaller orchestras, this job is often combined with the duties of other jobs. There are only a limited number of orchestras in the country in which to seek positions. Orchestra jobs in this specialty area are so hard to locate that there is not a high turnover rate.

Advancement Prospects

An individual in the position of Director of Educational Activities may advance his or her career in a number of ways. The person may seek a job in the same field with a more prestigious orchestra. The person may move up in the organization and become a director of public relations, development, fund-raising, etc.

Advancement opportunities are poor. There is not a high turnover rate in any of the jobs in the orchestra. This makes it difficult to advance to another position.

Education and Training

Educational requirements for the Director of Educational Activities in an orchestra vary. In some jobs—mainly in the larger major orchestras—individuals are either required or preferred to hold college degrees. Other positions—those in smaller orchestras—do not require anything over a high school diploma.

Experience, Skills, and Personality Traits

People in this position must be knowledgeable about the working of the orchestra and music in general. They must have the ability to write clearly and creatively.

Individuals working in this job must be articulate, congenial, and able to relate well to young people.

Some individuals working as Directors of Educational Activities obtain the position soon after leaving college. Other individuals work in various capacities with the orchestra or at arts councils. There are other people who work as reporters, publicists, or musicians before entering the field.

Unions and Associations

The Director of Educational Activities of an orchestra may belong to the American Symphony Orchestra League (ASOL). This association offers seminars, information, and other help to individuals working with orchestras.

Tips for Entry

1. Look for seminars and courses on orchestral management and administration. These are given by colleges, universities, associations, organizations, and orchestras.
2. Internships—paid, unpaid, and credit-bearing—are sometimes available. Check with your college, various orchestras, and the American Symphony Orchestra League (ASOL).
3. Openings for these positions are often listed in the ASOL newsletter as well as in various arts council newsletters.
4. If you're still in school, you might volunteer your services or look for a summer job in this career area, either in an orchestra or in a similar position with arts council projects.
5. Surf the Web for openings. Check out Web sites of orchestras. Opportunities may also be located on job search sites such as hotjobs.com, monster.com, and simplyhired.com.

PERSONNEL DIRECTOR

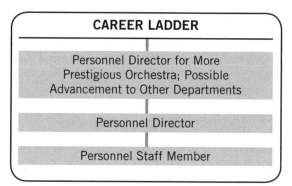

Position Description

The Personnel Director of an orchestra is responsible for all the hirings and firings of personnel in that orchestra. He or she is in charge of sending out notices whenever openings occur in either the business end or the talent end of the operation. These notices are usually sent to schools, colleges, conservatories, newsletters, associations, and organizations. In addition to notices, the Personnel Director writes ads and places them in newspapers or magazines to alert people to these openings.

The Personnel Director screens all applications that come to the orchestra. In the case of talent positions (section members, leaders, etc.), he or she will usually work in conjunction with the conductor, the concertmaster, and the section leaders who will be doing the auditioning.

In cases where the position is on the business side, the Personnel Director would not only screen the applications, but also give preliminary interviews. After the first interviews are held, the Personnel Director calls back the best candidates for further interviews.

Substitute musicians are often required by orchestras. It is the duty of the Personnel Director to hire these substitutes. As these individuals are often needed on the spur of the moment, the Personnel Director must maintain a list of backups for each instrument in the orchestra.

Before an individual is hired, the Personnel Director usually explains orchestra policies, rules, regulations, and salaries. He or she must see that all forms are filled out and all information needed by the orchestra is supplied.

In the event that an individual must be fired, this job usually falls to the Personnel Director, too. The Personnel Director keeps track of employee attendance and, in the case of musicians, punctuality.

This individual works with all the other departments of the orchestra. He or she must have the ability to put people into jobs for which they are best suited.

Salaries

Salaries for the Personnel Director of an orchestra vary according to the size of the orchestra, its budget, and its location. Earnings will also depend on the qualifications of the individual and his or her duties. The Personnel Director has a salary between $26,000 and $65,000 plus annually.

Employment Prospects

There are only limited positions open for Personnel Directors in orchestras. Employment prospects for this job are not good. There are more and more people with personnel training that want to get into work involving music and/or orchestras, and there are not enough positions to go around. Additionally, there is not a high turnover of people in these positions.

Advancement Prospects

Advancement in this job is difficult. Finding a position as a Personnel Director with a more prestigious organization is very hard. As competition is tough and people don't leave these jobs often, it is almost impossible.

Personnel Directors may, however, advance to other departments in the orchestra if they are qualified. Personnel Directors with the correct training may also go into labor relations and negotiating.

Education and Training

Educational requirements for the position of Personnel Director vary from orchestra to orchestra. Some do not require a college degree, while others do. Certain positions require at least some college background.

Major orchestras often require their Personnel Directors to have degrees in personnel administration.

There are colleges around the country that grant degrees in the field of personnel.

Experience, Skills, and Personality Traits

Personnel Directors need the ability to put the right people in the right jobs. In the symphony orchestra, Personnel Directors must have at least a basic knowledge of music and of the other business positions in the organization.

The individual must be skilled at interviewing potential employees, screening applications, etc.

In addition, the Personnel Director must be extremely articulate, able to communicate ideas well, and organized.

Unions and Associations

The Personnel Director of an orchestra may be a member of the American Symphony Orchestra League (ASOL), the Associated Council of the Arts, or other arts councils in the area.

Tips for Entry

1. Try to find an internship program. Internships help you get a foot in the door.
2. Openings for these positions are sometimes listed in the American Symphony Orchestra League (ASOL) newsletter, the Associated Council of the Arts newsletter, regional arts organizations' publications, and local newspaper advertisements.
3. No matter what educational requirement an orchestra has for this position, it doesn't hurt to be overtrained. It makes it easier to get a job and easier to advance if you have the education beforehand.
4. Check out some of the more popular job search sites such as hotjobs.com, monster.com, and simplyhired.com, and go from there.
5. Don't forget to check out orchestra Web sites. Many list job openings.

ORCHESTRAL MUSIC LIBRARIAN

Duties: Catalog and order music for orchestra; assist conductor copying scores and parts
Alternate Title(s): None
Salary Range: $27,000 to $62,000+
Employment Prospects: Poor
Advancement Prospects: Poor
Best Geographical Location(s) for Position: Cities that host larger orchestras, such as New York City, Boston, Memphis, Phoenix, Syracuse, Pittsburgh, Philadelphia, etc.
Prerequisites:
  Education or Training—Bachelor's degree in music history or theory and library sciences; master's degree in music or library science often required

CAREER LADDER

Music Librarian for Major Orchestra

Music Librarian

Music Librarian Assistant

Experience—Position as music librarian assistant; library experience
Special Skills and Personality Traits—Interest in orchestral music; extensive knowledge of music; ability to copy musical notations; organization

Position Description

Orchestral Music Librarians combine their skills as librarians with their love for and comprehensive knowledge of music. An Orchestral Music Librarian has many duties. He or she catalogs the orchestra's printed music. The individual is also responsible for ordering new music. If the orchestra decides not to purchase certain pieces of music, the music librarian is in charge of locating the music, renting it, and seeing that it gets back when it is no longer needed.

The Orchestral Music Librarian must be competent in copying musical markings. The individual often assists the conductor after he or she has looked at a piece of music and made changes in it. The music librarian may copy parts for the different section members, making the necessary corrections and adding bowings and/or phrasings where indicated.

During rehearsals or concerts, it is the Orchestral Music Librarian's job to hand out the music to the section members. These are collected after the rehearsal or performance has concluded.

The music librarian travels with the orchestra when it goes on tour or performs special concerts. On the road, the individual is totally responsible for the sheet music. The music librarian also makes contact with any guest conductor the orchestra might be hosting. It is his or her duty to question the conductor about his or her music requirements.

The Orchestral Music Librarian has more contact with live music than a music librarian working at a school or a library. Although many of the responsibilities are the same, there are some differences. The music librarian must decide what type of setting he or she prefers.

The Orchestral Music Librarian does not work regular hours, as music librarians in other places of employment usually do. He or she is usually responsible to the orchestra conductor.

Salaries

As with all orchestral positions, salaries depend on the type of orchestra. A music librarian working for a major orchestra makes between $27,000 and $62,000 or more annually.

A music librarian working for a regional or metropolitan orchestra might make between $25,000 and $35,000 or more annually. In local orchestras, the music librarian is often a section member who works gratis.

Employment Prospects

Employment prospects are poor for individuals seeking positions as Orchestral Music Librarians. There are a limited number of orchestras in the country and not every orchestra employs a paid individual in this position. The best possibilities for opportunities will be in areas hosting major, regional, and metropolitan orchestras, such as New York City, Boston, Memphis, Phoenix, Syracuse, Pittsburgh, Philadelphia, etc.

Advancement Prospects

The possibility for advancement is poor as a result of the small number of music librarian positions available in orchestras. There are more candidates than there are jobs to fill.

An individual in an orchestral setting might find that he or she wants to move into another type of position, such as one in a library or educational setting. However, these, too, may be limited.

Education and Training

The education needed for a music librarian working in an orchestra is much the same as for any music librarian. All positions require at least an undergraduate degree in music theory or history. Some positions require a dual major in music and library sciences. Still others require a master's degree in either music or library sciences.

Additionally, the Orchestral Music Librarian in this setting needs training in copying parts and scores.

Experience, Skills, and Personality Traits

Orchestral Music Librarians often work as music librarian assistants prior to becoming full-fledged music librarians. These positions are usually available only in larger symphonies. However, there are internship programs to help the aspiring music librarian gain experience.

The Orchestral Music Librarian must have neat handwriting. The individual must also be able to copy conductor's markings on scores.

In addition, the Orchestral Music Librarian must be extremely organized and very personable.

Unions and Associations

The Orchestral Music Librarian might belong to a number of associations. These include the American Library Association (ALA), the Special Libraries Association (SLA), and the American Symphony Orchestra League (ASOL). These organizations help the individual to maintain contacts and they provide seminars, newsletters, and other valuable information. The Orchestral Music Librarian might additionally belong to the American Federation of Musicians (AFM).

Tips for Entry

1. Try to find an internship as a music librarian in a major, regional, or metropolitan orchestra.
2. Act as the music librarian of your college or school orchestra or band for experience.
3. Send your résumé and a short cover letter to orchestras. Remember to request that your résumé be kept on file if there are no current openings.
4. Openings may be advertised in the classified section of newspapers. Look under headings such as "Orchestras," "Orchestral Music Librarian," and "Music Librarian."
5. Openings may also be listed on Web sites of orchestras as well as on job search sites such as hotjobs.com, monster.com, and simplyhired.com.

ARENAS, FACILITIES, HALLS, AND CLUBS

CONCERT HALL MANAGER

Position Description

A Concert Hall Manager is in charge of managing the hall and overseeing all activities that occur in the facility. The individual has diverse duties to perform depending on the facility and the position.

One of the functions of the hall manager is to supervise all employees of the facility. These workers include electricians, sound people, lighting people, ticket sellers, ushers, security, clean-up people, and a host of others. In some situations, the person might also hire a publicist, public relations firm, or advertising agency to handle hall promotion. In other circumstances, the hall owner might handle this project. As a rule, the Concert Hall Manager has the authority to hire people and fire them. In directing the activities of all these workers, the manager tries to ensure the most efficient operations possible for the theater.

Another function of the Concert Hall Manager is to oversee the financial business of the hall. The individual must try to keep the hall or theater booked.

Sometimes the manager will buy the talent; other times he or she will rent out the hall to various promoters. Whichever system is used, the individual must negotiate to get the best price. When promoters rent the hall, the individual must attempt to obtain the best rental fee, giving away the fewest possible extras.

The Concert Hall Manager may be responsible for payroll. In some cases, if a union is involved (and they frequently are), the individual must see that all union regulations are enforced at the hall. Unions involved might include the musicians union, the electricians union, and others.

After an event has been planned, the manager is in charge of advertising it and publicizing it to maximize the attendance. This might be accomplished with the assistance of an advertising agency and a public relations firm. The hall may have its own in-house advertising agency and/or publicist. The Concert Hall Manager must be knowledgeable about obtaining the most exposure for an event for the least amount of money.

It is the responsibility of the Concert Hall Manager to make sure that the facility is in good condition and clean at all times. If there are things that need repair, the individual oversees the work. On occasion, the hall may be refurbished or completely done over. The hall manager, once again, is in charge of these work projects.

The hall manager must be ready to handle all types of crises effectively and without panicking. Potential problems include an act not showing up for a performance, union workers going on strike before a show, inclement weather on the night of a performance when tickets are being sold at the door, or a patron getting unruly during a show. There are, of course, many other things that can occur.

The Concert Hall Manager must see to it that the money that is to be paid to acts is available on the night of a show. He or she must also be sure to fulfill any contract riders exactly as they are written.

The individual must work closely with all the media in the immediate area. Most of the time these press people will be offered press passes or backstage passes. Maintaining a good relationship with the press and other media goes a long way toward helping the theater become successful.

The Concert Hall Manager works long, irregular hours. He or she is responsible to the owner of the theater, hall, or arena.

Salaries

The salary of a Concert Hall or Arena Manager or Director varies greatly depending on the size of the venue, the location, the prestige of the hall, qualifications of the individual, and the duties.

A person managing a small concert theater in an out-of-the-way location will not make as much as one who is managing a large, prestigious hall in a major metropolitan area. The individual managing a small theater might earn from $26,000 to $33,000 yearly. Those who manage larger, more prestigious halls in major metropolitan areas can earn from $45,000 to $90,000 or more annually.

Employment Prospects

Employment prospects for a Concert Hall Manager are fair. There are different types of halls, a range of sizes, and various locations. Major cities have the greatest number of concert halls and/or arenas. However, it may be more difficult to obtain a job in these locations.

Smaller cities have fewer opportunities, but jobs are usually easier to obtain.

Advancement Prospects

Advancement prospects are fair for Concert Hall Managers. The most common path to career advancement is landing a similar job in a larger, more prestigious hall. In order to do this, individuals may need to relocate to obtain a better position. Some individuals also move into corporate positions in large arenas.

Education and Training

Educational requirements vary for positions as Concert Hall Managers. While there are some jobs that require only a high school diploma, most employers now demand or prefer that a candidate hold a minimum of a bachelor's degree. Good choices for majors include music, theater, business, marketing or a related field.

Courses, workshops, and seminars in theater management, business, bookkeeping, accounting, communications, marketing, and other music business–oriented subjects will be useful.

Experience, Skills, and Personality Traits

Concert Hall Managers come from a variety of backgrounds. Some individuals may originally have aspired to be musicians, actors, or actresses, but when that was not possible, they went into managing concert halls as a way of maintaining contact with the industry.

Experience requirements vary depending on the size and prestige of the facility. Larger, more prestigious facilities generally require three to five years of experience in the field. This may be obtained through positions as concert hall assistant managers. Smaller halls generally have less stringent experience requirements.

Concert Hall Managers must be responsible, organized individuals who can multitask successfully. They must be adept at reading concert contracts and the long riders that often are part of them. The ability to handle crises calmly and effectively is critical.

Individuals should have excellent verbal and written communication skills. Concert Hall Managers must additionally be totally knowledgeable about the music business and concert hall and arena affairs.

Unions and Associations

Concert Hall Managers may belong to the International Association of Assembly Managers (IAAM). Concert Hall Managers may have to deal with a variety of unions, including the American Federation of Musicians (AFM).

Tips for Entry

1. Your chances of obtaining a job, if you are not experienced, are better in a smaller facility and/or a smaller city.
2. Jobs for theater or Concert Hall Managers are often advertised in the classified or display sections of newspapers. They can also be located online via many of the job search sites such as hotjobs.com, monster.com, and simplyhired.com.
3. Try to find a job as an assistant manager in a small venue. The employee turnover is higher in these halls, and you will have a better chance of promotion in a shorter span of time.
4. Many openings are advertised in a word-of-mouth fashion. Get friendly with Hall Managers in other facilities.

CONCERT HALL MARKETING DIRECTOR

CAREER PROFILE

Duties: Develop and implement marketing campaigns; oversee all aspects of concert hall marketing efforts; oversee public relations and advertising departments; develop budgets; design and develop marketing materials

Alternate(s) Title: Director of Marketing; Marketing Manager

Salary Range: $25,000 to $100,000+

Employment Prospects: Fair

Advancement Prospects: Fair

Best Geographical Location(s) for Position: Positions located throughout the country; greatest number of positions are located in culturally active cities hosting large numbers of concert halls and similar venues

Prerequisites:

Education or Training—Minimum of bachelor's degree in marketing, advertising, public relations, communications or related industry

Experience—Experience working in marketing, advertising and public relations generally necessary; experience in music or entertainment industry helpful

Special Skills and Personality Traits—Creativity; good verbal and written communication skills; knowledge and understanding of music and entertainment industry; people skills; marketing skills; publicity skills; ability to conceptualize ideas

CAREER LADDER

Marketing Director for Larger or More Prestigious Concert Hall or Vice President of Marketing at Large Arena or Venue

Marketing Director—Concert Hall

Assistant Marketing Director—Concert Hall, Assistant Public Relations Director—Concert Hall or Marketing Director in Other Industry

Position Description

Concert halls, like other entertainment venues, may present a wide array of music and other entertainment. Depending on the facility, this might include concerts in various genres, such as rock, pop, folk, country, hip hop, R&B, and classical. Some halls also host comedy shows, specialty acts, and ballet and other types of dance performances.

Whether a concert hall is in a large city or in the suburbs, it usually offers a variety of entertainment options for its public. Whatever the options, in order to remain viable, concert halls must constantly vie to attract people who will buy tickets and fill their seats.

The challenge for concert halls is finding ways to market their facility so that people will be aware that they exist and then attend concerts and other events there. The individual in charge of this task is the marketing director.

The Concert Hall Marketing Director is expected to develop and implement concepts and campaigns to successfully market the venue and promote its events. Within the scope of the job, the individual may have varied duties.

The Concert Hall Marketing Director is responsible for determining the most effective techniques and programs to promote the concert hall. As part of the job, he or she must plan, coordinate, and implement all of the venue's marketing goals and objectives. If the concert hall is a large one, the marketing director may oversee a staff of people, including those in the public relations, publicity, and advertising departments. If the concert hall is smaller, the individual may handle many of the tasks of those departments him- or herself.

A great deal of the marketing strategy the director develops is focused on the demographics of the people the venue is attempting to attract. Are concerts geared toward older adults? What about younger adults? How about families? What about teens? How about senior citizens?

What types of acts are booked into the facility? Are the acts established? Are some of the acts hot commodities that can almost sell themselves? Should the hall be booking different types of entertainment? Determining the answers to these questions can help the marketing director choose just the right strategies and campaigns.

The director must do a great deal of research to learn the precise demographics of the people attending events at the concert hall. He or she must also do research on other entertainment venues in the area. Knowing the competition can often prove critical to success.

Research might be accomplished by utilizing surveys, questionnaires, focus groups, and so on. Information may be obtained in person at events or may be obtained from people who are purchasing tickets. In many cases, this information is obtained through direct mail. It might also be gathered via the Internet.

The individual may come up with simple, traditional marketing ideas such as two-for-one promotions, whereby people can buy two tickets for the price of one, or discount promotions for seniors or children. The marketing director might work with local restaurants putting together promotions allowing people who buy tickets to concerts at the hall to get discounts on dinner before the show or dessert or snacks after the concert.

Some Concert Hall Marketing Directors plan opening night parties, lunches with the musical artists who are performing at the hall, or meet-and-greets. Others work with local radio stations, television stations, or newspapers, putting together promotions, contests, and sweepstakes offering tickets as prizes. Some marketing directors develop promotions based on holidays.

Very successful Concert Hall Marketing Directors constantly come up with new, innovative, and creative ways of attracting people and prompting them to purchase tickets to events. These may include a wide array of promotions and special events.

The Concert Hall Marketing Director is responsible for overseeing all of the advertising for concerts held at the hall, as well as special promotions and events. The director may work with the public relations and advertising departments to publicize, advertise, and implement promotions. In smaller halls, the marketing director might be responsible for handling the public relations and advertising functions as well as their implementation. In some cases, the marketing director may also work with an outside advertising agency.

The Concert Hall Marketing Director must determine the most effective places to advertise the hall in general, as well as particular concerts and other events. In order to do this, he or she may meet with representatives from the various media outlets, including newspapers, periodicals, television, cable, radio, and the Internet. Once the director selects where to advertise, he or she must decide how much adverting to purchase.

Concert halls may produce their own events or may bring in outside promoters. Often, when an outside promoter will pay for all or part of the advertising. This can save the concert hall thousands of dollars.

An important responsibility of the Concert Hall Marketing Director is to develop annual budgets that detail projected spending for the implementation of all marketing campaigns, advertising, promotion, publicity, and department staffing. Once this is completed and approved, the marketing director must do everything he or she can to stay within budget.

Another function of the marketing director is to design and develop marketing materials for the concert hall. These might include pamphlets, brochures, posters, newsletters, etc. The individual might do this him- or herself or assign the tasks to a staff member or an outside vendor.

The Concert Hall Marketing Director uses every avenue possible to get publicity for the concert hall and the concerts being held there. Once again, depending on the size and structure of the concert hall, he or she may handle this task, assign it to a marketing staff member, or hand it over to the public relations department or a publicist. The marketing director may often do interviews on radio, television, or in the newspaper to keep the concert hall in the public eye in a positive manner. He or she may also arrange for interviews or feature stories on the hall or the entertainment being provided there.

The Internet has changed the way everyone does business, and concert halls are no exception. People often go online to check out upcoming concerts, consult schedules of shows, purchase tickets, or just to see what is happening. Marketing the site is essential. The marketing director may handle the marketing of the site or may oversee a Web site marketing manager.

As part of the job, the marketing director must plan and coordinate the Web site's marketing goals and objectives. How will people know the Web site is online? How will they know the Web address? How will they find it? Who is the site being marketed to? What will bring people to it? The marketing director must find ways to attract people to the site who wish to learn more about what is happening at the concert hall.

No matter who is in charge of the concert hall's Web site, the marketing director must always be sure that the hall's Web address is in as many places as possible. This includes all advertising, brochures, newsletters, and so on. If the Concert Hall Marketing Director can get the Web address known, people will be able to find it easily when they are looking for information on the hall.

The marketing director will also work to develop e-mail blasts and other forms of e-mail marketing. Utilizing e-mail and the Internet means that with the click of a mouse, the Concert Hall Marketing Director can, for example, let people know there are tickets available for an event or that the hall is holding a special promotion.

The Concert Hall Marketing Director must continually monitor the effectiveness of the marketing campaigns. If it is working, he or she will continue with the campaign. If not, the director must revamp the program.

Salaries

Earnings for Concert Hall Marketing Directors can range from approximately $25,000 to $100,000 or more. Variables affecting earnings include the size, location, and prestige of the concert hall and the experience, qualifications, and responsibilities of the director.

Those with a great deal of experience, handling the marketing for larger, more prestigious halls in major cities will have higher earnings than their counterparts working in smaller facilities.

Employment Prospects

Employment prospects are fair for individuals seeking to become Concert Hall Marketing Directors. Concert halls are located throughout the country. Halls range in size and prestige. The greatest number of opportunities will exist in culturally active areas hosting a large number of concert halls.

Those just starting their careers may have an easier time breaking in at a smaller hall where they can obtain experience and then climb the career ladder.

Advancement Prospects

Advancement prospects are fair for marketing directors working in concert halls. The most common method of climbing the career ladder is for a prospective director to locate similar positions in larger or more prestigious halls. This generally results in increased responsibilities and earnings. Depending on the specific facility, some individuals may also be promoted to vice president of

marketing. In general, this type of position exists only in large concert halls. Still others become marketing directors in other industries.

Education and Training

Concert Hall Marketing Directors usually are required to hold a minimum of a bachelor's degree. Good choices of majors include marketing, public relations, advertising, business, communications, music business management, or a related field.

Courses, seminars, or workshops in publicity, marketing, advertising, public relations, promotion, music, or the entertainment industry will be helpful for their educational value and opportunities to establish contacts.

Experience, Skills, and Personality Traits

Experience requirements for Concert Hall Marketing Directors vary depending on the specific facility, its prestige, size, and location. Generally, the larger or more prestigious the concert hall, the more experience is required. Concert halls in smaller areas may require only one or two years of marketing experience. More prestigious concert halls in larger cities may require applicants to have five years of experience or more.

Concert Hall Marketing Directors need to be extremely creative individuals. The ability to develop and conceptualize unique ideas is essential. Individuals must be highly articulate in this type of job. Excellent verbal and written communication skills are critical.

A working knowledge of publicity, promotion, public relations, advertising, and research techniques is necessary, as is a thorough understanding of the inside workings of the music and entertainment industries.

The Concert Hall Marketing Director must be organized with the ability to multitask effectively. Supervisory skills and interpersonal skills are also a must.

Unions and Associations

Concert Hall Marketing Directors may belong to a number of trade associations that provide professional support and guidance. These might include the American Marketing Association (AMA), the Marketing Research Association (MRA), and the Public Relations Society of America (PRSA). They might also belong to the International Association of Assembly Managers (IAAM) or various organizations in the music industry.

Tips for Entry

1. Send your résumé and a short cover letter to concert halls inquiring about opportunities. Request that your résumé be kept on file if there are no current openings. Just because you don't see a

job advertised, doesn't mean one doesn't exist. The "hidden job market" is an opportunity to let people know you are available.

2. Openings may be advertised in the classified section of newspapers. Look under such headings as "Concert Hall," "Marketing Director," "Director of Marketing," "Marketing Manager," "Marketing," "Entertainment," "Music," or "Concert Hall Marketing Director."

3. Openings may also be located online. Check out some of the more traditional job search sites, such as monster.com and hotjobs.com. Then surf the Web for other options. Use keywords such as "Concert Hall Marketing Director."

4. If you are still in school, consider finding an internship in the marketing or management office of a concert hall. Contact concert halls in your area to check into the possibilities.

5. Look for seminars, workshops, and courses on all aspects of marketing, publicity, public relations, promotion, and music/entertainment events. In addition to the educational value, these courses can help you to hone your skills and provide the opportunity to make valuable contacts.

STAGE MANAGER

CAREER PROFILE

Duties: Supervise and oversee all activities occurring onstage in a theater, club, concert hall, arena, etc.; may be responsible for lighting, curtain changes, etc.; in charge of backstage area

Alternate Title(s): None

Salary Range: $24,000 to $75,000+

Employment Prospects: Fair

Advancement Prospects: Poor

Best Geographical Location(s) for Position: Large metropolitan cities offer the most opportunities

Prerequisites:

Education or Training—No formal education required; training in lighting, sound, and/or electronics helpful

Experience—Lighting technician; sound person; assistant stage manager

CAREER LADDER

Stage Manager in Large, Prestigious Concert Hall, Club, Theater, etc.; Hall or Club Manager

Stage Manager

Sound Technician; Lighting Technician; Assistant Stage Manager; Student

Special Skills and Personality Traits—Responsibility; dependability; enjoyment of music; knowledge of lighting technology; cognizance of sound and/or electronics; supervisory skills; ability to get along with people

Position Description

The Stage Manager is the individual in charge of much that occurs onstage in a concert hall, theater, arena, club, etc. Depending on the situation, he or she may work alone or oversee the work of an assistant and/or an entire staff.

The Stage Manager must be present during rehearsals and concerts. His or her duties depend on the type of venue, its size, and the kind of concert.

If the Stage Manager is working in a very large concert hall or theater, he or she might be responsible for supervising or controlling the lighting of the stage and the room. For example, during a show the Stage Manager might have the house or room lights off and the stage lit brightly. Or the stage may be dark, illuminated by a spotlight. The Stage Manager must find out during the rehearsal exactly when the act wants each kind of lighting. He or she probably will go over the show concept with the act or its management, road management, or lighting technician.

Many of the top rock acts travel with their own lighting technician and/or light show. In these instances the Stage Manager works with the act's technician, helping and advising. The Stage Manager may or may not be responsible for the lighting in these circumstances.

The Stage Manager may also be responsible for controlling the volume on the microphones. Once again, if an act comes in with its own sound people, the Stage

Manager may just help and advise these people. In other situations, the Stage Manager might oversee a resident sound technician.

The Stage Manager is in charge of curtain changes. This includes making sure that the curtains are opened at the proper times and closed when there is an intermission or the show is finished.

The Stage Manager is also responsible for keeping the backstage area as clear as possible. Many times, with very well-known acts, the backstage area gets crowded and noisy. It is up to the individual to check for backstage passes and enforce any rules and regulations necessary to clear the area of unnecessary people.

At times, the Stage Manager may have the responsibility of making sure that the act has water, soda, juice, towels, etc., in their dressing room.

The Stage Manager might be the one who tells the act when to begin or when they should go onstage. He or she may also signal to the act when their show should be over.

The individual works late hours in this job. He or she is usually responsible to the facility manager or owner.

Salaries

Salaries of Stage Managers vary according to the type of venue, the geographical location, and the qualifications and duties of the individual.

Generally, the larger and more prestigious a theater, club, concert hall, arena, etc., is, the larger the Stage Manager's salary.

Individuals working as Stage Managers may earn from $24,000 to $75,000 plus annually.

Employment Prospects

Employment prospects for Stage Managers are fair. Almost every theater, concert hall, and arena hires a Stage Manager. Clubs might hire individuals for this position or may delegate their responsibilities to other people.

If an individual works in a smaller venue, he or she may be hired as a Stage Manager and also have additional duties.

Metropolitan areas tend to have more positions.

Advancement Prospects

It is difficult for a Stage Manager to advance his or her career. The individual may obtain a position in a larger or more prestigious concert hall, club, theater, etc. In some situations, the individual may go on to become a club or theater manager or talent buyer. In other situations, the Stage Manager is just working in that position to be close to the live music business. He or she may be an aspiring musician, songwriter, etc.

Education and Training

No formal education is required for the position of Stage Manager. The individual may require training in sound, lighting, electronics, etc., depending on the position. If he or she is hoping to advance to club or theater manager, the Stage Manager may consider taking some business classes.

Experience, Skills, and Personality Traits

The Stage Manager must enjoy music. He or she will probably have to listen to quite a bit of it. The individual must be dependable and reliable. He or she needs the ability to get along with others. Supervisory skills may be necessary.

The Stage Manager should also know as much as possible about electronics, lighting, and sound equipment.

The individual in this position may have been a sound technician, a lighting technician, or an assistant Stage Manager, or might just have finished school.

Unions and Associations

Stage Managers may belong to the International Alliance of Theatrical Stage Employees (IATSE). They may also belong to the American Guild of Musical Artists (AGMA) under certain conditions.

Tips for Entry

1. Stage Manager jobs are often advertised in the classified sections of newspapers. Look under headings such as "Stage Manager," "Concert Hall," "Arena," and "Night Club."
2. You might consider visiting clubs, theaters, concert halls, etc. Speak to the manager of any of these venues. Tell him or her of your qualifications and leave a résumé. Follow up by writing a letter thanking the person for talking to you.
3. Volunteer your services as a Stage Manager in a community, school, or church concert or play. It will give you useful experience.
4. The more skills you have, the better your chances are to find a job. Learn all you can about lighting, sound, electronics, stage techniques, etc.
5. You might consider taking a theater course to learn concepts that might be helpful to you.
6. Job openings may also be located online. Check out some of the more popular job seach sites such as monster.com, hotjobs.com, and simplyhired.com and go from there. Don't forget to check out the Web sites of theaters, concert halls, arenas, and night clubs.

RESIDENT SOUND TECHNICIAN

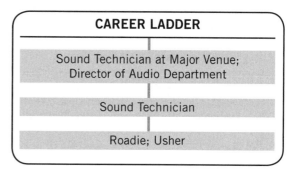

Position Description

The Resident Sound Technician of a hall is responsible for the basic sound engineering of a concert. The technician may work in a club, theater, concert hall, arena, school, or any similar location. The individual may be a full-time or a part-time employee.

The Sound Technician oversees the set-up of the sound equipment. The objective is to have everything in just the right place in order to produce the best possible sound. As the Resident Sound Technician, the individual must be aware of any acoustical problems in the room. Understanding the acoustical problems is just the beginning of a sound technician's job. Solving the problem is the prime responsibility. The more familiar the person is with the room and its problems, the better he or she can counsel the touring technician employed by the act or the act's road manager.

In the position of Resident Sound Technician, the individual must attend all sound checks scheduled before a concert. During these sound checks, the individual will talk to the act's road manager or act members in order to determine exactly what type of sound they require. The technician will also discuss any special effects the act likes to have during the show.

The Resident Sound Technician might ask questions involving how the act wants its music balanced. The individual might advise the act on the volume requirement of the hall and should be prepared to regulate the sound.

During a concert or show the Resident Sound Technician is responsible for running the sound board. The sound board is usually set up somewhere in the middle of the front of the stage. From this location the technician can best hear the sound and make the proper adjustments.

After the concert, the Resident Sound Technician will go over the equipment and check for any problems. If repairs are required, the technician will either make them or arrange for others to take care of them immediately.

The Resident Sound Technician works closely with the act's road manager. In some cases, the act appearing at the club or hall will travel with their own sound technician. Under these circumstances, the Resident Sound Technician will act as an advisor and overseer.

People in these positions must usually work late evening hours. Work schedules do not begin, however, until the afternoon.

Salaries

Resident Sound Technicians may work either part time or full time. On a part-time basis, they will probably be paid by the hour or the show. Rates can vary from minimum wage to approximately $100 per hour.

Sound technicians who work full time may earn $25,000 to $60,000 or more annually, depending on the type and size of the club, hall, etc., that they are involved with. Other factors affecting earnings include the experience and responsibilities of the individual. Resident Sound Technicians working in unionized facilities have minimum earnings set by the union.

Employment Prospects

Employment prospects for Resident Sound Technicians are fair. Qualified individuals may find employment in a variety of clubs, halls, arenas, schools, or theaters. Some of these positions may be part time. People seeking employment in this type of job category may have to relocate to areas where there are greater opportunities.

Advancement Prospects

Advancement prospects are fair for Resident Sound Technicians. Some individuals climb the career ladder by locating similar positions at larger, more prestigious facilities. Others are promoted to the director of the theater or hall's audio department.

Some Resident Sound Technicians working in concert halls, arenas, or clubs are picked up by major touring artists seeking qualified sound people to work for them on the road.

Education and Training

There is no formal educational requirement for a position as a Resident Sound Technician. Different halls or clubs may require that applicants have some training, either formal or informal, in electronics and sound recording. There are a variety of technical and vocational schools that teach electronics. Most people, however, pick up the basics of sound engineering by watching and listening to others.

Experience, Skills, and Personality Traits

A Resident Sound Technician working in a hall, club, arena, etc., must be able to work well with people.

Many times the sound technician who travels with an act will accompany the group to the hall. The Resident Sound Technician may have to advise or consult with this individual. It is imperative that the individual be a responsible type of person. He or she must be at sound checks on time to oversee things, even if there is another technician hired by the group working the sound equipment at a concert.

The Resident Sound Technician must have a good knowledge of electronics, the sound board, and other sound equipment. The individual must have a good musical "ear" and enjoy music.

Unions and Associations

Resident Sound Technicians may belong to the International Alliance of Theatrical Stage Employees (IATSE). This is a bargaining union for individuals working in theater situations.

Tips for Entry

1. Sound technician positions are often advertised in the help wanted sections of newspapers. Check under "Sound Technician," "Sound Engineer," and "Audio Technician."
2. Check the clubs and theaters in your area that employ Resident Sound Technicians. Talk to the managers of these clubs and theaters and tell them of your qualifications. Follow up the discussion by sending them your résumé to keep on file.
3. You might consider a short stint as an apprentice to a Resident Sound Technician. This will provide you with added on-the-job experience. The sound technician may leave the job or know of other openings. All this can be useful to you.
4. Check out Web sites of concert halls, arenas, and theaters. Many post openings.

NIGHTCLUB MANAGER

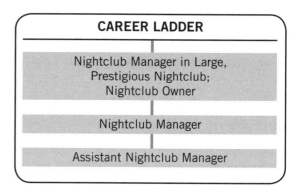

CAREER LADDER

Nightclub Manager in Large, Prestigious Nightclub; Nightclub Owner

Nightclub Manager

Assistant Nightclub Manager

the entertainment and/or music business, booking acts, negotiating, and contracts; ability to deal under pressure

Position Description

A Nightclub Manager is responsible for overseeing the day-to-day (or night-to-night) functions of a nightclub. Duties may differ depending on the type of club an individual manages. In many instances, the Nightclub Manager is also the club owner.

As the Nightclub Manager, a person may be responsible for not only hiring the entertainment, but deciding what type of entertainment the club will use. For example, should the club cater to country fans, dance-music fans, or rock-and-rollers? The Manager must also decide whether the club should use live entertainment, D.J.'s, or jukeboxes. In making these decisions, the individual must often do research. Other clubs in the area may be checked out. Clubs that have been unsuccessful as well as those that are doing well may be looked into. Often, if a Nightclub Manager sees why a certain club isn't doing well, he or she knows what to avoid to make his or her club successful.

The Nightclub Manager must choose what types of advertising to use. In certain areas, radio works well. In other areas, TV advertising or the print media may work better. The individual must develop an advertising budget and decide where his or her advertising dollar can best be spent.

The Nightclub Manager may call local media, trying to build good relationships between editors, disc jockeys, TV producers, and the club.

When the club hires live entertainment, the Nightclub Manager may be responsible for negotiating and signing contracts, or this responsibility may fall to the club owner.

The individual must run the nightclub. This includes hiring and training personnel. The Nightclub Manager may hire bartenders, waitresses, hosts, hostesses, chefs, cooks, security people, lighting technicians, sound people, etc., depending on the type of establishment.

As the Nightclub Manager, the individual may be responsible for buying food and liquor. He or she may also be in charge of controlling the liquor and making sure that all state and local alcohol laws are observed.

The Nightclub Manager must make sure that all accounts are paid. The individual may be responsible for tallying nightly totals and receipts.

If there are any problems in the club, the manager is in charge of taking care of them. The Nightclub Manager works long hours. He or she may begin working in the afternoon and not get home until 4:00 or 5:00 A.M. The Nightclub Manager is responsible to the club owner.

Salaries

Salaries for Nightclub Managers depend on the type of club, its location, its popularity, and the experience and duties of the individual.

Salaries run from around $27,000 to $150,000 plus. If the club manager is also the club owner, he or she may receive a salary plus a share of profits from the club or the individual might just receive a share of the profits.

Employment Prospects

Employment prospects for Nightclub Managers are fair. The individual might have to work in a very small club, or an establishment specializing in a different form of entertainment or music than the manager's choice. He or she might have to move to another location to find a job.

There are nightclubs all over the country. However, many of these are so small they don't use the services of a Manager.

Advancement Prospects

Advancement prospects are fair for a Nightclub Manager. After obtaining some experience in a small nightclub, an individual may move into a job as Nightclub Manager in a larger, more prestigious club. The Nightclub Manager might also open up his or her own nightclub.

Education and Training

There is no formal educational requirement to become a Nightclub Manager. Some training in business is helpful. Training in food service or the hospitality field might also be useful.

Experience, Skills, and Personality Traits

Any type of experience in running a business is a plus. Usually a Nightclub Manager has worked as either an assistant manager or a supervisor in a nightclub, bar, or restaurant.

The individual must be knowledgeable about the music business, booking talent, negotiating, and contracts. Much of this is learned on the job.

The Nightclub Manager needs the ability to deal well with people and to deal effectively under pressure.

Being aggressive and personable helps. The individual in this position needs good supervisory skills.

Unions and Associations

Nightclub Managers may work with any number of local unions, depending what variety of club they manage. Individuals may also represent their clubs in the National Federation of Music Clubs.

Tips for Entry

1. You might begin by working as a bartender, host, or hostess. Then move on to a job as an assistant nightclub manager.
2. These jobs are often listed in the help wanted sections of newspapers.
3. The more skills you have, the better your position. If you have managed a restaurant or bar and have an understanding of the entertainment business, put these things in your résumé.
4. You may consider sending a résumé and cover letter to a number of nightclubs. Ask them to keep your résumé on file.
5. Think about trying to obtain a job as a Nightclub Manager in a hotel/motel club. These clubs can be found all over the country and turnover is high. You may go directly to the hotel/motel or send a letter and résumé to the main office of a hotel/motel chain.
6. If you live in an area hosting casinos, check out openings in casino clubs.

EDUCATION

MUSIC SUPERVISOR

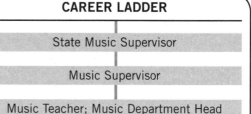

CAREER LADDER

State Music Supervisor

Music Supervisor

Music Teacher; Music Department Head

Position Description

The school Music Supervisor may work in a variety of situations. He or she may work as a school supervisor, a district supervisor, or a state Music Supervisor.

In this position, the individual is responsible for directing and coordinating activities of teaching personnel who are engaged in instructing students in vocal and instrumental music in a specific school or school system.

As a Music Supervisor, the person probably will not teach on a day-to-day basis. There are, however, positions in which the person teaches a few days a week and administers a program the remaining days.

One of the duties of a Music Supervisor is to plan and develop the music education curriculum for the school, district, or state. This is accomplished by meeting and consulting with teachers and others on the administrative staff to get input. Working closely with these people, the supervisor can tell which programs work, which do not, and which should be eliminated.

The Music Supervisor will visit classrooms while other teachers are giving classes and observe and evaluate them. If the supervisor has any comments on their teaching, he or she may set up a meeting. During this meeting, the supervisor will talk about the evaluation and recommend possible changes in teaching methods.

The supervisor will analyze the music education program in the school, district, or state. The individual may evaluate both the instructional methods and/or the materials used in teaching.

As many schools are currently experiencing cutbacks in funds, the supervisor may have to decide which programs to continue and which to cut out.

The Music Supervisor might order any instructional materials, books, supplies, equipment, and/or visual aids needed by the music department. In this position, he or she is authorized to order and purchase musical instruments required for instruction or for the school band.

Additionally, the school Music Supervisor would help establish interschool bands, choruses, and orchestras to represent the various schools at civic and community events.

The Music Supervisor's hours are usually regular working or school hours. He or she is responsible to either the principal, the superintendent, or the commissioner of education.

Salaries

Salaries of Music Supervisors depend largely on the location of the school district and the position. Supervisors generally have salaries that parallel those of teachers in the area. If, for example, teachers' salaries are low in a particular community, the supervisor's salary, too, will be low. Conversely, if the supervisor works in a district in which teachers' salaries are relatively high, his or hers will be correspondingly higher.

The salary range for Music Supervisors runs from approximately $32,000 to $79,000 plus annually.

Employment Prospects

Employment prospects are fair for Music Supervisors. Jobs may be available throughout the country. Individuals will, however, need to be licensed in the state in which they work.

Advancement Prospects

Individuals in the position of school Music Supervisor can be promoted to district Music Supervisor. District Supervisors can be promoted to state Music Supervisor positions.

Individuals with education in supervision and administration may additionally go on to positions as assistant principal or principal.

Education and Training

Music Supervisors are required to have bachelors' degrees with a major in music education. As a rule, they would have to complete a semester of student teaching in order to become a music teacher.

Music Supervisors are generally required to have additional courses in supervision and administration and/or master's degrees depending on the state regulations.

Special Requirements

Music Supervisors must be licensed or certified by the state in which they work. Individuals in this position generally have moved up the ranks, starting as music teachers. In order to teach in a public school, an individual must hold a state teaching license, certificate, or similar credential. Each state has its own requirements regarding licensure. In addition, Music Supervisors may be required to hold some sort of administrative license or credentialing. Individuals should contact their state department of education to determine the type of licensure or credentialing necessary.

Experience, Skills, and Personality Traits

Music Supervisors must like music. Generally, they have held positions as music teachers for a few years prior to applying for a job as a Music Supervisor.

As a Music Supervisor, an individual must know how to teach and be able to evaluate others. He or she must also have the ability to lead others, administer a program, and, most important, enjoy music and instructing others in it.

Unions and Associations

Music Supervisors may belong to the National Federation of Teachers (NFT). Individuals may also belong to the National Council of State Supervisors of Music (NCSSM).

Tips for Entry

1. There are specialty employment agencies that deal specifically with educational jobs. These are usually located in larger cities.
2. Openings may be advertised in the classified section of newspapers. Many newspapers have sections specifically dedicated to job openings in education.
3. Check with your local school district for openings.
4. Check out openings online. Start with some of the major job sites, such as www.monster.com and www.hotjobs.com, and go from there.

COLLEGE, CONSERVATORY, OR UNIVERSITY MUSIC EDUCATOR

CAREER PROFILE

Duties: Teach music instruction, theory, history, composition, and/or instrumental or vocal training and performance; coach chamber music groups

Alternate Title(s): Music Teacher; Professor; Instructor

Salary Range: $27,000 to $75,000+

Employment Prospects: Fair

Advancement Prospects: Fair

Best Geographical Location(s) for Position: Locations with colleges, conservatories, and/or universities may have positions available

Prerequisites:

Education or Training—Minimum of master's degree; many positions require doctoral degree

Experience—Teaching at some level; instrumental or vocal performance experience (if applicable)

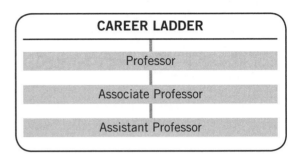

CAREER LADDER

Professor

Associate Professor

Assistant Professor

Special Skills and Personality Traits—Knowledge of many facets of music; desire to continue learning, studying, and researching; ability to communicate ideas to students

Position Description

College, Conservatory, or University Music Educators may be hired for a variety of different positions. They may be brought into a school as a general music educator to teach areas of music theory, music arranging, and/or music history, or they may teach vocal or instrumental performance. Educators are also hired to coach chamber music groups or to conduct choruses or orchestras.

Applicants for positions that require some performance skills are usually given auditions. These types of positions may include any area of instrumental instruction, coaching, or conducting.

Educators at higher learning institutions, especially those which specialize in music degrees, generally teach students who want to learn all they can. Most of these students are seriously considering professional careers in music.

It is the duty of the educator to be as knowledgeable and informed about his or her subject matter as possible. He or she must help the students learn all they can during their educational careers.

Most educators also delve into research areas of special interest to them. They take the research and write papers for publication. Published works help Educators advance their careers and increase the demand for their services.

Working in a school setting, the educator may participate in many of the cultural and educational programs, events, and benefits available.

The educator cannot walk into a classroom or lecture hall and begin teaching without preparation. Preparation for classes takes a great deal of time. This is especially true for the beginning educator or for the individual who is teaching a course for the first time.

Educators who solely teach voice or instrumental performance or coach or conduct music groups usually require less preparation time.

The educator must have specific hours set aside each week to meet with his or her students. He or she must read student's papers and grade any tests or exams.

The educator working in a community college setting will probably teach about eighteen hours a week. An educator working at a four-year university, college, or conservatory spends considerably fewer hours teaching. Teaching time usually runs from nine to twelve hours per week. Keep in mind, though, the amount of time that is spent in preparation, student meetings, and grading. Total working time may be more than 45 hours per week.

The educator is responsible to the head of his or her department or to the administrator of the school.

Salaries

Salaries for College, Conservatory, or University Music Educators depend on the school, its reputation, and its location. Salaries also depend on the professional status of the educator.

Salaries for assistant professors at small schools can start at $27,000 yearly. As the Educator gains more experience, earnings go up.

Professors' salaries range from $30,000 to $75,000 or more yearly. As noted above, however, salaries depend heavily on the school where an educator is employed. A professor working at a prestigious university would undoubtedly earn more than a professor teaching at a small college.

Employment Prospects

There is a fair chance for employment as a music educator at a conservatory, college, or university. Applicants, however, must be willing to relocate to areas that have openings.

Applicants additionally must be willing to teach in more than one specialization.

Advancement Prospects

Educators in higher learning institutions can advance their careers in a number of ways. they can start out as assistant professors and teach for a few years. Eventually they may be promoted to associate professors. During the years as an assistant professor, the educator is evaluated. He or she may or may not receive tenure. Associate professors can also be promoted to full professors.

The educator can also advance his or her career by taking a position in a college and then seeking a better position in a more prestigious university.

Education and Training

The majority of positions as College, Conservatory, or University Music Educators require at least a master's degree. Many of the positions also demand a doctoral degree.

There are educators currently teaching at conservatories and universities who hold no degree. Individuals such as symphony orchestra members are accepted as Educators on the basis of exceptional musical acclaim.

Experience, Skills, and Personality Traits

Most educators have some type of teaching experience previous to their appointment at a college, university, or conservatory.

The individual must have a tremendous knowledge of many facets of music, not only his or her specialization. He or she usually has an ongoing desire to learn more, whether through study or research.

Most important, the College, University, or Conservatory Music Educator must be able to effectively communicate ideas and theories to their students.

Unions and Associations

College, University, or Conservatory Educators may belong to the College Music Society and the American Musicological Society. These organizations sponsor a number of conferences and programs during the year. They also publish newsletters.

Individuals may also be members of the College Band Directors National Association, the College Music Society, and/or the National Association of College Wind and Percussion Instructors.

Tips For Entry

1. Openings are often advertised in the classified section of the newspaper. Sundays generally have the most listings. Look under headings such as "Education," "Colleges," "Universities," "Music Educator," and "Conservatories." In many newspapers, there is a separate section for jobs in education. Jobs may also be listed within boxed display ads in the classified section of the paper.
2. Openings may also be located online. Consult college, university, and conservatory Web sites. Many list their openings.
3. Don't forget to check out job search sites such as monster.com, hotjobs.com, or education-specific sites.
4. Send your résumé and a short cover letter directly to colleges and universities and ask to have it kept on file in case openings occur.
5. The College Music Society (CMS) and American Musicological Society (AMS) publishes a listing called the "Music Faculty List" of openings at a variety of schools, colleges, and universities.

SECONDARY SCHOOL MUSIC TEACHER

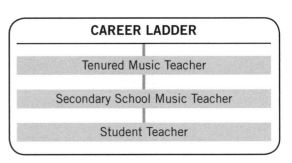

Position Description

Secondary School Music Teachers can work in junior highs or high schools and at public, private, or parochial institutions. Their duties vary depending on the type of job they are hired for.

A Secondary School Music Teacher might fill a position in instrumental teaching. This teacher would be responsible for giving lessons to students, organizing and conducting a school band and/or orchestra, and teaching basic music theory. The instrument teacher is also responsible for putting on school concerts. He or she might work with students to get them ready for competitions or auditions for summer music festivals. In addition, the instrumental music teacher could be in charge of putting together a marching band. In this case, he or she would not only be responsible for rehearsals and conducting, but also for performances in parades and at various events after school hours and on weekends or holidays.

A Secondary School Music Teacher might conversely fill a position in vocal instruction. This teacher would be responsible for giving vocal lessons, putting together and conducting school choruses and choirs, and teaching basic music theory. The vocal teacher is usually in charge of putting on all vocal concerts. He

or she might be involved in musicals or plays put on by the school.

The vocal teacher works with students preparing them for school and state vocal competitions. He or she might also be in charge of a school glee club.

Secondary School Music Teachers, like all teachers, usually go through a period of student teaching. Through student teaching they can better evaluate what area of specialization they prefer. They get the important chance for hands-on training with students while they are still under supervision.

The Secondary School Music Teacher is evaluated after a certain number of years in a school system. If his or her evaluation is positive, he or she will receive tenure. After receiving tenure, the teacher cannot be fired from the school system under normal conditions and circumstances. This gives the job a great degree of security. The school system can, however, terminate the teacher's position and move him or her to another area of music specialization.

In addition to the Secondary School Music Teacher's teaching and leading responsibilities, he or she must be available for parent/teacher/student conferences.

He or she is responsible for making up lesson plans and grading student work.

Teachers usually work only ten months a year. If they work in summer school positions, they are paid extra. Teachers do not work during school vacations.

Music teachers are responsible to the music department head, the school principal, or the superintendent of the school system.

Salaries

Salaries for teachers depend on the location of the school, the type of school, and the teacher's qualifications.

Teachers working in large metropolitan areas earn more than teachers in small communities.

Teachers usually start out at around $30,000 per school year. Their salary can go up to $70,000 or more annually. In addition, most school systems have fringe benefits and pension plans.

Salaries in public schools are usually paid on a system called "steps." Each time an individual reaches a certain step, his or her salary is raised. Steps relate to the amount of education (degrees, credits, etc.) a teacher has accumulated. Steps also relate to the amount of experience that a teacher has.

Employment Prospects

Employment prospects are not good, but positions may be found if the applicant is willing to relocate to other areas. Teachers who get tenure often do not leave their jobs, so school system turnover is not great. Once a teacher gets tenure, he or she is likely to stay in the system until retirement.

Advancement Prospects

Teachers advance their careers in a number of ways. First, there is the monetary advancement. This is attained through the step system noted above.

Second, teachers who have proven themselves are given tenures. This means that they cannot be fired under normal circumstances. This gives the individual a great deal of security.

Third, teachers can take additional courses and become department heads, district music supervisors, or state music supervisors.

Education and Training

Secondary School Music Teachers are required to have at least a bachelor's degree with a major in music education. They are usually required to complete a semester of student teaching.

The individual who plans on teaching in a public school must have a teaching certificate or license. These are granted to qualified individuals by state education departments.

In order to get permanent certification, many states require additional credits or even a master's degree.

Special Requirements

In order to teach in a public school, Secondary School Music Teachers, like all other teachers working in public schools, must hold a state teaching license, certificate, or similar credential. Each state has its own requirements regarding licensure.

Individuals should contact their specific state department of education to find out what type of licensure or credentialing is necessary.

Experience, Skills and Personality Traits

Secondary School Music Teachers generally obtain experience through a period of student teaching. Individuals must like to teach and have good teaching skills.

Secondary School Music Teachers specialize in either vocal or instrumental music. Whichever they choose, they must have a broad background and knowledge of all areas of music. They must have at least a limited knowledge of conducting either a vocal or band ensemble.

Successful Secondary School Music Teachers must have the ability to inspire and motivate young people to utilize their musical talents. Verbal and written communications skills are essential. Teachers need to be responsible people who can serve as role models to their students.

Unions and Associations

Teachers may belong to the National Education Association (NEA) or the National Federation of Teachers (NFT). Both of these organizations work on behalf of the teacher to obtain better benefits, working conditions, and salaries.

Teachers may also belong to the Music Educators National Conference, the Music Teachers National Associations, Inc., the National Association of Schools of Music, the American Choral Directors Association, and a host of others. These associations work toward good music education in the schools and offer seminars, conferences, booklets, and other information on various subjects.

Tips for Entry

1. There are employment agencies (usually located in major cities) that specialize in locating positions for teachers. Check these out.

2. College placement offices receive notices of openings at schools.
3. Get letters of recommendation from several of your professors at school as well as your student teaching supervisor.

4. Apply for summer school positions. These are often easier to obtain, and they help you get your foot in the door of a school system.

ELEMENTARY SCHOOL MUSIC TEACHER

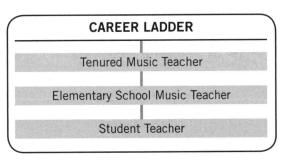
Position Description

Elementary School Music Teachers work in public, private, and parochial schools. Their duties vary depending on the school and the ages and grades they teach.

Music teachers must often follow guidelines for what they teach students. These are set up by the school music department heads, district music supervisors, and state music supervisors.

Very young children, such as those in kindergarten and the first grade, are often taught simple things, like singing songs or rhythmic movements. This singing, clapping, and stamping is considered fun by most children. The teacher also might play records or show films about music.

As the age and grade of the children increases the Elementary School Music Teacher can teach such things as music theory, singing fundamentals, and group singing. He or she might also get the students interested in instruments and possibly give lessons.

Music teachers learn many of the teaching methods that they use as student teachers. Student teaching gives the individual a chance for hands-on training with supervision.

A Music teacher is evaluated after a certain number of years working in the school system (usually three or four), and he or she may receive tenure. After receiving tenure, a teacher cannot be fired from the school system under normal circumstances. This gives the job a tremendous amount of stability.

Good Elementary School Music Teachers are creative and enthusiastic. They come up with unique ways of teaching. For example, the teacher might have the class make instruments out of everyday materials or have the students write their own lyrics and music for a song.

In addition to the normal teaching responsibilities, music teachers might also direct the school's choral group, be involved in plays, shows, concerts, etc., in the school.

Teachers usually work only 10 months a year. If they work in summer school, they receive additional remuneration. Teachers also have time off during all school vacations.

Teachers are responsible to the department head, principal, or superintendent of the school system.

Salaries

Salaries for Elementary School Music Teachers depend on the location of the school, the type of school, and the teacher's qualifications.

Teachers in large metropolitan areas earn more than teachers in small communities.

Teachers usually start out at around $30,000 per school year. Their salary can go up to $75,000 or more annually.

Salaries in public schools are usually paid on a system called "steps." Each time a teacher reaches a certain step, his or her salary is raised. Steps relate to the amount of education (degrees, credits, etc.) a teacher accumulates. Steps also relate to the amount of experience a teacher has.

Employment Prospects

Employment prospects for music teachers aspiring to work in elementary school education are fair. Positions may be available throughout the country. Individuals may need to relocate for available jobs. It should be noted that in order to land a specific job, individuals must be licensed and/or certified within that state.

Positions generally become available as teachers leave for other jobs or retire.

Advancement Prospects

Teachers advance their careers in a number of ways. First, there is a monetary advancement. This is attained through the step system mentioned above. Second, Teachers who have proven themselves are given tenure. This means that they cannot, under normal circumstances, be fired. This provides job stability.

Third, teachers can take additional courses and become department heads, district music supervisors, or state music supervisors.

Education and Training

Elementary School Music Teachers must have a minimum of a bachelor's degree. Most individuals pursuing careers in this area major in music education. Aspiring Elementary School Music Teachers usually go through a semester of student teaching.

Special Requirements

As a rule, individuals teaching in public schools must obtain a teaching certificate or license. These are granted by state education departments to qualified individuals who have complete a specific course of study.

In order to receive permanent certification, many states require individuals to take continuing education in music education or to get a master's degree in music education.

Experience, Skills, and Personality Traits

Elementary School Music Teachers must have both the ability and the patience to teach children. They are usually required to play at least one instrument, either piano or guitar.

The Elementary School Music Teacher must also be able to read music and must have a broad knowledge of the subject.

Elementary School Music Teachers must be creative and enthusiastic in order to guide children into an interest in this subject.

Unions and Associations

Teachers may belong to the National Education Association (NEA) or the National Federation of Teachers (NFT). Both of these organizations work on behalf of the teacher to obtain better benefits, working conditions, and salaries.

Teachers may also belong to a host of associations, depending on their interests. These include the Music Educators National Conference, the Music Teachers National Association, Inc., the National Association of Schools of Music, the American Choral Directors Association, and others. These groups work toward having good music education in the schools and offer seminars, conferences, pamphlets, booklets, and other valuable information.

Tips for Entry

1. There are employment agencies (usually located in major cities) that specialize in locating positions for teachers. Check these out.
2. Colleges usually have placement offices that receive notices of openings at schools.
3. Get letters of recommendation from several of your professors at college as well as your student teacher supervisor.
4. Check out openings in the newspaper classified section as well as online via the Internet.
5. Consider sending your résumé and a short cover letter to the human resources department of schools in which you hope to work. Be sure to ask that your résumé be kept on file if there are no current openings.

PRIVATE INSTRUMENT TEACHER

Duties: Instruct and teach a student how to play a specific instrument on a private or semiprivate basis

Alternate Title(s): Studio Teacher

Salary Range: $23,000 to $60,000+

Employment Prospects: Good

Advancement Prospects: Fair

Best Geographical Location(s) for Position: Cities and metropolitan areas with large enough populations to support a number of private teachers

Prerequisites:

Education or Training—Extensive training and/or study in specific instrument

CAREER LADDER

Owner of Private Teaching Studio

Private Instrument Teacher

Performer; Schoolteacher; Student

Experience—Playing instrument

Special Skills and Personality Traits—Ability to teach; ability to play one or more instruments; patience; enthusiasm

Position Description

A Private Instrument Teacher teaches students how to play a specific instrument. Sometimes the student is eager to learn the instrument; at other times he or she is being forced to take lessons. This can be quite frustrating for the teacher.

Good instrument teachers have the ability to make the instrument exciting and make learning to play a good experience. Expertise in a certain instrument alone does not make a good teacher.

Private Instrument Teachers can teach in a number of different locations, including their home, the student's home, a music instrument store, a private studio, or a commodity room.

Private Instrument Teachers often teach groups of three or four students at one time in addition to giving private lessons to individual students. Lessons run from 45 minutes to an hour and are usually scheduled once a week. Students must be encouraged not to miss lessons and to practice in between.

Instructors may teach beginners or advanced students. There are also expert instructors who teach professionals.

Private Instrument Teachers must be reliable and dependable. Nothing hurts a new teacher's reputation more than forgetting a lesson or habitually cancelling.

If the Private Instrument Teacher is self-employed (as opposed to working on staff in a studio or shop), he or she must decide how much will be charged per lesson, how and when the fee will be paid, and what policies to develop on the way his or her business will be run.

If the instructor is teaching in a studio or shop, he or she might put the students together for a group recital or a program of solo performances.

The Private Instrument Teacher is responsible directly to the student (or, in the case of children, to the parents). To be successful, the teacher must be easy to get along with, congenial, and professional, as well as being a good teacher.

Most often, a successful teacher is one who struggled through technical problems in his or her own training. These individuals have frequently developed new and easier ways to conquer these problems and can pass the methods on to their students.

Private Instrument Teachers usually have irregular working hours because of students' jobs and/or school times.

Salaries

Salaries vary depending on the instrument being taught and the expertise of the teacher. Fees usually range from $10 to $50 per hour. Fees naturally go up for experts in the field, such as jazz greats, orchestra musicians, etc. These fees can run from $50 to $500 and up per lesson.

Private Instrument Teachers are often on staff in music stores or studios. In cases such as this, the instructor is either paid a fee per student, a weekly salary, or a combination of the two. Studio teachers may earn from $25,000 to $60,000 plus annually.

Employment Prospects

A talented Private Instrument Teacher is always in demand on staff at a studio or music store or as a self-employed private instructor. Once a teacher obtains a few students who are satisfied, word travels fast.

There are many Private Instrument Teachers who work full-time as schoolteachers and part-time giving lessons after school. The individual may obtain quite a few private students as a result of the school position.

Advancement Prospects

Advancement prospects are fair for a Private Instrument Teacher. As noted above, it doesn't take long for word to travel about a good teacher.

Eventually, the teacher may have so many students that he or she wants to open a private teaching studio. The individual may employ other private music teachers of the same instrument or diversify, offering instruction in other instruments. When hiring other teachers, the owner must screen the teachers carefully in order to uphold the reputation of the studio.

Education and Training

The main requirement for a Private Instrument Teacher is the ability to play an instrument well enough to show a student the techniques of playing. Extensive training and/or study in the specific instrument or group of instruments is necessary. This may be professional training from a conservatory or college, private lessons, or self-taught skills.

Experience, Skills, and Personality Traits

Private Instrument Teachers must have the ability to play an instrument or instruments and to teach it as well. If an individual plays an instrument he or she cannot always teach someone else to play it.

One of the most important traits a teacher can have is patience. Often, it takes new students a while to pick up new techniques on an instrument. The teacher must be enthusiastic enough to communicate the excitement of new techniques to the student.

Unions and Associations

Private Music Teachers do not have a union. They can belong to the American Federation of Musicians (AFM) if they are also performers.

Private Music Teachers might also belong to the Music Teachers National Association, Inc., the Music Educators National Conference, or the National Association of Schools of Music. These organizations promote music education of all varieties.

Tips for Entry

1. Talk to all the music, record, and instrument shops in the area. Discuss your credentials and the instrument or instruments you can teach.
2. Leave business cards and/or flyers in all the music, record, and instrument shops. Include information such as your name, phone number, any accomplishment with your instrument, and any other pertinent information.
3. Contact the churches, temples, and synagogues in your area as well as all the school systems and colleges. It is usually best to visit all the places in person instead of calling or writing. Have your credentials with you.

MUSIC THERAPIST

CAREER PROFILE

Duties: Use music or musical activities to treat physical, mental, and/or emotional disabilities in patients

Alternate Title(s): None

Salary Range: $24,000 to $135,000+

Employment Prospects: Excellent

Advancement Prospects: Good

Best Geographical Location(s) for Position: Positions may be found in every major city in the country as well as in smaller communities.

Prerequisites:

Education or Training—Undergraduate degree in music therapy required; master's degree may be required

Experience—Some experience working with handicapped or disabled individuals

Special Skills and Personality Traits—Ability to work with handicapped and/or disabled individuals; compassion; ability to play piano and/or guitar; emotional stability

Special Requirements—license and certification required

Position Description

The Music Therapist works to restore a patient's health, working with a number of other individuals. These might include doctors, nurses, teachers, physical therapists, psychologists, psychiatrists, and/or the patient's family. Together the team decides what course of action to take for the patient's therapy.

Often, when all else has failed, the Music Therapist can make a breakthrough with a patient. The Music Therapist uses different forms of music as therapy for patients who have physical, mental, or emotional disabilities or illnesses.

The Music Therapist plans musical activities for an individual or a group. For example, the therapist may teach a group of elderly patients a new song or play a record or tape of tunes that were popular when they were younger. This often helps a withdrawn nursing home patient remember and reminisce. The patient might start talking about what was going on in his or her life when the song was popular.

The Music Therapist might teach a blind child how to play an instrument. This gives the child a sense of accomplishment that he or she might not have had before. Once again, the therapist has accomplished something of value.

The Music Therapist is often responsible for selecting pieces to be used as background music in certain rooms in a facility. Through training, the therapist

knows what type of music might evoke a reaction and what type might be soothing.

The Music Therapist in a hospital might put together a group of patients to sing or play instruments for hospital staff and other patients.

He or she works with a patient on either a one-to-one basis or in a group, depending on the patient and his or her needs. Conferences are often held with other members of the team. At these conferences the Music Therapist discusses the patient's needs and progress. The Music Therapist is usually happy if the patient makes even the slightest amount of progress. Progress is usually slow, and the therapist must be extremely patient.

The therapist hopes to reach his or her patient through music and have the patient become healthier emotionally, mentally, and/or physically.

Salaries

Salaries for Music Therapists vary, depending on experience, education, and the responsibilities of the individual. Earnings are also dependent on the size, prestige, and geographic location of the specific facility and job. A Music Therapist just entering the field usually makes from $24,000 to $39,000 yearly. A more experienced therapist at a larger institution or facility may command a salary of $35,000 to $54,000 or more annually. Supervisory positions in the field of music therapy often offer yearly salaries of $80,000 and up. Experienced individuals working at large facilities may earn $135,000 or more.

Employment Prospects

With the growing number of health-care facilities, the music therapy field is wide open. There are currently more positions than there are Music Therapists. A qualified individual should have no problem finding a job.

Individuals may work in a variety of locations including hospitals, psychiatric facilities, outpatient clinics, mental health centers, nursing homes, correctional facilities, schools, etc., as well as working in private practice.

Advancement Prospects

Music Therapists can move up to supervisory or administrative positions. These positions, however, usually reduce the contact Therapists have with patients. They also require additional training and education.

Other Music Therapists move into research or university teaching. These positions also limit contact with patients.

Many Therapists go into private practice and consulting after working in institutions or facilities for a period of time.

Education and Training

Music Therapists need bachelor's degrees in music therapy. There are many colleges that offer this degree program. Courses usually include music theory, voice studies, instrument lessons, psychology, sociology, and biology in addition to the general courses. A Music Therapist who plans on working in a public school system must also have a teaching degree.

Many positions require a master's degree. These too, can be obtained at colleges and universities around the country.

In addition, Music Therapists must go through a six-month internship before getting their licenses.

Special Requirements

Music Therapists must be licensed by the state in which they practice. Certification is also available.

Certification by the Certification Board for Music Therapists (CBMT) requires competition of academic and clinical training approved by the American Music Therapy Association (AMTA) and passing a national, written examination.

Experience, Skills, and Personality Traits

A good Music Therapist must be able to work with handicapped and/or disabled people. He or she must have patience, compassion, and emotional stability.

A Music Therapist must be able to play the piano and/or guitar. Ability to play other instruments is a plus. He or she must also be able to teach others to either play an instrument or sing. A good knowledge of music is essential.

Many Music Therapists work at a health facility or school as a summer job or as a volunteer before deciding to become a therapist. This gives them the opportunity to gain some experience in the field.

Unions and Associations

Two associations that Music Therapists may belong to are the National Association for Music Therapy, Inc. and the American Association for Music Therapy. These organizations help place qualified Music Therapists, do research, and act as liaisons for colleges that have music therapy programs.

Tips for Entry

1. Go to the college job placement office. Often facilities or schools looking for Music Therapists will send a list of openings to colleges and universities that grant degrees in music therapy.
2. Both the National Association for Music Therapy, Inc. and the American Association for Music Therapy have registration and placement services for their members. Join the organizations. In addition, their newsletters list various openings.
3. Many positions for Music Therapists are available through the Federal Government. These civil service positions can be located through your state employment service.
4. Check out openings via the Internet.
5. There are many civil-service positions throughout the country for qualified Music Therapists. Contact state employment services for information.

MUSIC LIBRARIAN

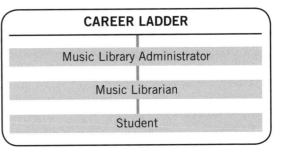

Position Description

A Music Librarian combines his or her skills as a librarian with an extensive knowledge of music. Duties vary depending on the type of position. Usually, however, the Music Librarian is responsible for cataloging all musical materials. These might include records, tapes, printed music, books on music-oriented subjects, etc.

The Music Librarian must do all reference work. He or she often looks up or finds information for a student, library patron, or professor. The individual must constantly be reading reviews of new music books, records, and tapes. The person in this position often writes reviews of books and music. The Music Librarian is in charge of ordering or recommending new materials for the library to purchase.

At times, the Music Librarian's duties also include arranging for courses on music-related subjects or lecturing on music. Depending on the position, the Music Librarian might also be responsible for putting together concerts, recitals, and other music-related activities or locating sponsors for these activities.

A Music Librarian may work in a library or school, for an orchestra, or at a television or radio station. At a TV station, the Music Librarian is not only responsible for cataloging the music, but is also often responsible for helping choose music for programs.

The Music Librarian working at a radio station must catalog all the station's records and tapes. He or she is usually responsible for pulling the records that the disc jockey or program director has chosen prior to a show. At stations that have live request shows, the Music Librarian may be on hand to pull the requested records from the library. The radio station Music Librarian is usually responsible for putting used records and tapes back in their proper places. He or she keeps track of any broken, scratched, or warped records that need replacement. In addition, the librarian works with the program director choosing and purchasing new music.

The Music Librarian must be an extremely organized individual. His or her memory must be good enough to remember vintage tapes, records, books, etc.

The Music Librarian usually works regular hours. If the Music Librarian works in a public library, conservatory, or university library position, he or she is usually responsible to the library director. If the position is in a TV or radio station, the individual is usually responsible to the program director and/or station manager. Music Librarians working in music stores or record shops are responsible to the store manager or owner.

Salaries

A Music Librarian at a mid-sized radio station might make a starting salary of $23,000 yearly. His or her salary at a larger station might range to $38,000 annually.

Music Librarians working in libraries, schools, conservatories, etc., can make from $23,000 for a beginning position to $60,000 or more in a position that requires experience. Positions in orchestras, bands, etc. may pay $70,000 or more annually.

Employment Prospects

There are more Music Librarians than there are jobs to fill. A Music Librarian can choose from a variety of different settings, including schools, conservatories, colleges, universities, public libraries, sheet music stores, record stores, radio or TV stations, orchestras, and music research libraries.

Positions in symphonies and/or choirs are limited. There is a low rate of turnover of Music Librarians in schools, conservatories, colleges, universities, and public libraries. The best place to look for a job is in a mid-sized radio station. Individuals in these stations often leave for jobs with bigger stations.

Advancement Prospects

There is almost no possibility for advancement as a Music Librarian. The competition for jobs in this field is very tough. The main way to advance as a Music Librarian is to find a job at a bigger radio station, better college or university, or more extensive library.

Music Librarians can also be promoted to administrative positions at the facility or institution for which they work.

Education and Training

The education required of a Music Librarian varies according to the type of position desired. All positions require at least an undergraduate degree in music theory or history. Some positions require a dual major in music and library sciences. Other positions require a master's degree in either music or library sciences. Jobs at very large libraries often require a master's in both disciplines.

Experience, Skills, and Personality Traits

Most Music Librarians work in libraries before and during their training. Picking up the basic library science skills makes training for the position easier. Prior experience in a sheet music store or large record store is also helpful.

Music Librarians must like to do research and have a great interest in music, recordings, and books.

This position also requires an ability to get along with people. Depending on the type of position, some Music Librarians must also be knowledgeable in a foreign language.

Unions and Associations

There are a number of associations for Music Librarians to belong to. These include the American Library Association (ALA) and the Special Libraries Association (SLA). Music Librarians might additionally belong to the Music Library Association (MLA) and the American Federation of Musicians (AFM).

Tips for Entry

1. As competition is very stiff, secure as much education as possible.
2. In addition to required courses, take specialized classes in specific areas such as ethnic music. Become an expert in at least one specialty.
3. Try to obtain a job as a library assistant while you're still in school.
4. Check out openings online. www.monster.com and www.hotjobs.com are good places to start your search.
5. Jobs may also be advertised in the classified section of the newspaper. Look under headings such as "Music Librarian," "Record Librarian," "Librarian," etc.

TALENT AND WRITING

RECORDING GROUP

Duties: Record tunes for singles and albums

Alternate Title(s): Recording Act; Recording Artist(s)

Salary Range: It is impossible to estimate earnings

Employment Prospects: Fair

Advancement Prospects: Fair

Best Geographical Location(s) for Position: New York City, Los Angeles, and Nashville, for major record labels; independent labels located throughout country

Prerequisites:

Education or Training—No formal educational requirement; musical and/or vocal training may be helpful

Experience—Writing songs; playing music; singing

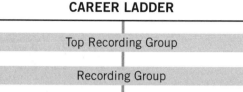

Special Skills and Personality Traits—Musical and/or vocal talent; creativity; understanding of music and recording industry; professionalism; good stage appearance; charisma; perseverance; luck

Position Description

A Recording Group is a group that is currently recording their music professionally or one that has done so in the past. For the sake of this section, Recording Group will mean a group or an individual artist.

Recording Groups may be involved with any type of music, including rock, pop, folk, country, jazz, R&B, rap, classical, or orchestral.

The Recording Group may evolve in a number of ways. Many groups start out as bar bands, lounge groups, show groups, etc. Other groups begin their careers by writing music and making demos, never really setting foot on stage.

Once the group receives a recording contract, it needs to find something to record. A Recording Group may or may not write its own material. If not, the group must find suitable songs to record. These might be located through the help of an A & R person, a music publisher, the Recording Group's manager, etc.

After a group finds songs that might be potential hits, it learns them, rehearses until perfect, and records. This is done with the help of engineers, arrangers, studio musicians, and/or background vocalists.

At this point, the group may also make a music video to help sell and market the record and the act.

The Recording Group will work with all the different departments in a record company to get ready for the release of the record. The group and/or their representative may sit down with the publicity and press department to give them information for press kits, news releases, etc. It may work with the promotion department setting up promotional appearances. The Recording Group may talk to the art department about ideas for the album cover.

Once the record is released, one or more members of a Recording Group may visit key radio stations and meet with program directors, music directors, and disc jockeys. A concert tour to promote the release of the record will probably be scheduled. The group may give interviews to various print media and appear on TV talk and variety shows.

The Recording Group must set aside time for rehearsals both before concert tours and while on the road. Once it has made it, the group must always sound their best.

As a successful Recording Group, the members may enjoy some fame and fortune. To keep the fame and build up the fortune, the group must constantly come up with new tunes to record that become hits.

Becoming a top Recording Group is the ultimate goal for most musical artists. Staying at the top is never easy.

Salaries

Earnings for Recording Groups are impossible to estimate. There are too many factors that can influence finances: how the group splits up the money, how popular the group is, the type of recording contract, etc.

Many groups do not make big money on their first recording, even if it is a hit. It depends how much was spent making the record. Record companies usually recoup their expenses from the record's profits.

Successful Recording Groups can make hundreds of thousands or even millions of dollars. Some of these monies are earned from the sale of the record. Other monies might come from concert tours, public appearances, and merchandising of the group's name and products.

Employment Prospects

The goal of most music acts is to become recording groups. A number of years ago, this was a very difficult, if not impossible, goal. Today, however, there are many more independent record labels. Additionally, with new technology, individuals can record their material and sell it themselves via the Internet.

Getting signed by a major record label is another story. And while it is difficult, it is not impossible. Realistically, it is very difficult to become a top Recording Group. For every group that signs a major recording deal, there are hundreds that don't. However, a group with talent, perseverance, and a lot of luck can eventually make it. The problem is that many groups give up too soon.

Advancement Prospects

Once a group has obtained a bona fide recording contract, they have a fair chance of advancing their career. The first step in advancement for a Recording Group is getting a record on the charts. The second is moving it up the charts. Moving into the top ten on the charts is next. A Recording Group whose record holds the number one position for one or more weeks is achieving the goal. Having a string of tunes hit this position is even better.

None of this is easy, but it is possible.

Education and Training

Members of Recording Groups are not required to have any educational training, although many individuals do have a college background. Some type of music and/or vocal training is necessary. This might come through private study or schooling or be self-taught.

Experience, Skills, and Personality Traits

Members of Recording Groups should have good stage presence and charisma. This is important for the Group when they do promotional tours and appearances. Members should be talented musically and/or vocally. An understanding of the music and recording industry is necessary. An ability to deal with business situations is helpful. Perseverance, luck, and being at the right place at the right time are all factors.

Unions and Associations

Recording Groups may be members of the American Federation of Musicians (AFM). They might also belong to the National Academy of Recording Arts and Sciences (NARAS). This is the association which gives out the Grammy awards each year. Depending on the type of music the group records, they might belong to the Country Music Association (CMA) or the Gospel Music Association (GMA).

Tips for Entry

1. Make the most professional demo possible.
2. Try to have original songs on the demo.
3. Many members of successful Recording Groups start out as session musicians. After being recognized as having talent, the individuals can strike out on their own.
4. Never send your demos out without first querying interest. Either call the record company or write them a note. Try to send your demo to a specific person, not just a title. For example, address it to "Mr. John Jones, A&R Director," not just "A&R Director."
5. Look for opportunities to showcase your act.
6. Many acts have been successful uploading videos of them perfroming their tunes to YouTube. You might consider this as well.

FLOOR SHOW GROUP

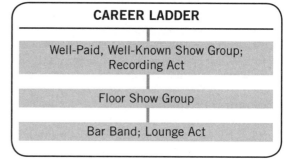

Position Description

Floor Show Groups work in nightclubs, hotels, cruise ships, cafés, bars, and concert halls putting on shows for patrons. They not only perform, they entertain. Show Groups may perform all different types of music in their act.

Floor Show Groups have to play a specific number of sets per night. Generally, show groups will be required to perform two shows. They may also have to play one or two dance sets during the course of the engagement.

The dance set will consist of popular and old tunes the group plays so that patrons can get out on the floor and dance. Shows, on the other hand, must be developed and put together. During show sets, members of the audience stay seated and watch and listen to the act on stage. The act may include any number of songs, melodies, skits, jokes, etc. The show may also contain dancers, light shows, sound effects, or any number of other special effects.

Floor Show Groups have pizzazz. The show set is usually planned quite extensively. Ad-libs may sound like ad-libs to the audience, but they have usually been repeated time and time again. The show must be flexible. At times, a show group will change its opening and closing and leave the rest of the act as is. As new songs become hits, the group may wish to take out some of their old material and replace it. Usually, Floor Show Groups have exciting finales. They wear costumes on stage. Key members of the group may change costumes for each set.

Between sets or after the engagement, the musicians and vocalists may mingle with patrons.

Floor Show Groups may work in one place for two or three weeks before moving on to the next gig.

Fees are paid weekly or semi-weekly for this type of work. Hotel rooms and, on occasion, food may be part of the deal.

The Floor Show Group travels quite a lot. If the club manager likes their show, they will be booked back again. This is how show groups build up followings in specific areas. Individuals must not only be free to travel, but also like living out of a suitcase for months at a time.

The Floor Show Group must appear professional at all times. They must arrive at the correct times for their sets, dressed appropriately. Working hours are usually at night. In order to attain success, it helps for the group to develop good working relationships with managers and agents of clubs where they work. The group is responsible directly to the club manager. It is he or she who controls whether or not the group is invited back. Members of Floor Show Groups often acquire a bit of stardom, at least on the club circuit where they perform.

Salaries

It is difficult to determine a salary range for members of Floor Show Groups. There are quite a number of factors that can affect salaries: the way the group splits up fees, how popular the act is, whether they are working under a union contract, how many members are in the act, expenses, etc.

As a rule, Floor Show Groups earn more per engagement than lounge acts. According to the American Federation of Musicians (AFM) union, leaders earn more than the other members of groups.

There are show groups that work sporadically and earn minimum fees (according to union contracts). There are also Floor Show Groups that tour fifty weeks a year, zipping back and forth across the country (or sections of it) earning large fees.

Fees for Floor Show Groups run from $250 to $15,000+ per engagement.

Employment Prospects

Once a group attracts a following, employment prospects are fair. Until a show group has a following, employment is difficult. Show groups usually work with agents who book them in specific areas of the country. Some Floor Show Groups also try to book themselves, but this task can be extremely difficult. There are agents who work specifically with show groups and have contracts with various rooms around the country. Groups of this type may also open for better-known acts.

Advancement Prospects

It is difficult to advance as a Floor Show Group. Most groups of this kind aspire to be recording artists. This transition is tough to make.

Show groups can, however, build up a tremendous following. By doing this, they assure themselves of constant bookings and larger fees.

Advancement in any part of the music business depends on talent, the ability to persevere, and a lot of luck.

Education and Training

There are no educational requirements for members of Floor Show Groups. What is required is the ability to play an instrument and/or sing very well. This may be acquired through high school training, college or university education, private study, or self-teaching.

Experience, Skills, and Personality Traits

Floor Show Groups must be exciting. Their members need to have a good stage presence and charisma. It goes without saying that members of these groups must have musical and/or vocal skills.

Show groups must not only perform, but also entertain. They need the ability to play dance sets and show sets. In order to do this, someone in the group or their entourage must put shows together creatively. The group needs to keep in mind the current musical trends. It is often required that the group have a variety of different sets, enabling patrons to come back to the club, see the show, and not be bored.

Unions and Associations

Members of Floor Show Groups may belong to the American Federation of Musicians (AFM). This union bargains for musicians on fees, terms of contracts, etc. It also helps protect the musician from being fired unjustly, treated badly, etc.

Not all musicians belong to the union. However, most major clubs work with the union and do not hire any nonunion groups.

Tips for Entry

1. Join the union. They often know of openings. Hanging around their offices or talking to other union members helps build a contact list.
2. Be professional. If you have an interview with a club manager or agent, show up on time. If you cannot get to an interview on time, chances are you will be late for gigs.
3. Have a professional photographer take pictures of the group. Make sure the group is shown in the picture as they will be on stage (e.g., don't take pictures in costumes and go on stage in jeans).
4. Have the group's name printed on the picture. Don't forget to include your agent's or manager's phone number. If you don't have either yet, use a number where you know someone will answer the phone most of the time. If you don't answer, someone else will get a call for the job.
5. Print up a list of clubs where you have worked previously. You might want to get recommendations in writing from club owners you have worked for.
6. Print up a list of tunes you can perform for both dance sets and show sets.
7. You might want to make up a small brochure (or a letter with the group's picture) letting people know that you are available. Send this to clubs, agents, organizations, etc.
8. When you do get gigs, get the commitment in writing in the form of a contract. Make sure dates, times, monies, and any other pertinent information are included. Make sure that the contract is signed by both parties.
9. Consider utilizing the new karaoke hardware and software in your act. Successful Floor Show Groups often have a segment of their show dedicated to audience involvement.

DANCE BAND

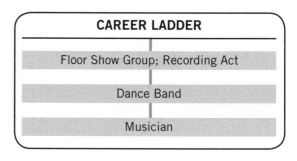

Position Description

Dance Bands may work in schools, bars, clubs, cafés, or hotels, or for private parties. The Dance Band's main function is to provide music for people to dance to and listen to.

When Dance Bands are employed by a specific person, they contract to play a certain number of sets. These sets are usually from forty-five minutes to one hour in length. The band may play from two to five sets nightly, taking breaks in between.

Dance Bands may consist of guitarists, bass players, pianists, organists or synthesizer players, drummers, singers, horn players, etc. They may have any number of people in them.

Dance Bands usually specialize in one or two varieties of music. Rock, pop, Top 40, disco, jazz, country, swing, etc., are all possibilities. When the band, is hired the leader, manager, or booking agent must ask what type of music will be required for the engagement.

Dance Bands must set aside specific periods of time for rehearsals. Good Dance Bands know most of the current hits in their variety of music. Additionally, most Dance Bands know an assortment of other tunes. It is important for the Dance Band to have a big playlist. This will enable them to perform sets without repeating songs.

Dance Bands may take requests from the audience. These requests may be made in a written form or face-to-face. Dance Bands often have specific parts of their sets in which they take requests. In this way, the structure of their show will not be disturbed.

It is usual for Dance Bands to know ahead of time which songs will be played at what time during the set. There may be a group leader who calls out the songs during the show. The sets may be peppered with ad-libs by members of the group.

Dance Bands may work on either a part-time or a full-time basis. Frequently, the first paying job a musician has is in a Dance Band. Dance Bands usually work nights, although they may be hired for affairs and functions in the daytime.

Members of Dance Bands often hold day jobs or teach on the side in order to earn additional income.

When working, the group is responsible to the individual or club who has hired them. The Dance Band may work with an agent, manager, road manager, or other personnel. They may perform popular tunes as well as their own compositions.

Salaries

Salaries and/or fees for Dance Bands and their members vary greatly depending on the popularity of the group, their location, experience, etc.

Groups playing in school situations earn from $250 to $3,000 plus per engagement. Dance Bands with large followings may earn considerably more.

If the members of the band belong to the musicians union (AFM), their base pay will be set by the union.

Dance Bands working in bars earn between $250 and $1,500 plus per night. A group playing in a lounge or nightclub setting might earn from $500 to $15,000 plus per engagement.

Employment Prospects

Dance Bands looking for part-time work on weekends have a fair chance of finding gigs if they are good. These groups usually have fairly large followings within their community.

Dance Bands seeking full-time employment have a more difficult time. There are many more bands looking for work than there are openings.

Advancement Prospects

Advancement prospects are fair for talented Dance Bands. While it can be difficult for Dance Bands to climb the career ladder, it is not impossible. Dance Bands that attract large followings can obtain more bookings and demand and receive larger fees.

Some acts decide to put together a show and try to work as a show group. One of the problems with this is that, in many cases, bands tend to break up before this happens.

If the band is very talented, very lucky, and in the right place at the right time, they may become a top recording group.

Education and Training

Members of Dance Bands are not required to have any type of specialized education. The ability to play an instrument or sing well is essential. Training for this may be picked up in school or in private study, or it may be self-taught.

This is not to indicate that members of Dance Bands are uneducated. Many are highly educated. Some have degrees or backgrounds in music, while others hold degrees in other majors. Some Dance Band members are still in school.

Experience, Skills, and Personality Traits

Dance Bands must have, or be able to build, large followings. The group must have musical talent and ability. Members of the group should be able to work well together, giving and taking. They must want to persevere and stay together. Dance Bands that play during their college years know that they will probably only be together until graduation. Other groups may stay together for years on end. As long as all the members want the same thing, it usually works out.

Many members of Dance Bands begin playing their instrument or singing while in school. They find that they can earn money while enjoying themselves playing in a school group for a dance or prom.

Members of Dance Bands need a good stage presence. Professional behavior at all times is important. Bands that are familiar with all types of music will have more flexibility in finding jobs.

Unions and Associations

Members of Dance Bands may belong to the American Federation of Musicians (AFM), which is a bargaining union. It helps the musician in all phases of his or her career, from setting guidelines on base salaries for performing to providing health insurance plans.

Tips for Entry

1. Openings for Dance Bands may be found in local papers in the help wanted section.
2. Other openings are learned about by word-of-mouth through members of organizations, schools, associations, firms, etc.
3. Be as professional as possible. Show up on time for all interviews and gigs.
4. Have pictures taken by a professional photographer.
5. Have the group's name, representative, and phone number printed on the pictures so that people know how to locate you for jobs.
6. Set up adequate time for rehearsals *before* a job, not during it.
7. You may consider making up a small brochure or printed piece to mail to potential talent buyers (schools, clubs, agents, etc.).
8. Try to get job commitments in writing in the form of contracts. There are standard contract forms available if you don't have one. Read the contract thoroughly before signing and make sure all information is correct.
9. Make up business cards and give them out. Tell everyone you have a group. Put cards on bulletin boards in stores, schools, malls, etc.
10. You might want to put an ad in a local paper indicating your group's availability. Make sure to put down a phone number where people can locate you or your representative.
11. Develop a press kit to give to the media and potential talent buyers.

SESSION MUSICIAN

Duties: Play background music for a recording artist in a studio

Alternate Title(s): Studio Musician; Session Player; Sideman or Woman; Freelance Musician; Backup Musician

Salary Range: Up to $100,000+

Employment Prospects: Fair

Advancement Prospects: Fair

Best Geographical Location(s) for Position: New York, Los Angeles, and Nashville; other cities may also have opportunities

Prerequisites:

    Education or Training—Musical training helpful

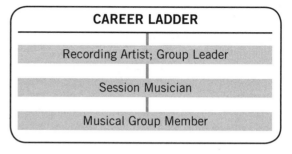

CAREER LADDER

Recording Artist; Group Leader

Session Musician

Musical Group Member

Experience—Performing in bands and groups

Special Skills and Personality Traits—Proficiency in at least one instrument; dependability; ability to read music; versatility

Position Description

The Session Musician may be known as a studio musician, a session player, a sideman or woman, a freelance musician, or a backup musician. The job, however, stays the same.

The main responsibility of a Session Musician is to back up the leader of a group in the recording studio. He or she might also play music for commercials. At times, the individual may back up the leader of the group in a live concert.

It is important for the Session Musician to have the ability to sight-read. There is usually not a lot of time for rehearsals, and because of the high cost of studio personnel and time, mistakes are not tolerated.

In order for the Session Musician to get as much work as possible, it is in his or her best interest to know how to play a number of different styles and to be proficient in more than one instrument.

Session Musicians are usually hired by a contractor. This individual most often calls musicians he or she knows and has worked with before. The contractor tells the individual the date, time, and whom they will be backing up. The Session Musician either accepts the job or rejects it. After a few job rejections, the contractor probably won't call that particular Session Musician back, no matter what the reason for the rejections.

It is the responsibility of the Session Musician to play what he or she is told and in the manner that the leader of the group or the producer wants it played.

He or she must be responsible, reliable, and easy to get along with, in addition to being a good musician.

Session Musicians are usually paid by the hour. Their minimum fee is set by the union (AFM). If they are in great demand, they can usually negotiate higher fees. Session Musicians often work with a number of different groups over a short time span. Each job is called a gig or a session.

A Session Musician can make a good living. However, one thing that bothers many studio musicians is that this job stifles their creativity. Another problem for some is that the individual playing on the recording does not always get credit for his or her work. This means that the studio musician works in the shadow of another musician.

Salaries

Salaries of Session Musicians depend on a number of factors. These include the type of recording, how much work they do, their geographical location, and whether they are in great demand.

The American Federation of Musicians (AFM) specifies the minimum rate Session Musicians should receive. The union has different rates depending on the specific recording situation. Individuals are urged to check with the local AFM for specific rates.

When Session Musicians are in demand and well known, they can negotiate for more than the minimum rates. Individuals who play more than one instrument during a session will usually be paid additional monies.

Talented Session Musicians who are in constant demand may earn $100,000 or more annually. Naturally, those who are called less frequently will make considerably less.

Employment Prospects

Employment prospects for Session Musicians are fair if the musician is extremely talented. He or she needs a lot of contacts to get his or her foot in the door. Unfortunately, talent alone doesn't make it.

Session Musicians are often hired through contractors. If an individual is hired and turns out to be not only talented, but responsible and easy to work with, too, he or she will continue receiving assignments from the contractor.

The majority of studio work is found in New York, Los Angeles and Nashville, although there are studios located all over the country.

Advancement Prospects

Session Musicians can advance their careers in a number of ways. They can become group leaders—not always an easy move—or they can become top Session Musicians. To become a top studio musician, one must be more talented, more versatile, and better connected than other musicians around.

Although there are many who have moved from being Session Musicians to top positions in the music business, it is a tough hill to climb.

Another option for career advancement for Session Musicians is for individuals to be called in to play for sessions more frequently, resulting in increased earnings.

Education and Training

There is no formal educational requirement for Session Musicians. Individuals have usually had extensive private study in their instruments. However, there are also many successful Session Musicians who are self-taught. The ability to read music is not always necessary, but makes the musician more flexible.

Many musicians have college degrees in music or an unrelated subject. This way, they feel they have something to fall back on in case they can't make a living in music.

Experience, Skills, and Personality Traits

It is essential for the Session Musician to be a great musician. Most Session Musicians begin their careers playing in local bands while in high school. Any performance experience at all is useful for a Session Musician.

As noted above, it is not always necessary to read music, but the ability to do so is a plus. Another advantage is the ability to play more than one instrument.

Unions and Associations

Session Musicians may be members of the American Federation of Musicians (AFM). This union stipulates the minimum wages that can be paid to musicians in addition to performing a variety of other functions.

Tips for Entry

1. Begin your career by working in a local band.
2. When you feel experienced enough, put an ad for work as a Session Musician in either a music-oriented newspaper or one of the trade magazines.
3. If you want to get into recording studio work and no one will let you put your foot in the door musically, try to get a job doing anything in the studio (studio assistant, receptionist, gofer, etc). You will learn a lot and make the contacts you need.
4. Join the American Federation of Musicians; your affiliation will help you locate jobs and make contacts.

BACKGROUND VOCALIST

Position Description

Background Vocalists back up other singers or musicians on recordings, in jingles, on television commercials, or in live performance. Background Vocalists may have full-time jobs or may freelance.

An individual working as a Background Vocalist in a lounge or show group travels with the act to all their performances. He or she is responsible for singing background music in all the shows. The person must also learn all the songs in the repertoire and attend all the rehearsals.

Background Vocalists working in the theater may sing in the chorus. They must attend all rehearsals, learn parts, and sing in shows.

Background Vocalists who freelance on recordings, jingles, or television commercials have slightly different functions. Such an individual must build up a reputation as a great singer and be flexible, responsible, and available when needed.

The world of singing backup on recordings is unique. A Background Vocalist must be able to walk into a studio, pick up some music, go over it quickly, and be ready to record without a mistake. The vocalist may be asked to harmonize with other singers with whom he or she has never sung. The individual may also be asked to improvise. The singer who can pick up on what the producers want and sound good is the one who will be called on again.

The Background Vocalist must be versatile. An individual may have a job in the morning doing the background vocals for a pop tune and another gig that night singing background for an R & B tune. The more flexible the singer is, the more opportunities there are.

The Background Vocalist who works on television commercials or radio jingles performs much the same as when doing a recording. Individuals in this type of work often have more time to rehearse the tunes.

People involved in singing background vocals may work long, irregular hours on some days and not at all on others. As a matter of fact, Background Vocalists who rely only on recording dates might not work for weeks or months at a time.

Jobs are often obtained through contractors or producers in the recording field. The Background Vocalist needs many contracts to become successful.

The Background Vocalist working in a group or chorus finds work either through an agent or by auditioning.

Salaries

Salaries of Background Vocalists depend on a number of variables. These include how much the singer works, what type of work he or she performs, geographical location of the singer, and general success. Base salaries of union members are set by the various unions. Background Vocalists who work as singers with bands may not belong to a union.

Background Vocalists working in recording studios are paid according to how long the finished product will be, what day and time the individual works, how long the vocalist is in the studio, etc. Rates are also based on the number of vocalists singing on the recording. The Background Vocalist will earn additional monies for overtime, other songs, etc. If the completed song is more than three and one-half minutes, the individual is paid extra.

It is impossible to estimate the earnings of a Background Vocalist because of the variables involved. Those who are successful may earn up to $100,000 plus in the studio.

Employment Prospects

Employment prospects are fair for a Background Vocalist working as a singer within a band. Employment opportunities become more difficult for vocalists seeking work with very well-known acts or in recordings or jingles.

Generally, Background Vocalists must audition for a position in a major act. Competition is keen. Some Background Vocalists audition for agents who find them jobs.

Locating jobs as Background Vocalists for recordings or jingles is much more difficult. One must develop a reputation in order to get a foot in the door.

Advancement Prospects

Advancement prospects depend to a great extent on the career aspirations of the individuals. For those seeking to become soloists or major recording artists, advancement can be difficult. That does not mean that it is impossible, only challenging.

Advancement prospects are more promising for those who get their foot in the door as Background Vocalists for recording sessions or jingles. Many of these individuals are offered more than they can handle. Those who do background vocals for jingles can achieve success and financial security.

Education and Training

There is a school of thought that says that individuals who aspire to be musicians or singers should be educated in a field other than music in order to have something to fall back on. This is up to the individual.

There is no formal education needed to become a singer. Some singers have a broad background in music and others do not. Many Background Vocalists have graduated from conservatories. Still others go to vocal coaches or other private teachers. Many singers are self-taught.

Experience, Skills, and Personality Traits

A Background Vocalist needs a good voice and the ability to sing. This is not as silly as it sounds, for many great singers do not possess the confidence to sing well in front of others.

Other qualifications for a good Background Vocalist include the ability to harmonize, possession of a good vocal range, and the ability to sing all styles of music. This permits the Background Vocalist to obtain more jobs.

Although it is not always necessary, it is helpful for a Background Vocalist to be able to sight-read. Many recording jobs specify this.

Additionally, the person in this position must be reliable, show up on time for jobs, and have the perseverance necessary to make a living in this type of job.

Unions and Associations

Background Vocalists may belong to a number of different unions, depending on where they are working. If the Singer is doing a recording session or a radio jingle, he or she may belong to the American Federation of Television and Radio Artists (AFTRA). Individuals singing in theatrical jobs will belong to the American Guild of Musical Artists (AGMA) or the Actors Equity Association, commonly referred to as Equity (AEA). The singer who works on a television commercial may belong to either the Screen Actors Guild (SAG) or AFTRA. Individuals may belong to more than one union.

Tips for Entry

1. Background Vocalists often advertise their specialty in the trades or in the classified sections of newspapers.
2. Read the trades on a regular basis. See what is happening and where there are possible openings.
3. Local groups may advertise for a Background Vocalist in the newspaper's classified section.
4. The various union offices are full of information on openings. You might have to hang around there or become friendly with the people who run the office.
5. Visit different recording studios. Get to know people who book studio time, producers, engineers, etc. These people can help you find work. Make sure you tell them what you do and leave a phone number.
6. The telephone is your lifeline, especially if you are looking for freelance recording dates. Make

sure someone answers your phone at all times. If this isn't possible, use voice mail, an answering service, or answering machine. Don't keep the line busy with unnecessary talking if you don't have call waiting. If your number is busy, important people may call someone else for a job.

7. Sing at every possible opportunity. Get your name (and your voice) around.

SONGWRITER

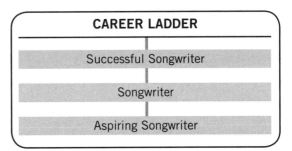

CAREER LADDER

Successful Songwriter

Songwriter

Aspiring Songwriter

Position Description

A Songwriter writes songs. He or she may write the lyrics, the melody, or both. Songwriters who work with others are called collaborators.

Songwriters work in many different ways. Some people sit down at the same time every day and try to create music and/or lyrics. Others wait until they are inspired by an idea, a person, a thought, an occasion, a feeling, etc. Some may write the music first, then try to create or find the perfect lyrics. Others develop lyrics and then try to find the perfect tune.

Songwriters may also be called composers, writers, or lyricists. Once the individual has finished a song, either alone or with another person, he or she must find a way to market it. The main goal of most professional Songwriters is to write a song that is not only recorded, but also turns into a number one hit or a standard.

Before the Songwriter does anything, he or she should make sure that the song is protected. This can be done in a number of ways. The individual can copyright the song. Another method of protection is to put the finished music and words into an envelope, address it, and send it to him- or herself via certified registered mail. Once the person receives the song back from the post office, he or she should put it away without opening it. The official postmark is a type of protection. Some individuals feel that if they are dealing with reputable music publishers these procedures are not necessary. However, it is better to be safe than sorry. Many

industry professionals feel that the only real protection is to copyright.

The Songwriter must find a music publisher or recording act to work with the song. The person should use any contracts he or she has to get the song listened to. As many publishers, recording acts, producers, A & R people, managers, etc., as possible should be contacted. If the Songwriter does not know such people, he or she must make calls, knock on doors, and write letters.

In order for the song to be listened to, the Songwriter must make up a demo record or cassette. These demos should accurately showcase the song. There is no need to make a very elaborate demo, although it should be as professional as possible. After a demo master is made, copies must be made to send to the important listeners. If the Songwriter makes his or her own demo, the individual should be sure that the tapes are clean and of good quality. Each tape should be labeled with the Songwriter's name, address, phone number, and the names and times of each song included on the demo. Incidentally, if there is more than one song on a tape, the person should note where each song ends and the next begins. There shouldn't be more than three or four songs on a tape.

It is always better to send a query letter prior to sending a demo. Many music publishers and A & R people don't accept unsolicited material. When the Songwriter does send tapes, they should always be sent first class.

The Songwriter may get lucky and have one of his or her songs accepted by a music publisher, recording group, A & R person, etc. Depending on the deal made, the Songwriter may sell the song outright or just sell the rights to it. At this point, the individual should seek the advice of an attorney to go over any details, contracts, etc.

Although the Songwriter receives credit on a record, he or she does not often receive a lot of attention for writing a song.

The individual may work long hours trying to create something unique. The Songwriter may develop a block. Some people write one hit song and are never heard from again. Others have a long stream of hits and standards. There are also many people who write good songs but are never discovered.

Salaries

Earnings of Songwriters depend on a number of factors. These include the number of songs published and/or sold, the number of times each song is played, used, etc., the general popularity of the tune, and the type of agreement made for each song. For example, songs may be sold outright, pay writer's royalties, and/or pay publisher's royalties.

Songwriters may write the tune, the lyrics, or both. If individuals collaborate on songs, monies must be shared. The split will differ depending on the individuals and the tunes.

Songwriters may write songs for years and never sell or publish them. On the other hand, one of these individuals might wake up one day, write a song, have a recording act record it, and have it turn into a monster hit. Financial success can occur at any time in this profession. Once a song is published, a Songwriter may receive royalties from it for the rest of his or her life.

Successful Songwriters can earn $500,000 plus yearly. Very successful individuals may earn over a million dollars each year.

Employment Prospects

Almost anyone can write a song. Selling it or publishing it is a different matter. Songwriters may write songs for performers to sing in concert or on records. They may write radio or television jingles or music for plays, films, or TV.

The exciting thing about being a Songwriter is that an individual can write a song that will turn into a hit at any time.

In this profession, a person can work full- or part-time. He or she might be a musician who prefers to write his or her own tunes.

Songwriters usually work for themselves or work with a collaborator. There are numerous opportunities for an individual to be employed by a record company, producer, recording group, etc., as a staff Songwriter. Competition for these jobs is tough.

Advancement Prospects

The way a Songwriter advances is by writing songs that turn into hits. As noted before, this can happen at any time in a Songwriter's career.

Education and Training

There is no formal education needed to be a Songwriter. Depending on whether one writes lyrics, music, or both, he or she might study music theory, harmony, orchestration, and/or ear training. The individual may have studied one or more instruments through private lessons or be self-taught.

The Songwriter might take courses in lyric writing. Again, this is not a requirement.

There are many Songwriter workshops, seminars, and books that may be helpful and provide inspiration.

Experience, Skills, and Personality Traits

Songwriters need to be talented, creative people. A knowledge of the music business is helpful in marketing, selling, or publishing the song. The ability to play one or more instruments and/or musical talent is helpful, although not necessary for every Songwriter.

As most Songwriters work on their own, good work habits are useful in getting things accomplished. Persistence is a must in writing new songs and selling and/or publishing them.

Luck and being in the right place at the right time are important factors.

Unions and Associations

Songwriters may belong to a variety of organizations, including the American Society of Composers, Authors, and Publishers (ASCAP), Broadcast Music, Inc. (BMI), and/or SESAC. These performing rights organizations pay Songwriters royalties for public performances of their song.

An individual might be a member of the Songwriters Guild of America (SGA). This association represents composers and lyricists. The Songwriter may be a member of the Nashville Songwriters Association International, the Country Music Association (CMA), or the Gospel Music Association (GMA). Songwriters might additionally be members of the National Academy of Recording Arts and Sciences (NARAS).

Tips for Entry

1. Write as much as you can. Practice does not always make perfect, but it helps develop the craft.

2. Try to find some songwriting workshops. These not only give helpful advice and tips, but also provide inspiration.

3. Protect your songs. Either copyright them or send them to yourself by registered, certified mail. Copyrighting is best.

4. Do not get involved with any individual who wants you to pay to publish your songs. Publishers are supposed to pay *you* for the songs.

5. Learn as much as possible about every aspect of the music business. It will help you sell, publish, and market your songs more effectively.

6. Try to get your songs listened to by as many people as possible. You might consider letting local club acts, disc jockeys, and music directors hear your tunes. Get their opinions and advice on how to better your work.

7. Have persistence and perseverance.

CHURCH MUSIC

CHOIR DIRECTOR

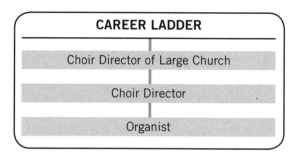

Duties: Recruit and direct choirs; develop and maintain music budget; plan music programs

Alternate Title(s): Music Director; Minister of Music; Administrator of Music Program; Church Musician

Salary Range: $22,000 to $85,000+

Employment Prospects: Good

Advancement Prospects: Fair

Best Geographical Location(s) for Position: Cities with a number of large churches tend to have more positions available

Prerequisites:

Education or Training—Bachelor's degree in church music usually required; master's degree in church music preferred

Experience—Experience working in church music situations helpful

Special Skills and Personality Traits—Ability to work well within the congregational hierarchy and politics; knowledge of choral techniques; familiarity with liturgical practice

Position Description

The Choir Director's prime responsibility is to prepare the church's choir for services. In some jobs, the Choir Director may be the only paid person involved in the music department of the church. In this situation, the Choir Director might not be only in charge of the choir, but might also be the organist accompanying the group during services.

In other positions, the Choir Director acts as the music director, supervising others in the music department of the church and coordinating their efforts.

As a Choir Director, an individual must conduct and lead the choir. This may include auditioning members of the congregation who would like to sing in the choir as well as soliciting potential members who would be assets to the group. The director also auditions singers to act as section leaders, assistant conductors, or soloists.

The Choir Director sets times each week for rehearsals. He or she is responsible for leading and supervising rehearsals so that time is spent most effectively.

Another duty of the director is to choose the music that will be used during services, making sure that it is appropriate to the sermon, holiday, or special occasion. As director, the individual will be in charge of the church's music library and might recruit a volunteer to act as music librarian. The Choir Director must often recruit volunteers to care for vestments and help with music programs as well.

Special programs, concerts, and other musical activities are the responsibility of the Choir Director. He or she must plan them, orchestrate them, and rehearse them.

The Choir Director works closely with all the members of the music department of the church as well as with the minister of the congregation. If any of them have a particular musical need, they will go to the Director. The Choir Director is, in essence, the music resource person for the church.

The music or Choir Director must work out a budget for the music program. This budget is presented to the appropriate members of the congregation for approval. It then becomes the responsibility of the Choir Director to stay within the budget. The budget might include items such as robes for the choir, music for the group, trips for special concerts, staging for plays, etc. The director analyzes the needs and sets budget priorities.

Certain churches have more than one choir. For example, the church may have a regular choir and a children's choir. The director must provide leadership for both. At times, the Choir Director will be asked to have extra concerts or lead the choir at special events, weddings, funerals, etc. The director may also be required to coordinate additional music-oriented activities in the church and community.

In addition to his or her music responsibilities, the Choir Director is usually expected to maintain office hours each week to discuss problems, work with small groups of singers, help the organist, write music, and handle administrative chores. The music or Choir Director may be expected to attend a variety of workshops, conferences, and seminars each year.

The Choir Director is responsible to a church committee or to the minister of the church. Whatever the case, the Choir Director works very closely with the minister and the congregation to help fulfill their musical requirements.

Salaries

Salaries of church musicians vary depending on their experience, the type of position held, and the size, location, and budget of the church. Salaries for full-time Choir Directors begin at around $22,000 yearly. Salaries go up to $85,000 or more per year, and may be slightly higher at very large metropolitan churches.

Employment Prospects

Employment prospects for church musicians are good. The Choir Director must have sound training to get into any major position. A bachelor's degree in church music helps land a job; a master's or doctorate in church music makes a person even more employable in this field.

While educational qualifications are helpful, an applicant must also demonstrate an enthusiastic, positive attitude to pass the interview process many church committees require.

Advancement Prospects

Depending on the job a Choir Director holds, he or she has a fair chance of advancement. Small churches do not usually have large music departments. An individual who holds a position in such a church has limited upward mobility in that institution.

In larger metropolitan churches, however, the Choir Director may have a lot of money to put into a music program. The director can build up the music department of the church and may gain some recognition for doing so. He or she may then move on to a position in an even larger and more prestigious church.

This is not to say that a church musician cannot do well in a smaller church. He or she may institute and supervise a number of music programs, choirs, etc., for the church and be quite happy doing so.

Education

Education requirements for the position of Choir Director differ from church to church. Most churches, however, require at least a bachelor's degree in music with a major in church music. Some churches are now requiring that a Choir Director hold a master's degree.

Experience, Skills, and Personality Traits

Church musicians, as a rule, work in churches in one capacity or another throughout most of their lives. The aspiring Choir Director was probably a member of the choir at his or her own church.

It is important that the music or Choir Director have the ability to work well within the politics of the congregational hierarchy. From the time the person is interviewed, and throughout his or her tenure the Choir Director will be working closely with these people.

The Choir Director must be familiar with liturgical practice. A knowledge of choral techniques and an ability to teach and/or lead is essential. Additionally, most church musicians know how to play the organ, piano, and/or guitar.

Unions and Associations

Among the helpful and useful groups a Choir Director may belong to are the AGO (The American Guild of Organists), the Choristers Guild, the American Choral Directors Association, the National Association of Pastoral Musicians, the Association of Anglican Musicians, and various other denominational groups.

Tips for Entry

1. Schools of religious music have placement centers at which graduates may register. Churches in need of musical personnel usually advise these placement agencies about openings and opportunities.
2. Your church's music/Choir Director may know of openings in other churches. Ask around.
3. In certain positions, auditions are necessary (especially if organ playing is part of the job). Check the requirements before an interview so that you can prepare properly.
4. Positions are often advertised in the classified section of the newspaper. Look under heading such as "Choir Director," "Music Director," "Minister of Music," and "Church Musician."

CANTOR

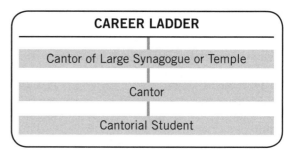

CAREER LADDER

Cantor of Large Synagogue or Temple

Cantor

Cantorial Student

Position Description

The Cantor of a temple or synagogue has a very important position. The prime responsibility of the individual is to present liturgical music that will help clarify the prayers and studies of the religion. The objective is to enrich the religious experience of the worshippers.

As the Cantor of a temple or synagogue, the individual leads the congregation in prayer during services. The Cantor's cultured and melodic voice can usually be heard clearly above everyone else's.

The Cantor may teach music in the religious school of the synagogue. If the temple has a choir, the Cantor will lead them, supervise their rehearsals, etc. The Cantor is responsible for preparing the choir for all services. Special attention is given to the Jewish High Holy Days services. Any musical activity that occurs in the synagogue becomes the Cantor's responsibility.

In the Cantorial position, the individual may teach various courses in the synagogue's adult education classes. One of the main teaching responsibilities is that of preparing youngsters to sing or chant their Bar or Bat Mitzvah services. This responsibility is often shared with other members of the synagogue, depending on how many young people must be trained at any one time.

The Cantor is, in essence, a minister of his or her faith. Although the job is structured in part by the Cantor's duties at all Sabbath worship services, it is unstructured in other ways. Many Cantors maintain schedules that give them time for additional study of the Jewish religion and liturgical music.

The Cantor works closely with the rabbi of the congregation. At times, he or she will be involved in pastoral duties, which might include visiting members of the congregation who are sick or comforting members who are in mourning. The individual may officiate at weddings and funerals as well as at regular weekly services and holidays.

Before becoming a Cantor, one usually chooses the branch of Judaism in which he or she will study and officiate. Individuals may select the Reform branch, the Conservative branch, or the Orthodox branch. Training varies slightly in the various Judaic philosophies.

The job is generally a service position in that the Cantor helps and guides people. Cantors in both small and large congregations are, in fact, public figures in the community. On occasion, they will be asked to serve on community boards, as members of associations, and as speakers at functions.

Cantors additionally have the option during their career of becoming concert artists. In this position, Cantors sing liturgical music in a variety of concert settings, ranging from local functions to full-scale concerts at major halls.

Salaries

Cantors' salaries depend on the location and size of the synagogue or temple. Salaries usually range from $25,000 to $80,000 plus yearly. Most Cantors also receive living allowances from the congregation.

Cantors may have an opportunity to earn additional income by performing at concerts.

Employment Prospects

The employment prospects for Cantors are excellent. As of this writing, there is a shortage of qualified individuals to fill cantorial positions.

As a rule, Cantors work with congregations close to their branch of Judaic preference. They may work with either Reform, Conservative, or Orthodox congregations.

Advancement Prospects

As noted above, there is a shortage of trained Cantors. Individuals who have gained experience in the cantorate can move into positions in larger synagogues or temples.

Cantors who have established themselves as great singers may become guest Cantors for special services and/or give concerts of Jewish music. There are a number of Cantors who have attained great prestige in this way.

Education and Training

In order to become a trained Cantor one must obtain a college degree. A degree in music is, of course, preferable. There are a limited number of schools available to prepare the individual for a position as a Cantor. Schools differ in the branch of Judaism they follow. One may become a Cantor in the Reform, Conservative, or Orthodox branch of the religion.

Study in one of these schools varies in length from three to five years. As a graduate of a Cantorial college, an individual will receive a diploma certifying him or her a Cantor or hazan.

Incidentally, both secular and religious studies must be completed before graduation.

Experience, Skills, and Personality Traits

An individual aspiring to become a Cantor must possess a cultured voice. They must have a knowledge of Hebrew and all Hebraic disciplines. Cantors need to be adept at reading Torah.

Musical knowledge is a must and the ability to play an instrument is a plus.

Before an individual decides to become a Cantor, he or she generally participates in a variety of synagogue functions, taking part in various Jewish youth groups and junior congregational services.

Unions and Associations

Depending on the branch of Judaism the Cantor is involved with, he or she may belong to different organizations. These include the Jewish Ministers Cantors' Association of America (JMCA) and the American Conference of Cantors.

Tips for Entry

1. Talk to the Cantor at a synagogue or temple in the branch of Judaism with which you hope to be involved. Ask questions you have about the occupation.
2. The B'nai B'rith Vocational Service has trained people to counsel you in a career as a Cantor.
3. If you require financial aid for your education in this field, there are a number of options. Check out the college of your choice for financial assistance, scholarships, etc. Local community groups and synagogues often offer financial help in this area.
4. There are part-time cantorial positions available for cantorial students. Check synagogues, temples, and the school you attend for positions.

ORGANIST

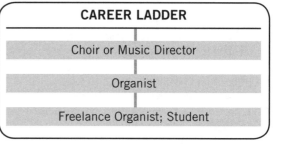

Position Description

An Organist working for a religious institution provides the music during the services. The Organist may be in charge of choosing the music to accompany prayers or may work closely with the choir or music director in accomplishing this task. In some houses of worship, the individual may act as both the Organist and the choir director.

Depending on the size and the budget of the hiring institution, the job may be either full time or part time. In a small, rural church, for instance, the Organist may work only on Sunday. In a larger metropolitan church, the Organist might be responsible not only for Sunday service music, but also for accompanying choirs, rehearsals, or playing for church services for TV or radio broadcasts.

The Organist may also be required to play for special services, including weddings and funerals. If the individual is working on a part-time basis, he or she is usually paid for the extra workload.

In this position, a person may teach other students the instrument as a way of earning additional income. The Organist is usually allowed to use the organ and the space at no charge. Occasionally, the Organist will find musically talented youngsters in the congregation. It is up to him or her to encourage the students and possibly have them participate in services.

The Organist may be responsible for giving recitals. These are mainly presented as part of the institu-

tion's music program. However, it is not unusual to find Organists performing in a setting totally apart from their job.

In a full-time position, the Organist is expected to supervise the maintenance of the organ and make sure that it is always in proper working order.

As a member of the house of worship's music committee, the Organist might advise the congregation on music-related matters. He or she usually has regular office hours or at least time in which practice and rehearsal take place.

The Organist working for a house of worship may play in a church, synagogue, or temple. The individual need not be of the same religious belief as the congregation for which he or she is providing music. The Organist is responsible to the institution's music or choir director, the music committee, or directly to the minister, priest, or rabbi.

Salaries

Organists working in religious institutions command a range of salaries. Some organists are part-time employees and some work full time. Part-time positions are usually paid by the service. Fees range from $25 to $250 or more per service.

Organists working full time may earn between approximately $30,000 and $110,000 or more a year. Factors affecting earnings include the number of hours the individual works and his or her duties and educational level. Other factors affecting earnings include the geographic location of the religious institution and its budget. In general, those who have doctoral degrees in organ or sacred music who work in large religious institutions command the highest salaries.

Employment Prospects

There are quite a few opportunities to work as an Organist in a church, temple, or synagogue. Many of these positions are only part time. (A number of churches, temples, and synagogues have Organists within the congregation who donate their services.)

Full-time positions are available in larger metropolitan areas. The more education and experience an individual has, the better opportunity he or she will have to obtain a full-time position.

Advancement Prospects

Advancement for an Organist is possible. In this position, an individual may be promoted in a number of directions. For example, the Organist may go from a part-time to a full-time position. The individual may find a position at a larger institution that pays a higher salary. An Organist might advance to the position of Organist/choir director or to that of music director.

Education and Training

Educational requirements for Organists vary according to the position. In a small town church or temple, often all that is required is the ability to play the organ well.

Conversely, Organists who are hired to work in large metropolitan houses of worship in full-time positions may be required to hold not only a bachelor's degree, but possibly a master's degree or even a doctoral degree in organ or sacred music. If the Organist's position is one which also encompasses the duties of a musical or choir director, a degree will generally be required.

In lieu of college education (although training is most certainly needed), Organists may apply for an Associates Certificate. This is given by the American Guild of Organists. The organization gives a series of tests and certifies church musicians at various levels.

Experience, Skills, and Personality Traits

The Organist must be accomplished on the instrument. He or she must be able to read and write music. A knowledge of religious music is a must.

The Organist may need to know how to maintain the organ or at least be able to supervise service on it.

Organists must get along well with the congregation and be reliable.

Unions and Associations

Organists may belong to the American Federation of Musicians (AFM) if they play outside the church, synagogue, or temple. They may also belong to a number of organizations, including the AGO (the American Guild of Organists), the Choristers Guild, the American Choral Directors Association, or a host of denominational groups.

Tips for Entry

1. There are often ads in the classified sections of newspapers from religious institutions looking for organists. Most of these jobs are part time.
2. The American Guild of Organists has a placement service for church Organists. Churches let the organization know of any openings they have.
3. The music director or choir director of any institution usually knows about job openings or opportunities in other institutions. Speak to these individuals.

APPENDIXES

APPENDIX I
DEGREE AND NONDEGREE PROGRAMS

A. FOUR-YEAR COLLEGES AND UNIVERSITIES OFFERING MAJORS RELATED TO THE MUSIC INDUSTRY

Although a college degree does not guarantee a job in the music industry, it may be in your best interest to pursue further education after high school. This gives you the opportunity to learn additional information, gain new skills, and make important contacts. Because the music industry is so competitive, higher education might give one person an advantage over another who does not have one.

The following is a listing of four-year schools granting degrees related to the music industry. They are grouped by state. The author does not endorse any one school over another. Use this list as a start. Check out the reference section of your local library or guidance counseling center to learn about additional schools.

ALABAMA

Spring Hill College
4000 Dauphin Street
Mobile, AL 36608
Phone: (251) 380-3030
Fax: (251) 460-2186
E-mail: admit@shc.edu
http://www.shc.edu

ARIZONA

Northern Arizona University
Box 4084
Flagstaff, AZ 86011
Phone: (928) 523-5511
E-mail: undergraduate.
    admissions@nau.edu
http://home.nau.edu

University of Arizona
P.O. Box 210040
Tucson, AZ 85721
Phone: (520) 621-3237
Fax: (520) 621-9799
E-mail: appinfo@arizona.edu
http://www.arizon.edu

CALIFORNIA

California Institute of the Arts
24700 McBean Parkway
Valencia, CA 91355
Phone: (661) 255-1050
E-mail: admiss@calarts.edu
http://www.calarts.edu

California State University, Chico
400 West First Street
Chico, CA 95929
Phone: (800) 542-4426
Fax: (530) 898-6456
E-mail: info@csuchico.edu
http://www.csuchico.edu

California State University, East Bay
25800 Carlos Bee Boulevard
Hayward, CA 94542
Phone: (510) 885-3248
Fax: (510) 885-4059
E-mail: admissions@csueastbay.edu
http://www.csueastbay.edu

Claremont McKenna College
890 Columbia Avenue
Claremont, CA 91711
Phone: (909) 621-8088
Fax: (909) 621-8516
E-mail: admission@
    claremontmckenna.edu
http://www.claremontmckenna.edu

San Diego State University
5500 Campanile Drive
San Diego, CA 92182
Phone: (619) 594-6336
E-mail: admissions@sdsu.edu
http://www.sdsu.edu

University of California, Riverside
1120 Hinderaker Hall
Riverside, CA 92521
Phone: (951) 827-4531
Fax: (951) 827-6344
E-mail: discover@ucr.edu
http://ww.ucr.edu

University of San Francisco
2130 Fulton Street
San Francisco, CA 94117
Phone: (415) 422-6563
Fax: (415) 422-2217
E-mail: admission@usfca.edu
http://www.usfca.edu

University of the Pacific
Stockton, CA 95211
Phone: (209) 946-2211
E-mail: admission@pacific.edu
http://www.pacific.edu/
    admission

COLORADO

Fort Lewis College
1000 Rim Drive
Durango, CO 81301
Phone: (970) 247-7184
http://www.fortlewis.edu

University of Denver
2197 South University Boulevard
Denver, CO 80208
Phone: (303) 871-2036
E-mail: admission@du.edu
http://www.du.edu/admission

Western State College of Colorado
600 North Adams Street
Gunnison, CO 81231
Phone: (800) 876-5309
E-mail: admissions@western.edu
http://www.western.edu

CONNECTICUT

Connecticut College
270 Mohegan Avenue
New London, CT 06320
Phone: (860) 439-2200
Fax: (860) 439-4301
E-mail: admission@conncoll.edu
http://www.conncoll.edu

University of Hartford
West Hartford, CT 06117
Phone: (860) 768-4296
Fax: (860) 768-4961
E-mail: admission@hartford.edu
http://admission.hartford.edu

University of New Haven
300 Boston Post Road
West Haven, CT 06516
Phone: (203) 932-7319
E-mail: adminfo@newhaven.edu
http://www.newhaven.edu

DELAWARE

Delaware State University
1200 North DuPont Highway
Dover, DE 19901
Phone: (302) 857-6351

Fax: (302) 857-6908
E-mail: gcheatha@desu.edu
http://www.desu.edu

FLORIDA

Florida Atlantic University
777 Glades Road
Boca Raton, FL 33431
Phone: (800) 299-4FAU
E-mail: admissions@fau.edu
http://www.fau.edu

Florida Southern College
111 Lake Hollingsworth Drive
Lakeland, FL 33801
Phone: (800) 274-4131
E-mail: fscadm@flsouthern.edu
http://www.flsouthern.edu

Jacksonville University
2800 University Boulevard North
Jacksonville, FL 32211
Phone: (904) 256-7000
E-mail: admissions@ju.edu
http://www.ju.edu

Southeastern University
1000 Longfellow Boulevard
Lakeland, FL 33801
Phone: (863) 667-5000
Fax: (863) 667-5200
E-mail: admission@seuniversity.edu
http://www.seuniversity.edu

University of Miami
P.O. Box 248025
Coral Gables, FL 33146
Phone: (305) 284-4472
Fax: (305) 284-2507
E-mail: admission@miami.edu
http://www.miami.edu

GEORGIA

Berry College
P.O. Box 490159
2277 Martha Berry Highway, NW
Mount Berry, GA 30149
Phone: (706) 236-2215
Fax: (706) 290-2178
E-mail: admissions@berry.edu
http://www.berry.edu

Brenau University
500 Washington Street, SE
Gainesville, GA 30501
Phone: (770) 531-6100
Fax: (770) 538-4701
E-mail: wcadmissions@brenau.edu
http://www.brenau.edu

Georgia State University
P.O. Box 4009
Atlanta, GA 30302
Phone: (404) 651-4110
Fax: (404) 651-4811
E-mail: dniccum@gsu.edu
http://www.gsu.edu

Mercer University
1400 Coleman Avenue
Macon, GA 31207
Phone: (478) 301-2650
E-mail: admissions@mercer.edu
http://www.mercer.edu

Savannah College of Art and Design
P.O. Box 2072
Savannah, Georgia 31402
Phone: (912) 525-5100
Fax: (912) 525-5986
E-mail: admission@scad.edu
http://www.scad.edu

IDAHO

Boise State University
Boise, ID 83725
Phone: (208) 426-1177
E-mail: bsuinfo@boisestate.edu
http://www.boisetate.edu

University of Idaho
P.O. Box 444264
Moscow, ID 83844
Phone: (208) 885-6326
Fax: (208) 885-9119
E-mail: admissions@uidaho.edu
http://www.uidaho.edu

ILLINOIS

Benedictine University
5700 College Road
Lisle, IL 60532

Phone: (630) 829-6300
Fax: (630) 829-6301
E-mail: admissions@ben.edu
http://www.ben.edu

Columbia College Chicago
600 South Michigan Avenue
Chicago, IL 60605
Phone: (312) 344-7130
Fax: (312) 344-8024
E-mail: admissions@colum.edu
http://www.colum.edu

DePaul University
1 East Jackson Boulevard
Chicago, IL 60604
Phone: (312) 362-8300
E-mail: admission@depaul.edu
http://www.depaul.edu

Elmhurst College
190 Prospect Avenue
Elmhurst, IL 60126
Phone: (630) 617-3400
E-mail: admit@elmhurst.edu
http://www.elmhurst.edu

Greenville College
315 East College Avenue
Greenville, IL 62246
Phone: (618) 664-7100
Fax: (618) 664-9841
E-mail: admissions@greenville.edu
http://www.greenville.edu

Illinois Wesleyan University
P.O. Box 2900
Bloomington, IL 61702
Phone: (309) 556-3031
Fax: (309) 556-3820
E-mail: iwuadmit@iwu.edu
http://www.iwu.edu

Lewis University
One University Parkway
Romeoville, IL 60446
Phone: (800) 897-9000
E-mail: admissions@lewisu.edu
http://www.lewisu.edu

Millikin University
1184 West Main Street
Decatur, IL 62522-2084

Phone: (217) 424-6210
Fax: (217) 425-4669
E-mail: admis@millikin.edu
http://www.millikin.edu

Northwestern University
P.O. Box 3060
Evanston, IL 60204
Phone: (847) 491-7271
E-mail: ug-admission@
   northwestern.edu
http://northwestern.edu

Quincy University
Quincy, IL 62301
Phone: (217) 228-5210
E-mail: admissions@quincy.edu
http://www.quncy.edu

Roosevelt University
Schaumburg Campus
1400 North Roosevelt Boulevard
Schaumburg, IL 60173
Phone: (877) APPLY-RU
Fax: (312) 341-4316
E-mail: applyRU@roosevelt.edu
http://www.roosevelt.edu

School of the Art Institute of Chicago
36 South Wabash
Chicago, IL 60603
Phone: (312) 629-6100
Fax: (312) 629-6101
E-mail: admiss@saic.edu
http://www.saic.edu

Trinity International University
2065 Half Day Road
Deerfield, IL 60015
Phone: (847) 317-7000
Fax: (847) 317-8097
E-mail: tcadmissions@tiu.edu
http://www.tiu.edu

Western Illinois University
1 University Circle
Macomb, IL 61455
Phone: (309) 298-3157
Fax: (309) 298-3111
E-mail: admissions@wiu.edu
http://www.wiu.edu

Wheaton College
Wheaton, IL 60187
Phone: (630) 752-5005
E-mail: admissions@wheaton.edu
http://www.wheaton.edu

INDIANA

Anderson University
1100 East Fifth Street
Anderson, IN 46012
Phone: (765) 641-4080
Fax: (765) 641-3851
E-mail: info@anderson.edu
http://www.anderson.edu

Butler University
4600 Sunset Avenue
Indianapolis, IN 46208
Phone: (317) 940-8100
Fax: (317) 940-8150
E-mail: admission@butler.edu
http://go.butler.edu

DePauw University
101 East Seminary Street
Greencastle, IN 46135
Phone: (765) 658-4006
Fax: (765) 658-4007
E-mail: admission@depauw.edu
http://www.depauw.edu

Huntington University
2303 College Avenue
Huntington, IN 46750
Phone: (260) 356-6000
Fax: (260) 356-9448
E-mail: admissions@huntington.
   edu
http://www.huntington.edu

Indiana State University
Terre Haute, IN 47809
Phone: (812) 237-2121
E-mail: admissions@indstate.edu
http://www.indstate.edu

Indiana University Bloomington
300 North Jordan Avenue
Bloomington, IN 47405
Phone: (812) 855-0661
Fax: (812) 855-5102

E-mail: iuadmit@indiana.edu
http://www.indiana.edu

Indiana University South Bend

1700 Mishawaka Avenue
P.O. Box 7111
South Bend, IN 46634
Phone: (574) 237-4480
Fax: (574) 237-4834
E-mail: admissio@iusb.edu
http://www.iusb.edu

Marian College

3200 Cold Spring Road
Indianapolis, IN 46222
Phone: (317) 955-6300
Fax: (317) 955-6401
E-mail: admissions@marian.edu
http://www.marian.edu

Taylor University

236 West Reade Avenue
Upland, IN 46989
Phone: (765) 998-5511
E-mail: admissions@taylor.edu
http://www.taylor.edu

University of Evansville

1800 Lincoln Avenue
Evansville, IN 47722
Phone: (812) 488-2468
Fax: (812) 488-4076
E-mail: admission@evansville.edu
http://www.evansville.edu

Valparaiso University

1700 Chapel Drive
Valparaiso, IN 46383
Phone: (219) 464-5011
Fax: (219) 464-6898
E-mail: undergrad.admissions@
valpo.edu
http://www.valpo.edu

IOWA

Buena Vista University

610 West Fourth Street
Storm Lake, IA 50588
Phone: (712) 749-2235
E-mail: admissions@bvu.edu
http://www.bvu.edu

Drake University

2507 University Avenue
Des Moines, IA 50311
Phone: (515) 271-3181
Fax: (515) 271-2831
http://www.choose.drake.edu

University of Iowa

107 Calvin Hall
Iowa City, IA 52242
Phone: (319) 335-3847
Fax: (319) 335-1535
E-mail: admissions@uiowa.edu
http://www.uiowa.edu

Upper Iowa University

Box 1859
Fayette, IA 52142
Phone: (563) 425-5393
Fax: (563) 425-5323
E-mail: admission@uiu.edu
http://www.uiu.edu

Waldorf College

106 South Sixth Street
Forest City, IA 50436
Phone: (641) 585-8119
E-mail: admissions@waldorf.edu
http://www.waldorf.edu

Wartburg College

100 Wartburg Boulevard
P.O. Box 1003
Waverly, IA 50677
Phone: (319) 352-8264
Fax: (319) 352-8579
E-mail: admissions@wartburg.edu
http://www.wartburg.edu

KANSAS

Benedictine College

1020 North Second Street
Atchison, KS 66002
Phone: (913) 367-5340
Fax: (913) 367-5462
E-mail: bcadmiss@benedictine.edu
http://www.benedictine.edu

Bethany College

421 North First Street
Lindsborg, KS 67456
Phone: (785) 227-3311

Fax: (785) 227-8993
E-mail: admissions@bethanylb.edu
http://www.bethanylb.edu

Bethel College

300 East 27th Street
North Newton, KS 67117
Phone: (316) 284-5230
Fax: (316) 284-5870
E-mail: admissions@bethelks.edu
http://www.bethelks.edu

Kansas Wesleyan University

100 East Claflin Avenue
Salina, KS 67401
Phone: (785) 827-5541
Fax: (785) 827-0927
E-mail: admissions@kwu.edu
http://www.kwu.edu

Tabor College

400 South Jefferson
Hillsboro, KS 67063
Phone: (620) 947-3121
Fax: (620) 947-6276
E-mail: rustya@tabor.edu

KENTUCKY

Asbury College

Wilmore, KY 40390
Phone: (859) 858-3511
Fax: (859) 858-3921
http://www.asbury.edu

Bellarmine University

2001 Newburg Road
Louisville, KY 40205
Phone: (502) 452-8131
Fax: (502) 452-8002
E-mail: admissions@bellarmine.edu
http://www.bellarmine.edu

Transylvania University

300 North Broadway
Lexington, KY 40508
Phone: (859) 233-8242
E-mail: admissions@transy.edu
http://www.transy.edu

University of Kentucky

100 W. D. Funkhouser Building
Lexington, KY 40506

Phone: (859) 257-2000
E-mail: admissio@uky.edu
http://www.uky.edu

Western Kentucky University
Potter Hall 117
1906 College Heights Boulevard
Bowling Green, KY 42101
Phone: (270) 745-2551
Fax: (270) 745-6133
E-mail: admission@wku.edu
http://www.wku.edu

LOUISIANA

Dillard University
2601 Gentilly Boulevard
New Orleans, LA 70122
Phone: (504) 816-4670
Fax: (504) 816-4895
E-mail: mreed@dillard.edu
http://www.dillard.edu

Loyola University
6363 St. Charles Avenue, Box 18
New Orleans, LA 70118
Phone: (504) 865-3240
Fax: (504) 865-3383
E-mail: admit@loyno.edu
http://www.loyno.ed

Southeastern Louisiana University
SLU 10752
Hammond, LA 70402
Phone: (985) 549-2066
Fax: (985) 549-5632
E-mail: admissions@selu.edu
http://www.selu.edu

University of Louisiana at Lafayette
PO Drawer 41210
Lafayette, LA 70504
Phone: (337) 482-6473
Fax: (337) 482-1317
E-mail: admissions@louisiana.edu
http://www.louisiana.edu

MARYLAND

St. Mary's College of Maryland
18952 East Fisher Road

St. Mary's City, MD 20686
Phone: (240) 895-5000
Fax: (240) 895-5001
E-mail: admissions@smcm.edu
http://www.smcm.edu

MASSACHUSETTES

Berklee College of Music
1140 Boylston Street
Boston, MA 02215
Phone: (617) 266-1400
Fax: (617) 747-2047
E-mail: admissions@berklee.edu
http://www.berklee.edu

New England Institute of Art
10 Brookline Place West
Brookline, MA 02445
Phone: (617) 739-1700
Fax: (617) 582-4500
http://www.artinstitutes.edu/boston

Northeastern University
150 Richards Hall
360 Huntington Avenue
Boston, MA 02115
Phone: (617) 373-2200
E-mail: admissions@neu.edu
http://www.northeastern.edu/admissions

Simmons College
300 The Fenway
Boston, MA 02115
Phone: (800) 345-8468
Fax: (617) 521-3190
E-mail: ugadm@simmons.edu
http://www.simmons.edu

MICHIGAN

Adrian College
110 South Madison Street
Adrian, MI 49221
Phone: (800) 877-2246
Fax: (517) 264-3331
E-mail: admissions@adrian.edu
http://www.adrian.edu

Aquinas College
1607 Robinson Road, SE
Grand Rapids, MI 49506

Phone: (616) 632-2900
E-mail: admissions@aquinas.edu
http://www.aquinas.edu

Central Michigan University
Warriner Hall 102
Mt. Pleasant, MI 48859
Phone: (989) 774-3076
Fax: (989) 774-7267
E-mail: cmuadmit@cmich.edu
http://www.cmich.edu

Eastern Michigan University
400 Pierce Hall
Ypsilanti, MI 48197
Phone: (734) 487-3060
Fax: (734) 487-1484
E-mail: admissions@emich.edu
http://www.emich.edu

Ferris State University
1201 South State Street
Big Rapids, MI 49307
Phone: (231) 591-2000
Fax: (231) 591-3944
E-mail:admissions@ferris.edu
http://www.ferris.edu

MINNESOTA

McNally Smith College of Music
19 Exchange Street East
St. Paul, MN 55101
Phone: (651) 291-0177
Fax: (651) 291-0366
E-mail: khawks@mcnallysmith.edu
http://www.mcnallysmith.edu

Minnesota School of Business–Rochester
2521 Pennington Drive, NW
Rochester, MN 55901
Phone: (507) 536-9500
Fax: (507) 535-8011
http://www.msbcollege.edu

Minnesota State University Mankato
122 Taylor Center
Mankato, MN 56001
Phone: (507) 389-1822
Fax: (507) 389-1511

E-mail: admissions@mnsu.edu
http://www.mnsu.edu

Minnesota State University Moorhead

Owens Hall
Moorhead, MN 56563
Phone: (218) 477-2161
Fax: (218) 477-4374
E-mail: dragon@mnstate.edu
http://www.mnstate.edu

North Central University

910 Elliot Avenue
Minneapolis, MN 55404
Phone: (612) 343-4460
Fax: (612) 343-4146
E-mail: admissions@northcentral.
edu
http://www.northcentral.edu

Saint Mary's University of Minnesota

700 Terrace Heights
Winona, MN 55987
Phone: (507) 457-1700
Fax: (507) 457-1722
E-mail: admissions@smumn.edu
http://www.smumn.edu

Southwest Minnesota State University

1501 State Street
Marshall, MN 56258
Phone: (507) 537-6286
Fax: (507) 537-7145
E-mail: shearerr@southwestmsu.
edu
http://www.southwestmsu.edu

St. Olaf College

1520 St. Olaf Avenue
Northfield, MN 55057
Phone: (507) 786-3025
Fax: (507) 786-3832
E-mail: admissions@stolaf.edu
http://www.stolaf.edu

Winona State University

P.O. Box 5838
Winona, MN 55987
Phone: (507) 457-5100
Fax: (507) 457-5620

E-mail: admissions@winona.edu
http://www.winona.edu

MISSISSIPPI

Belhaven College

150 Peachtree Street
Jackson, MS 39202
Phone: (601) 968-5940
Fax: (601) 968-8946
E-mail: admission@belhaven.edu
http://www.belhaven.edu

University of Southern Mississippi

118 College Drive, # 5166
Hattiesburg, MS 39406-1000
Phone: (601) 266-5000
Fax: (601) 266-5148
E-mail: admissions@usm.edu
http://www.usm.edu

MISSOURI

College of the Ozarks

P.O. Box 17
Point Lookout, MO 65726
Phone: (417) 334-6411
Fax: (417) 335-2618
E-mail: admiss4@cofo.edu
http://www.cofo.edu

Culver-Stockton College

One College Hill
Canton, MO 63435
Phone: (800) 537-1883
E-mail: admissions@culver.edu
Whttp://www.culver.edu

Drury University

900 North Benton
Springfield, MO 65802
Phone: (417) 873-7205
Fax: (417) 866-3873
E-mail: druryad@drury.edu
http://www.drury.edu

Fontbonne University

6800 Wydown Boulevard
St. Louis, MO 63105
Phone: (314) 889-1400
Fax: (314) 889-1451
E-mail: pmusen@fontbonne.edu
http://www.fontbonne.edu

Northwest Missouri State University

800 University Drive
Maryville, MO 64468
Phone: (660) 562-1146
E-mail: admissions@nwmissouri.
edu
http://www.nwmissouri.edu

NEBRASKA

Peru State College

P.O. Box 10
Peru, NE 68421
Phone: (402) 872-2221
Fax: (402) 872-2296
E-mail: mwillis@oakmail.peru.edu
http://www.peru.edu

NEW HAMPSHIRE

Keene State College

Elliot Hall
Keene, NH 03435
Phone: (603) 358-2276
Fax: (603-358-2767
E-mail: admissions@keene.edu
http://www.keene.edu

NEW JERSEY

William Paterson University of New Jersey

Wayne, NJ 07470
Phone: (973) 720-2125
E-mail: admissions@wpunj.edu
http://www.wpunj.edu

NEW MEXICO

College of Santa Fe

1600 Saint Michael's Drive
Santa Fe, NM 87505
Phone: (505) 473-6133
Fax: (505) 473-6129
E-mail: admissions@csf.edu
http://www.csf.edu

NEW YORK

Baruch College of the City University of New York

One Bernard Baruch Way
Box H-0720

New York, NY 10010
Phone: (646) 312-1400
Fax: (646) 312-1363
E-mail: admissions@baruch.cuny.edu
http://www.baruch.cuny.edu

Fashion Institute of Technology
Seventh Avenue at 27th Street
New York, NY 10001
Phone: (212) 217-3760
E-mail: fitinfo@fitnyc.edu
http://www.fitnyc.edu

Five Towns College
305 North Service Road
Dix Hills, NY 11746
Phone: (631) 424-7000
Fax: (631) 656-2172
E-mail: admissions@ftc.edu
http://www.ftc.edu

Hofstra University
100 Hofstra University
Hempstead, NY 11549
Phone: (516) 463-6700
Fax: (516) 463-5100
http://www.hofstra.edu

Ithaca College
100 Job Hall
Ithaca, NY 14850
Phone: (607) 274-3124
Fax: (607) 274-1900
http://www.ithaca.edu/admission

Long Island University, Brooklyn Campus
1 University Plaza
Brooklyn, NY 11201
Phone: (718) 488-1011
Fax: (718) 797-2399
E-mail: admissions@brooklyn.liu.edu
http://www.brooklyn.liu.edu/apply

Long Island University, C.W. Post Campus
720 Northern Boulevard
Brookville, NY 11548
Phone: (516) 299-2900
Fax: (516) 299-2137

E-mail: enroll@cwpost.liu.edu
http://www.liu.edu/cwpost

New York University
Office of Undergraduate Admissions
22 Washington Square North
New York, NY 10011
Phone: (212) 998-4500
http://admissions.nyu.edu

State University of New York at Fredonia
Fenner House
Fredonia, NY 14063
Phone: (716) 673-3251
E-mail: admissions.office@fredonia.edu
http://www.fredonia.edu

State University of New York College at Oneonta
Oneonta, NY 13820
Phone: (607) 436-2524
Fax: (607) 436-3074
E-mail: admissions@oneonta.edu
http://www.oneonta.edu

State University of New York College at Potsdam
44 Pierrepont Avenue
Potsdam, NY 13676
Phone: (315) 267-2180
Fax: (315) 267-2163
E-mail: admissions@potsdam.edu
http://www.postdam.edu

Wagner College
Admissions Office
1 Campus Road
Staten Island, NY 10301
Phone: (718) 390-3411
Fax: (718) 390-3105
E-mail: admissions@wagner.edu
http://www.wagner.edu

NORTH CAROLINA

Appalachian State University
Boone, NC 28608
Phone: (828) 262-2120
http://www.appstate.edu

Bennett College For Women
Campus Box H
Greensboro, NC 27401
Phone: (336) 517-8624
E-mail: admiss@bennett.edu
http://www.bennett.edu

Chowan University
200 Jones Drive
Murfreesboro, NC 27855
Phone: (252) 398-6298
http://www.chowan.edu

Elizabeth City State University
P.O. Box 901 ECSU
Elizabeth City, NC 27909
Phone: (252) 335-3305
http://www.ecsu.edu

Johnson C. Smith University
100 Beatties Ford Road
Charlotte, NC 28216
Phone: (704) 378-1010
Fax: (704) 378-1242
E-mail: admissions@jcsu.edu
http://www.jcsu.edu

Lenoir-Rhyne College
P.O. Box 7227
Hickory, NC 28603
Phone: (828) 328-7300
Fax: (828) 328-7378
E-mail: admission@lrc.edu
http://www.lrc.edu

Methodist University
5400 Ramset Street
Fayetteville, NC 28311
Phone: (910) 630-7027
http://www.methodist.edu

Montreat College
P.O. Box 1267
Montreat, NC 28757
Phone: (828) 669-8012
Fax: (828) 669-0120
E-mail: admissions@montreat.edu
http://www.montreat.edu

North Carolina State University
Box 7103
112 Peele Hall
Raleigh, NC 27695

Phone: (919) 515-2434
Fax: (919) 515-5039
E-mail: undergrad_admissions@
ncsu.edu
http://www.ncsu.edu

Pfeiffer University
P.O. Box 960
Highway 52 North
Misenheimer, NC 28109
Phone: (704) 463-1360
Fax: (704) 463-1363
E-mail: admiss@pfeiffer.edu
http://www.pfeiffer.edu

Salem College
Dean of Admissions
601 South Church Street
Winston-Salem, NC 27101
Phone: (336) 721-2621
E-mail: admissions@salem.edu
http://www.salem.edu

University of North Carolina at Asheville
117 Lipinsky Hall
CPO 2210
One University Heights
Asheville, NC 28804
Phone: (828) 251-6481
Fax: (828) 251-6482
E-mail: admissions@unca.edu
http://www.unca.edu

OHIO

Bowling Green State University
110 McFall Center
Bowling Green, OH 43403
Phone: (419) 372-BGSU
Fax: (419) 372-6955
E-mail: choosebgsu@bgsu.edu
http://www.bgsu.edu

Capital University
1 College and Main
Columbus, OH 43209
Phone: (614) 236-6101
Fax: (614) 236-6926
E-mail: admissions@capital.edu
http://www.capital.edu

Heidelberg College
310 East Market Street
Tiffin, OH 44883
Phone: (419) 448-2330
Fax: (419) 448-2334
E-mail: adminfo@heidelberg.edu
http://www.heidelberg.edu

Ohio Northern University
Ada, OH 45810
Phone: (888) 408-4668
Fax: (419) 772-2821
E-mail: admissions-ug@onu.edu
http://www.onu.edu

Ohio University
Athens, OH 45701-2979
Phone: (740) 593-4100
Fax: (740) 593-0560
E-mail: admissions@ohio.edu
http://www.ohio.edu

Otterbein College
One Otterbein College
Westerville, OH 43081
Phone: (614) 823-1500
E-mail: uotterb@otterbein.edu
http://www.otterbein.edu

Tiffin University
155 Miami Street
Tiffin, OH 44883
Phone: (419) 448-3423
Fax: (419) 443-5006
E-mail: admiss@tiffin.edu
http://www.tiffin.edu

University of Akron
277 East Buchtel Avenue
Akron, OH 44325
Phone: (330) 972-6427
Fax: (330) 972-7022
E-mail: admissions@uakron.edu
http://www.uakron.edu

Wright State University
3640 Colonel Glenn Highway
Dayton, OH 45435
Phone: (937) 775-5700
E-mail: admissions@wright.edu
http://www.wright.edu/admissions

OKLAHOMA

Oklahoma City University
2501 North Blackwelder
Oklahoma City, OK 73106
Phone: (405) 208-5340
Fax: (405) 208-5916
E-mail: mlockhart@okcu.edu
http://www.okcu.edu

Southwestern Oklahoma State University
100 Campus Drive
Weatherford, OK 73096
Phone: (580) 774-3009
Fax: (580) 774-3795
E-mail: ropers@swosu.edu
http://www.swosu.edu

OREGON

Northwest Christian University
828 East 11th Avenue
Eugene, OR 97401
Phone: (541) 684-7201
Fax: (541) 684-7317
E-mail: admissions@nwcc.edu
http://www.nwcc.edu

Southern Oregon University
1250 Siskiyou Boulevard
Ashland, OR 97520
Phone: (541) 552-6411
E-mail: admissions@sou.edu
http://www.sou.edu

Warner Pacific College
2219 Southeast 68th Avenue
Portland, OR 97215
Phone: (503) 517-1020
Fax: (503) 517-1352
E-mail: admissions@warnerpacific.
edu
http://www.warnerpacific.edu

PENNSYVLVANIA

Chatham University
Woodland Road
Pittsburgh, PA 15232
Phone: (412) 365-1290
Fax: (412) 365-1609
E-mail: admissions@chatham.edu
http://www.chatham.edu

Clarion University of Pennsylvania
840 Wood Street
Clarion, PA 16214
Phone: (814) 393-2306
E-mail: admissions@clarion.edu
http://www.clarion.edu/admiss/

Duquesne University
600 Forbes Avenue
Pittsburgh, PA 15282
Phone: (412) 396-5002
Fax: (412) 396-5644
E-mail: admissions@duq.edu
http://www.duq.edu

Geneva College
3200 College Avenue
Beaver Falls, PA 15010
Phone: (724) 847-6500
E-mail: admissions@geneva.edu
http://www.geneva.edu

Grove City College
100 Campus Drive
Grove City, PA 16127
Phone: (724) 458-2100
Fax: (724) 458-3395
E-mail: admissions@gcc.edu
http://www.gcc.edu

Lebanon Valley College
101 North College Avenue
Annville, PA 17003
Phone: (866) 582-423
Fax: (717) 867-6026
E-mail: admission@lvc.edu
http://www.lvc.edu

Mansfield University of Pennsylvania
Beecher House
Mansfield, PA 16933
Phone: (570) 662-4813
E-mail: admissions@mnsfld.edu
http://www.mnsfld.edu

Marywood University
2300 Adams Avenue
Scranton, PA 18509
Phone: (570) 348-6234
Fax: (570) 961-4763

E-mail: yourfuture@marywood.edu
http://www.mymarywood.com

Mercyhurst College dmissions
501 East 38th Street
Erie, PA 16546
Phone: (814) 824-2202
E-mail: admissions@mercyhurst.edu
http://admissions.mercyhurst.edu

Point Park University
201 Wood Street
Pittsburgh, PA 15222
Phone: (412) 392-3430
Fax: (412) 392-3902
E-mail: enroll@pointpark.edu
http://www.pointpark.ed

Seton Hill University
Box 991
One Seton Hill Drive
Greensburg, PA 15601
Phone: (800) 826-6234
Fax: (724) 830-1294
E-mail: admit@setonhill.edu
http://www.setonhill.

RHODE ISLAND

Brown University
Box 1876
Providence, RI 02912
Phone: (401) 863-2378
Fax: (401) 863-9300
E-mail: admission_undergraduate@brown.edu
http://www.brown.edu

SOUTH CAROLINA

South Carolina State University
300 College Street Northeast
Orangeburg, SC 29117
Phone: (803) 536-7186
Fax: (803) 536-8990
E-mail: admissions@scsu.edu
http://www.scsu.edu

SOUTH DAKOTA

South Dakota State University
P.O. Box 2201
Brookings, SD 57007

Phone: (605) 688-4121
Fax: (605) 688-6891
E-mail: sdsu.admissions@sdstate.edu
http://www.sdstate.edu

TENNESSEE

Belmont University
1900 Belmont Boulevard
Nashville, TN 37212
Phone: (615) 460-6785
Fax: (615) 460-5434
E-mail: buadmission@mail.belmont.edu
http://www.belmont.edu

Bryan College
P.O. Box 7000
Dayton, TN 37321
Phone: (423) 775-2041
Fax: (423) 775-7199
E-mail: admissions@bryan.edu
http://www.bryan.edu

Middle Tennessee State University
1301 East Main Street
Murfreesboro, TN 37132
Phone: (615) 898-2111
Fax: (615) 898-5478
E-mail: admissions@mtsu.edu
http://www.mtsu.edu

Trevecca Nazarene University
333 Murfreesboro Road
Nashville, TN 37210
Phone: (615) 248-1320
Fax: (615) 248-7406
E-mail: admissions_und@trevecca.edu
http://www.trevecca.edu

Union University
1050 Union University Drive
Jackson, TN 38305
Phone: (731) 661-5100
E-mail: info@uu.edu
http://www.uu.edu

University of Memphis
101 John Wilder Tower
Memphis, TN 38152

Phone: (901) 678-2169
http://www.memphis.edu

TEXAS

Dallas Baptist University
3000 Mountain Creek Parkway
Dallas, TX 75211
Phone: (214) 333-5360
Fax: (214) 333-5447
E-mail: admiss@dbu.edu
http://www.dbu.edu

Hardin-Simmons University
Box 16050
Abilene, TX 79698
Phone: (325) 670-5890
Fax: (325) 671-2115
E-mail: breynolds@hsutx.edu
http://www.hsutx.edu

University of Texas at San Antonio
6900 North Loop 1604 West
San Antonio, TX 78249

Phone: (210) 458-4536
Fax: (210) 458-2001
E-mail: prospects@utsa.edu
http://www.utsa.edu

VERMONT

Vermont State College
337 College Hill
Johnson, VT 05656
Phone: (802) 635-1219
Fax: (802) 635-1230
E-mail: jscadmissions@jsc.vsc.edu
http://www.vsc.edu

WASHINGTON

Central Washington University
400 East University Way
Ellensburg, WA 98926
Phone: (509) 963-1211
Fax: (509) 963-3022
E-mail: cwuadmis@cwu.edu
http://www.cwu.edu

Northwest University
P.O. Box 579
Kirkland, WA 98083
Phone: (425) 889-5212
Fax: (425) 889-5224
E-mail: admissions@northwestu.edu
http://www.northwestu.edu

University of Puget Sound
1500 North Warner Street, #1062
Tacoma, WA 98416
Phone: (253) 879-3211
E-mail: admission@ups.edu
http://www.ups.edu

WISCONSIN

Marian College of Fond du Lac
45 South National Avenue
Fond du Lac, WI 54935
Phone: (800) 262-7426
Fax: (920) 923-8755
E-mail: admit@mariancollege.edu
http://www.mariancollege.edu

B. TWO-YEAR COLLEGES OFFERING DEGREES IN MUSIC MANAGEMENT

The following is a listing of two-year schools offering degrees in music management. They are grouped by state. The author does not endorse any one school over another. Use this list as a start. Check out the reference section of your local library or guidance counseling center to locate other schools.

ARIZONA

Glendale Community College
6000 West Olive Avenue
Glendale, AZ 85302
Phone: (623) 435-3305
Fax: (623) 845-3303
E-mail: info@gc.maricopa.edu
http://www.gc.maricopa.edu

CALIFORNIA

American River College
4700 College Oak Drive
Sacramento, CA 95841
Phone: (916) 484-8171
http://www.arc.losrios.edu

Los Medanos College
2700 East Leland Road

Pittsburgh, CA 94565
Phone: (925) 439-2181 Ext. 7500
http://www.losmedanos.net/

Orange Coast College
2701 Fairview Road
Costa Mesa, CA 92926
Phone: (714) 432-5788
Fax: (714) 432-5072
E-mail: kclark@occ.cccd.edu
http://www.cccd.edu

ILLINOIS

Lincoln College
300 Keokuk Street
Lincoln, IL 62656
Phone: (800) 569-0556
Fax: (217) 732-7715

E-mail: information@
   lincolncollege.com
http://www.lincolncollege.com

KANSAS

Independence Community College
P.O. Box 708
Independence, KS 67301
Phone: (620) 332-5400
Fax: (620) 331-0946
E-mail: sciufulescu@indycc.edu
http://www.indycc.edu

NEBRASKA

Northeast Community College
801 East Benjamin Avenue

P.O. Box 469
Norfolk, NE 68702
Phone: (402) 844-7258
Fax: (402) 844-7400
E-mail: admission@northeast.edu
http://www.northeast.edu

NEW YORK

**Schenectady County
   Community College**
78 Washington Avenue
Schenectady, NY 12305
Phone: (518) 381-1370
E-mail: sampsodg@gw.sunysccc.
   edu
http://www.sunysccc.edu

Villa Maria College of Buffalo
240 Pine Ridge Road
Buffalo, NY 14225
Phone: (716) 896-0700
Fax: (716) 896-0705
E-mail: admmissions@villa.edu
http://www.villa.edu

TEXAS

Austin Community College
5930 Middle Fiskville Rd.
Austin, TX 78752
Phone: (512) 223-7503
Fax: (512) 223-7665
E-mail: admission@austincc.edu
http://www.austincc.edu

**Collin County Community
   College**
28 E Spring Creek Parkway
Plano, TX 75074
Phone: (972) 881-5174
Fax: (972) 881-5175
E-mail: tfields@ccccd.edu
http://www.ccccd.edu

Houston Community College
3100 Main Street
P.O. Box 667517
Houston, TX 77266
Phone: (713) 718-8500
Fax: (713) 718-2111
http://houstoncc.edu

C. COLLEGES AND UNIVERSITIES THAT OFFER DEGREES IN ARTS MANAGEMENT AND ADMINISTRATION

ALABAMA

Spring Hill College
4000 Dauphin Street
Mobile, AL 36608
Phone: (251) 380-3030
Fax: (251) 460-2186
E-mail: admit@shc.edu
http://www.shc.edu

ARIZONA

Northern Arizona University
Box 4084
Flagstaff, AZ 86011
Phone: (928)523-5511
E-mail: undergraduate.
   admissions@nau.edu
http://home.nau.edu

CALIFORNIA

**California State University,
   East Bay**
25800 Carlos Bee Boulevard
Hayward, CA 94542
Phone: (510) 885-3248
Fax: (510) 885-4059
E-mail: admissions@csueeastbay.edu
http://www.csueeastbay.edu

University of San Francisco
2130 Fulton Street
San Francisco, CA 94117
Phone: (415) 422-6563
Fax: (415) 422-2217

COLORADO

Fort Lewis College
1000 Rim Drive
Durango, CO 81301
Phone: (970) 247-7184
E-mail: admission@usfca.edu
http://www.usfca.edu

CONNECTICUT

University of Hartford
West Hartford, CT 06117
Phone: (860) 768-4296
Fax: (860) 768-4961
E-mail: admission@hartford.edu
http://admission.hartford.edu

DELAWARE

Delaware State University
1200 North DuPont Highway
Dover, DE 19901-2277

Phone: (302) 857-6351
Fax: (302) 857-6908
E-mail: gcheatha@desu.edu
http://www.desu.edu

FLORIDA

Barry University
11300 N.E. Second Avenue
Miami Shores, FL 33161
Phone: (305) 899-3000
E-mail: admissions@mail.barry.
   edu
http://www.barry.edu

GEORGIA

Brenau University
500 Washington Street, SE
Gainesville, GA 30501
Phone: (770) 531-6100
Fax: (770) 538-4701
E-mail: wcadmissions@brenau.edu
http://www.brenau.edu

**Savannah College of Art and
   Design—Atlanta**
P.O. Box 77300
Atlanta, Georgia 30357

Phone: (404) 253-2700
Fax: (404) 253-3466
E-mail: scadatl@scad.edu
http://www.scad.edu

ILLINOIS

Benedictine University

5700 College Road
Lisle, IL 60532
Phone: (630) 829-6300
Fax: (630) 829-6301
E-mail: admissions@ben.edu
http://www.ben.edu

Columbia College Chicago

600 South Michigan Avenue
Chicago, IL 60605
Phone: (312) 344-7130
Fax: (312) 344-8024
http://www.colum.edu

DePaul University

1 East Jackson Boulevard
Chicago, IL 60604
Phone: (312) 362-8300
E-mail: admission@depaul.edu
http://www.depaul.edu

Millikin University

1184 West Main Street
Decatur, IL 62522
Phone: (217) 424-6210
Fax: (217) 425-4669
E-mail: admis@millikin.edu
http://www.millikin.edu

Quincy University

1800 College Avenue
Quincy, IL 62301
Phone: (217) 228-5210
E-mail: admissions@quincy.edu
http://www.quincy.edu

INDIANA

Butler University

4600 Sunset Avenue
Indianapolis, IN 46208
Phone: (317) 940-8100
Fax: (317) 940-8150
E-mail: admission@butler.edu
http://go.butler.edu

Indiana University, Bloomington

300 North Jordan Avenue
Bloomington, IN 47405
Phone: (812) 855-0661
Fax: (812) 855-5102
E-mail: iuadmit@indiana.edu
http://www.indiana.edu

Marian College

3200 Cold Spring Road
Indianapolis, IN 46222
Phone: (317) 955-6300
Fax: (317) 955-6401
E-mail: admissions@marian.edu
http://www.marian.edu

IOWA

Buena Vista University

610 West Fourth Street
Storm Lake, IA 50588
Phone: (712) 749-2235
E-mail: admissions@bvu.edu
http://www.bvu.edu

University of Iowa

107 Calvin Hall
Iowa City, IA 52242
Phone: (319) 335-3847
Fax: (319) 335-1535
E-mail: admissions@uiowa.edu
http://www.uiowa.edu

Upper Iowa University

Box 1859
Fayette, IA 52142
Phone: (563) 425-5393
Fax: (563)425-5323
E-mail: admission@uiu.edu
http://www.uiu.edu

Wartburg College

100 Wartburg Boulevard
P.O. Box 1003
Waverly, IA 50677
Phone: (319) 352-8264
Fax: (319) 352-8579
E-mail: admissions@wartburg.edu
http://www.wartburg.edu

KANSAS

Benedictine College

1020 North Second Street
Atchison, KS 66002

Phone: (913) 367-5340
Fax: (913) 367-5462
E-mail: bcadmiss@benedictine.edu
http://www.benedictine.edu

Bethany College

421 North First Street
Lindsborg, KS 67456
Phone: (785) 227-3311
Fax: (785) 227-8993
E-mail: admissions@bethanylb.edu
http://www.bethanylb.edu

Kansas Wesleyan University

100 East Claflin Avenue
Salina, KS 67401
Phone: (785) 827-5541
Fax: (785) 827-0927
E-mail: admissions@kwu.edu
http://www.kwu.edu

KENTUCKY

University of Kentucky

100 W. D. Funkhouser Building
Lexington, KY 40506
Phone: (859) 257-2000
E-mail: admissions@uky.edu
http://www.uky.edu

LOUISIANA

Dillard University

2601 Gentilly Boulevard
New Orleans, LA 70122
Phone: (504) 816-4670
Fax: (504) 816-4895
E-mail: mreed@dillard.edu
http://www.dillard.edu

Southeastern Louisiana University

SLU 10752
Hammond, LA 70402
Phone: (985) 549-2066
Fax: (985) 549-5632
E-mail: admissions@selu.edu
http://www.selu.edu

MASSACHUSSETTS

Simmons College

300 The Fenway

Boston, MA 02115
Phone: (800) 345-8468
Fax: (617) 521-3190
http://www.simmons.edu

MICHIGAN

Aquinas College
1607 Robinson Road, SE
Grand Rapids, MI 49506
Phone: (616) 632-2900
E-mail: admissions@aquinas.edu
http://www.aquinas.edu

Eastern Michigan University
Ypsilanti, Michigan 48197
Phone: (734) 487-3060
Fax: (734) 487-6559
E-mail: admissions@emich.edu
http://www.emich.edu

MISSISSIPPI

Belhaven College
150 Peachtree Street
Jackson, MS 39202
Phone: (601) 968-5940
Fax: (601) 968-8946
E-mail: admission@belhaven.edu
http://www.belhaven.edu

MISSOURI

Culver-Stockton College
One College Hill
Canton, MO 63435
Phone: (800) 537-1883
E-mail: admissions@culver.edu
http://www.culver.edu

Drury University
900 North Benton
Springfield, MO 65802
Phone: (417) 873-7205
Fax: (417) 866-3873
E-mail: druryad@drury.edu
http://www.drury.edu

Fontbonne University
6800 Wydown Boulevard
St. Louis, MO 63105
Phone: (314) 889-1400
Fax: (314) 889-1451

E-mail: pmusen@fontbonne.edu
http://www.fontbonne.edu

NEW YORK

Baruch College of the City University of New York
One Bernard Baruch Way
Box H-0720
New York, NY 10010
Phone: (646) 312-1400
Fax: (646) 312-1363
E-mail: admissions@baruch.cuny.edu
http://www.baruch.cuny.edu

Fashion Institute of Technology
Seventh Avenue at 27th Street
New York, NY 10001
Phone: (212) 217-3760
E-mail: fitinfo@fitnyc.edu
http://www.fitnyc.edu

Ithaca College
100 Job Hall
Ithaca, NY 14850
Phone: (607) 274-3124
Fax: (607) 274-1900
http://www.ithaca.edu/admission

Long Island University, C. W. Post Campus
720 Northern Boulevard
Brookville, NY 11548
Phone: (516) 299-2900
Fax: (516) 299-2137
E-mail: enroll@cwpost.liu.edu
http://www.liu.edu

Parsons The New School for Design
65 Fifth Avenue
New York, NY 10011
Phone: (212) 229-8989
Fax: (212) 229-8975
E-mail: parsadm@newschool.edu
http://www.parsons.newschool.edu

State University of New York at Fredonia
Fenner House
Fredonia, NY 14063
Phone: (716) 673-3251

E-mail: admissions.office@ fredonia.edu
http://www.fredonia.edu

Wagner College
1 Campus Road
Staten Island, NY 10301
Phone: (718) 390-3411
Fax: (718) 390-3105
E-mail: admissions@wagner.edu
http://www.wagner.edu

NORTH CAROLINA

Appalachian State University
Boone, NC 28608
Phone: (828) 262-2000
E-mail: admissions@appstate.edu
http://www.appstate.edu

Bennett College For Women
Campus Box H
Greensboro, NC 27401
Phone: (336) 517-8624
E-mail: admiss@bennett.edu
http://www.bennett.edu

Lenoir-Rhyne College
P.O. Box 7227
Hickory, NC 28603
Phone: (828) 328-7300
Fax: (828) 328-7378
E-mail: admission@lrc.edu
http://www.lrc.edu

North Carolina State University
Box 7103
112 Peele Hall
Raleigh, NC 27695
Phone: (919) 515-2434
Fax: (919) 515-5039
E-mail: undergrad_admissions@ ncsu.edu
http://www.ncsu.edu

Pfeiffer University
P.O. Box 960
Highway 52 North
Misenheimer, NC 28109
Phone: (704) 463-1360
Fax: (704) 463-1363
E-mail: admiss@pfeiffer.edu
http://www.pfeiffer.edu

Salem College
601 South Church Street
Winston-Salem, NC 27101
Phone: (336) 721-2621
E-mail: admissions@salem.edu
http://www.salem.edu

OHIO

Tiffin University
155 Miami Street
Tiffin, OH 44883
Phone: (419) 448-3423
Fax: (419) 443-5006
E-mail: admiss@tiffin.edu
http://www.tiffin.edu

Wright State University
3640 Colonel Glenn Highway
Dayton, OH 45435
Phone: (937) 775-5700
E-mail: admissions@wright.edu
http://www.wright.edu/admissions

OKLAHOMA

Oklahoma City University
2501 North Blackwelder
Oklahoma City, OK 73106
Phone: (405) 208-5340
Fax: (405) 208-5916
E-mail: mlockhart@okcu.edu
http://www.okcu.edu

University of Tulsa
800 South Tucker Drive
Tulsa, OK 74104
Phone: (918) 631-2307
Fax: (918) 631-5003
E-mail: admission@utulsa.edu
http://www.utulsa.edu/admission

OREGON

University of Portland
5000 North Willamette Boulevard
Portland, OR 97203
Phone: (503) 943-7147
Fax: (503) 943-7315
E-mail: admissions@up.edu
http://www.up.edu

PENNSYLVANIA

Chatham University
Woodland Road
Pittsburgh, PA 15232
Phone: (412) 365-1290
Fax: (412) 365-1609
E-mail: admissions@chatham.edu
http://www.chatham.edu

Marywood University
2300 Adams Avenue
Scranton, PA 18509
Phone: (570) 348-6234
Fax: (570) 961-4763
E-mail: yourfuture@marywood.edu
http://www.mymarywood.com

Mercyhurst College Admissions
501 East 38th Street
Erie, PA 16546
Phone: (814) 824-2202
E-mail: admissions@mercyhurst.edu
http://admissions.mercyhurst.edu

Point Park University
201 Wood Street
Pittsburgh, PA 15222
Phone: (412) 392-3430
Fax: (412) 392-3902
E-mail: enroll@pointpark.edu
http://www.pointpark.ed

Seton Hill University
Box 991
One Seton Hill Drive
Greensburg, PA 15601
Phone: (800) 826-6234
Fax: (724) 830-1294
E-mail: admit@setonhill.edu
http://www.setonhill.edu

Waynesburg University
51 West College Street
Waynesburg, PA 15370
Phone: (724) 852-3333
Fax: (724) 627-8124
E-mail: admissions@waynesburg.edu
http://www.waynesburg.edu

SOUTH CAROLINA

College of Charleston
66 George Street
Charleston, SC 29424
Phone: (843) 953-5670
Fax: (843) 953-6322
E-mail: admissions@cofc.edu
http://www.cofc.edu

UTAH

Westminster College
1840 South 1300 East
Salt Lake City, UT 84105
Phone: (801) 832-2200
http://www.westminstercollege.edu

VIRGINIA

Hollins University
P.O. Box 9707
Roanoke, VA 24020
Phone: (540) 362-6401
E-mail: huadm@hollins.edu
http://hollins.edu

Mary Baldwin College
Frederick and New Streets
Staunton, VA 24401
Phone: (540) 887-7260
Fax: (540) 887-7229
E-mail: lbranson@mbc.edu
http://www.mbc.edu

Randolph-Macon College
P.O. Box 5005
Ashland, VA 23005
Phone: (804) 752-7305
E-mail: admissions@rmc.edu
http://www.rmc.edu

Shenandoah University
1460 University Drive
Winchester, VA 22601
Phone: (540) 665-4581
Fax: (540) 665-4627
E-mail: admit@su.edu
http://www.su.edu

WASHINGTON

Whitworth University
West 300 Hawthorne Road

Spokane, WA 99251
Phone: (509) 777-3212
E-mail: admission@whitworth.edu
http://www.whitworth.edu

WISCONSIN

**University of Wisconsin–
Stevens Point**
2100 Main Street

Stevens Point, WI 54481
Phone: (715) 346-2441
Fax: (715) 346-3296
E-mail: admiss@uwsp.edu
http://www.uwsp.edu

Viterbo University
900 Viterbo Drive
LaCrosse, WI 54601
Phone: (608) 796-3085

Fax: (608) 796-3020
E-mail: admission@viterbo.edu
http://www.viterbo.edu

D. COLLEGES AND UNIVERSITIES THAT OFFER DEGREES IN MUSIC THERAPY

The following is a listing of colleges and universities offering bachelor's degree programs approved by the American Music Therapy Association (AMTA). They are grouped by state. Asterisks (*) following college names indicate that graduate degrees are available.

Contact the American Music Therapy Association (AMTA) to find out about any new programs that may have been approved.

Names, addresses, phone numbers, and Web sites have been included when available to make it easier to get information regarding a specific school.

ALABAMA

University of Alabama
School of Music
P.O. Box 870366
Tuscaloosa, AL 35487
Phone: (205) 348-1432
http://www.ua.edu

ARIZONA

Arizona State University*
School of Music
P.O. Box 870113
Tempe, AZ 85287
Phone: (480) 965-7788
E-mail: ugradinq@asu.edu
http://www.asu.edu

CALIFORNIA

**California State University,
Northridge**
18111 Nordhoff Street
Northridge, CA 91330
Phone: (818) 677-3174
http://www.csun.edu

University of the Pacific*
Conservatory of Music
3601 Pacific Avenue
Department of Music Therapy

Stockton, CA 95211
Phone: (209) 946-2419
E-mail: admission@pacific.edu
http://www.pacific.edu

COLORADO

Colorado State University*
School of the Arts
Department of Music, Theatre, and
Dance
Fort Collins, CO 80523
Phone: (970) 491-5888
E-mail: admissions@colostate.edu
http://www.colostate.edu

DISTRICT OF COLUMBIA

Howard University
Department of Music–Division of
Fine Arts
College of Arts & Sciences
Childers Hall, Room 3030
Washington, DC 20059
Phone: (202) 806-7136

FLORIDA

Florida State University*
School of Music
Tallahassee, FL 32306
Phone: (850) 644-4565

E-mail: admissions@admin.fsu.edu
http://www.fsu.edu

University of Miami*
Frost School of Music
Music Therapy Program
P.O. Box 248165
Coral Gables, FL 33124
Phone: (305) 284-3943
E-mail: admission@miami.edu
http://www.miami.edu

GEORGIA

**Georgia College & State
University***
Department of Music Therapy
CBX 067
Milledgeville, GA 31061
Phone: (478) 445-2645
E-mail: info@gcsu.edu
http://www.gcsu.edu

University of Georgia*
School of Music
250 River Road
Athens, GA 30602-3153
Phone: (706) 542-2801
E-mail: undergrad@admissions.
uga.edu
http://www.uga.edu

ILLINOIS

Illinois State University*
5660 School of Music
Normal, IL 61790
Phone: (309) 438-8803
http://www.ilstu.edu

Western Illinois University
School of Music
1 University Circle
Macomb, IL 61455
Phone: (309) 298-1187
http://www.wiu.edu

INDIANA

Indiana-Purdue University Fort Wayne
Department of Music
2101 Coliseum Boulevard East
Classroom Medical Building
Fort Wayne, IN 46805
Phone: (260) 481-6716
E-mail: ask@ipfw.edu
http://www.ipfw.edu

Indiana University—Purdue, University of Indianapolis*
School of Music, IT 379
535 West Michigan Street
Indianapolis, IN 46202
Phone: (317) 278-2014
http://www.iupui.edu

Saint Mary-of-the-Woods College*
Department of Music Therapy
SMWC Conservatory
3301 St. Mary's Road
St. Mary-of-the-Woods, IN 47876
Phone: (812) 535- 5154
E-mail: smwcadms@smwc.edu
http://www.smwc.edu

University of Evansville
Department of Music
1800 Lincoln Ave.
Evansville, IN 47722
Phone: (812) 488- 2754
E-mail:admission@evansville.edu
http://www.evansville.edu

IOWA

University of Iowa*
School of Music
1006 Voxman Music Building
Iowa City, IA 52242
Phone: (319) 335-1643
E-mail: admissions@uiowa.edu
http://www.uiowa.edu

Wartburg College
School of Music
222 Ninth Street
Waverly, IA 50677
Phone: (319) 352-8401
E-mail: admissions@wartburg.edu
http://www.wartburg.edu

KANSAS

University of Kansas*
MEMT Division
Room 448 Murphy Hall
1530 Naismith Drive
Lawrence, KS 66045
Phone: (785) 864-9635
http://www.ku.edu

KENTUCKY

University of Louisville
School of Music
Cardinal Boulevard
Louisville, KY 40292
Phone: (502) 852-2316
E-mail: admitme@gwise.louisville.edu
http://www.loisville.edu

LOUISIANA

Loyola University*
College of Music
6363 St. Charles Avenue
Box 8
New Orleans, LA 70118
Phone: (504) 865-2142
http://www.loyno.edu

MASSACHUSSETTS

Anna Maria College
Music Therapy Program
Box 45

50 Sunset Lane
Paxton, MA 01612
Phone: (508) 849-3454
E-mail: admissions@annamaria.edu
http://www.annamaria.edu

Berklee College of Music
Chair Music Therapy Department
1140 Boylston Street
Boston, MA 02215
Phone: (617) 747-2639
E-mail: admissions@berklee.edu
http://www.berklee.edu

Lesley University*
Division of Expressive Therapies
29 Everett Street
Cambridge, MA 02138
Phone: (617) 349-8166
http://web.lesley.edu

MICHIGAN

Eastern Michigan University
Department of Music
Ypsilanti, MI 48197
Phone: (734) 487-0292
E-mail: admissions@emich.edu
http://www.emich.edu

Michigan State University*
School of Music
East Lansing, MI 48824
Phone: (517) 353-9856

Western Michigan University*
School of Music
1903 West Michigan Avenue
Kalamazoo, MI 49008
Phone: (269) 387-4724
http://www.wmich.edu/admissions

MINNESOTA

Augsburg College
2211 Riverside Avenue
Minneapolis, MN 55454
Phone: (612) 330-1273
E-mail: admissions@augsburg.edu
http://www.augsburg.edu

University of Minnesota*
School of Music

2106 Fourth Street South
100 Ferguson Hall
Minneapolis, MN 55455
Phone: (612) 624-1091
E-mail: admissions@tc.umn.edu
http://www.umn.edu

MISSISSIPPI

Mississippi University for Women
Fine & Performing Arts Division
Box W-70
Columbus, MS 39701
Phone: (662) 241-7897
http://www.muw.edu

William Carey University
498 Tuscan Avenue
Hattiesburg, MS 39401
Phone: (601) 318-6416
E-mail: admissions@wmcarey.edu
http://www.wmcarey.edu

MISSOURI

Drury University
900 North Benton Avenue
Springfield, MO 65802
Phone: (417) 873-7370
http://www.drury.edu

Maryville University of Saint Louis*
School of Health Professions
13550 Conway Road
St. Louis, MO 63141
Phone: (314) 529-9441
Fax: (314) 529-9927
E-mail: admissions@maryville.edu
http://www.maryville.edu

University of Missouri-Kansas City*
Conservatory of Music
4949 Cherry
316 Grant Hall
Kansas City, MO 64110
Phone: (816) 235-2920
http://www.umkc.edu

NEW JERSEY

Montclair University*
Music Department

1 Normal Avenue
Upper Montclair, NJ 07043
Phone: (973) 655-5268
http://www.montclair.edu

NEW YORK

Molloy College
Music Department
1000 Hempstead Avenue
P.O. Box 5002
Rockville Centre, NY 11571
Phone: (516) 678-5000
http://www.molloy.edu

Nazareth College
4245 East Avenue
Rochester, NY 14618
Phone: (585) 389-2702
Fax: (555) 586-2452
http://www.naz.edu

New York University*
777 Education Building
Music Therapy Program
35 West Fourth Street
New York, NY 10012
Phone: (212) 998-5452
http://admissions.nyu.edu

State University of New York at Fredonia
School of Music
Mason Hall
Fredonia, NY 14063
Phone: (716) 673-4648
E-mail: admissions.office@ fredonia.edu
http://www.fredonia.edu

State University of New York at New Paltz
Music Therapy Program
1 Hawk Drive
New Paltz, NY 12561
Phone: (845) 257-2709
Fax: (845) 257-3209
E-mail: adminssions@newpaltz.edu
http://www.newpaltz.edu

NORTH CAROLINA

Appalachian State University*
Hayes School of Music

813 Rivers Street
P.O. Box 32096
Boone, NC 28608
Phone: (828) 262-6444
http://www.appstate.edu

East Carolina University*
212 Fletcher Music Center
Greenville, NC 27858
Phone: (252) 328-6343
http://www.ecu.edu

Queens University of Charlotte
Music Department
1900 Selwyn Avenue
Charlotte, NC 28274
Phone: (704) 337-2570
Fax: (704) 337-2403
E-mail: admissions@queens.edu
http://www.queens.edu

NORTH DAKOTA

University of North Dakota
Department of Music
P.O. Box 7125
Grand Forks, ND 58202
Phone: (701) 777-2828
Fax: (701) 777-2721
E-mail: enrollmentservices@mail. und.nodak.edu
http://www.und.nodak.edu

OHIO

Baldwin-Wallace College
Cleveland Consortium
275 Eastland Road
Berea, OH 44017
Phone: (440) 826-3176
Fax: (440) 826-3830
E-mail: info@bw.edu
http://www.bw.edu/admission

Cleveland State University
Department of Music
2121 Euclid Avenue
Cleveland, OH 44115
Phone: (216) 687-2033
http://www.csuohio.edu

College of Wooster
Department of Music

1189 Beall Avenue
Wooster, OH 44691
Phone: (330) 263-2000
Fax: (330) 263-2621
E-mail: admissions@wooster.edu
http://www.wooster.edu

Ohio University*
School of Music
440 Music Building
Athens, OH 45701
Phone: (740) 593-4249
http://www.ohio.edu

University of Dayton
Department of Music
300 College Park
Dayton, OH 45469
Phone: (937) 229-3908
E-mail: admission@udayton.edu
http://www.dayton.edu

OKLAHOMA

**Southwestern Oklahoma State
University**
Department of Music
100 Campus Drive
Weatherford, OK 73096
Phone: (580) 774-774-3218
Fax: (580) 774-3795
E-mail: ropers@swosu.edu
http://www.swosu.edu

OREGON

Marylhurst University
17600 Pacific Highway-Highway 43
P.O. Box 261
Marylhurst, OR 97036
Phone: (503) 636-8141
Fax: (503) 635-6585
E-mail: admissions@marylhurst.
    edu
http://www.maryhurst.edu

PENNSYLVANIA

Drexel University*
Hahnemann Creative Arts in
    Therapy Program–Music
    Therapy
245 North 15th Street

Philadelphia, PA 19102
Phone: (215) 762-6927
http://www.drexel.edu

Duquesne University
School of Music
600 Forbes Avenue
Pittsburgh, PA 15282
Phone: (412) 396-5578
Fax: (412) 396-5644
E-mail: admissions@duq.edu
http://www.duq.edu

Elizabethtown College
Department of Fine and Performing
    Arts
One Alpha Drive
Elizabethtown, PA 17022
Phone: (717) 361-1991
Fax: (717) 361-1365
E-mail: admissions@etown.edu
http://www.etown.edu

Immaculata University*
Department of Music
P.O. Box 654
1145 King Road
Immaculata, PA 19345
Phone: (610) 647-4400
Fax: (610) 640-0836
E-mail: admis@immaculata.edu
http://www.immaculata.edu

Marywood University
2300 Adams Avenue
Scranton, PA 18509
Phone: (570) 348-6211
E-mail: ugadm@ac.marywood.edu
http://www.marywood.edu

Seton Hill University
Seton Hill Drive
Greensburg, PA 15601
Phone: (724) 830-1062
http://www.setonhill.edu

**Slippery Rock University of
Pennsylvania**
Department of Music
1 Morrow Way
Slippery Rock, PA 16057
Phone: (724) 738-2447
Fax: (724) 738-2913

E-mail: asktherock@sru.edu
http://www.sru.edu

Temple University*
Music Therapy, TU-012-00
East Boyer College of Music
2001 N 13th Street
Philadelphia, PA 19122
Phone: (215) 204-8314
E-mail: tuadm@temple.edu
http://www.temple.edu

SOUTH CAROLINA

**Charleston Southern
University**
9200 University Boulevard
P.O. Box 118087
Charleston, SC 29423
Phone: (843) 863-7782
http://www.csuniv.edu

Converse College
Petrie School of Music
580 East Main Street
Spartanburg, SC 29302
Phone: (864) 596-9166
Fax: (864) 596-9225
E-mail: admissions@converse.edu
http://www.converse.edu

TEXAS

Sam Houston State University
School of Music
SHSU Box 2208
Huntsville, TX 77341
Phone: (936) 294-1376
E-mail: admissions@shsu.edu
http://www.shsu.edu

Southern Methodist University
Meadows School of the Arts
P.O. Box 750356
Department of Music Therapy,
    Division of Music
Dallas, TX 75275
Phone: (214) 768-3175
E-mail: ugadmission@smu.edu
http://www.smu.edu

Texas Woman's University*
P.O. Box 425768

Denton, TX 76204
Phone: (940) 898-2514
E-mail: admissions@twu.edu
http://www.twu.edu

University of the Incarnate Word

Music Therapy Department
4301 Broadway
Box 340
San Antonio, TX 78209
Phone: (210) 829-3856
Fax: (210) 829-3921
E-mail: admis@uiwtx.edu
http://www.uiw.edu

West Texas A&M University

Department of Music & Dance
WTAMU Box 60879
Canyon, TX 79016
Phone: (806) 651-2822
Fax: (806) 651-5285
E-mail: sthomas@mail.wtamu.edu
http://www.wtamu.edu

UTAH

Utah State University

Music Therapy Program
4015 Old Main Hill

Logan, UT 84322
Phone: (435) 797-3009
Fax: (435) 797-3708
E-mail: admit@usu.edu
http://www.usu.edu

VIRGINIA

Radford University*

Department of Music
Radford, VA 24142
Phone: (540) 831-5024
http://www.radford.edu

Shenandoah University*

1460 University Drive
Winchester, VA 22601
Phone: (540) 665-4560
Fax: (540) 665-4627
E-mail: admit@su.edu
http://www.su.edu

WISCONSIN

Alverno College

3400 South 43 Street
P.O. Box 343922
Milwaukee, WI 53234
Phone: (414) 382-6135
Fax: (414) 382-6354

E-mail: admissions@alverno.edu
http://www.alverno.edu

University of Wisconsin–Eau Claire

P.O. Box 4004
Eau Claire, WI 54702
Phone: (715) 836-5415
Fax: (715) 836-2409
E-mail: admissions@uwec.edu
http://www.uwec.edu

University of Wisconsin–Milwaukee

P.O. Box 413
Milwaukee, WI 53201
Phone: (414) 229-4397
Fax: (414) 229-6940
E-mail: uwmlook@uwm.edu
http://www.uwm.edu

University of Wisconsin–Oshkosh

800 Algoma Boulevard
Oshkosh, WI 54901
Phone: (920) 424-0202
E-mail: oshadmuw@uwosh.edu
http://www.uwosh.edu

E. COLLEGES AND UNIVERSITIES OFFERING DEGREES IN MUSIC EDUCATION

The following is a listing of selected four-year schools offering majors in music education. They are grouped by state. School names, addresses, phone numbers, Web addresses, and e-mail addresses are included when available.

The author does not endorse any one school over another. Use this list as a beginning. Check the reference section of libraries or guidance counseling centers for additional schools offering degrees in this field.

ALABAMA

Alabama Agricultural and Mechanical University

P.O. Box 908
Normal, AL 35762
Phone: (256) 372-5245
Fax: (256) 851-9747
http://www.aamu.edu

Alabama State University

915 South Jackson Street

Montgomery, AL 36104
Phone: (334) 229-4291
Fax: (334) 229-4984
E-mail: mpettway@alasu.edu
http://www.alasu.edu

Auburn University

202 Mary Martin Hall
Auburn, AL 36849
Phone: (334) 844-6446
E-mail: admissions@auburn.edu
http://www.auburn.edu

Birmingham-Southern College

900 Arkadelphia Road
Birmingham, AL 35254
Phone: (2O5) 226-4696
E-mail: admission@bsc.edu
http://www.bsc.edu

Jacksonville State University

700 Pelham Road North
Jacksonville, AL 36265
Phone: (256) 782-5363
Fax: (256) 782-5291

E-mail: info@jsu.edu
http://www.jsu.edu

Judson College
P.O. Box 120
302 Bibb Street
Marion, AL 36756
Phone: (334) 683-5110
Fax: (334)683-5282
E-mail: admissions@judson.edu
http://www.judson.edu

Oakwood University
7000 Adventist Boulevard, NW
Huntsville, AL 35896
Phone: (256) 726-7354
Fax: (256) 726-7154
E-mail: admission@oakwood.edu
http://www.oakwood.edu

Samford University
Birmingham, AL 35229
Phone:(205)726-3673
E-mail: admission@samford.edu
http://www.samford.edu

Talladega College
627 West Battle Street
Talladega, AL 35160
Phone: (256) 761-6219
Fax: (205) 362-0274
http://www.talladega.edu

University of Alabama
Box 870132
Tuscaloosa, AL 35487
Phone: (205) 348-5666
Fax: (205) 348-9046
E-mail: admissions@ua.edu
http://www.ua.edu

ALASKA

University of Alaska Anchorage
3211 Providence Drive
Anchorage, AK 99508
Phone: (907) 786-1480
Fax: (907) 786-4888
E-mail: enroll@uaa.alaska.edu
http://www.alaska.edu

ARIZONA

Arizona State University
P.O. Box 1630

State University, AR 72467
Phone: (870) 972-3024
Fax: (870) 910-3406
E-mail: admissions@astate.edu
http://www.astate.edu

Northern Arizona University
Box 4084
Flagstaff, AZ 86011
Phone: (928)523-5511
E-mail: undergraduate.
    admissions@nau.edu
http://home.nau.edu

Prescott College
220 Grove Avenue
Prescott, AZ 86301
Phone: (928) 350-2100
E-mail: admissions@prescott.edu
http://www.prescott.edu

Southwestern College
2625 E. Cactus Road
Phoenix, AZ 85032
Phone: (602) 386-4106
Fax: (602) 404-2159
E-mail: rebekah@swcaz.edu
http://www.swcaz.edu

University of Arizona
P.O. Box 210040
Tucson, AZ 85721
Phone: (520) 621-3237
Fax: (520) 621-9799
E-mail: appinfo@arizona.edu
http://www.arizona.edu

ARKANSAS

Arkansas State University
P.O. Box 1630
State University, AR 72467
Phone: (870) 972-3024
Fax: (870) 910-3406
E-mail: admissions@astate.edu
http://www.astate.edu

Arkansas Tech University
L. L. Doc Bryan Student Services
    Building
Russellville, AR 72801
Phone: (479) 968-0343
Fax: (479) 964-0522

E-mail: tech.enroll@atu.edu
http://www.atu.edu

Harding University
Box 12255
Searcy, Arkansas 72149
Phone: (501) 279-4407
Fax: (501) 279-4129
E-mail: admissions@harding.edu
http://www.harding.edu

Henderson State University
1100 Henderson Street
P.O. Box 7560
Arkadelphia, AR 71999
Phone: (870) 230-5028
Fax: (870) 230-5066
E-mail: hardwrv@hsu.edu
http://www.hsu.edu

John Brown University
200 West University Street
Siloam Springs, AR 72761
Phone: (479) 524-7454
Fax: (479) 524-4196
E-mail: dcrandal@jbu.edu
http://www.jbu.edu

Ouachita Baptist University
OBU Box 3776
Arkadelphia, AR 71998
Phone: (870) 245-5110
Fax: (870) 245-5500
E-mail: pittmank@obu.edu
http://www.obu.edu

Southern Arkansas University–
   Magnolia
P.O. Box 9382
100 East University
Magnolia, AR 71754
Phone: (870) 235-4040
E-mail: addanna@saumag.edu
http://www.saumag.edu

University of Arkansas at Fort
   Smith
5210 Grand Avenue
P.O. Box 3649
Fort Smith, AR 72913
Phone: (479) 788-7104
Fax: (479) 788-7016

E-mail: information@uafortsmith.edu

http://www.uaforsmith.edu

University of Arkansas at Monticello

P.O. Box 3600
Monticello, AR 71656
Phone: (870) 460-1026
E-mail: admissions@uamont.edu
http://www.uamont.edu

University of Arkansas at Pine Bluff

UAPB Box 17
1200 University Drive
Pine Bluff, AR 71601
Phone: (870) 575-8487
http://www.uapb.edu

CALIFORNIA

Bethany University

800 Bethany Drive
Scotts Valley, CA 95066
Phone: (831) 438-3800
Fax: (831) 438-4517
E-mail: info@bethany.edu
http://www.bethany.edu

California Lutheran University

60 West Olsen Road
Thousand Oaks, CA 91360
Phone: (805) 493-3135
Fax: (805) 493-3114
E-mail: admissions@CalLutheran.edu
http://www.CalLutheran.edu

California State University, Chico

400 West First Street
Chico, CA 95929
Phone: (530) 898-4879
Fax: (530) 898-6456
E-mail: info@csuchico.edu
http://www.csuchico.edu

California State University, Dominguez Hills

1000 East Victoria Street
Carson, CA 90747

Phone: (310) 243-4696
Fax: (310) 217-6800
http://www.csudh.edu

California State University, Fresno

5150 North Maple Avenue
Fresno, CA 93740
Phone: (559) 278-6115
Fax: (559) 278-4812
E-mail: yolandad@csufresno.edu
http://www.csufresnu.edu

California State University, Fullerton

P.O. Box 6900
800 North State College Boulevard
Fullerton, CA 92834
Phone: (714) 278-2370
E-mail: admissions@fullerton.edu
http://www.fullerton.edu

Chapman University

One University Drive
Orange, CA 92866
Phone: (714) 997-6711
Fax: (714) 997-6713
E-mail: admit@chapman.edu
http://www.chapman.edu

Fresno Pacific University

1717 South Chestnut Avenue
Fresno, CA 93727
Phone: (800) 660-6089
Fax: (559) 453-2007
E-mail: ugadmis@fresno.edu
http://www.fresno.edu

Hope International University

2500 East Nutwood Avenue
Fullerton, CA 92831
Phone: (714) 879-3901
Fax: (714) 681-7423
E-mail mfmadden@hiu.edu
http://www.hiu.edu

Humboldt State University

1 Harpst Street
Arcata, CA 95521
Phone: (707) 826-6221
Fax: (707) 826-6190
E-mail: hsuinfo@humboldt.edu
http://www.humboldt.edu

La Sierra University

45 Riverwalk Parkway
Riverside, CA 92515
Phone: (951) 785-2176
Fax: (951) 785-2477
E-mail admissions@lasierra.edu
http://www. lasierra.edu

Pacific Union College

One Angwin Avenue
Angwin, CA 94508
Phone: (707) 965-6425
Fax: (707) 965-6432
E-mail: enroll@puc.edu
http://www.puc.edu

Pepperdine University

24255 Pacific Coast Highway
Malibu, CA 90263
Phone: (310) 506-4392
Fax: (310) 506-4861
E-mail: admission-seaver@pepperdine.edu
http://www.pepperdine.edu

San Diego State University

5500 Campanile Drive
San Diego, CA 92182
Phone: (619) 594-6886
Fax: (619) 594-1250
E-mail: admissions@sdsu.edu
http://www.sdsu.edu

Simpson University

2211 College View Drive
Redding, CA 96003
Phone: (530) 224-5600
Fax: (530) 226-4861
E-mail: admissions@simpsonuniversity.edu
http://www.simpsonuniversity.edu

Sonoma State University

1801 East Cotati Avenue
Rohnert Park, CA 94928
Phone: (707) 664-2778
E-mail gustavo.flores@sonoma.edu
http://www.sonoma.edu

University of Redlands

P.O. Box 3080
Redlands, CA 92373

Phone: (800) 455-5064
Fax: (909) 335-4089
E-mail: admissions@redlands.edu
http://www.redlands.edu

University of Southern California
University Park
Los Angeles, CA 90089
Phone: (213) 740-1111
E-mail: admitusc@usc.edu
http://www.usc.edu

University of the Pacific
Stockton, CA 95211
Phone: (209) 946-2211
E-mail: admission@pacific.edu
http://www.pacific.edu/admission

COLORADO

Adams State College
208 Edgemont Boulevard
Alamosa, CO 81102
Phone: (719) 587-7712
Fax: (719) 587-7522
E-mail: ascadmit@adams.edu
http://www.adams.edu

Colorado State University
Fort Collins, CO 80523
Phone: (970) 491-6909
Fax: (970) 491-7799
E-mail: admissions@colostate.edu
http://www.colostate.edu/

Fort Lewis College
1000 Rim Drive
Durango, CO 81301
Phone: (970) 247-7184
http://www.fortlewis.edu

Metropolitan State College of Denver
P.O. Box 173362
Denver, CO 80217
Phone: (303) 556-2615
http://www.mscd.edu

University of Colorado at Boulder
552 UCB
Boulder, CO 80309

Phone: (303) 492-6301
http://www.colorado.edu

University of Northern Colorado
Campus Box 10
Carter Hall 3006
Greeley, CO 80639
Phone: (970) 351-2881
Fax: (970) 351-2984
E-mail: admissions.help@unco.edu
http://www.unco.edu

Western State College of Colorado
600 North Adams Street
Gunnison, CO 81231
Phone: (800) 876-5309
E-mail: admissions@western.edu
http://www.western.edu

CONNECTICUT

Connecticut College
270 Mohegan Avenue
New London, CT 06320
Phone: (860) 439-2200
Fax: (860) 439-4301
E-mail: admission@conncoll.edu
http://www.conncoll.edu

Fairfield University
1073 North Benson Road
Fairfield, CT 06824
Phone: (203) 254-4100
Fax: (203) 254-4199
E-mail: admis@mail.fairfield.edu
http://www.fairfield.edu

University of Connecticut
2131 Hillside Road
Box Unit 3088
Storrs, CT 06269
Phone: (860) 486-3137
E-mail: beahusky@uconn.edu
http://www.uconn.edu

University of Hartford
West Hartford, CT 06117
Phone: (860) 768-4296
Fax: (860) 768-4961
E-mail: admission@hartford.edu
http://admission.hartford.edu

Western Connecticut State University
181 White Street
Danbury, CT 06810
Phone: (203) 837-9000
E-mail: admissions@wcsu.edu
http://www.wcsu.edu

DELAWARE

Delaware State University
1200 North DuPont Highway
Dover, DE 19901-2277
Phone: (302) 857-6351
Fax: (302) 857-6908
E-mail: gcheatha@desu.edu
http://www.desu.edu

University of Delaware
116 Hullihen Hall
Newark, DE 19716
Phone: (302) 831-8123
Fax: (302) 831-6905
E-mail admissions@udel.edu
http://www.udel.edu

DISTRICT OF COLUMBIA

Catholic University of America
Washington, D.C. 20064
Phone: (202) 319-5305
Fax: (202) 319-6533
E-mail: cua-admissions@cua.edu
http://www.cua.edu

University of the District of Columbia
4200 Connecticut Avenue, NW
Building 39
Washington, DC 20008
Phone: (202) 274-6110
Fax: (202) 274-5553
http://www.udc.edu

FLORIDA

Bethune-Cookman University
640 Dr. Mary McLeod Bethune Boulevard
Daytona Beach, FL
Phone: (386) 481-2600
Fax: (386) 481-2601
E-mail: admissions@cookman.edu
http://www.bethune.cookman.edu

Florida Agricultural and Mechanical University
Tallahassee, FL 32307
Phone: (850) 599-3796
E-mail: admissions@famu.edu
http://www.famu.edu

Florida Atlantic University
777 Glades Road
Boca Raton, FL 33431
Phone: (800) 299-4FAU
E-mail: admissions@fau.edu
http://www.fau.edu

Florida International University
P.O. Box 659003
Miami, FL 33265
Phone: (305) 348-2363
Fax: (305) 348-3648
http://www.fiu.edu

Florida Memorial University
15800 NW 42nd Avenue
Miami-Dade, FL 33054
Phone: (305) 626-3147
http://www.fmuniv.edu

Florida Southern College
111 Lake Hollingsworth Drive
Lakeland, FL 33801
Phone: (800) 274-4131
E-mail: fscadm@flsouthern.edu
http://www.flsouthern.edu

Florida State University
Tallahassee, FL 32306
Phone: (850) 644-2525
E-mail: admissions@admin.fsu.edu
http://www.fsu.edu

Jacksonville University
2800 University Boulevard North
Jacksonville, FL 32211
Phone: (904) 256-7000
E-mail: admissions@ju.edu
http://www.ju.edu

Miami Dade College
300 NE Second Avenue
Miami, FL 33132
Phone: 305-237-8888
Fax: (305) 237-2964
http://www.mdc.edu

Palm Beach Atlantic University
P.O. Box 24708
West Palm Beach, FL 33416
Phone: (561) 803-2000
E-mail: admit@pba.edu
http://www.pba.edu

Southeastern University
1000 Longfellow Boulevard
Lakeland, FL 33801
Phone: (863) 667-5000
Fax: (863) 667-5200
E-mail: admission@seuniversity.edu
http://www.seuniversity.edu

Stetson University
Unit 8378
Griffith Hall
DeLand, FL 32723
Phone: (386) 822-7100
Fax: (386) 822-7112
E-mail: admissions@stetson.edu
http://www.stetson.edu

University of Central Florida
P.O. Box 160111
Orlando, FL 32816
Phone: (407) 823-3000
E-mail: admission@mail.ucf.edu
http://www.ucf.edu

University of Florida
P.O. Box 114000
Gainesville, FL 32611
Phone: (352) 392-3261
E-mail: freshman@ufl.edu
http://www.ufl.edu

University of Miami
P.O. Box 248025
Coral Gables, FL 33124
Phone: (305) 284-2211
E-mail: admission@miami.edu
http://www.miami.edu

University of North Florida
4567 St. Johns Bluff Road South
Jacksonville, FL 32224
Phone: (904) 620-2624
Fax: (904) 620-2014
E-mail: admissions@unf.edu
http://www.unf.edu

University of South Florida
4202 East Fowler Avenue
Tampa, FL 33620
Phone: (813) 974-3350
Fax: (813) 974-9689
E-mail: bullseye@admin.usf.edu
http://www.usf.edu

University of Tampa
401 West Kennedy Boulevard
Tampa, FL 33606
Phone: (813) 253-6211
Fax: (813) 254-4955
E-mail: : admissions@ut.edu
http://www.ut.edu

Warner University
Warner Southern Center
13895 Highway 27
Lake Wales, FL 33859
Phone: (863) 638-7212
Fax: (863) 638-1472
E-mail: admissions@warner.edu
http://www.warner.edu

GEORGIA

Albany State University
504 College Drive
Albany, GA 31705
Phone: (229) 430-4645
Fax: (229) 430-3936
E-mail: admissions@asurams.edu
http://www.asurams.edu

Armstrong Atlantic State University
11935 Abercom Street
Savannah, GA 31419
Phone: (912) 921-5425
Fax: (912) 921-5462
E-mail: craig.morrison@armstrong.edu
http://www.armstrong.edu

Augusta State University
2500 Walton Way
Augusta, GA 30904
Phone: (706) 737-1632
Fax: (706) 667-4355
E-mail: admissions@aug.edu
http://www.aug.edu

Berry College
P.O. Box 490159
2277 Martha Berry Highway, NW
Mount Berry, GA 30149
Phone: (706) 236-2215
Fax: (706) 290-2178
E-mail: admissions@berry.edu
http://www.berry.edu

Brenau University
500 Washington Street, SE
Gainesville, GA 30501
Phone: (770) 531-6100
Fax: (770) 538-4701
E-mail: wcadmissions@brenau.edu
http://www.brenau.edu

Columbus State University
4225 University Avenue
Columbus, GA 31907
Phone: (706) 568-2035
Fax: (706) 568-5272
E-mail: mail: admissions@colstate.
edu
http://www.colstate.edu

Georgia College & State University
C.P.O. Box 023
Milledgeville, GA 31061
Phone: (478) 445-1284
Fax: (478) 445-3653
E-mail: info@gcsu.edu
http://www.gesu.edu

Georgia Southern University
Forest Drive
Statesboro, GA 30460
Phone: (912) 681-5391
Fax: (912) 486-7240
E-mail: admissions@
georgiasouthern.edu
http://www.georgiasouthern.edu

Kennesaw State University
1000 Chastain Road
Kennesaw, GA 30144
Phone: (770) 423-6300
Fax: (770) 420-4435
E-mail: ksuadmit@ksumail.
kennesaw.edu
http://www.kennesaw.edu

Mercer University
1400 Coleman Avenue
Macon, GA 31207
Phone: (478) 301-2650
E-mail: admissions@mercer.edu
http://www.mercer.edu

North Georgia College & State University
Dahlonega, GA 30533
Phone: (706) 864-1800
Fax: (706) 864-1478
E-mail: admissions@ngcsu.edu
http://www.ngcsu.edu

Shorter College
315 Shorter Avenue
Rome, GA 30165
Phone: (706) 233-7319
Fax: (706) 233-7224
E-mail: admissions@shorter.edu
http://www.shorter.edu

Toccoa Falls College
P.O. Box 800–899
Toccoa Falls, GA 30598
Phone: (706) 886-7299
Fax: (706) 282-6012
E-mail: admissions@tfc.edu
http://www.tfc.edu

University of Georgia
Athens, GA 30602
Phone: (706) 542-8776
Fax: (706) 542-1466
E-mail: undergrad@admissions.
uga.edu
http://www.uga.edu

University of West Georgia
Carrollton, GA 30118
Phone: (678) 839-4000
E-mail: admiss@westga.edu
http://www.westga.edu/~admiss

Valdosta State University
1500 North Patterson Street
Valdosta, GA 31698
Phone: (229) 333-5791
Fax: (229) 333-5482
E-mail: admissions@valdosta.edu
http://www.valdosta.edu

HAWAII

Brigham Young University– Hawaii
55-220 Kulanui Street
Oahu, HI 96762
Phone: (808) 293-3731
Fax: (808) 293-3741
E-mail: admissions@byuh.edu
http://www.byuh.edu

IDAHO

Boise State University
1910 University Drive
Boise, ID 83725
Phone: (208) 426-1177
E-mail: bsuinfo@boisestate.edu
http://www.boisestate.edu

University of Idaho
P.O. Box 444264
Moscow, ID 83844
Phone: (208) 885-6326
Fax: (208) 885-9119
E-mail: carolynl@uidaho.edu
http://www.uidaho.edu

ILLINOIS

Augustana College
639 38th Street
Rock Island, IL 61201
Phone: (309) 794-7341
Fax: (309) 794-7422
E-mail: admissions@augustana.
edu
http://www.augustana.edu

Bradley University
1501 W. Bradley Avenue
Peoria, IL 61625
Phone: (309) 676-7611
E-mail: admissions@bradley.edu
http://www.bradley.edu

Chicago State University
95th Street at King Drive
Chicago, IL 60628
Phone: (773) 995-2513
Fax: (773) 995-3820
E-mail: ug-admissions@csu.ed
http://www.csu.edu

Concordia University Chicago
7400 Augusta Street
River Forest, IL 60305
Phone: (708) 209-3100
Fax: (708) 209-3473
E-mail: crfadmis@cuchicago.edu
http://www.cuchicago.edu

DePaul University
1 East Jackson Boulevard
Chicago, IL 60604
Phone: (312) 362-8300
E-mail: admitdpu@depaul.edu
http://www.depaul.edu

Elmhurst College
190 Prospect Avenue
Elmhurst, IL 60126
Phone: (630) 617-3400
E-mail: admit@elmhurst.edu
http://www.elmhurst.edu

Illinois State University
Campus Box 2200
Normal, IL 61790-2200
Phone: (309) 438-2181
Fax: (309) 438-3932
E-mail: admissions@ilstu.edu
http://www.ilstu.edu

Judson University
1151 North State Street
Elgin, IL 60123
Phone: (847) 695-2522
Fax: (847) 628-2526
E-mail: bdean@judsoncollege.edu
http://wwwjudsoncollege.edu

MacMurray College
447 East College Avenue
Jacksonville, IL 62650
Phone: (217) 479-7056
Fax: (217) 291-0702
E-mail: admiss@mac.edu
http://www.mac.edu

Millikin University
1184 West Main Street
Decatur, IL 62522
Phone: (217) 424-6210
Fax: (217) 425-4669
E-mail: admis@millikin.edu
http://www.millikin.edu

North Central College
30 North Brainard Street
Naperville, IL 60540
Phone: (630) 637-5800
Fax: (630) 637-5819
E-mail: ncadm@noctrl.edu
http://www.northcentralcollege.edu

Northern Illinois University
DeKalb, IL 60445
Phone: (815) 753-0446
E-mail: admission-info@niu.edu
http://www.niu.edu

North Park University
3225 West Foster Avenue
Chicago, IL 60625
Phone: (773) 244-5500
http://www.northpark.edu/focus

Northwestern University
P.O. Box 3060
Evanston, IL 60204
Phone: (847) 491-7271
E-mail: ug-admission@
   northwestern.edu
http://www.northwestern.edu

Roosevelt University
430 South Michigan Avenue
Chicago, IL 60605
Phone: (877) APPLY-RU
Fax: (312) 341-4316
E-mail: applyRU@roosevelt.edu
http://www.roosevelt.edu

**University of Illinois–Urbana-
   Champaign**
901 W. Illinois
Urbana, IL 61801
Phone: (217) 333-1000
E-mail: admissions@oar.uiuc.edu
http://www.uiuc.edu

Wheaton College
Wheaton, IL 60187
Phone: (630) 752-5005
E-mail: admissions@wheaton.edu
http://www.wheaton.edu

INDIANA

Anderson University
1100 East Fifth Street

Anderson, IN 46012
Phone: (765) 641-4080
Fax: (765) 641-3851
E-mail: info@anderson.edu
http://www.anderson.edu

Ball State University
2000 University Avenue
Muncie, IN 47306
Phone: (765) 285-8300
E-mail: askus@bsu.edu
http://www.bsu.edu

Bethel College
1001 West McKinley Avenue
Mishawaka, IN 46545
Phone: (574) 257-3339
Fax: (574) 257-3335
E-mail: admissions@bethelcollege.
   edu
http://www.bethelcolleg.edu

Butler University
4600 Sunset Avenue
Indianapolis, IN 46208
Phone: (317) 940-8100
Fax: (317) 940-8150
E-mail: admission@butler.edu
http://go.butler.edu

DePauw University
Greencastle, IN 46135
Phone: (765) 658-4006
Fax: (765)658-4007
E-mail: admission@depauw.edu
http://www.depauw.edu

Huntington College
2303 College Avenue
Huntington, IN 46750
Phone: (260) 356-6000
Fax: (260) 356-9448
E-mail: admissions@huntington.edu
http://www.huntington.edu

**Indiana University
   Bloomington**
300 North Jordan Avenue
Bloomington, IN 47405
Phone: (812)855-0661
Fax: (812) 855-5102
E-mail: iuadmit@indiana.edu
http://www.indiana.edu

Indiana University–Purdue University Fort Wayne
2101 East Coliseum Boulevard
Fort Wayne, IN 46805
Phone: (260) 481-6812
Fax: (260) 481-6880
E-mail: ipfwadms@ipfw.edu
http://www.ipfw.edu

Indiana University South Bend
1700 Mishawaka Avenue
P.O. Box 7111
South Bend, IN 46634
Phone: (574)237-4480
Fax: (574)237-4834
E-mail: admissio@iusb.edu
http://www.iusb.edu

Manchester College
North Manchester, IN 46962
Phone: (800) 852-3648
E-mail: admitinfo@manchester.edu
http://www.manchester.edu

University of Evansville
1800 Lincoln Avenue
Evansville, IN 47722
Phone: (812) 479-2468
E-mail: admission@evansville.edu
http://www.evansville.edu

University of Indianapolis
1400 East Hanna Avenue
Indianapolis, IN 46227
Phone: (317) 788-3216
Fax: (317) 788-3300
E-mail: admission@uindy.edu
http://uindy.edu

Valparaiso University
Valparaiso, IN 46383
Phone: (219) 464-5011
Fax: (219) 464-6898
E-mail: undergrad.admissions@
    valpo.edu
http://www.valpo.edu

IOWA

Ashford University
400 North Bluff Boulevard
P.O. Box 2967
Clinton, IA 52733

Phone: (563) 242-4023
E-mail: admissns@tfu.edu
http://www.tfu.edu

Central College
812 University Street
Pella, IA 50219
Phone: (641) 628-7600
Fax: (641) 628-5316
E-mail: admissions@central.edu
http://www.central.edu

Clarke College
1550 Clarke Drive
Dubuque, IA 52001
Phone: (563) 588-6316
Fax: (319)588-6789
E-mail: admissions@clarke.edu
http://www.clarke.edu

Coe College
1220 First Avenue, NE
Cedar Rapids, IA 52402
Phone: ((319) 399-8500
Fax: (319) 399-8816
E-mail: admission@coe.edu
http://www.coe.edu

Cornell College
600 First Street West
Mount Vernon, IA 52314
Phone: (319) 895-4477
E-mail: admissions@cornellcollege.
    edu
http://www.cornellcollege.edu

Dordt College
498 4th Avenue, NE
Sioux Center, IA 51250
Phone: (712) 722-6080
Fax: (712) 722-1967
E-mail: admissions@dordt.edu
http://www.dordt.edu

Drake University
2507 University Avenue
Des Moines, IA 50311
Phone: (515) 271-3181
Fax: (515) 271-2831
http://www.choose.drake.edu

Graceland University
Lamoni, IA 50140

Phone: (641) 784-5196
Fax: (641) 784-5480
E-mail: admissions@graceland.edu
http://www.graceland.edu

Iowa State University of Science and Technology
Ames, IA 50011
Phone: (515) 294-3094
Fax: (515) 294-2592
E-mail: admissions@iastate.edu
http://www.iastate.edu

Morningside College
1501 Morningside Avenue
Sioux City, IA 51106
Phone: (712)274-5111
E-mail: mscadm@morningside.
    edu
http://www.morningside.edu

Mount Mercy College
1330 Elmhurst Drive, NE
Cedar Rapids, IA 52402
Phone: (319) 368-6460
E-mail: admission@mtmercy.edu
http://www.mtmercy.edu

Simpson College
701 North C Street
Indianola, IA 50125
Phone: (515) 961-1624
E-mail: admiss@simpson.edu
http://www.simpson.edu

St. Ambrose University
518 West Locust Street
Davenport, IA 52803
Phone: (563) 333-6300
E-mail: admit@sau.edu
http://www.sau.edu

University of Iowa
Iowa City, IA 52242
Phone: (319) 335-3847
Fax: (319) 335-1535
E-mail: admissions@uiowa.edu

University of Northern Iowa
Cedar Falls, IA 50614
Phone: (319) 273-2281
Fax: (319) 273-2885
E-mail: admissions@uni.edu

Waldorf College
106 South Sixth Street
Forest City, IA 50436
Phone: (641) 585-8119
Fax: (641) 585-8125
E-mail: admissions@waldorf.edu
http://www.waldorf.edu

KANSAS

Baker University
Baldwin City, KS 66006
Phone: (800) 873-4282
E-mail: admission@bakeru.edu
http://www.bakeru.edu

Bethany College
421 North First Street
Lindsborg, KS 67456
Phone: (785) 227-3311
Fax: (785) 227-8993
E-mail: admissions@bethanylb.edu
http://www.bethanylb.edu

Emporia State University
1200 Commercial Street
Emporia, KS 66801
Phone: (620) 341-5465
Fax: (620) 341-5599
E-mail: go2esu@emporia.edu
http://www.emporia.edu

Fort Hays State University
600 Park Street
Hays, KS 67601
Phone: (785) 628-5830
E-mail: tigers@fhsu.edu
http://www.fhsu.edu

Friends University
2100 West University Street
Wichita, KS 67213
Phone: (316) 295-5512
E-mail: sexson@friends.edu
http://www.friends.edu

Kansas State University
119 Anderson Hall
Manhattan, KS 66506
Phone: (785) 532-6250
Fax: (785) 532-6393
E-mail: kstate@ksu.edu
http://www.ksu.edu

MidAmerica Nazarene University
2030 East College Way
Olathe, KS 66062
Phone: (913) 791-3380
Fax: (913) 791-3481
E-mail: admissions@mnu.edu
http://www.mnu.edu

Ottawa University
1001 South Cedar #17
Ottawa, KS 66067
Phone: (785) 242-5200
Fax: (785)242-7429
E-mail: admiss@ottawa.edu
http://www.ottawa.edu

Pittsburg State University
Pittsburg, KS 66762
Phone: (620) 235-4251
Fax: (620) 235-6003
E-mail: psuadmit@pittstate.edu
http://www.pittstate.edu

Southwestern College
100 College Street
Winfield, KS 67156
Phone: (620) 229-6236
Fax: (620) 229-6344
E-mail: scadmit@sckans.edu
http://www.sckans.edu

Sterling College
P.O. Box 98
Sterling, KS 67579
Phone: (620) 278-4364
Fax: (620) 278-4416
E-mail: admissions@sterling.edu
http://www.sterling.edu

University of Kansas
1502 Iowa
Lawrence, KS 66045
Phone: (785) 864-2700
E-mail: adm@ukans.edu
http://www.ukans.edu

Washburn University
1700 SW College Avenue
Topeka, KS 66621
Phone: (785) 231-1010
Fax: (785) 231-1089
http://www.washburn.edu

Wichita State University
1845 North Fairmount
Wichita, KS 67260
Phone: (316) 978-3085
Fax: (316) 978-3174
E-mail: admissions@wichita.edu
http://www.withita.edu

KENTUCKY

Asbury College
Wilmore, KY 40390
Phone: (859) 858-3511
Fax: (859) 858-3921
http://www.asbury.edu

Eastern Kentucky University
521 Lancaster Avenue
Richmond, KY 40475
Phone: (859) 622-2106
Fax: (859) 622-8024
E-mail: admissions@eku.edu
http://www.eku.edu

Georgetown College
400 East College Street
Georgetown, KY 40324
Phone: (502) 863-8009
E-mail: admissions@
   georgetowncollege.edu
http://www.georgetowncollege.edu

Murray State University
P.O. Box 9
Murray, KY 42071
Phone: (270) 762-3035
Fax: 270) 762-3050
E-mail: admissions@murraystate.
   edu
http://www.murraystate.edu

University of Kentucky
100 W. D. Funkhouser Building
Lexington, KY 40506
Phone: (859) 257-2000
E-mail: admissio@uky.edu
http://www.uky.edu

University of Louisville
2211 South Brook
Louisville, KY 40292
Phone: (502)852-6531
Fax: (502) 852-4776

E-mail: admitme@gwise.louisville.
edu
http://www.louisville.edu

Transylvania University
300 North Broadway
Lexington, KY 40508
Phone: (859) 233-8242
E-mail: admissions@transy.edu
http://www.transy.edu

University of the Cumberlands
Williamsburg, KY 40769
Phone: (606) 539-4241
E-mail: admiss@ucumberlands.
edu
http://www.ucumberlands.edu

LOUISIANA

Centenary College of Louisiana
2911 Centenary Boulevard
P.O. Box 41188
Shreveport, LA 71134
Phone: (318) 869-5134
Fax: (318) 869-5005
E-mail: egregory@centenary.edu
http://www.centenary.edu

Grambling State University
P.O. Drawer 1165
100 Main Street
Grambling, LA 71245
Phone: (318) 274-6183
E-mail: bingamann@medgar.gram.
edu
http://www.gram.edu

Louisiana College
1140 College Drive
Pineville, LA 71359
Phone: (318) 487-7439
Fax: (318) 487-7550
E-mail: admissions@lacollege.edu
http://www.lacollege.edu

**Louisiana State University and
Agricultural and Mechanical
College**
Baton Rouge, LA 70803
Phone: (225) 578-1175
E-mail: admissions@lsu.edu
http://www.lsu.edu

Louisiana Tech University
P.O. Box 3178
Ruston, LA 71272
Phone: (318) 257-3036
E-mail: bulldog@latech.edu
http://www.latech.edu

Loyola University
6363 St. Charles Avenue
New Orleans, LA 70118
Phone: (504) 865-3240
Fax: (504) 865-3383
E-mail: admit@loyno.edu
http://www.loyno.edu

McNeese State University
P.O. Box 92895
Lake Charles, LA 70609
Phone: (337) 475-5238
E-mail: info@mail.mcneese.edu
http://www.mcneese.edu

**Northwestern State University
of Louisiana**
Natchitoches, LA 71497
Phone: (318) 357-4503
Fax: (318) 357-5567
E-mail: recruiting@nsula.edu
http://www.nsula.edu

**Southern University and
Agricultural and Mechanical
College**
P.O. Box 9901
Baton Rouge, LA 70813
Phone: (225) 771-2430
Fax: (225) 771-2500

**University of Louisiana at
Lafayette**
P.O. Box 44652
Lafayette, LA 70504
Phone: (800) 752-6553
E-mail: enroll@louisiana.edu
http://www.louisiana.edu

MAINE

University of Maine
Orono, ME 04469
Phone: (207) 581-1561
Fax: (207) 581-1213
E-mail: um-admit@maine.edu
http://www.maine.edu

University of Southern Maine
37 College Avenue
Gorham, ME 04038
Phone: (207) 780-5724
Toll-free: (800) 800-4USM
Ext. 5670
Fax: (207) 780-5640
E-mail: usmadm@usm.maine.edu
http://www.usm.maine.edu

MARYLAND

**College of Notre Dame of
Maryland**
Office of Admissions
4701 North Charles Street
Baltimore, MD 21210
Phone: (410) 532-5330
E-mail: admiss@ndm.edu
http://www.ndm.edu

Columbia Union College
7600 Flower Avenue
Takoma Park, MD 20912
Phone: (301) 891-4502
Toll-free: (800) 835-4212
Fax: (301) 971-4230
E-mail: enroll@cuc.edu
http://www.cuc.edu

University of Maryland
College Park, MD 20742
Phone: (301) 314-8385
Fax: (301) 314-9693
http://www.uga.umd.edu

MASSACHUSETTS

Atlantic Union College
P.O. Box 1000
South Lancaster, MA 01561
Phone: (978) 368-2239
Fax: (978) 368-2015
E-mail: rosita.lashley@auc.edu
http://www.auc.edu

Berklee College of Music
1140 Boylston Street
Boston, MA 02215
Phone: (617) 266-2222
Fax: (617) 747-2047
E-mail: admissions@berklee.edu
http://www.berklee.edu

Boston College
Chestnut Hill, MA 02467
Phone: (617) 552-3100
Fax: (617) 552-0798
http://www.bc.edu

BOSTON CONSERVATORY
8 the Fenway
Boston, MA 02215
Phone: (617) 912-9153
Fax: (617) 536-3176
E-mail: admissions@
    bostonconservatory.edu
http://www.bostonconservatory.edu

Bridgewater State College
Bridgewater, MA 02325
Phone: (508) 531-1237
Fax: (508) 531-1746
E-mail: admission@bridgew.edu
http://www.bridgew.edu

Eastern Nazarene College
Quincy, MA 02170
Phone: (617) 745-3711
E-mail: admissions@enc.edu
http://www.enc.edu

Gordon College
255 Grapevine Road
Wenham, MA 01984
Phone: (978) 867-4218
Fax: (978) 867-4682
E-mail: admissions@gordon.edu
http://www.gordon.edu

Westfield State College
577 Western Avenue
Westfield, MA 01086
Phone: (413) 572-5218
http://www.wsc.ma.edu

MICHIGAN

Adrian College
110 South Madison Street
Adrian, MI 49221
Phone: (517) 265-5161
E-mail: admissions@adrian.edu
http://www.adrian.edu

Alma College
614 West Superior Street

Alma, MI 48801
Phone: (800) 321-ALMA
E-mail: admissions@alma.edu
http://www.alma.edu

Andrews University
Berrien Springs, MI 49104
Phone: (800) 253-2874
Fax: (269) 471-3228
E-mail: enroll@andrews.edu
http://www.andrews.edu

Calvin College
3201 Burton Street, SE
Grand Rapids, MI 49546
Phone: (616) 526-6106
Fax: (616) 526-6777
E-mail: admissions@calvin.edu
http://www.calvin.edu

Central Michigan University
Mt. Pleasant, MI 48859
Phone: (989) 774-3076
Fax: (989) 774-7267
E-mail: cmuadmit@cmich.edu
http://www.cmich.edu

Concordia University
4090 Geddes Road
Ann Arbor, MI 48105
Phone: (734) 995-7450
Fax: (734) 995-4610
E-mail: admissions@cuaa.edu
http://www.cuaa.edu

Eastern Michigan University
400 Pierce Hall
Ypsilanti, MI 48197
Phone: (734) 487-3060
Fax: (734) 487-1484
E-mail: admissions@emich.edu
http://www.emich.edu

Grand Valley State University
1 Campus Drive
Allendale, MI 49401
Phone: (616) 331-2025
E-mail: go2qvsu@qvsu.edu
http://www.gvsu.edu

Hope College
69 East 10th Street
P.O. Box 9000

Holland, MI 49422
Phone: (616) 395-7850
E-mail: admissions@hope.edu
http://wwwhope.edu

Northern Michigan University
1401 Presque Isle Avenue
Marquette, MI 49855
Phone: (906) 227-2650
Fax: (906) 227-1747
E-mail: admiss@nmu.edu
http://www.nmu.edu

**Saginaw Valley State
    University**
7400 Bay Road
University Center, MI 48710
Phone: (989) 964-4200
Fax: (517) 790-0180
E-mail: admissions@svsu.edu
http://www.svsu.edu

University of Michigan
515 East Jefferson
Ann Arbor, MI 48109
Phone: (734) 764-7433
Fax: (734) 936-0740
E-mail: ugadmiss@umich.edu
http://www.umich.edu

University of Michigan–Flint
303 East Kearsley Street
Flint, MI 48502
Phone: (810) 762-3434
Fax: (810) 762-3272
E-mail: admissions@umflint.edu
http://www.umflint.edu

MINNESOTA

Augsburg College
2211 Riverside Avenue
Minneapolis, MN 55454
Phone: (612) 330-1001
Fax: (612) 330-1590
E-mail: admissions@augsburg.edu
http://www.augsburg.edu

Bemidji State University
1500 Birchmont Drive, NE
Bemidji, MN 56601
Phone: (218) 755-2040
Fax: (218) 755-2074

E-mail: admissions@bemidjistate.
edu
http://wwwbemidjistate.edu

Bethel University
3900 Bethel Drive
St. Paul, MN 55112
Phone: (651) 638-6242
Fax: (651) 635-1490
E-mail: BUadmissions-cas@bethel.
edu
http://www.bethel.edu

Concordia College
901 Eighth Street South
Moorhead, MN 56562
Phone: (218) 299-3004
Fax: (218) 299-3947
E-mail: admissions@cord.edu
http://www.cord.edu

Concordia University-St. Paul
275 Syndicate North
St. Paul, MN 55104
Phone: (651) 641-8230
Fax: (651) 659-0207
E-mail: admiss@csp.edu
http://www.csp.edu

Gustavus Adolphus College
800 West College Avenue
Saint Peter, MN 56082
Phone: (507) 933-7676
Fax: (507) 933-7474
E-mail: admission@gustavus.edu
http://www.gustavus.edu

Hamline University
1536 Hewitt
St. Paul, MN 55104
Phone: (651) 523-2207
Fax: (651) 523-2458
E-mail: cla-admiss@gw.hamline.edu
http://www.gw.hamline.edu

Minnesota State University Mankato
122 Taylor Center
Mankato, MN 56001
Phone: (507) 389-6670
Fax: (507) 389-1511
E-mail: admissions@mnsu.edu
http://www.mnsu.edu

Minnesota State University Moorhead
Moorhead, MN 56563
Phone: (218) 477-2161
Fax: (218) 236-2168

Northwestern College
3003 Snelling Avenue North
St. Paul, MN 55113
Phone: (651) 631-5209
Fax: (651) 631-5680
E-mail: admissions@nwc.edu
http://www.nwc.edu

Saint Cloud State University
720 Fourth Avenue South
St. Cloud, MN 56301
Phone: (320) 308-2244
Fax: (320) 308-2243
E-mail: scsu4u@stcloudstate.edu
http://www.stcloudstate.edu

Saint Mary's University of Minnesota
700 Terrace Heights
Winona, MN 55987
Phone: (507) 457-1700
Fax: (507) 457-1722
E-mail: admissions@smumn.edu
http://www.smumn.edu

Southwest Minnesota State University
1501 State Street
Marshall, MN 56258
Phone: (507) 537-6286
Fax: (507) 537-7154
E-mail: shearerr@southwest.msus.
edu
http://www.southwest.msus.edu

University of Minnesota-Duluth
1117 University Drive
Duluth, MN 55812
Phone: (218) 726-7171
Fax: (218) 726-7040
E-mail: umdadmis@d.umn.edu
http://www.d.umn.edu

University of Minnesota-Twin Cities Campus
240 Williamson Hall

Minneapolis, MN 55455
Phone: (612) 625-2008
Fax: (612) 626-1693
E-mail: admissions@tc.umn.edu
http://www.tc.umn.edu

Western Michigan University
1903 West Michigan Avenue
Kalamazoo, MI 49008
Phone: (269) 387-2000
http://www.wmich.edu/admissions

Winona State University
P.O. Box 5838
Winona, MN 55987
Phone: (507) 457-5100
Fax: (507) 457-5620
E-mail: admissions@winona.edu
http://www.winona.edu

MISSISSIPPI

Blue Mountain College
P.O. Box 160
Blue Mountain, MS 38610
Phone: (662) 685-4161 Ext. 176
E-mail: tbarkley@bmc.edu
http://www.bmc.edu

Jackson State University
P.O. Box 17330
1400 John R. Lynch Street
Jackson, MS 39217
Phone: (601) 979-2911
E-mail: schatman@ccaix.jsums.edu
http://www.jsums.edu

Mississippi College
P.O. Box 4026
200 South Capitol Street
Clinton, MS 39058
Phone: (601) 925-3800
Fax: (601) 925-3804
E-mail: enrollment-services@
mc.edu
http://www.mc.edu

Mississippi University for Women
P.O. Box 1613
Columbus, MS 39701
Phone: (601) 329-7106
Fax: (601) 241-7481

E-mail: admissions@muw.edu
http://www.muw.edu

University of Southern Mississippi

118 College Drive
Hattiesburg, MS 39406
Phone: (601) 266-5000
Fax: (601) 266-5148
E-mail: admissions@usm.edu
http://www.usm.edu

William Carey College

498 Tuscan Avenue
Hattiesburg, MS 39401
Phone: (601) 318-6051
E-mail: admissions@wmcarey.edu
http://www.wmcarey.edu

MISSOURI

Central Missouri State University

1401 Ward Edwards
Warrensburg, MO 64093
Phone: (660) 543-4170
E-mail: admit@cmsuvmb.cmsu.edu
http://www.cmsu.edu

College of the Ozarks

P.O. Box 1
Point Lookout, MO 65726
Phone: (417) 334-6411
Fax: (417) 335-2618
E-mail: admiss4@cofo.edu
http://www.cofo.edu

Culver-Stockton College

Canton, MO 63435
Phone: (800) 537-1883
E-mail: enrollment@culver.edu
http://www.culver.edu

Drury University

900 North Benton
Springfield, MO 65802
Phone: (417) 873-7205
Fax: (417) 866-3873
E-mail: druryad@drury.edu
http://www.drury.edu

Lincoln University

820 Chestnut Street

Jefferson City, MO 65102
Phone: (573) 681-5599
Fax: (573) 681-5889
E-mail: enroll@lincolnu.edu
http://www.lincolnu.edu

Lindenwood University

209 South Kings Highway
St. Charles, MO 63301
Phone: (636) 949-4949
Fax: (636) 949-4989

Missouri Western State University

4525 Downs Drive
St. Joseph, MO 64507
Phone: (816) 271-4267
Fax: (816) 271-5833
E-mail: admissn@mwsc.edu
http://www.mwsc.edu

Northwest Missouri State University

800 University Drive
Maryville, MO 64468
Phone: (660) 562-1146
Fax: (660) 562-1121
E-mail: admissions@acad. nwmissouri.edu
http://www.nwmissouri.edu

Southeast Missouri State University

Cape Girardeau, MO 63701
Phone: (573) 651-2590
Fax: (573) 651-5936
E-mail: admissions@semo.edu
http://www.semo.edu

University of Central Missouri

1400 Ward Edwards
Warrensburg, MO 64093
Phone: (660) 543-4170
Fax: (660) 543-8517
E-mail: admit@ucmo.edu
http://www.ucmo.edu

University of Missouri–Columbia

230 Jesse Hall
Columbia, MO 65211
Phone: (573) 882-7786
Fax: (573) 882-7887

E-mail: mu4u@missouri.edu
http://www.missouri.edu

University of Missouri–Kansas City

5100 Rockhill Road
Kansas City, MO 64110
Phone: (816) 235-1111
Fax: (816) 235-5544
E-mail: admit@umkc.edu
http://ww.unkc.edu

Webster University

470 E. Lockwood Avenue
St. Louis, MO 63119
Phone: (314) 961-2660
Fax: (314) 968-7115
E-mail: admit@webster.edu
http://www.webster.edu

William Jewell College

500 College Hill

Liberty, MO 64068
Phone: (816) 781-7700
Fax: (816) 415-5040
E-mail: admission@william.jewell. edu
http//www.william.jewell.edu

MONTANA

Montana State University–Billings

1500 University Drive
Billings, MT 59101
Phone: (406) 657-2158
Fax: (406) 657-2302
E-mail: admissions@msubillings. edu
http://www.subillings.edu

Rocky Mountain College

1511 Poly Drive
Billings, MT 59102
Phone: (406) 657-1026
Fax: (406) 259-9751
E-mail: admissions@rocky.edu
http://www.rocky.edu

University of Montana–Missoula

Missoula, MT 59812

Phone: (406) 243-6266
Fax: (406) 243-5711
E-mail: admiss@selway.umt.edu
http://www.selway.umt.edu

University of Montana–Western
710 South Atlantic Street
Dillon, MT 59725
Phone: (406) 683-7331
Fax: (406) 683-7493
E-mail: admissions@umwestern.edu
http://www.umwester.edu

NEBRASKA

Chadron State College
1000 Main Street
Chadron, NE 69337
E-mail: inquire@csc.edu
http://www.csc.edu

Concordia University
800 North Columbia Avenue
Seward, NE 68434
Phone: (402) 643-7233
Fax: (402) 643-4073
E-mail: admiss@cune.edu
http://www.cune.edu

Dana College
2848 College Drive
Blair, NE 68008
Phone: (402) 426-7220
Fax: (402) 426-7386
E-mail: admissions@dana.edu
http://www.dana.edu

Grace University
1311 South Ninth Street
Omaha, NE 68108
Phone: (402) 449-2831
Fax: (402) 341-9587
E-mail: admissions@
    graceuniversity.com
http://www.graceuniversity.com

Hastings College
710 North Turner Avenue
Hastings, NE 68901
Phone: (402) 461-7320
Fax: (402) 461-7490
E-mail: mmolliconi@hastings.edu
http://www.hastings.edu

Midland Lutheran College
Fremont, NE 68025
Phone: (402) 941-6504
Fax: (402) 941-6513
E-mail: admissions@admin.mlc.edu
http://www.mlc.edu

Nebraska Wesleyan University
5000 Saint Paul Avenue
Lincoln, NE 68504
Phone: (402) 465-2218
Fax: (402) 465-2177
E-mail: admissions@nebrwesleyan.
    edu
http://www.nebrwesleyan.edu

Peru State College
P.O. Box 10
Peru, NE 68421
Phone: (402) 872-2221
Fax: (402) 872-2296
E-mail: mwillis@oakmail.peru.ed
http://www.peru.edu

Union College
3800 South 48th Street
Lincoln, NE 68506
Phone: (402) 486-2504
Fax: (402) 486-2566
E-mail: ucenroll@ucollege.edu
http://www.ucolle.edu

University of Nebraska at Omaha
6001 Dodge Street
Omaha, NE 68182
Phone: (402) 554-2416
Fax: (402) 554-3472
http://www.unomaha.edu

Wayne State College
1111 Main Street
Wayne, NE 68787
Phone: (402) 375-7234
Fax: (402) 375-7204
E-mail: admit1@wsc.edu
http://www.wsc.edu

NEVADA

University of Nevada, Reno
Reno, Nevada 89557
Phone: (775) 784-4700

E-mail: asknevada@unr.edu
http://www.unr.edu

NEW HAMPSHIRE

Keene State College
Keene, NH 03435
Phone: (603) 358-2276
Fax: (603) 358-2767
E-mail: admissions@keene.edu
http://www.keene.edu

Plymouth State University
17 High Street
Plymouth, NH 03264
Phone: (603) 535-2237
Fax: (603) 535-2714
http://www.plymouth.edu

University of New Hampshire
4 Garrison Avenue
Durham, NH 03801
Phone: (603) 862-1360
Fax: (603) 862-0077
http://www.unh.edu

NEW JERSEY

College of New Jersey
P.O. Box 7718
Ewing, NJ 08628
Phone: (609) 771-2131
http://www.tcnj.edu

Kean University
1000 Morris Avenue
Union, NJ 07083
Phone: (908) 737-7100
Fax: (908) 737-7105
E-mail: admitme@kean.edu
http://www.kean.edu

New Jersey City University
2039 Kennedy Boulevard
Jersey City, NJ 07305
Phone: (201) 200-3234
E-mail: admissions@njcu.edu
http://www.njcu.edu

Rider University
2083 Lawrenceville Road
Lawrenceville, NJ 08648
Phone: (609) 896-5000

E-mail: admissions@rider.edu
http://www.rider.edu

Rutgers, the State University of New Jersey
65 Davidson Road
Piscataway, NJ 08854
Phone: (732) 932-INFO
http://admissions.rutgers.edu

William Paterson University of New Jersey
Wayne, NJ 07470
Phone: (973) 720-2125
E-mail: admissions@wpunj.edu
http://www.wpunj.edu

NEW MEXICO

Eastern New Mexico University
Station #7 ENMU
Portales, NM 88130
Phone: (505) 562-2178
Fax: (505) 562-2118
E-mail: donna.kittrell@enmu.edu
http://www.enmu.edu

University of New Mexico
P.O. Box 4895
Albuquerque, NM 87196
Phone: (505) 277-2447
Fax: (505) 277-6686
E-mail: apply@unm.edu
http://www.unm.edu

Western New Mexico University
College Avenue
Silver City, NM 88062
Phone: (505) 538-6106
Fax: (505) 538-6127
E-mail: tresslerd@wnmu.edu
http://www.wnmu.edu

NEW YORK

Brooklyn College
City University of New York
1103 James Hall
2900 Bedford Avenue
Brooklyn, NY 11210
Phone: (718) 951-5001

E-mail: adminqry@brooklyn.cuny.edu
http://www.brooklyn.cuny.edu

Buffalo State College-State College of New York
1300 Elmwood Avenue
Buffalo, NY 14222
Phone: (716) 878-4017
Fax: (716) 878-6100
E-mail: admissions@buffalostate.edu
http://www.buffalostate.edu

City College of the City University of New York
Office of Admissions
160 Convent Avenue
New York, NY 10031
Phone: (212) 650-6977
E-mail: admissions@ccny.cuny.edu
http://www.ccny.cuny.edu/admissions

College of Saint Rose
432 Western Avenue
Albany, NY 12203
Phone: (518) 454-5150
Fax: (518) 454-2013
E-mail: admit@strose.edu (admissions)
http://www.strose.edu

Five Towns College
305 North Service Road
Dix Hills, New York 11746
Phone: (631) 424-7000
Fax: (631) 656-2172
E-mail: admissions@ftc.edu
http://www.ftc.edu

Hartwick College
Oneonta, NY 13820
Phone: (607) 431-4150
E-mail: admissions@hartwick.edu
http://www.hartwick.edu

Hofstra University
Hempstead, NY 11549
Phone: (516) 463-6700
Fax: (516) 463-5100

Houghton College
P.O. Box 128

Houghton, NY 14744
Phone: (585) 567-9353
Fax: (585) 567-9522
E-mail: admission@houghton.edu
http://www.houghton.edu

Ithaca College
100 Job Hall
Ithaca, New York 14850
Phone: (607) 274-3124
Fax: (607) 274-1900
E-mail: admission@ithaca.edu
http://www.ithaca.edu

Long Island University, C. W. Post Campus
720 Northern Boulevard
Brookville, NY 11548
Phone: (516) 299-2900
Fax: (516) 299-2137
E-mail: enroll@cwpost.liu.edu
http://www.cwpost.lin.edu

Manhattanville College
2900 Purchase Street
Purchase, NY 10577
Phone: (914) 323-5464

New York University
22 Washington Square North
New York, NY 10011
Phone: (212) 998-4500
http://admissions.nyu.edu

Queens College of the City University of New York
65-30 Kissena Boulevard
Flushing, NY 11367
Phone: (718) 997-5600
E-mail: admissions@qc.edu
http://www.qc.edu

State University of New York at Fredonia
Fredonia, NY 14063
Phone: (716) 673-3251
http:///www.fredonia.edu

State University of New York College at Potsdam
44 Pierrepont Avenue
Potsdam, NY 13676
Phone: (315) 267-2180

E-mail: admissions@potsdam.edu
http://www.potsdam.edu

Syracuse University
Syracuse, NY 13244
Phone: (315) 443-3611
http://admissions.syr.edu
http://www.syr.edu

University of Rochester
P.O. Box 270251
Rochester, NY 14627
Phone: (585) 275-3221
http://www.enrollment.rochester.
    edu/admissions

NORTH CAROLINA

Appalachian State University
Boone, NC 28608
Phone: (828) 262-2000
E-mail: admissions@appstate.edu
http://www.appstate.edu

Bennett College For Women
Campus Box H
Greensboro, NC 27401
Phone: (336) 517-8624
E-mail: admiss@bennett.edu
http://www.bennett.edu

Brevard College
400 North Broad Street
Brevard, NC 28712
Phone: (800) 527-9090
E-mail: admission@brevard.edu
http://www.brevard.edu

Campbell University
P.O. Box 546
Buies Creek, NC 27506
Phone: (910) 893-1320
E-mail: adm@mailcenter.campbell.
    edu
http://www.campbell.edu

Catawba College
Salisbury, NC 28144
Phone: (704) 637-4402
E-mail: admissions@catawba.edu

Chowan University
200 Jones Drive

Murfreesboro, NC 27855
Phone: (252) 398-6298
http://www.chowan.edu

East Carolina University
Greenville, NC 27858
Phone: (252) 328-6640
Fax: (252) 328-6945
E-mail: admis@mail.ecu.edu
http://www.ecu.edu

Elon University
Elon, NC 27244
Phone: (336) 278-3566
E-mail: admissions@elon.edu
http://www.elon.edu

Fayetteville State University
1200 Murchison Road
Fayetteville, NC 28301
Phone: (910) 486-1371
http://www.uncfsu.edu

Gardner-Webb University
Boiling Springs, NC 28017
Phone: (704) 406-4GWU
http://www.gardner-webb.edu

Greensboro College
815 West Market Street
Greensboro, NC 27401
Phone: (800) 346-8226
E-mail: admissions@gborocollege.
    edu
http://ww.gborocollege.edu

Lenoir-Rhyne College
P.O. Box 7227
Hickory, NC 28603
Phone: (828) 328-7300
Fax: (828) 328-7378
E-mail: admission@lrc.edu
http://www.lrc.edu

Mars Hill College
Mars Hill, NC 28754
Phone: (828) 689-1201
Fax: (828) 689-1473
E-mail: admissions@mhc.edu
http://www.mhc.edu

Meredith College
3800 Hillsborough Street

Raleigh, NC 27607
Phone: (919) 760-8581
Fax: (919) 760-2348
E-mail: admissions@meredith.edu
http://www.meredith.edu

Methodist University
5400 Ramset Street
Fayetteville, NC 28311
Phone: (910) 630-7027
http://www.methodist.edu

North Carolina Central University
P.O. Box 19717
Durham, NC 27707
Phone: (919) 530-6298
Fax: (919) 530-7625
E-mail: admissions@nccu.edu
http://www.nccu.edu

Pfeiffer University
P.O. Box 960
Highway 52 North
Misenheimer, NC 28109
Phone: (704) 463-1360
Fax: (704) 463-1363
E-mail: admiss@pfeiffer.edu
http://www.pfeiffer.edu

Salem College
601 South Church Street
Winston-Salem, NC 27101
Phone: (336) 721-2621
E-mail: admissions@salem.edu
http://www.salem.edu

University of North Carolina at Charlotte
9201 University City Boulevard
Charlotte, NC 28223
Phone: (704) 687-2213
Fax: (704) 687-6483
http://wwwuncc.edu

University of North Carolina at Greensboro
1400 Spring Garden Street
P.O. Box 26170
Greensboro, NC 27402
Phone: (336) 334-5243
Fax: (336) 334-4180

E-mail: undergrad_admission@
uncg
http://www.uncg.edu

University of North Carolina at Pembroke

One University Drive
Pembroke, NC 28372
Phone: (910) 521-6262
Fax: (910) 521-6497
E-mail: admissions@uncp.edu
http://www.uncp.edu

University of North Carolina at Wilmington

601 South College Road
Wilmington, NC 28403
Phone: (910) 962-4198
Fax: (910) 962-3038
E-mail: admissions@uncwil.edu
http://www.uncwil.edu

Western Carolina University

Cullowhee, NC 28723
Phone: (828) 227-7317
Fax: (828) 227-7319
E-mail: admiss@wcu.edu
http://www.poweryourmind.com

Wingate University

Wingate, NC 28174
Phone: (704) 233-8200
Fax: (704) 233-8110
E-mail: admit@wingate.edu
http://www.wingate.edu

NORTH DAKOTA

Dickinson State University

Dickinson, ND 58601
Phone: (701) 483-2175
http://www.dickinsonstate.edu

Jamestown College

6081 College Lane
Jamestown, ND 58405
Phone: (701) 252-3467
Fax: (701) 253-4318
E-mail: admissions@jc.edu
http://www.jc.edu

Minot State University

500 University Avenue West

Minot, ND 58707
Phone: (701) 858-3126
Fax: (701) 858-3825
E-mail: askmsu@minotstateu.edu
http://www.minotstateu.edu

North Dakota State University

P.O. Box 5454
Fargo, ND 58105
Phone: (701) 231-8643
Fax: (701) 231-8802
E-mail: ndsu.admission@ndsu.edu
http://www.ndsu.edu

OHIO

Ashland University

Ashland, OH 44805
Phone: (419) 289-5052
Fax: (419) 289-5999
E-mail: enrollme@ashland.edu
http://www.ashland.edu

Baldwin-Wallace College

275 Eastland Road
Berea, OH 44017
Phone: (440) 826-2222
Fax: (440) 826-3830
E-mail: info@bw.edu
http://www.bw.edu

Bowling Green State University

Bowling Green, OH 43403
Phone: (419) 372-BGSU
E-mail: choosebgsu@bgnet.bgsu.
edu
http://www.bgsu.edu

Capital University

1 College and Main
Columbus, OH 43209
Phone: (614) 236-6101
Fax: (614) 236-6926
E-mail: admissions@capital.edu
http://www.capital.edu

Case Western Reserve University

10900 Euclid Avenue
Cleveland, OH 44106
Phone: (216) 368-4450

E-mail: admission@case.edu
http://admission.case.edu

Cedarville University

251 North Main Street
Cedarville, OH 45314
Phone: (800) 233-2784
E-mail: admissions@cedarville.edu
http://www.cedarville.edu

College of Wooster

Wooster, OH 44691
Phone: (330) 263-2000
Fax: (330) 263-2621
E-mail: admissions@wooster.edu
http://www.wooster.edu

Heidelberg College

310 East Market Street
Tiffin, OH 44883
Phone: (419) 448-2330
Fax: 419-448-2334
E-mail: adminfo@heidlberg.edu
http://www.heidlberg.edu

Kent State University

P.O. Box 5190
Kent, OH 44242
Phone: (330) 672-2444
E-mail: kentadm@kent.edu
http://www.kent.edu

Mount Union College

1972 Clark Avenue
Alliance, OH 44601
Phone: (330) 823-2590
E-mail: admissn@muc.edu
http://www.muc.edu

Oberlin College

Oberlin, OH 44074
Phone: (440) 775-8411
E-mail: college.admissions@
oberlin.edu
http://www.oberlin.edu

Ohio State University

154 West 12th Avenue
Columbus, OH 43210
Phone: (614) 247-6281
Fax: (614) 292-4818
E-mail: askabuckeye@osu.edu

Ohio Wesleyan University
Delaware, OH 43015
Phone: (800) 922-8953
Fax: (740) 368-3314
E-mail: owadmit@owu.edu
http://www.owu.edu

Ohio University
Athens, OH 45701
Phone: (740) 593-4100
E-mail: admissions.freshmen@
    ohiou.edu
http://www.ohio.edu

University of Akron
277 E. Buchtel Avenue
Akron, OH 44325
Phone: (330) 972-6425
Fax: (330) 972-7022
E-mail: admissions@uakron.edu
http://www.uakron.edu

University of Cincinnati
P.O. Box 210091
Cincinnati, OH 45221
Phone: (513) 556-1100
Fax: (513) 556-1105
E-mail: admissions@uc.edu
http://www.uc.edu

University of Dayton
300 College Park
Dayton, OH 45469
Phone: (937) 229-4411
E-mail: admission@udayton.edu
http://www.udayton.edu

University of Rio Grande
Rio Grande, OH 45674
Phone: (740) 245-7208
Fax: (740) 245-7260
http://www.rio.edu

University of Toledo
2801 West Bancroft
Toledo, OH 43606
Phone: (419) 530-5728
Fax: (419) 530-5872
E-mail: enroll@utnet.utoledo.edu
http://www.utoledo.edu

Wilmington College
251 Ludovic Street

Wilmington, OH 45177
Phone: (937) 382-6661
Fax: (937) 382-7077
E-mail: admission@wilmington.edu
http://www.wilmington.edu

Wright State University
Dayton, OH 45435
Phone: (937) 775-5700
E-mail: admission@wright.edu
http://www.wright.edu

Youngstown State University
One University Plaza
Youngstown, OH 44555
Phone: (330) 941-2000
Fax: (330) 941-3674
E-mail: enroll@ysu.edu
http://www.ysu.edu

OKLAHOMA

East Central University
1100 East 14th Street
Ada, OK 74820
Phone: (580) 310-5233
E-mail: pdenny@ecok.edu
http://www.ecok.edu

Langston University
P.O. Box 728
Langston, OK 73120
Phone: (405) 466-2984
Fax: (405) 466-3391
http://www.lunet.edu

**Northwestern Oklahoma State
    University**
709 Oklahoma Boulevard
Alva, OK 73717
Phone: (580)327-8550
Fax: (580)327-8699
E-mail: smmurrow@nwosu.edu
http://www.nwosu.edu

Oklahoma Baptist University
Box 61174
Shawnee, OK 74804
Phone: (405) 878-2033
Fax: (405) 878-2046
E-mail: admissions@mail.okbu.edu
http://www.okbu.edu

Oklahoma City University
2501 North Blackwelder
Oklahoma City, OK 73106
Phone: (405) 521-5050
E-mail: uadmissions@okcu.edu
http://www.youatocu.com

Oklahoma State University
Stillwater, OK 74078
Phone: (405) 744-6858
Fax: (405) 744-5285
E-mail: admit@okstate.edu
http://www.okstate.edu

Oral Roberts University
7777 South Lewis Avenue
Tulsa, OK 74171
Phone: (918) 495-6518
Fax: (918) 495-6222
E-mail: admissions@oru.edu
http://www.oru.edu

**Southeastern Oklahoma State
    University**
1405 North Fourth Avenue
Durant, OK 74701
Phone: (580) 745-2060
Fax: (580) 745-7502
E-mail: admissions@sosu.edu
http://www.sosu.edu

**Southwestern Oklahoma State
    University**
100 Campus Drive
Weatherford, OK 73096
Phone: (580) 774-3009
Fax: (580) 774-3795
E-mail: ropers@swosu.edu
http://www.swosu.edu

**University of Central
    Oklahoma**
100 North University Drive
Edmond, OK 73034
Phone: (405) 974-2338
Fax: (405) 341-4964
E-mail: admituco@ucok.edu
http://ecok.edu

University of Oklahoma
1000 Asp Avenue
Norman, OK 73019
Phone: (405) 325-2151

Fax: (405) 325-7124
E-mail: admrec@ou.edu
http://www.ou.edu

OREGON

Corban College
5000 Deer Park Drive, SE
Salem, OR 97301
Phone: (503) 375-7115
Fax: (503) 585-4316
E-mail: admissions@corban.edu
http://www.corban.edu

George Fox University
Newberg, OR 97132
Phone: (800) 765-4369
E-mail: admissions@georgefox.edu
http://www.georgefox.edu

University of Oregon
1217 University of Oregon
Eugene, OR 97403
E-mail: uoadmit@oregon.uoregon.edu
http://www.uoregon.edu

Portland State University
P.O. Box 751
Portland, OR 97207
Phone: (503) 725-3511
Fax: (503) 725-5525
E-mail: admissions@pdx.edu
http://www.pdx.edu

PENNSYLVANIA

Bucknell University
Lewisburg, PA 17837
Phone: (570) 577-1101
Fax: (570) 577-3538
E-mail: admissions@bucknell.edu
http://www.bucknell.edu

Chestnut Hill College
9601 Germantown Avenue
Philadelphia, PA 19118
Phone: (215) 248-7001
E-mail: chcapply@chc.edu
http://www.chc.ed

Clarion University of Pennsylvania
840 Wood Street

Clarion, PA 16214
Phone: (814) 393-2306
E-mail: admissions@clarion.edu
http://www.clarion.edu/admiss

Duquesne University
600 Forbes Avenue
Pittsburgh, PA 15282
Phone: (412) 396-5000
Fax: (412) 396-5644
E-mail: admissions@duq.edu
http://www.duq.edu

Geneva College
3200 College Avenue
Beaver Falls, PA 15010
Phone: (724) 847-6500
E-mail: admissions@geneva.edu
http://www.geneva.edu

Grove City College
Grove City, PA 16127
Phone: (724) 458-2100
Fax: (724) 458-3395
E-mail: admissions@gcc.edu
http://www.gcc.edu

Kutztown University of Pennsylvania
Kutztown, PA 19530
Phone: (610) 683-4000
E-mail: admission@kutztown.edu
http://www.kutztown.edu

Lincoln University
P.O. Box 179
Lincoln University, PA 19352
Phone: (484) 365-8000
E-mail: admiss@lu.lincoln.edu
http://www.lincoln.ed

Mansfield University of Pennsylvania
Beecher House
Mansfield, PA 16933
Phone: (570) 662-4813
E-mail: admissions@mnsfld.edu
http://www.mnsfld.edu

Marywood University
2300 Adams Avenue
Scranton, PA 18509
Phone: (570) 348-6211

E-mail: ugadm@ac.marywood.edu
http://www.marywood.edu

Mercyhurst College Admissions
501 East 38th Street
Erie, PA 16546
Phone: (814) 824-2202
E-mail: admissions@mercyhurst.edu
http://www.mercyhurst.edu

Messiah College
Box 3005
One College Avenue
Grantham, PA 17027
Phone: (717) 691-6000
Fax: (717) 796-5374
E-mail: admiss@messiah.edu

Millersville University of Pennsylvania
P.O. Box 1002
Millersville, PA 17551
Phone: (717) 872-3371
E-mail: admissions@millersville.edu
http://www.millersville.edu

Pennsylvania State University-University Park Campus
201 Shields Building
Box 3000
University Park, PA 16804
Phone: (814) 865-5471
Fax: (814) 863-7590
E-mail: admissions@psu.edu
http://www.psu.edu

Seton Hill University
Box 991
One Seton Hill Drive
Greensburg, PA 15601
Phone: (800) 826-6234
Fax: (724) 830-1294
E-mail: admit@setonhill.edu
http://www.setonhill.edu

Susquehanna University
514 University Avenue
Selinsgrove, PA 17870
Phone: (570) 372-4260
Fax: (570) 372-2722
E-mail: suadmiss@susqu.edu
http//www.susqu.edu

Temple University (041-09)
Philadelphia, PA 19122
Phone: (215) 204-7200
E-mail: tuadm@temple.edu
http://www.temple.edu

York College of Pennsylvania
York, PA 17405
Phone: (717) 849-1600
Fax: (717) 849-1607
E-mail: admissions@ycp.edu

RHODE ISLAND

Providence College
549 River Avenue
Providence, RI 02918
Phone: (401) 865-2535
Fax: (401) 865-2826
E-mail: pcadmiss@providence.edu
http://www.providence.edu

Rhode Island College
600 Mount Pleasant Avenue
Providence, RI 02908
Phone: (401) 456-8234
Fax: (401) 456-8817
E-mail: admission@ric.edu
http://www.ric.edu

Salve Regina University
100 Ochre Point Avenue
Newport, RI 02840
Phone: (401) 341-2908
Fax: (401) 848-2823
E-mail: sruadmis@salve.edu
http://www.salve.edu

SOUTH CAROLINA

Anderson University
316 Boulevard
Anderson, SC 29621
Phone: (864) 231-2030
Fax: (864) 231-2033

Charleston Southern University
9200 University Boulevard
P.O. Box 118087
Charleston, SC 29423
Phone: (843) 863-7050
http://www.charlestonsouthern.edu

Coker College
300 East College Avenue
Hartsville, SC 29550
Phone: (843) 383-8050
Fax: (843) 383-8056
E-mail: admissions@coker.edu
http://www.coker.edu

Columbia College
1301 Columbia College Drive
Columbia, SC 29203
Phone: (803) 786-3765
Fax: (803) 786-3674
E-mail: admission@collacoll.edu
http://www.colacoll.edu

Converse College
580 East Main Street
Spartanburg, SC 29302
Phone: (864) 596-9040
E-mail: admissions@converse.edu
http://www.converse.edu

Furman University
3300 Poinsett Highway
Greenville, SC 29613
Phone: (864) 294-2034
Fax: (864) 294-3127
E-mail: admissions@furman.edu
http://www.furman.edu

Limestone College
1115 College Drive
Gaffney, SC 29340
Phone: (864) 488-4554
Fax: (864) 488-8206
E-mail: admiss@limestone.edu
http://www.limestone.edu

Newberry College
2100 College Street
Newberry, SC 29108
Phone: (803) 321-5127
E-mail: admissions@newberry.edu
http://www.newberry.ed

South Carolina State University
300 College Street Northeast
Orangeburg, SC 29117
Phone: (803) 536-8408
Fax: (803) 536-8990
E-mail: admissions@scsu.edu
http://www.scsu.edu

University of South Carolina
Columbia, SC 29208
Phone: (803) 777-7700
E-mail: admissions-ugrad@sc.edu
http://www.sc.edu

University of South Carolina Aiken
471 University Parkway
Aiken, SC 29801
Phone: (803) 648-6851
Fax: (803) 641-3727
E-mail: admit@usca.edu
http://www.usca.edu

Winthrop University
Rock Hill, SC 29733
Phone: (803) 323-2191
E-mail: admissions@winthrop.edu
http://www.winthrop.edu

SOUTH DAKOTA

Augustana College
2001 South Summit Avenue
Sioux Falls, SD 57197
Phone: (605) 274-5516
Fax: (605) 274-5518
E-mail: admission@augie.edu
http://www.audie.edu

Dakota Wesleyan University
1200 West University Avenue
Mitchell, SD 57301
Phone: (605) 995-2650
Fax: (605) 995-2699
E-mail: admissions@dwu.edu
http://www.dwu.edu

Northern State University
1200 South Jay Street
Aberdeen, SD 57401
Phone: (605) 626-2544
Fax: (605) 626-2587
E-mail: admissions1@northern.edu
http://www.northern.edu

South Dakota State University
P.O. Box 2201
Brookings, SD 57007
Phone: (605) 688-4121
Fax: (605) 688-6891

E-mail: sdsu_admissions@sdstate.
edu
http://www.sdstate.edu

University of Sioux Falls
1101 West 22nd Street
Sioux Falls, SD 57105
Phone: (605) 331-6600
Fax: (605) 331-6615
E-mail: admissions@usiouxfalls.edu
http://www.usioxfalls.edu

University of South Dakota
414 East Clark Street
Vermillion, SD 57069
Phone: (605) 677-5434
Fax: (605) 677-6753
E-mail: admiss@usd.edu
http://www.usd.edu

TENNESSEE

Belmont University
1900 Belmont Boulevard
Nashville, TN 37212
Phone: (615) 460-6785
Fax: (615) 460-5434
E-mail: buadmission@mail.
belmont.edu
http://www.belmont.edu

Bethel College
325 Cherry Avenue
McKenzie, TN 38201
Phone: (731) 352-4030
Fax: (731) 352-4069
E-mail: admissions@bethel-college.
edu
http://www.bethel-college.edu

Bryan College
P.O. Box 7000
Dayton, TN 37321
Phone: (423) 775-2041
Fax: (423) 775-7199
E-mail: admissions@bryan.edu
http://www.bryan.edu

Carson-Newman College
Jefferson City, TN 37760
Phone: (865) 471-3223
E-mail: thuebner@cn.edu
http://www.cn.edu

Cumberland University
One Cumberland Square
Lebanon, TN 37087
Phone: (615) 444-2562 Ext. 1280
Fax: (615) 444-2569
E-mail: admissions@cumberland.
edu
http://www.cumberland.edu

Fisk University
1000 17th Avenue North
Nashville, TN 37208
Phone: (615) 329-8666
Fax: (615) 329-8774
E-mail: admit@fisk.edu
http://www.fisk.edu

Freed-Hardeman University
158 East Main Street
Henderson, TN 38340
Phone: (731) 989-6651
Fax: (731) 989-6047
E-mail: admissions@fhu.edu
http://www.fhu.edu

Lambuth University
705 Lambuth Boulevard
Jackson, TN 38301
Phone: (731) 425-3223
E-mail: admit@lambuth.edu
http://www.lambuth.edu

Lipscomb University
3901 Granny White Pike
Nashville, TN 37204
Phone: (615) 269-1000
Fax: (615) 269-1804
E-mail: admissions@lipscomb.edu
http://www.lipscomb.edu

Maryville College
502 East Lamar Alexander Parkway
Maryville, TN 37804
Phone: (865) 981-8092
Fax: (865) 981-8005
E-mail: admissions@
maryvillecollege.edu
http://www.maryvillecollege.edu

Milligan College
P.O. Box 210
Milligan College, TN 37682
Phone:: (423) 461-8730

Fax: (423) 461-8982
E-mail: admissions@milligan.edu
http://www.milligan.edu

Union University
1050 Union University Drive
Jackson, TN 38305
Phone: (800) 33-UNION
E-mail: info@uu.edu
http://www.uu.edu

TEXAS

Baylor University
One Bear Place #97056
Waco, TX 76798
Phone: (254) 710-3435
http://www.baylor.edu

Hardin-Simmons University
Box 16050
Abilene, TX 79698
Phone: (325) 670-5890
Fax: (325) 671-2115
E-mail: breynolds@hsutx.edu
http://www.hsutx.edu

Howard Payne University
1000 Fisk Avenue
Brownwood, TX 76801
Phone: (325) 649-8027
Fax: (325) 649-8901
E-mail: enroll@hputx.edu
http://www.hputx.edu

Lamar University
P.O. Box 10009
Beaumont, TX 77710
Phone: (409) 880-8888
Fax: (409) 880-8463
E-mail: admissions@hal.lamar.edu
http://www.hal.lamar.edu

Midwestern State University
Wichita Falls, TX 76308
Phone: (940) 397-4334
Fax: (940) 397-4672
E-mail: admissions@mwsu.edu
http://www.mwsu.edu

Sam Houston State University
P.O. Box 2418
Huntsville, TX 77341

Phone: (936) 294-1828
Fax: (936) 294-3758

Southern Methodist University
P.O. Box 750296
Dallas, TX 75275
Phone: (214) 768-2000
E-mail: ugadmission@smu.edu
http://www.smu.edu

Southwestern University
Georgetown, TX 78626
Phone: (512) 863-1200
Fax: (512) 863-9601
E-mail: admission@southwestern.
edu
http://www.southwestern.edu

Tarleton State University
Tarleton Station
Stephenville, TX 76402
Phone: (254) 968-9125
Fax: (254) 968-9951
E-mail: uadm@tarleton.edu
http://www.tarleton.edu

Texas A&M University
College Station, TX 77843
Phone: (979) 845-3741
Fax: (979) 845-8737
E-mail: admissions@tamu.edu
http://www.tamu.edu

Texas Christian University
2800 South University Drive
Fort Worth, TX 76129
Phone: (817) 257-7490
Fax: (817) 257-7268
E-mail: frogmail@tcu.edu
http://www.tcu.edu

Texas Southern University
3100 Cleburne Street
Houston, TX 77004
Phone: (713) 313-7472
http://www.tsu.edu

Wiley College
711 Wiley Avenue
Marshall, TX 75670
Phone: (903) 927-3222
Fax: (903) 923-8878
E-mail: ajones@wileyc.edu
http://www.wileyc.edu

UTAH

Brigham Young University
Provo, UT 84602
Phone: (801) 422-2507
Fax: (801) 422-0005
E-mail: admissions@byu.edu
http://www.byu.edu

Southern Utah University
351 West Center Street
Cedar City, UT 84720
Phone: (801) 586-7740
Fax: (435) 865-8223
E-mail: adminfo@suu.edu
http://www.suu.edu

Utah State University
Logan, UT 84322
Phone: (435) 797-1079
Fax: (435) 797-3708
E-mail: admit@cc.usu.edu
http://www.usu.edu

Utah Valley State College
800 West University Parkway
Orem, UT 84058
Phone: (801) 863-8460
Fax: (801) 225-4677
E-mail: info@uvsc.edu
http://www.uvsc.edu

Weber State University
1137 University Circle
3750 Harrison Boulevard
Ogden, UT 84408
Phone: (801) 626-6050
Fax: (801) 626-6744
E-mail: admissions@weber.edu
http://www.weber.edu

VERMONT

Castleton State College
Castleton, VT 05735
Phone: (802) 468-1213
Fax: (802) 468-1476
E-mail: info@castleton.edu
http://www.castleton.edu

Johnson State College
337 College Hill
Johnson, VT 05656

Phone: (802) 635-1219
Fax: (802) 635-1230
http://www.jsc.vsc.edu

University of Vermont
194 South Prospect Street
Burlington, VT 05401
Phone: (802) 656-3370
Fax: (802) 656-8611
E-mail: admissions@uvm.edu
http://www.uvm.edu

VIRGINIA

Bluefield College
3000 College Drive
Bluefield, VA 24605
Phone: (276) 326-4214
Fax: (276) 326-4288
E-mail: admissions@mail.bluefield.
edu
http://www.bluefield.edu

Hampton University
Hampton, VA 23668
Phone: (757) 727-5328
Fax: (757) 727-5095
E-mail: admit@hamptonu.edu
http://www.hamptonu.edu

Longwood University
Farmville, VA 23909
Phone: (434) 395-2060
Fax: (434) 395-2332
E-mail: admit@longwood.edu
http://www.longwood.edu

Old Dominion University
108 Rollins Hall
Norfolk, VA 23529
Phone: (757) 683-3685
E-mail: admit@odu.edu
http://www.odu.edu

Shenandoah University
1460 University Drive
Winchester, VA 22601
Phone: (540) 665-4581
Fax: (540) 665-4627
E-mail: admit@su.edu
http://www.su.edu

University of Mary Washington
1301 College Avenue
Fredericksburg, VA 22401
Phone: (540) 654-2000
Fax: (540) 654-1857
E-mail: admit@umw.edu
http://www.umw.edu

WASHINGTON

Central Washington University
400 East University Way
Ellensburg, WA 98926
Phone: (509) 963-1211
Fax: (509) 963-3022
E-mail: cwuadmis@cwu.edu
http://www.cwu.edu

Eastern Washington University
Cheney, WA 99004
Phone: (509) 359-2397
Fax: (509) 359-6692
E-mail: admission@mail.ewu.edu
http://www.ewu.edu

Gonzaga University
Spokane, Washington 99258
Phone: (800) 322-2584
E-mail: admissions@gu.gonzaga.
edu
http://www.gonzaga.edu

Northwest University
P.O. Box 579
Kirkland, WA 98083
Phone: (425) 889-5598
Fax: (425) 889-5224
E-mail: admissions@northwestu.
edu
http://www.northwestu.edu

Seattle Pacific University
3307 Third Avenue West, Suite 115
Seattle, WA 98119
Phone: (206) 281-2021
E-mail: admissions@spu.edu
http://www.spu.edu

University of Puget Sound
1500 North Warner Street, #1062
Tacoma, WA 98416
Phone: (253) 879-3211

E-mail: admission@ups.edu
http://www.ups.edu

University of Washington
Seattle, WA 98195
Phone: (206) 543-9686

Walla Walla College
204 South College Avenue
College Place, WA 99324
Phone: (509) 527-2327
Fax: (509) 527-2397
E-mail: info@wwc.edu
http://www.wwe.edu

Washington State University
French Administration Building
Pullman, WA 99164
Phone: (509) 335-5586
Fax: (509) 335-7468
E-mail: admiss@wsu.edu
http://www.wsu.edu

Western Washington University
516 High Street
Bellingham, WA 98225
Phone: (360) 650-3440
Fax: (360) 650-7369
E-mail: admit@wwu.edu
http://www.wwu.edu

Whitworth College
West 300 Hawthorne Road
Spokane, WA 99251
Phone: (509) 777-3212
E-mail: admission@whitworth.edu
http://www.whitworth.edu

WEST VIRGINIA

Alderson-Broaddus College
Philippi, WV 26416
Phone: (800) 263-1549 (toll-free)
E-mail: admissions@ab.edu
http://www.ab.edu

Concord University
1000 Vermillion Street
Athens, WV 24712
Phone: (304) 384-5248
Fax: (304) 384-9044

E-mail: admissions@concord.edu
http://www.concord.edu

Davis & Elkins College
100 Campus Drive
Elkins, WV 26241
Phone: (304) 637-1230
E-mail: admiss@davisandelkins.edu
http://www.davisandelkins.edu

Fairmont State University
1201 Locust Avenue
Fairmont, WV 26554
Phone: (304) 367-4892
E-mail: fscinfo@mail.fscwv.edu
http://www.fscwv.edu

University of Charleston
2300 MacCorkle Avenue, SE
Charleston, WV 25304
Phone: (304) 357-4750
Fax: (304) 357-4781
E-mail: admissions@ucwv.edu
http://www.ucwv.edu

West Virginia State University
Campus Box 197
P.O. Box 1000
Institute, WV 25112
Phone: (304) 766-3032
Fax: (304) 766-4158
E-mail: sweeneyt@wvstateu.edu
http://www.wvstateu.edu

West Virginia Wesleyan College
59 College Avenue
Buckhannon, WV 26201
Phone: (304) 473-8510
E-mail: admission@wvwc.edu
http://www.wvwc.edu

WISCONSIN

Beloit College
700 College Street
Beloit, WI 53511
Phone: (608) 363-2500
Fax: (608) 363-2075
E-mail: admiss@beloit.edu
http://www.beloit.edu

Carroll College
100 North East Avenue
Waukesha, WI 53186
Phone: (262) 524-7220
E-mail: ccinfo@cc.edu
http://www.cc.edu

Carthage College
2001 Alford Park Drive
Kenosha, WI 53140
Phone: (262) 551-6000
E-mail: admissions@carthage.edu
http://www.carthage.edu

Lawrence University
P.O. Box 599
Appleton, WI 54912
Phone: (920) 832-6500
E-mail: excel@lawrence.edu
http://www.lawrence.edu

Ripon College
300 Seward Street
P.O. Box 248
Ripon, WI 54971
Phone: (800) 94RIPON
E-mail: adminfo@ripon.edu
http://www.ripon.edu

University of Wisconsin–Madison
716 Langdon Street
Madison, WI 53706
Phone: (608) 262-3961
Fax: (608) 262-7706
http://www.wisc.edu

University of Wisconsin–Milwaukee
P.O. Box 749
Milwaukee, WI 53201
Phone: (414) 229-4397
Fax: (414) 229-6940
E-mail: uwmlook@uwm.edu
http://www.uwm.edu

University of Wisconsin–Oshkosh
Oshkosh, WI 54901
Phone: (920) 424-0202
E-mail: oshadmuw@uwosh.edu
http://www.uwosh.edu

University of Wisconsin–River Falls
410 South Third Street
River Falls, WI 54022
Phone: (715) 425-3500
Fax: (715) 425-0676
E-mail: admit@uwrf.edu
http://www.uwrf.edu

University of Wisconsin–Stevens Point
2100 Main Street
Stevens Point, WI 54481
Phone: (715) 346-2441
Fax: (715) 346-3296
E-mail: admiss@uwsp.edu
http://www.uwsp.edu

University of Wisconsin–Superior
P.O. Box 2000
Superior, WI 54880
Phone: (715) 394-8217
Fax: (715) 394-8407
E-mail: admissions@uwsuper.edu
http://www.uwsuper.edu

University of Wisconsin–Whitewater
800 West Main Street
Whitewater, WI 53190
Phone: (262) 472-1440 Ext. 1512
Fax: (262) 472-1515
E-mail: uwwadmit@uww.edu
http://www.uww.edu

Viterbo University
900 Viterbo Drive
LaCrosse, WI 54601
Phone: (608) 796-3010
Fax: (608) 796-3020
E-mail: admission@viterbo.edu
http://www.viterbo.edu

WYOMING

University of Wyoming
1000 East University Avenue
Laramie, WY 82071
Phone: (307) 766-5160
E-mail: why-wyo@uwyo.edu
http://www.uwyo.edu

F. COLLEGES AND UNIVERSITIES OFFERING MAJORS IN PUBLIC RELATIONS

The following is a listing of selected four-year schools offering majors in public relations. They are grouped by state. School names, addresses, phone numbers, Web addresses, and e-mail addresses are included when available.

The author does not endorse any one school over another. Use this list as a beginning. Check the reference section of libraries or guidance counseling centers for additional schools offering degrees in this field.

ALABAMA

Alabama State University
915 South Jackson Street
Montgomery, AL 36104
Phone: (334) 229-4291
E-mail: mpettway@alasu.edu
http://www.alasu.edu

Auburn University
202 Martin Hall
Auburn University, AL 36849
Phone: (334) 844-4080
E-mail: admissions@auburn.edu
http://www.auburn.edu

Spring Hill College
4000 Dauphin Street

Mobile, AL 36608
Phone: (251) 380-3030
Fax: (251) 460-2186
E-mail: admit@shc.edu
http://www.shc.edu

University of Alabama
Box 870132
Tuscaloosa, AL 35487
Phone: (205) 348-5666
Fax: (205) 348-9046
E-mail: admissions@ua.edu
http://www.ua.edu

ARIZONA

Grand Canyon University
3300 West Camelback Road
Phoenix, AZ 85017
Phone: (800) 486-7085
E-mail: admissionsground@gcu.edu
http://www.gcu.edu

Northern Arizona University
P.O. Box 4084
Flagstaff, AZ 86011
Phone: (928) 523-5511
E-mail: undergraduate.admissions@
nau.edu
http://www.nau.edu

ARKANSAS

Harding University
Box 12255
Searcy, Arkansas 72149
Phone: (501) 279-4407
Fax: (501) 279-4129
E-mail: admissions@harding.edu
http://www.harding.edu

John Brown University
200 West University Street
Siloam Springs, AR 72761
Phone: (479) 524-7454
Fax: (479) 524-4196
E-mail: dcrandal@jbu.edu
http://www.jbu.edu

CALIFORNIA

California State Polytechnic University
3801 West Temple Avenue

Pomona, CA 91768
Phone: (909) 869-3210
http://www.csupomona.edu

California State University, Chico
400 West First Street
Chico, CA 95929
Phone: (530) 898-4879
Fax: (530) 898-6456
E-mail: info@csuchico.edu
http://www.csuchico.edu

California State University, Dominguez Hills
1000 East Victoria Street
Carson, CA 90747
Phone: (310) 243-4696
Fax: (310) 217-6800
http://www.csudh.edu

California State University, Fresno
5150 North Maple Avenue
Fresno, CA 93740
Phone: (559) 278-6115
Fax: (559) 278-4812
E-mail: yolandad@csufresno.edu
http://www.csufresnu.edu

California State University, Fullerton
P.O. Box 6900
800 North State College Boulevard
Fullerton, CA 92834
Phone: (714) 278-2370
E-mail: admissions@fullerton.edu
http://www.fullerton.edu

California State University, Hayward
25800 Carlos Bee Boulevard
Hayward, CA 94542
Phone: (510) 885-3248
Fax: (510) 885-3816
E-mail: adminfo@csuhayward.edu
http://www.csuhayward.edu

Chapman University
One University Drive
Orange, CA 92866
Phone: (714) 997-6711
Fax: (714) 997-6713

E-mail: admit@chapman.edu
http://www.chapman.edu

Pacific Union College
One Angwin Avenue
Angwin, CA 94508
Phone: (707) 965-6425
Fax: (707) 965-6432
E-mail: enroll@puc.edu
http://www.puc.edu

Pepperdine University
24255 Pacific Coast Highway
Malibu, CA 90263
Phone: (310) 506-4392
Fax: (310) 506-4861
E-mail: admission-seaver@
pepperdine.edu
http://www.pepperdine.edu

San Diego State University
5500 Campanile Drive
San Diego, CA 92182
Phone: (619) 594-6886
Fax: (619) 594-1250
E-mail: admissions@sdsu.edu
http://www.sdsu.edu

San Jose State University
One Washington Square
San Jose, CA 95192
Phone: (408) 924-1000
E-mail: contact@sjsu.edu
http://www.sjsu.edu

University of Southern California
University Park
Los Angeles, CA 90089
Phone: (213) 740-1111
E-mail: admitusc@usc.edu
http://www.usc.edu

COLORADO

Colorado State University
Fort Collins, Colorado 80523
Phone: (970) 491-6909
E-mail: admissions@colostate.edu
http://www.colostate.edu

Johnson & Wales University
8 Abbott Park Place
Providence, RI 02903

Phone: (977) 598-3368
Fax: (303) 256-9333
E-mail: den.admissions@jwu.edu
http://www.jwu.edu

CONNECTICUT

Quinnipiac University
Hamden, Connecticut 06518
Phone: (203) 582-8600
Fax: (203) 582-8906
E-mail: admissions@quinnipiac.edu
http://www.quinnipiac.edu

DELAWARE

Delaware State University
1200 North DuPont Highway
Dover, DE 19901-2277
Phone: (302) 857-6351
Fax: (302) 857-6908
E-mail: gcheatha@desu.edu
http://www.desu.edu

University of Delaware
Newark, DE 19716
Phone: (302) 831-8123
Fax: (302) 831-6905
E-mail: admissions@udel.edu
http://www.udel.edu

DISTRICT OF COLUMBIA

American University
4400 Massachusetts Avenue, NW
Washington, D.C. 20016
Phone: (202) 885-6000
Fax: (202) 885-1025
E-mail: afa@american.edu
http://admissions.american.edu

FLORIDA

Barry University
11300 N.E. Second Avenue
Miami Shores, FL 33161
Phone: (305) 899-3000
E-mail: admissions@mail.barry.edu
http://www.barry.edu

Florida Agricultural and Mechanical University
Tallahassee, FL 32307

Phone: (850) 599-3796
E-mail: admissions@famu.edu
http://www.famu.edu

Florida Southern College
111 Lake Hollingsworth Drive
Lakeland, FL 33801
Phone: (800) 274-4131
E-mail: fscadm@flsouthern.edu
http://www.flsouthern.edu

Florida State University
Tallahassee, FL 32306
Phone: (850) 644-2525
E-mail: admissions@admin.fsu.edu
http://www.fsu.edu

University of Florida
P.O. Box 114000
Gainesville, FL 32611
Phone: (352) 392-3261
E-mail: freshman@ufl.edu
http://www.ufl.edu

University of Miami
P.O. Box 248025
Coral Gables, FL 33124
Phone: (305) 284-2211
E-mail: admission@miami.edu
http://www.miami.edu

University of Tampa
401 West Kennedy Boulevard
Tampa, FL 33606
Phone: (813) 253-6211
Fax: (813) 254-4955
E-mail: : admissions@ut.edu
http://www.ut.edu

GEORGIA

Georgia Southern University
Forest Drive
Statesboro, GA 30460
Phone: (912) 681-5391
Fax: (912) 486-7240
E-mail: admissions@ georgiasouthern.edu
http://www.georgiasouthern.edu

Paine College
1235 15th Street
Augusta, GA 30901

Phone: (706) 821-8320
E-mail: tinsleyj@mail.paine.edu
http://www.paine.edu

Shorter College
315 Shorter Avenue
Rome, GA 30165
Phone: (706) 233-7319
Fax: (706) 233-7224
E-mail: admissions@shorter.edu
http://www.shorter.edu

University of Georgia
212 Terrell Hall
Athens, GA 30602
Phone: (706) 542-3000
E-mail: undergrad@admissions. uga.edu
http://www.uga.edu

HAWAII

Hawaii Pacific University
1164 Bishop Street
Honolulu, HI 96813
Phone: (808) 544-0200
E-mail: admissions@hpu.edu
http://www.hpu.edu

IDAHO

Northwest Nazarene University
623 Holly Street
Nampa, ID 83686
Phone: (208) 467-8000
Fax: (208) 467-8645
E-mail: admissions@nnu.edu

University of Idaho
P.O. Box 444264
Moscow, ID 83844
Phone: (208) 885-6326
Fax: (208) 885-9119
E-mail: carolynl@uidaho.edu
http://www.uidaho.edu

ILLINOIS

Bradley University
1501 W. Bradley Avenue
Peoria, IL 61625
Phone: (309) 676-7611
E-mail: admissions@bradley.edu
http://www.bradley.edu

Columbia College Chicago
600 South Michigan Avenue
Chicago, IL 60605
Phone: (312) 344-7130
Fax: (312) 344-8024
http://www.colum.edu

Greenville College
315 East College Avenue
Greenville, IL 62246
Phone: (618) 664-7100
Fax: (618) 664-9841
E-mail: admissions@greenville.edu

Illinois State University
Normal, IL 61790
Phone: (309) 438-2181
Fax: (309) 438-3932
E-mail: ugradadm@ilstu.edu
http://www.ilstu.edu

Lewis University

One University Parkway
Romeoville, IL 60446
Phone: (800) 897-9000
E-mail: admissions@lewisu.edu
http://www.lewisu.edu

McKendree University
701 College Road
Lebanon, IL 62254
Phone: (618) 537-6833
Fax: (618) 537-6496
E-mail: inquiry@mckendree.edu
http://www.mckendree.edu

Monmouth College
700 East Broadway
Monmouth, IL 61462
Phone: (309) 457-2140
Fax: (309) 457-2141
E-mail: admit@monm.edu

Quincy University
1800 College Avenue
Quincy, IL 62301
Phone: (217) 228-5210
E-mail: admissions@quincy.edu
http://www.quincy.edu

Roosevelt University
Chicago Campus
430 South Michigan Avenue

Chicago, IL 60605
Phone: 877-APPLY-RU
http://www.roosevelt.edu

INDIANA

Ball State University
2000 University Avenue
Muncie, IN 47306
Phone: (765) 285-8300
E-mail: askus@bsu.edu
http://www.bsu.edu

Goshen College
1700 South Main Street
Goshen, IN 46526
Phone: (574) 535-7535
Fax: (574) 535-7609
E-mail: lynnj@goshen.edu
http://www.goshen.edu

Purdue University
475 Stadium Mall Drive
Schleman Mall
West Lafayette, IN 47907
Phone: (765)494-1776
Fax: (765) -494-0544
E-mail: admissions@purdue.edu
http://www.purdue.edu

University of Southern Indiana
8600 University Boulevard
Evansville, IN 47712
Phone: (812) 464-8600
E-mail: enroll@usi.edu
http://www.usi.edu

IOWA

Clarke College
1550 Clarke Drive
Dubuque, IA 52001
Phone: (563) 588-6300
E-mail: admissions@clarke.edu
http://www.clarke.edu

Coe College
1220 First Avenue, NE
Cedar Rapids, IA 52402
Phone: (319) 399-8500
Fax: (319) 399-8816
E-mail: admission@coe.edu
http://www.coe.edu

Drake University
2507 University Avenue
Des Moines, IA 50311
Phone: (515) 271-2011
E-mail: admitinfo@acad.drake.edu
http://www.drake.edu

St. Ambrose University
518 West Locust Street
Davenport, IA 52803
Phone: (563) 333-6300
E-mail: admit@sau.edu
http://www.sau.admissions

University of Northern Iowa
Cedar Falls, IA 50614
Phone: (319) 273-2281
Fax: (319) 273-2885
E-mail: admissions@uni.edu

Wartburg College
100 Wartburg Boulevard
P.O. Box 1003
Waverly, IA 50677
Phone: (319) 352-8264
Fax: (319) 352-8579

KANSAS

Fort Hays State University
600 Park Street
Hays, KS 67601
Phone: (785) 628-5830
E-mail: tigers@fhsu.edu
http://www.fhsu.edu

MidAmerica Nazarene University
2030 East College Way
Olathe, KS 66062
Phone: (913) 791-3380
Fax: (913) 791-3481
E-mail: admissions@mnu.edu

Pittsburg State University
Pittsburg, KS 66762
Phone: (620) 235-4251
Fax: (620) 235-6003
E-mail: psuadmit@pittstate.edu
http://www.pittstate.edu

KENTUCKY

Eastern Kentucky University
521 Lancaster Avenue

Richmond, KY 40475
Phone: (859) 622-2106
Fax: (859) 622-8024
E-mail: admissions@eku.edu

Murray State University
P.O. Box 9
Murray, KY 42071
Phone: (270) 762-3035
Fax: 270) 762-3050
E-mail: admissions@murraystate.
edu
http://www.murraystate.edu

Northern Kentucky University
Highland Heights, KY 41099
Phone: (859) 572-5220
E-mail: admitnku@nku.edu
http://www.nku.edu

Western Kentucky University
One Big Red Way
Bowling Green, KY 42101
Phone: (270) 745-2551
Fax: (270) 745-6133
E-mail: admission@wku.edu
http://www.wku.edu

LOUISIANA

University of Louisiana at Lafayette
P.O. Box 44652
Lafayette, LA 70504
Phone: (337) 482-6473
E-mail: admissionsl@louisiana.edu
http://www.louisiana.edu

MAINE

New England School of Communications
1 College Circle
Bangor, ME 04401
Phone: (207) 941-7176
Fax: (207) 947-3987
E-mail: info@nescom.edu
http://www.nescom.edu

MARYLAND

Bowie State University
Bowie, MD 20715

Phone: (301) 860-3415
Fax: (301) 860-3518
E-mail: undergraduateadmissions@
bowiestate.edu
http://www.bowiestate.edu

MASSACHUSETTES

Boston University
121 Bay State Road
Boston, MA 02215
Phone: (617) 353-2000
E-mail: admissions@bu.edu
http://www.bu.edu

Curry College
Milton, MA 02186
Phone: (617) 333-2210
Fax: (617) 333-2114
E-mail: curryadm@curry.edu
http://www.curry.edu

Emerson College
120 Boylston Street
Boston, MA 02116
Phone: (617) 824-8500
E-mail: admission@emerson.edu
http://www.emerson.edu

Salem State College
352 Lafayette Street
Salem, MA 01970
Phone: (978) 542-6200

Simmons College
300 the Fenway
Boston, MA 02115
Phone: (800) 345-8468
Fax: (617) 521-3190
http://www.simmons.edu

Suffolk University
8 Ashburton Place
Boston, MA 02108
Phone: (800) 6-SUFFOLK
Fax: (617) 742-4291
E-mail: admission@suffolk.edu
http://www.suffolk.edu

MICHIGAN

Andrews University
Berrien Springs, MI 49104

Phone: (800) 253-2874
Fax: (269) 471-3228
E-mail: enroll@andrews.edu
http://www.andrews.edu

Central Michigan University
Mt. Pleasant, MI 48859
Phone: (989) 774-3076
Fax: (989) 774-7267
E-mail: cmuadmit@cmich.edu
http://www.cmich.edu

Eastern Michigan University
Ypsilanti, Michigan 48197
Phone: (734) 487-3060
Fax: (734) 487-6559
E-mail: admissions@emich.edu
http://www.emich.edu

Ferris State University
901 State Street
Big Rapids, MI 49307
Phone: (231) 591-2000
E-mail: admissions@ferris.edu
http://www.ferris.edu

Grand Valley State University
One Campus Drive
Allendale, MI 49401
Phone: (616) 895-6611
E-mail: go2gvsu@gvsu.edu
http://www.gvsu.edu

Madonna University
36600 Schoolcraft Road
Livonia, MI 48150
Phone: (734) 432-5317
Fax: (734) 432-5393
E-mail: muinfo@madonna.edu
http://www.madonna.edu

Northern Michigan University
1401 Presque Isle Avenue
Marquette, MI 49855
Phone: (906) 227-2650
Fax: (906) 227-1747
E-mail: admiss@nmu.edu
http://www.nmu.edu

Spring Arbor University
106 East Main Street
Spring Arbor, MI 49283
Phone: (517) 750-1200

Fax: (517) 750-6620
E-mail: admissions@arbor.edu
http://www.arbor.edu

Wayne State University
Detroit, MI 48202
Phone: (313) 577-3581
Fax: (313) 577-7536
E-mail: admissions@wayne.edu
http://www.wayne.edu

MINNESOTA

Concordia College–Moorhead
901 S. Eighth Street
Moorhead, MN 56562
Phone: (218) 299-4000
E-mail: admissions@cord.edu
http://www.cord.edu

**Minnesota State University
Mankato**
Mankato, MN 56001
Phone: (507) 389-6670
Fax: (507) 389-1511
E-mail: admissions@mnsu.edu
http://www.mnsu.edu

**Minnesota State University
Moorhead**
Owens Hall
Moorhead, MN 56563
Phone: (218) 477-2161
Fax: (218) 477-4374
E-mail: dragon@mnstate.edu
http://www.mnstate.edu

Northwestern College
3003 Snelling Avenue North
St. Paul, MN 55113
Phone: (651) 631-5209
Fax: (651) 631-5680
E-mail: admissions@nwc.edu
http://www.nwc.edu

Saint Cloud State University
720 Fourth Avenue South
St. Cloud, MN 56301
Phone: (320) 308-2244
Fax: (320) 308-2243
http://www.stcloudstate.edu

**Saint Mary's University of
Minnesota**
700 Terrace Heights #2

Winona, MI 55987
Phone: (507) 457-1700
Fax: (507) 457-1722
E-mail: admissions@smumn.edu
http://www.smumn.edu

Winona State University
P.O. Box 5838
Winona, MN 55987
Phone: (507) 457-5100
E-mail: admissions@winona.edu
http://www.winona.edu

MISSISSIPPI

Mississippi College
P.O. Box 4026
200 South Capitol Street
Clinton, MS 39058
Phone: (601) 925-3800
Fax: (601) 925-3804
E-mail: enrollment-services@mc.edu
http://www.mc.edu

MISSOURI

Lindenwood University
209 South Kings Highway
St. Charles, MO 63301
Phone: (636) 949-4949
Fax: (636) 949-4989
http://www.lindenwood.edu

**Northwest Missouri State
University**
800 University Drive
Maryville, MO 64468
Phone: (660) 562-1146
Fax: (660) 562-1121
E-mail: admissions@nwmissouri.
edu
http://www.nwmissouri.edu

Stephens College
Columbia, MO 65215
Phone: (573) 876-7207
Fax: (573) 876-7237
E-mail: apply@stephens.edu
http://www.stephens.edu

University of Central Missouri
1400 Ward Edwards
Warrensburg, MO 64093

Phone: (660) 543-4170
Fax: (660) 543-8517
E-mail: admit@ucmo.edu
http://www.ucmo.edu

Webster University
470 E. Lockwood Avenue
St. Louis, MO 63119
Phone: (314) 961-2660
Fax: (314) 968-7115
E-mail: admit@webster.edu
http://www.webster.edu

William Woods University
1 University Avenue
Fulton, MO 65251
Phone: (573) 592-4221
E-mail: admissions@williamwoods.
edu
http://www.williamwoods.edu

MONTANA

Carroll College
1601 North Benton Avenue
Helena, MT 59625
Phone: (406) 447-4384
E-mail: admit@carroll.edu
http://www.carroll.edu

**Montana State University–
Billings**
1500 University Drive
Billings, MT 59101
Phone: (406) 657-2158
Fax: (406) 657-2302
E-mail: admissions@msubillings.
edu
http://www.msubillings.edu

NEBRASKA

Hastings College
710 North Turner Avenue
Hastings, NE 68901
Phone: (402)461-7320
Fax: (402) 461-7490
E-mail: mmolliconi@hastings.edu
http://www.hastings.edu

Union College
3800 South 48th Street
Lincoln, NE 68506

Phone: (402) 486-2504
Fax: (402) 486-2566
E-mail: ucenroll@ucollege.edu

NEVADA

University of Nevada, Reno
Reno, NV 89557
Phone: (775) 784-4700
E-mail: asknevada@unr.edu
http://www.unr.edu

NEW HAMPSHIRE

New England College
26 Bridge Street
Henniker, NH 03242
Phone: (800) 521-7642
Fax: (603) 428-3155
E-mail: admission@nec.edu
http://www.nec.edu

Southern New Hampshire University
2500 North River Road
Manchester, NH 03106
Phone: (603) 645-9611
Fax: (603) 645-9693
http://www.snhu.edu

NEW JERSEY

Rider University
2083 Lawrenceville Road
Lawrenceville, NJ 08648
Phone: (609) 896-5000
E-mail: admissions@rider.edu
http://www.rider.edu

NEW YORK

Buffalo State College
1300 Elmwood Avenue
Buffalo, NY 14222
Phone: (716) 878-4017
Fax: (716) 878-6100
E-mail: admissions@buffalostate.edu
http://www.buffalostate.edu

Hofstra University
100 Hofstra University
Hempstead, NY 11549
Phone: (516) 463-6700

Fax: (516) 463-5100
http://www.hofstra.edu

Iona College
715 North Avenue
New Rochelle, NY 10801
Phone: (914) 633-2502
Fax: (914) 637-2778
E-mail: admissions@iona.edu
http://www.iona.edu

Ithaca College
Ithaca, NY 14850
Phone: (607) 274-3124
E-mail: admission@ithaca.edu
http://www.ithaca.edu

Long Island University, C. W. Post Campus
720 Northern Boulevard
Brookville, NY 11548
Phone: (516) 299-2900
Fax: (516) 299-2137
E-mail: enroll@cwpost.liu.edu
http://www.liu.edu

Marist College
3399 North Road
Poughkeepsie, NY 12601
Phone: (845) 575-3226
E-mail: admissions@marist.edu
http://www.marist.edu

Mount Saint Mary College
330 Powell Avenue
Newburgh, NY 12550
Phone: (845) 569-3248
E-mail: mtstmary@msmc.edu
http://www.msmc.edu

Rochester Institute of Technology
Director of Undergraduate Admissions
60 Lomb Memorial Drive
Rochester, NY 14623
Phone: (585) 475-6631
Fax: (585) 475-7424
E-mail: admissions@rit.edu
http://www.rit.edu

State University of New York College at Brockport
350 New Campus Drive

Brockport, NY 14420
Phone: (585) 395-2751
Fax: (585) 395-5452
E-mail: admit@brockport.edu

State University of New York at Oswego
229 Sheldon Hall
Oswego, NY 13126
Phone: (315) 312-2250
Fax: (315)312-3260
E-mail: admiss@oswego.edu
http://www.oswego.edu

St. John's University
8000 Utopia Parkway
Queens, NY 11439
Phone: (718) 990-2000
Fax: (718) 990-2160
E-mail: admhelp@stjohns.edu
http://www.stjohns.edu

Utica College
1600 Burrstone Road
Utica, NY 13502
Phone: (315) 792-3006
E-mail: admiss@ucsu.edu
http://www.utica.edu

NORTH CAROLINA

Appalachian State University
Boone, NC 28608
Phone: (828) 262-2000
E-mail: admissions@appstate.edu
http://www.appstate.edu

Campbell University
P.O. Box 546
Buies Creek, NC 27506
Phone: (910) 893-1320
E-mail: adm@mailcenter.campbell.edu
http://www.campbell.edu

North Carolina State University
Box 7103
112 Peele Hall
Raleigh, NC 27695
Phone: (919) 515-2434
Fax: (919) 515-5039
E-mail: undergrad_admissions@ncsu.edu
http://www.ncsu.edu

NORTH DAKOTA

University of Mary
7500 University Drive
Bismarck, ND 58504
Phone: (701) 355-8191
Fax: (701) 255-7687
E-mail: marauder@umary.edu
http://www.umary.edu

OHIO

Baldwin-Wallace College
275 Eastland Road
Berea, OH 44017
Phone: (440) 826-2222
Fax: (440) 826-3830
E-mail: info@bw.edu
http://www.bw.edu

Bowling Green State University
110 McFall Center
Bowling Green, OH 43403
Phone: (419) 372-BGSU
Fax: (419) 372-6955
E-mail: choosebgsu@bgnet.bgsu.edu
http://www.bgsu.edu

Capital University
1 College and Main
Columbus, OH 43209
Phone: (614) 236-6101
Fax: (614) 236-6926
E-mail: admissions@capital.edu
http://www.capital.edu

Cleveland State University
1806 East 22nd Street
Cleveland, OH 44114
Phone: (216) 687-2100
Fax: (216) 687-9210
E-mail: admissions@csuohio.edu
http://csuohio.edu

Heidelberg College
310 East Market Street
Tiffin, OH 44883
Phone: (419) 448-2330
Fax: (419) 448-2334
E-mail: adminfo@heidelberg.edu
http://www.heidelberg.edu

Kent State University
P.O. Box 5190
Kent, OH 44242
Phone: (330) 672-2121
E-mail: kentadm@kent.edu
http://www.kent.edu

Marietta College
Marietta, OH 45750
Phone: (800) 331-7896
E-mail: admit@marietta.edu
http://www.marietta.edu

Ohio Northern University
Ada, OH 45810
Phone: (888) 408-4668
Fax: (419) 772-2313
E-mail: admissions-ug@onu.edu
http://www.onu.edu

Ohio University
Athens, OH 45701
Phone: (740) 593-4100
E-mail: admissions.freshmen@ohiou.edu
http://www.ohiou.edu

Otterbein College
One Otterbein College
Westerville, OH 43081
Phone: (614) 823-1500
E-mail: uotterb@otterbein.edu
http://uotterb@otterbein.edu

University of Dayton
300 College Park
Dayton, OH 45469
Phone: (937) 229-4411
E-mail: admission@udayton.edu
http://www.dayton.edu

University of Findlay
1000 North Main Street
Findlay, OH 45840
Phone: (419) 434-4732
E-mail: admissions@findlay.edu
http://www.findlay.edu

University of Rio Grande
P.O. Box 500
Rio Grande, OH 45674
Phone: (740) 245-7208
Fax: (740) 245-7260

E-mail: admissions@rio.edu
http://www.rio.edu

Ursuline College
2550 Lander Road
Pepper Pike, OH 44124
Phone: (440) 449-4203
Fax: (440) 684-6138
E-mail: admission@ursuline.edu
http://www.ursuline.edu

Xavier University
3800 Victory Parkway
Cincinnati, OH 45207
Phone: (513) 745-3301
E-mail: xuadmit@xavier.edu
http://www.xavier.edu

OKLAHOMA

East Central University
1100 East 14th Street
Ada, OK 74820
Phone: (580) 310-5233
E-mail: pdenny@ecok.edu
http://www.ecok.edu

Northeastern State University
601 North Grand
Tahlequah, OK 74464
Phone: (918) 444-2211
Fax: (918) 458-2342
E-mail: cain@nsuok.edu
http://www.nsuok.edu

Oklahoma City University
2501 North Blackwelder
Oklahoma City, OK 73106
Phone: (405) 521-5050
E-mail: mlockhart@okcu.edu
http://www.okcu.edu

University of Central Oklahoma
100 North University Drive
Edmond, OK 73034
Phone: (405)974-2338
Fax: (405)341-4964
E-mail: admituco@ucok.edu
http://ucok.edu

University of Oklahoma
1000 Asp Avenue

Norman, OK 73019
Phone: (405) 325-2151
Fax: (405) 325-7124
E-mail: admrec@ou.edu
http://www.ou.edu

OREGON

George Fox University
Newberg, OR 97132
Phone: (800) 765-4369
E-mail: admissions@georgefox.
edu
http://www.georgefox.edu

University of Oregon
1217 University of Oregon
Eugene, OR 97403
Phone: (541) 346-3201
http://www.uoregon.edu

PENNSYLVANIA

Keystone College
One College Green
La Plume, PA 18440
Phone: (570)945-8111
E-mail: admissions@keystone.edu
http://www.keystone.edu

La Salle University
1900 West Olney Avenue
Philadelphia, PA 19141
Phone: (215) 951-1500
Fax: (215) 951-1656
E-mail: admiss@lasalle.edu
http://www.lasalle.edu

**Mansfield University of
Pennsylvania**
Mansfield, PA 16933
Phone: (570) 662-4813
Fax: (570) 662-4121
E-mail: admissions@mansfield.edu
http://www.mansfield.edu

Marywood University
2300 Adams Avenue
Scranton, PA 18509
Phone: (570) 348-6211
E-mail: ugadm@ac.marywood.edu
http://www.marywood.edu

**Mercyhurst College
Admissions**
501 East 38th Street
Erie, PA 16546
Phone: (814) 824-2202
E-mail: admissions@mercyhurst.
edu
http://www.mercyhurst.edu

Susquehanna University
514 University Avenue
Selinsgrove, PA 17870
Phone: (570) 372-4260
Fax: (570) 372-2722
E-mail: suadmiss@susqu.edu
http://www.susqu.edu

Temple University
Philadelphia, PA 19122
Phone: (215) 204-7200
E-mail: tuadm@temple.edu
http://www.temple.edu

**University of Pittsburgh at
Bradford**
300 Campus Drive
Bradford, PA 16701
Phone: (814) 362-7555
http://www.upb.pitt.edu

Westminster College
319 South Market Street
New Wilmington, PA 6172
Phone: (724) 946-7100
E-mail: admis@westminster.edu
http://www.westminster.edu

York College of Pennsylvania
York, PA 17405
Phone: (717) 849-1600
Fax: (717) 849-1607
E-mail: admissions@ycp.edu

RHODE ISLAND

Johnson & Wales University
8 Abbott Park Place
Providence, RI 02903
Phone: (401) 598-1000
Fax: (401) 598-4901
E-mail: petersons@jwu.edu
http://www.jwu.edu

SOUTH CAROLINA

Columbia College
1301 Columbia College Drive
Columbia, SC 29203
Phone: (803) 786-3765
Fax: (803) 786-3674
E-mail: admissions@colacoll.edu
http://www.colacoll.edu

**University of South Carolina-
Columbia**
Columbia, SC 29208
Phone: (803) 777-7000
E-mail: admissions-ugrad@sc.edu
http://www.sc.edu

TENNESSEE

Belmont University
1900 Belmont Boulevard
Nashville, TN 37212,
Phone: (615) 460-6785
Fax: (615)460-5434
E-mail: buadmission@mail.
belmont.edu
http://www.belmont.edu

Freed-Hardeman University
158 East Main Street
Henderson, TN 38340
Phone: (731) 989-6651
Fax: (731) 989-6047
E-mail: admissions@fhu.edu
http://www.fhu.edu

Lambuth University
705 Lambuth Boulevard
Jackson, TN 38301
Phone: (731) 425-3223
E-mail: admit@lambuth.edu
http://www.lambuth.edu

Lipscomb University
3901 Granny White Pike
Nashville, TN 37204
Phone: (615) 269-1000
Fax: (615) 269-1804
E-mail: admissions@lipscomb.edu
http://www.lipscomb.edu

**Middle Tennessee State
University**
1301 East Main Street

Murfreesboro, TN 37132
Phone: (615) 898-2111
Fax: (615) 898-5478
E-mail: admissions@mtsu.edu
http://www.ntsu.edu

Union University
1050 Union University Drive
Jackson, TN 38305
Phone: (731) 661-5100
E-mail: info@uu.edu
http://www.uu.edu

TEXAS

Hardin-Simmons University
Box 16050
Abilene, TX 79698
Phone: (325) 670-5890
Fax: (325) 671-2115
E-mail: breynolds@hsutx.edu
http://www.hsutx.edu

Howard Payne University
1000 Fisk Avenue
Brownwood, TX 76801
Phone: (325) 649-8027
Fax: (325) 649-8901
E-mail: enroll@hputx.edu
http://www.hputx.edu

Sam Houston State University
P.O. Box 2418
Huntsville, TX 77341
Phone: (936) 294-1111
E-mail: admissions@shsu.edu
http://www.shsu.edu

Southern Methodist University
P.O. Box 750181
Dallas, TX 75275
Phone: (214) 768-2000
E-mail: ugadmission@smu.edu
http://www.smu.edu

Texas A&M University
217 John J. Koldus Building
College Station, TX 77843-1265
Phone: (979) 845-3741
Fax: (979) 845-8737
E-mail: admissions@tamu.ed
http://www.tamu.edu

Texas State University-San Marcos
San Marcos, TX 78666
Phone: (512) 245-2364
Fax: (512) 245-8044
E-mail: admissions@txstate.edu
http://www.txstate.edu

Texas Tech University
Box 45005
Lubbock, TX 7940
Phone: (806) 742-2011
E-mail: admissions@ttu.edu
http://www.ttu.edu

University of Houston
122 E. Cullen Building
Houston, Texas 77204
Phone: (713) 743-1010
E-mail: admissions@uh.edu
http://www.uh.edu

University of Texas at Arlington
P.O. Box 19111
701 South Nedderman Drive
Arlington, TX 76019
Phone: (817) 272-6287
Fax: (817) 272-3435
E-mail: admissions@uta.edu
http://www.uta.edu

University of Texas at Austin
Main Building, Room 7
Austin, TX 78712
Phone: (512) 471-3434
E-mail: frmn@uts.cc.utexas.edu
http://www.utexas.edu

UTAH

Brigham Young University
A-153 Abraham Smoot Building
Provo, UT 84602
Phone: (801) 422-2507
Fax: (801) 422-0005
E-mail: admissions@byu.edu
http://www.byu.edu

University of Utah
201 South
Salt Lake City, UT 84112
Phone: (801) 581-8761

Fax: (801) 585-7864
E-mail: admissions@sa.utah.edu

Weber State University
1137 University Circle
3750 Harrison Boulevard
Ogden, UT 84408-1137
Phone: (801) 626-6050
Fax: (801) 626-6744
E-mail: admissions@weber.edu
http://www.weber.edu

VERMONT

Castleton State College
Castleton, VT 05735
Phone: (802) 468-1213
Fax: (802) 468-1476
E-mail: info@castleton.edu
http://www.castleton.edu

Champlain College
163 South Willard Street
P.O. Box 670
Burlington, VT 05402
Phone: (802) 860-2727
Fax: (802) 860-2767
E-mail: admission@champlain.edu
http://www.champlain.edu

University of Vermont
194 South Prospect Street
Burlington, VT 05401
Phone: (802) 656-3370
Fax: (802) 656-8611
E-mail: admissions@uvm.edu
http://www.uvm.edu

VIRGINIA

Hampton University
Tyler Street
Hampton, VA 23668
Phone: (757) 727-5070
E-mail: admissions@hamptonu.edu
http://www.hamptonu.edu

Virginia State University
Petersburg, VA 23806
Phone: (804) 524-5902
Fax: (804) 524-5055
E-mail: ilogan@vsu.edu
http://www.vsu.edu

WASHINGTON

Central Washington University
400 East University Way
Ellensburg, WA 98926
Phone: (509) 963-1211
Fax: (509) 963-3022
E-mail: cwuadmis@cwu.edu
http://www.cwu.edu

Gonzaga University
Spokane, WA 99258
Phone: (800) 322-2584
E-mail: mcculloh@gu.gonzaga.edu
http://www.gonzaga.edu

Seattle University
900 Broadway
Seattle, WA 98122
Phone: (206) 296-2000
E-mail: admissions@seattleu.edu
http://www.seattleu.edu

Walla Walla College
204 South College Avenue
College Place, WA 99324
Phone: (509) 527-2327
Fax: (509) 527-2397
E-mail: info@wwc.edu

WEST VIRGINIA

West Virginia Wesleyan College
59 College Avenue
Buckhannon, WV 26201
Phone: (304) 473-8510
E-mail: admission@wvwc.edu
http://www.wvwc.edu

WISCONSIN

Cardinal Stritch University
6801 North Yates Road
Milwaukee, WI 53217
Phone: (414) 410-4040
E-mail: admityou@stritch.edu
http://www.stritch.edu

Carroll College
100 North East Avenue
Waukesha, WI 53186
Phone: (262) 524-7220
E-mail: ccinfo@cc.edu
http://www.cc.edu

Marquette University
P.O. Box 1881
Milwaukee, WI 53201
Phone: (414) 288-7250
E-mail: admissions@marquette.edu
http://www.marquette.edu

Mount Mary College
2900 North Menomonee River Parkway
Milwaukee, WI 53222
Phone: (414) 256-1219
Fax: (414) 256-0180
E-mail: admiss@mtmary.edu
http://www.mtmary.edu

University of Wisconsin–Madison
716 Langdon Street
Madison, WI 53706
Phone: (608) 262-3961
Fax: (608) 262-7706
E-mail: on.wisconsin@admissions.wisc.edu
http://www.wisc.edu

University of Wisconsin–River Falls
410 South Third Street
River Falls, WI 54022
Phone: (715) 425-3500
Fax: (715) 425-0676
E-mail: admit@uwrf.edu
http://www.urf.edu

The following is a listing of trade associations, unions, and other organizations discussed in this book. There are numerous other associations listed here that may also be useful to you in your career. The names, addresses, phone numbers, fax numbers, Web sites, and e-mail addresses are included to help you get in touch with any of the unions and associations for information.

Headquarters of unions and associations will be able to provide you with the phone numbers, addresses, and other contact information of the closest local office.

Use this list to help you find internships, explore job opportunities, and obtain other useful information.

Academy of Country Music (ACM)
4100 W Alameda
Burbank, CA 91505 USA
Phone: (818) 842-8400
Fax: (818) 842-8535
E-mail: info@acmcountry.com
http://www.acmcountry.com

Acoustical Society of America (ASA)
2 Huntington Quadrangle
Melville, NY 11747
Phone: (516)576-2360
Fax: (516) 576-2377
E-mail: asa@aip.org
http://asa.aip.org

Actors' Equity Association (AEA)
165 W 46th Street
New York, NY 10036
Phone: (212) 869-8530
Fax: (212) 719-9815
E-mail: info@actorsequity.org
http://www.actorsequity.org

American Academy of Teachers of Singing (AATS)
c/o Jan Eric Douglas, Chair
777 West End Avenue
New York, NY 10025
Phone: (212) 666-5951
E-mail: info@americanacademyof teachersofsinging.org

http://www.americanacademyof teachersofsinging.org

American Advertising Federation (AAF)
1101 Vermont Avenue, NW
Washington, DC 20005
Phone: (202) 898-0089
Fax: (202) 898-0159
E-mail: aaf@aaf.org
http://www.aaf.org

American Bandmasters Association (ABA)
c/o Dr. William J. Moody, Secretary
4250 Shorebrook Drive
Columbia, SC 29206
Phone: (803) 787-6540
E-mail: wmoody@sc.rr.com
http://www.americanbandmasters. org

American Bar Association (ABA)
321 N Clark Street
Chicago, IL 60610
Phone: (312) 988-5000
Fax: (312) 988-5177
E-mail: service@abanet.org
http://www.abanet.org

American Choral Directors Association (ACDA)
P.O. Box 2720
Oklahoma City, OK 73101

Phone: (405) 232-8161
Fax: (405) 232-8162
E-mail: acda@acdaonline.org
http://www.acdaonline.org

American College of Musicians (ACM)
P.O. Box 1807
Austin, TX 78767
Phone: (512) 478-5775
E-mail: ngpt@pianoguild.com
http://www.pianoguild.com

American Composers Alliance (ACA)
648 Broadway
New York, NY 10012
Phone: (212) 362-8900
Fax: (212) 925-6798
E-mail: info@composers.com
http://www.composers.com

American Conference of Cantors (ACC)
213 N Morgan Street
Chicago, IL 60607
Phone: (312) 491-1034
Fax: (312) 491-1087
E-mail: info@accantors.org
http://www.accantors.org

American Disc Jockey Association (ADJA)
20118 N 67th Avenue
Glendale, AZ 85308

Phone: (888) 723-5776
E-mail: office@adja.org
http://www.adja.org

American Federation of Jazz Societies (AFJS)

c/o Randolph Siple, President
6500 Casitas Pass Road
Ventura, CA 93001

American Federation of Musicians of the United States and Canada (AFM)

1501 Broadway
New York, NY 10036
Phone: (212) 869-1330
Fax: (212) 764-6134
E-mail: presoffice@afm.org
http://www.afm.org

American Federation of Teachers (AFT)

555 New Jersey Avenue, NW
Washington, DC 20001
Phone: (202) 879-4400
Fax: (202) 879-4545
E-mail: online@aft.org
http://www.aft.org

American Federation of Television and Radio Artists (AFTRA)

260 Madison Avenue
New York, NY 10016
Phone: (212) 532-0800
Fax: (212) 532-2242
E-mail: info@aftra.com
http://www.aftra.com

American Federation of Violin and Bow Makers (AFVBM)

1201 S Main Street
Mount Airy, MD 21771
E-mail: dvzviolins@comcast.net
http://www.afvbm.com

American Guild of Musical Artists (AGMA)

1430 Broadway
New York, NY 10018
Phone: (212) 265-3687
Fax: (212) 262-9088
E-mail: agma@musicalartists.org
http://www.musicalartists.org

American Guild of Organists (AGO)

475 Riverside Drive, Suite 1260
New York, NY 10115
Phone: (212) 870-2310
Fax: (212) 870-2163
E-mail: info@agohq.org
http://www.agohq.org

American Guild of Variety Artists (AGVA)

363 Seventh Avenue
New York, NY 10001
Phone: (212) 675-1003
Fax: (212) 633-0097

American Institute of Certified Public Accountants

1211 Avenue of the Americas
New York, NY 10036 USA
Phone: (212) 596-6200
Fax: (212) 596-6213
E-mail: center@aicpa.org
http://www.aicpa.org

American Institute of Musical Studies (AIMS)

6621 Snider Plaza
Dallas, TX 75205
Phone: (214) 363-2683
Fax: (214) 363-6474
E-mail: aims@airmail.net
http://www.aimsgraz.com

American Library Association (ALA)

50 E Huron Street
Chicago, IL 60611
Phone: (312)944-7298
Fax: (312)280-4380
E-mail: library@ala.org
http://www.ala.org

American Marketing Association (AMA)

311 S Wacker Drive
Chicago, IL 60606
Phone: (312) 542-9000
Fax: (312) 542-9001
http://www.marketingpower.com

American Musical Instrument Society (AMIS)

389 Main Street

Malden, MA 02148
Phone: (781) 397-8870
Fax: (781) 397-8887
E-mail: amis@guildassoc.com
http://www.amis.org

American Music Center (AMC)

30 W 26th Street
New York, NY 10010
Phone: (212) 366-5260
Fax: (212) 366-5265
E-mail: center@amc.net
http://www.amc.net/index.html

American Music Conference (AMC)

5790 Armada Drive
Carlsbad, CA 92008
Phone: (760) 431-9124
Fax: (760) 438-7327
E-mail: sharonm@amc-music.org
http://www.amc-music.org

American Music Festival Association (AMFA)

10 N Second Street
Harrisburg, PA 17101
Phone: (717) 255-3020
Fax: (717) 255-6554
E-mail: cschulz@harrisburgevents.
com
http://www.americanmusicfest.org

American Musicological Society (AMS)

201 S 34th Street
Philadelphia, PA 19104
Phone: (215) 898-8698
Fax: (215) 573-3673
E-mail: ams@sas.upenn.edu
http://www.ams-net.org

American Music Therapy Association (AMTA)

8455 Colesville Road
Silver Spring, MD 20910
Phone: (301) 589-3300
Fax: (301) 589-5175
E-mail: info@musictherapy.org
http://www.musictherapy.org

American Pianists Association (APA)

4603 Clarendon Road

Indianapolis, IN 46208
Phone: (317) 940-9945
E-mail: apainfo@americanpianists.
  org
http://www.americanpianists.org

American Recorder Society (ARS)

1129 Ruth Drive
St. Louis, MO 63122
Phone: (314) 966-4082
Fax: (314) 966-4649
E-mail: recorder@
  americanrecorder.org
http://www.americanrecorder.org

American School Band Directors Association (ASBDA)

P.O. Box 696
Guttenberg, IA 52052
Phone: (563) 252-2500
E-mail: asbda@alpinecom.net
http://home.comcast.net/~asbda

American Society for Jewish Music (ASJM)

15 W 16th Street
New York, NY 10011
Phone: (212) 294-8382
Fax: (212) 294-6161
E-mail: asjm@cjh.org
http://www.jewishmusic-asjm.org

American Society of Composers, Authors and Publishers (ASCA)

1 Lincoln Plaza
New York, NY 10023 USA
Phone: (212) 621-6000
Fax: (212) 724-9064
E-mail: info@ascap.com
http://www.ascap.com

American Society of Music Arrangers and Composers (ASMAC)

P.O. Box 17840
Encino, CA 91416
Phone: (818) 994-4661
Fax: (818) 994-6181
E-mail: syd@theproperimageevents.
  com
http://www.asmac.org

American String Teachers Association (ASTA)

4153 Chain Bridge Road
Fairfax, VA 22030
Phone: (703) 279-2113
Fax: (703) 279-2114
E-mail: asta@astaweb.com
http://www.astaweb.com

American Symphony Orchestra League (ASOL)

33 W 60th Street
New York, NY 10023
Phone: (212) 262-5161
Fax: (212) 262-5198
E-mail: league@symphony.org
http://www.symphony.org

American Theatre Organ Society (ATOS)

c/o Jim Merry, Executive Secretary
P.O. Box 5327
Fullerton, CA 92838
Phone: (714) 773-4354
Fax: (714) 773-4829
E-mail: merry@atos.org
http://www.atos.org

Amusement and Music Operators Association (AMOA)

33 W Higgins Road
South Barrington, IL 60010
Phone: (847) 428-7699
Fax: (847) 428-7719
E-mail: amoa@amoa.com
http://www.amoa.com

Association for Technology in Music Instruction (ATMI)

312 E Pine Stree
Missoula, MT 59802
Phone: (406) 721-1152
Fax: (406) 721-9419
E-mail: atmi@music.org
http://www.atmionline.org

Association for the Advancement of Creative Musicians (AACM)

410 S Michigan Avenue
Chicago, IL 60680
Phone: (312) 922-1900

Fax: (312) 922-1900
E-mail: greatblackmusic@
  aacmchicago.org
http://aacmchicago.org/aacmgoals.
  html

Association of Anglican Musicians (AAM)

28 Ashton Road
Fort Mitchell, KY 41017
Phone: (828) 274-2681
E-mail: cr273@aol.com
http://www.anglicanmusicians.org

Association of Concert Bands (ACB)

6613 Cheryl Ann Drive
Independence, OH 44131
Phone: (216) 524-1897
http://www.acbands.org

Association of Independent Music Publishers (AIMP)

P.O. Box 69473
Los Angeles, CA 90069
Phone: (818) 771-7301
E-mail: lainfo@aimp.org
http://www.aimp.org

Association of Theatrical Press Agents and Managers (ATPAM)

1560 Broadway
New York, NY 10036
Phone: (212) 719-3666
Fax: (212) 302-1585
E-mail: info@atpam.com
http://www.atpam.com

Black Rock Coalition (BRC)

P.O. Box 1054
Cooper Station
New York, NY 10276
Phone: (212) 713-5097
E-mail: ldavis@blackrockcoalition.
  org
http://www.blackrockcoalition.org

Bluegrass Music Association of Maine

c/o Jean Johnson, Secretary
P.O. Box 154
Troy, ME 04987

Phone: (207) 948-5819
E-mail: bluegrass@bmam.org
http://www.bmam.org

Blues Foundation

49 Union Avenue
Memphis, TN 38103
Phone: (901) 527-2583
Fax: (901) 529-4030
E-mail: jay@blues.org
http://www.blues.org

Blues Heaven Foundation (BHF)

2120 Michigan Avenue
Chicago, IL 60616
Phone: (312) 808-1286
Fax: (312) 808-0273
E-mail: infobluesheaven@
   bluesheaven.com
http://www.bluesheaven.com

Broadcast Music, Inc. (BMI)

320 W 57th Street
New York, NY 10019
Phone: (212) 586-2000
Fax: (212) 956-2059
E-mail: newyork@bmi.com
http://bmi.com

Certification Board for Music Therapists (CBMT)

506 E Lancaster Avenue
Downingtown, PA 19335
Phone: (610) 269-8900
E-mail: info@cbmt.com
http://www.cbmt.org

Chorister's Guild (CG)

c/o Jim Rindelaub, Executive
   Director
2834 W Kingsley Road
Garland, TX 75041
Phone: (972) 271-1521
Fax: (972) 840-3113
E-mail: choristers@choristersguild.
   org
http://www.choristersguild.org

Chorus America

1156 15th Street, NW
Washington, DC 20005

Phone: (202) 331-7577
Fax: (202) 331-7599
E-mail: service@chorusamerica.
   org
http://www.chorusamerica.org

Church Music Association of America (CMAA)

c/o Dr. Kurt Poterack, Ed.
Christendom College
134 Christendom Drive
Front Royal, VA 22630 USA
Phone: (540) 636-2900
Fax: (540) 636-1655
E-mail: kpoterack@hotmail.com
http://www.musicasacra.com

Church Music Publishers Association (CMPA)

P.O. Box 158992
Nashville, TN 37215
Phone: (615) 791-0273
Fax: (615) 790-8847
http://www.cmpamusic.org

Coalition for Disabled Musicians (CDM)

P.O. Box 1002M
Bay Shore, NY 11706
Phone: (631) 586-0366
Fax: (631) 586-0366
E-mail: cdmnews@aol.com
http://www.disabled-musicians.org

College Band Directors National Association (CBDA)

c/o Richard L. Floyd, Secretary
University of Texas
Box 8028
Austin, TX 78713
Phone: (512) 471-5883
Fax: (512) 471-6589
E-mail: rfloyd@mail.utexas.edu
http://www.cbdna.org

College Music Society (CMS)

312 E Pine Street
Missoula, MT 59802
Phone: (406) 721-9616
Fax: (406) 721-9419
E-mail: cms@music.org
http://www.music.org

Conductors Guild (CG)

5300 Glenside Drive
Richmond, VA 23228
Phone: (804) 553-1378
Fax: (804) 553-1876
E-mail: guild@conductorsguild.net
http://www.conductorsguild.org

Contemporary A Cappella Society of America (CASA)

325 Sharon Park Drive
Menlo Park, CA 94025
Phone: (415) 358-8067
E-mail: editor@casa.org
http://www.casa.org

Council for Research in Music Education (CRME)

School of Music, University of
   Illinois at Urbana–Champaign
1114 W Nevada Street
Urbana, IL 61801
Phone: (217) 333-1027
Fax: (217) 244-8136
E-mail: crme@uiuc.edu
http://www.crme.uiuc.edu

Country Dance and Song Society (CDSS)

132 Main St.
P.O. Box 338
Haydenville, MA 01039
Phone: (413) 268-7426
Fax: (413) 268-7471
E-mail: office@cdss.org
http://www.cdss.org

Country Music Association (CMA)

1 Music Circle, South
Nashville, TN 37203
Phone: (615) 244-2840
Fax: (615) 726-0314
E-mail: info@cmaworld.com
http://www.cmaworld.com

Country Music Foundation (CMF)

222 Fifth Avenue, South
Nashville, TN 37203
Phone: (615) 416-2001
E-mail: info@countrymusichallof
   fame.com
http://www.countrymusichallof
   fame.com

Country Music Showcase International (CMSI)
P.O. Box 368
Carlisle, IA 50047
Phone: (515) 989-3748
E-mail: haroldl@cmshowcase.org
http://www.cmshowcase.org

Dollywood Foundation (DF)
1020 Dollywood Lane
Pigeon Forge, TN 37863
Phone: (865) 428-9607
Fax: (865) 428-9612
E-mail: ccrouse@dollyfoundation.
com
http://www.dollywoodfoundation.
com

Electronic Industries Alliance (EIA)
2500 Wilson Boulevard
Arlington, VA 22201
Phone: (703) 907-7500
E-mail: dmccurdy@eia.org
http://www.eia.org

Electronic Music Foundation (EMF)
P.O. Box 8748
Albany, NY 12208
Phone: (518) 434-4110
Fax: (518) 434-0308
E-mail: emf@emf.org
http://www.emf.org

Equity
Actors' Equity Association (AEA)
165 W 46th Street
New York, NY 10036
Phone: (212) 869-8530
Fax: (212) 719-9815
E-mail: info@actorsequity.org
http://www.actorsequity.org

Financial Planning Association (FPA)
4100 E Mississippi Avenue
Denver, CO 80246
Phone: (303) 759-4910
Fax: (303) 759-0749
E-mail: marv.tuttle@fpanet.org
http://www.fpanet.org

Gospel Music Association (GMA)
1205 Division Street
Nashville, TN 37203
Phone: (615) 242-0303
Fax: (615) 254-9755
E-mail: info@gospelmusic.org
http://www.gospelmusic.org

Gospel Music Workshop of America (GMWA)
3908 W Warren
Detroit, MI 48208
Phone: (313) 898-6900
Fax: (313) 898-4520
E-mail: gmwa@ureach.com
http://www.gmwanational.org

GRAMMY Foundation
3402 Pico Boulevard
Santa Monica, CA 90405
Phone: (310) 392-3777
Fax: (310) 392-2188
Toll-Free: (877) GRAMMYED
E-mail: grammyfoundation@
grammy.com
http://www.grammy.com/
GRAMMY_Foundation

Guild of Church Musicians (GCM)
13938A Cedar Road
University Heights, OH 44118
E-mail: shirmidbar@cox.net
http://www.guildoftemplemusicians.
org

Guitar and Accessories Marketing Association (GAMA)
P.O. Box 757
New York, NY 10033
Phone: (212) 795-3630
Fax: (212) 795-3630
E-mail: assnhdqs@earthlink.net
http://www.discoverguitar.com

Guitar Foundation of America (GFA)
P.O. Box 4909
Garden Grove, CA 92842
Phone: (909) 624-7730
Toll-Free: 877-570-3409

E-mail: info@guitarfoundation.org
http://www.guitarfoundation.org

Institute of Internal Auditors (IIA)
247 Maitland Avenue
Altamonte Springs, FL 32701
Phone: (407) 937-1100
Fax: (407) 937-1101
E-mail: iia@theiia.org
http://www.theiia.org

Institute of the American Musical (IAM)
121 N Detroit Street
Los Angeles, CA 90036
Phone: (323) 934-1221
Fax: (323) 934-1221

International Alliance of Theatrical State Employees, Moving Picture Technicians, Artists and Allied Crafts of the United States, Its Territories and Canada
1430 Broadway
New York, NY 10018
Phone: (212) 730-1770
Fax: (212) 730-7809
E-mail: organizing@iatse-intl.org
http://www.iatse-intl.org

International Association of Administrative Professionals (IAAP)
10502 N W Ambassador Drive
P.O. Box 20404
Kansas City, MO 64195
Phone: (816) 891-6600
Fax: (816) 891-9118
E-mail: rstroud@iaap-hq.org
http://www.iaap-hq.org

International Association of Assembly Managers (IAAM)
635 Fritz Drive
Coppell, TX 75019
Phone: (972) 906-7441
Fax: (972) 906-7418
E-mail: dexter.king@iaam.org
http://www.iaam.org

International Brotherhood of Electrical Workers (IBEW)
900 Seventh Street, NW
Washington, DC 20001
Phone: (202) 833-7000
Fax: (202) 728-7676
E-mail: journal@ibew.org
http://www.ibew.org

Internet Professionals Publishers Association (IPPA)
c/o Digital Minute
P.O. Box 670446
Coral Springs, FL 33067
Phone: (954) 426-3507
E-mail: info@ippa.org
http://www.ippa.org

Marketing Research Association (MRA)
110 National Drive
Glastonbury, CT 06033
Phone: (860) 682-1000
Fax: (860) 682-1010
E-mail: E-mail@mra-net.org
http://www.mra-net.org

Meet The Composer (MTC)
75 9th Avenue
New York, NY 10011
Phone: (212) 645-6949
Fax: (212) 645-9669
E-mail: mtc@meetthecomposer.org
http://www.meetthecomposer.org

MENC-National Association for Music Education
1806 Robert Fulton Drive
Reston, VA 20191
Phone: (703) 860-4000
Fax: (703) 860-1531
Toll-Free: 800-336-3768
E-mail: info@menc.org
http://www.menc.org

Metropolitan Opera Association (MOA)
Lincoln Center
New York, NY 10023
Phone: (212) 799-3100
E-mail: metinfo@mail.metopera.org
http://www.metoperafamily.org/
    metopera/index.aspx

Metropolitan Opera Guild (MOG)
70 Lincoln Center Plaza
New York, NY 10023
Phone: (212) 769-7000
E-mail: info@metguild.org
http://www.metopera.org

MIDI Manufacturers Association (MMA)
P.O. Box 3173
La Habra, CA 90632
E-mail: info@midi.org
http://www.midi.org

Mid-State Music Teachers Association
c/o Betty Toombs, President
1417 Corner Oaks Drive
Brandon, FL 33510
Phone: (813) 684-5984
E-mail: toombstbjk@earthlink.net

Music and Entertainment Industry Educators Association (MEIEA)
c/o Debbie Forrest
1900 Belmont Boulevard
Nashville, TN 37212
Phone: (615) 460-6946
E-mail: office@meiea.org
http://www.meiea.org

Music Critics Association of North America (MCA)
722 Dulaney Valley Road
Baltimore, MD 21204
Phone: (410) 435-3881
Fax: (410) 435-3881
E-mail: musiccritics@aol.com
http://www.mcana.org

Music Library Association (MLA)
8551 Research Way
Middleton, WI 53562
Phone: (608) 836-5825
Fax: (608) 831-8200
E-mail: mla@areditions.com
http://www.musiclibraryassoc.org

Music Publishers' Association of the United States (MAP)
243 Fifth Avenue

New York, NY 10016
Phone: (212) 327-4044
Fax: (212) 327-4044
E-mail: mpa-admin@mpa.org
http://www.mpa.org

Music Teachers National Association (MTNA)
243 Fifth Avenue
New York, NY 10016
Phone: (212) 327-4044
Fax: (212) 327-4044
E-mail: mpa-admin@mpa.org
http://www.mpa.org

Nashville Songwriters Association International (NSAI)
1710 Roy Acuff Place
Nashville, TN 37203
Phone: (615) 256-3354
Fax: (615) 256-0034
E-mail: nsai@nashvillesongwriters.
    com
http://www.nashvillesongwriters.
    com

National Academy of Popular Music (NAPM)
330 W 58th Street
New York, NY 10019
Phone: (212) 957-9230
Fax: (212) 957-9227
E-mail: info@songhall.org
http://www.songwritershalloffame.
    org

National Academy of Recording Arts and Sciences (NARAS)
3402 Pico Boulevard
Santa Monica, CA 90405
Phone: (310) 392-3777
Fax: (310) 399-3090
E-mail: memservices@grammy.com
http://www.grammy.com

National Academy of Television Arts and Sciences (NATAS)
5220 Lankershim Boulevard
North Hollywood, CA 91601
Phone: (818) 754-2810,
    (818) 754-2800
Fax: (818) 761-2827

E-mail: pprice@emmyonline.tv
http://www.emmyonline.org

National Association for Campus Activities (NACA)
13 Harbison Way
Columbia, SC 29212
Phone: (803) 732-6222
Fax: (803) 749-1047
E-mail: info@naca.org
http://www.naca.org

National Association of Broadcast Employees and Technicians– Communications Workers of America (NABET-CWA)
501 Third Street, NW
Washington, DC 20001
Phone: (202) 434-1254
Fax: (202) 434-1426
Toll-Free: (800) 882-9174
E-mail: nabet-cwa@cwa-union.org
http://www.nabetcwa.org

National Association of Broadcasters (NAB)
1771 N Street, NW
Washington, DC 20036
Phone: (202) 429-5300
Fax: (202) 429-4199
E-mail: nab@nab.org
http://www.nab.org

National Association of College Wind and Percussion Instructors (NACWPI)
c/o Dr. Richard K. Weerts,
   Executive Secretary
308 Hillcrest Drive
Kirksville, MO 63501
Phone: (660) 785-4442
Fax: (660) 785-7463
E-mail: dweerts@sbcglobal.net
http://www.nacwpi.org

National Association of Composers, USA (NACUSA)
P.O. Box 49256, Barrington Station
Los Angeles, CA 90049
Phone: (818) 709-8534
Fax: (818) 709-8534

E-mail: nacusa@music-usa.org
http://www.music-usa.org/nacusa

National Association of Mobile Entertainers (NAME)
P.O. Box 144
Willow Grove, PA 19090
Phone: (215) 658-1193
http://www.djkj.com

National Association of Music Merchandisers (NAMM)
5790 Armada Drive
Carlsbad, CA 92008
Phone: (760) 438-8001
Fax: (760) 438-7327
E-mail: info@namm.com
http://www.namm.com

National Association of Orchestra Leaders (NAOL)
34 Metropolitan Oval
Bronx, NY 10462
Phone: (718) 863-8997

National Association of Pastoral Musicians (NAPM)
962 Wayne Avenue
Silver Spring, MD 20910
Phone: (240) 247-3000
Fax: (240) 247-3001
E-mail: npmsing@npm.org
http://www.npm.org

National Association of Professional Band Instrument Repair Technicians (NAPBIRT)
P.O. Box 51
Normal, IL 61761
Phone: (309) 452-4257
Fax: (309) 452-4825
E-mail: napbirt@napbirt.org
http://www.napbirt.org

National Association of Recording Merchandisers (NARM)
9 Eves Drive
Marlton, NJ 08053
Phone: (856) 596-2221
Fax: (856) 596-3268

E-mail: donio@narm.com
http://www.narm.com

National Association of School Music Dealers (NASMD)
14070 Proton Road
Dallas, TX 75244
Phone: (972) 233-9107
Fax: (972) 490-4219
E-mail: office@nasmd.com
http://www.nasmd.com

National Association of Teachers of Singing (NATS)
4745 Sutton Park Court
Jacksonville, FL 32224
Phone: (904) 992-9101
Fax: (904) 992-9326
E-mail: info@nats.org
http://www.nats.org

National Band Association (NBA)
118 College Drive
Hattiesburg, MS 39406
Phone: (601) 297-8168
Fax: (601) 266-6185
E-mail: info@
   nationalbandassociation.org
http://www.
   nationalbandassociation.org

National Catholic Band Association (NCBA)
c/o John Badsing, Secretary
3334 N Normandy Avenue
Chicago, IL 60634
E-mail: info@catholicbands.org
http://www.catholicbands.org

National Conference of Personal Managers
P.O. Box 50008
Henderson, NV 89016
Phone: (702) 837-1170
Fax: (702) 255-2256
E-mail: askncopm@ncopm.com
http://www.ncopm.com

National Council of Acoustical Consultants (NCAC)
7150 Winton Drive
Indianapolis, IN 46268

Phone: (317) 328-0642
Fax: (317) 328-4629
E-mail: info@ncac.com
http://www.ncac.com

National Federation of Independent Unions (NFIU)
1166 S 11th Street
Philadelphia, PA 19147
Phone: (215) 336-3300
E-mail: fjcnfiu@aol.com
http://www.nfiu.org

National Federation of Music Clubs (NFMC)
1336 N Delaware Street
Indianapolis, IN 46202
Phone: (317) 638-4003
Fax: (317) 638-0503
E-mail: info@nfmc-music.org
http://www.nfmc-music.org

National Foundation for Advancement in the Arts (NFAA)
444 Brickell Avenue
Miami, FL 33131
Phone: (305) 377-1140
Fax: (305) 377-1149
E-mail: info@nfaa.org
http://www.artsawards.org

National Guild of Piano Teachers (NGPT)
c/o American College of Musicians
P.O. Box 1807
Austin, TX 78767
Phone: (512) 478-5775
Fax: (512) 478-5843
E-mail: ngpt@pianoguild.com
http://www.pianoguild.com

National High School Band Directors Hall of Fame
4166 Will Rhoades Drive
Columbus, GA 31909
E-mail: oboone9007@mchsi.com
http://www.hsbdna.com/home.htm

National Music Council (NNMC)
425 Park Street
Upper Montclair, NJ 07043

Phone: (973) 655-7974
Fax: (973) 655-5432
E-mail: sandersd@mail.montclair.edu
http://www.musiccouncil.org

National Music Publishers' Association (NMPA)
101 Constitution Avenue, NW
Washington, DC 20001
Phone: (202) 742-4375
Fax: (202) 742-4377
E-mail: pr@nmpa.org
http://www.nmpa.org

National Music Theater Network (NMTN)
242 W 38th Street
New York, NY 10018
Phone: (212) 664-0979
Fax: (212) 664-0978
E-mail: info@nmtn.org
http://www.nmtn.org

National Opera Association (NOA)
P.O. Box 60869
Canyon, TX 79016
Phone: (806) 651-2857
Fax: (806) 651-2958
http://www.noa.org

National Orchestral Association (NOA)
P.O. Box 7016
New York, NY 10150
Phone: (212) 208-4691
Fax: (212) 208-4691
E-mail: info@nationalorchestral.org
http://www.nationalorchestral.org

National Piano Foundation (NPF)
5960 W Parker Road
Plano, TX 75093
Phone: (972) 625-0110
Fax: (972) 625-0110
E-mail: don@dondillon.com
http://www.pianonet.com

National Sheet Music Society (NSMS)
1597 Fair Park Avenue

Los Angeles, CA 90041
Phone: (805) 497-2212
E-mail: res0fek5@verizon.net
http://www.nsmsmusic.org

National Society of Accountants (NSA)
1010 N Fairfax Street
Alexandria, VA 22314
Phone: (703) 549-6400
Fax: (703) 549-2984
E-mail: members@nsacct.org
http://www.nsacct.org

National Symphony Orchestra Association (NSOA)
John F. Kennedy Center for the Performing Arts
2700 F Street, NW
Washington, DC 20566
Phone: (202) 416-8000
E-mail: comments@kennedy-center.org
http://www.kennedy-center.org/nso

National Traditional Country Music Association (NTCMA)
P.O. Box 492
Anita, IA 50020
Phone: (712) 762-4363
E-mail: bobeverhart@yahoo.com
http://www.oldtimemusic.bigstep.com

Opera America (OA)
330 Seventh Avenue
New York, NY 10001
Phone: (212) 796-8620
Fax: (212) 796-8631
E-mail: frontdesk@operaamerica.org
http://www.operaamerica.org

Piano Manufacturers Association International (PMAI)
c/o Donald W. Dillon, Executive Director
5960 W Parker Road
Plano, TX 75093
Phone: (972) 625-0110
Fax: (972) 625-0110

E-mail: don@dondillon.com
http://www.pianonet.com

Piano Technicians Guild (PTG)
4444 Forest Avenue
Kansas City, KS 66106
Phone: (913) 432-9975
Fax: (913) 432-9986
E-mail: ptg@ptg.org
http://www.ptg.org

Professional Women Singers Association (PWSA)
P.O. Box 884
New York, NY 10024
Fax: (520) 395-2560
E-mail: info@womensingers.org
http://www.womensingers.org

Public Relations Society of America (PRSA)
33 Maiden Lane
New York, NY 10038
Phone: (212) 460-1400
Fax: (212) 995-0757
E-mail: exec@prsa.org
http://www.prsa.org

Public Relations Student Society of America
33 Maiden Lane
New York, NY 10038
Phone: (212) 460-1400
Fax: (212) 995-0757
E-mail: exec@prsa.org
http://www.prsa.org

Radio Advertising Bureau (RAB)
1320 Greenway Drive
Irving, TX 75038
Phone: (972) 753-6822
Fax: (972) 753-6727
E-mail: dareeder@rab.com
http://www.rab.com

Recording Industry Association of America (RIAA)
1330 Connecticut Avenue, NW

Washington, DC 20036
Phone: (202) 775-0101
Fax: (202) 775-7253
http://www.riaa.org

Rhythm and Blues Rock and Roll Society (RBRRS)
P.O. Box 1949
New Haven, CT 06510
Phone: (203) 924-1079
http://www.blues.org/affiliates/
societies.php4

Screen Actors Guild (SAG)
5757 Wilshire Boulevard
Los Angeles, CA 90036
Phone: (323) 954-1600
Fax: (323) 549-6603
http://www.sag.org

SESAC, Inc.
55 Music Square East
Nashville, TN 37203
Phone: (615) 320-0055
http://www.sesac.com

Society for Music Teacher Education (SMTE)
c/o David J. Teachout, Chairman
P.O. Box 26170
Greensboro, NC 27402
E-mail: djteacho@uncg.edu
http://smte.iweb.bsu.edu

Society for Music Theory (SMT)
Department of Music
University of Chicago
1010 E 59th Street
Chicago, IL 60637
Phone: (773) 834-3821
E-mail: vlong@uchicago.edu
http://www.societymusictheory.org

Society of Professional Audio Recording Services (SPARS)
9 Music Square South
Nashville, TN 37203

Fax: (615) 846-5123
E-mail: spars@spars.com
http://www.spars.com

Songwriters Guild
1500 Harbor Boulevard
Weehawken, NJ 07086
Phone: (201) 867-7603
Fax: (201) 867-7535
E-mail: corporate@
songwritersguild.com
http://www.songwritersguild.com

Special Libraries Association (SLA)
331 S Patrick Street
Alexandria, VA 22314
Phone: (703) 647-4900
Fax: (703) 647-4901
E-mail: sla@sla.org
http://www.sla.org

Volunteer Lawyers for The Arts (VLA)
1 E 53rd Street
New York, NY 10022
Phone: (212) 319-2787
Fax: (212) 752-6575
E-mail: epaul@vlany.org
http://www.vlany.com

World Organization of Webmasters (WOW)
9580 Oak Avenue Parkway
Folsom, CA 95630
Phone: (916) 989-2933
Fax: (916) 987-3022
E-mail: info@joinwow.org
http://www.joinwow.org

World Piano Competition (WPC)
441 Vine Street
Cincinnati, OH 45202
Phone: (513) 421-5342
Fax: (513) 421-2672
E-mail: info@amsa-wpc.org
http://www.amsa-wpc.org

APPENDIX III
RECORD COMPANIES

The following is a listing of major and independent record companies. Most of the major companies are located in the music capitals of the country. Whenever possible, branch offices have been included. Many independent labels are currently beginning to experience a great deal of success in the music industry. They are, therefore, valuable resources for intern and job possibilities as well as for record deals. Due to space limitations, all record companies and labels have not been included. Inclusion or exclusion on this list does not indicate the recommendation or endorsement of one company over another.

A&M Records
2220 Colorado Avenue
Santa Monica, CA 90404
Phone: (310) 865-1000
http://www.amrecords.com

Allied Artists
273 West Allen Avenue
San Dimas, CA 90028
Phone: (626) 330-0600
Fax: (626) 961-0411
http://www.alliedartists.net

Alligator Records
1441 West Devon Avenue
Chicago, IL 60660
Phone: (773) 973-7736
Fax: (773) 973-2088
http://www.aliigator.com

Angel Records
150 Fifth Avenue
New York, NY 10011
Phone: (212) 786-8600
Fax: (212) 786-8649
http://www.angelrecords.com

Arista Records Nashville
1400 18th Avenue South
Nashville, TN 37212
Phone: (615) 301-4300
Fax: (615) 846-9195
http://www.aristanashville.com

Arkadia Records
34 East 23rd street
New York, NY 10010
Phone: (212) 533-0007

Fax: (212) 979-0266
http://www.arkadiarecords.com

Artists Direct Records
1601 Cloverfield Boulvard
Santa Monica, CA 90404
Phone: (310) 956-3300
Fax: (310) 956-3301
http://www.artistdirect.com

Astralwerks
101 Avenue of the Americas
New York, NY 10013
Phone: (212) 886-7500
Fax: (212) 643-5573
http://www.astralwerks.com

Asylum Records
1290 Avenue of the Americas
New York, NY 10104
Phone: (212) 707-3020
Fax: (212) 405-5408
http://www.asylumrecords.com

Atlantic Group
1290 Avenue of the Americas
New York, NY 10104
Phone: (212) 707-2000
Fax: (212) 405-5430
http://atlanticrecords.com

Atlantic Records (Classical Division)
1290 Avenue of the Americas
New York, NY 10104
Phone: (212) 707-2000
Fax: (212) 405-5430
http://atlantic-records.com

BAM Records Inc.
18352 North Dallas Parkway
Dallas, TX 75287
Phone: (214) 485-0001
Fax: (972) 820-8473
http://www.bamrecords.com

Bad Boy Entertainment
1710 Broadway
New York, NY 10019
Phone: (212) 381-1540
Fax: (212) 381-1599
http://www.badboyonline.com

Banner Records
P.O. Box 10440
Hamilton Square, NJ 08560
Phone: (609) 844-1031
Fax: (609) 844-1032
http://www.bannerrecords.com

Bar None Records
P.O. Box 1704
Hoboken, NJ 07030
Phone: (201) 770-9090
Fax: (201) 770-9920
http://www.bar-none.com

BeatOven Records
3312 Holmes Street
Kansas City, MO 64109
Phone: (816) 255-3762

Beggars Group
304 Hudson Avenue
New York, NY 10013
Phone: (212) 995-5882
Fax: (212) 995-5883
http://www.beggarsgroupusa.com

Big Heavy World
215 College Street
Burlington, VT 05402
Phone: (802) 865-1140
http://www.heavyworld.com

Blue Note Records
150 Fifth Avenue
New York, NY 10011
Phone: (212) 786-8600
Fax: (212) 786-8943
http://www.bluenote.com

BME Recordings
2144 Hills Avenue
Atlanta, GA 30318
Phone: (404) 367-8130
Fax: (404) 367-8637
http://www.bmerecordings.com

BNA Records
1400 18th Avenue South
Nashville, TN 37212
Phone: (615) 301-4300
Fax: (615) 301-4347
http://www.bnarecords.com

Boyd Records & Publishing
P.O. Box 226
Cincinnati, OH 45201
Phone: (513) 230-7084
Fax: (513) 729-0269
http://www.boydrec.com

Brainticket Records
P.O. Box 122048
Arlington, TX 76012
Phone: (817) 274-2332
Fax: (817) 274-2119
http://www.brainticket.com

Cadence Jazz Records Ltd.
Cadence Building
Redwood, NY 13679
Phone: (315) 287-2852
Fax: (315) 287-2860
http://www.cadencebuilding.com

Canyon Records
3131 West Clarendon Avenue
Phoenix, AZ 85107
Phone: (602) 279-5941
Fax: (602) 279-9233

http://www.canyonrecords.com

Capitol Nashville
3322 West End Avenue
Nashville, TN 37203
Phone: (615) 269-2000
Fax: (615) 269-2059
http://www.capitol-nashville.com

Capitol Records
1750 North Vine Street
Hollywood, CA 90028
Phone: (323) 462-6252
Fax: (323) 871-5185
http://www.hollywoodandvine.com

Carrot Top Records/CTD Ltd.
3716 West Fullerton Avenue
Chicago, IL 60647
Phone: (312) 432-1194
Fax: (312) 432-1351
http://www.carrottoprecords.com

Castle Records
30 Music Square West
Nashville, TN 37203
Phone: (615) 401-7111
Fax: (615) 401-7119
http://www.castlerecords.com

Century Media Recordings
2323 West El Segundo Boulevard
Hawthorne, CA 90250
Phone: (323) 418-1400
Fax: (323) 418-0118
http://www.centurymedia.com

Columbia Nashville
1400 18th Avenue South
Nashville, TN 37212
Phone: (615) 301-4300
Fax: (615) 301-4347
http://www.columbianashville.com

Columbia Records
550 Madison Avenue
New York, NY 10022
Phone: (212) 833-5212
Fax: (212) 833-5401
http://www.columbiarecords.com

Columbia Records
2100 Colorado Avenue

Santa Monica, CA 90404
Phone: (310) 449-2100
Fax: (310) 552-1350
http://www.columbiarecords.com

Compass Records
916 19th Avenue South
Nashville, TN 37212
Phone: (615) 320-7672
Fax: (615) 320-7378
http://www.compassrecords.com

Concord Records, Inc.
100 North Crescent Drive
Beverly Hills, CA 90210
Phone: (310) 385-4455
Fax: (310) 385-4466
http://www.concordmusicgroup.com

Copeland International Arts
1830 North Sierra Bonita Avenue
Los Angeles, CA 90046
Phone: (323) 512-4080
Fax: (323) 512-4080
http://www.milescopeland.net

Cordless Recordings
30 Irving Place
New York, NY 10003
Phone: (212) 287-6100
Fax: (212) 287-6169
http://www.cordless.com

Corporate Punishment Records
1314 South Oxford Avenue
Los Angeles, CA 90006
http://www.corporatepunishment.
  com

Curb Records
48 Music Square East
Nashville, TN 37203
Phone: (615) 321-5080
Fax: (615) 327-3003
http://www.curb.com

Deep South Entertainment
P.O. Box 17737
Raleigh, NC 27619
Phone: (919) 844-1515
Fax: (919) 847-5922
http://www.deepsouthentertain
  ment.com

Dionsysus Records
P.O. Box 1975
Burbank, CA 91507
Phone: (818) 848-2098
http://www.dionsusrecords.com

Disney Records
350 South Buena Vista Street
Burbank, CA 91532
Phone: (818) 973-4360
Fax: (818) 973-4322
http://www.disneyrecords.com

Domo Records Inc.
11340 West Olympic Boulevard
Los Angeles, CA 90064
Phone: (310) 966-4414
Fax: (310) 966-4420
http://www.domo.com

Drag City Records
P.O. Box 476867
Chicago, IL 60647
Phone: (312) 455-1015
Fax: (312) 455-1057
http://www.dragcity.com

Eagle Records
825 Eighth Avenue
New York, NY 10019
Phone: (212) 333-8000
Fax: (212) 445-3232
http://www.eaglerockent.com

**EMI Christian Music Group
(CMG) Label Group**
101 Winners Circle
Brentwood, TN 37024
Phone: (615) 371-4300
Fax: (615) 371-6915
http://www.emicmg.com

EMI Latin Music Group
303 Washington Avenue
Miami Beach, FL 33139
Phone: (305) 674-7529
Fax: (305) 674-7546
http://www.emilatin.com

Epic Records Group
550 Madison Avenue
New York, NY 10022
Phone: (212) 833-8000

Fax: (212) 833-4583
http://www.epicrecords.com

Epitaph Records
2798 Sunset Boulevard
Los Angeles, CA 90026
Phone: (213) 413-7353
Fax: (213) 413-9678
http://www.epitaph.com

Flyte Time Productions
8750 Wilshire Boulevard
Beverly Hills, CA 90211
Phone: (818) 753-0999
Fax: (818) 753-0906
http://www.flytime.com

Fountainbleu Records
P.O. Box 211246
Woodhaven, NY 11421
Phone: (718) 296-8122
Fax: (718) 296-8123
http://www.fountainbleu.com

Frontier Records
P.O. Box 22
Sun Valley, CA 91353
Phone: (818) 759-8279
http://www.fronteirrecords.com

Geffen Records
2222 Colorado Avenue
Santa Monica, CA 90404
Phone: (310) 865-1000
Fax: (310) 865-7096
http://www.geffen.com

Gotham Records
P.O. Box 7185
Santa Monica, CA 90406
Phone: (310) 393-0828
Fax: (310) 393-0829
http://www.gothamrecords.com

Higher Octave Music, Inc.
150 Fifth Avenue
New York, NY 10011
Phone: (212) 786-8600
Fax: (212) 786-8645
http://www.higheroctave.com

HighNote Records
106 West 71st Street

New York, NY 10023
Phone: (212) 873-2020
Fax: (212) 877-0407
http://www.jazzdepot.com

Hightone Records
110 Fourth Street
Oakland, CA 94607
Phone: (510) 763-8500
Fax: (510) 763-8558
http://www.hightone.com

Hollywood Records
400 South Buena Vista Street
Burbank, CA 91521
Phone: (816) 560-5670
Fax: (816) 560-3186
http://www.hollywoodrecords.com

Hollywood Records
825 Eighth Avenue
New York, NY 10019
Phone: (212) 445-3507
Fax: (212) 445-3850
http://www.hollywoodrecords.com

Idol Records and Publishing
P.O. Box 720044
Dallas, TX 75372
Phone: (214) 321-8890
Fax: (214) 321-8889
http://www.idolrecords.com

Immortal Entertainment
10585 Santa Monica Boulevard
Los Angeles, CA 90025
Phone: (310) 481-1800
Fax: (310) 474-6688
http://www.immortalrecords.com

Interscope
22220 Colorado Avenue
Santa Monica, CA 90404
Phone: (310) 865-1000
Fax: (310) 865-7083
http://www.interscope.com

Island Def Jam Music Group
825 Eighth Avenue
New York, NY 10019
Phone: (212) 333-8000
Fax: (212) 603-7931
http://www.islanddefjam.com

Jive/Silvertone/Verity/Volcano Records (Zomba Label Group)
137–139 West 25th Street
New York, NY 10001
Phone: (212) 727-0016
Fax: (212) 645-3783
http://www.jiverecords.com

JRecords/Arista
550 Madison Avenue
New York, NY 10022
Phone: (646) 840-5600
Fax: (646) 840-5619
http://www.jrecords.com

Just Us Records
P.O. Box 6822
Alexandria, VA 22306
Phone: (703) 765-3166
Fax: (703) 765-4882
http://www.justusrecords.com

Lamon Records Corp
7124-A Matthews Minto Hill Road
Charlotte, NC 28227
Phone: (704) 282-9910
Fax: (704) 282-0505
http://www.lamonrecords.com

Lanor Records
406 West Jefferson Street
Jennings, LA 70546
Phone: (337) 824-6063
Fax: (337) 824-6064
http://www.lanorrecords.com

Lava Records
1290 Avenue of the Americas
New York, NY 10104
Phone: (212) 707-2550
Fax: (212) 405-5661
http://www. atlanticrecords.com

Lazy Bones Recordings, Inc.
9594 First Avenue, Northeast
Seattle, WA 98115
Phone: (206) 447-0712
Fax: (425) 821-5720
http://www.lazybones.com

Lens Records
3023 North Clark Street

Chicago, IL 60657
Phone: (773) 404-2692
Fax: (773) 404-2976
http://www.lensrecords.com

Little Dog Records
2219 West Olive Avenue
Burbank, CA 91506
Phone: (818) 557-1595
Fax: (818) 557-0524
http://www.littledogrecrods.com

Lost Highway Records
401 Commerce Street
Nashville, TN 37219
Phone: (615) 524-7500
Fax: (615) 524-7850
http://www.losthighwayrecords.com

Lyric Street Records
1100 Demonbreun Street
Nashville, TN 37203
Phone: (615) 963-4848
Fax: (615) 963-4862
http://www.lyricstreeet.com

Matador Records
304 Hudson Street
New York, 10013
Phone: (212) 995-5882
Fax: (212) 995-5883
http://www.matadorrecords.com

MCA Nashville
31 Commerce Street
Nashville, TN 37219
Phone: (615) 244-8944
Fax: (615)
http://www.mcanashville.com

Megaforce Records
P.O. Box 1955
New York, NY 10113
Phone: (212) 741-8861
Fax: (212) 757-8602
http://www.megaforcerecords.com

Mercury Nashville
401 Commerce Street
Nashville, TN 37219
Phone: (615) 524-7500
Fax: (615) 524-7600
http://www.mercurynashville.com

Merge Records
P.O. Box 1235
Chapel Hills, NC 27514
Phone: (919) 688-9969
Fax: (919) 68809970
http://www.mergerecords.com

Motown Records
1755 Broadway
New York, NY 10019
Phone: (212) 841-8000
Fax: (212) 489-9096
http://www.motown.com

Music Mill Entertainment
1103 11th Avenue South
Nashville, TN 37212
Phone: (615) 254-5925
Fax: (615) 244-5928
http://www.musicmill.com

Mute Records
101 Sixth Avenue
New York, NY 10013
Phone: (212) 255-7670
Fax: (212) 255-6056
http://www.mute.com

Narada Productions, Inc.
150 Fifth Avenue
New York, NY 10011
Phone: (212) 786-8600
http://www.narada.com

Nashville Sound Records
P.O. Box 11
Pleasant View, TN 37146
Phone: (615) 746-4444
http://www.nashvillesoundrecord.
com

Nashville Underground
P.O. Box 120086
Nashville, TN 37212
Phone: (615) 673-7215
Fax: (615) 866-5928
http://www.nashvilleunderground.
com

Neurodisc Records, Inc.
2901 North University Drive
Fort Lauderdale, FL 33351
Phone: (954) 572-0289

Fax: (954) 572-2874
http://www.neurodisc.com

New West Records
8888 Olympic Boulevard
Beverly Hills, CA 90211
Phone: (310) 246-5767
http://www.newwestrecords.com

Octone Records
113 University Place
New York, NY 10003
Phone: (646) 845-1700
Fax: (646) 613-9096
http://site.amoctone.com

Outback Records
P.O. Box 1993
Mount Vernon, IL 62864
Phone: (618) 244-9410
Fax: (312) 628-7634
http://www.outbackrecords.com

Palmeto Records
67 Hill Road
West Redding, CT 06896
Phone: (203) 938-7054
http://www.palmetto-records.com

Peppermint Records
581 Old Highway
New Brighton, MN 55112
Phone: (651) 293-1010
http://www.pepermintcds.com

Philadelphia International Records
309 South Broad Street
Philadelphia, PA 19107
Phone: (215) 985-0900
Fax: (215) 985-1195
http://www.gamble-huffmusic.com

Pinecastle Records
P.O. Box 753
Columbus, NC 28722
Phone: (828) 894-0322
Fax: (828) 894-2810
http://www.pinecastle.com

Provident Music Group
741 Cool Springs Boulevard
Franklin, TN 37067

Phone: (615) 261-6500
Fax: (615) 261-5916
http://www.providentmusic.com

RCA Music Group-RCA Records-J Records
745 Fifth Avenue
New York, NY 10151
Phone: (646) 840-5600
Fax: (646) 840-5791
http://www.jrecords.com

RCA Records Nashville
1400 18th Avenue South
Nashville, TN 37212
Phone: (615) 301-4300
Fax: (615) 301-4356
http://www.jrecords.com

RCA Victor Group
1540 Broadway
New York, NY 10036
Phone: (212) 930-4941
Fax: (212) 930-4965
http://www.rcavictorgroup.com

Real Music
85 Libertyship Way
Sausalito, CA 94965
Phone: (415) 331-8273
Fax: (415) 331-8278
http://www.realmusic.com

Red Ink
76 Fifth Avenue
New York, NY 10003
Phone: (212) 404-0600
Fax: (212) 404-0640
http://www.redmusic.com/redink

Reprise Records
3300 Warner Boulevard
Burbank, CA 91505
Phone: (818) 846-9090
Fax: (818) 840-2409
http://www.repriserec.com

Republic Records
1775 Broadway
New York, NY 10019
Phone: (212) 841-5100
Fax: (212) 841-8012
http://www.republicrecords.com

Roadrunner Records
902 Broadway
New York, NY 10010
Phone: (212) 274-7500
Fax: (212) 505-7469
http://www.roadrunnerrecords.com

Robbins Entertainment
159 West 25th Street
New York, NY 10001
Phone: (212) 675-4321
Fax: (212) 675-4441
http://www.robbinsent.com

RPM Music Productions, Inc.
48 West 10th Street
New York, NY 10011
Phone: (212) 246-8126
Fax: (212) 397-1371
http://www.rpm-productions.com

Sanctuary Records Group
825 Eighth Avenue
New York, NY 10019
Phone: (212) 333-8000
http://www.sanctuaryrecordsgroup.
com

Scarab Records
7660 Beverly Boulevard
Los Angeles, CA 90036
Phone: (323) 954-9909
http://www.scarabrecords.com

Secret Records
1099 Wall Street West
Lyndhurst, NJ 08071
Phone: (212) 691-1200
Fax: (201) 438-1777
http://www.selectrecordsonline.com

Shangri-La Records
1916 Madison Avenue
Memphis, TN 38104
Phone: (901) 274-1916
http://www.shangri.com

Sony BMG Masterworks
1540 Broadway
New York, NY 10036
Phone: (212) 930-4941
Fax: (212) 930-4965
http://www.bmgclassics.com

Sony BMG Music
605 Lincoln Road
Miami Beach, FL 33139
Phone: (315) 695-3556
Fax: (315) 695-3664
http://www.sonydiscos.com

Sony BMG Music
   International-Latin America
605 Lincoln Road
Miami Beach, FL 33139
Phone: (305) 695-3500
Fax: (305) 695-3664
http://www.sonybmglatin.com

Spring Hill Music Group
101 Winners Circle
Brentwood, TN 37027
Phone: (615) 383-5535
Fax: (615) 383-6632
http://www.springhillmusic.com

Standard Recording Company
P.O. Box 441047
Indianapolis, IN 46244
Phone: (317) 362-1667
http://www.standardrecording.com

Star Trak Entertainment
1755 Broadway
New York, NY 100019
Phone: (212) 603-7850
http://www.startrakmusic.com

Strummer Records
2220 Colorado Avenue
Santa Monica, CA 90404
Phone: (310) 865-2711
Fax: (310) 865-2940
http://www.strummerrecords.com

Tommy Boy Entertainment LLC
120 Fifth Avenue
New York, NY 10011

Phone: (212) 388-8300
Fax: (212) 388-8431
http://www.tommyboy.com

Universal Classics
825 Eighth Avenue
New York, NY 10019
Phone: (212) 333-8000
Fax: (212) 333-8402
http://www.universalclassics.com

Universal Music Latino
420 Lincoln Road
Miami Beach, FL 33139
Phone: (305) 938-1300
Fax: (305) 938-1379
http://www.universalmusica.com

Universal Records
1755 Broadway
New York, NY 10019
Phone: (212) 373-0600
Fax: (212) 247-3594
http://www.universalmusic.com

Universal Records South
40 Music Square
Nashville, TN 37203
Phone: (615) 259-5300
Fax: (615) 259-5301
http://www.universal-south.com

Verve Music Group
1755 Broadway
New York, NY 10019
Phone: (212) 331-2000
Fax: (212) 331-2064
http://www.vervemusicgroup.com

Virgin Records
150 Fifth Avenue
New York, NY 10011
Phone: (212) 786-2000
http://www.virginrecords.com

Warner Brothers Records Inc.
3300 Warner Boulevard
Burbank, CA 91505
Phone: (818) 846-9090
Fax: (818) 840-2393
http://www.wbr.com

Warner Brothers Records, Inc.
20 Music Square East
Nashville, TN 37203
Phone: (615) 748-8000
Fax: (615) 214-1567
http://www.wbnashville.com

Warner Music International
75 Rockefeller Plaza
New York, NY 10019
Phone: (212) 275-2000
Fax: (212) 757-3985
http://www.wmg.com

Warner Music Latina
555 Washington Avenue
Miami Beach, FL 33139
Phone: (305) 702-2200
Fax: (305) 702-2264
http:://www.wmg.com

World Label Group/Warner
   Brothers Records (Christian
   Division)
25 Music Square West
Nashville, TN 37203
Phone: (615) 251-0600
http://www.wordentertainment.com

Zomba Label Group (Jive/
   Silvertone/Verity/Volcano
   Records)
137–139 West 25th Street
New York, NY 10001
Phone: (212) 727-0016
Fax: (212) 645-3783
http://www.jiverecords.com

APPENDIX IV
RECORD DISTRIBUTORS

This is a listing of selected record distributors in the United States. You might find it useful if you are looking for a job working with a distributor or are trying to distribute an independent record.

Use this list as a beginning. There are many more scattered throughout the country. Due to space limita-

tions, all distributors have not been included. Inclusion or exclusion on this list does not indicate that the author recommends or endorses any one distributor over another.

101 Distribution
2375 E. Camelback Road
Phoenix, AZ 85016
Phone: (602) 357-3288
Fax: (602) 357-3288
E-mail: support@101distribution.
  com
http://www.101distribution.com

AEC One Stop Group
4350 Coral Ridge Drive
Coral Springs, FL 44065
Phone: (954) 255-4000
Fax: (954) 255-4908
http://www.aent.com

Albany Music Distributors
915 Broadway
Albany, NY 12207
Phone: (518) 436-8814
Fax: (518) 436-0643
E-mail: mkalbanymusic@yahoo.com
http://www.albanyrecords.com

Alcione
12975 SW 132nd Avenue
Miami, FL 33186
Phone: (305) 378-9987
Fax: (305) 387-8890
E-mail: alcione@alcione.com
http://www.alcoione.com

Alliance Entertainment
4250 Coral Ridge Drive
Coral Springs, FL 33065
Phone: (954) 255-4429
Fax: (954) 255-4990

**Alternative Distribution
  Alliance**
72 Spring Street
New York, NY 10012
Phone: (212) 343-2485
Fax: (212) 343-7977
http://www.ada-music.com

**American Distribution
  Services**
462 NE 63rd Street
Miami, FL 33138
Phone: (305) 762-4225
Fax: (305) 759-4808
E-mail: info@adsdvds.com

Associated Distributors, Inc.
10 West McKinley Street
Phoenix, AZ 85003
Phone: (602) 278-5584
Fax: (602) 269-6356
E-mail: adimusic@aol.com

Baker & Taylor
501 South Gladiolus Street
Momence, IL 60954
Phone: (815) 802-2444
E-mail: btinfo@btol.com
http://www.btol.com

Big Bang Distribution
9420 Reseda Boulevard
Northridge, CA 91324
Phone: (818) 727-1127
Fax: (818) 727-1126
http://www.bigbangdist.com

**Big Daddy Music Distribution
  Company**
162 North Eighth Street
Kenilworth, NJ 07033
Phone: (908) 653-9110
Fax: (908) 653-9114
E-mail: info@bigdaddymusic.com
http://www.bigdaddymusic.com

**Big Easy Distributing
  Company**
134 Harbor Circle
New Orleans, LA 70126
Phone: (504) 241-9800
Fax: (504) 241-9866
E-mail: bnorton@
  bigeasydistributing.com
http://www.bigeasydistributing.
  com

Big World Distribution
2081 NW 24th Street
Miami, FL 33142
Phone: (305) 633-9963
Fax: (305) 634-3775
http://www.platanorecords.com

Breen Agency
3811 Bedford Avenue
Nashville, TN 37215
Phone: (615) 777-2227
Fax: (615) 321-4656
E-mail: info@thebreenagency.com
http://www.thebreenagency.com

Campus Records
5033 Transamerica Drive

Columbus, OH 43228
Phone: (614) 771-9222
Fax: (614) 771-9226

Caroline Distribution
101 Avenue of the Americas
New York, NY 10013
Phone: (212) 886-7500
Fax: (212) 643-5563
E-mail: sales@caroline.com
http://www.carolinedist.com

Caroline Distribution
6161 Santa Monica Boulevard
Los Angeles, CA 90038
Phone: (323) 468-8627
Fax: (323) 468-8626
E-mail: sales&caroline.com
http://www.carolinedist.com

Carrot Top Records
3716 West Fullerton Avenue
Chicago, IL 60622
Phone: (312) 432-1194
Fax: (312) 432-1351
E-mail: patric@carrottoprecords.com
http://www.carrottoprecords.com

Cisco Music - Los Angeles
6307 De Soto Avenue
Woodland Hills, CA 91367
Phone: (818) 884-2234
Fax: (818) 884-1268
http://www.ciscomusic.com

Cisco Music NYC
386 Park Avenue South
New York, NY 10016
Phone: (212) 213-8197
Fax: (212) 213-8559
http://www.ciscomusic.com

City Hall Records
101 Glacier Point
San Rafael, CA 94901
Phone: (415) 457-9080
Fax: (415) 457-0780
E-mail: info@cityhallrecords.com
http://www.cityhallrecords.com

Crosstalk Distributors
650 West Lake Street
Chicago, IL 60661

Phone: (312) 715-1230
Fax: (312) 715-1251
http://www.crosstalkchicago.com

Crystal Clear Distribution
10486 Brockwood Road
Dallas, TX 75238
Phone: (214) 349-5707
Fax: (214) 349-3819
E-mail: info@
  crystalcleardistribution.com
http://www.crystalcleardistribution.
  com

Dico-O-Rama Music World Distributors
186 West Fourth Street
New York, NY 10014
Phone: (212) 206-8417
Fax: (212) 741-0809
E-mail: discman@discorama.com
http://www.discorama.com

EMI Music Distribution
501 Flynn Road
Camarillo, CA 93012
Phone: (805) 384-1102
Fax: (805) 384-5607
http://www.emigroup.com

Empire Music Group LLC
170 West 74th Street
New York, NY 10023
Phone: (212) 580-5959
Fax: (212) 874-8605
http://www.empiremusic.com

Eurpac Warehouse Sales
3001 Skyway Circle North
Chula Vista, CA 75038
Phone: (972) 257-1945
http://www.eurpac.com

Floyd's Wholesale Distributors
434 East Main Street
Ville Platte, LA 70586
Phone: (337) 363-2184
Fax: (337) 363-5622
E-mail: info@floydsrecordshop.com
http://www.floydsrecordshop.com

Groove Distribution
346 North Justine Street

Chicago, IL 60607
Phone: (773) 435-0250
Fax: (312) 997-2382
E-mail: sales@groovedis.com
http://www.groovedis.com

Horseshoe Distributors
2937 Harline Drive
Nashville, TN 37211
Phone: (615) 331-1125

Ingram Entertainment, Inc.
382 East Lies Road
Carol Stream, IL 60188
Phone: (630) 871-0222
Fax: (630) 871-7806
http://www.ingramentertainment.
  com

Koch Entertainment Distribution
7059 Illinois Court
Fontana, CA 92336
Phone: (909) 944-7788

Koch Entertainment Distribution
26592 Heather Brook
Lake Forest, IL 92630
Phone: (949) 597-8464
Fax: (949) 597-8469
http://www.kochdistribution.com

Koch Entertainment Distribution
1803 Westridge Drive
Austin, TX 78704
Phone: (512) 442-5570
Fax: (512) 442-5730
http://www.kochent.com

Koch Entertainment Distribution
22 Harbor Park Drive
Port Washington, NY 11050
Phone: (516) 484-1000
Fax: (516) 484-4746
http://www.kochent.com

Koch Entertainment Distribution
740 Broadway
New York, NY 10003

Phone: (212) 979-2856
Fax: (212) 353-3797
http://www.kochent.com

Music City Record Distribution, Inc.
25 Lincoln Street
Nashville, TN 37210
Phone: (615) 255-7315
Fax: (615) 255-7329
http://www.mcrd.com

Music Video Distributors
H840 North Circle Drive
Business Center
Oaks, PA 19456
Phone: (610) 650-8200
Fax: (610) 650-9102
E-mail: customerservice@
    musicvideodistributors.com
http://www.musicvideodistibutors.
    com

Navarre Corporation
7400 49th Avenue North
New Hope, MN 55428
Phone: (763) 535-8333

Fax: (763) 533-2156
http://www.navarre.com

Oarfin Distribution, Inc.
12229 Nicollet Avenue South
Saint Louis Park, MN 55426
Phone: (612) 673-0508
Fax: (612) 673-0776
E-mail: admin@oarfindistribution.
    com
http://www.oarfindistribution.
    com

Off-Beat Records, Inc.
165 Front Street
Chicopee, MA 01013
Phone: (413) 594-5299
Fax: (413) 594-5299
E-mail: sales@offbeatrec.com
http://www.offbeatrec.com

Reyes Records, Inc.
140 NW 22nd Avenue
Miami, FL 33125
Phone: (305) 541-6686
Fax: (305) 642-2785
http://www.reyesrecords.com

RND Distribution
P.O. Box 540102
Houston, TX 77254
Phone: (713) 521-2616
Fax: (713) 529-4914
http://www.rnddistribution.com

SONY BMG Music Entertainment Sales Group
550 Madison Avenue
New York, NY 10022
Phone: (212) 833-8000
Fax: (212) 883-8620
http://www.sonybmg.com

Super Marketing Distributors
65 Richard Road
Ivyland, PA 18974
Phone: (215) 674-5410
Fax: (215) 674-5459
http://www.supermtkg.com

Universal Music Group Distribution
1660 South Highway 100
Saint Louis Park, MN 55416
Phone: (952) 828-6060
Fax: (952) 828-9494
http://www.universalmusic.com

APPENDIX V
BOOKING AGENCIES

The following is a listing of booking agencies located throughout the country. Although many of the agencies listed are major companies, smaller regional agencies have also been included which may be helpful in your career.

Due to space limitations, every booking agency could not be included. Inclusion or exclusion in this listing does not indicate any one agency is endorsed or recommended over another.

A Cappella Central
1450 Southgate Avenue
Daly City, CA 94015-4021
Phone: (650) 550-0062
E-mail: acappella@princesf.com
http://www.princesf.com

Access Talent
P.O. Box 24372
Nashville, TN 37202
Phone: (615) 790-0660
Fax: (615) 794-2328
E-mail: Shauna@accesstalentnow.
      com
http://www.accesstalentnow.com

Adams & Green Entertainment Agency
P.O. Box 17376
Sugarland, TX 77496
Phone: (281) 835-6400
Fax: (281) 835-6004
E-mail: info@entertainment
      houston.com
http://www.entertainmenthouston.
      com

The Agency Group, Ltd.
1775 Broadway
New York, NY 10019
Phone: (212) 581-3100
Fax: (212) 581-0015
http://www.theagencygroup.com

The Agency Group, Ltd.
1880 Century Park East
Los Angeles, CA 90067
Phone: (310) 385-2800
Fax: (310) 385-1220
http://www.theagencygroup.com

Agent 0007, Inc.
P.O. Box 117
Hopkinton, MA 01748
Phone: (781) 259-0007
Fax: (508) 544-1407
E-mail: info@agent0007.com
http://www.agent0007.com

AIF Music Productions
P.O. Box 691
Mamaroneck, NY 10543
Phone: (914) 510-9022
E-mail: aifrecords@verizon.net

American Artists
315 South Beverly Drive
Beverly Hills, CA 90212
Phone: (310) 277-7877
Fax: (310) 277-9697
http://www.americanartists.net

APA (Agency for the Performing Arts)
405 S Beverly Drive
Beverly Hills, CA 90212
Phone: (310) 888-4200
Fax: (310) 888-4242
E-mail: jgosnell@apa-agency.com
http://www.apa-agency.com

APA (Agency for the Performing Arts)
3017 Poston Avenue
Nashville, TN 37203
Phone: (615) 297-0200
http://www.apa-agency.com

Artists Worldwide
2911 Wilshire Boulevard

Los Angeles, CA 90010
Phone: (213) 368-2112
Fax: (213) 368-2110
E-mail: artistsworldwide@aol.com
http://www.artists-worldwide.com

Associated Booking Corp.
501 Madison Avenue
New York, NY 10022
Phone: (212) 874-2400
Fax: (212) 769-3649
E-mail: musicbiz@mindspring.com
http://www.abcbooking.com

Backstreet Booking
700 West Pete Rose Way
Cincinnati, OH 45203
Phone: (513) 542-9544
Fax: (513) 542-9595
E-mail: info@backstreetbooking.com
http://www.backstreetbooking.com

Berkeley Agency
2608 Ninth Street
Berkeley, CA 94710
Phone: (510) 843-4902
Fax: (510) 843-7271
http://www.berkeleyagency.com

Big J Productions, Inc.
558 Brockenbraught Court
Metarie, LA 70005
Phone: (985) 867-8821
http://www.bigjprod@aol.com

Billons Corp.
833 West Chicago Avenue
Chicago, IL 60622
Phone: (312) 997-9999
Fax: (312) 997-2287

E-mail: boche@billons.com
http://www.billons.com

Capitol International Productions

47829 Tomahawk Drive
Negley, OH 44441
Phone: (330) 227-2000
Fax: (330) 227-2207
E-mail: info@capitolint.com
http://www.capitolint.com

Capitol Management Group

118 Curtiswood Drive
Hendersonville, TN 37075
Phone: (615) 321-0600
Fax: (615) 338-4497
E-mail: capitolmanagement.com
http://www.capitolmanagment.com

Carmel Music and Entertainment

701 Main Street
Evanston, IL 60202
Phone: (847) 864-5969
Fax: (847) 864-6149
http://www.carmelme.com

Keith Case & Associates

1025 17th Avenue South
Nashville, TN 37212
Phone: (615) 327-4636
Fax: (615) 327-4949
http://www.keithcase.com

Creative Artists Agency, Inc.

2000 Avenue of the Stars
Los Angeles, CA 90067
Phone: (424) 288-2000
Fax: (424) 288-2900
http://www.caatouring.com

Creative Entertainment Group

505 Eighth Avenue
New York, NY 10018
Phone: (212) 634-0427
Fax: (212) 634-0432
http://www.cegmusic.com

DMR Booking Agency

215 Walton Street
Syracuse, NY 13202
Phone: (315) 475-2500

E-mail: music@dmrbooking.com
http://sss.drmbooking.com

Do It Booking

P.O. Box 522016
Salt Lake City, UT 84512
Phone: (801) 466-8374
Fax: (801) 466-8376
http://www.doitbooking.com

East Coast Entertainment

P.O. Box 11283
Richmond, VA 23230
Phone: (804) 355-2178.
Fax: (804) 353-3407
http://www.eastcoastentertainment.com

Entertainment Artists Nashville

2409 21st Avenue South
Nashville, TN 37212
Phone: (615) 320-7041
Fax: (615) 320-0856
E-mail: entartnash@aol.com

Entourage Talent Associates, Ltd.

236 West 27th Street
New York, NY 10001
Phone: (212) 633-2600
Fax: (212) 633-1818
http://www.entouragetalent.com

Fat City Artists

1906 Chet Atkins Plaza
Nashville, TN 37212
Phone: (615) 320-7678
Fax: (615) 321-5832
http://www.fatcityartists.com

Five Star Talent and Entertainment

1410 Palo Duro Road
Austin, TX 78757
Phone: (303) 635-1210
Fax: (303) 438-8212
E-mail: terri@5staractc.om
http://www.5staracts.com

Full House Entertainment Agency

3268 Belmont Street

Bellaire, OH 43906
Phone: (740) 676-5259
Fax: (740) 676-5921
E-mail: agent@
fullhouseentertainment.com
http://www.fullhouseentertainment.com

Gami/Simonds

42 County Road
Morris, CT 06763
Phone: (860) 567-2500
Fax: (925) 396-7046

Gary Good Entertainment & Speakers Bureau

1105 North West 63rd Street
Oklahoma City, OK 73116
Phone: (405) 840-2020
Fax: (404) 842-5451
http://www.garygood.com

Gemini Talent Associates

P.O. Box 261322
Littleton, CO 80163
Phone: (303) 721-6060
Fax: (303) 721-6188

GMA Agency

400 W Peachtree Street, NW
Atlanta, GA 30308
Phone: (404) 961-5373
Fax: (404) 961-5373
http://www.gmeagency.com/

Great American Talent

P.O. Box 2476
Hendersonville, TN 37077
Phone: (615) 452-7878
Fax: (615) 452-7887
http://www.gatalent.com

Green Light Talent Agency

P.O. Box 3172
Beverly Hills, CA 90212
Phone: (323) 655-4407
Fax: (323) 655-4406
E-mail: greentunes@aol.com

Harmony Artists

8455 Beverly Boulevard
Los Angeles, CA 90048
Phone: (323) 655-5007

Fax: (323) 655-5154
E-mail: contact_us@
   harmonyartists.com
http://www.harmonyartists.com

Heavy Hitter
3709 North Southport Avenue
Chicago, IL 6613
Phone: (773) 281-6369
Fax: (773) 281-6586
http://www.heavyhitter.com

Innovative Entertainment
2525 16th Street
San Francisco, CA 94103
Phone: (415) 552-4276
Fax: (415) 552-3545
http://www.inn-entertainment.com

International Creative Management
10250 Constellation Boulevard
Los Angeles, CA 90067
Phone: (310) 550-4000
Fax: (310) 550-4100
E-mail: contemporary@icmtalent.
   com
http://www.icmtalent.com

Buddy Lee Attractions
38 Music Square East
Nashville, TN 37203
Phone: (615) 244-4336
Fax: (615) 726-0428
http://www.buddyleeattractions.com

MAC Presents
P.O. Box 58773
Nashville, TN 37205
Phone: (615) 662-3522
Fax: (615) 366-2099
E-mail: info@macpresents.com
http://www.macpresents.com

Metro Talent Group
4514 Chamblee Dunwoody Road
Atlanta, GA 30338
Phone: (770) 395-1000
Fax: (770) 395-1095
http://www.metrotalentgroup.com

M.O.B. Agency
6404 Wilshire Boulevard
Los Angeles, CA 90048

Phone: (323) 653-0427
Fax: (323) 653-0428
E-mail: mobster411@verizon.net
http://www.mobagency.com

William Morris Agency
150 El Camino Drive
Beverly Hills, CA 90212
Phone: (310) 859-4000
Fax: (310) 859-4440
http://www.wma.com

William Morris Agency
1325 Avenue of the Americas
New York, NY 10019
Phone: (212) 586-5100
Fax: (212) 246-3583
http://www.wma.com

William Morris Agency
1600 Division Street
Nashville, TN 37203
Phone: (615) 963-3000
Fax: (615) 963-3091
http://www.wma.com

William Morris Agency
119 Washington Avenue
Miami Beach, FL 33139
Phone: (305) 938-2000
Fax: (305) 938-2002
http://www.wma.com

Music City Artists
2723 Berrywood Drive
Nashville, TN 37204
Phone: (615) 383-4862
Fax: (615) 383-4791
http://www.musiccityartists.com

Music Group International
5001 Fifth Street, NW
Washington, DC 20011
Phone: (615) 383-4862
Fax: (615) 383-4791
http://www.musiccityartists.com

Nightside Entertainmnet
10 Crabapple Lane
Greenville, RI 02828
Phone: (401) 949-2004
http://www.nightsideentertainment.
   com

Noteworthy Talent
124 1/2 Archwood Avenue
Annapolis, MD 21401
Phone: (410) 268-8232
Fax: (410) 268-2167
http://www.mcnote.com/

Ozark Talent
718 Schwarz Road
Lawrence, KS 66049
Phone: (785) 760-3143
Fax: (785) 841-0707
E-mail: oztalent@aol.com

Peppermint Booking
P.O. Box 7098
Minneapolis, MN 55407
Phone: (612) 729-3322
E-mail: info@peppermintbooking.
   com
http://www.peppermintbooking.com

Pinacle Entertainment Company
30 Glenn Street
White Plains, NY 10603
Phone: (914) 686-7100
Fax: (914) 686-4085

Pretty Polly Productions
397 Moody Street
Waltham, MA 02453
Phone: (781) 894-9600
Fax: (781) 894-9696
E-mail: info@prettypolly.com
http://www.prettypolly.com

Prince/SF Productions
1450 Southgate Avenue
Daly City, CA 94015-4021
Phone: (650) 550-0062
E-mail: info@princesf.com
http://www.princesf.com

Producers, Inc.
11806 North 56th Street
Tampa, FL 33613
Phone: (813) 988-8333
Fax: (813) 985-3293
http://www.producersinc.com

Pyramid Entertainment Group
377 Rector Place
New York, NY 10280

Phone: (212) 242-7274
Fax: (212) 242-6932
E-mail: info@pyramid-ent.com
http://www.pyramid-ent.com

Rainbow Talent Agency
146 Round Pond Lane
Rochester, NY 14626
Phone: (585) 723-3334
Fax: (585) 720-6172
http://www.rainbowtalentagency.com

Bobby Roberts Co, Inc.
P.O. Box 1547
Goodlesttsville, TN 37070
Phone: (615) 859-8899
Fax: (615) 859-2200
E-mail: info@bobbyroberts.com
http://www.bobbyroberts.com

Rosebud Agency
P.O. Box 170429
San Francisco, CA 94117
Phone: (415) 386-3456
Fax: (415) 386-0599
E-mail: info@rosebudus.com
http://www.rosebudus.com

Sound of New Orleans
P.O. Box 701157
Houston, TX 77270
Phone: (504) 352-1303
Fax: (713) 688-2293
http://www.soundofneworleans.com

Spectrum Talent Agency
520 W 43rd Street
New York, NY 10036
Phone: (212) 268-0404
Fax: (212) 268-1114
E-mail: marc@spectrumtalentagency.com
http://www.spectrumtalentagency.com

Starrleigh Entertainment
205 East Joppa Road
Baltimore, MD 21286
Phone: (410) 828-9400
Fax: (410) 823-5519
http://www.starleigh.com

Steiner Talent
2733 E Battlefield Road
Springfield, MO 65804

Phone: (417) 889-9909
http://www.steinertalent.com

Ted Kurland Associates
173 Brighton Avenue
Boston, MA 02134
Phone: (617) 254-0007
Fax: (617) 782-3577
http://www.tedkurland.com

Third Coast Artists Agency
2021 21st Avenue South
Nashville, TN 2021
Phone: (615) 297-2021
Fax: (615) 297-2776
http://www.tcaa.biz

Third Coast Talent LLC
P.O. Box 110225
Nashville, TN 37222
Phone: (615) 333-7235
Fax: (615) 333-7236
http://www.thirdcoasttalent.com

Triangle Talent
10424 Watterson Trerrace
Louisville, KY 40299
Phone: (502) 267-5466
Fax: (502) 267-8244
http://www.triangletalent.com

Ujaama Talent Agency
501 Seventh Avenue
New York, NY 10018
Phone: (212) 629-4454
Fax: (212) 629-4484
http://www.ujaamatalent.com

United Talent Coordinators
P.O. Box 38
Lombard, IL 60148
Phone: (630) 620-1154
Fax: (630) 620-1189
E-mail: Joey@unitedtalentco.com
http://www.unitedtalentco.com

Universal Attractions
145 W 57th Street
New York, NY 10019
Phone: (212) 582-7575
Fax: (212) 333-4508
E-mail: info@universalattractions.com
http://www.universalattractions.com

Unknown Legends Artists
P.O. Box 2781
Hot Springs, AR 71914
E-mail: info@unkownlegendsbooking.com
http://www.unknownlegendsbooking.com/

Unlimited Myles
6 Imaginary Place
Matawan, NJ 07747
Phone: (732) 566-2881
Fax: (732) 566-8157
E-mail: myles@unlimitedmyles.com
http://www.unlimitedmyles.com

Utopia Artists
108 E Matilija Street
Ojai, CA 93024
Phone: (805) 646-8433
Fax: (805) 646-3367
E-mail: utopiaasst@aol.com
http://www.utopiaartists.com

Val Denn Agency
111 Congress Avenue
Austin, TX 78701
Phone: (512) 391-3855
Fax: (512) 279-2477
E-mail: valdenn@valdenn.com
http://www.valdenn.com

Variety Artists International
793 Higuera
San Luis Obispo, CA 93401
Phone: (805) 545-5550
Fax: (805) 545-5559
E-mail: info@varietyart.com
http://www.varietyart.com

White Oak Productions, Inc.
8428 Oak Street
New Orleans, LA 70118
Phone: (504) 314-6680
Fax: (504) 314-6685
http://www.whiteoakproductions.com

William Ware Agency
2508 Valleyview Lane
Farmer Branch, TX 75234
Phone: (972) 484-9736
Fax: (972) 484-9760
http://www.williamwareagency.com

APPENDIX VI
MUSIC PUBLISHERS

This is a listing of many of the larger music publishers as well as some of the smaller ones. Larger music publishers may take longer to get back to you because of the high volume of songs they work with. Smaller music publishers may work harder with the songs they have. Try sending your material to both.

Some music publishers may also hire staff songwriters. If this is something in you are interested in, consider calling or writing to inquire about possibilities.

Due to space limitations every music publisher could not be included here. Inclusion or exclusion in this list does not indicate any one publisher is recommended or endorsed over another.

ABCO Music, Inc.
1700 Broadway
New York, NY 10019
Phone: (212) 399-0300
Fax: (212) 582-5090
E-mail: ikeitel@abkco.com
http://www.abkco.com

Abilene Music Inc.
Songwriters Guild of America
1500 Harbor Boulevard
Weehawken, NJ 07087
Phone: (201) 867-7603

Acuff-Rose Music Publishing, Inc.
65 Music Square West
Nashville, TN 37203
Phone: (615) 726-8300
Fax: (615) 743-1700

Addax Music Company
3500 West Olive Avenue
Suite 1000
Burbank, CA 91505

Ahab Music
1707 Grand Avenue
Nashville, TN 37212

Alain Boublil Music Ltd.
1775 Broadway
Suite 708
New York, NY 10019

Phone: (212) 246-7203
Fax: (212) 246-7217

Albert E. Brumley & Sons
209 10th Avenue South
Nashville, NC 37203
Phone: (615) 843-1554
http://www.brumleymusic.com

Albion Leadbrook Music Publishing
3960 N. 480 East
Provo, UT 84604
Phone: (801) 224-1513
http://www.leadbrook.com

Alcove Music Publications
P.O. Box 2676
King, NC 27021
Phone: (866) 577-3669
Fax: (336) 983-3599
E-mail: alcovemus@aol.com
http://www.alcovemusic.com

Alfred Publishing Company
P.O. Box 10003
Van Nuys, CA 91410
Phone: (818) 891-5999
Fax: (818) 891-4875
E-mail: permissions@alfred.com
http://www.alfred.com

Allaire Music Publications
212 Second Avenue
Bradley Beach, NJ 07720

Phone: (732) 988-6188
Fax: (732) 223-5732
E-mail: timbroege@aol.com

Alliance Publications, Inc.
9171 Spring Road
Fish Creek, WI 54212
Phone: (920) 868-3100
Fax: (608) 748-4491
E-mail: apimusic@dcwis.com
http://www.apimusic.org

Almo/Irving Music
360 North La Cienega Boulevard
Los Angeles, CA 90048
Phone: (310) 289-3500
Fax: (310) 289-4000

American Composers Alliance
648 Broadway
New York, NY 10012
Phone: (212) 925-0458
Fax: (212) 925-6798
http://www.composers.com

Amherst Early Music
47 Prentiss Street
Watertown, MA 02472
Phone: (617) 744-1324
Fax: (617) 744-1327
http://www.amherstearlymusic.org

Author's Connection Music Publishing
777 College Park Drive, SW

Albany, OR 97322
Phone: (541) 928-4188
http://www.acpublish.com

Bad Brains Publishing
52 Carmine Street
New York, NY 10014
Phone: (212) 741-3083
Fax: (212) 924-0333
E-mail: brains@ix.netcom.com
http://www.badbrains.com

Ballerbach Music
6602 Arbor Meadow Drive
San Antonio, TX 78265
Phone: (210) 698-9738
Fax: (210) 698-1521
E-mail: JamesSyler@aol.com
http://www.ballerbach.com

Balmur Corus Music
1105 17th Avenue South
Nashville, TN 37212
Phone: (615) 329-1431
Fax: (615) 321-0240

Barton Music Corporation
4200 West Magnolia Boulevard
Burbank, CA 91505
Phone: (818) 842-5691
Fax: (818) 842-5763
E-mail: bartonmusic@earthlink.net

Beethoven Music
ACF Music Group
P.O. Box 1770
Hendersonville, TN 37077
Phone: (615) 824-9439
Fax: (615) 824-6691

Belmont Music Publishers
P.O. Box 231
Pacific Palisades, CA 90272
Phone: (310) 454-1867
Fax: (310) 573-1925
E-mail: belmontmusic90272@
    yahoo.com

Belwin-Mills Publishing Corp.
c/o Alfred Publishing Company
P.O. Box 10003
Van Nuys, CA 91410
Phone: (818) 891-5999

Fax: (818) 891-4875
http://www.alfred.com

Big Fish Music
11927 Magnolia Boulevard
North Hollywood, CA 91607
Phone: (818) 984-0377
Fax: (818) 984-0377

BMG Gospel Division
1400 18th Avenue South
Nashville, TN 372
Phone: (615) 858-1300
Fax: (615) 858-1330
E-mail: jan.simenson@bmg.com
http://www.bmg.com

**BMG Music Publishing,
    Licensing**
8750 Wilshire Boulevard
Beverly Hills, CA 90211
Phone: (310) 358-4700

Bob-A-Lew Music
5217 Lankershim Boulevard
North Hollywood, CA 91607
Phone: (818) 506-6331
Fax: (818) 506-4735
E-mail: bobalewmus@aol.com

**Brentwood-Benson Music
    Publishing, Inc.**
741 Cool Springs Boulevard
Franklin, TN 37067
Phone: (615) 261-3300
Fax: (615) 261-3386
E-mail: brentwoodbenson@
    musicservices.org
http://www.brentwood-
    bensonmusic.com

Brichtmark Music, Inc.
200 East 27th Street
Suite 10-V
New York, NY 10016
Phone: (212) 685-9048
http://www.brichtmarkmusic.com

Bright Tunes Music Corp.
7 Sheridan Road
Chappaqua, NY 10514
Phone: (914) 241-4529

Bug Music
7750 Sunset Boulevard
Los Angeles, CA 90046
Phone: (323) 969-0988
http://www.bugmusic.com

Burt Bachrach Music Group
9320 Wilshire Boulevard
Beverly Hills, CA 90212
Phone: (310) 550-1500

Cahn Music Company
704 North Canon Drive
Beverly Hills, CA 90210
Phone: (213) 274-7616

Cherry Lane Music Company
6 East 32nd Street
New York, NY 10016
Phone: (212) 561-3000
Fax: (212) 683-2040
E-mail: pprimont@cherrylane.com
http://www.cherrylane.com

Chesley Music Corp.
P.O. Box 340
Radio City Station
New York, NY 10101
Phone: (212) 227-4714
Fax: (212) 475-6345
E-mail: jandcdeknatel@yahoo.com

Choctaw Music Publishing Co.
224 Ridgedale Drive
Jackson, TN 38305
Phone: (901) 422-4277
E-mail: choctawpub@hotmail.com

Chrysalis Music Group
8500 Melrose Avenue
Los Angeles, CA 90069
Phone: (310) 652-0066
Fax: (310) 652-2024
E-mail: mail@chrysalismusic.com
http://www.chrysalismusic.com

Concordia Publishing House
3558 South Jefferson Avenue
St. Louis, MO 63118
Phone: (314) 268-1000
Fax: (314) 268-1000
E-mail: cphmusic@cph.org
http://www.cph.org

Copperfield Music Group
1400 South Street
Nashville, TN 37212
Phone: (615) 726-3100
Fax: (615) 726-3172
http://www.copperfieldmusic.com

Country Classics Music Pub. Co.
P.O. Box 15222
Oklahoma City, OK 73155
Phone: (405) 677-6448
Fax: (405) 737-8619

Covitt Music
c/o Benchmark Recordings Inc.
254 West 54th Street
New York, NY 10019
Phone: (212) 996-6439
Fax: (516) 726-5929

CPP/Belwin Music
c/o Alfred Publishing Company
P.O. Box 10003
Van Nuys, CA 91410
Phone: (818) 891-5999
Fax: (818) 891-4875
http://www.alfred.com

Creative Entertainment Music
P.O. Box 2586
Toluca Lake, CA 91610
Phone: (323) 860-7074
http://www.transitionmusic.com

Curnow Music Press, Inc.
100 John Sutherland Drive
Nicholasville, KY 40356
Phone: (859) 881-9454
Fax: (859) 881-5171
E-mail: Timjims@inetmail.att.net

The Copyright Company
P.O. Box 128139
Nashville, TN 37212
Phone: (615) 244-9848
Fax: (615) 244-9850
http://www.thecopyrightco.com

Dana Publishing Co.
826 83rd Street
Miami Beach, FL 33141
Phone: (305) 861-2308

Darcey Press
P.O. Box 5018
Vernon Hills, IL 60061
Phone: (847) 816-1468
Fax: (847) 816-1468
E-mail: darceypress@compuserve.com
http://www.darceypress.com

Davandon Music
c/o Charlotte Reid
50 Stratford Road
Harrison, NY 10528
Phone: (914) 967-4771

David Rose Publishing
12725 Ventura Boulevard
Studio City, CA 91604
Phone: (818) 623-8042
Fax: (818) 642-8065
http://www.davidrosepublishing.net

Deanna Yamman Publishing Company, Inc.
1105 McClelen Way
Decatur, GA 30033
Phone: (404) 355-4874

DeFeis Music
269 West 18th Street
Deer Park, NY 11729
Phone: (516) 667-7005
Fax: (516) 667-7005
E-mail: endyamon@vdot.net

Def Mix Music
928 Broadway
New York, NY 10010
Phone: (212) 505-7728
Fax: (212) 505-8041

Denton & Haskins Corp.
Box 340
Radio City Station
New York, NY 10101
Phone: (212) 227-4714
Fax: (212) 475-6345
E-mail: jandcdeknatel@yahoo.com

Disney Music Publishing
500 South Buena Vista Street
Burbank, CA 91521

Phone: (818) 569-3241
Fax: (818) 845-9705

DRC Music
P.O. Box 150693
Dallas, TX 75315
Phone: (214) 428-1839

The Dream Mill Music Company
1034 North Street
Mount Airy, NC 27030
Phone: (336) 280-0450
http://dreamhill.faithweb.com

Emerson Music
4650 Arrow Highway
Montclair, CA 91763
Phone: (800) 518-7214
Fax: (909) 482-2249
E-mail: parker@emersonenterprises.com
http://www.emersonenterprises.com

EMI Christian Music Publishing
P.O. Box 5085
Brentwood, TN 37024
Phone: (615) 371-4400

EMI Music Publishing
810 Seventh Avenue
New York, NY 10019
Phone: (212) 830-2000
Fax: (212) 830-5196

Famous Music Publishing
1633 Broadway
New York, NY 10019
Phone: (212) 654-7433
Fax: (212) 654-4748

Fancy Pants Music
441 East Main Street
Hazard, KY 41701
Phone: (606) 435-1234
E-mail: BernieFaulkner441@yahoo.com

FEMA Music Publications
Box 395
Naperville, IL 60566
Phone: (312) 357-0207

Five Jays Music
4146 Weslin Avenue
Sherman Oaks, CA 91423
Phone: (818) 995-7220

Fur Dixon Publishing
41 Harwood Avenue
White Plains, NY 10603
Phone: (914) 961-8570

Gaither Copyright Management
1703 South Park Avenue
Alexandria, IN 46001
Phone: (765) 724-8233
Fax: (765) 724-8290

Gamble-Huff Music
309 South Broad Street
Philadelphia, PA 19107
Phone: (215) 546-3510

Gems Music Publications
2751 Southeast 24th Place
Gainesville, FL 32641
Phone: (352) 367-2772
http://www.gemsmusicpublications.
    com

Gene Autry Music Group
4383 Colfax Avenue
Studio City, CA 91604
Phone: (818) 752-7770
Fax: (818) 752-7779
E-mail:kbuhlman@autry.com
http://www.autry.com

Glen Campbell Music Group
Gursey, Schneider & Co., LLP
10351 Santa Monica Boulevard
Los Angeles, CA 90025
Phone: (310) 552-0960
Fax: (310) 552-0960
E-mail: amurray@gursey.com

Golden Unlimited Music Inc.
200 West 51 Street
Suite 1009
New York, NY 10019
Phone: (212) 582-8995
Fax: (212) 977-5253

Good Ol' Guitar Music
    Publishing Company
6009 Mckinney Drive, NE

Albuquerque, NM 87109
Phone: (505) 571-9359

Gospel Music Roundup
    Publishing
P.O. Box 752373
Houston, TX 77275
Phone: (281) 468-1154

Grinere Publishing
P.O. Box 815
Brentwood, NY 11717
Phone: (516) 273-3494
Fax: (516) 273-6353

Goodman Group Music
    Publishers
254 West 54th Street
New York, NY 10022
Phone: (212) 246-3333
Fax: (212) 262-6299
E-mail: info@arcmusic.com
http://www.arcmusic.com

Hal Leonard Corporation
7777 West Bluemound Road
Milwaukee, WI 53213
Phone: (414) 774-3630
Fax: (414) 774-3259

Hallmark Music Co. Inc.
14 Elm Street
Brookline, MA 02445
Phone: (617) 277-9460
Fax: (617) 277-5065
E-mail: dlsongtime@aol.com

Hampshire House Pub Corp
c/o The Richmond Organization
266 West 37th Street
New York, NY 10018
Phone: (212) 594-9795

Handy Brothers Music Co. Inc.
1697 Broadway
New York, NY 10019
Phone: (212) 247- 0362
Fax: (212) 247-6179

Harrison Music Corp.
3808 Riverside Drive
Burbank, CA 91505
Phone: (818) 238-9394
Fax: (818) 238-0749

Harlem Music/Halwill Music
1762 Main Street
Buffalo, NY 14208
Phone: (716) 883-9520
Fax: (716) 884-1432

Hits Only Music
P.O. Box 151144
San Francisco, CA 94115
Phone: (414) 922-2622

HOUSE OF FAME, LLC.
P.O. Box 2527
603 East Avalon Avenue
Muscle Shoals, AL 35662
Phone: (256) 381-0801
Fax: (256) 381-6337
http://famestudios.com

IDG Publishing
c/o Padell, Nadell, Fine, Weinberger
    & Company
156 West 56th Street
New York, NY 10019
Phone: (212) 957-0900

Indigo Mood Music
15128 Burbank Boulevard
Sherman Oaks, CA 91411
Phone: (818) 909-9338

Island Music/Ackee Music, Inc.
8920 Sunset Boulevard
Los Angeles, CA 90069
Phone: (213) 276-4500
Fax: (213) 276-0029

J & H Publishing Co.
3865 Kings Way
Boca Raton, FL 33434
Phone: (561) 482-0400
Fax: (561) 482-0600

Jerry Lee Lewis Music
P.O. Box 384
Nesbit, MS 38651
Phone: (601) 429-1290
Fax: (601) 429-9830
E-mail: Kileret@aol.com

Kings Road Music
2828 Donald Douglas Loop North
Santa Monica, CA 90405

Phone: (310) 314-1140
Fax: (310) 314-1136

Kreiselman Music Publishing
215 East 95th Street
New York, NY 10128
Phone: (212) 410-5059
http://kreiselmanmusicpublishing.
    com

Largo Music, Inc.
425 Park Avenue
New York, NY 10022
Phone: (212) 756-5080
Fax: (212) 207-8167
E-mail: largomp@aol.com
http://www.largo.com

Latitunes Music Publishing
Box 94040
Cleveland, OH 44101
Phone: (440) 331-0700
http://www.latitunesmusic.com

Lawrence E. Berry Music
P.O. Box 196
Upper Marlboro, MD 20773
Phone: (301) 574-1350
Fax: (301) 574-5009

Lee Magid, Inc.
P.O. Box 532
Malibu, CA 90265
Phone: (213) 463-5998

Leiber & Stoller
9000 Sunset Boulevard
Suite 1107
Los Angeles, CA 90069
Phone: (310) 273-6401
Fax: (310) 273-1591

Leonard Bernstein Music
   Publishing Company
25 Central Park West
New York, NY 10023

M & I Music Publishing
630 Ninth Avenue
New York, NY 10036
Phone: (212) 582-0210
Fax: (212) 581-1370

Madlands Publishing
P.O. Box 78423
Los Angeles, CA 90016
Phone: (213) 732-4610

Makin' It Up Music Inc.
Makin Music, Inc.
1230 17th Avenue South
Nashville, TN 37212
Phone: (615) 269-6770
Fax: (615) 385-9310

Manhattan Beach Music
1595 East 46th Street
Brooklyn, NY 11234
Phone: (718) 338-4137
Fax: (718) 338-1151
E-mail: mbmband@aol.com
http://www.manhattanbeachmusic.
    com

MusicPlace Publishing
247 Shafer Road
Coraopolis, PA 15108
Phone: (412) 264-5382
http://nanmusic.com

Northeastern Music
   Publications
Roncorp, Inc.
P.O. Box 517
Glenmoore, PA 19343
Phone: (610) 942-2370
Fax: (610) 942-2370
E-mail: info@nemusicpub.com
http://www.nemusicpub.com

Octave Music Publishing
   Corp.
521 Fifth Avenue
Suite 1700
New York, NY 1017
Phone: (212) 265-5475
Fax: (212) 268-8864

Peermusic Classical
810 Seventh Avenue
New York, NY 10019
Phone: (212) 265-3910
Fax: (212) 489-2465
E-mail: tvunderink@peermusic.
    com
http://www.peermusic.com

PerMus Percussion
   Publications, Inc.
P.O. Box 218333
Columbus, OH 43221
Phone: (614) 529-0085
Fax: 614) 529-0085
E-mail: Permus@aol.com

Polygram International
2220 Colorado Avenue
Santa Monica, CA 90404
http://new.umusic.com

The PRI Music Publishing
   Companies
810 Seventh Avenue
New York, NY 10019
Phone: (212) 333-8381
Fax: (212) 333-8194

Roncorp, Inc.
P.O. Box 724
Cherry Hill, NJ 08003
Phone: (856) 722-5993
Fax: (856) 722-9252
E-mail: roncorp@comcast.net

Santa Barbara Music
   Publishing
260 Loma Media
Santa Barbara, CA 93103
Phone: (805) 962-5800
Fax: (805) 966-7711
http://www.sbmp.com

Schaffner Publishing Co.
224 Penn Avenue
Westmont, NJ 08108
Phone: (856) 854-3760
Fax: (856) 854-5584

A. Schroeder International LLC
297 Kinderkamack Road
Oradell, NJ 07649
Phone: (201) 262-1225
Fax: (201) 262-1229

Sony / ATV Music Publishing
8 Music Square West
Nashville, TN 37203
Phone: (615) 726-8300
Fax: (615) 743-1700

Sony Pictures Music Group
10202 Washington Boulevard
Culver City, CA 90233
Phone: (310) 244-7754
Fax: (310) 244-7754

StarNET Music
P.O. Box 3717
Teaneck, NJ 07666
Phone: (201) 836-0799
Fax: (201) 836-4440

The Sparrow Corp.
P.O. Box 5010
Brentwood, TN 37024
Phone: (615) 371-6800

Tempo Music Publications, Inc.
3773 West 95th Street
Leawood, KS 66206
Phone: (913) 381-5088
Fax: (913) 381-5081

Third Story Music, Inc.
Cohen & Cohen
740 North La Brea Avenue
Los Angeles, CA 90038
Phone: (323) 938-5000
Fax: (323) 936-6354

Thorpe Music Publishing
28 Dwight Street
Boston, MA 02118
Phone: (617) 426-8806
http://www.thorpemsic.com

Transcontinental Music Publications
633 Third Avenue
New York, NY 10017
Phone: (212) 650-4103
Fax: (212) 650-4119
http://www.etranscon.com

TRO Inc. (The Richmond Organization)
266 West 37th Street
New York, NY 10018
Phone: (212) 594-9795
Fax: (212) 594-9782
E-mail: copyright@songways.com

Universal Edition, Inc.
254 West 31st Street
New York, NY 10001
Phone: (212) 461-6953
Fax: (212) 810-4565
http://www.universaledition.com

Universal Music Publishing Group
2440 Sepulveda Boulevard
Los Angeles, CA 90064
Phone: (310) 235-4700
http://www.umusicpub.com

Warner/Belwin
P.O. Box 10003
Van Nuys, CA 91410
Phone: (818) 891-5999
http://www.alfred.com

Warner/Chappell Music, Inc.
10585 Santa Monica Boulevard
Los Angeles, CA 90025
http://www.warnerchappell.com

Waylon Jennings Music
1117 17th Avenue South
Nashville, TN 37212
Phone: (615) 329-9180
Fax: (615) 321-5747

Wild Cherry Music
5602 East Oakhurst Way
Scottsdale, AZ 85254
Phone: (602) 483-8551
Fax: (602) 438-8482

APPENDIX VII
RIGHTS SOCIETIES

A. RECORDING RIGHTS SOCIETIES

The following is a listing of societies that secure recording rights to music. Addresses, phone and fax numbers, e-mail addresses, and Web sites have been included when available to make it easier for you to obtain information.

American Mechanical Rights Association (AMRA)
149 South Barrington Avenue
Los Angeles, CA 90049
Phone: (310) 440-8778
Fax: (310) 440-0059
E-mail: info@amermechrights.com
http://www.amermechrights.com

Harry Fox Agency, Inc
601 West 26th Street
New York, NY 10001
Phone: (212) 370-5330
Fax: (646) 487-6779
E-mail: scotte@harryfox.com
http://www.harryfox.com

SESAC (Headquarters)
55 Music Square East
Nashville, TN 37203
Phone: (615) 320-0055
Fax: (615) 329-9627

E-mail: aperez@sesac.com
http://www.sesac.com

SESAC—Atlanta
981 Joseph East Lowery Boulevard, NW
Atlanta, GA 30318
Phone: (404) 897-1330
http://www.sesac.com

SESAC—Los Angeles
501 Santa Monica Boulevard
Santa Monica, CA 90401
Phone: (310) 393-9671
Fax: (310) 393-6497

SESAC—Miami
420 Lincoln Road ,
Miami, FL 33139
Phone: (305) 534-7500
E-mail: kcordova@sesac.com
http://www.sesac.com

SESAC—New York
152 West 57th Street
New York, NY 10019
Phone: (212) 586-3450
Fax: (212) 489-5699
E-mail: LLorence@sesac.com
http://www.sesac.com

SESAC, Inc.
510 Santa Monica Boulevard
Santa Monica, CA 90401
Phone: (310) 393-9671
Fax: (310) 393-6497
http://www.sesac.com/

SESAC International
67 Upper Berkeley Street
London W1H 7QX
England
Phone: 0207 616 9284
Fax: 0207 563 702

B. PERFORMING RIGHTS SOCIETIES

The following is a listing of societies that secure performance rights for music.

ASCAP (American Society of Composers, Authors and Publishers)—Atlanta
541 10th Street Northwest
Atlanta, GA 30318
Phone: (404) 635-1758
Fax: (404) 627-2404
E-mail: info@ascap.com
http://www.ascap.com

ASCAP (American Society of Composers, Authors and Publishers)—Chicago
1608 North Milwaukee
Chicago, IL 60647
Phone: (773) 394-4286
Fax: (773) 394-5639
E-mail: info@ascap.com
http://www.ascap.com

ASCAP (American Society of Composers, Authors and Publishers)—Los Angeles
7920 West Sunset Boulevard
Los Angeles, CA 90046
Phone: (323) 883-1000
Fax: (323) 883- 1049
E-mail: info@ascap.com
http://www.ascap.com

ASCAP (American Society of
Composers, Authors and
Publishers)—Miami
420 Lincoln Road
Miami Beach, FL 33139
Phone: (305) 673-3446
Fax: (305) 673-2446
E-mail: info@ascap.com
http://www.ascap.com

ASCAP (American Society of
Composers, Authors and
Publishers)—Nashville
2 Music Square West
Nashville, TN 37203
Phone: (615) 742-5000
Fax: (615) 742- 5020
E-mail: info@ascap.com
http://www.ascap.com

American Society of Composers,
Authors and Publishers
(ASCAP)—New York
1 Lincoln Plaza
New York, NY 10023
Phone: (212) 621-6000
Fax: (212) 724-9064
E-mail: info@ascap.com
http://www.ascap.com

ASCAP (American Society of
Composers, Authors and
Publishers)—Puerto Rico
623 Hillside St. Martinez Nadal
    Avenue
San Juan, Puerto Rico 00920
Phone: (787) 707-0782
Fax: (787) 707-0783
E-mail: info@ascap.com
http://www.ascap.com

BMI (Broadcast Music Inc.)—
Atlanta
3340 Peachtree Road, NE
Suite 570
Atlanta, GA 30326
Phone: (404) 261-5151
Fax: (404) 261-5152
E-mail: atlantaintern@bmi.com
http://www.bmi.com

BMI (Broadcast Music Inc.)—
London
84 Harley House
Marylebone Road
London NW1 5HN
England
Phone: 44-207-486-2036
Fax: 44-207-224-1046
E-mail: london@bmi.com
http://www.bmi.com

BMI (Broadcast Music Inc.)—
Los Angeles
8730 Sunset Boulevard
West Hollywood, CA 90069
Phone: (310) 659-9109
Fax: (310) 657-6947
E-mail: losangeles@bmi.com
http://www.bmi.com

BMI (Broadcast Music Inc.)—
Miami
5201 Blue Lagoon Drive
Miami, FL 33126
Phone: (305) 266-3636
Fax: (305) 266-2442
E-mail: latin@bmi.com
http://www.bmi.com

BMI (Broadcast Music, Inc.)—
Nashville
10 Music Square East
Nashville, TN 37203
Phone: (615) 401-2000
Fax: (615) 401-2707
E-mail: nashville@bmi.com
http://www.bmi.com

BMI (Broadcast Music Inc.)—
New York
320 West 57th Street
New York, NY 10019
Phone: (212) 586-2000
Fax: (212) 582-5972
E-mail: newyork@bmi.com
http://www.bmi.com

SESAC (Headquarters)
55 Music Square East
Nashville, TN 37203
Phone: (615) 320-0055
Fax: (615) 329-9627
E-mail: aperez@sesac.com
http://www.sesac.com

SESAC, Inc.
510 Santa Monica Boulevard
Santa Monica, CA 90401
Phone: (310) 393-9671
Fax: (310) 393-6497
http://www.sesac.com/

SESAC—New York
152 West 57th Street
New York, NY 10019
Phone: (212) 586-3450
Fax: (212) 489-5699
E-mail: LLorence@sesac.com
http://www.sesac.com

APPENDIX VIII
PUBLIC RELATIONS AND PUBLICITY FIRMS

The following is a listing of selected public relations and publicity firms handling music and/or entertainment clients. This list is just a beginning. There are many other public relations companies and independent publicists located throughout the country.

For additional names either surf the net or check the Yellow Pages of your local phone book under "Public Relations" or "Publicists." Due to space limitations every public relations and publicity firm could not be included here. Inclusion or exclusion in this list does not indicate any one public relations or publicity firm is recommended or endorsed over another.

Asbury Communications
9615 Brighton Way
Beverly Hills, CA 90210
Phone: (310) 859-1831
Fax: (310) 859-9658
E-mail: asburypr@aol.com
http://www.asburypr.com

Alison Aurbach Public Relations
3314 West End Avenue
Nashville, TN 37203
Phone: (615) 259-6440
Fax: (615) 259-8979
E-mail: alisonapr@aol.com

D Baron Media Relations, Inc.
1411 Cloverfield Boulevard
Santa Monica, CA 90404
Phone: (310) 315-5444
Fax: (310) 315-5474
E-mail: info@dbaronmedia.com
http://www.dbaronmedia.com

Bender/Helper Impact
11500 West Olympic Boulevard
Los Angeles, CA 90064
Phone: (310) 473-4147
Fax: (310) 689-6601
E-mail: info@bhimpact.com
http://www.bhimpact.com

Bender/Helper Impact
115 West 30th Street

New York, NY 10001
Phone: (212) 689-6360
Fax: (212) 689-6601
E-mail: info@bhimpact.com
http://www.bhimpact.com

Biz 3 Publicity
1321 North Milwaukee Avenue
Chicago, IL 60622
Phone: (773) 384-0426
Fax: (773) 384-0426
E-mail: info@biz3.net
http://www.biz3.net

Michael Bloom Media Relations
P.O. Box 41380
Los Angeles, CA 90041
Phone: (323) 258-6342
E-mail: musicpr@earthlink.net

Eric Bollinger Associates
P.O. Box 57227
Sherman Oaks, CA 91413
Phone: (818) 784-0534
Fax: (818) 789-8862
E-mail: henri@bollingerpr.com
http://www.bollingerpr.com

Brokaw Company
9255 Sunset Boulevard
Los Angeles, CA 90069
Phone: (310) 273-2060
Fax: (310) 276-4037

E-mail: brokaw@aol.com
http://www.brokawcompany.com

Catalano Public Relations
1 Central Street
Stoneham, MA 02180
Phone: (781) 438-4640
Fax: (781) 438-4643
E-mail: catalanopr#aol.com

DMG Public Relations
P.O. Box 2888
Malibu, CA 90265
Phone: (818) 506-8534
Fax: (818) 506-8534
E-mail: dmgpublicrelations@
    ppzmi.com
http://www.ppizmi.com

Dassinger Creative
172 Second Avenue
Little Falls, NJ 07424
Phone: (973) 890-1008
Fax: (973) 890-1009
E-mail: gdassinger@yahoo.com

Edelman
5670 Wilshire Boulevard
Los Angeles, CA 90036
Phone: (323) 857-9117
Fax: (323) 857-9117
E-mail: los.angeles@edelman.com
http://www.edelman.com

Front Page Publicity
4505 Indiana Avenue
Nashville, TN 37209
Phone: (615) 523-1347
Fax: (615) 523-1347
E-mail: kathyfrontpagepublicity.
com
http://www.frontpagepublicity.com

Glodow Nead Communications
1700 Montgomery Street
San Francisco, CA 94111
Phone: (415) 394-6500
Fax: (415) 403-9060
E-mail: info@glodownead.com
http://www.glodownead.com

Gurley & Company
P.O. Box 150657
Nashville, TN 37215
Phone: (615) 269-0474
E-mail: cathy@gurleybiz.com
http://www.gurleybiz.com

Gurtman & Murtha Associates
450 Seventh Avenue
New York, NY 10123
Phone: (212) 967-7350
Fax: (212) 967-7341
E-mail: gmartusts@aol.com
http://www.gurtmanandmurtha.
com

Hill & Knowlton, Inc.
607 14th Street, NW
Washington, DC 20005
Phone: (202) 333-7400
Fax: (202) 333-1638
http://www.hillandknowlton.
com/us

The Holley-Guidry Company
P.O. Box 121661
Nashville, TN 37212
Phone: (615) 460-9550
Fax: (615) 460-9553
E-mail: Debbie@holleyguidry.com

The Honig Company, Inc.
3500 West Olive Avenue
Burbank, CA 91505
Phone: (818) 986-4300
Fax: (818) 981-3141

E-mail: info@honigcompany.com
http://www.honigcompany.com

Hot Schatz Public Relations
1024 16th Avenue South
Nashville, TN 37212
Phone: (615) 782-0078
Fax: (615) 782-0088
E-mail: info@hotschatzpr.com
http://www.hotschatzpr.com

Jenson Communications
709 East Colorado Boulevard
Pasadena, CA 91101
Phone: (626) 585-9575
Fax: (626) 564-920
E-mail: info@jensen.com
http://www.jensencom.com

Little Ritchie Johnson Agency
318 Horizon Vista Boulevard
Belen, NM 87002
Phone: (505) 864-7441
Fax: (505) 864-7442

Dan Klores Communications
388 Park Avenue South
New York, NY 10016
Phone: (212) 685-4300
Fax: (212) 685-9024
E-mail: contact@dkcnews.com
http://www.dkcnews.com

Levinson Associates
1440 Veteran Avenue
Los Angeles, CA 90024
Phone: (323) 663-6940
Fax: (323) 663-2820
E-mail: levinc@aol.com
http://www.robertslevinson.com

The Lippin Group
6100 Wilshire Boulevard
Los Angeles, CA 90048
Phone: (323) 965-1990
Fax: (323) 525-1929
E-mail: losangeles,@lippingroup.
com
http://www.lippingroup.com

The Lippin Group
369 Lexington Avenue
New York, NY 10017

Phone: (212) 986-7080
Fax: (212) 986-2354
E-mail: newyork@lippingroup.com
http://www.lippingroup.com

Magnup PR
32 East 31st Street
New York, NY 10016
Phone: (212) 532-4650
Fax: (212) 532-6535
E-mail: office@magnumpr.net
http://www.magnumpr.net

McCain & Co Public Relations
1318 Riverwood Drive
Nashville, TN 37216
Phone: (615) 262-1727
Fax: (615) 262-0058
E-mail: mccainprnews@mccainpr.
com
http://www.mccainpr.com

**Miller Wright & Associates,
Inc.**
1650 Broadway
New York, NY 10019
Phone: (212) 977-7800
Fax: (212) 977-7963
E-mail: miller@millerwright.com
http://www.millerwright.com

Mixed Media
20 Lockmere Road
Cranston, RI 02910
Phone: (401) 942-8025
Fax: (401) 943-1915
E-mail: mixedmediapromo@cox.
net
http://www.mixedmediapromo.com

Nashville Publicity Group
P.O. Box 291705
Nashville, TN 37229
Phone: (615) 417-8149
Fax: (615) 523-1831
E-mail: brian@nashvillepublicity.
com
http://www.nashvillepublicity.com

**Porter/Novelli Public
Relations**
10960 Wilshire Boulevard
Los Angeles, CA 90024

Phone: (310) 444-7000
Fax: (310) 444-7004
E-mail: bkolberg@porternovelli.com

The Press Office
1009 16th Avenue South
Nashville, TN 37212
Phone: (615) 750-5938
Fax: (615) 810-9492
http://www.thepressofice.com

PRP
12701 Landale Street
Studio City, CA 91604
Phone: (818) 766-0442
Fax: (818) 766-1644
E-mail: prgroup@aol.com
http://www.prgroup.net

Rogers & Cowan
919 Third Avenue
New York, NY 10022
Phone: (212) 445-8400

Fax: (212) 445-8406
E-mail: inquires@rogersandcowan.
com
http://www.rogersandcowan.com

Rogers & Cowan
Pacific Design Center
8687 Mellrose Avenue
Hollywood, CA 90069
Phone: (310) 854-8100
Fax: (310) 854-8101
E-mail: inquires@rogersandcowan.
com
http://www.rogersandcowan.com

Rubinstein Associates, Inc.
1345 Avenue of the Americas
New York, NY 10105
Phone: (212) 843-8000
Fax: (212) 843-9200
E-mail: info@rubenstein.com
http://www.rubenstein.com

Shelly Field Organization
P.O. Box 711
Monticello, NY 12701
Phone: (845) 794-7312
http://www.shellyfield.com

Solters & Digney
1680 North Vine Street
Hollywood, CA 90028
Phone: (323) 993-3000
Fax: (323) 469-2115
E-mail: lee&solterspr.com
http://www.solterspr.com

**Webster & Associates Public
Relations**
P.O. Box 23015
Nashville, TN 37202
Phone: (615) 777-6995
Fax: (615) 369-2515
E-mail: info@websterpr.com
http://www.websterpr.com

APPENDIX IX
ENTERTAINMENT INDUSTRY ATTORNEYS AND LAW FIRMS

The following is a listing of attorneys and law firms handling music and/or entertainment issues and clients. There are many other law firms and attorneys who specialize in music and entertainment law throughout the country. Check out the Yellow Pages of the phone book, surf the net, or contact your local or state bar association for other names.

This listing is provided for informational purposes only. Inclusion or exclusion does not constitute the recommendation or endorsement of any one attorney or law firm by the author.

Daniel J. Aaron, PC
437 Madison Avenue
New York, NY 10022
Phone: (212) 684-4466
Fax: (212) 684-5566
http://www.djaaronlaw.com

Abrams Garfinkel Margolis Bergson, LLP
237 West 35th Street
New York, NY 10001
Phone: (212) 201-1170
Fax: (212) 201-1171
http://www.agmblaw.com

Ira Abrams
5692B Fox Hollow Drive
Boca Raton, FL 33486
Phone: (828) 262-9944
Fax: (828) 262-9901

Adams & Reece, LLP
One Shell Square
Poydras Streeet
New Orleans, LA 70139
Phone: (504) 581-3234
Fax: (504) 566-0210
http://www.adamsandreece.com

Akin Gump Strauss Hauer & Feld, LLP
2029 Century Park East
Los Angeles, CA 90067
Phone: (310) 229-1000

Fax: (310) 229-1001
http://www.akingump.com

Stephen Baerwitz
10940 Wilshire Boulevard
Los Angeles, CA 90024
Phone: (310) 443-4243
Fax: (310) 443-4263

Baker & Hosteller, LLP
12100 Wilshire Boulevard
Los Angeles, CA 90025
Phone: (310) 820-8800
Fax: (310) 820-8859
http://www.bakerlaw.com

Baker and Kelley
1227 17th Avenue South
Nashville, TN 37212
Phone: (615) 329-0900
Fax: (615) 329-2148
http://www.rowlawyers.com

Barnes Morris Klein Mark York Barnes & Levine
2000 Avenue of the Stars
Los Angeles, CA 90067
Phone: (310) 319-3900
Fax: (310) 319-3999
http://www.brnkylaw.com

Beitchman & Hudson
215 14th Street, NW
Atlanta, GA 30318

Phone: (404) 897-5252
Fax: (404) 897-5677
http://www.arts-entertainmentlaw. com

Beldock, Levine & Hoffman, LLP
99 Park Avenue
New York, NY 0016
Phone: (212) 490-0400
Fax: (212) 557-0565
http://www.blhny.com

Berger Kahn
4551 Glencoe Avenue
Marina del Rey, CA 90292
Phone: (310) 821-9000
Fax: (310) 775-8775
http://www.bergerkahn.com

Berliner, Corcoran & Rowe, LLP
1101 17th Street, NW
Washington, DC 20036
Phone: (202) 293-5555
Fax: (202) 293-9035
http://www.bcr.us

Berman Entertainment and Technology Law
235 Montgomery Street
San Francisco, CA 94104
Phone: (415) 421-0730
Fax: (415) 421-2355
http://www.beat-law.com

Blecher & Collins, PC
515 South Figueroa
Los Angeles, CA 90071
Phone: (213) 622-4222
Fax: (213) 622-1656
http://www.blechercollins.com

Blindman & Uram
630 Third Avenue
New York, NY 10017
Phone: (212) 867-9595
Fax: (212) 949-1857

Boles, Schiller & Flexner, LLP
100 Southeast Second Street
Miami, FL 33131
Phone: (305) 539-8400
Fax: (305) 539-1307
http://www.bsflip.com

Boult, Cummings, Conners & Berry, PLC
100 Division Street
Nashville, TN 37203
Phone: (615) 244-2582
Fax: (615) 252-6380
http://www.bccb.com

Joel Brooks & Associates, P.C.
1500 Broadway
New York, NY 10036
Phone: (212) 730-8015

California Lawyers for the Arts
1641 18th Stret
Santa Monica, CA 90404
Phone: (310) 998-5590
Fax: (310) 998-5594
http://www.calalawyersforthearts.
    org

Carroll, Guildo & Groffman, LLP
9111 Sunset Boulevard
West Hollywood
Los Angeles, CA 90069
Phone: (310) 271-0241
Fax: (310) 271-0775
http://www.ccgglaw.com

Robert A. Celestin, Esquire
250 West 57th Street
New York, NY 100107

Phone: (212) 262-1103
Fax: (212) 262-1173
http://www.raclawfirm.com

Cowan, Liebowitz, & Latman, PC
1133 Avenue of the Americas
New York, NY 10026
Phone: (212) 790-9200
Fax: (212) 575-0671
http://www.cll.com

DLA Piper US, LLP
1251 Avenue of the Americas
New York, NY 10020
Phone: (212) 835-6000
Fax: (212) 335-4501
http://www.dapiper.com

Davis Shapiro Lewit Montone & Hayes, LLP
150 South Road
Beverly Hills, CA 90212
Phone: (310) 248-3400
Fax: (310) 278-4457
http://www.davisshapiro.com

Davis Shapiro Lewit Montone & Hayes LLP
689 Fifth Avenue
New York, NY 10022
Phone: (212) 813-1204
Fax: (212) 230-5500
http://www.davisshapiro.com

Day & Blair, PC
5300 Maryland Way
Brentwood, TN 37027
Phone: (615) 742-4880
Fax: (615) 742-4881
http://www.dayblair.com

DeFree & Fiske, LLC
200 South Michigan Avenue
Chicago, IL. 60604
Phone: (312) 372-4000
Fax: (312) 939-5617
http://www.defrees.com

Dewey & LeBouf, LLP
125 West 55th Street
New York, NY 10019
Phone: (212) 424-8000

Fax: (212) 424-8500
http://www.deweyleboeuf.com

Diamond & Wilson
12304 Santa Monica Boulevard
Los Angeles, CA 90025
Phone: (312) 820-7808

DiJulio Law Group
100 West Broadway
Glendale, CA 91210
Phone: (818) 502-1700
Fax: (818) 500-8799
http://www.jijuliolawgroup.com

Edelstein, Laird & Sobel, LLP
9255 Sunset Boulevard
Los Angels, CA 90069
Phone: (310) 274-6184
Fax: (310) 274-6185
http://www.elsentlaw.com

Entertainment Law Chicago, PC
915 West Carmen Avenue
Chicago, IL 60640
Phone: (773) 682-4912
http://www.
    enterertainmentlawchicao.com

Epstein, Levinson, Bodine, Hurwitz& Weinstein, LLP
1790 Broadway
New York, NY 10019
Phone: (212) 262-5022
http://www.entlawfirm.com

Eris Weisman Music Licensing, Inc.
500 Seventh Avenue
New York, NY 10018
Phone: (212) 707-8804
Fax: (212) 707-8952

Eskridge & Eskridge
100 North Main Street
Memphis, TN 38103
Phone: (901) 522-9600
Fax: (901) 276-3800
http://www.eskridgelaw.com

Fish & Richardson, PC
225 Franklin Street

Boston, MA 02110
Phone: (617) 368-2121
Fax: (617) 542-8906

Fox Law Group, PC
14724 Ventura Boulevard
Sherman Oaks, CA 91403
Phone: (818) 461-1740
Fax: (818) 461-1744
http://www.foxlawgroup.com

Frankfurt Kurnit Klein & Selz
488 Madison Avenue
New York, NY 10022
Phone: (212) 980-0120
Fax: (212) 593-9175
http://www.fkks.com

Franklin, Weinrib, Rudell & Vassallo, PC
488 Madison Avenue
New York, NY 10022
Phone: (212) 935-5500
Fax: (212) 308-0642
http://www.fwrv.com

Gang, Tyre, Ramer & Brown, Inc.
132 South Rodeo Drive
Beverly Hills, CA 90212
Phone: (310) 777-4800
Fax: (310) 777-4801

Norman Gillis & Associates Law Offices
11 Music Circle South
Nashville, TN 37203
Phone: (615) 320-1332
Fax: (615) 320-8651
http://www.musicrowlaw.com

Goldring, Hertz, Lichenstein, LLP
450 North Roxbury Drive
Beverly Hills, CA 90210
Phone: (310) 271-8777
Fax: (310) 550-5232

Steve Gordon Law
41 River Terrace
New York, NY 10282
Phone: (212) 924-1166

Fax: (212) 924-4150
http://www.stevegordon.law.com

Green & Green
1 Embarcadero Center
San Francisco, CA 94111
Phone: (415) 457-8300
Fax: (415) 457-8757
http://www.musiclawyer.com

Green & Green
Courthouse Square
1000 Fourth Street
San Rafael, CA 94901
Phone: (415) 457-8300
Fax: (415) 457-8757
http://www.musiclawyer.com

Greenberg Glusker
1900 Avenue of the Stars
Los Angeles, CA 90067
Phone: (310) 553-3610
Fax: (310) 553-0687
http://www.ggfirm.com

Greenberg Traurig, LLP
The Forum
3290 Northside Parkway
Atlanta, GA 30327
Phone: (678) 553-2199
Fax: (678) 553-0687
http://www.gtlaw.com

Greenberg Traurig, LLP
2450 Colorado Avenue
Santa Monica, CA 90404
Phone: (310) 586-7700
Fax: (310) 586-7800
http://www.gtlaw.com

Greenberg Traurig, LLP
Met Life Building
200 Park Avenue
New York, NY 10166
Phone: (212) 801-9200
Fax: (212) 801-6400
http://www.gtlaw.com

Greenberg Traurig, LLP
3773 Howard Hughes Parkway
Las Vegas, NV 89169
Phone: (702) 792-3773
Fax: (702) 792-9002
http://www.gtlaw.com

Gruman Indurksy & Shire, PC
152 West 57th Street
New York, NY 10019
Phone: (212) 554-0400
Fax: (212) 554-0444

Hall, Booth, Smith & Slover, PC
Atlantic Center Plaza
1180 West Peachtree, NW
Atlanta, GA 30309
Phone: (404) 954-5000
Fax: (404) 954-5020
http://www.hbss.net

Hall, Booth, Smith & Slover, PC
The Tower
611 Commerce Street
Nashville, TN 38203
Phone: (615) 313-9913
Fax: (615) 313-8008

Hamburg, Karic, Edwards & Martin, LLP
1900 Avenue of the Stars
Los Angeles, CA 90067
Phone: (310) 552-9292
Fax: (310) 552-9291
http://www.hkemlaw.com

Harke & Clasby, LLP
155 South Miami Avenue
Miami, FL 33130
Phone: (305) 536-8220
Fax: (305) 536-8229
http://www.harkeclasby.com

Harris, Martin, Jones, Shrum, Bradford & Wommack, PA
49 Music Square West
Nashville, TN 37303
Phone: (615) 321-5400
Fax: (615) 321-5469
http://www.rowlaw.com

Heller Ehrman, LLP
333 South Hope Street
Los Angeles, CA 90071
Phone: (213) 689-0200
Fax: (213) 614-1868
http://www.hellerehrman.com

Holland & Knight, LLP
131 South Dearborn Street
Chicago, IL 60603
Phone: (312) 263-3600
Fax: (312) 578-6666
http://www.hklaw.com

Holland & Knight, LLP
701 Bricknell Avenue
Miami, FL 33131
Phone: (305) 374-8500
Fax: (305) 374-789-7799
http://www.hkklaw.com

HRbek Law
60 Broad Street
New York, NY 10004
Phone: (212) 480-2553
Fax: (212) 480-2353
http://www.hrbeklaw.com

Paul W. Isinna, Esquire
286 Hall Avenue
White Plains, NY 10604
Phone: (914) 686-3414

Isaacman, Kaufman& Painter, PC
8484 Wilshire Boulevard
Beverly Hills, CA 90211
Phone: (323) 782-7700
Fax: (323) 782-7744
http://www.ikplaw.com

Jacobson & Colfin, PC
60 Madison Avenue
New York, NY 10010
Phone: (212) 691-5830
Fax: (212) 645-5038
http://www.thefirm.com

Janvey, Gordon, Herlands, Randolph & Cox, LLP
355 Lexington Avenue
New York, NY 10017
Phone: (212) 986-1200
Fax: (212) 983-0772
http://www.janveygordon.com

Jenner & Block
1099 New York Avenue
Washington, DC 20001
Phone: (202) 639-6000

Fax: (202) 639-6066
http://www.jenner.com

Johnson & Johnson, LLP
439 North Canon Drive
Beverly Hills, CA 90210
Phone: (310) 975-1090
Fax: (310) 975-1095
http://www.jillplaw.com

Johnston Barton Proctor & Rose, LLP
569 Brookwood Village
Birmingham, AL 35209
Phone: (205) 458-9400
Fax: (205) 458-9500
http://www.johstonbarton.com

Kauff, McClain & McGuire
950 Third Avenue
New York, NY 10022
Phone: (212) 644-1010
Fax: (212) 644-1946
http://www.kmm.com

Kenyon & Kenyon, LLP
1 Broadway
New York, NY 10004
Phone: (212) 425-7200
Fax: (212) 425-6288
http://www.kenyon.com

King & Ballow
1100 Union Street Plaza 315
Union Street
Nashville, TN 37201
Phone: (615) 259-3456
Fax: (615) 254-7907
http://www.kingballow.com

LaPolt Law, PC
9000 Sunset Boulevard
West Hollywood, CA 90069
Phone: (310) 858-0922
Fax: (310) 858-0933
http://www.lapoltlaw.com

Lassiter, Tidwell, Davis, Keller & Hogan, PLC
150 Fourth Avenue North
Nashville, TN 37219
Phone: (615) 259-9344
Fax: (615) 690-4768
http://www.lassiterlaw.com

Jerry Lastelick, Esquire
8111 Preston Road
Dallas, TX 75225
Phone: (214) 360-0338
Fax: (214) 360-9038

Lathrop & Gage
10 South Broadway
Saint Louis, MO 63102
Phone: (314) 613-2500
Fax: (314) 613-2559
http://www.lathropgage.com

Lawrence Lighter, Attorney at Law
488 Madison Avenue
New York, NY 10022
Phone: (212) 371-8730
Fax: (212) 753-3630

Loeb & Loeb
321 North Clark Street
Chicago, IL 60654
Phone: (312) 464-3100
Fax: (312) 464-3111
http://www.loeb.com

Loeb & Loeb
10100 Santa Monica Boulevard
Los Angeles, CA 90067
Phone: (310) 282-2000
Fax: (310) 282-2200
http://www.loeb.com

Loeb & Loeb
1906 Acken Avenue
Nashville, TN 37212
Phone: (615) 749-8300
Fax: (615) 749-8308
http://www.loeb.com

Loeb & Loeb
345 Park Avenue
New York, NY 10154
Phone: (212) 407-4000
Fax: (212) 407-4990
http://www.loeb.com

Lyon & Phillips, PLC
11 Music City Circle South
Nashville, TN 37203
Phone: (615) 259-4664
Fax: (615) 259-4668

Manatt, Phelps & Phillips, LLP
11355 West Olympic Boulevard
Los Angeles, CA 90064
Phone: (310) 312-4000
Fax: (310) 312-4224
http://www.manatt.com

Manatt, Phelps, & Phillips, LLP
7 Times Square
New York, NY 10036
Phone: (212) 790-4500
Fax: (212) 790-4545
http://www.manatt.com

Mason Miller, LLP
2121 Avenue of the Stars
Los Angeles, CA 90067
Phone: (310) 424-1120
Fax: (310) 424-1121
http:///www.masonmillerllp.com

Masur & Associates
101 East 15th Street
New York, NY 10003
Phone: (212) 931-8220
Fax: (212) 931-8221
http://www.masurlaw.com

Mayer & Glassman Law Corporation
12400 Wilshire Boulevard
Los Angeles, CA 90025
Phone: (310) 207-0007
Fax: (310) 207-3578
http://www.mglawcorp.com

McLaughlin & Stern, LLP
260 Madison Avenue
New York, NY 10016
Phone: (212) 448-1100
Fax: (212) 448-0066
http://www.mclaughlinstern.com

Alexander Murphy, Jr., Esquire
912 Adams Way
West Chester, PA 19382
Phone: (810) 399-9033
Fax: (810) 399-4417

Ober Kaier
120 East Baltimore Street
Baltimore, MD 21202
Phone: (410) 347-7388

Fax: (410) 547-0699
http://www.ober.com

Olshan Grundman Fromo Rosenzweig & Wolosky, LLP
65 East 55th Street
New York, NY 10022
Phone: (212) 451-2321
Fax: (212) 451-2222
http://www.olshanlaw.com

O'Melveny & Myers, LLP
Times Square Tower
7 Times Square
New York, NY 10036
Phone: (212) 326-2000
Fax: (212) 326-2061
http://www.omm.com

O'Melveny & Myers, LLP
1999 Avenue of the Stars
Los Angeles, CA 90067
Phone: (310) 553-6700
Fax: (310) 246-6779
http://www.omm.com

The Music Law Group, LLC
250 West 57th Street
New York, NY 10107
Phone: (212) 245-4125
Fax: (212) 245-6293
http://www.themusiclawgroup.com

Orrick, Harrington & Sutcliffe, LLP
777 South Figueroa Street
Los Angeles, CA 90017
Phone: (213) 629-2020
Fax: (213) 612-2499
http://www.orrick.com

Orrick, Harrington & Sutcliffe, LLP
666 Fifth Avenue
New York, NY 10103
Phone: (212) 506-5000
Fax: (212) 506-5151
http://www.orick.com

Paul Weiss, Rifkind, Wharton & Garrison
1285 Avenue of the Americas
New York, NY 10019
Phone: (212) 373-3000
Fax: (212) 757-3990
http://www.paulweiss.com

Tobias Pieniek, PC
515 Madison Avenue
New York, NY 10022
Phone: (212) 339-8930
Fax: (212) 339-8927

Pullman Group, LLC
1370 Avenue of the Americas
New York, NY 100019
Phone: (212) 750-0210
Fax: (212) 750-0464
http://www.pullmanbonds.com

Reed Smith, LLP
1901 Avenue of the Stars
Century City, CA 09967
Phone: (310) 734-5200
Fax: (310) 734-5299
http://www.reedsmith.com

Glenn C. Romano, PC
7948 Oxford Avenue
Philadelphia, PA 19111
Phone: (215) 742-0592
Fax: (215) 742-3892
http://www.glennromano.com

Matthew G. Rosenberger, Esquire
1 Summit Street
Philadelphia, PA 19118
Phone: (215) 242-9510
Fax: (215) 242-9421

Scott D. Sanders, PC
21 Eighth Street, NE
Atlanta, GA 30309
Phone: (404) 873-4422
Fax: (404) 873-4480
http://www.entlaw.com

Daniel Schiffman, Esquire
903 Park Avenue
New York, NY 10075
Phone: (212) 628-6433
http://www.schiffman.us

Serling, Rooks & Ferrara, LLP
119 Fifth Avenue
New York, NY 10003
Phone: (212) 245-7300
Fax: (212) 586-5175
http://www.srslip.com

Shaheen & Gordon, PA
107 Storrs Street
Concord, NH 03302
Phone: (603) 225-7262
Fax: (603) 225-5112
http://www.shaheengordon.com

Steele & Utz
1700 Pennsylvania Avenue, NW
Washington, DC 20006
Phone: (202) 785-2130
Fax: (202) 351-6866

Bernard Stollman Esquire
646 East 14th Street
New York, NY 10009
Phone: (212) 979-0590
Fax: (212) 995-5422

Sullivan & Worcester
1290 Avenue of the Americas
New York, NY 10104
Phone: (212) 660-3000
Fax: (212) 660-3001

Weil, Gotshal & Manges, LLP
767 Fifth Avenue
New York, NY 10153
Phone: (212) 310-8000
Fax: (212) 310-8007
http://www.weil.com

White, Fleischner & Fine
61 Broadway
New York, NY 10006
Phone: (212) 487-9700
Fax: (212) 487-9777
http://www.wff-law.com

Ziffren, Brittenham, Branca, Fischer, Gilbert-Lurie, Stieffelman, Cook, Johnson, Lande & Wolf, PLC
1801 Century Park West
Los Angeles, CA 90067
Phone: (310) 552-3388
Fax: (310) 553-7068

APPENDIX X
MUSIC-RELATED WEB SITES

The Internet is a premier resource for information. Surfing the net can help you locate almost anything you want. Throughout the appendixes of this book, whenever possible, Web site addresses have been included to help you find information quicker. This listing contains an assortment of various music-related sites that may be of value to you in your career.

Use this list as a start. There are literally thousands of sites related to the music business and more emerging every day. This listing is for your information. The author is not responsible for any site content. Inclusion or exclusion in this listing does not signify any one site is endorsed or recommended over another by the author.

A&R Worldwide
http://www.anrworld.com

AccessMyMusic
http://www.accessmymusic.com

Aiding & Abetting
http://www.aidabet.com

All Indies
http://www.allindies.com

All Media Guide
http://www.allmediaguide.com

All Music Industry Contacts
http://www.allmusicindustry
    contacts.com

Allied Artists
http://www.alliedartists.com

Amazon.com
http://www.amazon.com

American Federation of Musicians
http://www.afm.org

American Music Showcase
http://www.americanmusicshow
    case.com

ARTISTdirect
http://www.artistdirect.com

ASCAP
http://www.ascap.com

Association of Music Writers and Photographers
http://www.musicjournlists.com

Backstagecommerce.com
http://www.backstagecommerce.com

Backstage World
http://www.backstageworld.com

Bandname.com
http://www.bandname.com

Bands 4 Bands
http://www.bands4bands.com

bandsforlabels.com
http://www.bandsforlabels.com

Bandzoogle.com
http://www.banzoogle.com

Bathtub Music
http://www.bathtubmusic.com

Berklee Music
http://www.berkleemusic.com

Billboard
http://www.billboard.com

Billboard.biz
http://www.billboard.biz

BlackVibes.com
http://www.blackvibes.com

Blue Coupe
http://www.bluecoupe.com

BMI (Broadcast Music International)
http://www.bmi.org

CafePress.com
http://www.cafepress.com

CD Army
http://www.cdarmy.com

CDBaby.com
http://www.cdbaby.com

CD Replic8.com
http://www.cdreplic8.com

CDreview.com
http://www.cdreview.com

CDReviews.com
http://www.cdreviews.com

CD Street
http://www.cdstreet.com

Clickspin.com
http://www.clickspin.com

Cornerband.com
http://www.cornerband.com

CornerWorld, Inc.
http:// www1.cornerworld.com

Cosmic Radio
http://www.cosmicradio.com

CountryInterviewsOnline.net
http://www.countryinterviews online.net

Creative Musicians Coalition
http://www.aimcmc.com

degyshop.com
http://www.degyshop.com

Demoshoppers.com
http://www.demoshoppers.com

Digital Club Network
http://www.digitalclubnetwork.com

Digital Music Company
http://www.audiosurge.com

Disc Jockey 101
http://www.discjockey101.com

Disc Makers
http://www.discmakers.com

Discogs
http://www.disogs.com

Drummers World
http://www.drummersworld.org

Earbuzz.com
http://www.earbuzz.com

Entertainmentcareers.net
http://www.entertainmentcareers. net

Entertainment World Music
http://www.entertainmentworld.us

Festival Finder
http://www.festivalfinder.com

Festival Network Online
http://www.festivalnet.com

Figgle.com
http://www.figgle.com

4 Front Media and Music
http://www.4frontmusic.com

Future of Music Coalition
http://www.futureofmusic.org

Gajoob
http://www.gajoob.com

Garageband
http://www.garageband.com

Getindie.com
http://www.getindie.com

Getsigned.com
http://www.getsigned.com

Harry Fox Agency, Inc.
http://www.harryfox.com

GigAmerica.com
http://www.gigamerica.com

Gigmasters.com
http://www.gigmasters.com

Global Music Project
http://www.globalmusicproject.org

H.E.A.R. (Hearing Education and Awareness for Rockers)
http://www.hearnet.com

Harmony-Central
http://www.harmony-central.com

Hit Quarters
http://www.hitquarters.com

Host Baby
http://www.hostbaby.com

House Concerts
http://www.houseconcerts.com

iMusicWorks
http://www.imusicworks.com

Independent Distribution Network
http://www.idnmusic.com

Independent Music Network
http://www.imntv.com

Independent Online Distribution Alliance
http://www.iodalliance.com

Independent Songwriter
http://www.independent songwriter. com

Independentbands.com
http://www.independentbands.com

Indie Monkey
http://www.indiemonkey.com

Indie Music
http://www.indie-music.com

Indie Performer
http://www.indieperformer.com

Indiebiz.com
http://www.indiebiz.com

Indiepower.com
http://www.indiepower.com

Indiespace
http://www.indiespace.com
Inside Sessions
http://www.insidesessions.com

Kings of A&R
http://www.kingsofar.com

Launch Media, Inc.
http://www.launch.com

Localeyez
http://www.localeyez.com

Locals Online
http://www.localsonline.com

Los Angeles Music Productions
http://www.lamusicproductions.com

Lyrical Line
http://www.lyricalline.com

Lyrics.com
http://www.lyrics.com

Magatune
http://www.magatune.com

MHZ Networks
http://www.mhznetworks.org

Marketing Your Music
http://www.marketingyourmusic.com

ModernRock.com
http://www.modernrock.com

Mojam.com
http://www.mojam.com

Muse's Muse Songwriting Resource
http://www.musemuse.com

Music Biz Advice
http://www.musicbizadvice.com

Music Books Plus
http://www.musicbooksplus.com

MusicContracts.com
http://www.musiccontracts.com

Music Office
http://www.musicoffice.com

Music Pages
http://www.musicpages.com

Music Player Network
http://www.musicplayer.com

Music Review
http://www.musreview.com

Musician.com
http://www.guitarcenter.com

Musician's Assistance Program
http://www.map200.org

Musicians.com
http://www.musicains.com

Musicians Contact Service
http://www.musicianscontact.com

Musicians National Referral
http://www.musicianreferral.com

Musiclink
http://www.musiclink.com

Musictoday
http://wwwmusictoday.com

MusicWire
http://www.musicwire.com

National Music Publishers Association
http://www.nmpa.org

New Music Times
http://www.nmtinc.com

Nolo.com
http://www.nolo.com

Nova Music Productions
http://www.novamusic.com

Outersound
http://www.outersound.com

PasteMusic.com
http://www.pastemusic.com

Performing Biz
http://www.performingbiz.com

Pollstar.com
http://www.pollstar.com

Poplife.net
http://www.poplife.net

PowerGig
http://www.powergig.com

Professional Musicians Referral
http://www.pmr-musicians.com

Promosquad
http://www.promosquad.com

Radio and Records
http://www.radioandrecords.com

Rane Corporation
http://www.rane.com

Record Store Review
http://www.recordstorereview.com

Rock & Read Magazine
http://www.rocknread.com

Rock & Roll Library
http://www.rocklibrary.com

Roots Music Report
http://www.rootsmusicreport.com

SESAC, Inc.
http://www.sesac.com

Shelly Field
http://www.shellyfield.com

sideRoad music group
http://www.sideroadmusic.com

Society of Singers, Inc.
http://www.singers.org

Songwriter Universe
http://www.songwriteruniverse.com

Song Quarters
http://www.songquarters.com

Sonicbids
http://www.sonicbids.com

Sputnik7.com
http://www.sputnik7.com

StarPolish
http://www.starpolish.com

Stress Free Success
http://www.shellyfield.com

Studiofinder.com
http://www.studiofinder.com

Summit Artists
http://www.summitartists.com

Talkguitar
http://www.talkguitar.com

Taxi
http://www.taxi.com

The Orchard
http://www.theorchard.com

USA Musician
http://www.usamusician.com

U.S. Copyright Office
http://www.copywright.gov

U.S. Patent and Trademark Office
http://www.uspto.gov

U.S. Small Business Administration (SBA)
http://www.sba.gov

Undercurrents, Inc.
http://www.undercurrents.com

Uniform Code Council
http://www.uc-council.org

Virtual Radio.com
http://www.virtualradio.com

Westlake Audio
http://www.westlakeaudio.com

Worldwide Internet Music Resources
http://www.music.indiana.edu/
music_resources

APPENDIX XI
CAREER AND JOB WEB SITES

The Internet is a premier resource for information, no matter what you need. Surfing the Web can help you locate almost anything including valuable career information and job openings.

This listing contains an assortment of career and job oriented Web sites. Some are geared specifically to music industry while others are more general.

Use this list as a start. More sites are emerging every day. This listing is for your information. The author is not responsible for any site content. Inclusion or exclusion in this listing does not imply any one site is endorsed or recommended over another by the author.

Americas Job Bank
http://www.americasjobbank.com

Ascap Jobline
http://www.ascap.com/jobline

Careerbuilder.com
http://www.careerbuilder.com

Entertainment careers.net
http://www.entertainmentcareers.net

GetGigs.com
http://www.getgigs.com

Gigmasters
http://www.gigmasters.com

Hollywoodentertainmentjobs
http://www.hollywoodentertainmentjobs.com

Hotjobs.com
http://www.hotjobscom

Indeed.com
http://www.indeed.com

Job Monkey
http://www.jobmonkey.com

Job Openings.net
http://www.jobopenings.net

Jobster.com
http://www.jobster.com

Lawjobs.com
http://www.lawjobs.com

MENC: The National Association for Music Careers Education
http://www.menc.org/careers/view_public

Monster.com
http://www.monster.com

MTV Jobhunt
https://jobhuntweb.viacom.com/jobhunt/main/jobhome.asp

Music-Careers.com
http://www.music-careers.com

Musicians Contact
http://www.musicianscontact.com

Music Jobs Board
http://mediawebsource.com/jobsboard.htm

MyMusicjob.com
http://www.mymusicjob.com

MySpaceJobs.com
http://www.myspacejobs.com

NBC/Universal Jobs
http://www.nbcunicareers.com

Showbizjobs.com
http://www.showbizjobs.com

Simplyhired.com
http://www.simplyhired.com

SONY Music Jobs
http://jobs-sonymusic.icims.com/jobs/intro

TopUSAJobs.com
http://www.topusajobs.com

US Music Jobs
http://us.music-jobs.com

Warner Brothers Careers
http://www.warnerbroscareers.com

Warner Brothers Intern Careers
http://www.wbjobs.com/intern.html

APPENDIX XII
WORKSHOPS, SEMINARS, CONFERENCES, AND CONVENTIONS

The following is a selected listing of workshops, seminars, conferences, and conventions. This is by no means a complete listing. It is offered for your information to help you locate programs of interest to you. Inclusion or exclusion does not indicate the author endorses any one program over another. The author is additionally not responsible for subject content.

American Society of Composers, Authors and Publishers (ASCA)
1 Lincoln Plaza
New York, NY 10023
Phone: (212) 621-6000
Fax: (212) 724-9064
E-mail: info@ascap.com
http://www.ascap.com
ASCAP offers a variety of workshops for songwriters in New York City, Los Angeles, and Nashville

American Symphony Orchestra League (ASOL)
33 West 60th Street
New York, NY 10023
Phone: (212) 262-5161
Fax: (212) 262-5198
E-mail: league@symphony.org
http://www.symphony.org
The American Symphony Orchestra League offers regional workshops, seminars and symposiums in every aspect of the orchestra business and craft including orchestra management, marketing, fundraising and conducting. Their annual conferences present a variety of informative programs.

Atlantis Music Conference
Barrett Parkway
Marietta, GA 30066
Phone: (770) 499-8600
Fax: (770) 499-8650
http://www.atlanticmusic.com

The Atlantic Music Conference brings together industry professionals and artists.

Billboard Latin Music Conference & Awards
770 Broadway
New York, NY 10003
Phone: (646) 654-4660
Fax: (646) 654-4674
E-mail: bbevents@billboard.com
http://www.billboardevents.com
Billboard Latin Music Conference and Awards is held annually.

Billboard Music & Money Symposium
770 Broadway
New York, NY 10003
Phone: (646) 654-4660
Fax: (646) 654-4674
E-mail: bbevents@billboard.com
http://www.billboardevents.com
The Billboard Music and Money Symposium focuses on finances in the music industry. The event brings together entrepreneurs, key decision makers, and companies interested in providing funding for entertainment ventures.

Billboard Touring Conference and Awards
770 Broadway
New York, NY 10003
Phone: (646) 654-4660
Fax: (646) 654-4674

E-mail: bbevents@billboard.com
http://www.billboardevents.com
The Billboard Touring Conference and Awards is an annual event bringing together industry professionals. It offers informative panels and networking opportunities. The awards ceremony targets promoters, agents, managers, venues, sponsors, and individuals working in production.

Broadcast Music, Inc. (BMI)
320 West 57th Street
New York, NY 10019
Phone: (212) 586-2000
Fax: (212) 956-2059
E-mail: newyork@bmi.com
http://bmi.com
BMI conducts a multitude of workshops and seminars throughout the country for songwriters.

Career Opp Seminars & Speakers
P.O. Box 711
Monticello, NY 12701
Phone: (845) 794-7312
http://www.shellyfield.com
Career Opp Seminars and Speakers offers programs throughout the country on a variety of career-oriented subjects including how to enter and succeed in the music industry.

Dallas Songwriters Association
Sammons Center for the Arts

3630 Harry Hines Boulevard
Dallas, TX 75219
Phone: (214) 750-0916
E-mail: info@dallassongwriters.org
http://www.dallassongwriters.com

The Dallas Songwriters Association offers a variety of educational workshops on both the business and craft of songwriting.

Electronic Industries Alliance (EIA)

2500 Wilson Boulevard
Arlington, VA 22201
Phone: (703) 907-7500
E-mail: dmccurdy@eia.org
http://www.eia.org

The Electronic Industries Alliance offers annual fall and spring conferences.

Florida Music Festival and Conference

116 South Orange Avenue
Orlando, FL 32801
Phone: (407) 839-0039
E-mail: sean@floridamusicfestival. com
http://www.floridamusicfestival.com

The Florida Music Festival and Conference offers a variety of showcasing and networking opportunities.

Glitter, Glamour & Gold Seminars

P.O. Box 711
Monticello, NY 12701
Phone: (845) 794-7312
http://www.shellyfield.com

Glitter, Glamour & Gold Seminars provide helpful programs for those aspiring to work in the music industry as well as for those already in it.

Gospel Music Workshop of America (GMWA)

3908 West Warren
Detroit, MI 48208
Phone: (313) 898-6900
Fax: (313) 898-4520
E-mail: gmwa@ureach.com
http://www.gmwanational.org

The Gospel Music Workshop of America offers musical instruction in a variety of areas encompassing composition and performance.

Making It in Music Seminars & Speakers

P.O. Box 711
Monticello, NY 12701
Phone: (845) 794-7312
http://www.shellyfield.com

Making It in Music Seminars & Speakers offers programs throughout the country for individuals in both the business and talent ends of the music industry.

Metropolitan Opera Association (MOA)

Lincoln Center
New York, NY 10023
Phone: (212) 799-3100
E-mail: metinfo@mail.metopera.org
http://www.metoperafamily.org/
metopera/index.aspx

The Metropolitan Opera Association sponsors a number of seminars and training programs.

Metropolitan Opera Guild (MOG)

70 Lincoln Center Plaza
New York, NY 10023
Phone: (212) 769-7000
E-mail: info@metguild.org
http://www.metopera.org

The Metropolitan Opera Guild Offers a variety of educational programs and lectures relating to opera.

Mid Atlantic Music Conference

Wholeteam Enterprises
5588 Chamblee Dunwoody Road
Dunwoody, GA 30338
Phone: (770) 300-0175
E-mail: info@wholteam.com
http://www.midatlanticmusic.com

The Mid-Atlantic Music Conference is an annual event for those seeking to succeed in the music industry. The event offers offers educational and networking opportunities. Conference includes panel discussions with industry professionals.

Music Critics Association of North America (MCANA)

722 Dulaney Valley Road
Baltimore, MD 21204
Phone: (410) 435-3881
Fax: (410) 435-3881
E-mail: musiccritics@aol.com
http://www.mcana.org

The Music Critics Association of North America holds an annual convention for those involved in music journalism.

Nashville Songwriters Association International (NSAI)

1710 Roy Acuff Place
Nashville, TN 37203
Phone: (615) 256-3354
Fax: (615) 256-0034
E-mail: nsai@nashvillesongwriters. com
http://www.nashvillesongwriters. com

The Nashville Songwriters Association International holds weekly workshops for songwriters.

National Academy of Popular Music (NAPM)

330 West 58th Street
New York, NY 10019
Phone: (212) 957-9230
Fax: (212) 957-9227
E-mail: info@songhall.org
http://www.songwritershalloffame. org

The National Academy of Popular Music holds seminars and workshops in a variety of areas for those interested in songwriting and music.

National Association for Campus Activities (NACA)

13 Harbison Way
Columbia, SC 29212
Phone: (803) 732-6222
Fax: (803) 749-1047

E-mail: Gordons@naca.org
http://www.naca.org

The National Association for Campus Activities offers workshops and education sessions of interest to those seeking careers in the music business. The association also holds a variety of workshops on concert management and promotion in various locations through the country. The organization also holds an annual conference.

National Association of College Wind and Percussion Instructors (NACWPI)

c/o Dr. Richard K. Weerts,
   Executive Secretary
308 Hillcrest Drive
Kirksville, MO 63501
Phone: (660) 785-4442
Fax: (660) 785-7463
E-mail: dweerts@sbcglobal.net
http://www.nacwpi.org

The National Association of College Wind and Percussion Instructors holds programs, clinics, and workshops at the annual Music Educators National Conference.

National Association of Music Merchandisers (NAMM)

5790 Armada Drive
Carlsbad, CA 92008
Phone: (760) 438-8001
Fax: (760) 438-7327
E-mail: info@namm.com
http://www.namm.com

The National Association of Music Merchants offers a variety of seminars at their conventions and expositions. Programs change every year but always revolve around better business methods, selling, and so on. NAMM also hosts professional development seminars throughout the country.

National Academy of Recording Arts and Sciences (NARAS)

3402 Pico Boulevard
Santa Monica, CA 90405

Phone: (310) 392-3777
Fax: (310) 399-3090
E-mail: memservices@grammy.com
http://www.grammy.com

The National Academy of Recording Arts and Sciences offers seminars and discussion on a variety of subject of interest to those in the recording industry.

National Association of Recording Merchandisers (NARM)

9 Eves Drive
Marlton, NJ 08053
Phone: (856) 596-2221
Fax: (856) 596-3268
E-mail: donio@narm.com
http://www.narm.com

The National Association of Recording Merchandisers holds an annual convention with educational seminars on various subjects of interest to those working in all areas of recording merchandise.

National Music Publishers' Association (NMPA)

101 Constitution Avenue, NW
Washington, DC 20001
Phone: (202) 742-4375
Fax: (202) 742-4377
E-mail: pr@nmpa.org
http://www.nmpa.org

The National Music Publishers Association holds periodic forums for people involved in music publishing. Forums are put together by the Los Angeles, Nashville, and New York chapters.

Piano Technicians Guild (PTG)

4444 Forest Avenue
Kansas City, KS 66106
Phone: (913) 432-9975
Fax: (913) 432-9986
E-mail: ptg@ptg.org
http://www.ptg.org

The Piano Technicians Guild holds an annual convention featuring technical sessions. Seminars for piano technicians are also offered at various times throughout the year.

Public Relations Society of America

Public Relations Society of America
   (PRSA)
33 Maiden Lane
New York, NY 10038
Phone: (212) 460-1400
Fax: (212) 995-0757
E-mail: exec@prsa.org
http://www.prsa.org

The Public Relations Society of America hosts an annual convention as well sponsoring a variety of workshops and seminars throughout the year.

Recording Industry Association of America (RIAA)

1330 Connecticut Avenue, NW
Washington, DC 20036
Phone: (202)775-0101
Fax: (202)775-7253
http://www.riaa.org

The Recording Industry Association of America sponsors conferences on a variety of issues including anti-piracy.

Songwriters Guild

1500 Harbor Boulevard
Weehawken, NJ 07086
Phone: (201) 867-7603
Fax: (201) 867-7535
E-mail: corporate@
   songwritersguild.com
http://www.songwritersguild.com

The Songwriters Guild of America offers workshops in both the business and craft of songwriting. These are held throughout the year. The guild has an "Ask a Pro" workshop, song critique workshop, and courses in all phases of songwriting.

Special Libraries Association (SLA)

331 South Patrick Street
Alexandria, VA 22314
Phone: (703) 647-4900
Fax: (703) 647-4901
E-mail: sla@sla.org
http://www.sla.org

The Special Libraries Association conducts an array of continuing education courses of interest to those working in music libraries.

Volunteer Lawyers for the Arts (VLA)

1 East 53rd Street
New York, NY 10022
Phone: (212) 319-2787
Fax: (212) 752-6575

E-mail: epaul@vlany.org
http://www.vlany.com

The Volunteer Lawyers for the Arts runs educational programs, seminars, and workshops throughout the year in a multitude of areas.

West Coast Songwriters Conference

West Coast Songwriters
1724 Laurel Street

San Carlos, CA 94070
Phone: (650) 654-3966
Fax: (650) 654-2156
E-mail: info@westcoastsongwriters. org
http://www.westcoastsongwriters. org

The West Coast Songwriters Conference is chockfull of seminars, lyric reviews, showcases, and networking opportunities.

GLOSSARY

The following is a list of abbreviations, acronyms, and music business lingo that should prove helpful to individuals interested in the music industry. Entries are listed alphabetically.

AAF   American Advertising Federation

AAMT   American Association for Music Therapy

A & R   Artist & Repertoire (the department in a record company that finds new songs, signs new artists, etc.)

ABA   American Bar Association

A/C   Adult contemporary music

ACC   American Conference of Cantors

ACDA   American Choral Directors Association

ACM   Academy of Country Music

advance   A prepayment of monies against future royalties or fees

affiliate   A broadcast station that belongs to a network. For example, WABC in New York and KABC in Los Angeles are both affiliates of the ABC network.

AFM   American Federation of Musicians of the United States and Canada (the union that most musicians belong to)

AFT   American Federation of Teachers

AFTRA   American Federation of Television and Radio Artists

AGAC   American Guild of Authors and Composers (now known as The Songwriters Guild)

agent   The person who obtains work for an act or artist

AGM   American Guild of Music

AGMA   American Guild of Musical Artists

AGO   American Guild of Organists

AGVA   American Guild of Variety Artists

AICPA   American Institute of Certified Public Accountants

airplay   The broadcasting of records by radio stations

ALA   American Library Association

AMA   American Marketing Association

AMC   American Music Conference

AOR   Album-oriented rock (a type of music played by radio stations)

arbitron ratings   A television and radio rating service that indicates what percentage of the people are viewing or listening to a particular show or station. They may be referred to as the "arbitrons." Rates for commercial air time are often based on these ratings.

arrangement   The adaptation of a song for a performance or recording

ASCAP   American Society of Composers, Authors & Publishers

A-side   The side of a single record that is promoted more actively

ASMA   American Society of Music Arrangers

ASMC   American Society of Music Copyists

ASOL   American Symphony Orchestra League

assignment   The transfer of rights from a songwriter to publisher

ATPAM   Association of Theatrical Press Agents & managers

bar code   The black stripes that encode product information. Bar codes are assigned according to the Universal Product Code (UPC).

bio   Biography of artist or act, most commonly used in press kits and for other publicity

BMA   Black Music Association

BMI   Broadcast Music Incorporated

B-side   The flip side of a single

booking agent   Individual responsible for seeking and soliciting work for entertainers

bootlegging   The unauthorized selling of records, tapes, CDs, videos, etc.

bullet   A printed mark designating songs that have potential on the charts; used in trade magazines, they may look like a bullet, a rocket, or a star

B & W glossy   Black and white glossy photograph, also known as an 8 × 10 glossy

B/W   Backed with. The opposite of the A-side of a record.

catalog   The collection of songs to which a publisher owns the rights

C & W   Country and Western

CARP   Copyright Arbitration Royalty Panel; this is a panel appointed to arbitrate copyright and/or royalty disputes

CBDNA   College Band Directors National Association

CD   Compact Disc

CDG   Compact disc with graphics

chart action   The movement of a specific record on the charts

charts   Lists of the current hits, found in the trade magazines

CHR   Contemporary Hit Radio; a radio format

CMA   Country Music Association

commission   A percentage of money paid to an agent, manager, etc. for services

compact disc   Disc containing encoded music read by laser beam in CD or compact disc player

contractor   The person who hires session members for a recording session

co-publish   Agreement whereby two individuals or companies open the publishing rights to a song

copyright   A legal protection granted to an author or composer for the exclusive rights to his or her works

cover record   Another version of a tune that has already been recorded

CPA   Certified public accountant

CPM   Conference of Personal Managers

crossover record   A record that is popular in one type of music and then becomes popular in one or more other markets of music (e.g., a song that becomes a Top 40 hit and then becomes a hit on the country and/or R & B charts)

cut   A specific selection on an album or CD; to record a song

day job   The job many individuals work to pay the bills while waiting for their "big break" in the music business.

demo   Demonstration record used for selling a record, tune, or act

demographics   Information—such as age, gender, sex, marital status, education level, etc.—used to target buyers; radio stations also use this information to target listeners and advertisers.

distributor   Individual or company who moves records, CDs, etc. from the manufacturer to retail outlets

D.J.   Disc jockey

door   the revenue obtained from admission fees; may also be referred to as the "gate"

EIA   Electronic Industry Association

E.P.   Extended play record

Equity   Actors Equity Association, the actors' union

exploit   The process of finding legitimate uses of songs or acts for income

fan club   A club made up of people devoted to a specific artist or act

FCC   Federal Communications Commission

format   The style of programming that a radio station uses (e.g., all talk, country, Top 40, etc.)

GAMMA   Guitar and Accessories Music Marketing Association

gig   A job for musicians

GMA   Gospel Music Association

gold album   An LP that has sold 500,000 units as certified by the R.I.A.A.

Gold Music Video Single   A music video containing not more than two songs which has sold 25,000 units

gold single   A single record or CD single that has sold 500,000 units as certified by the R.I.A.A.

Grammy   One of the most prestigious awards in the music business; given by the NARAS

gross income   Total income before expenses and taxes are deducted

headliner   The main act people come to see in a concert

hip-hop   Musical style combining rap, R&B, and disco music

hit   A record that is popular and sells a lot of copies

hook   The repetitive part of a song that is most remembered when people think about that tune

hype   Extensive publicity used to promote acts, new records, etc. (Incidentally, hype is not always true.)

IAAM   International Association of Auditorium Managers

IAFP   International Association of Financial Planning

IATSE   International Alliance of Theatrical Stage Employees

ICFP   Institute of Certified Financial Planners

IIA   Institute of Internal Auditors

independent record label   Record label not owned by major company

indie   Independent record label

IRC   International reply coupon. These are used when requesting the return of materials from other countries.

jingle   A musical tune in a commercial

key man clause   A contract provision allowing artists to terminate a contract if a specific person integral to the individual's career leaves the company; may apply to management contracts, booking agency contracts, publishing contracts, recording contracts, etc.

K.J.   Karaoke Jockey

label   Record company

LD   Laser disc

lead sheet   Written version of a song containing the melody, lyrics, and chords, etc.

local   The local in a union is the local affiliation in a particular geographic area of a national or international union.

log The list of music played by radio stations used to determine performance royalties; logs also contain additional programming information

LP Long-playing record, commonly known as an album

lyrics The words of a song

Major A major record label, such as EMI, Sony, BMG, Universal Music, or Warner Music

market Can refer to geographical location, such as the East Coast market, the West Coast market, etc., or may refer to a type of musical market, such as Top 40, R&B, country, etc.

master The finished tape that is turned into a record

MCA Music Critics Association

MD Mini disc; these are used for recording and playing digitally encoded music

mechanical license A license obtained from a song publisher, needed to record the song

MENC Music Educators National Conference

MIEA Music Industry Educators Association

mix Putting all the different tracts for a record together electronically

MLA Music Library Association

MOR Middle of the road music, also called easy listening music

multi-platinum single A single which has sold 2 million units as certified by the RIAA

music video A video used by musical acts and singers to promote their songs on television

Muzak Canned music such as that heard in dentist's offices, department stores, elevators, etc.

NAA National Association of Accountants

NAB National Association of Broadcasters

NABET National Association of Broadcast Employees and Technicians

NACA National Association for Campus Activities

NACWPI National Association of College Wind and Percussion Instructors

NAMM National Association of Music Merchants

NAMT National Association for Music Therapy, Inc.

NARAS National Academy of Recording Arts & Sciences

NARM National Association of Record Merchandisers

NASM National Association of Schools of Music

NASSM National Association of State Supervisors of Music

Net The Internet

network A group of television or radio stations affiliated and interconnected for simultaneous broadcast of the same programming

NFMC National Federation of Music Clubs

NMPA National Music Publishers Association

NOA National Orchestra Association

NPMA National Piano Manufacturers Association

NPR National Public Radio

NSPA National Society of Public Accountants

oldies Songs that were hits some years ago

one-stop Wholesale distributor of records and video products and accessories

on-line Connecting to the Internet

overdub Adding another part (vocal or instrument) to a basic multi-track recording

payola Money or other "gratuities" given to D.J.'s or program directors in order to have certain records played more often (this is illegal)

P.D. Public domain; program director

performing rights The right to license music and collect monies for use by anyone playing that music

personal manager Person who directs the career of a performer

platinum single or album A single record, album, cassette, CD, etc. that has sold 1,000,000 units

playlist A list of songs that a radio station compiles designating which songs it will play

portfolio A collection of sample pieces done by someone in the creative field (either a writer or artist), which is put together into a book so that prospective employers can get an idea of a person's potential

P.R. Public relations

press kit A promo kit containing publicity, photos, and other promotional materials on an act

print rights Permission granted to reproduce the printed sheet music of a copyrighted song or other work

promo Promotion

PRSA Public Relations Society of America

PSA Public service announcements on radio or television given to not-for-profit organizations

public domain Songs or other works that have no copyright or whose copyright has expired

R & B Rhythm and blues

R & R Rock 'n' roll

release date The actual date a manufacturer releases a product

repertoire A list of songs that an act performs or records, etc.

RIA Recording Institute of America

RIAA Recording Industry Association of America, Inc.

royalties Monies paid periodically for the sales of records, sheet music, etc.

royalty statement   An itemized accounting of earnings for songwriters or recording artists

SAG   Screen Actors Guild

scale   The minimum union wages

search the Net   Look for information on the Internet

self-contained act   A group that has all members included and needs no outside augmentation

SESAC   Society of European Songwriters, Authors and Composers

ship date   The actual date a manufacturer physically ships a product

short form   A music video with only one song

Short Form Albums   Short form albums have a minimum of three songs and a maximum of five. They run approximately 30 minutes.

single   A record with one tune on each side

site   Website

SLA   Special Libraries Association

SPARS   Society of Professional Audio Recording Studios

S.R.O.   Standing room only—all seats for a concert or show are sold out

standard   A song that becomes popular in all markets and then becomes timeless, it may also be known as a classic.

street date   The actual date a CD, cassette, record, etc. arrives in retail stores (or other markets for sale).

superstar   Act that is famous, talented, rich, and well known

supporting act   Act that opens the show before the main event

surf the net   Going on-line, visiting various sites on the Internet

TEIA   Touring Entertainment Industry Association

tip sheet   A newspaper, newsletter, or magazine that lists new records and fast-moving tunes (Tip sheets are used by program directors and/or music directors at radio stations to help make up the station's playlists.)

Top 40   The forty songs in the country that are selling the best and/or requested the most on radio stations (The Top 40 may be found in the trades. Often there is a Top 40 for different categories of music, such as Country, R & B, Albums, etc.)

Top Ten   The top ten songs on the charts

tour   A series of concerts, usually in different geographic areas

tour support   Monies paid to acts to offset the high cost of tours (Tour support is most often paid by the act's label. However, many companies are now underwriting concert tours, including soft drink companies, beer companies, perfume companies, etc.)

trades   Magazines and newspapers that deal with the music/record/entertainment industry

turntable hit   a record that experiences airplay success but limited or no sales success

12″ single   A 12-inch recording of one or more mixes of a tune, usually played in dance clubs

U/C   Urban contemporary music

UPC   Universal Product Code

union card   A card that is used to identify members of specific unions

V.J.   Video Jockey

VeeJay   Video Jockey

venue   A hall, auditorium, or club where an act performs

Web   The World Wide Web

Website   A place on the World Wide Web

Work for Hire   A work (song, press release, book, etc.) done by an employee as part of his or her job. The work is owned and copyrightable by the employer, not the employee.

WTO   World Trade Organization

WWW   World Wide Web

YCA   Young Concert Artists

BIBLIOGRAPHY

A. BOOKS

There are thousands and thousands of books covering all aspects of music. The books listed below are separated into general categories. The subject matter of many of these books overlaps.

These books can be found in bookstores, online, and in libraries. If your local library does not have the book you want, ask your librarian to order it for you through the interlibrary loan system.

This list is meant to be a starting point. For other books that might interest you, look in the music section of bookstores, check out *Books in Print* (found in the reference section of libraries or available online by subscription), or surf the Internet for other possibilities.

ARTIST MANAGEMENT

Allen, Paul. *Artist Management for the Music Business.* Burlington, Mass.: Elsevier Science & Technology Books, 2007.

Marcone, Stephen. *Managing Your Band: Artist Management: The Ultimate Responsibility.* Wayne, N.J.: HiMarks Publishing Company, 2006.

BIOGRAPHIES, AUTOBIOGRAPHIES, MUSICAL ARTISTS, ETC.

Collins, Jeff. *Rock Legends at Rockfield.* Cardiff: University of Wales Press, 2008.

Gable, Christopher. *The Words and Music of Sting.* Portsmouth, N.H.: Greenwood Publishing Group, 2008.

Goldberg, Danny. *Bumping into Geniuses: My Life Inside the Rock and Roll Business.* New York: Penguin, 2008.

Jones, Quincy. *The Complete Quincy Jones: My Journey and Passions—Photos. Letters, Memories and More from Q's Personal Collection.* San Rafael, Calif.: Palace Publishing Group, 2008.

CHURCH MUSIC

Acker, Mark. *The Passion-Driven Youth Choir: A Guide for Directors of Youth Choirs with 10 to 100 Members.* Nashville: Abingdon Press, 2007.

Bullard, Alan. *The Oxford Book of Flexible Anthems: A Complete Resource for Every Church Choir.* New York: Oxford University Press, 2008.

Wilson, Eli, Jr. *Equipping the Church Choir for Ministry: A Resource for Church Music Leaders and Choir Members.* Bloomington, Ind.: Authorhouse, 2008.

CONCERT PROMOTION

Berry, Jake. *This Business of Concert Promotion and Touring: A Practical Guide to Creating, Selling, Organizing, and Staging Concerts.* New York: Watson-Guptill Publications, 2007.

EDUCATION: MUSIC

Blanchard, Bonnie. *Making Music and Enriching Lives: A Guide for All Music Teachers.* Bloomington: Indiana University Press, 2008.

Conway, Colleen Marie. *Teaching Music in Higher Education.* New York: Oxford University Press, 2008.

Flohr, John. *Music in Elementary Education.* Boston: Prentice Hall, 2008.

Houlahan, Michael. *Kodály Today: A Cognitive Approach to Elementary Music Education.* New York: Oxford University Press, 2008.

Kelly, Steven. *Teaching Music in American Society: A Social and Cultural Understanding of Music Education.* New York: Routledge, 2008.

Mark, Michael, L. *A Concise History of American Music Education.* Lanham, Md.: Rowman & Littlefield, 2008.

Sobol, Elise S. *An Attitude and Approach for Teaching Music to Special Learners.* Lanham, Md.: Rowman & Littlefield, 2008.

EDUCATION—MUSIC THERAPY

Koen, Benjamin D. *Beyond the Roof of the World: Music, Prayer, and Healing in the Pamir Mountains.* New York: Oxford University Press, 2008.

Lewis, Cathleen. *Rex: A Mother, Her Autistic Child, and the Music That Transformed Their Lives.* Nashville: Thomas Nelson, 2008.

Odell-Miller, Helen. *Supervision of Music Therapy.* New York: Routledge, 2008.

Oldfield, Amelia. *Music Therapy with Children and Their Families*. London: Jessica Kingsley, 2008.

INSTRUMENT REPAIR AND DESIGN

Bogdanovich, John S. *Classical Guitar Making: A Modern Approach to Traditional Design*. New York: Sterling Publishing, 2007.

Willis, Alex. *Step by Step Guitar Making*. East Petersburg, Pa.: Fox Chapel Publishing, 2007.

MUSIC AND THE INTERNET

Hustwit, Gary. *Musician's Guide to the Internet*. Milwaukee, Wisc.: Hal Leonard Corp., 2002.

Hutchison, Tom. *Web Marketing for the Music Business*. Saint Louis, Mo.: Elsevier Science & Technology Books, 2008.

Kalliongis, Nicky. *Myspace Music Profit Monster!: Proven Online Marketing Strategies!* New York: PowerHouse Cultural Entertainment, 2008.

Nevue, David. *How to Promote Your Music Successfully on the Internet, 2007 Ed.* North Charleston, N.C.: BookSurge, 2008.

MUSIC BUSINESS

Bordowitz, Hank. *Dirty Little Secrets of the Record Business: Why So Much Music You Hear Sucks*. Chicago: A Cappella Books, 2007.

Brabec, Jeffrey, and Todd Brabec. *Music, Money and Success*. New York: Music Sales Corporation, 2008.

Ford, Cecil. *Your Guide to the Music Business*. Chicago: Independent Publisher, 2007.

Gordon, Steve. *The Future of the Music Business: How to Succeed with the New Digital Technologies*. Milwaukee: Hal Leonard Corp., 2008.

Hawkins, Martin. *A Shot in the Dark: Making Records in Nashville 1945–1955*. Nashville: Vanderbilt University Press, 2006.

Krasilovsky, M. William, and Sidney Shemel. *This Business of Music: The Definitive Guide to the Music Industry*. New York: Watson-Guptill Publications, 2007.

Passman, Donald. *All You Need to Know about the Music Business*. New York: Simon & Schuster, 2006.

Stiernberg, John. *Succeeding in Music: Business Chops for Performers and Songwriters*. Milwaukee, Wisc.: Hal Leonard Publishing, 2008.

Walker, James L., Jr. *This Business of Urban Music: A Practical Guide to Achieving Success in the Industry, from Gospel to Funk to R&B to Hip-Hop*. New York: Watson-Guptill Publications, 2008.

Williams, Wheat. *Complete Music Business Office*. Boston: Course Technology, 2008.

MUSIC BUSINESS LAW

Aczon, Michael A. *The Musician's Legal Companion*. Boston: Course Technology, 2008.

Forest, Greg. *The Music Business Contract Library*. Milwaukee, Wisc.: Hal Leonard Corp., 2008.

Halloran, Mark. *Musician's Business and Legal Guide*. East Rutherford, N.J.: Musician's Business and Legal Guide, 2007.

Reece-Davies, Patrisha. *Unconscionable Contracts in the Music Industry: The Need for New Legal Relationships*. Lewiston, N.Y.: Edwin Mellen Press, 2006.

Stim, Richard. *Music Law: How to Run Your Band's Business*. Berkeley, Calif.: NOLO, 2006.

MUSIC, GENERAL

Boyd, Joe. *White Bicycles: Making Music in the 1960s*. London: Serpent's Tail Limited, 2007.

Courrier, Kevin. *Artificial Paradise: The Dark Side of the Beatles' Utopian Dream*. Portsmouth, N.H.: Greenwood Publishing Group, 2008.

Goldberg, Danny. *Bumping into Geniuses: My Life Inside the Rock and Roll Business*. New York: Penguin Group, 2008.

Ilson, Bernie. *Sundays with Sullivan: How the Ed Sullivan Show Brought Elvis, the Beatles, and Culture to America*. Lanham, Md.: Taylor Trade Publishing, 2008.

McWhorter, John. *All about the Beat: Why Hip-Hop Can't Save Black America*. New York: Penguin Group, 2008

Thompson, Gordon Ross. *Please Please Me: Sixties British Pop, Inside Out*. New York: Oxford University Press, 2008.

THE MUSIC INDUSTRY

Beattie, Will. *The Rock and Roll Times: Guide to the Music Industry*. Oxford: How to Books, 2008.

Espejo, Roman. *What Is the Future of the Music Industry?* Farmington, Mich.: Cengage Gale, 2008.

Field, Shelly. *Ferguson Career Coach: Managing Your Career in the Music Industry*. New York: Facts On File, 2008.

Nottingham, David. *The Art of Developing Fans for Life: Circle of Competence Discussion Topics*. Philadelphia: Xlibris Corporation, 2008.

MUSIC MARKETING AND PROMOTION

Baker, Bob. *Guerrilla Music Marketing Handbook: 201 Self-Promotion Ideas for Songwriters, Musicians and Bands on a Budget*. Saint Louis, Mo.: Spotlight Publications, 2007.

———. *MySpace Music Marketing: How to Promote & Sell Your Music on the World's Biggest Networking Web Site*. Saint Louis, Mo.: Spotlight Publications, 2006.

———. *Guerrilla Music Marketing, Encore Edition: 201 More Self-Promotion Ideas, Tips and Tactics for Do-It-Yourself Artists*. Saint Louis, Mo.: Spotlight Publications, 2006.

Fisher, Jeffrey P. *Ruthless Self-Promotion in the Music Industry*. Boston: Course Technology, 2005.

Gelfand, Michael. *Strategies for Success: Self-Promotion Secrets for Musicians*. Chester, N.Y.: Music Sales Corp., 2005.

Kalliongis, Nickey. *Myspace Music Profit Monster!: Proven Online Marketing Strategies!*. New York: powerHouse Cultural Entertainment, 2008.

Lathrop, Tad. *This Business of Global Music Marketing: Global Strategies for Maximizing Your Music's Popularity and Profits*. New York: Watson-Guptill Publications, 2007.

Slichter, Jacob. *So You Wanna Be a Rock and Roll Star: How I Machine-Gunned a Roomful of Record Executives and Other True Tales from a Drummer's Life*. New York: Broadway Books, 2005.

Spellman, Peter. *The Self-Promoting Musician: Strategies for Independent Music Success*. Milwaukee, Wisc.: Hal Leonard Corp., 2008.

MUSIC PUBLISHING

Poe, Randy. *New Songwriter's Guide to Music Publishing: Everything You Need to Know to Make the Best Publishing Deals for Your Songs*. Cincinnati, Ohio: F&W Media, 2005.

Whitsett, Tim. *The Business of Music Publishing*. Boston: Course Technology, 2008.

Williams, Wheat. *Complete Music Business Office*. Boston: Course Technology, 2008.

Wixen, Randal. *The Plain and Simple Guide to Music Publishing*. Milwaukee, Wis.: Hal Leonard Corp., 2006.

MUSIC VIDEOS & MUSIC TELEVISION

Pegley, Kip. *Coming to You Wherever You Are: MuchMusic, MTV, and Youth Identities*. Middletown, Conn.: Wesleyan University Press, 2008.

Temporal, Paul. *The Branding of MTV: Will Internet Kill the Video Star?* Hoboken, N.J.: John Wiley & Sons, 2008.

PUBLICITY, PUBLIC RELATIONS, AND PROMOTION

Basic Books. *Stylebook and Briefing on Media Law*. New York: Basic Books, 2007.

Field, Shelly. *Career Opportunities in Advertising and Public Relations*. New York: Facts On File, 2005.

Hartunian, Paul. *Power Publicity for Musicians*. Upper Montclair, N.J.: Clifford Publishing, 2006.

———. *Power Publicity for Entertainers*. Upper Montclair, N.J.: Clifford Publishing, 2006.

Yudkin, Marcia. *Six Steps to Free Publicity*. Franklin Lakes, N.J.: Career Press, 2008.

RADIO

Apple, Terri. *Making Money in Voice-Overs: Winning Strategies to a Successful Career in TV, Commercials, Radio and Animation*. New York: Watson-Guptill Publications, 2008.

Broughton, Frank. *Last Night a DJ Saved My Life: The History of the Disc Jockey*. New York: Grove/Atlantic, 2008.

Zemon, Stacy. *The DJ Sales and Marketing Handbook: How to Make Big Profits as a Disc Jockey*. Burlington, Mass.: Elsevier, 2005.

RECORDING AND THE RECORD BUSINESS

Brown, Jake. *Jay Z and the Roc-A-Fella Records Dynasty*. Phoenix, Ariz.: Amber Books, 2006

Elementary Media. *Introduction to the Recording Studio and the Music Industry: A Course Workbook*. New York: Elementary Media, 2007.

Foster, David. *Hitman: Forty Years Making Music, Topping the Charts, and Winning Grammys*. Riverside, N.J.: Simon and Schuster, 2008.

George, Nelson. *Where Did Our Love Go?: The Rise and Fall of the Motown Sound*. Chicago: University of Illinois Press, 2007.

Gilchrist, Auvil. *How to Get Rich Selling Your Own CD's by Running Your Own Record Label—the Music*

BluePrint. Lawrenceville, Ga.: ADG Music Group, 2006.

Goodridge, Walt F. J. *Change the Game: How to Start, Run, and Really Make Money with Your Own Independent Hip Hop Record Label.* New York: Passion Profit Company, 2004.

Kahn, Ashley. *The House That Trane Built: The Story of Impulse Records.* New York: W. W. Norton & Company, 2007.

Marmorstein, Gary. *The Label: The Story of Columbia Records.* Cambridge, Mass.: Da Capo Press, 2007.

O'Connor, Alan. Punk *Record Labels and the Struggle for Autonomy: The Emergence of DIY.* Lanham, Md.: Lexington Books, 2008.

Prial, Dunstan. *The Producer: John Hammond and the Soul of American Music.* New York: Farrar, Straus and Giroux, 2006.

Ramone, Phil. *Making Records: The Scenes Behind the Music.* New York: Hyperion Press, 2007.

Roberson, Kawani. *The Indie Record Label Guide: All U Need to Succeed.* Sandy, Utah: Aardvark Global Publishing, 2006.

Stubbs, David. *Ace Records: Labels Unlimited.* London: Black Dog Publishing, 2008.

Toussaint, Simone. *The Music Business Fine Prints: (Everything an Artist Need, Want and Should Know about the Music Business).* Parker, Colo.: Outskirts Press, 2007.

Wild, David. *And the Grammy Goes To . . . : The Official Story of Music's Most Coveted Award.* Ann Arbor, Mich.: Borders Group, Inc, 2007.

RECORD PRODUCTION

Farquharson, Michael. *Writer. Producer. Engineer: A Handbook for Creating Contemporary Commercial Music.* Milwaukee, Wis.: Hal Leonard Corp., 2007.

One Omik Music. *Applied Music Theory for Managers, Engineers, Producers and Artists 2nd Edition: What You Should Know and Why You Should Know It.* Chicago: One Omik Music, 2008.

Perry, Megan. *How to Be a Record Producer in the Digital Era.* New York: Watson-Guptill Publications, 2008.

SYMPHONY ORCHESTRAS AND OPERAS

Bourne, Joyce. *Opera: The Great Composers and Their Masterworks.* New York: Oxford University Press, 2008.

Brown, Susan C. *String Players' Guide to the Orchestra: Orchestral Repertoire Excerpts, Scales, and Studies for String Orchestra and Individual Study.* Oriskany, N.Y.: Alfred Publishing Company, 2008.

Cowen, Tyler. *Good and Plenty: The Creative Successes of American Arts Funding.* Princeton, N.J.: Princeton University Press, 2008.

North, James H. *Boston Symphony Orchestra: An Augmented Discography.* Lanham, Md.: Scarecrow Press, Incorporated, 2008.

Streatfeild, Richard Alexander. *The Opera.* Charleston, S.C.: BiblioBazaar, 2008.

TALENT & SONGWRITING

Appleby, Amy. *You Can Write a Song.* Collingdale, Pa.: Diane Publishing, 2008.

Aschmann, Lisa. *1000 Songwriting Ideas.* Milwaukee, Wis.: Hal Leonard, 2008.

Blume, Jason. *Six Steps to Songwriting Success: The Comprehensive Guide to Writing and Marketing Hit Songs.* New York: Watson-Guptill Publications, 2008.

Burnett, Gene. *Songwriting for Geniuses: 25 Tips for the Genius in Everyone.* Bloomington, Ind.: I-Universe, 2008.

Dion, Frank. *Fingers Bleed: Learn How to Write a Song in about 15 Minutes and Increase Your Chances of Becoming a Rock 'n' Roll Superstar.* North Charleston, S.C.: BookSurge, 2006.

Ford, Jerry Lee Jr. *Righting Wrongs in Writing Songs.* Boston: Course Technology, 2008.

Hawks, Tony. *One Hit Wonderland.* London: Ebury Publishing, 2008.

Leikin, Molly-Ann. *How to Write a Hit Song.* Milwaukee, Wis.: Hal Leonard Corp., 2008.

Market Books Team. *2009 Songwriter's Market.* Cincinnati, Ohio: Writer's Digest Books, 2008.

Redfield, Bessie G. *Nothing Rhymes with Orange: Perfect Words for Poets, Songwriters, and Rhymers.* New York: Penguin Group, 2008.

Swanson, Stan. *The Songwriter's Journal: 52 Weeks of Songwriting Ideas and Inspiration.* Daytona Beach, Fla.: Stony Meadow Publishing, 2007.

TALENT AND MUSIC

Carr, Daphne. *Best Music Writing 2008.* New York: Perseus Books Group, 2008.

Smirnoff, Marc. *The Oxford American Book of Great Music Writing.* Fayetteville: University of Arkansas Press, 2008.

B. PERIODICALS

Magazines, newspapers, membership bulletins, newsletters, and e-magazines may be helpful in finding a job in a specific field. As with the books, this list should serve only as a guide. Because of space limitations, many periodicals are not listed. Look in your local library or a newspaper/magazine shop for other periodicals that may interest you. You might also want to check for online versions of periodicals.

The periodicals in this section are listed in general categories. Subject matter may overlap. Check all categories relevant to the type of career you are interested in pursuing.

THE TRADES

Billboard
770 Broadway
New York, NY 10003
Phone: (646) 654-4500
Fax: (646) 654-4682
E-mail: info@billboard.com
http://www.billboard.com

Billboard Los Angeles
5055 Wilshire Boulevard
Los Angeles, CA 90036
Phone: (323) 525-2300
Fax: (323) 525-2394
E-mail: info@billboard.com
http://www.billboard.com

Billboard Nashville
49 Music Square West
Nashville, TN 37203
Phone: (615) 321-4290
Fax: (615) 320-0454
E-mail: info@billboard.com
http://www.billboard.com

The Hollywood Reporter
5055 Wilshire Boulevard
Los Angeles, CA 90036
Phone: (323) 525-2000
Fax: (323) 525-2377
E-mail: contactcommuncations@nielsen.com
http://www.hollywoodreporter.com

Variety
5700 Wilshire Boulevard
Los Angeles, CA 90036
Phone: (323) 857-6600
Fax: (323) 965-2475
http://www.variety.com

CHURCH MUSIC

American Organist Magazine
American Guild of Organists
475 Riverside Drive
New York, NY 10115
Phone: (212) 870-2310
Fax: (212) 870-2163
http://www.agohq.org

Church Music Report
P.O. Box 1179
Grapevine, TX 76099
Phone: (817) 488-0141
Fax: (817) 481-4191
http://www.tcmr.com

Gospel Voice
Gottem Entertainment Publications Inc.
P.O. Box 682427
Franklin, TN 37068
Phone: (615) 859-7239
www.gospelvoice.com

The Hymn
Hymn Society in the United States and Canada
Boston University School of Theology
745 Commonwealth Avenue
Boston, MA 02215
Phone: (617) 353-6493
Fax: (617) 353-7322
E-mail: hymneditor@aol.com
http://www.thehymnsociety.org

Pastoral Music
National Association of Pastoral Musicians
962 Wayne Avenue
Silver Spring, MD 20910
Phone: (202) 723-5800
Fax: (202) 723-2262
E-mail: NPMSING@npm.org
http://www.npm.org

Singing News
Salem Publishing
104 Woodmont Boulevard
Nashville, TN 37205

CONCERT INDUSTRY

Pollstar
4697 West Jacquelyn Avenue
Fresno, CA 93722
Phone: (559) 271-7900
Fax: (559) 27107979
http://www.pollstar.com

EDUCATION

American Music Teacher
Music Teachers National Association
441 Vine Street
Cincinnati, OH 45202
Phone: (888) 512-5278
E-mail: mtnanet@mtna.org
http://www.mtna.org

Journal of Music Teacher Education Online
2455 Teller Road
Thousand Oaks, CA 91320
Phone: (805) 499-0721
Fax: (805) 499-0871
http://www.sagepublications.com

Journal of Research In Music Education
2455 Teller Road
Thousand Oaks, CA 91320
Phone: (805) 499-0721

Fax: (805) 499-0871
http://jrm.sagepub.com

MEIEA
Music & Entertainment Industry
    Educators Association (MEIEA)
1900 Belmont Boulevard
Nashville, TN 37212
Phone: (615) 460-6946
http://www.meiea.org

Music Educators Journal
2455 Teller Road
Thousand Oaks, CA 91320
Phone: (805) 499-0721
Fax: (805) 499-0871
http://mej.sagepub.com

Teaching Music
1806 Robert Fulton Drive
Reston, VA 20191
Phone: (703) 860-4000
Fax: (703) 860-9443
E-mail: info@menc.org
http://www.menc.org

FACILITY MANAGEMENT

Building Operating Management
2100 West Florist Avenue
Milwaukee, WI 53209
Phone: (414) 228-7701
Fax: (414) 228-1134
http://www.tradepress.com

Facility Manager
International Association of
    Assembly Managers
635 Fritz Drive
Coppell, TX 75019
Phone: (972) 906-7441
Fax: (972) 906-7418
http://www.iaam.org

GENERAL

Cream Magazine
33076 Ann Arbor Trail
Westland, MI 48185
http://www.creemmagazine.com

USA Today
7950 Jones Branch Drive

McLean, VA 22108
http://www.usatoday.com

INSTRUMENT REPAIR, RESTORATION, DESIGN, AND BUILDING

Piano Technicians Journal
Piano Technicians' Guild
4444 Forest Avenue
Kansas City, KS 66106
Phone: (913) 432-9975
Fax: (913) 432-9986
E-mail: ptg@ptg.org
http://www.ptg.org

MISCELLANEOUS MUSIC MAGAZINES

*Bam: The California Music
    Magazine*
1351 Apple Drive
Concord, CA 94518

Blender
1040 Avenue of the Americas
New York, NY 10018
Phone: (212) 302-2626
Fax: (212) 302-2635
http://www.blender.com

Country Weekly
1000 American Media Way
Boca Raton, FL 33464
Phone: (561) 989-1227
http://www.americanmediainc.com

Entertainment Today
10701 Riverside Drive
Toluca Lake, CA 91602
Phone: (818) 762-2171
Fax: (818) 980-1900

Entertainment Weekly
Time-Life Building
Rockefeller Plaza
New York, NY 10020
Phone: (212) 522-4482
http://www.ew.com

Gig Magazine
2800 Campus Drive
San Mateo, CA 94403

Phone: (650) 513-4300
Fax: (650) 513-4642

Rolling Stone
1290 Avenue of the Americas
New York, NY 10104
Phone: (212) 484-1616
Fax: (212) 484-1713
http://www.rollingstone.com

Vibe
215 Lexington Avenue
New York, NY 10016
Phone: (212) 448-7300
Fax: (212) 448-7400
http://www.vibe.com

Voxonline.com (E-magazine)
P.O. Box 712412
Los Angeles, CA 90071
E-mail: vox@voxonline.com
http://www.voxonline.com

XXL Magazine
111 Broadway
New York, NY 10010
Phone: (212) 807-7100
Fax: (212) 620-7787
http://www.xxlmag.com

MUSIC GENERAL

Alternative Press
1305 West 80th Street
Cleveland, OH 44102
Phone: (216) 631-1510
Fax: (216) 631-1016
E-mail: editorial@altpress.com
http://www.altpress.com

Spin
205 Lexington Avenue
New York, NY 10016
Phone: (212) 231-7400
Fax: (212) 231-7300
http://www.spin.com

MUSIC BUSINESS

*Cutting Edge/Music Business
    Institute*
1524 North Clairborne Avenue
New Orleans, LA 70116

Phone: (504) 945-1800
Fax: (504) 945-1873
http://www.cuttingedgemusic
business.com

Entertainment Law
Thomson West
610 Opperman Drive
Eagan, MN 55123
Phone: (651) 687-7000
Fax: (651) 687-6674
http://west.thomson.com

MUSICIANS

International Musician
American Federation of Musicians
of the United States and Canada
(AFM)
1501 Broadway
New York, NY 10036
Phone: (212) 869-1330
Fax: (212) 764-6134
E-mail: presoffice@afm.org
http://www.afm.org

Performer Magazine
24 Dane Street
Somerville, MA 02143
Phone: (617) 627-9200
Fax: (617) 627-9930
http://www.performermag.com

1340 Magazine (E-magazine)
67 East Main Street
Mount Jewett, PA 16740
http://www.1340mag.com

20th Century Guitar
135 Oser Avenue
Hauppauge, NY 11788
Phone: (800) 291-9687
Fax: (631) 434-905
http://www.tcguitar.com

Under the Radar
238 South Tower Drive
Beverly Hills, CA 91211
Phone: (323) 653-8705
Fax: (323) 658-5738
http://www.undertheradermag.
com

Unsigned : The Magazine
P.O. Box 165166
Irving, TX 75016
Phone: (214) 459-3199
E-mail: unsignedthemagazine.com
http://www.unsignedthemagazine.
com

MUSIC JOURNALISM

Critical Review
722 Dulaney Valley Road
Baltimore, MD 21204
Phone: (410) 435-3881
Fax: (410) 435-3881
E-mail: musiccritics@aol.com
http://www.mcana.org

ORCHESTRAS AND OPERAS

Classical Singer
P.O. Box 1710
Draper, UT 84020
Phone: (801) 254-1025
E-mail: subscriptions@
classicalsinger.com
http://www.classicalsinger.com

Conductors Guild Journal
5300 Glenside Drive
Richmond, VA 23228
Phone: (804) 553-1378
Fax: (804) 553-1876
http://www.conductorsguild.net

Lyric Opera News
Lyric Opera of Chicago
20 North Wacker Drive
Chicago, IL 60606
Phone: (312) 332-2244
Fax: (312) 332-2633

NOA Newsletter
National Opera Association, Inc.
P.O. Box 60869
Canyon, TX 79016
Phone: (806) 651-2857
Fax: (806) 651-2958
http://www.noa.org

Opera America Newsline
1156 15th Street, NW
Washington, DC 20005

Phone: (202) 293-4466
Fax: (202) 393-0735
http://www.

Opera News
Metropolitan Opera Guild, Inc.
70 Lincoln Center Plaza
New York, NY 10023
Phone: (212) 769-7080
http://www.metguild.org

Symphony
American Symphony Orchestra
League (ASOL)
33 West 60th Street
New York, NY 10023
Phone: (212) 262-5161
Fax: (212) 262-5198
E-mail: league@symphony.org
http://www.symphony.org

The Woman Conductor
Woman Band Directors National
Association
C/O Carol Nendza
10611 Ridgewood Drive
Palos Park, IL 60464
E-mail: carolnen@aol.com
http://womenbanddirectors.org

PUBLIC RELATIONS AND PUBLICITY

Bulldog Reporter Business Media
124 Linden Street
Oakland, CA 94607
Phone: (510) 596-9300
http://www.bulldogreporter.com

Expert PR
MediaMap, Inc.
311 Arsenal Street
Watertown, MA 02472
Phone: (617) 393-3200
Fax: (617) 393-3250

PR News
Access Intelligence, LLC
4 Choke Cherry Road
Rockville, MD 20850
Phone: (301) 354-2000
Fax: (301) 738-8153
http://www.accessintel.com

PR Reporter
Lawrence Ragan Communications,
    Inc.
111 East Wacker Drive
Chicago, IL 60601
Phone: (312) 861-3592

Public Relations Quarterly
Hudson Associates
44 West Market Street
Box 311
Rhinebeck, NY 12572
Phone: (845) 876-2081
Fax: (845) 876-2561
E-mail: hphudson@aol.com
http://www.newsletter-clearinghse.
    com

**Public Relations Society of
    America (PRSA)**
33 Maiden Lane
New York, NY 10038
Phone: (212) 460-1400
Fax: (212) 995-0757
E-mail: exec@prsa.org
http://www.prsa.org

Ragan's Public Relations Review
Lawrence Ragan Communications,
    Inc.
111 East Wacker Drive
Chicago, IL 60601
Phone: (312) 861-3592
http://www.ragan.com

RADIO

Broadcasting and Cable
360 Park Avenue South
New York, NY 10010
Phone: (646) 746-6400
Fax: (646) 746-7131
http://www.broadcastingcable.com

Country Airplay Monitor
770 Broadway
New York, NY 10003
Phone: (800) 745-8922

Radio and Records
Radio & Records, Inc.
2049 Century Park East
Los Angeles, CA 90067

Phone: (310)788-1625
Fax: (310) 203-8727
E-mail: radioandrecords@espcomp.
    com
http://www.radioandrecords.com

R&B Airplay Monitor
770 Broadway
New York, NY 10003
Phone: (800) 745-8922

R&R Directory
Radio & Records, Inc.
2049 Century Park East
Los Angeles, CA 90067
Phone: (310)788-1625
Fax: (310) 203-8727
E-mail: radioandrecords@espcomp.
    com
http://www.radioandrecords.com

Rock Airplay Monitor
770 Broadway
New York, NY 10003
Phone: (800) 745-8922

Radio Journal
365 Union Street
Littleton, NH 03561
Phone: (603) 444-5720
Fax: (603) 444-2872
E-mail: streaming@insideradio.com
http://www.mstreet.net

RECORDING AND THE
RECORDING INDUSTRY

Mix Magazine
6400 Hollist Street
Emeryville, CA 94608
Phone: (510) 653-3307
Fax: (510) 653-5142
http:///www.mixonline.com

Pro Sound News
810 Seventh Avenue
New York, NY 10019
Phone: (212) 378-0400
Fax: (212) 378-0470
http://www.prosoundnews.com

Recording
5412 Idylwild Trail

Boulder, CO 80301
Phone: (303) 516-9118
Fax: (303) 516-9119

Recording Magazine
5408 Idlywild Trail
Boulder, CO 80301
Phone: (303) 516-9118
Fax: (303) 516-9119
http://www.recordingmag.com

RETAILING AND
WHOLESALING

Musical Merchandise Review
Symphony Publishing, LLC
26202 Detroit Road
Westlake, OH 44145
Phone: (440) 871-1300
Fax: (440) 835-8306
http://www.symphonypublishing.
    com

NAPRA Review
109 North Beach Road
P.O. Box 9
Eastsound, WA 98245
Phone: (360) 376-2702
Fax: (360) 376-2704
E-mail: napra@napra.com
http://www.napra.com

TALENT AND WRITING

Acoustic Guitar
225 West End Avenue
San Anselmo, CA 94979
Phone: (415) 485-6946
Fax: (415) 485-0831
E-mail: editors.ag@stringletter.com
http://www.acousticguitar.com

American Songwriter Magazine
1303 16th Avenue South
Nashville, TN 37212
Phone: (615) 321-6096
Fax: (615) 321-6097
http://www.americansongwriter.com

Amplifier
5 Callista Terrace
Westford, MA 02886

E-mail: joej@amplifiermagazine.
    com
http://www.amplifiermagazine.
    com

AMP Magazine
American Music Press
P.O. Box 1070
Martinez, CA 94553
Phone: (925) 227-1423
E-mail: info@ampmagazine.com
http://www.ampmagazine.com

Bass Player
111 Bayhill Drive
San Bruno, CA 94066
Phone: (650) 238-0293
Fax: (650) 238-0261
E-mail: bassplayer@musicplayer.
    com
http://www.bassplayer.com

Big Takeover Magazine
1713 Eighth Avenue
Brooklyn, NY 11215
E-mail: jrabid@bigtakeover.com
http://www.bigtakeover.com

BMI Music World
Broadcast Music, Inc.
320 West 57th Street
New York, NY 10019
Phone: (212) 586-2000
http://www.bmi.org

Composer USA
National Association of Composers
P.O. Box 49256
Barrington Station
Los Angeles, CA 90049
Phone: (310) 541-8213
http://www.music-usa.org/nacusa

Down Beat
102 North Haven Road
Elmhurst, IL 60126
Phone: (630) 941-2030
Fax: (630) 941-3210
E-mail: jasonk@downbeatjazz.com
http://www.downbeat.com

Electronic Musician
6400 Hollis Street

Emeryville, CA 94608
Phone: (510) 653-3307
Fax: (510) 653-5142
http://www.emusician.com

Guitar Player
810 Seventh Avenue
New York, NY 10019
Phone: (212) 378-0400
Fax: (212) 378-0470
http://www.guitarplayer.com

Guitar Review
Albert Augustine, Ltd.
151 West 26th Street
New York, NY 10001
Phone: (971) 661-0220
Fax: (971) 661-0223

Guitar World
149 Fifth Avenue
New York, NY 10010
Phone: (212) 768-2966
Fax: (212) 944-9279
E-mail: soundingboard@
    guitarworld.com
http://ww.guitarworld.com

Hit Parader
210 Route 4E
Suite 211
Paramus, NJ 07652
Phone: (201) 843-4004
Fax: (201) 843-8636
http://www.hardradio.com

Keyboard
810 Seventh Avenue
New York, NY 10019
Phone: (212) 378-0400
Fax: (212) 378-0470
E-mail: keyboard@musicplayer.com
http://www.keyboardmag.com

Music Connection
Music Connection Inc.
14654 Victory Boulevard
Van Nuys, CA 91411
Phone: (818) 995-0101
Fax: (818) 995-9235
E-mail: ContactMC@
    musicconnection.com
http://www.musicconection.com

Musician Hotline
Heartland Construction Group, Inc.
1003 Central Avenue
Fort Dodge, IA 50501

Music Monitor
107 East Aycock Street
Raleigh, NC 27608
Phone: (919) 460-1941
http://www.musicmonitor.net

Music Trades
80 West Street
P.O. Box 432
Englewood, NJ 07631
Phone: (201) 871-1965
Fax: (201) 871-0455

Piano Today
333 Adams Street
Bedford, NY 10507
Phone: (914) 244-8500
Fax: (914) 244-8560

Sing Out!
P.O. Box 5460
Bethlehem, PA 18015
Phone: (610) 865-5366

Songwriter's Market
4700 East Galbraith Road
Cincinnati, OH 45236
Phone: (513) 531-2690
Fax: (513) 531-0798
E-mail: wds@fwpubs.com
http://www.fwpublications.com

STRINGS
255 West End Avenue
San Rafael, CA 94901
Phone: (415) 485-6946
Fax: (415) 485-0831
http://www.stringletter.com

Vintage Guitar
Orion Research
14555 North Scottsdale Road
Scottsdale, AZ 85254
Phone: (800) 844-0759
E-mail: orion@bluebook.com
http://www.netzone.com/orion

INDEX

music shop salesperson 80, **82–83**
music store manager 80
music supervisor **210–211**
music teacher 210
music teacher, college 212
Music Teachers National
　　Association, Inc. 215, 218, 220
music therapist **221–222**
music therapist consultant 221, 222
music therapy supervisor 221, 222
MySpace xi

N

NAAISC (North American
　　Association of Independent
　　Security Consultants) 163
NAB (National Association of
　　Broadcasters) 59, 61, 63
NABET (National Association
　　of Broadcast Employees and
　　Technicians) 59, 61, 63, 65
NACA (National Association for
　　Campus Activities) 33
NAMM (National Association of
　　Music Merchants) 81, 83, 89, 91
NAMT (National Association for
　　Music Therapy) 222
NARAS (National Academy of
　　Recording Arts and Sciences) 3,
　　5, 7, 9, 11, 14, 17, 19, 23, 35, 37,
　　52, 54, 65, 101, 105, 107, 114, 154,
　　227, 238
NARM (National Association of
　　Recording Merchandisers) 25, 27,
　　29, 85, 91, 114
National Academy of Recording
　　Arts and Sciences (NARAS) 3, 5,
　　7, 9, 11, 14, 17, 19, 23, 35, 37, 52,
　　54, 65, 101, 105, 107, 114, 154,
　　227, 238
National Association for Campus
　　Activities (NACA) 33
National Association for Music
　　Therapy (NAMT) 222
National Association of Broadcast
　　Employees and Technicians
　　(NABET) 59, 61, 63, 65
National Association of Broadcasters
　　(NAB) 59, 61, 63
National Association of Music
　　Merchants (NAMM) 81, 83, 89,
　　91

National Association of Recording
　　Merchandisers (NARM) 25, 27,
　　29, 85, 91, 114
National Association of Schools of
　　Music 215, 218, 220
National Conference of Personal
　　Managers 96, 109
National Council of Acoustical
　　Consultants (NCAC) 119, 121,
　　125
National Council of Investigation
　　and Security Services (NCISS)
　　163
National Council of State Supervisors
　　of Music (NCSSM) 211
National Educators Association
　　(NEA) 215, 218
National Federation of Music Clubs
　　207
National Federation of Teachers
　　(NFT) 211, 215, 218
National Music Publishers'
　　Association (NMPA) 107
National Orchestra Association
　　(NOA) 169, 171, 173
national sales director, record label
　　24, 25
NCAC (National Council of
　　Acoustical Consultants) 119, 121,
　　125
NCISS (National Council of
　　Investigation and Security
　　Services) 163
NCSSM (National Council of State
　　Supervisors of Music) 211
NEA (National Educators
　　Association) 215, 218
new in the sixth edition xii
NFT (National Federation of
　　Teachers) 211, 215, 218
nightclub manager **206–207**
nightclub owner 206, 207
NMPA (National Music Publisher's
　　Association) 107
NOA (National Orchestra
　　Association) 169, 171, 173
non-music-oriented advance person
　　76
non-music oriented publicist 13,
　　137
nonmusic-oriented publicity
　　position 131
nonmusic-oriented reporter 138

North American Association of
　　Independent Security Consultants
　　(NAAISC) 163

O

on-air personality 62
on-air position in television 64
on the road, career opportunities
　　67–77
operas, orchestras, symphonies, etc,
　　careers in **165–193**
opera singer **174–175**
operatic singer 174
operations manager, orchestra 178
orchestral music librarian **192–193**
orchestra manager 176, **178–179,**
　　180, 181, 182, 183
orchestras, symphonies, operas, etc,
　　careers in **165–193**
orchestrator **43–44**, 45, 46
organist, church 242, **246–247**
organization of material xii

P

partner in law firm 110, 112
P.D. 58
performer 219
performing rights societies **330–331**
PERL 48
personal assistant to recording artist
　　156–159
personal manager 68, 69, **94–96**
personnel director, orchestra
　　190–191
personnel manager 190
personnel staff member, orchestra
　　190
Piano Technicians Guild (PTG) 119,
　　121, 123
piano tuner-technician **122–123**
piano tuner technician apprentice
　　122
position description, explanation
　　of xix
P.R. counselor 16, 128
P.R. director 10
P.R. director, orchestra 184
press agent 13, 133
press agent trainee 136
principal player 170
print media journalist 131

ABOUT THE AUTHOR

Shelly Field is a nationally recognized motivational speaker, career expert, stress-management specialist, personal career and life coach, and author of more than 35 best-selling books in the business and career fields.

Her books help people find careers in a variety of areas, including the music, sports, hospitality and communications industries, casinos and casino hotels, advertising and public relations, theater, the performing arts, entertainment, animal rights, heath care, writing, and art. She is a frequent guest on local, regional, and national radio, cable, and television talk, information, and news shows and has been the subject of numerous print interviews for articles and news stories.

Field is a featured speaker at conferences, conventions, expos, corporate functions, spouse programs, employee-training and development sessions, career fairs, casinos, and other events nationwide. A former comedienne, she adds a humorous spin whether speaking on empowerment, motivation, stress management, staying positive, the power of laughter, careers, and attracting, retaining, and motivating employees or improving customer service. Her popular presenta-

tions, "STRESS BUSTERS: Beating The Stress in Your Work and Your Life" and The De-Stress Express" are favorites around the country.

A career consultant to businesses, educational institutions, employment agencies, women's groups, and individuals, Field is sought out by executives, celebrities, and sports figures for personal-life and career coaching and stress management.

In her role as a corporate consultant to businesses throughout the country, she provides assistance related to human-resources issues, such as attracting, retaining, and motivating employees, customer service training, and stress management in the workplace

President and CEO of The Shelly Field Organization, a public relations, marketing, and management firm handling national clients, she has represented celebrities in the sports, music, and entertainment industries, as well as authors, businesses, and corporations.

For media inquiries, information about personal appearances, seminars or workshops, stress-management or personal coaching, please contact The Shelly Field Organization at P.O. Box 711, Monticello, NY 12701, or visit Shelly on the Web at www.shellyfield.com